Studies in Soviet
Input-Output Analysis

edited by
Vladimir G. Treml
foreword by
Wassily Leontief

The Praeger Special Studies program—
utilizing the most modern and efficient book
production techniques and a selective
worldwide distribution network—makes
available to the academic, government, and
business communities significant, timely
research in U.S. and international economic, social, and political development.

Studies in Soviet Input-Output Analysis

PRAEGER SPECIAL STUDIES IN INTERNATIONAL ECONOMICS AND DEVELOPMENT

Praeger Publishers New York London

Library of Congress Cataloging in Publication Data
Main entry under title:

Studies in Soviet input-output analysis.

   (Praeger special studies in international economics
and development)
   Includes bibliographical references and index.
   1.   Russia—Industries—Mathematical models.
2.   Interindustry economics.   I.   Treml, Vladimir G.
HC336.24.S8   1977   338'.0947   77-2739
ISBN 0-275-56550-5

0-275-56550-5

PRAEGER SPECIAL STUDIES
200 Park Avenue, New York, N.Y., 10017, U.S.A.

Published in the United States of America in 1977
by Praeger Publishers,
A Division of Holt, Rinehart and Winston, CBS, Inc.

789   038   987654321

Printed in the United States of America

The input-output method has evolved over the last 30 years into one of the standard, routinely used tools of economic analysis. In many countries construction of national and regional input-output tables became a regular responsibility of the central statistical offices, along with compilation of national income accounts. "Inversion" of structural matrixes and other more sophisticated kinds of input-output computations are being performed routinely by forecasters and economic planners in developed and developing, in free market and socialist countries.

Soviet experts have taken an active part in four of the six international input-output conferences held at regular intervals since 1952. Nevertheless, while the U.S. input-output table and those of many other developed and developing countries have been published and analyzed again and again, a description of the input-output structure of the Soviet economy--the second largest industrialized country in the world--has been available only in a very incomplete, fragmentary form. This volume represents a major step toward filling that gap. Combining systematic alignment of figures presented in Russian statistical publications with painstaking analytical reconstruction of the missing data, Professor Treml and his colleagues have produced the first detailed--75-sector--input-output table of the Soviet economy for the year 1966. Moreover, they have presented it in a form securing the greatest possible comparability with a corresponding input-output table of the U.S. economy. To be sure, as the authors repeatedly emphasize, the numbers they present are subject to a great amount of uncertainty. Much additional work will be required to improve them and, needless to say, Soviet statisticians and input-output experts can make a major contribution to the successful accomplishment of that task.

With the steady growth of international economic interdependence, the development of any one country cannot be properly understood unless its external economic relationships are examined in the context of a reasonably detailed description of the economic structure of all other parts of the world. The picture of the world economy presently available looks like a sixteenth-century map with the outlines of most continents traced out fairly accurately, but with some of the inside areas filled in only very sketchily or even left entirely blank. This volume makes a major contribution to the completion of a detailed input-output map of the world.

v

Those of us who do not have access to Russian economic and statistical literature will find in this book a description of important contributions in the general area of input-output analysis and, in particular, in the field of regional input-output analysis by our Soviet colleagues. Professor Treml and his collaborators have also made a number of valuable methodological contributions of their own.

Wassily Leontief

Input-output techniques and input-output tables are rapidly becoming a ubiquitous tool of Soviet economists, statisticians, and planners for micro- and macromodeling, national and regional planning, determination of prices, management of labor resources, and a variety of other analytical and administrative purposes. The widespread popularity and utilization of input-output analysis and data can easily be understood when considered against the background of poor and often nonexisting statistical data, and the restrictively dogmatic interpretation of economic theory that the Soviet economic profession had to work with until well into the 1950s. Input-output analysis thus appears to increasingly dominate the economic scene in the Soviet Union, both in terms of resources devoted to construction of numerous tables and models, and in terms of their applications.

The nine studies that comprise this volume can hardly match the scope of development and application of input-output analysis in the Soviet Union, but they give some idea of its range and a sampling of its analytical potential.

The volume is focused on the 1966 Soviet input-output table and related data. As explained in Chapter 1, despite all the widespread use and interest in input-output as reflected in an ever-growing body of literature, Soviet statistical agencies do not publish the complete tables but only segments of them, omitting key blocks of data. Thus it is necessary to reconstruct these tables by filling in the missing parts through the use of a variety of estimating techniques. The national table presented in Chapter 1 incorporates new data not previously available, including relevant statistics from regional input-output tables. It is thus, in the opinion of the authors, the definitive reconstruction of that table, superseding all previously published versions.

The selection of subjects for this volume was dictated by a desire to offer as many different insights into the Soviet economy based on input-output analysis as possible. Chapters 2, 3, and 4 are focused on economywide applications of input-output and related techniques in such areas as planning, scale of production, and transportation. Chapter 5 offers a set of price indexes and a conversion of the 1966 table to 1970 prices to facilitate intertemporal comparisons of economic structures revealed in input-output tables. Chapters 6 and 7 are devoted to Soviet explorations of regional input-output analysis, including a case study of a republic input-output table. Chapter 8 is concerned with U.S.-Soviet comparisons based on input-output tables, and Chapter 9 develops the methodology for integration of input-output tables with an econometric model.

Most of the studies included in this volume were originally undertaken under a Ford Foundation grant to Duke University, which established a research project on Soviet input-output analysis. In fact, Chapters 2, 3, 4, 5, 6, and 7 are updated and revised studies that were published earlier in the mimeographed series of <u>Duke University-University of North Carolina Occasional Papers on Soviet Input-Output Analysis</u>. The authors gratefully acknowledge the generous financial support of the Ford Foundation.

Of the nine authors of this volume, seven are or were associated with Duke University as faculty, graduate students, or visiting researchers, and the University, particularly Professor Allen C. Kelley, the Chairman of the Economics Department, should be thanked for assistance and encouragement. Several Duke University students have contributed in a significant way to the various aspects of the research; specific mention should be made of John Barnett, Mason Barnett, Julie Blum, Rosemary Klemfus, Paul Messner, Richard Mintzer, Olga Sheinman, and Patti Velasquez. The contributions of Marion Salinger, administrative assistant of the Center for International Studies of Duke University, and of Eleanor Simon and Patricia Calebaugh, research secretaries, must also be acknowledged.

All errors, avoidable and inadvertent, are, of course, the responsibility of the authors and the editor.

Vladimir G. Treml

CONTENTS

LIST OF TABLES AND FIGURES

LIST OF ABBREVIATIONS USED IN TABLES

ABRASV	abrasives
AGRIC M&E	tractors and agricultural machinery and equipment
ANIL DYE PR	aniline dye products
ANIMAL HUSB	animal husbandry
AUTOS	automobiles
BASIC CHEM	basic chemistry
BEARNG	bearings
BLDGS & STRUCT	buildings, structures, and transmission facilities
CABLE PROD	cable products
CAST M&E	casting machinery and equipment
COKE PROD	coke products
CONMAT M&E	construction materials machinery and equipment
CONST	construction
CONST MAT	construction materials
CONST M&E	construction machinery and equipment
DAIRY PROD	dairy products
ELEC POWER	electric power and steam
ELTECH M&E	electrotechnical machinery and equipment
EN&POW M&E	energy and power machinery and equipment
FD IND M&E	food industry machinery and equipment
FER METALS	ferrous metals
FER ORES	ferrous ores
FISH PROD	fish products
FLOUR & BREAD	flour, bread, and confections
FOREST	forestry
FORG-PR M&E	forging-pressing machinery and equipment
GENERAL M&E	general machinery and equipment
GLASS	glass and porcelain
GVO	gross value of output
HOIST-TRAN E	hoisting-transporting machinery and equipment
INDMET PROD	industrial metal products
IND NEC	industry not elsewhere classified
INTIND USE	interindustry use
LOG&PA M&E	logging and paper machinery and equipment
LOGGNG	logging
LT IND M&E	light industry machinery and equipment
MACH TOOLS	machine tools
MEAT PROD	meat products

METAL STRUCT	metal structures
MI&MET M&E	mining and metallurgical machinery and equipment
MINRL CHEM	mineral chemistry products
NATIONAL INC	national income
NONFER METAL	nonferrous metals
NONFER ORES	nonferrous ores
OIL EXTRAC	oil extraction
OIL REF	oil refining
ORGSYN PROD	organic synthetic products
OTH CAPITAL	other fixed capital stock
OTH NET INC	other net income
OTHER BRANCH	other branches of material production
OTHER CHEM	other chemicals
OTHER FD	other final demand
OTHER LT IND	other light industry products
OTHER METWRS	other metal wares
OTHER WDWK	other woodworking
PAINT & LAC	paints and lacquers
POWER M&E	power machinery and equipment
PRECIS INST	precision instruments
PRINT M&E	printing machinery and equipment
PRIVAT CONSUM	private consumption
PUBLIC CONSUM	public consumption
PUMPS&CHEM E	pumps and chemical equipment
RADIO&OTH MB	radio and other machinebuilding
REFRAC MAT	refractory materials
REPAIR	repair of machinery and equipment
RUBBER PROD	rubber and asbestos products
SANIT ENG PR	sanitary engineering products
SAW&LUM PR	sawmills and lumber products
SPECIAL M&E	specialized machinery and equipment
SYN FIBERS	synthetic fibers
SYN R&PLAST	synthetic resins and plastics
TAX ON PURCH	turnover taxes on purchases
TEXTLS	textiles
TOTAL FD	total final demand
TOTAL PURCH	total purchases
TOTL CAPITAL	total fixed capital stock
TRADE&DIST	trade and distribution
TRANS&COM	transportation and communications
TRANS M&E	transportation machinery and equipment
WOOD CHEM	wood chemistry products

Studies in Soviet
Input-Output Analysis

1

1966 EX POST INPUT-OUTPUT TABLES FOR THE USSR: A SURVEY

Vladimir G. Treml
Dimitri M. Gallik
Barry L. Kostinsky

INTRODUCTION

The 1966 input-output table is the second national ex post table constructed in the USSR. In terms of statistical coverage, sophistication of data collection and processing, and the accuracy of primary and supplementary statistics it appears to be superior to its 1959 predecessor and therefore of particular interest to Western scholars.

Soviet statistical sources publish only fragmentary data on their input-output tables and the authors of this chapter have been engaged in several rounds of "reconstruction" of Soviet input-output tables, that is, preparation of complete three-quadrant tables by estimating and filling in the segments omitted from the published data.

Earlier variants of the reconstructed tables and related supplementary statistics have appeared elsewhere.[1] The purpose of this chapter is to make available corrected and revised versions of the 1966 purchasers' and producers' price tables. Also presented are supplementary statistics that have not been published before. Limitations on space made it necessary to include only the most essential summary notes on the methodology, documentation, statistical concepts, and classification systems employed in the reconstructed tables.

THE ORIGINAL SOVIET TABLE[2]

The description of the original 1966 Soviet input-output table in this study is restricted to a brief summary of its major features. A detailed and comprehensive description can be found in Treml et al. (1972, Ch. 3).

Like the other Soviet national ex post input–output tables in value terms produced to date (1959 and 1972), the 1966 table is of the conventional static, open, Leontief type. The basic flow table is composed of three principal quadrants: quadrant I--a square matrix of interindustry transactions, which depicts the commodity flows among all the producing sectors in the economy; quadrant II-- the final-demand quadrant, which shows the distribution of output among various categories of final or end users; and quadrant III-- the value-added quadrant, which shows depreciation and income (labor income, profits, taxes, and other payments) originating in each of the producing sectors. The flows are measured in current purchasers' prices of the given year (1966), that is, the prices paid by the purchasers of the products, including transportation and distribution charges and turnover taxes when applicable, as well as producers' costs and profits.

The first quadrant divides the economy into 110 producing sectors: 95 in industry, 5 in construction, 2 in agriculture, and 1 each for forestry, railroad transportation, other transportation, communications, trade, supply, agricultural procurement, and a sector called other branches of material production. A detailed description of each of these sectors is given in Treml et al. (1972, Ch. 5). Input-output tables adhere to the material product concept used in Soviet national income accounts in that the sectors that define the first quadrant encompass all productive activities, including the services indicated in the above list as well as equipment repair and certain consumer services such as clothing, furniture and appliance repair, and dry cleaning. Nonproductive activities are shown in the final-demand quadrant as claimants against end output. Since the 1966 table has been described as having 131 rows and columns (Volodarskii and Eidel'man 1969, p. 20) and the first quadrant is 110 x 110, there are possibly 21 elements of final demand. However, it is likely that subtotals have been counted in the 131 and that there are somewhat fewer separate elements of final demand. Similarly the value-added quadrant has a maximum of 21 separate categories.

The scope and analytical importance of the 1966 table have also been greatly enhanced by two complementary sets of data--one on labor and one on the capital utilized in production during the year. In this respect Soviet input-output tables compare favorably with their Western counterparts, few of which have such vectors for these primary resources. The labor data show employment in man-years averaged over the year for each of the 110 sectors in the flow table. The capital matrix shows the stock of fixed capital (valued in constant 1955 prices) employed in the productive sectors as an average for the year. In this case, however, the original has only 105 productive sectors instead of the 110 in the other tables. The capital assets are broken down into 30 types, of which 25 represent machinery and equipment.

The sectors in Soviet input-output tables are supposed to be "pure"--that is, each reflects the production of only those commodities that come within its defined scope. Since in practice the enterprises included in any given sector usually also produce some output that by definition belongs in some other sector, the data in both the rows and columns of all Soviet tables (outputs and inputs) are adjusted to reflect only the proper activities of each sector.

Several aspects of Soviet input-output tables differ from Western tables. Because Soviet tables are in purchasers' prices that include all transportation and distribution costs, these costs are reflected only in the first quadrant; the entries for these sectors in the final-demand quadrant are zero. On the other hand, because all construction activity, including repair and maintenance, is considered investment, the entries of the construction row in the first quadrant are zeros and construction output is shown in the investment categories of final demand.

The final-demand quadrant also includes the exports and imports. As is generally the case, exports in the Soviet table are shown simply as one of the claimants on final output. Recording imports in input-output tables is more complex and procedures vary. Flows in the Soviet table include both imported and domestically produced goods, so that the sum of all sales in a row would equal total supply--that is, domestic production plus imports. In order to preserve the row-column equality that is necessary in input-output tables, imports must either be added to each sector's inputs (which relate only to domestic production), as an element of value-added, or must be subtracted from its sales, as a negative element of final demand. Since shifting the import vector between final demand and value-added is a simple procedure, the same table can be readily available in both formats. However, for the calculation of direct and total coefficients imports are included in the final-demand quadrant so that the calculations are based on domestic output. It should also be noted that Soviet tables do not distinguish between competing and noncompeting imports. Another special feature of the treatment of foreign trade flows in Soviet input-output tables is that industrial imports are recorded in industry prices--that is, prices that include turnover taxes--while exports are measured in enterprise prices net of taxes.

A vexing puzzle to all users of Soviet input-output tables is the treatment of defense industries and defense-related activities. Since Soviet input-output tables agree with national income and gross social product (GSP) accounts, the material purchases of the military as

well as the production and distribution of military hardware must be
somehow included in the transaction flows of the input-output tables.
However, neither the published fragmentary blocks of input-output
statistics nor the numerous methodological, descriptive, and analytical sources on Soviet input-output ever refer to defense.

Our conjectures on the location of defense in Soviet input-
output tables agree basically with the Western understanding of the
treatment of defense in national income and product accounting
(Becker 1969, pp. 16, 28, 33, 163-64).

The final-demand quadrant includes all end-use material components of the defense bill. The private consumption column includes
all items of material consumption by military personnel, such as
food, clothing, fuel and electricity used in military housing, and the
like. Current material expenditures of defense activities are shown
in the public and state consumption columns: materials used in research and development, munitions and fuel consumed in military
operations, electrical power used in military communications and
military facilities, and similar items. The bulk of military hardware and civilian machinery delivered to the military establishment
is found under two categories of gross investment. Hardware that
is permanently mounted or affixed to or in buildings and structures
(for example, radar systems and other electronic gear, missile
launching mechanisms) is in the gross fixed investment column,
while all other weapons and hardware are shown in the "increase in
reserves and stocks" column. However, even the most detailed
input-output commodity description available (TsSU 1971) makes no
mention of defense-related production activities. The list of commodities omits not only weapons, tanks, and ammunition, but even
such products as aircraft, some of which, of course, go to the civilian sector. It must be assumed, however, that the production of
military hardware has not been omitted. Soviet input-output tables
are completely integrated and agree fully with Soviet national income
and product accounting. Thus, any sector generating material output must be included in the table.

The most reasonable explanation of the method of concealment
of military production is that the several defense sectors were simply
aggregated with selected civilian sectors. For example, the aircraft
industry may have been incorporated with the automobile sector. Another possible but a less likely explanation is that the entire defense
sector was distributed proportionally or on some other basis within
the machinery block of the table.

THE RECONSTRUCTION PROCESS

The reconstruction of the 1966 national table is an intricate
process involving literally thousands of estimates. The description

of this process here must perforce be sketchy. Except for a few
modifications dictated by new data, it is basically the same as that
described in detail in Treml et al. (1972).

There are three basic stages in this process, the principle involved being that of establishing as accurate a set of control totals
as possible and then disaggregating these totals on the basis of other
data that may be less reliable. The first of these stages is construction of a table in which the economy is divided into six sectors: industry, construction, agriculture and forestry, transportation and
communications, trade and distribution, and other branches of
material production. The second is expansion of the single industry
sector in this table into 13, in a complete 18-sector table. The
final stage is to expand these 18 sectors into the 75 shown in Table 1.1.

The original table described above has never been published as a
complete table in any form, not even highly aggregated. The data that
have been published are incomplete and fragmentary; without reconstruction of the table, they would be of little value in analyzing the
Soviet economy. The officially published table is an 85-sector portion of the first quadrant of the original. The 85 sectors include 75
of the original 110, with another 29 of the original sectors being
aggregated into 10, and 6 omitted completely. This published table
is the basic block of data upon which the reconstructed table is built.
Published with it were some selected direct and total coefficients
that are based, not on the published flows, but on the original table.
Although these coefficients are important in the reconstruction, they
represent only a small portion of the total number of coefficients in
the original table. Other large blocks of input-output data that have
appeared in subsequent statistical yearbooks include a matrix of embodied labor flows corresponding to the published ruble flows and
expressed in terms of man-years (Narkhoz 68, pp. 74-121); a matrix
of fixed capital stock showing 27 types of capital and corresponding
generally to the sectors in the published flow table, but also including a single sector that encompasses those omitted from the flow
table (Narkhoz 68, pp. 51-71); and a set of direct capital input coefficients for 45 of the original 110 sectors (Narkhoz 69, pp. 47-73).
No other national input-output data have appeared in official publications.

The officially published data are supplemented by a variety of
input-output and input-output-based data that have appeared in more
or less authoritative, but not official, government publications.
Some of these data come directly from the original table, others are
based on the published table, and still others correspond neither to
the original nor the published versions. All such data must be analyzed and evaluated for reliability before they can be used in the reconstruction process. They are first checked against available

official input-output data and then subjected to additional quantitative
and qualitative tests.

In the current version of the reconstructed table, the 6-sector
table, to a large extent, is estimated on the basis of data in a source
not available for the earlier reconstruction (Shatalin and Serebrennikova 1974). This source gives a table of total input coefficients at the
6-sector level which provides more reliable estimates of flows and
GVOs than were previously possible. Several other sources of new
data under lie the revised gross value of output (GVO) estimates in the
18-sector table (Belkin 1972, Granberg 1975, Mazanova 1974, Savinskii 1972, Slepov 1976, Velkov 1976). The estimates for unpublished
first-quadrant flows in this table were significantly improved by new
coefficient data on total purchases by most sectors (Granberg 1975,
pp. 21-22) and new data on sales and purchases by the complete
machinebuilding and metalworking (MBMW) industry (Buzunov 1975,
pp. 114-18). Outside the first quadrant, the consumption estimates
were greatly improved by being based directly on new input-output-
related data (Shatalin and Serebrennikova 1974, p. 6). With some
important exceptions, the expansion of the 18-sector to the 75-
sector table remains, as it was previously, a mechanical process of
distributing the unpublished entries in the smaller table among the
disaggregated sectors in proportion to a pattern based on specific
sectors selected to represent the unpublished sectors. Important
new exceptions to this are the flows between radio and other machinebuilding (the combined unpublished MBMW sectors) and the published
MBMW sectors (Buzunov 1975, pp. 114-18), and the flows between
synthetic rubber (the unpublished chemical sector) and the published
chemical sectors, which were calculated from detailed input-output-
based data not previously available (Savinskii 1972, pp. 33, 93).
Regional input-output tables were also used in making judgments
about some of the estimates of unpublished flows. In short, the
present table is believed to represent a significant improvement
over the earlier table because of the new, primarily input-output-
related, data that are used in its reconstruction.

CONVERSION TO PRODUCERS' PRICES

There are two principal types of input-output tables in value
terms with respect to the type of prices used in the valuation of
product flows--tables in purchasers' prices and tables in producers'
prices. Purchasers' prices include transportation and distribution
costs and any applicable sales or excise taxes and customs duties,
as well as the direct costs of production. Producers' prices can
best be described as "factory gate" prices; that is, they encompass

only direct production costs (including profits) and are net of transportation and distribution charges and excise taxes.

For most analytical purposes, tables in producers' prices are
generally considered to be superior to those in purchasers' prices.
In fact, virtually all Western input-output tables are constructed in
terms of producers' prices. The analytical superiority of this type
of table stems from the fact that its flows reflect more closely the
real movement of goods throughout the economy and correspond to
the flows measured in physical quantities. The flow entries in tables
in purchasers' prices, on the other hand, include not only the value
of the goods shipped from the producer to the user but also the costs
of shipment, distribution margins, and taxes as appropriate. Since
all of these are highly differentiated, the real movement of goods is
distorted. Thus, the purchase of a product by a distantly located
buyer is shown as a larger flow than the purchase of the same quantity of the same product by a closer buyer because of higher transportation costs. Similarly, purchases by final consumers at retail
appear as larger flows than the same purchases at wholesale. Also,
excise taxes inflate the value of taxed goods as compared with un-
taxed goods. Such distortions violate the assumption of constant re-
turns to scale necessary in input-output analysis. Generally, it is
assumed that proportional increases in the levels of use of all inputs
into a given producing sector will result in a proportional increase
in the gross output of that sector. If, however, the input flows for
the sector are measured in purchasers' prices, the increase in output will not necessarily be proportional to the increase in inputs because of differences in the distribution patterns. Furthermore, the
input coefficients will display greater instability over time, since in
general the basic technology of production is more stable than patterns of distribution. Thus, even in the absence of any changes in
technology or prices, matrixes of input coefficients for different
periods may show changes that are due entirely to shifts in distribution patterns.

The distortions intrinsic to purchasers' prices tables in general are probably more pronounced in tables for the Soviet Union
than in those for most other countries. It would appear that each of
the three major elements making for such distortion is aggravated
in the Soviet case.

1. The sheer size of the country and a differentiated structure of freight rates result in great disparity in transportation costs.
2. There are at least three separate and distinct distribution
systems, each serving a different sector of the economy. The retail trade system serves private consumers and handles primarily
final consumer goods. The system of material-technical supply

distributes all kinds of materials, intermediate products, and supplies to producing enterprises and government organizations. Agricultural procurement organizations handle unprocessed agricultural commodities. All three systems have substantially different scales of service charges.

    3. The Soviet turnover tax is a form of excise tax that constitutes a very significant and volatile element in the Soviet price system. This tax is highly differentiated both by product and by purchaser of the same product, and in many instances the tax rate is quite high in relation to the price of the product. In all probability, the distortive effects of the turnover tax are even more pronounced than those of the other two elements noted above.

    In addition to the distortive effects of these elements of purchasers' prices, in Soviet input-output practice, transportation and distribution services are shown as separate activities in the interindustry matrix, while at the same time the costs of these services are also incorporated as an intrinsic part of each flow entry in the table. The result is doublecounting of all transportation and distribution costs for the table as a whole. Thus, the sum of the GVO of all the sectors of a table in purchasers' prices exceeds the gross social product (GSP) of the economy by the value of the GVOs of the transportation and distribution sectors.

    All these considerations make it highly desirable, if indeed not essential, to use tables in producers' prices in various analytical studies. Nonetheless, most Soviet tables in value terms completed to date, including the national ex post table for 1966, have been constructed in terms of current purchasers' prices. It appears that in the Soviet context the construction of tables in producers' prices is not practicable. Selection of the type of prices to be used is usually not a matter of choice open to those preparing the tables but is dictated by the nature of the basic economic statistics available. In the Soviet case, input-output data are prepared on the basis of information supplied by producing enterprises. The latter, however, do not know the producer's value of their various material purchases. At the same time, although they know the value of their output in producers' prices, they rarely know the ultimate destinations of their products. Thus, because of the nature of the primary data, Soviet tables are constructed by columns rather than by rows.

    The methodology for converting a Soviet purchasers' prices table into producers' prices consists basically of the removal and reallocation of turnover taxes, transportation and communications costs, and trade and distribution charges. The details of this methodology as applied to the 1966 table are expounded in Treml et al. (1973). Suffice it to say here that transportation and com-

munication costs are taken from the published table, removed
proportionally from all sales, and reallocated in a new transportation
and communications row, which represents the delivery costs of inputs rather than outputs. The trade and distribution costs in the published table must be broken down into the three separate forms of distribution (trade, supply, and procurement) and removed as applicable.
They are then reallocated to a new trade and distribution row, as in
the case of transportation and communications. Turnover taxes are
not given in the published table; they must be estimated independently
and removed selectively.[3] They are then reallocated to a new row in
the first quadrant.

In addition to being based on an improved purchasers' prices
table, the revised producers' prices table presented here reflects
previously unavailable turnover tax data, primarily that given in
Borovik and Plashchinskii (1972, p. 179).

THE RECONSTRUCTED TABLES

The complete reconstructed table in purchasers' prices is presented in Table 1.1.[4] The 75 producing sectors of the first quadrant
are described in terms of the commodities or activities they encompass in an appendix to this chapter. Column 76 and row 76 give the
totals for this quadrant, that is, total interindustry sales and purchases, respectively.

The final-demand categories in the second quadrant, in column order, are as follows:

1. Private consumption, which encompasses all goods purchased by individuals (including consumer durables) and home-
grown produce; private consumption of military personnel is also
included.
2. Public consumption, which incorporates all material
products consumed by state and public organizations, such as defense, science, health, education, utilities, and passenger transportation and communications serving the population.
3. Commodity exports.
4. Commodity imports.
5. Other final-demand categories, including net increments
in fixed capital, inventories, replacements and repair of capital,
losses, and other elements. Column 82 shows the total for the
final-demand quadrant, and column 83 gives the full row total
or the gross output for each sector.

TABLE 1.1

The Reconstructed Soviet 1966 Input-Output Table in Purchasers' Prices
(thousands of rubles; employment in thousands of man-years)

SEQ NO.	110 ORDER NO.		FER ORES 1	FER METALS 2	NONFER ORES 3	NONFER METAL 4	COKE PROD 5	REFRAC MAT 6	INDOMET PROD 7	COAL 8	OIL EXTRAC 9
1	1	FER ORES	1491	806143	0	17160	0	37514	2915	330	53
2	2	FER METALS	11640	1551650	23700	70000	1703	0	498000	27564	2539
3	6	NONFER ORES	0	0	1000	1240159	0	0	0	0	0
4	7	NONFER METAL	0	1015211	0	1834514	868	0	23338	4290	539
5	3	COKE PROD	5150	630500	5000	127276	81320	5473	1268	448	90
6	4	REFRAC MAT	10000	100964	0	0	514	3405	1355	186	46
7	5	INDOMET PROD	5000	50618	0	2718	954	894	18742	20843	1098
8	8	COAL	18600	429600	6686	26450	927552	6799	3538	1289087	74
9	9	OIL EXTRAC	0	0	0	0	0	0	0	0	9410
10	10	OIL REF	13166	120615	10830	67740	2443	8187	8976	12178	19012
11	11	GAS	0	212538	0	9685	13419	10171	4727	817	2877
12	12	PEAT	0	640	0	1536	878	11	11	402	1
13	13	OIL SHALES	298	2734	246	256	21354	11	14	207	97
14	14	ELEC POWER	85050	195388	78000	367039	37	8900	25769	211303	76277
15	15	ENSPOW M&E	149	1684	382	7595	875	27	1617	398	272
16	16	ELTECH M&E	5737	19068	7306	2363	290	928	620	12586	1604
17	17	CABLE PROD	3136	9410	3286	65	64	366	80	29945	1278
18	20	MACH TOOLS	107	872	355	387	12	2	215	159	18
19	21	FORG- PR M&E	147	470	694	454	4	0	63	63	0
20	22	CAST M&E	343	791	437			3	5	7	0
21	23	TOOLS & DIES	2526	2556	3217	3344	116	144	752	5249	590
22	24	PRECIS INST	1175	3549	934	2116	203	105	147	2663	470
23	25,26,27	MISMT M&E	28514	96161	23761	23965	1328	972	2136	82297	8376
24	28,29	PUMPS&CHEM E	549	1907	1200	333	517	38	11	379	1149
25	30	LOG&PA M&E	36		30						
26	31	LT IND M&E	0	3	0	0	0	4	0	0	0
27	32	FD IND M&E	0	7	0	0	1	0	1	1	1
28	33	PRINT M&E	0	30	0	0	2	0	0	2	0
29	34	HOIST&TRAN E	243	1392	402	142	81	70	67	1186	23
30	35	CONST M&E	5696	965	2136	352	8	353	2	1451	4
31	36	CONMAT M&E	136	602	173	180	0	566	0	6	0
32	37,38	TRANS M&E	2472	1707	1462	1162	190	138	70	1032	3
33	39	AUTOS	6105	4216	3613	2870	75	226	227	919	744
34	40	AGRIC M&E	2237	648	2164	851	28	139	9	1505	590
35	41	BEARNG M&E	1380	5904	919	2014	123	210	479	1333	187
36	18,19,42,43	RADIO&OTH MB	5399	17681	6436	7586	842	807	1378	8423	1144
37	44	SANIT ENG PR	332	1345	319	706	132	59	133	679	44
38	45	OTHER METWRS	6826	15706	6955	7819	569	391	2763	13518	953
39	46	METAL STRUCT	371	854	378	426	119		3	904	10
40	47	REPAIR	21320	91218	14191	31115	10327	3916	3357	20873	2940
41	48	ABRASV	2619	11203	1743	3821	27	1483	850	395	215
42	49	MINRL CHEM	450	4126	371	2317	88	468	496	439	27
43	50	BASIC CHEM	13561	127902	11484	71832	16040	4263	12812	50561	3380
44	51	ANIL DYE PR	33	306	28	172	2	2	2	113	3
45	52	SYN R& PLAST	355	3257	292	1829	73	23	499	229	290

Idx	Code	Name	(1)	(2)	(3)	(4)	(5)	(6)	(7)	(8)	(9)
46	53	SYN FIBERS	54	495	44	278	0	0	88	0	0
47	55	ORGSYN PROD	724	6630	595	3724	143	572	81	2939	3251
48	56	PAINT & LAC	655	5998	538	3369	1132	213	508	2063	531
49	57	RUBBER PROD	4051	37114	3333	20844	1549	1104	868	30908	1496
50	54.58.59	OTHER CHEM	115	1053	94	591	9	29	16	4906	98
51	60	LOGGNG	21937	0	13280	0	236	1149	1569	293761	525
52	61.62	SAW & LUM PR	5922	13625	6034	6783	460	831	13198	67040	832
53	63	FURNITURE	459	1710	441	975	103	103	340	1325	172
54	64	OTHER WDWK	167	1530	137	860	35	49	294	743	80
55	65	PAPER & PULP	478	4381	393	2460	412	415	1831	422	147
56	66	WOOD CHEM	293	2681	241	1505	913	470	11	29	126
57	67-73	CONST MAT	5472	12591	5576	6269	725	1181	1611	27163	803
58	74	GLASS	1096	4441	1051	2325	214	105	553	798	180
59	75-80	TEXTLS	3296	15188	1678	9271	680	613	43187	5009	1239
60	81	SEWN GOODS	8472	39031	4312	23827	1010	1748	4859	43245	2235
61	82	OTH LT IND	1619	7461	824	4555	353	231	406	6725	729
62	83	FISH PROD	3	13	40	8	0	1	4	2	0
63	84	MEAT PROD	80	366	1552	224	4	26	0	0	3
64	85	DAIRY PROD	3051	14054	3	8580	906	188	334	659	739
65	86	SUGAR	5	23	24	14	0	13	0	0	0
66	87-89	FLOUR&BREAD	47	220	695	134	0	0	1	4	0
67	90-94	OTHER FOOD	1367	6296		3844	161	397	3646	3564	365
68	95	IND NEC	42367	144805	36194	63252	10791	6117	13998	46029	2011
69	96-100	CONST	0	0	0	0	0	0	0	0	0
70	101	CROPS	155	712	79	435	0	48	18	716	65
71	102	ANIMAL HUSB	61	279	31	170	0	0	0	0	0
72	103	FOREST	302169	926705	131963	0	0	0	0	0	0
73	104-106	TRANS &COM	29646	255745	25089	268815	121363	62294	66773	1539377	536823
74	107-109	TRADE & DIST	0	203070	0	152758	7091	422	32845	208470	137800
75	110	OTHER BRANCH				114227	50	10	2356	0	17
76		TOTAL PURCH	597110	7262378	459373	4640451	1231518	175391	806779	4091000	828156
77		DEPRECIATION	233825	674003	234551	293133	64696	30035	41837	877955	439227
78		WAGES	276163	1266419	179482	983016	77400	84521	172138	2786540	118292
79		TURNOVER TAX	112509	112509	126594	0	0	0	42491	0	0
80		OTH NET INC	-7098	1784691	306076	321840	88386	67313	138755	1026495	509525
81		NATIONAL INC	269065	3163619		1304856	165786	151834	353384	1760045	627817
82		TOTAL OUTLAY	1200000	11100000	1000000	6238440	1462000	357560	1202000	6729000	1895200
83		EMPLOYMENT	178.4	818.1	91.2	499.5	50.0	54.6	111.2	1189.0	92.3
84		TOTL CAPITAL	3293316	9493000	2969000	3710548	911211	427250	589258	9145370	5779301
85		BLDGS&STRUCT	2018579	4557200	1978039	2270653	419941	220803	300580	6943256	5068324
86		POWER M&E	23954	267300	50704	41276	27427	4102	8603	79565	33520
87		GENERAL M&E	193680	669300	242332	258965	38726	56995	140534	308253	91760
88		SPECIAL M&E	813150	3863800	572209	1057368	414729	137140	131405	1753054	566027
89		TRANS MSE	154446	104900	87022	71470	7361	4059	3889	33715	10981
90		OTH CAPITAL	84477	30900	27694	10816	3007	4145	4243		8669

(Table 1.1 continued)

SEQ NO.	110 ORDER NO.		OIL REF 10	GAS 11	PEAT 12	OIL SHALES 13	ELEC POWER 14	EN&POW M&E 15	ELTECH M&E 16	CABLE PROD 17	MACH TOOLS 18
1	1	FER ORES	528	7	31	5	699	2580	6790	27	1421
2	2	FER METALS	8807	865	1417	600	9568	240700	309300	9487	63000
3	6	NONFER ORES	0	0	0	0	0	0	0	0	0
4	7	NONFER METAL	0	0	0	175	0	50238	391240	545508	10426
5	3	COKE PROD	9582	1	47		51	1244	10716	97	3250
6	4	REFRAC MAT	298	18	42	3	1709	1079	3811	15	823
7	5	INDMET PROD	1129	142	1126	512	6664	7704	32385	27180	6239
8	8	COAL	323		670	2396	1542408	2598	12341	2006	1653
9	9	OIL EXTRAC	1208540	2079			11233	0	0	0	0
10	10	OIL REF	490124	8688	12052	1368	450405	8203	22666	7094	3291
11	11	GAS	21797	15281	10	2	444147	8224	12898	618	2086
12	12	PEAT	0	8	59790	0	174506	63	45	0	5
13	13	OIL SHALES	931	7509	178	9286	33483	33412	1225	632	167
14	14	ELEC POWER	244789	10509	7449	7117	11456	22994	68396	15759	18908
15	15	EN&POW M&E	23	47	175	10	13064	96575	37193	6	39
16	16	ELTECH M&E	1670	269	538	570	8746	4894	559475	4695	77473
17	17	CABLE PROD	823	173	351	878	2753	433	189208	9968	2707
18	20	MACH TOOLS	11	0	30	3	1		2042	103	14805
19	21	FORG- PR M&E	3	0	64	0	13		1258	104	21
20	22	CAST M&E	1		45	1	4	9	303	0	38
21	23	TOOLS & DIES	482	112	527	59	995	3112	12475	594	9473
22	24	PRECIS INST	1915	137	85	51	3585	11744	37629	199	5844
23	25,26,27	MI&MET M&E	11916	671	7399	1226	19	137	23	11	11
24	28,29	PUMPS&CHEM E	1326	210	13	36	925	6774	3042	56	5659
25	30	LOG&PA M&E	0	0	0	0	4	0	1	0	0
26	31	LT IND M&E	1	0	2	0	0	0	0	423	55
27	32	FD IND M&E	0	0	0	0	0	0	2	0	0
28	33	PRINT M&E	0	0	0	0	0	0		0	0
29	34	HOIST&TRAN E	19	9	189	14	267	66	454	98	1049
30	35	CONST M&E	2	0	275	94	21	0	16	0	0
31	36	CONMAT M&E	2	0	1	6	17	0	725	0	1
32	37,38	TRANS M&E	1	0	0	42	195	208	220	0	20
33	39	AUTOS	454	217	872	170	1208	9431	28694	201	340
34	40	AGRIC M&E	145	115	800	26	559	1723	2060	32	215
35	41	BEARNG	181	224	5666	75	725	3909	18182	184	10420
36	18,19,42,43	RADIO&OTH MB	1978	12	640	343	3528	142176	53838	7002	73189
37	44	SANIT ENG PR	67	285	344	18	246	661	829	47	98
38	45	OTHER METWRS	1679	558	100	183	2342	6558	21941	2983	14834
39	46	METAL STRUCT			1076	3	8	1070	949		106
40	47	REPAIR	9008		911	366	40123	3074	7742	1304	1770
41	48	ABRASV	127	18	53	13	452	1787	73471	512	2922
42	49	MINRL CHEM	499	5	44		473	64	440	163	22
43	50	BASIC CHEM	77054	5972	1901	5383	13866	3401	39712	4098	1374
44	51	ANIL DYE PR	222	3	8	2	59	172	313	1325	23
45	52	SYN R& PLAST	263	18	12	6	3008	1439	131686	101882	2334

Code	Industry	1	2	3	4	5	6	7	8	9
46	SYN FIBERS	0	4	0	0	0	0	9200	3200	0
47	ORGSYN PROD	381C7	3110	27	7	605	632	8421	5761	1024
48	PAINT & LAC	1238	139	355	38	2152	4177	37467	13047	6203
49	RUBBER PROD	2530	429	724	1554	3025	3599	63256	12929	3625
50 54.58.59	OTHER CHEM	1565	117	57	7	183	298	6025	47660	88
51 60	LOGGNG	582	43	1755	1518	801	2018	1748	382	1270
52 61.62	SAW & LUM PR	4037	118	1237	319	1735	8115	33594	19635	7738
53 63	FURNITURE	562	36	220	42	747	1835	2571	265	658
54 64	OTHER WDWK	58	30	22	32	381	136	2320	162	115
55 65	PAPER & PULP	1743	42	68	11	672	1141	38313	6124	831
56 66	WOOD CHEM	5257	1111	12	4	48	201	4912	1509	171
57 67-73	CONST MAT	2096	305	1000	129	3295	2223	7429	405	1587
58 74	GLASS	1923	55	90	18	1176	940	80246	3057	612
59 75-80	TEXTLS	2345	202	826	164	2842	3931	39692	56142	2542
60 81	SEWN GOODS	4670	619	3647	590	5030	3898	17978	1300	2353
61 82	OTH LT IND	1C41	168	636	172	1377	1233	5429	532	592
62 83	FISH PROD	16	0	0	0	1	0	3	0	0
63 84	MEAT PROD	94	0	2	0	18	13	194	9	45
64 85	DAIRY PROD	4090	439	38	60	2090	1192	8271	1649	1063
65 86	SUGAR	0	0	0	0	0	0	23	0	13
66 87-89	FLOUR&BREAD	8	0	0	0	5	0	53	1	4
67 90-94	OTHER FOOD	9415	68	171	68	3311	877	6747	2567	490
68 95	IND NEC	10728	916	779	367	29662	9794	92356	12367	12274
69 96-100	CONST	0	0	0	0	0	0	0	0	0
70 101	CROPS	25	15	142	0	0	0	77	0	11
71 102	ANIMAL HUSB	0	29	0	0	0	0	38	0	0
72 103	FOREST			0	5607		0	0	0	0
73 104-106	TRANS &COM	1507477	722593	63144	0	4119	30268	213683	87911	72977
74 107-109	TRADE & DIST	56C8C6	68	0	39	400	15713	102885	10895	24327
75 110	OTHER BRANCH	50		0		790	2206	3475	0	1199
76	TOTAL PURCH	4457204	605940	179909	41791	2848000	772981	2882352	1031922	477925
77	DEPRECIATION	248442	57021	54935	9448	1159410	74224	140669	27552	56532
78	WAGES	148281	27170	144949	32937	836367	303908	843224	89843	250871
79	TURNOVER TAX	2703000	580000		0	1458000	0	183189	0	0
80	OTH NET INC	705073	183869	61007	38924	1225523	334887	1376566	232683	191872
81	NATIONAL INC	3556354	791039	205956	71861	3519890	638795	2402979	322526	442743
82	TOTAL OUTLAY	8262000	1654000	440800	123100	7527300	1486000	5426000	1382000	977200
83	EMPLOYMENT	115.7	21.2	113.1	25.7	615.7	237.8	659.8	70.3	196.3
84	TOTL CAPITAL	2853202	803118	716846	123290	23661429	976627	1850909	362521	743840
85	BLDGS&STRUCT	1460174	625777	363965	71681	15408323	512730	1034473	171255	361728
86	POWER M&E	33870	18391	8674	542	540858	21876	27393	6163	7066
87	GENERAL M&E	98047	16302	19282	5425	2428135	367114	651890	105893	319407
88	SPECIAL M&E	1196422	136142	240718	42758	456667	59086	97543	74932	39051
89	TRANS M&E	4517	4257	40501	2034	119253	4981	8884	761	3571
90	OTH CAPITAL	10164	2249	37706	850	45193	10840	30726	3517	13017

(Table 1.1 continued)

SEQ NO.	110 ORDER NO.		FORG-PR M&E 19	CAST M&E 20	TOOLS & DIES 21	PRECIS INST 22	MI&MET M&E 23	PUMPS& CHEM E 24	LOG&PA M&E 25	LT IND M&E 26	FD IND M&E 27
1	1	FER ORES	376	50	541	1323	6471	1738	117	684	1040
2	2	FER METALS	19470	1948	119700	48090	239216	163687	12620	33210	44830
3	6	NONFER ORES									0
4	7	NONFER METAL	2574	1499	19615	76224	81927	52666	1881	14004	17515
5	3	COKE PROD	662	145	139	527	3048	2086	269	1944	691
6	4	REFRAC MAT	378	28	117	745	3650	980	47	352	125
7	5	INDMET PROD	1082	256	2204	18106	13734	9008	1545	7717	3603
8	8	COAL	250	320	600	3845	5780	2743	206	1455	772
9	9	OIL EXTRAC				154					0
10	10	OIL REF	1038	180	2148	5165	10296	6674	1272	1964	1336
11	11	GAS	571	75	416	3275	11506	3698	369	1501	342
12	12	PEAT	0	0	17	41	106	0	0	14	1
13	13	OIL SHALES	7	4	20	136	64	178	8	115	100
14	14	ELEC POWER	5658	897	11241	22276	36003	27540	2382	9271	4641
15	15	EN&POW M&E	3	11	13	2020	1459	1377	139	1	274
16	16	ELTECH M&E	9342	1735	4940	67271	12379	155841	6277	11426	21384
17	17	CABLE PROD	477	55	2988	20745	4470	14981	361	942	997
18	20	MACH TOOLS	159	41	639	1140	1128	663	70	211	100
19	21	FORG- PR M&E	1068		45	56	96	26		11	22
20	22	CAST M&E	7	622	306	13	200	10	2	42	18
21	23	TOOLS & DIES	983	294	2771	13489	5871	5454	368	2783	1662
22	24	PRECIS INST	1031	175	168	135420	2500	21262	947	1235	2787
23	25,26,27	MI&MET M&E	70	362	0	71	44666	8		3	4
24	28,29	PUMPS&CHEM E	1196	1	137	501	9986	31482	852	1456	3864
25	30	LOG&PA M&E	0	0	0	4	152	0	3202	2	1
26	31	LT IND M&E	0	0	0	2	1	0	0	21804	196
27	32	FD IND M&E	0	0	0	3	2	46	0	0	4078
28	33	PRINT M&E	0	0	0	7	0			70	4
29	34	HOIST&TPAN E	7	9	22	10	2213	229	194	131	330
30	35	CONST M&E	0	1	0	0	243	1	11	0	1
31	36	CONMAT M&E	0	0	0	0	18	3	4	0	8
32	37,38	TRANS M&E	9	0	4	11	3771	26	0	5	17833
33	39	AUTOS	102	11	85	11147	27782	7888	602	374	6270
34	40	AGRIC M&E	50	3	17	138	14651	2828	5109	50	2266
35	41	BEARNG	831	179	2944	5474	20657	4162	1383	3166	12116
36	18,19,42,43	RADIO&OTH MB	9112	1678	4487	185269	105884	83203	13789	6346	220
37	44	SANIT ENG PR	38	5	117	181	257	633	41	134	3500
38	45	OTHER METWRS	1900	571	7492	3339	18365	13684	779	3891	0
39	46	METAL STRUCT	649	0	0	0	716	52	0	515	357
40	47	REPAIR	511	6	969	1857	5394	1886	209	648	
41	48	ABRASV CHEM	307	73	4120	3445	2076	2351	225	1196	346
42	49	MINRL CHEM	54	0	9	125	56	31	0	114	3
43	50	BASIC CHEM	529	163	1238	10685	4668	8202	273	936	676
44	51	ANIL DYE PR	5	0	16	335	8	375	1	28	3
45	52	SYN R& PLAST	149	36	1333	19367	2008	16915	136	5010	406

#	Code	Branch									
46	53	SYN FIBERS	0	0	0	289	0	0	0	0	37
47	55	ORGSYN PROD	152	17	143	3366	790	2070	31	1148	183
48	56	PAINT & LAC	958	220	713	7154	4831	7418	517	4114	2556
49	57	RUBBER PROD	1054	257	803	5988	16914	10058	981	3501	5684
50	54,58,59	OTHER CHEM	8	11	74	3227	889	217	98	411	261
51	60	LOGGNG	4.8	48	165	2695	2356	2136	357	715	521
52	61,62	SAW & LUM PR	1445	277	2691	17259	5287	9639	1410	10481	4652
53	63	FURNITURE	118	16	88	1589	523	2898	71	13944	121
54	64	OTHER WDWK	16	38	353	4184	198	241	19	159	47
55	65	PAPER & PULP	176	13	1011	6135	796	1781	103	182	223
56	66	WOOD CHEM	48		22	578	67	113	74		29
57	67-73	CONST MAT	321	81	637	3344	2736	3065	253	939	554
58	74	GLASS	181	23	126	16520	1316	4860	96	609	121
59	75-80	TEXTLS	331	64	1241	14430	3118	3368	371	14746	1045
60	81	SEWN GOODS	791	101	1109	5949	4110	3772	444	1841	1132
61	82	OTH LT IND	168	20	858	8103	1036	807	111	1426	515
62	83	FISH PROD	0	0	0	6	2	1	0	6	9
63	84	MEAT PROD	13	4	46	364	37	38	7	102	28
64	85	DAIRY PROD	189	80	348	9109	3910	1370	94	903	174
65	86	SUGAR	0	0		1	21	0	0		3
66	87-89	FLOUR&BREAD	0	1	1	10	7	0	0	8	
67	90-94	OTHER FOOD	101	23	229	1882	719	839	73	748	156
68	95	IND NEC	1704	375	2601	39160	13499	7879	713	3793	3357
69	96-100	CONST	0	0	0	0	0	0	0	0	0
70	101	CROPS	0	0	80	37	67	0	0	49	0
71	102	ANIMAL HUSB	0	0	0	59	0	0	0	0	0
72	103	FOREST	0	0	0	0	0	0	0	0	0
73	104-106	TRANS &COM	10322	5122	37597	148484	121336	69523	2018	32638	26521
74	107-109	TRADE & DIST	1702	443	20206	68230	20980	19600	1808	14040	3559
75	110	OTHER BRANCH	1187	246	122	1822	4293	2702	208	1609	857
76		TOTAL PURCH	82058	18923	262690	1031914	912416	799603	65549	243885	207073
77		DEPRECIATION	14420	2180	22084	76552	99661	61575	9575	22940	13247
78		WAGES	46647	11246	130739	642706	498292	259562	25432	135212	73996
79		TURNOVER TAX	0	0	0	311561	0	158202	0	46986	0
80		OTH NET INC	65075	9351	150487	717267	1189631	521058	26144	153677	121184
81		NATIONAL INC	111722	20597	281226	1671534	1687923	938822	51576	335875	195180
82		TOTAL OUTLAY	208200	41700	566000	2780000	2700000	1800000	126700	602700	415500
83		EMPLOYMENT	36.5	8.8	102.3	502.9	389.9	203.1	19.9	105.8	57.9
84		TOTL CAPITAL	189740	28630	290574	1007268	1311334	810191	125981	301843	174306
85		BLDGS&STRUCT	95647	16118	120153	542817	685500	465069	73787	154604	95851
86		POWER M&E	1803	384	3545	13699	16796	12424	1625	6067	3521
87		GENERAL M&E	73002	9029	153975	389007	475871	260575	39167	118745	62402
88		SPECIAL M&E	11499	2557	7206	30319	104063	51653	8668	17809	8610
89		TRANS M&E	702	173	668	6043	10807	5001	655	875	1098
90		OTH CAPITAL	2087	419	5027	25383	18217	15469	2079	3743	2824

15

(Table 1.1 continued)

SEQ NO.	110 ORDER NO.		PRINT M&E 28	HOIST& TRAN E 29	CONST M&E 30	CONMAT M&E 31	TRANS M&E 32	AUTOS 33	AGRIC M&E 34	BEARNG 35	RADIO& OTH MB 36
1	1	FER ORES	46	1342	1444	725	8117	4967	8927	494	69651
2	2	FER METALS	2230	81500	67680	34550	286289	451200	640200	107200	751323
3	6	NONFER ORES	0	0	0	0	0	0	0	0	0
4	7	NONFER METAL	1201	3741	6274	2975	108630	142147	80232	5765	290370
5	3	COKE PROD	121	695	876	497	1856	6787	12272	12	15602
6	4	REFRAC MAT	42	586	1066	530	4578	2466	5921	116	6001
7	5	INDMET PROD	237	8358	7496	1042	41425	51168	39418	10771	67209
8	8	COAL	148	1213	1651	604	6448	11587	8896	270	26412
9	9	OIL EXTRAC	0	0	0	0	0	0	0	0	401
10	10	OIL REF	452	2047	3694	1388	17327	28137	22641	4149	72420
11	11	GAS	90	2474	2076	827	13378	17796	14383	789	42085
12	12	PEAT	0	0	58	33	454	454	10	0	66
13	13	OIL SHALES	6	107	170	0	194	988	529	482	1040
14	14	ELEC POWER	976	11641	12877	5634	68419	62833	92130	15857	240210
15	15	EN&POW M&E	1	3754	7519	62	263743	1116	3069	9	21000
16	16	ELTECH M&E	2222	73919	22763	11492	277002	76152	64678	1113	291965
17	17	CABLE PROD	247	5411	2340	379	30098	15309	10085	453	248711
18	20	MACH TOOLS	1	529	1021	200	3721	5078	6503	1707	7526
19	21	FORG-PR M&E	22	94	5	54	552	2122	2082	69	3108
20	22	CAST M&E	0	87	30	212	288	1050	2364	0	747
21	23	TOOLS & DIES	336	2384	2881	410	14191	14581	24122	2894	61409
22	24	PRECIS INST	72	2047	2239	827	60444	4331	7037	93	937640
23	25,26,27	MI&MET INST	87	9	0	8	956	37	21	0	91
24	28,29	PUMPS&CHEM E	0	656	5539	338	111916	6590	5818	26	34454
25	30	LOG&PA M&E	0	0	0	0	134	0	0	0	125
26	31	LT IND M&E	0	0	0	0	5	6	0	0	573
27	32	FD IND M&E	0	3	0	0	1165	0	231	0	5161
28	33	PRINT M&E	20	0	0	0	0	9	1	0	0
29	34	HOIST&TRAN E	0	27940	1478	223	27773	2276	282	61	3357
30	35	CONST M&E	0	545	19966	647	129	73	4	0	0
31	36	CONMAT M&E	0	0	2330	2700	23	7	4	0	1627
32	37,3B	TRANS M&E	0	2019	45	10	79849	263	306	122	0
33	39	AUTOS	33	94577	37543	454	9016	962299	51784	54	151050
34	40	AGRIC M&E	1	2565	210392	32	1101	1378	896083	5476	116773
35	41	BEARNG	159	10347	8205	1769	24126	45145	81963	0	31000
36	18,19,42,43	RADIO&CTH MB	0	55865	58692	24970	481726	150593	212128	37	4390864
37	44	SANIT ENG PR	15	353	219	51	3795	1092	3629	3469	14521
38	45	OTHER METWRS	604	5671	6363	1655	28180	30260	44534	1	246377
39	46	METAL STRUCT	0	2531	65	44	2052	8	34	0	3095
40	47	REPAIR	524	2174	1643	640	9326	5376	7250	1122	26400
41	48	ABRASV	86	588	719	168	11163	5650	9338	6665	96572
42	49	MINRL CHEM	0	0	35	63	54	237	58	12	877
43	50	BASIC CHEM	59	1094	1836	722	13848	10693	8388	863	78217
44	51	ANIL DYE PR	0	6	0	0	371	176	3561	68	1005
45	52	SYN R& PLAST	275	1362	1002	34	11211	12694	3071	761	234438

16

Code	Detail	Sector	1	2	3	4	5	6	7	8	9
46		SYN FIBERS	0	0	0	0	738	205	0	0	14727
47	53	ORGSYN PROD	41	745	447	52	2331	6016	4147	257	18294
48	55	PAINT & LAC	253	4847	3814	795	22952	37720	29787	240	69253
49	56	RUBBER PROD	413	21677	35667	1335	17529	461187	179906	2222	338045
50	57 54,58,59	OTHER CHEM	10	79	55	13	2906	353	538	40	6255
51	60	LOGGNG	127	627	609	140	5278	3855	2734	165	9931
52	61,62	SAW & LUM PR	662	5715	3028	1591	34576	33015	48068	2962	113668
53	63	FURNITURE	20	353	337	66	7970	2077	1803	530	9299
54	64	OTHER WDWK	96	198	515	118	241	915	491	331	14538
55	65	PAPER & PULP	9	548	52	23	2067	9287	5142	1983	99351
56	66	WOOD CHEM	66	102	1660	818	638	337	464	52	12271
57	67-73	CONST MAT	66	1357	743	95	19112	7309	4006	457	65785
58	74	GLASS	19	821	1799	1195	10220	21074	3460	103	4452
59	75-80	TEXTILS	227	1657	2130	698	20641	33266	14094	2312	133992
60	81	SEWN GOODS	105	2069	514	148	22966	14086	14328	1715	59128
61	82	OTH LT IND	91	642	38	20	4684	16682	6843	553	33440
62	83	FISH PROD	0	32	595	310	4	6	0	1	13
63	84	MEAT PROD	5	342	0	0	179	225	62	18	831
64	85	DAIRY PROD	512	0	2	17	25848	2373	6133	110	25872
65	86	SUGAR	0	0	230	74	0	2	302	0	36
66	87-89	FLOUR&BREAD	0	292	4962	859	32	13	0	3	94
67	90-94	OTHER FOOD	41	2857	0	0	3402	3141	1676	386	12846
68	95	IND NEC	0	0	0	0	10901	24456	25168	0	40064
69	96-100	CONST	0	0	0	0	0	0	0	0	0
70	101	CROPS	0	0	0	0	47	78	106	0	0
71	102	ANIMAL HUSB	0	0	0	0	0	0	0	0	0
72	103	FOREST	0	0	0	0	10	28	96	0	0
73	104-106	TRANS &COM	2122	39157	47733	12087	51417	292146	302145	70627	325740
74	107-109	TRADE & DIST	1065	5140	6456	2394	19695	120070	36170	17906	266635
75	110	OTHER BRANCH	181	1603	4079	753	2954	6704	16547	0	6557
76		TOTAL PURCH	16580	501097	615789	120581	2314413	3231716	3078215	273954	10272690
77		DEPRECIATION	3029	26773	27338	15012	155838	146862	189025	30288	1049895
78		WAGES	13930	115787	132145	42557	534459	691142	833384	145692	4867007
79		TURNOVER TAX						591680			706382
80		OTH NET INC	18361	187743	222928	64650	795290	703600	659376	98066	607526
81		NATIONAL INC	32291	302930	355073	107207	1329749	1986422	1492760	243758	6180915
82		TOTAL OUTLAY	51900	830800	998200	242800	3800000	5365000	4760000	548000	17503500
83		EMPLOYMENT	10.9	90.6	103.4	33.3	418.2	540.8	652.1	114.0	3808.3
84		TOTL CAPITAL	39857	352273	359714	197530	2050497	1932930	2487177	398526	13814412
85		BLDGS&STRUCT	20135	194490	196368	114192	1300353	885615	1124204	142632	9833188
86		POWER M&E	654	3805	7986	1501	27880	44252	50738	2511	428864
87		GENERAL M&E	15133	119596	122209	63782	484288	870543	1109978	232979	2465855
88		SPECIAL M&E	3201	26104	24857	12642	186879	98937	163160	11837	792999
89		TRANS M&E	68	3029	2122	2035	11507	12367	15420	1633	90628
90		OTH CAPITAL	666	5249	4172	3378	39590	20676	23877	6934	182878

17

(Table 1.1 continued)

SEQ NO.	110 ORDER NO.		SANIT ENG PR 37	OTHER METWRS 38	METAL STRUCT 39	REPAIR 40	ABRASV 41	MINRL CHEM 42	BASIC CHEM 43	ANIL DYE PR 44	SYN R& PLAST 45
1	1	FER ORES	3916	1617	4486	10828	285	41	1635	117	7
2	2	FER METALS	203400	426779	322100	380000	4923	3363	55588	2315	2614
3	6	NONFER ORES	60659	0	0	90478	21416	0	0	0	0
4	7	NONFER METAL	13468	214800	4268	12829	143	305	42265	1024	4300
5	3	COKE PROD	1788	4992	606	7116	161		89090	14633	8149
6	4	REFRAC MAT	7202	912	92	41385	317	45	922	66	4
7	5	INDMET PROD	4208	50366	8136	53145	1531	4088	4905	201	1556
8	8	COAL	0	9378	1440	0		3298	22199	858	2251
9	9	OIL EXTRAC		0	0				1186	0	0
10	10	OIL REF	4248	7778	2722	78237	3043	14690	40546	2341	21244
11	11	GAS	4834	2849	1715	14393	987	3133	47692	2157	1822
12	12	PEAT	0	127	40	29	0		2	0	39
13	13	OIL SHALES	413	648	7	1556	79	3	893	717	67
14	14	ELEC POWER	20211	41814	13532	114336	12146	22408	334347	9546	35657
15	15	EN&POW M&E	424	1623	79	94951	5	22	214	0	3
16	16	ELTECH M&E	7697	20275	3145	159908	964	1623	5759	282	945
17	17	CABLE PROD	749	2636	1401	47603	176	1426	2118	128	271
18	20	MACH TOOLS	267	1077	153	11716	14	29	101	6	4
19	21	FORG- PR M&E	50	1071	82	1384	0	22	36	0	71
20	22	CAST M&E	1054	146	1	358		9	12	0	6
21	23	TOOLS & DIES	1295	5049	1020	21369	345	180	2200	140	366
22	24	PRECIS INST	1569	2087	79	35795	99	182	1925	125	517
23	25,26,27	MI&MET M&E	354	3159	1	36237	1	1968	323	0	0
24	28.29	PUMPS&CHEM E	782	461	26	24855	52	518	7191	606	1723
25	30	LOG&PA M&E	0	4	0	7	0	0	0	0	0
26	31	LT IND M&E	0	1965	0	745	0	0	0	0	0
27	32	FD IND M&E	0	96	0	6779	0	0	6	0	0
28	33	PRINT M&E	0	5	0	48	0	0	0	0	0
29	34	HOIST&TRAN E	13	116	230	5031	5	140	160	5	5
30	35	CONST M&E	0	14	7	77570	7	426	202	0	2
31	36	CONMAT M&E	3	444	5	331	0	55	14	0	0
32	37,38	TRANS M&E	4	1		127286	0	244	139	0	2
33	39	AUTOS	540	6566	369	336847	64	1632	1332	61	141
34	40	AGRIC M&E	317	6468	1330	687192	26	500	201	1	5
35	41	BEARING	527	1982	643	60845	186	221	579	31	74
36	18,19,42,43	RADIO&OTH MB	24476	9525	5344	356788	0		266107	0	6132
37	44	SANIT ENG PR	1061338	4504	3240	6293	54	90	351	31	72
38	45	OTHER METWRS	6650	75367	2477	59053	1660	510	6829	407	1487
39	46	METAL STRUCT	10	96	4364	38547		54	2		
40	47	REPAIR	2270	5787	1501	37063	812	1520	15370	1666	3983
41	48	ABRASV	1307	5934	228	18132	102130	41	380	52	178
42	49	MINRL CHEM	273	805	70	62	41	3732	194926	592	184
43	50	BASIC CHEM	11882	9396	2440	21947	2103	21425	303394	28051	35378
44	51	ANIL DYE PR	118	111	25	267	0	41	3265	60301	1627
45	52	SYN R& PLAST	4116	10733	153	14811	7482	294	4568	348	129409

#	Code	Name									
46	53	SYN FIBERS	0	0	0	0	0	0	0	0	0
47	55	ORGSYN PROD	211	1731	329	6023	1325	7297	61279	23721	281083
48	56	PAINT & LAC	11050	14597	3469	55857	226	297	5411	327	2371
49	57	RUBBER PROD	6223	25032	1053	63247	276	2742	10328	467	3440
50	54,58,59	OTHER CHEM	52	1562	15	2253	38	158	177	118	109
51	60	LOGGNG	522	930	163	12026	60	1336	2240	104	257
52	61,62	SAW & LUM PR	8820	31235	822	95152	658	812	31729	2046	9973
53	63	FURNITURE	304	2319	207	1750	58	122	721	135	209
54	64	OTHER WDWK	57	5100	30	1482	274	67	728	54	344
55	65	PAPER & PULP	1838	24049	124	6314	1001	737	34201	249	13463
56	66	WOOD CHEM	94	224	28	2048	25	809	7956	396	34300
57	67-73	CONST MAT	2617	4545	931	27913	1300	869	10747	564	906
58	74	GLASS	5644	15984	250	10382	296	1390	4923	149	14529
59	75-80	TEXTLS	4394	26841	396	55819	6768	1296	14946	2134	37115
60	81	SEWN GOODS	4361	16194	3200	23746	822	1634	12267	1529	2966
61	82	OTH LT IND	1276	19772	448	14283	146	464	1702	279	673
62	83	FISH PROD	41	5	0	42	7	3	314	393	546
63	84	MEAT PROD	597	251	390	410	924	315	5347	1494	539
64	85	DAIRY PROD	4	3559	0	11482	434	1831	10682	976	2673
65	86	SUGAR	86	0	0	26	0	0	31	1	0
66	87-89	FLOUR&BREAD	897	7	662	45	1	1	21	0	3
67	90-94	OTHER FOOD	3290	2766	1635	6189	954	702	14215	4534	7568
68	95	IND NEC	47	27477	38	63959	0	2697	82288	965	5482
69	96-100	CONST		913		537	0	0	0	0	0
70	101	CROPS					0	14	192	0	0
71	102	ANIMAL HUSB	0	32	0	192	0	0	55	0	0
72	103	FOREST	15253	122945	42408	12306	28786	83828	296452	10575	86392
73	104-106	TRANS &COM	3139	37135	4710	0	522	1400	30372	2473	9648
74	107-109	TRADE & DIST	929	2912	0	14771	15	101	0	0	16
75	110	OTHER BRANCH			14771						
76		TOTAL PURCH	568892	1427680	449118	3582406	206178	199200	2098300	180500	774900
77		DEPRECIATION	40425	79861	38421	470850	14301	67220	290522	18483	43383
78		WAGES	192339	518296	123199	2557789	70290	74976	420684	29832	85404
79		TURNOVER TAX	4000	100000	0	0	0	0	12000	0	41000
80		OTH NET INC	195344	1174163	75162	1614955	84131	81604	601494	55485	287313
81		NATIONAL INC	391683	1792459	198361	4172744	154421	156580	1034178	85317	413717
82		TOTAL OUTLAY	1001000	3300000	685900	8226000	374900	423000	3423000	284300	1232000
83		EMPLOYMENT	150.5	483.8	96.4	2001.4	55.0	56.8	318.7	22.6	64.7
84		TOTL CAPITAL	531902	1050798	505541	6195397	188172	884637	4046296	276176	551656
85		BLDGS&STRUCT	318024	567642	317783	3945440	118265	616503	2316908	178630	313451
86		POWER M&E	9096	19545	9302	142494	3462	12650	53816	7650	4579
87		GENERAL M&E	161006	378286	120177	1450130	44844	36800	330177	13919	42919
88		SPECIAL M&E	34893	59476	48330	381019	17939	181174	1284296	72690	182157
89		TRANS M&E	3245	9772	4296	157363	1600	34679	38844	1574	5681
90		OTH CAPITAL	5638	16077	5359	118951	1994	2931	22255	1713	2869

(Table 1.1 continued)

SEQ NO.	110 ORDER NO.		SYN FIBERS 46	ORGSYN PROD 47	PAINT & LAC 48	RUBBER PROD 49	OTHER CHEM 50	LOGGNG 51	SAW & LUM PR 52	FURNIT URE 53	OTHER WDWK 54
1	1	FER ORES	184	1092	943	1150	121	0	0	0	4
2	2	FER METALS	3747	13746	3417	11073	4599	4023	26945	2984	1510
3	6	NONFER ORES	6	0	85500	0	0	1305	0	788	0
4	7	NONFER METAL	343	21089	21964	446	10517	4	4549	80	439
5	3	COKE PROD	174	110029	532	31	20848	77	67661	46	1
6	4	REFRAC MAT	104	616	486	26890	68		374	26722	682
7	5	INDMET PROD	446	1006	2213	3761	644	17077	17799	10996	1222
8	8	COAL	4397	17884	0	180	2824	4785	23044	0	0
9	9	OIL EXTRAC	0	9252		0	0		0		
10	10	OIL REF	4159	121603	19043	17255	99650	152713	27298	6257	4030
11	11	GAS	1237	37258	1957	3826	5586	5	5424	4459	380
12	12	PEAT	503	6	7	0	228	943	325	211	884
13	13	OIL SHALES	6	45	1071	350	231	17009	4475	614	137
14	14	ELEC POWER	67810	101804	7374	65992	89217	1580	90128	28384	3991
15	15	EN&POW M&E	72	72	389		40	2120	217	24	0
16	16	ELTECH M&E	2030	1875	130	2283	3126	2654	5801	1887	415
17	17	CABLE PROD	352	544	6	916	258	881	2994	810	90
18	20	MACH TOOLS	713	3		55	197	153	6194	1648	53
19	21	FORG-PR M&E	3	7		48	3	13	4	17	0
20	22	CAST M&E	0	0		52					
21	23	TOOLS & DIES	237	193	201	1439	309	5084	2309	1550	108
22	24	PRECIS INST	539	914	107	618	794	377	396	142	0
23	25,26,27	MI&MET M&E	178	178	193	769	1349	63	323	21	35
24	28,29	PUMPS&CHEM E	4153	1759	1	4985	1	24053	2737	103	0
25	30	LOG&PA M&E	0	3		5	6	2		18	111
26	31	LT IND M&E	13403	0		381	24			24	1
27	32	FD IND M&E	0	0		2	16			38	0
28	33	PRINT M&E	0	0		1	2				0
29	34	HOIST&TRAN E	10	9	18	121		1680	765		0
30	35	CONST M&E	2	4	4	0		1256	29		0
31	36	CONMAT M&E	1	1	0	0	11	109	21	11	0
32	37,38	TRANS M&E	8	3	117	90	209	5770	64	843	2
33	39	AUTOS	168	277	13	853	446	55051	5348	208	286
34	40	AGRIC M&E	30	72	78	145	97	44458	2404	239	217
35	41	BEARNG	362	186	4834	366	49126	2728	2045	1322	52
36	18,19,42,43	RADIO&OTH MB	4452	10095	100	17399	116	1627	4038	449	272
37	44	SANIT ENG PR	98	163		192		63	1433		771
38	45	OTHER METWRS	1764	5021	11369	10902	2003	10949	29545	74146	1771
39	46	METAL STRUCT	0	0				13	9348	943	0
40	47	REPAIR	2458	7012	2432	6032	3345	12220	12300	4493	1088
41	48	ABRASV	54	631	90	300	104	687	2271	12461	1336
42	49	MINRL CHEM	2616	2668	9673	3707	2921	22	22	8	128
43	50	BASIC CHEM	75650	99590	24449	29975	141575	773	13143	1794	6504
44	51	ANIL DYE PR	7036	3166	18269	3033	4396	47	370	3222	1
45	52	SYN R& PLAST	188061	6468	60179	11199	7382	9	55147	43728	1192

#	Code	Sector									
46		SYN FIBERS	0	0	0	256672	0	0	0	0	22
47	53	ORGSYN PROD	9736	135975	22053	138286	137271	137	9092	12560	668
48	55	PAINT & LAC	1654	10416	170255	14636	32614	1611	20965	78348	4476
49	56	RUBBER PROD	2685	1799	687	706673	36482	36127	9706	7910	2239
50	57 / 54.58.59	OTHER CHEM	96	2162	296	942819	243770	371	153	3415	56
51	60	LOGGNG	79	1729	574	198	129	230508	2117714	52547	42296
52	61.62	SAW & LUM PR	619	8640	7098	4816	3396	18706	836671	388753	50310
53	63	FURNITURE	268	524	178	473	293	1518	926	29278	15
54	64	OTHER WDWK	102	523	224	331	1700	2153	2699	4737	10861
55	65	PAPER & PULP	117153	17367	5799	3217	15208	285	4328	4839	7440
56	66	WOOD CHEM	916	16156	42442	7746	112705	5976	4478	1366	413
57	67-73	CONST MAT	814	1576	1091	1430	1011	650	12125	2764	233
58	74	GLASS	639	12550	10967	1086	28664	8189	9541	87747	162
59	75-80	TEXTLS	18278	4648	1150	410853	51098	39975	16961	227522	4224
60	81	SEWN GOODS	1854	6111	1597	7728	5322		16853	6303	905
61	82	OTH LT IND	532	972	415	1205	662	9938	4342	8224	2944
62	83	FISH PROD	0	96	785	7	11126	2	7567	42	0
63	84	MEAT PROD	281	2407	1755	586	9568	17	13328	6022	3666
64	85	DAIRY PROD	2203	2968	3445	3921	8150	194		4399	189
65	86	SUGAR	0	8650	0	0	13288	3	0	20	0
66	87-89	FLOUR&BREAD	271	4001	234	48	4343	6	5	2	1008
67	90-94	OTHER FOOD	823	28934	368863	11369	121814	704	3532	1364	290
68	95	IND NEC	1832	2995	11601	8434	32716	2560	17289	25160	720
69	96-100	CONST	0	0	0	0	0	7675	1305	360	0
70	101	CROPS	0	532	510	0	25447				0
71	102	ANIMAL HUSB	0	260	82	0	7863	121	96	0	0
72	103	FOREST	0	0	0	0	170556	192402	0	0	15716
73	104-106	TRANS &COM	92523	74081	71613	137335	290116	1394602	559878	136695	5000
74	107-109	TRADE & DIST	7448	18664	11910	16135	7225	68741	263846	152300	38
75	110	OTHER BRANCH	14	0	0	478		0	0	408	
76		TOTAL PURCH	648000	941900	1112900	2267310	1826990	2396086	4360694	1474775	180908
77		DEPRECIATION	76904	89603	15559	62016	76888	419004	205812	79662	12418
78		WAGES	141758	114312	61776	269148	184272	1649282	1129652	457331	88134
79		TURNOVER TAX	0	27000	22000	205612	141000	481628	339842	200000	116600
80		OTH NET INC	284328	509185	223765	810914	324550	2130910	1469494	157232	-13160
81		NATIONAL INC	426096	650497	307541	1285674	649822			814563	191574
82		TOTAL OUTLAY	1151000	1682000	1436000	3615000	2553700	4946000	6036000	2369000	384900
83		EMPLOYMENT	107.4	86.6	46.8	203.9	139.6	1170.7	1003.3	406.3	78.3
84		TOTL CAPITAL	1051004	1184659	217041	883948	1150383	2831109	2638615	813630	127070
85		BLDGS&STRUCT	577469	689627	142075	462836	683778	1505300	1672870	550989	66941
86		POWER M&E	8292	21551	1671	8486	43971	56339	118489	18958	1919
87		GENERAL M&E	33712	74515	12849	52241	57677	90904	559690	197305	31375
88		SPECIAL M&E	464440	385251	55345	346418	342308	774560	195543	26037	20940
89		TRANS M&E	1309	7345	1888	3448	9040	344262	65971	7404	3265
90		OTH CAPITAL	5782	6160	3213	10519	13609	59736	25052	12937	2630

(Table 1.1 continued)

SEQ NO.	110 ORDER NO.		PAPER & PULP 55	WOOD CHEM 56	CONST MAT 57	GLASS 58	TEXTLS 59	SEWN GOODS 60	OTH LT IND 61	FISH PROD 62	MEAT PROD 63
1	1	FER ORES	372	0	27763	14835	28	5	145	90	90
2	2	FER METALS	3204	731	486449	16472	7320	511	4709	46938	45854
3	6	NONFER ORES	0		0		0	0	0		
4	7	NONFER METAL	6726	676	61183	1482	3377	182	12119	2551	3324
5	3	COKE PROD	115	137	21753	9646	341	1	310	49	5
6	4	REFRAC MAT	210	49	13111	4529	222		82	51	51
7	5	INDMET PROD	2730	265	86820	7893	10658	3	5936	9689	1170
8	8	COAL	67288	12321	244286		23386	484	10122	9964	14236
9	9	OIL EXTRAC	0		0			4462			
10	10	OIL REF	12666	3005	225205	24854	22099	2410	15604	204961	7963
11	11	GAS	5324	2692	150777	25208	14318	807	6763	453	6889
12	12	PEAT	3476	1	7896	4512	4805	377	1233	104	207
13	13	OIL SHALES	914	345	16405	4998	1696	136	568	1314	351
14	14	ELEC POWER	71410	9648	366931	28913	180940	29397	39162	10279	30447
15	15	ENSPOW M&E	222	131	1726	43	582	35	28	6637	85
16	16	ELTECH M&E	1971	295	20699	2630	14100	2874	3317	3666	1716
17	17	CABLE PROD	708	163	11518	780	3484	692	880	4225	849
18	20	MACH TOOLS	25	21	985	117	203	126	216	5	35
19	21	FORG- PR M&E	2	2	586	21	17	0	183	16	11
20	22	CAST M&E	14	1	76	70	31		1	1	3
21	23	TOOLS & DIES	654	83	8611	813	2994	1681	2804	4707	909
22	24	PRECIS INST	594	109	2435	2191	1186	148	371	1049	379
23	25,26,27	MI&MET M&E	27	0	6290	640	209	0	1556	0	0
24	28,29	PUMPS&CHEM E	360	242	1248	22	6	13		938	455
25	30	LOG&PA M&E	3301	43	0	620		0		1	6
26	31	LT IND M&E	4		0	23	83386	6141	8605		13
27	32	FD IND M&E	1	0			1	1	5	8746	2839
28	33	PRINT M&E	20	0		1	2	42	71		0
29	34	HOIST&TRAN E	146	20	3634	111	174	0	3	2204	85
30	35	CONST M&E	9	3	13260	52	4	0		1	5
31	36	CONMAT M&E	1	2	61557	296	27	0	2	0	0
32	37,38	TRANS M&E	68	17	1477	35	18	998	25	1253	6
33	39	AUTOS	560	183	17073	851	1647	5	572	2590	1076
34	40	AGRIC M&E	111	52	8412	204	480	101	314	266	80
35	41	BEARNG	520	53	5283	380	1846	532	332	192	209
36	18,19,42,43	RADIO&OTH MB	1671	262	3620	289	2692	165	649	2430	1080
37	44	SANIT ENG PR	168	31	9818	7758	1013		374	128	266
38	45	OTHER METWRS	1801	300	38770	3280	19417	13944	31388	40911	6851
39	46	METAL STRUCT	14		1250	48	89		22		44
40	47	REPAIR	5339	929	46253	12247	12781	4532	6225	59849	5675
41	48	ABRASV	338	21	1361	3479	823	125	2083	82	78
42	49	MINRL CHEM	14338	182	5909	8764	229	0	2036	7	64
43	50	BASIC CHEM	26380	8424	32314	47239	32919	173	25098	5412	3322
44	51	ANIL DYE PR	1891	4	982	1095	87611	175	17516	13	28
45	52	SYN R& PLAST	1272	343	26452	22155	10688	7484	33319	541	3225

Data table (branch codes, names, and nine value columns):

#	Code	Branch	1	2	3	4	5	6	7	8	9
46	53	SYN FIBERS	0	0	0	0	920194	0	48	1734	0
47	55	ORGSYN PROD	2584	1031	41340	471	29033	177	76731	469	677
48	56	PAINT & LAC	1011	180	7365	3673	5812	1318	10978	4164	1538
49	57	RUBBER PROD	1790	384	46696	2028	27895	11498	35221	5106	1373
50	54.58.59	OTHER CHEM	542	220	2351	556	2351	1234	112402	799	625
51	60	LOGGNG	328121	152182	19264	11972	4942	1212	35267	2767	3694
52	61.62	SAW & LUM PR	5445	13723	89030	30242	17705	2879	18660	148556	24785
53	63	FURNITURE	378	49	3297	607	2690	2621	1353	369	745
54	64	OTHER WDWK	169	79	2747	2687	8760	315	2068	2773	2028
55	65	PAPER & PULP	202488	283	63154	7402	2763	5756	26908	9668	9392
56	66	WOOD CHEM	16935	26157	3369	334	3450	39	9515	250	311
57	67-73	CONST MAT	5003	1759	1937386	18300	7470	1428	3417	3455	3358
58	74	GLASS	2339	508	46381	37812	5357	364	2389	4693	1191
59	75-80	TEXTLS	34746	413	34852	7690	16863387	6802796	678915	151958	7520
60	81	SEWN GOODS	2449	724	43387	5846	18516	12269	8666	29884	7864
61	82	OTH LT IND	2126	281	12875	1026	19369	214245	2340430	11150	2143
62	83	FISH PROD	164	1027	176	4	1336	5	7564	1959049	1287
63	84	MEAT PROD	1513	207	200	44	1704	33	620256	1072	3656762
64	85	DAIRY PROD	7274	295	12939	1044	5361	57	8780	310	5691
65	86	SUGAR	6	396	3	3	25	3	1469	5417	2362
66	87-89	FLOUR&BREAD	7	770	24	21	2219	198	16243	2548	18484
67	90-94	OTHER FOOD	2718	1185	47080	824	35446	663	24426	110618	26308
68	95	IND NEC	3407		105906	12260	90035	4591		694	7181
69	96-100	CONST	0	0	0	0	0	0	1614	0	0
70	101	CROPS	936	454	1125	237	3388572	330		5592	11350
71	102	ANIMAL HUSB	0	51	67	0	1579706	0	474276	896	12419148
72	103	FOREST	0	0	0	0	268161	0	69895	152425	106057
73	104-106	TRANS &COM	133037	22654	3861450	133227	858148	95164	320107	275917	1055745
74	107-109	TRADE & DIST	92778	773	135620	71842	551	501239	24533	478	11208
75	110	OTHER BRANCH	46082	27	22721	2253		306			
76		TOTAL PURCH	1130663	277674	8605000	612000	24742812	7739310	5166878	3325125	17528808
77		DEPRECIATION	120003	25070	781680	55515	274159	94881	71318	273435	72456
78		WAGES	191033	37529	2062637	328427	1796806	1390804	672767	620791	338831
79		TURNOVER TAX	6000	0	38510	195490	8065000	1515005	2804388	432856	0
80		OTH NET INC	195101	51827	1464173	560568	264223	2905809	21649	321793	-3380095
81		NATIONAL INC	402134	89356	3585320	1084485	12506029		3498804	1375440	-3041264
82		TOTAL OUTLAY	1653000	392100	12992000	1752000	37523000	10740000	8737000	4974000	14560000
83		EMPLOYMENT	149.9	29.7	1648.0	284.5	1786.8	1523.0	658.8	285.5	326.1
84		TOTL CAPITAL	1621664	256071	9894681	750204	4153929	1416135	1033592	3255183	1317378
85		BLDGS&STRUCT	784723	140634	6224602	425441	1748866	942177	552243	614904	1015185
86		POWER M&E	88867	23559	132073	11853	59095	6797	15401	19531	16072
87		GENERAL M&E	55656	16337	412168	143514	116756	37103	37107	243246	24504
88		SPECIAL M&E	676093	71855	2889370	152906	2173796	351604	404448	112546	226840
89		TRANS M&E	12325	2355	111567	6452	13777	20534	4651	2240217	20418
90		OTH CAPITAL	4000	1331	124901	9978	41639	57920	19742	24739	14359

23

(Table 1.1 continued)

SEQ NO.	110 ORDER NO.		DAIRY PROD 64	SUGAR 65	FLOUR& BREAD 66	OTHER FOOD 67	IND NEC 68	CONST 69	CROPS 70	ANIMAL HUSB 71	FOREST 72
1	1	FER ORES	138	2284	74	345	2373	0	0	0	0
2	2	FER METALS	29929	5583	4653	44325	100004	1608469	13197	11350	281
3	6	NONFER ORES		0	0	0	0		3739	1455	116
4	7	NONFER METAL	7677	8096	3535	10090	45256	122557			0
5	3	COKE PROD	7	855	83	72	8475	0			0
6	4	REFRAC MAT	78	1341	309	195	1356	138735			
7	5	INDMET PROD	1184	35179	2890	5164	12035	169274			
8	8	COAL	29494	0	46114	41910	61042	71331	11990	8556	342
9	9	OIL EXTRAC			0		1221	873	53152	75546	144
10	10	OIL REF	18176	69900	12635	64941	48834	585478	997945	288786	10196
11	11	GAS	4014	9510	15960	14943	7325	8289	0	0	0
12	12	PEAT	1114	2369	2239	1230	1221	5672	72812	11524	
13	13	OIL SHALES	982	912	434	3602	2442	6980			
14	14	ELEC POWER	36081	20221	55057	72479	113938	297565	86546	99334	890
15	15	EN&POW M&E	199	102	83	454	5292	20505			
16	16	ELTECH M&E	1762	1557	3598	4558	21373	453069	14448	12871	
17	17	CABLE PROD	707	1144	1359	2050	4692	551885	6136	5940	
18	20	MACH TOOLS	2	17	29	87	763	5017			
19	21	FORG- PR M&E	2	25		119	134	0			
20	22	CAST M&E		4	12	17	88				
21	23	TOOLS & DIES	1131	739	1689	1462	2072	51100	15225	12814	379
22	24	PRECIS INST	522	615	670	733	4147	51044	3143	2141	
23	25,26,27	MI&MET M&E					1131	111686			
24	28,29	PUMPS&CHEM E	625	283	144	629	2935	11125			
25	30	LOG&PA M&E	0	0	9	12	403				
26	31	LT IND M&E	408	7		1	470				
27	32	FD IND M&E	8558	4349	10248	7259	147				
28	33	PRINT M&E			96	80	9583				
29	34	HOIST&TRAN E	27	114	555	158	915	30539			
30	35	CONST M&E	0	5	0	1	1358	99688			
31	36	CONMAT M&E	231	1	0	3	814	7417			
32	37,38	TRANS M&E	11	58	10	87	2633	8507			
33	39	AUTOS	4153	1412	458	2415	20042	118884	148641	55881	7512
34	40	AGRIC M&E	163	2140	68	484	22502	62823	583447	128942	4557
35	41	BEAR-G	202	509	439	473	3895	186313	12545	2933	
36	18,19,42,43	RADIO&OTH MB	1177	1120	2200	2727	6042	713800	12893	11003	
37	44	SANIT ENG PR	230	81	456	425	1823	374048			
38	45	OTHER METWRS	8992	1936	11481	64062	6722	590059			
39	46	METAL STRUCT	802	6	50	65	753	199813	118573	90550	
40	47	REPAIR	8244	5432	10260	17204	2834		348949	162572	1191
41	48	ABRASV	87	90	79	206	3306	10034	4379	1535	
42	49	MINRL CHEM	14	1587	99	379	14092	0		67500	
43	50	BASIC CHEM	4797	3687	1541	46862	55144	44282	818236	21409	1190
44	51	ANIL DYE PR	97	136	84	593	6285	7635			
45	52	SYN R& PLAST	663	262	781	6552	191599	17233			

#	Code	Sector	(1)	(2)	(3)	(4)	(5)	(6)	(7)	(8)	(9)
46	53	SYN FIBERS	0	0	0	0	15097	1309	0	0	0
47	55	ORGSYN PROD	274	265	391	51950	52742	41606	13582	2290	0
48	56	PAINT & LAC	1601	1406	2340	5915	33563	419040	7149	5908	0
49	57	RUBBER PROD	2675	2051	3237	5369	26580	138517	153552	55079	0
50	54.58.59	OTHER CHEM	921	48	1166	3705	14675	0	7860	111530	0
51	60	LOGGNG	5152	1088	2559	3334	170	646060	29546	53215	3634
52	61.62	SAW & LUM PR	22422	2846	73075	116901	71523	2312730	55328	83173	1442
53	63	FURNITURE	423	144	987	1089	120055	11998	2335	1570	0
54	64	OTHER WDWK	940	66	2359	12100	17424	23105	2985	7349	34
55	65	PAPER & PULP	17519	5052	43533	96394	213505	3708	2113	1927	0
56	66	WOOD CHEM	159	56	1227	12691	2295	9656129	71892	7504	1208
57	67-73	CONST MAT	3487	22862	4352	8295	45054	501108	9175	111320	0
58	74	GLASS	11355	312	800	97109	7854	183689	87755	13592	0
59	75-80	TEXTILS	5936	12423	16108	218675	243250	346978	34681	40766	0
60	81	SEWN GOODS	6442	4846	28175	14725	63311			65552	2987
61	82	OTH LT IND	1920	1322	3592	3100	26657	39718	25641	38341	0
62	83	FISH PROD	143	37	7809	43564	852	0	1666	88354	0
63	84	MEAT PROD	1993	669	26143	212974	2573	0	0	68230	0
64	85	DAIRY PROD	686147	190	217542	53893	9107	0	0	162590	0
65	86	SUGAR	158509	934084	1033070	846051	1316	0	0	116099	0
66	87-89	FLOUR&BREAD	14655	1394	4625052	81412	264978	1309	6786	322857	0
67	90-94	OTHER FOOD	20586	33821	50564	6608637	32913	146806	8967	131688	968
68	95	IND NEC	32976	0	59405	167626	61584	587317	0	635204	0
69	96-100	CONST	0		0	0	0	0		0	
70	101	CROPS	4221	2413353	6157764	4027612	615522	24300	3617525	11609725	1494
71	102	ANIMAL HUSB	6089364	0	53812	5410	0	6200	298475	2055275	0
72	103	FOREST	118920	183341	225083	658975	130981	47693	800860	114815	12890
73	104-106	TRANS &COM	824502	559007	1394256	2877096	352840	0	2160000	656800	9074
74	107-109	TRADE & DIST	30	15	1250	23230	59008	529500	40740	17460	0
75	110	OTHER BRANCH									
76		TOTAL PURCH	8207164	4364366	14892252	16679285	3284740	22422093	10772349	17650855	60529
77		DEPRECIATION	114744	130072	137617	230345	456384	1837900	2833510	1944575	2015
78		WAGES	303945	150749	796243	885250	1029115	15800000	19861322	18779304	409374
79		TURNOVER TAX	0	3850234	4455024	11681886	382300	0	9826819	0	0
80		OTH NET INC	373147	-632421	-913136	4559234	1884061	3300007		1681266	-31918
81		NATIONAL INC	677092	3368562	4338131	17126370	3295476	19100007	29688141	20460570	377456
82		TOTAL OUTLAY	8999000	7863000	19368000	34036000	7036600	43360000	43294000	40056000	440000
83		EMPLOYMENT	308.7	154.9	808.7	899.1	970.0	9450.0	16183.1	17189.4	427.5
84		TOTL CAPITAL	1365997	1646475	2074742	3472682	6067904	11830000	34858600	32251400	21480
85		BLDGS&STRUCT	824158	880007	1358417	2040494	3455427	3779992	16227389	15013726	9011
86		POWER M&E	40843	140044	32869	83295	196459	153005	286537	265107	154
87		GENERAL M&E	29803	82781	44353	87545	1091898	2329467	1105365	2803498	7466
88		SPECIAL M&E	418329	513606	605593	1190082	506895	4569350	10831922	1052332	2136
89		TRANS M&E	37565	15477	10493	25996	671495	596444	1137400	12094054	570
90		OTH CAPITAL	15299	14160	23017	44670	145630	309682	5269987	1022693	2143

(Table 1.1 continued)

SEQ NO.	110 ORDER NO.		TRANS &COM 73	TRADE & DIST 74	OTHER BRANCH 75	INT IND USE 76	PRIVAT CONSUM 77	PUBLIC CONSUM 78	EXPORT 79	IMPORT 80	GROSS INV 81
1	1	FER ORES	0	0		1060715	0	0	139285	0	0
2	2	FER METALS	41683	7035	224	9807530	4600	341400	1338813	-257974	-214369
3	6	NONFER ORES	20032			1241159	0	0	82071	-323230	0
4	7	NONFER METAL		3416	156	5656955	0	251000	593551	-140419	-122647
5	3	COKE PROD	41018			1336056	0	0	24194		101750
6	4	REFRAC MAT	246966	11724	1312	329939	0	0	13312	-6905	21214
7	5	INDMET PROD		60535	1289	1067346	14400	65600	26609	-10137	38182
8	8	COAL				5635154	166000	681000	222921	-168580	192505
9	9	OIL EXTRAC				1264529	0	0	585709	0	44962
10	10	OIL REF	1516114	98189	4742	6311006	18000	770000	362542	-60089	690541
11	11	GAS	2123	50709	45	1340811	139000	72000	6607		95582
12	12	PEAT	607	5036		365017	0	9200		0	-16217
13	13	OIL SHALES	152	324		118483	0	0		0	4617
14	14	ELEC POWER	457683	154041	9165	5385200	1162000	963000	16474	0	626
15	15	EN&POW M&E	2060			519792	0	0	78607	-41670	929271
16	16	ELTECH M&E	14423	32469	1042	2752210	708000	230000	47526	-68582	1756846
17	17	CABLE PROD	17863	13318	708	1315855	7000	71000	11661	-52497	20981
18	20	MACH TOOLS	1087			81754	0	25000	56945	-54548	868549
19	21	FORG- PR M&E				18300	0	0	8307	-18535	200128
20	22	CAST M&E			1145	10415	0	0	1125	-4707	34867
21	23	TOOLS & DIES	20562	7043	616	384688	0	0	4420	-1365	178257
22	24	PRECIS INST	7320	7996	161	1380047	570000	122000	53711	-68682	716924
23	25.26.27	MI&MET M&E	637		1	497131	0	0	148863	-94596	2148602
24	28.29	PUMP&CHEM E	4993	13446		324035	285000	90000	34854	-186140	1252251
25	30	LOG&PA M&E				39633	0	0	4009	-26143	100201
26	31	LT IND M&E		915		139227	113000	0	8216	-82879	425136
27	32	FD IND M&E				60690	0	0	19228	-57957	393539
28	33	PRINT M&E				10083	0	0	2855	-15372	54334
29	34	HOIST&TRAN E	16154	15105		150915	0	0	44993	-76266	711158
30	35	CONST M&E	1061	92	247	228061	0	0	61305	-14308	723142
31	36	CONMAT M&E	128516			80474	0	41000	10304	-20433	172455
32	37.38	TRANS M&E	276807	20781		372483	0	305000	47050	-509641	3849108
33	39	AUTOS	10631	1881	2890	2529342	1154000	9000	218242	-91971	1250387
34	40	AGRIC M&E	12020	3921		2847602	0	0	143342	-50168	1819024
35	41	BEARING	59369		15	419811	0	0	21150	-3942	101981
36	18.19.42.43	RADIO&OTH MB		16704		7203350	2047000	547000	47602	-171410	7829958
37	44	SANIT ENG PR	22069	2905	59	894123	0	55000	143	-3543	55277
38	45	OTHER METWRS		75987	1124	1763322	885000	228000	5105	-13291	431864
39	46	METAL STRUCT	125839			661553	0	0		-123	24470
40	47	REPAIR				1466734	0	28000		0	6711266
41	48	ABRASV	1169	237	23	422670	0	0	1810	-3606	-45974
42	49	MINRL CHEM				349881	0	78000	99008	-6471	-19418
43	50	BASIC CHEM	17555	3397	8140	2645276	44000	0	128965	-122316	649075
44	51	ANIL DYE PR				238187	5000	0	4676	-6565	41002
45	52	SYN R& PLAST	1000	1000	178	1426929	85000	32000	24401	-58617	-277713

#	Sector	Code	Col1	Col2	Col3	Col4	Col5	Col6	Col7	Col8	Col9
46	SYN FIBERS	53	0	0	9	1224444	135000	0	2378	-44108	-31714
47	ORGSYN PROD	55	8096	1958	271	1401158	10000	30000	21108	-63918	156652
48	PAINT & LAC	56	38367	39815	1174	1298872	74000	172000	11099	-67933	11962
49	RUBBER PROD	57	457943	52105	2164	2607653	542000	408000	36586	-39547	528308
50	OTHER CHEM	54,58,59	535	1519	15126	1555600	137000	749000	66255	-361881	2726
51	LOGGNG	60	83552	35361	351	4267306	59000	346000	226976	-1410	-29872
52	SAW & LUM PR	61,62	68415	137505	1358	5285679	208000	126000	400415	-56801	221707
53	FURNITURE	63	6364	22323	3252	276334	175000	27000	891	-174674	159449
54	OTHER WDWK	64	0	8414	92	138443	0	16000	1772	0	53685
55	PAPER & PULP	65	6890	177114	16722	1555876	153000	88000	103881	-103622	8865
56	WOOD CHEM	66	1965	55	12	359362	425000	0	11000	-15891	37629
57	CONST MAT	67-73	35004	59961	1038	12272000	11544000	288000	29733	-21538	250805
58	GLASS	74	7499	66098	282	1185600	9712000	44000	5255	-8585	100730
59	TEXTLS	75-80	50891	94177	21597	26893020	6493000	504000	641031	-2718540	659489
60	SEWN GOODS	81	77164	124113	2665	1360409	2397000	372000	6235	-1178592	467948
61	OTH LT IND	82	24512	6519	25503	2982571	8973000	81000	83172	-985753	83010
62	FISH PROD	83	0	21000	0	2146193	5900000	266000	61761	-36913	139859
63	MEAT PROD	84	0	156000	28	4796510	4671000	528000	23354	-54612	293748
64	DAIRY PROD	85	0	28969	0	1399237	13644000	886000	48431	-19269	784601
65	SUGAR	86	0	13738	0	3137042	25873000	244000	50861	-377427	137524
66	FLOUR&BREAD	87-89	55	40240	2	5386043	3525000	529000	32952	-129973	-94022
67	OTHER FOOD	90-94	14044	8269	211	8637975	0	311000	162189	-730112	-218052
68	IND NEC	95	30670	219761	286461	3386900	7853000	538000	57538	-140174	-326664
69	CONST	9G-100	0	0	0	0	13488000	124000	0	0	43360000
70	CROPS	101	6154	79930	0	32005492	0	370000	270920	-961991	4002579
71	ANIMAL HUSB	102	1	1474	0	22993657	0	0	69080	-251509	3386772
72	FOREST	103	0	0	15900	221194	0	0			218806
73	TRANS &COM	104-106	53577	144145	47096	19100000	2208000	214000			
74	TRADE &DIST	107-109	0	0	264700	15730000			38177	-16698	44624
75	OTHER BRANCH	110	0	92978	12619	1291897					
76	TOTAL PURCH		4038232	2317827	902415	257156640	127640000	12360000	7213561	-11455049	88379848
77	DEPRECIATION		2845900	1186000	35000	22310000	5560000	4440000	0	0	0
78	WAGES		5045359	6552046	1187424	105339696					
79	TURNOVER TAX		6170509	5664127	1655161	39580904					
80	OTH NET INC		12215868	12226173	2842585	56907764					
81	NATIONAL INC		19100000	15750000	3780000	201826360					
82	TOTAL OUTLAY					481295000					
83	EMPLOYMENT		4588.7	6896.6	977.5	84377.9					
84	TOTL CAPITAL		4144000	1938200	537520	298000000					
85	BLDGS&STRUCT		2694173	14420569	248697	172529890					
86	POWER M&E		126017	120626	2456	8864747					
87	GENERAL M&E		4295903	1003568	90763	29976514					
88	SPECIAL M&E		715507	1482781	79472	48870390					
89	TRANS M&E		9115661	445417	87239	17254616					
90	OTH CAPITAL		236739	1009039	28893	20583843					

(Table 1.1 continued)

SEQ NO.	110 ORDER NO.		TOTAL FD 82	GVO 83
1	1	FER ORES	139285	1200000
2	2	FER METALS	1212470	11100000
3	6	NONFER ORES	-241159	1000000
4	7	NONFER METAL	581485	6238440
5	3	COKE PROD	125944	1462000
6	4	REFRAC MAT	27621	357560
7	5	INDMET PROD	134654	1202000
8	8	COAL	1093846	6729000
9	9	OIL EXTRAC	630671	1895200
10	10	OIL REF	1950994	8262000
11	11	GAS	313189	1654000
12	12	PEAT	75783	440800
13	13	OIL SHALES	4617	123100
14	14	ELEC POWER	2142100	7527300
15	15	EN&POW M&E	966208	1486000
16	16	ELTECH M&E	2673790	5426000
17	17	CABLE PROD	66145	1382000
18	20	MACH TOOLS	895946	977200
19	21	FORG- PR M&E	189900	208200
20	22	CAST M&E	31285	41700
21	23	TOOLS & DIES	181312	566000
22	24	PRECIS INST	1393953	2780000
23	25,26,27	MI&MET M&E	2202869	2700000
24	28,29	PUMPS&CHEM E	1475965	1800000
25	30	LOG&PA M&E	87067	126700
26	31	LT IND M&E	463473	602700
27	32	FD IND M&E	354810	415500
28	33	PRINT M&E	41817	51900
29	34	HOIST&TRAN E	679885	830800
30	35	CONST M&E	770139	998200
31	36	CONMAT M&E	162326	242800
32	37,38	TRANS M&E	3427517	3800000
33	39	AUTOS	2835658	5365000
34	40	AGRIC M&E	1912198	4760000
35	41	BEAR&G	128169	548000
36	18,19,42,43	RADIO&OTH MB	10300150	17503500
37	44	SANIT ENG PR	106877	10010000
38	45	OTHER METWRS	1536678	3300000
39	46	METAL STRUCT	24347	685900
40	47	REPAIR	6739266	8226000
41	48	ABRASV	-47770	374900
42	49	MINRL CHEM	73119	423000
43	50	BASIC CHEM	777724	3423000
44	51	ANIL DYE PR	46113	284300
45	52	SYN R& PLAST	-194929	1232000

46	53	SYN FIBERS	-73444	1151000
47	55	ORGSYN PROD	280842	1682000
48	56	PAINT & LAC	137128	1436000
49	57	RUBBER PROD	1007347	3615000
50	54.58.59	OTHER CHEM	998100	2553700
51	60	LOGGNG	678694	4946000
52	61.62	SAW & LUM PR	750321	6036000
53	63	FURNITURE	2092666	2369000
54	64	OTHER WDWK	246457	384900
55	65	PAPER & PULP	97124	1653000
56	66	WOOD CHEM	32738	392100
57	67-73	CONST MAT	700000	12972000
58	74	GLASS	566400	1752000
59	75-80	TEXTLS	10629980	37523000
60	81	SEWN GOODS	9379591	10740000
61	82	OTH LT IND	5754429	8737000
62	83	FISH PROD	2827807	4974000
63	84	MEAT PROD	9763490	14560000
64	85	DAIRY PROD	7599763	8999000
65	86	SUGAR	4725958	7863000
66	87-89	FLCUR&BREAD	13981957	19368000
67	90-94	OTHER FOOD	25398025	34036000
68	95	IND NEC	3651700	7038600
69	96-100	CONST	43360000	43360000
70	101	CROPS	11288508	43294000
71	102	ANIMAL HUSB	17062343	40056000
72	103	FOREST	218806	440000
73	104-106	TRANS &COM	0	19100000
74	107-109	TRADE & DIST	0	15730000
75	110	OTHER BRANCH	2488103	3780000
76		TOTAL PURCH	224138360	481295000
77		DEPRECIATION	10000000	32310000
78		WAGES		
79		TURNOVER TAX		
80		OTH NET INC		
81		NATIONAL INC		
82		TOTAL OUTLAY		
83		EMPLOYMENT		
84		TOTL CAPITAL		
85		BLDGS&STRUCT		
86		POWER M&E		
87		GENERAL M&E		
88		SPECIAL M&E		
89		TRANS M&E		
90		OTH CAPITAL		

Source: B. Kostinsky, The Reconstructed 1966 Soviet Input–Output Table: Revised Purchasers' and Producers' Price Table, U.S. Department of Commerce, F.D.A.D., Foreign Economic Report No. 13, Washington, D.C.: Government Printing Office, 1976 (as revised by the authors).

Quadrant III shows value-added in four separate categories: depreciation charges; wages and salaries, including premia and bonuses; turnover taxes collected; and other net income, which incorporates social security payments, income-in-kind and money income of kolkhoz members, profits of state enterprises, net income of kolkhozes and other cooperatives, and miscellaneous elements of income. Row 81 shows the sum of the value-added elements excluding depreciation or total national income; and row 82 gives the total outlays of the producing sectors, which equal their gross outputs.

The table also includes an employment vector and a fixed capital stock matrix. Row 83 shows employment in each producing sector in terms of man-years. The total value of fixed capital in each sector is given in row 84, and this is broken down by types of capital in the subsequent rows. A description of these categories is given in Treml et al. (1972, Ch. 11). In brief, the six categories listed here incorporate the following types in the published matrix:

1. Buildings, specialized structures, and transmission facilities used for production purposes;
2. Power-generating equipment and machinery;
3. General machinery and equipment, which includes such general purpose industrial equipment as electrical apparatus, instruments, machine tools, forging, pressing, and casting equipment, and other general purpose tools;
4. Specialized machinery and equipment, which incorporates specialized equipment for specific industries such as mining, metallurgy, chemical, printing, food industry, and so on;
5. Transportation machinery and equipment, for railway, highway, and waterway transport;
6. Other fixed capital such as livestock and long-term plantings.

The format of the producers' prices table (Table 1.2) is the same as that of the purchasers' prices table except for the recording of turnover taxes and foreign trade. Turnover taxes removed from each sector's purchases are placed in a newly created row, turnover taxes on purchases, which is shown in the first quadrant, and these values are included in the total purchases subtotal for each sector. The turnover tax row in the value-added quadrant is retained but with zero entries for all 75 producing sectors and a single entry in column 76 showing the total value of turnover taxes. The other entries in column 76 are zeros. The only purpose of the turnover tax row and column is to retain the value of turnover taxes in total national income. Exports and imports are not shown in the

TABLE 1.2

The Reconstructed Soviet 1966 Input-Output Table in Producers' Prices
(thousands of rubles; employment in thousands of man-years)

SEQ NO.	110 ORDER NO.		FER ORES 1	FER METALS 2	NONFER ORES 3	NONFER METAL 4	COKE PROD 5	REFRAC MAT 6	INDMET PROD 7	COAL 8	OIL EXTRAC 9
1	1	FER ORES	1491	581895	0	12386	0	27078	2104	230	38
2	2	FER METALS	10392	1385408	21160	62500	1520	0	44645	24610	2266
3	6	NONFER ORES	0	0	1000	1092505	810	0	21788	4005	0
4	7	NONFER METAL	4704	947804	4567	1712707	74282	4999	1158	409	82
5	3	COKE PROD	8284	575932	0	116260	425	2820	1122	154	38
6	4	REFRAC MAT	4622	83642			681	826			
7	5	INDMET PROD	12840	46791	4615	2512		4693	17325	19267	1014
8	8	COAL	0	296572		18259	640031	0	2442	1289087	51
9	9	OIL EXTRAC		0			0		0	0	9410
10	10	OIL REF	5515	46802	3654	25385	958	3213	3523	4780	11294
11	11	GAS	0	41695	0	1899	2632	1995	927	160	2877
12	12	PEAT	0	533	0	1460	834	0	0	335	0
13	13	OIL SHALES	283	2599	233			10	10	190	92
14	14	ELEC POWER	105638	242685	96880	455887	26523	11054	32007	176112	65238
15	15	EN&POW M&E	545	1642	372	249	36	26	13	388	265
16	16	ELTECH M&E	5480	18235	6979	7255	835	886	1544	12024	1532
17	17	CABLE PROD	2925	8778	3065	2204	270	341	578	27934	1192
18	20	MACH TOOLS	96	790	321	58	57	1	72	144	16
19	21	FORG- PR M&E	139	446	658	367	11	0	204	59	0
20	22	CAST M&E	301	695	384	399	3	2	4	6	0
21	23	TOOLS & DIES	2269	2295	2690	3004	104	129	675	4716	530
22	24	PRECIS INST	1105	3339	878	1990	190	98	138	2524	442
23	25,26,27	MI&MET M&E	27144	91543	22620	22814	1264	925	2033	78440	7973
24	28,29	PUMPS&CHEM E	525	1825	1148	323	494	36	10	362	1099
25	30	LOG&PA M&E	35		29	0	0	0	0	6	0
26	31	LT IND M&E	0		0	0	0	3	0	0	0
27	32	FD IND M&E	0	6	0	0	1	0	0	0	0
28	33	PRINT M&E	0	28	0	0	0	0	0	1	0
29	34	HOIST&TRAN E	231	1326	382	135	77	66	63	1129	21
30	35	CONST M&E	5405	915	2026	334	7	334	1	1376	3
31	36	CONMAT M&E	128	569	163	170	187	535	0	5	0
32	37,38	TRANS M&E	2437	1663	1441	1145	69	136	69	1017	2
33	39	AUTOS	5696	3953	3370	2677	26	210	211	857	694
34	40	AGRIC M&E	2080	602	2012	791	103	129	8	1399	548
35	41	BEARNG	1157	4954	771	1689	821	176	401	1118	156
36	18,19,42,43	RADIO&OTH MB	5267	17250	6279	7401	129	787	1344	8218	1116
37	44	SANIT ENG PR	325	1320	313	693	544	57	130	666	43
38	45	OTHER METWRS	6528	15021	6651	7478	110	373	2642	12928	911
39	46	METAL STRUCT		795	352	396		2	2	841	9
40	47	REPAIR	2288	91081	14169	31068	10311	3910	3351	20841	2935
41	48	ABRASV	2418	10344	1609	3528	24	1369	784	364	198
42	49	MINAL CHEM	359	3300	295	1853	70	374	396	351	21
43	50	BASIC CHEM	12668	116244	10437	65284	14578	3874	11664	45952	3071
44	51	ANIL DYE PR	31	293	26	164	1	1	1	108	2
45	52	SYN R& PLAST	328	3013	270	1692	67	21	461	211	268

31

(Table 1.2 continued)

No.	Code	Item									
46	53	SYN FIBERS	49	453	40	254	0	0	80	0	0
47	55	ORGSYN PROD	689	6312	566	3545	136	544	77	2798	3095
48	56	PAINT & LAC	621	5690	510	3196	1074	202	481	1957	503
49	57	RUBBER PROD	3879	35539	3191	19959	1483	1057	831	29596	1432
50	54.58.59	OTHER CHEM	95	878	78	492	7	24	13	4091	81
51	60	LOGGNG	15579	0	12982	0	167	816	1114	208629	372
52	61.62	SAW & LUM PR	5184	11929	5282	5938	402	727	11555	58695	728
53	63	FURNITURE	402	1499	386	854	90	90	298	1161	150
54	64	OTHER WDWK	154	1411	126	793	32	45	271	685	73
55	65	PAPER & PULP	415	3808	341	2138	358	360	1591	366	127
56	66	WOOD CHEM	276	2526	227	1418	860	442	10	27	118
57	67-73	CONST MAT	3809	8765	3881	4364	504	822	1121	18910	559
58	74	GLASS	995	4033	954	2111	194	95	502	724	163
59	75-80	TEXTLS	3264	15043	1662	9182	673	607	42776	4961	1227
60	81	SEWN GOODS	8386	38635	4268	23585	999	1730	4809	42806	2212
61	82	OTH LT IND	1598	7368	813	4498	348	228	400	6641	719
62	83	FISH PROD	2	12	1	7	3	0	0	0	0
63	84	MEAT PROD	79	363	39	222	3	25	3	1	2
64	85	DAIRY PROD	3007	13854	1529	8458	893	185	329	649	728
65	86	SUGAR	4	21	2	13	0	12	0	0	0
66	87-89	FLOUR&BREAD	45	213	23	130	0	0	0	3	0
67	90-94	OTHER FOOD	1217	5610	618	3425	145	371	3219	3320	327
68	95	IND NEC	41751	140709	35170	61463	10485	5943	13602	44727	1954
69	96-100	CONST	0	0	0	0	0	0	16	0	
70	101	CROPS	145	669	74	409	0	45	0	673	61
71	102	ANIMAL HUSB	59	272	30	165	0	0	0	0	0
72	103	FOREST	0	0	0	0	0	0	0	0	0
73	104-106	TRANS &COM	25900	720491	18754	263513	270703	20478	53997	119225	7767
74	107-109	TRADE & DIST	3711	134841	2950	89506	33521	2130	15388	9578	2631
75	110	OTHER BRANCH	-7064	182829	158887	102841	88416	66524	2121		15
76		TAX ON PURCH	-16698	65494	-14230	-60557	327	4167	-1305	39557	13011
77		TOTAL PURCH	365261	6065893	302287	4218843	1103034	112644	707129	2343118	153502
78		DEPRECIATION	233825	674003	234551	293133	64646	30335	41837	877955	439227
79		WAGES	276163	1266419	179482	983016	77400	84521	172138	2786540	118292
80		TURNOVER TAX	0	0	0	0	0	0	0		
81		OTH NET INC	-7064	1805984	158887	327792	88416	66524	139365	-980190	509556
82		NATIONAL INC	269099	3072403	338369	1310808	165816	153045	311503	1806350	627848
83		TOTAL OUTLAY	868185	9812299	875207	5822784	1333546	296024	1060469	5027423	1220577
84		EMPLOYMENT	178.4	818.1	91.2	499.5	50.0	54.6	111.2	1189.0	92.3
85		TOTL CAPITAL	3293316	9493000	296000	3710548	911211	427250	589256	9145370	5779301
86		BLDGS&STRUCT	2018579	4557200	1970039	2270653	419941	220803	300580	6943256	5061324
87		POWER M&E	23954	267300	5704	41276	27427	4102	8803	79565	33520
88		GENERAL M&E	198660	669000	242332	250065	38726	569995	140538	308253	91780
89		SPECIAL M&E	813160	3663800	574209	1057368	414729	137146	131405	1753054	566027
90		TRANS M&E	154446	104800	87022	71470	7381	4059	3889	27527	10981
91		OTH CAPITAL	84477	30900	27694	10816	3007	4145	4243	33715	8669

SEQ NO.	110 ORDER NO.		OIL REF 10	GAS 11	PEAT 12	OIL SHALES 13	ELEC POWER 14	EN&POW M&E 15	ELTECH M&E 16	CABLE PROD 17	MACH TOOLS 18
1	1	FER ORES	381	5	22	3	504	1862	4901	19	1025
2	2	FER METALS	7863	772	1265	535	8542	214911	276162	8470	56250
3	6	NONFER ORES	0	0	0	163	0	0	0	0	0
4	7	NONFER METAL	8752	0	0	0	0	46902	365262	509287	9733
5	3	COKE PROD	246	14	42	0	46	1136	9788	88	2968
6	4	REFRAC MAT	1643	131	34	473	1415	893	3157	12	681
7	5	INDMET PROD	222	744	1040	1654	6160	7121	29936	25125	5767
8	8	COAL			462	537	6961	1793	8519	1384	1141
9	9	OIL EXTRAC	749305	13683			1064793	0	0	0	0
10	10	OIL REF	291161	5161	4731		176805	3251	8897	2784	1292
11	11	GAS	21797	15281	2	0	87131	1613	2530	121	409
12	12	PEAT	0	6	59790	0	145585	3	37	600	4
13	13	OIL SHALES	885	7139	69	9286	31833	59	1164	15165	158
14	14	ELEC POWER	204015	8758	6208	5931	9547	32154	65820	5	18196
15	15	EN&POW M&E	22	45	170	9	12739	22422	36268	4485	38
16	16	ELTECH M&E	1595	256	513	544	6355	92262	534494	9298	74013
17	17	CABLE PROD	767	161	327	819	2568	4565	176506	93	2525
18	20	MACH TOOLS	9	0	27	0	11	392	1850	98	13413
19	21	FORG- PR M&E	2	0	60	0	1	0	1194	0	19
20	22	CAST M&E	0	0	39	0	3	7	266		33
21	23	TOOLS & DIES	433	100	473	53	893	2796	11208	533	8511
22	24	PRECIS INST	1801	128	79	47	3373	11049	35403	187	5498
23	25,26,27	MI&MET M&E	11343	638	7043	1167	18	130	21	10	10
24	28,29	PUMPS&CHEM E	268	200	12	34	885	6482	2911	53	5415
25	30	LOG&PA M&E	0	0	2	2	3	0	0	0	53
26	31	LT IND M&E	0	0	0	0	0	0	9	397	0
27	32	FD IND M&E	0	0	1	0	0	0	0	0	0
28	33	PRINT M&E	0	0	0	0	0	0	1	0	0
29	34	HOIST&TRAN E	18	8	180	13	254	62	432	93	999
30	35	CONST M&E	1	0	260	89	19	0	15	0	0
31	36	CONMAT M&E	1	0	0	5	16		686	0	0
32	37,38	TRANS M&E	0	0	859	41	192	205	216	0	19
33	39	AUTOS	423	202	746	158	1127	8799	26771	187	317
34	40	AGRIC M&E	134	106	5270	24	519	1602	1916	29	199
35	41	BEARNG	151	34	537	62	608	3280	15256	154	8743
36	18,19,42,43	RADIO&OTH MB	1929	218	335	334	3442	138717	52528	6831	71408
37	44	SANIT ENG PR	65	11	98	17	241	648	813	46	96
38	45	OTHER METWRS	1605	272	1029	175	2239	6272	20984	2852	14187
39	46	METAL STRUCT	0	0	0	0	0	996	883	0	98
40	47	REPAIR	8994	557	909	365	40062	3069	7730	1302	1767
41	48	ABRASV	117	16	48	12	417	1650	67840	472	2698
42	49	MINRL CHEM	399	3	35	0	378	51	351	130	17
43	50	BASIC CHEM	70030	5427	1727	4892	12602	3091	36092	3724	1248
44	51	ANIL DYE PR	212	2	7	1	56	164	300	1270	22
45	52	SYN R& PLAST	243	16	11	5	2782	1331	121833	94259	2159

(Table 1.2 continued)

No.	Code	Industry									
46	53	SYN FIBERS	0	2961	0	3	0	0	8430	2932	0
47	55	ORGSYN PROD	36282	131	25	6	576	601	8017	5485	974
48	56	PAINT & LAC	1174	410	336	36	2041	3963	35548	12379	5885
49	57	RUBBER PROD	2422	693	693	1488	2896	3446	60572	12380	3471
50	54,58,59	OTHER CHEM	1305	97	47	5	152	248	5024	39746	73
51	60	LOGGNG	413	30	1246	1078	568	1433	1241	271	901
52	61,62	SAW & LUM PR	3534	103	1083	279	1519	7104	29412	17191	6774
53	63	FURNITURE	492	31	192	36	654	1608	2253	232	576
54	64	OTHER WDWK	62	27	38	29	351	125	2140	149	106
55	65	PAPER & PULP	1515	36	59	3	584	992	33310	5324	722
56	66	WOOD CHEM	4964	1047	11	89	45	189	4629	1422	161
57	67-73	CONST MAT	1459	212	696	16	2293	1547	5171	281	1104
58	74	GLASS	1746	49	81	162	1068	853	72691	2776	555
59	75-80	TEXTLS	2322	200	818	584	2814	3893	39512	55607	2517
60	81	SEWN GOODS	4622	612	3610	584	4979	3858	17795	1286	2329
61	82	OTH LT IND	1028	165	628	169	1359	1217	5361	525	584
62	83	FISH PROD	15	0	0	0	17	12	2	0	1
63	84	MEAT PROD	93	0	0	0	0	0	192	8	44
64	85	DAIRY PROD	4031	432	37	59	2060	1175	8153	1625	1047
65	86	SUGAR	0	0	0	0	0	0	21	0	12
66	87-89	FLOUR&BREAD	7	0	0	0	4	0	51	0	3
67	90-94	OTHER FOOD	8836	62	158	63	2577	797	6175	2409	452
68	95	IND NEC	10424	890	756	356	28823	9517	89744	12017	11926
69	96-100	CONST	0	0	0	0	0	0	0	0	0
70	101	CROPS	23	14	133	0	0	0	72	0	10
71	102	ANIMAL HUSB	0	28	0	0	0	0	0	0	0
72	103	FOREST	0	0	0	0	0	0	37	0	0
73	104-106	TRANS &COM	498189	10538	4889	2227	751701	42973	147781	44497	20737
74	107-109	TRADE & DIST	176214	3335	1302	325	92375	10744	33162	21741	4859
75	110	OTHER BRANCH	45	61	0	35	711	1986	3128	0	1079
76		TAX ON PURCH	40754	1746	5331	1647	310148	6950	14971	3239	2556
77		TOTAL PURCH	2188883	83314	116732	36157	2843446	726971	2565745	933085	380587
78		DEPRECIATION	248442	57021	54935	9448	1159410	74224	140669	27552	56532
79		WAGES	148281	27170	144949	32937	836367	303908	843224	89643	250871
80		TURNOVER TAX	0	0	0	0	1225558	335741	1379364	235931	195764
81		OTH NET INC	722300	183902	61040	38951	0	0	0	200	0
82		NATIONAL INC	870581	211072	205989	71888	2061925	639649	2222588	325774	446635
83		TOTAL OUTLAY	3307906	351407	377656	117493	6064781	1440844	4929002	1286411	883754
84		EMPLOYMENT	115.7	21.2	113.1	25.7	615.7	237.8	659.8	70.3	196.3
85		TOTL CAPITAL	2823202	803118	716846	123290	23661429	976627	1850909	362521	743840
86		BLDGS&STRUCT	1480174	625777	369965	71681	15408323	512730	1034473	171255	361728
87		POWER M&E	33878	18391	8674	542	5203858	21076	27393	6163	7066
88		GENERAL M&E	98047	16302	19282	5425	2428135	367114	651890	105893	319407
89		SPECIAL M&E	1196422	136142	240718	42758	456667	59046	97543	74932	39051
90		TRANS M&E	4517	4257	40501	2034	119253	4901	8884	761	3571
91		OTH CAPITAL	10164	2249	37706	850	45193	10840	30726	3517	13017

SEQ NO.	110 ORDER NO.		FORG-FR M&E 19	CAST M&E 20	TOOLS & DIES 21	PRECIS INST 22	MI&MET M&E 23	PUMPS& CHEM E 24	LOG&PA M&E 25	LT IND M&E 26	FD IND M&E 27
1	1	FER ORES	271	36	390	954	4670	1254	84	493	750
2	2	FER METALS	17384	1739	106875	42937	213586	146149	11267	29651	40026
3	6	NONFER ORES	2403	0	0	0		0	0	0	0
4	7	NONFER METAL	604	1399	18312	71162	76487	49169	1756	13074	16352
5	3	COKE PROD	313	132	126	481	2784	1905	245	1775	631
6	4	REFRAC MAT	1000	236	96	617	3023	811	38	291	103
7	5	INDMET PROD	172	220	2037	16737	12695	8327	1428	7133	3330
8	8	COAL	0	0	414	2654	3990	1893	142	1004	532
9	9	OIL EXTRAC				95		0	0	0	0
10	10	OIL REF	407	70	842	2027	4041	2619	499	771	524
11	11	GAS	112	14	61	642	2257	725	72	294	67
12	12	PEAT	6	0	14	34	88	0	0	11	0
13	13	OIL SHALES		3	19	129	60	169	7	109	95
14	14	ELEC POWER	5444	863	10817	21437	34647	26503	2292	8922	4466
15	15	EN&POW M&E	444	10	12	1977	1422	1342	135	0	267
16	16	ELTECH M&E	8924	1657	4719	64267	11826	148882	5996	10915	20429
17	17	CABLE PROD	444	51	2787	19352	4169	13975	336	878	930
18	20	MACH TOOLS	144	37	578	1032	1021	600	63	191	90
19	21	FORG-PR M&E	1014		42	53	91	24	0	10	20
20	22	CAST M&E		547	269	11	175	8	1	36	15
21	23	TOOLS & DIES	883	264	2489	12119	5274	4900	330	2500	1493
22	24	PRECIS INST	970	164	158	127412	2352	20004	891	1161	2622
23	25,26,27	MI&MET M&E	66	2	0	67	42521	7	815	1393	3697
24	28,29	PUMPS&CHEM E	1144	346	131	479	9956	30128			
25	30	LOG&PA M&E	0	0	0	3	148	0	3135		
26	31	LT IND M&E	0	0	0	1	0	0	0	2048	184
27	32	FD IND M&E	0	0	1	2	1	0	0		3825
28	33	PRINT M&E	0	0	0	6		44	0	67	3
29	34	HOIST&TRAN E	6	8	20	9	2108	218	184	124	314
30	35	CONST M&E	0	0	0	0	230	0	10		0
31	36	CONMAT M&E	0	0	0	0	17	2	3	0	7
32	37,38	TRANS M&E	8	0	3	10	3718	25		4	0
33	39	AUTOS	95	10	79	10400	25920	7359	561	348	16638
34	40	AGRIC M&E	46	2	15	128	13628	2630	4752	46	5832
35	41	BEARNG	697	150	2470	4593	17333	3492	1160	2656	1901
36	18,19,42,43	RADIO&OTH MB	8890	1637	4377	180762	103308	81179	13453	6191	11821
37	44	SANIT ENG PR	37	4	114	177	252	621	40	131	215
38	45	OTHER NETWRS	1817	546	7155	3193	17564	13087	745	3721	3347
39	46	METAL STRUCT	604	0	0	0	666	48	0	479	3
40	47	REPAIR	510	5	957	1854	5385	1883	208	647	356
41	48	ABRASV	283	67	3804	3180	1916	2170	207	1104	319
42	49	MINRL CHEM	43	0	7	99	44	24	0	91	2
43	50	BASIC CHEM	480	148	1125	9711	4242	7454	248	850	614
44	51	ANIL DYE PR	4	0	15	321	7	359	0	26	2
45	52	SYN R& PLAST	137	33	1233	17918	1857	15649	125	4635	375

(Table 1.2 continued)

No.	Code	Item									
46	53	SYN FIBERS	0	0	0	264	0	0	0	0	33
47	55	ORGSYN PROD	144	16	136	3204	752	1970	29	1093	174
48	56	PAINT & LAC	908	208	676	6787	4583	7038	490	3903	2425
49	57	RUBBER PROD	1009	246	773	5733	15334	9640	939	3352	5442
50	54,58,59	OTHER CHEM	6	9	61	2691	741	180	81	342	217
51	60	LOGGNG	296	34	117	1913	1673	1516	253	507	370
52	61,62	SAW & LUM PR	1265	242	2356	15110	4628	8439	1234	9176	4072
53	63	FURNITURE	103	14	77	1393	458	2540	62	12224	106
54	64	OTHER WDWK	14	5	325	3860	182	222	17	146	43
55	65	PAPER & PULP	153	33	878	5333	692	1548	89	878	193
56	66	WOOD CHEM	45	12	20	544	63	106	69	171	27
57	67-73	CONST MAT	223	56	443	2327	1904	2133	176	653	385
58	74	GLASS	164	20	114	15005	1195	4414	87	553	109
59	75-80	TEXTLS	327	63	1229	14193	3088	3335	367	14605	1035
60	81	SEWN GOODS	782	99	1097	5888	4068	3733	439	1822	1120
61	82	OTH LT IND	165	19	847	8002	1023	797	109	1408	508
62	83	FISH PROD	12	3	45	5	1	37	6	5	8
63	84	MEAT PROD	186	78	343	361	3854	1843	92	101	27
64	85	DAIRY PROD	0	0	0	8979	19	0	0	890	171
65	86	SUGAR	0	0	0	0	6	0	0	0	0
66	87-89	FLOUR&BREAD	0	21	212	9	658	724	65	7	2
67	90-94	OTHER FOOD	93	364	2527	1620	13117	7656	692	0	0
68	95	IND NEC	1655	0	75	38052	63		0	601	143
69	96-100	CONST	0	0	0	34				3685	3262
70	101	CROPS	0	0	0					46	0
71	102	ANIMAL HUSB	0	0	0	57	0	0	0	0	0
72	103	FOREST	0	0	0	0	0	0	0	0	0
73	104-106	TRANS &COM	4193	818	14447	40584	51489	40466	3468	11968	10710
74	107-109	TRADE & DIST	1061	205	4250	8634	12630	9310	841	3723	2653
75	110	OTHER BRANCH	1068	221	109	1640	3865	2432	187	1448	771
76		TAX ON PURCH	763	120	1295	3897	8861	4648	652	1647	748
77		TOTAL PURCH	70005	13329	205055	815161	770062	710365	61692	197170	176954
78		DEPRECIATION	14420	2180	22084	76552	99661	61575	9575	22940	13247
79		WAGES	46647	11246	130739	642706	498292	259562	25432	135212	73996
80		TURNOVER TAX	0			0	0	0	0	0	0
81		OTH NET INC	65947	9899	150608	721325	1193776	528172	26520	157949	124469
82		NATIONAL INC	112594	21145	281347	1364031	1692068	787734	51952	293161	198465
83		TOTAL OUTLAY	197019	36654	508486	2255744	2561791	1559674	123219	513271	388666
84		EMPLOYMENT	36.5	8.8	102.3	502.9	389.9	203.1	19.9	105.0	57.9
85		TOTL CAPITAL	189740	20680	290574	1007268	1311334	810191	125981	301843	174306
86		BLDGS&STRUCT	95647	16118	120153	542817	685500	465069	73787	154604	95851
87		POWER M&E	1803	384	3545	13699	16790	12424	1625	6067	3521
88		GENERAL M&E	78002	9029	153975	389007	475071	260575	39167	118745	62402
89		SPECIAL M&E	11499	2557	7206	30319	104063	51653	8668	17809	8610
90		TRANS M&E	702	173	668	6043	10087	5001	655	875	1098
91		OTH CAPITAL	2087	419	5027	25383	18217	15469	2079	3743	2824

SEQ NO.	110 ORDER NO.		PRINT M&E 28	HOIST& TRAN E 29	CONST M&E 30	CONMAT M&E 31	TRANS M&E 32	AUTOS 33	AGRIC M&E 34	BEARNG 35	RADIO& OTH MB 36
1	1	FER ORES	33	958	1042	523	5859	3585	6443	356	50275
2	2	FER METALS	1991	72758	60428	30848	255616	402859	571610	95714	670827
3	6	NONFER ORES	0	0	0	0	0	0	0	0	0
4	7	NONFER METAL	1121	3492	5857	2777	101417	132708	74904	5382	271090
5	3	COKE PROD	110	634	800	453	1695	6199	11209	10	14251
6	4	REFRAC MAT	34	485	863	439	3792	2042	4905	96	4971
7	5	INDMET PROD	219	7726	6929	963	38293	47299	36438	9956	62128
8	8	COAL	102	837	1139	416	4451	7999	6141	186	18233
9	9	OIL EXTRAC	0	0	0	0	0	0	0	0	248
10	10	OIL REF	177	803	1450	544	6801	11045	8887	1628	28182
11	11	GAS	17	485	407	162	2624	3491	2821	154	7328
12	12	PEAT	0	0	48	0	378	8	8	0	55
13	13	OIL SHALES	5	101	161	31	184	939	502	458	988
14	14	ELEC POWER	939	11202	12391	5421	65842	60467	88661	15259	226477
15	15	EN&POW M&E	0	3660	7332	60	257189	1088	2992	8	20478
16	16	ELTECH M&E	2122	70616	21746	10978	264633	72751	61790	1063	278928
17	17	CABLE PROD	230	5047	2182	353	28077	14281	9407	422	232014
18	20	MACH TOOLS	0	479	925	181	3371	4600	5891	1546	6818
19	21	FORG- PR M&E	20	89	4	51	524	2014	1976	65	2950
20	22	CAST M&E	0	76	26	186	253	923	2079	0	657
21	23	TOOLS & DIES	301	2141	2588	368	12750	13100	21672	2600	55174
22	24	PRECIS INST	67	1925	2106	778	58869	4074	6620	87	882197
23	25,26,27	MI&MET M&E	0	8	0	7	910	35	19	0	86
24	28,29	PUMPS&CHEM E	83	627	5300	323	107104	6306	5567	24	33068
25	30	LOG&PA M&E	0	0	0	0	131	2	0	0	122
26	31	LT IND M&E	0	0	0	0	4	5	216	0	538
27	32	FD IND M&E	0	2	0	0	1092	0	0	0	4841
28	33	PRINT M&E	19	0	0	0	0	8	268	0	0
29	34	HOIST&TRAN E	0	26619	1408	212	26460	2168	3	58	3198
30	35	CONST M&E	0	517	18946	613	122	69	0	0	0
31	36	CONMAT M&E	0	1990	2204	2554	21	6	3	0	1539
32	37,38	TRANS M&E	0	88241	44	9	78741	259	301	1	0
33	39	AUTOS	30	2385	35028	423	8412	897635	48315	113	140931
34	40	AGRIC M&E	0	8682	195706	29	1024	1281	833535	50	108622
35	41	BEARNG	133	54506	6884	1484	20244	37881	68776	4594	26012
36	18,19,42,43	RADIO&OTH MB	0	346	57264	24362	470008	146930	206968	0	4284062
37	44	SANIT ENG PR	14	5423	214	50	3725	1072	3562	36	14255
38	45	OTHER METWRS	577	2357	6085	1582	26951	28941	42592	3317	235638
39	46	METAL STRUCT	0	2170	60	40	1911	7	31	0	2882
40	47	REPAIR	523		1540	639	9312	5367	7239	1120	26360
41	48	ABRASV	79	542	663	155	10307	5217	8622	6154	89171
42	49	MINRL CHEM	0	1	27	50	43	189	46	9	701
43	50	BASIC CHEM	53	994	1668	656	12585	9900	7623	784	71087
44	51	ANIL DYE PR	0	5	0	0	355	168	3415	65	963
45	52	SYN R& PLAST	254	1260	927	31	10372	11929	2841	704	216698

(Table 1.2 continued)

#	Code										
46	53	SYN FIBERS	0	0	0	0	676	187	0	0	13495
47	55	ORGSYN PROD	39	709	425	49	2219	5727	3948	244	17417
48	56	PAINT & LAC	240	4598	3618	754	21776	35788	28262	227	65707
49	57	RUBBER PROD	395	20757	34154	1278	16785	441623	172274	2127	323705
50	54.58.59	OTHER CHEM	8	65	45	10	2423	294	448	33	5216
51	60	LOGGNG	90	445	432	99	3748	2737	1941	117	7052
52	61.62	SAW & LUM PR	579	5003	2651	1392	30272	28905	42085	2593	99519
53	63	FURNITURE	17	309	295	57	6987	1820	1580	464	8152
54	64	OTHER WDWK	1	182	84	9	222	844	453	305	13415
55	65	PAPER & PULP	83	476	447	102	1797	8074	4470	1724	86378
56	66	WOOD CHEM	8	96	49	21	601	317	437	49	11565
57	67-73	CONST MAT	45	944	1155	569	13305	5088	2788	318	45797
58	74	GLASS	108	745	674	86	9283	19142	3142	93	4043
59	75-80	TEXTLS	224	1641	1781	1183	20444	32949	13959	2289	132716
60	81	SEWN GOODS	103	2048	2108	690	22733	13943	14182	1697	58528
61	82	OTH LT IND	89	634	507	146	4626	16475	6758	546	33026
62	83	FISH PROD	0	0	0	0	3	5	61	0	12
63	84	MEAT PROD	4	31	37	19	177	223	6045	17	824
64	85	DAIRY PROD	603	337	586	305	25481	2339	283	108	25504
65	86	SUGAR	0	0	0	0	1	1	0	0	33
66	87-89	FLOUR&BREAD	0	0	1	16	31	12	210	0	91
67	90-94	OTHER FOOD	35	266	207	70	3061	2904	1526	2	9843
68	95	IND NEC	0	2776	4821	834	10592	23764	24456	349	38930
69	96-100	CONST	0	0	0	0	0	0	0	0	0
70	101	CROPS	0	0	0	0	44	73	99	0	0
71	102	ANIMAL HUSB	0	0	0	0	9	27	93	0	0
72	103	FOREST	0	0	0	0	0	0	0	0	0
73	104-106	TRANS &COM	838	26054	33017	6421	106445	171880	177001	13797	434998
74	107-109	TRADE & DIST	218	5000	5826	1562	23163	33082	37594	3988	84365
75	110	OTHER BRANCH	162	1443	3672	677	2659	6035	14897	0	5903
76		TAX ON PURCH	224	1999	2465	967	13255	18159	16170	2287	58004
77		TOTAL PURCH	13366	456769	561569	106067	2243270	2819464	2739860	185393	9680281
78		DEPRECIATION	3029	26773	27338	15012	155838	146862	189025	30288	1049995
79		WAGES	13930	115787	132145	42557	534459	691142	833384	145692	4867007
80		TURNOVER TAX	0	0	0	0	0	0	0	0	0
81		OTH NET INC	18872	190466	223633	65621	801401	709158	662567	98598	610850
82		NATIONAL INC	32802	306253	355778	108178	1335860	1400300	1495951	244290	5477857
83		TOTAL OUTLAY	49197	789795	944685	229257	3734968	4366626	4424836	459971	16200033
84		EMPLOYMENT	10.9	90.6	103.4	33.3	418.2	540.8	652.1	114.0	3808.3
85		TOTL CAPITAL	39857	352273	359714	197530	2050497	1932390	2487177	398526	13814412
86		BLDGS&STRUCT	20135	194490	196368	114192	1300353	885615	1124204	142632	9033188
87		POWER M&E	654	3805	7986	1501	27880	44252	50738	2511	428864
88		GENERAL M&E	15133	119596	124209	63782	484288	989937	1109778	232379	2465855
89		SPECIAL M&E	3201	26104	24057	12642	186879	99937	163160	11837	792939
90		TRANS M&E	68	3029	2122	2035	11507	12367	15420	1633	90628
91		OTH CAPITAL	666	5249	4172	3378	39590	20676	23077	6934	182678

SEQ NO.	110 ORDER NO.		SANIT ENG PR 37	OTHER METWRS 38	METAL STRUCT 39	REPAIR 40	ABRASV 41	MINRL CHEM 42	BASIC CHEM 43	ANIL DYE PR 44	SYN R& PLAST 45
1	1	FER ORES	2826	1167	3238	7815	205	29	1180	84	5
2	2	FER METALS	816C8	381054	287590	339287	4395	3002	49632	2066	2333
3	6	NONFER ORES	56601	200537	0	84470	19994	0	39458	956	4014
4	7	NONFER METAL	12302	4559	553	11718	130	278	81379	13366	7443
5	3	COKE PROD	1481	755	76	5895	763	37	763	54	3
6	4	REFRAC MAT	6657	46558	7520	38256	293	3773	4534	185	1438
7	5	INDMET PROD	2904	6474	954	36688	1056	2276	15324	592	1553
8	8	COAL									
9	9	OIL EXTRAC								0	0
10	10	OIL REF	1667	3053	1068	30712	1194	5766	15916	919	8339
11	11	GAS	948	559	336	2823	193	614	9356	423	357
12	12	PEAT	332	105	33	24	0	0	1	0	32
13	13	OIL SHALES		616	6	1479	75	21563	849	681	63
14	14	ELEC POWER	19450	40240	13032	110032	11688	21	321760	9186	34314
15	15	ENSPOW M&E	413	1502	77	92591	4	1550	208	0	2
16	16	ELTECH M&E	7353	19369	3004	152768	920	1350	5501	269	902
17	17	CABLE PROD	698	975	1306	44407	164	26	1975	119	252
18	20	MACH TOOLS	241	1016	138	10614	5	20	91	5	3
19	21	FORG- PR M&E	47		77	1314	13		34	0	67
20	22	CAST M&E	927	128	0	314	0	7	10	0	5
21	23	TOOLS & DIES	1163	4636	916	19199	309	161	1976	125	328
22	24	PRECIS INST	1476	1563	74	33678	93	171	1811	117	486
23	25.26.27	MISMET M&E	537	3007	0	34497	0	1873	307	0	0
24	28.29	PUMPS&CHEM E	748	441	24	23786	49	495	6881	579	1648
25	30	LOG&PA M&E	0	3	0	6	0	0	0	0	0
26	31	LT IND M&E	0	1845	0	699	0	0	0	0	0
27	32	FD IND M&E	0	90	0	6359	0	0	5	0	0
28	33	PRINT M&E		4		45					4
29	34	HOIST&TRAN E	12	710	219	4793	4	133	152	4	1
30	35	CONST M&E	0	13	6	73607	6	404	191	0	0
31	36	CONMAT M&E	2	420	4	313	0	52	13	0	0
32	37.38	TRANS M&E	3	0	3	125519	0	240	137	8	1
33	39	AUTOS	503	6126	344	314281	59	1522	1242	56	131
34	40	AGRIC M&E	294	6016	1237	639225	24	465	186	26	4
35	41	BEARNG	442	1563	539	51055	156	185	485		62
36	18.19.42.43	RADIO&OTH NB	23380	9293	5214	348109	53	88	259634	30	5982
37	44	SANIT ENG PR	104194	4421	3180	6177	1587	487	344	389	70
38	45	OTHER METWRS	6360	72082	2369	56479	0	50	6531	1	1422
39	46	METAL STRUCT	9	89	4064	35899			1		
40	47	REPAIR	2266	5778	1498	37007	810	1517	15347	1663	3977
41	48	ABRASV	1206	5479	210	16742	94303	37	350	48	164
42	49	MINRL CHEM	218	643	55	49	32	3732	155904	473	147
43	50	BASIC CHEM	10799	8539	2217	19946	1911	19472	275741	25494	32153
44	51	ANIL DYE PR	113	106	23	256	0	39	3131	57836	1560
45	52	SYN R& PLAST	3808	5929	141	13702	6922	272	4226	321	119727

(Table 1.2 continued)

	Code		C1	C2	C3	C4	C5	C6	C7	C8	C9
46	53	SYN FIBERS	0	0	0	0	0	0	0	0	0
47	55	ORGSYN PROD	200	1648	313	5734	1261	6947	58344	22585	267622
48	56	PAINT & LAC	10484	13849	3291	52997	214	281	5133	310	2249
49	57	RUBBER PROD	5959	23970	1008	60564	264	2625	9889	447	3294
50	54.58.59	OTHER CHEM	43	1302	12	1878	31	131	147	98	90
51	60	LOGGNG	370	660	115	8540	42	948	1590	73	182
52	61.62	SAW & LUM PR	7722	27347	719	83308	576	710	27779	1791	8731
53	63	FURNITURE	266	2033	181	1534	50	106	632	118	183
54	64	OTHER WDWK	52	4706	27	1367	252	61	671	49	317
55	65	PAPER & PULP	1598	20908	107	5489	870	640	29735	216	11705
56	66	WOOD CHEM	88	211	26	1930	23	762	7498	373	32328
57	67-73	CONST MAT	1821	3164	682	19432	905	604	7481	392	630
58	74	GLASS	5126	14518	227	9430	268	1262	4471	135	13197
59	75-80	TEXTLS	4352	26585	392	52287	6703	1283	14803	2113	36761
60	81	SEWN GOODS	4316	16029	3167	23505	813	1617	12142	1513	2935
61	82	OTH LT IND	1260	19527	442	14106	144	458	1680	275	664
62	83	FISH PROD	0	4	0	40	6	2	301	377	524
63	84	MEAT PROD	40	249	0	406	916	312	5304	1482	534
64	85	DAIRY PROD	588	3508	384	11319	427	1805	10530	962	2635
65	86	SUGAR	0	0	0	24	0	0	29	0	0
66	87-89	FLOUR&BREAD	3	6	0	43	0	0	20	0	2
67	90-94	OTHER FOOD	817	2376	801	5629	706	575	10616	4110	6514
68	95	IND NEC	3196	26699	1588	62150	0	2620	79960	937	5326
69	96-100	CONST	0	0	0	0	0	0	0	0	0
70	101	CROPS	44	859	35	505	0	13	180	0	0
71	102	ANIMAL HUSB	0	31	0	187	0	0	53	0	0
72	103	FOREST	31	0	0	0	0	0	0	0	0
73	104-106	TRANS &COM	34319	72910	32133	219908	12305	9517	137471	9714	37724
74	107-109	TRADE & DIST	8682	22601	8919	42768	1236	1874	15885	1167	5790
75	110	OTHER BRANCH	836	2621	0	13298	13	90	0	0	14
76		TAX ON PURCH	3910	5445	2041	36054	2037	7001	45792	2115	9883
77		TOTAL PURCH	550470	1167568	401968	3570067	176642	113938	1771437	167426	678826
78		DEPRECIATION	40425	79861	38421	470850	14301	67220	290522	18483	43383
79		WAGES	192339	618296	123199	2557789	70290	74976	420684	29832	85404
80		TURNOVER TAX	0	0	0	0	0	0	0	0	0
81		OTH NET INC	199427	1174688	75201	1614988	84433	82912	611795	55749	291399
82		NATIONAL INC	391766	1792984	198400	4172777	154723	157888	1032479	85581	376803
83		TOTAL OUTLAY	982661	3040413	638789	8213694	345866	339046	3094438	271490	1099012
84		EMPLOYMENT	150.5	483.8	96.4	2001.4	55.0	56.8	318.7	22.6	64.7
85		TOTL CAPITAL	531902	1050798	505541	6195397	188172	804637	4046296	276176	551656
86		BLDGS&STRUCT	318024	567642	317783	3945440	110285	616503	2316908	176630	313451
87		POWER M&E	9096	19545	9302	142494	3462	12650	5816	7650	4579
88		GENERAL M&E	161006	378286	120471	1450130	44842	36800	330177	13919	42919
89		SPECIAL M&E	34893	59476	48330	381019	17989	181174	1284296	72690	182157
90		TRANS M&E	3245	9772	4296	157363	1600	34679	38844	1574	5681
91		OTH CAPITAL	5638	16077	5359	118951	1994	2831	22255	1713	2869

SEQ NO.	110 ORDER NO.		SYN FIBERS 46	ORGSYN PROD 47	PAINT & LAC 43	RUBBER PROD 49	OTHER CHEM 50	LOGGNG 51	SAW & LUM PR 52	FURNIT URE 53	OTHER WDWK 54
1	1	FER ORES	132	788	630	830	87	0	0	0	2
2	2	FER METALS	3545	12273	3050	9886	4106	3591	24058	2664	1348
3	6	NONFER ORES	320	19668	79823	0	0	1218	4246	735	0
4	7	NONFER METAL	158	103506	20063	407	9818	3	61805	42	409
5	3	COKE PROD	86	510	440	25	19043	63	309	66	1
6	4	REFRAC MAT	412	929	449	24857	56	15786	16453	24701	630
7	5	INDMET PROD	3035	12346	1527	2596	595	3303	15908	7591	843
8	8	COAL		5733		111	1949				0
9	9	OIL EXTRAC									
10	10	OIL REF	1632	47735	7475	6773	39117	59946	10715	2456	1581
11	11	GAS	242	7305	384	750	1095	0	1064	874	74
12	12	PEAT	419	5	5	0	190		271	176	737
13	13	OIL SHALES	5	42	1018	332	219	896	4254	583	130
14	14	ELEC POWER	65257	97971	7096	63507	84843	14175	75116	23656	3326
15	15	EN&POW M&E	1939	70	371	2181	39	1540	211		396
16	16	ELTECH M&E	328	179	121	854	2986	2025	5541	1802	83
17	17	CABLE PROD	645	507	0	49	240	2475	2793	755	48
18	20	MACH TOOLS	2	2	0	45	6	798	5611	1493	0
19	21	FORG- PR M&E	0	6	0	45	187	145	3	16	0
20	22	CAST M&E		0			2	11			0
21	23	TOOLS & DIES	212	173	180	1292	277	4567	2074	1392	97
22	24	PRECIS INST	507	659	100	581	747	354	372	133	1
23	25.26.27	MI&MET M&E	0	169	184	732	1291	60	309	0	33
24	28.29	PUMPS&CHEM E	3974	1683	0	4770	0	23356	2680	20	108
25	30	LOG&PA M&E	0	0	0	4	5	2	1		
26	31	LT IND M&E	12590	0	0	357	22	0	0	16	0
27	32	FD IND M&E	0	0	0	1	15	0		0	0
28	33	PRINT M&E	0			0	6			22	0
29	34	HOIST&TRAN E	9	8	17	115	1	1600	728	36	0
30	35	CONST M&E	1	3	3	0		1191	27		0
31	36	CONMAT M&E	0	0	0	0	0	103	19	0	0
32	37.38	TRANS M&E	7	2	0	88	10	5689	63	10	266
33	39	AUTOS	156	258	109	795	194	51363	4989	786	201
34	40	AGRIC M&E	27	66	12	134	414	41354	2236	193	43
35	41	BEAR-NG	303	156	65	307	81	2289	1715	200	265
36	18,19,42,43	RADIO&OTH MB	4343	9849	4716	16975	47931	1587	3939	1289	69
37	44	SANIT ENG PR	96	160	98	188	113	61	1406	440	1693
38	45	OTHER METWRS	1687	4802	10873	10426	1915	10471	28257	70914	0
39	46	METAL STRUCT	0	0				12	8705	878	1086
40	47	REPAIR	2454	7001	2428	6022	3339	12201	12281	4486	
41	48	ABRASV	49	582	83	277	96	634	2096	11506	1233
42	49	MINRL CHEM	2092	2149	7736	2964	2336	8	17		102
43	50	BASIC CHEM	68754	90512	22220	27242	128671	702	11945	1630	5911
44	51	ANIL DYE PR	6748	3036	17522	2909	4216	45	354	3090	
45	52	SYN R& PLAST	173990	5984	55676	10361	6829	8	51021	40456	1102

(Table 1.2 continued)

#	Code		1	2	3	4	5	6	7	8	9
46	53	SYN FIBERS	0	0	0	235201	0	0	0	0	20
47	55	ORGSYN PROD	9326	129463	116208	131663	130697	130	8656	11958	636
48	56	PAINT & LAC	1578	9682	161538	13886	30944	1528	19891	74336	4246
49	57	RUBBER PROD	2571	1722	657	67675	34934	34594	9294	7574	2144
50	54.58.59	OTHER CHEM	80	1803	246	786269	204961	309	127	2847	46
51	60	LOGGNG	56	1227	407	140	91	163706	1504001	37318	30038
52	61.62	SAW & LUM PR	541	7564	6214	4216	2973	16377	732532	340365	44048
53	63	FURNITURE	234	459	156	414	256	1330	811	25667	13
54	64	OTHER WDWK	94	482	206	305	1568	1986	2490	4371	10022
55	65	PAPER & PULP	101856	15099	5041	2796	13222	247	3762	4207	6468
56	66	WOOD CHEM	863	15227	40002	7300	106627	506	4220	1287	389
57	67-73	CONST MAT	566	1097	759	995	703	4160	8441	1924	162
58	74	GLASS	580	11399	1139	986	26036	590	8666	79704	147
59	75-80	TEXTLS	18104	4603	1580	406943	50611	8111	16799	225356	4183
60	81	SEWN GOODS	1835	6049	409	7649	5268	39569	16682	6239	895
61	82	OTH LT IND	525	959	753	1190	653	9815	4288	8122	2907
62	83	FISH PROD	278	92	1741	581	10686	16	0	40	0
63	84	MEAT PROD	1974	2388	3396	3865	9492	191	7507	5974	3637
64	85	DAIRY PROD	0	2925	15	15	8034	2	13138	4336	186
65	86	SUGAR	263	8122	227	46	12277	5	4	18	0
66	87-89	FLOUR&BREAD	665	3883	349756	10634	4214	648	3232	1	978
67	90-94	OTHER FOOD	1780	27134	11272	8195	89239	2487	16800	1180	221
68	95	IND NEC	0	2910	0	0	31790	7221	1227	24448	699
69	96-100	CONST	0	500	573	0	23942	118	93	338	0
70	101	CROPS	0	253	80		7672				0
71	102	ANIMAL HUSB									0
72	103	FOREST									0
73	104-106	TRANS &COM	34777	82632	49922	107641	79795	188436	714002	84459	20846
74	107-109	TRADE & DIST	9014	16353	13673	105163	42025	114884	50437	19566	3160
75	110	OTHER BRANCH	12		0	430	6522	17257	0	367	34
76		TAX ON PURCH	4470	58430	8886	9822	68135	54650	26244	8511	2218
77		TOTAL PURCH	547998	848322	1029346	2113804	1366254	932707	3536937	1185749	160162
78		DEPRECIATION	76904	89603	15559	62016	76888	419004	205812	79662	12418
79		WAGES	141768	114312	61776	269148	184272	1649282	1129652	457331	88134
80		TURNOVER TAX									0
81		OTH NET INC	287773	512002	227078	812524	346833	482061	345094	167450	-13130
82		NATIONAL INC	429541	626314	288854	1081672	531105	2131343	1474746	624781	75004
83		TOTAL OUTLAY	1054443	1564239	1333759	3257492	1974247	3483054	5217495	1890192	247584
84		EMPLOYMENT	107.4	86.6	46.8	203.9	139.6	1170.7	1003.3	406.3	78.3
85		TOTL CAPITAL	1091004	1184659	217041	803948	1150383	2831109	2638615	813630	127070
86		BLDGS&STRUCT	577469	689027	142075	462036	683378	1505300	1672870	550989	66941
87		POWER M&E	8292	21561	1671	8466	43971	56339	118489	18958	1919
88		GENERAL M&E	33712	74515	12849	52241	57677	90904	559690	197305	31375
89		SPECIAL M&E	464440	395251	55345	346418	342308	774568	196543	26037	20940
90		TRANS M&E	1309	7345	1808	3448	9040	344202	65971	7404	3265
91		OTH CAPITAL	5762	6160	3213	10519	13609	59736	25052	12937	2630

SEQ NO.	110 ORDER NO.		PAPER & PULP 55	WOOD CHEM 56	CONST MAT 57	GLASS 58	TEXTLS 59	SEWN GOODS 60	OTH LT IND 61	FISH PROD 62	MEAT PROD 63
1	1	FER ORES	268	0	20040	10708	20	3	104	64	64
2	2	FER METALS	2860	652	434331	14707	6535	456	4204	41909	40941
3	6	NONFER ORES	0	0	0	0	0	0	0	0	0
4	7	NONFER METAL	6279	631	57120	0	3152	169	11314	2381	3103
5	3	COKE PROD	105	125	19870	1353	311	2	283	44	4
6	4	REFRAC MAT	173	40	10861	7991	183	0	67	42	42
7	5	INDMET PROD	2523	244	80256	4186	9852	447	5407	8956	1081
8	8	COAL	46451	8505	168641	5448	17525	3080	6987	6878	9827
9	9	OIL EXTRAC	0	0	0	0	0	0	0	0	0
10	10	OIL REF	4972	1179	88403	9756	8675	946	6125	80457	3125
11	11	GAS	1044	527	29579	4945	2808	158	1326	88	1351
12	12	PEAT	2899	328	6587	3764	4008	314	1028	86	172
13	13	OIL SHALES	868	8041	15596	4751	1612	129	540	1249	333
14	14	ELEC POWER	59515	127	322481	24097	66921	10872	14484	3802	11260
15	15	EN&POW M&E	216	281	1683	41	567	34	27	6472	82
16	16	ELTECH M&E	1882	152	9774	2512	13470	2745	3168	3502	1639
17	17	CABLE PROD	660	19	10744	727	3250	645	820	3941	792
18	20	MACH TOOLS	22	0	892	106	183	114	195	4	31
19	21	FORG- PR M&E	1		556	19	16	5	173	15	10
20	22	CAST M&E	12		66	61	27	0		0	2
21	23	TOOLS & DIES	587	74	7736	730	2690	1510	2519	4229	816
22	24	PRECIS INST	558	102	2291	2061	1115	139	349	986	356
23	25,26,27	MI&MET M&E	25		5987	612	200	12		897	0
24	28,29	PUMPS&CHEM E	344	231	1194	21	5		1489	0	435
25	30	LOG&PA M&E	3232	42	55	582					5
26	31	LT IND M&E	0	0	0	0	78323	5768	8083	8204	12
27	32	FD IND M&E	15	0	0		1	39	4		2663
28	33	PRINT M&E	139						67		0
29	34	HOIST&TRAN E		19	3462	105	165		2	2099	80
30	35	CONST M&E		2	12582	49	3				4
31	36	CONMAT M&E	8	1	58246	260	25	0	0	0	0
32	37,38	TRANS M&E	6	16	1456	34	17	931	24	1235	5
33	39	AUTOS	522	170	15929	793	1536	4	533	2416	1003
34	40	AGRIC M&E	103	48	7824	189	446	84	292	247	74
35	41	BEARNG	435	44	4433	318	1549	519	278	161	175
36	18,19,42,43	RADIO&OTH MB	1630	255	3531	281	2626	161	633	2370	1053
37	44	SANIT ENG PR	164	30	9638	7615	954	13336	367	125	261
38	45	OTHER METWRS	1722	286	37080	3137	18510	0	30019	39127	6552
39	46	METAL STRUCT	13	0	1164	44	82	4525	20	0	40
40	47	REPAIR	5334	927	46183	12228	12761		6215	59759	5666
41	48	ABRASV	312	19	1256	3212	759	115	1923	75	72
42	49	MINRL CHEM	11467	145	4726	7009	183	157	1628	5	51
43	50	BASIC CHEM	23975	7656	29368	42933	29918	167	22810	4918	3019
44	51	ANIL DYE PR	1813		941	1050	84030		16800	12	26
45	52	SYN R& PLAST	1126	317	24472	20497	9838	6924	30826	500	2983

(Table 1.2 continued)

#	Code	Sector									
46	54.58.59	SYN FIBERS PROD	0	0	0	0	843219	0	43	1588	0
47	53	ORGSYN PROD	2269	10502	39360	448	27642	168	73056	446	644
48	55	PAINT & LAC	959	170	6987	3484	5514	1250	10415	3950	1459
49	56	RUBBER PROD	1714	367	44715	1941	26711	11010	33726	4889	1314
50	57	OTHER CHEM	452	183	1509	463	1960	1029	93738	666	521
51	60	LOGGING	233031	108079	13681	8502	3509	860	25046	1955	2623
52	61.62	SAW & LUM PR	4767	12014	77948	26677	15501	2520	16337	130065	21700
53	63	FURNITURE	331	42	2890	532	2358	2297	1186	323	653
54	64	OTHER WDWK	155	72	2534	2479	8083	290	1908	2558	1871
55	65	PAPER & PULP	176048	246	54907	6435	24142	5004	23394	8405	8165
56	66	WOOD CHEM	15961	24653	3175	314	3251	36	8968	235	293
57	67-73	CONST MAT	3482	1224	1348752	12739	5200	994	2378	2405	2337
58	74	GLASS	2124	461	42129	34346	4866	330	2170	4262	1081
59	75-80	TEXTLS	34415	409	34520	7616	13721728	5535431	672454	150511	7448
60	81	SEWN GOODS	2424	716	43442	5786	18328	12144	8578	29581	7784
61	82	OTH LT IND	2099	277	12715	1013	19129	211593	2311465	11012	2116
62	83	FISH PROD	157	986	169	43	1283	4	7264	1881597	1236
63	84	MEAT PROD	1501	205	198	1029	1690	32	615364	1063	3627923
64	85	DAIRY PROD	7170	290	12755	2	5284	56	8655	305	5610
65	86	SUGAR	5	371	2	20	2153	0	1379	5086	2217
66	87-89	FLOUR&BREAD	6	74	23	694	27820	591	192	2472	17938
67	90-94	OTHER FOOD	2036	677	44555	11913	87488	4461	14631	98241	20729
68	95	IND NEC	3310	1151	106797	0	0	0	23540	674	6977
69	96-100	CONST	0	0	0				0		
70	101	CROPS	927	427	1058	222	3185390	310	1518	5261	10673
71	102	ANIMAL HUSB	0	49	65	0	0	0	462756	874	12117491
72	103	FOREST	0	0	0	0	1541335	0	0	0	0
73	104-106	TRANS &COM	143050	53029	864690	51154	300374	55202	82943	137892	83133
74	107-109	TRADE & DIST	22151	2658	67377	6126	204484	8643	37244	39156	274915
75	110	OTHER BRANCH	41488	24	20456	2028	496	275	22087	430	10090
76		TAX ON PURCH	18581	3617	193451	22112	3142501	1233836	33192	83580	28814
77		TOTAL PURCH	905009	254211	4607894	406894	23616468	7142878	4776841	2896747	16366970
78		DEPRECIATION	120003	25070	781680	55515	274159	94881	71318	273435	72456
79		WAGES	191033	37529	2062637	320427	1796806	1390804	672767	620791	338831
80		TURNOVER TAX									
81		OTH NET INC	203059	52745	1490628	561335	2666914	1524444	31642	323054	-3379663
82		NATIONAL INC	394092	90274	3553265	889762	4463720	2915248	704409	943845	-3040632
83		TOTAL OUTLAY	1419104	369555	8942839	1352171	28354347	10153007	5552568	4114027	13398594
84		EMPLOYMENT	149.9	29.7	1648.0	284.5	1786.8	1523.0	658.8	285.5	326.1
85		TOTL CAPITAL	1621664	256071	9894681	750204	4153592	1416135	1033592	3255183	1317378
86		BLDGS&STRUCT	784723	140634	6224602	425441	1748446	942177	552243	614904	1015185
87		POWER M&E	88867	23559	132073	11853	59045	6797	15401	19531	14072
88		GENERAL M&E	55656	16337	412168	143514	116756	37107	37107	243246	24504
89		SPECIAL M&E	676093	71855	2889307	152966	2173796	351604	404448	112246	226840
90		TRANS M&E	12325	2355	111567	6452	13777	20534	4651	2240217	20418
91		OTH CAPITAL	4000	1331	124901	9978	41639	57920	19742	24739	14359

SEQ NO.	110 ORDER NO.		DAIRY PROD 64	SUGAR 65	FLOUR& BREAD 66	OTHER FOOD 67	IND NEC 68	CONST 69	CROPS 70	ANIMAL HUSB 71	FOREST 72
1	1	FER ORES	99	1648	53	249	1712	0	0	0	0
2	2	FER METALS	26722	4984	4154	39576	89289	1436140	11783	10133	250
3	6	NONFER ORES	0	0	0	0	0	0	3490	1358	108
4	7	NONFER METAL	7167	7395	3300	9420	42251	114419	0	0	0
5	3	COKE PROD	6	708	75	65	7741	114934	0	0	0
6	4	REFRAC MAT	64	255	255	161	1123	156477	11083	7909	316
7	5	INDMET PROD	1094	1239	2671	4773	1125	49243	36693	52152	99
8	8	COAL	20361	24285	3834	28932	42140	541	0	113362	4002
9	9	OIL EXTRAC	0	0	0	0	756	229828	391741	0	0
10	10	OIL REF	7135	27439	4959	25492	19003		0	0	0
11	11	GAS	787	1865	3130	2931	1275	1626	60745	9614	0
12	12	PEAT	929	1976	1867	1026	1018	4731	89015	102167	915
13	13	OIL SHALES	933	867	412	3424	2321	6636	13802	0	0
14	14	ELEC POWER	13344	7478	20362	26806	107423	242584	5724	12296	0
15	15	ENSPOW M&E	194	99	80	442	5160	19995	0	5541	0
16	16	ELTECH M&E	1683	1487	3437	4354	20418	432839	0	0	0
17	17	CABLE PROD	659	1067	1267	1912	4377	514836	0	0	0
18	20	MACH TOOLS	1	15	26	78	691	4545	0	0	0
19	21	FORG- PR M&E	1	23	10	112	127	0	0	0	0
20	22	CAST M&E	0	3		14	77		0	0	0
21	23	TOOLS & DIES	1016	663	1517	1313	1861	45911		11513	340
22	24	PRECIS INST	491	578	630	689	3901	48025		2014	0
23	25,26,27	MI&MET M&E	598	0	137	601	1076	106323			0
24	28,29	PUMPS&CHEM E	0	270	0	11	2808	10646			0
25	30	LOG&PA M&E	383	0	8	0	394				0
26	31	LT IND M&E	8028	6	9614	6809	441				0
27	32	FD IND M&E	1	4079	91	76	137				0
28	33	PRINT M&E	25	108	528	150	9181				0
29	34	HOIST&TRAN E	0	4	0		871	29095			0
30	35	CONST M&E					1288	94595			0
31	36	CONMAT M&E	218	0	0	2	770	7018			0
32	37,38	TRANS M&E	10	57	9	85	2596	8388			7008
33	39	AUTOS	3874	1317	427	2253	18699	110920	138683	52137	4238
34	40	AGRIC M&E	151	1990	63	450	20931	58437	542721	119941	0
35	41	BEARNG	169	427	368	396	3268	181781	10526	2461	0
36	18,19,42,43	RADIO&OTH MB	1148	1092	2146	2660	5895	700731	12579	10735	0
37	44	SANIT ENG PR	225	79	447	417	1789	357744			0
38	45	OTHER METWRS	8600	1851	10980	61269	6429	549532	113404	86603	1139
39	46	METAL STRUCT	746	5	46	60	701	199514			0
40	47	REPAIR	8231	5423	10244	17178	2829		348426	162328	0
41	48	ABRASV	80	63	72	190	3052	9265	4043	1417	0
42	49	MINRL CHEM	11	1269	79	303	11270			53987	0
43	50	BASIC CHEM	4359	3350	1400	42590	50117	40245	743657	19457	1081
44	51	ANIL DYE PR	93	130	80	568	6028	7322			0
45	52	SYN R& PLAST	613	242	722	6061	177264	15943			0

(Table 1.2 continued)

	code	label	1	2	3	4	5	6	7	8	9
46	53	SYN FIBERS	0	0	0	0	13834	1199	0	2180	0
47	55	ORGSYN PROD	260	252	372	49462	50216	39613	12931	5605	0
48	56	PAINT & LAC	1519	1334	2220	5612	31844	397586	6783	52742	0
49	57	RUBBER PROD	2561	1963	3099	5141	25452	132641	147038	93011	0
50	54.58.59	OTHER CHEM	768	40	972	3089	12238	0	6554	0	0
51	60	LOGGNG	3658	772	1817	2367	120	458832	20983	37793	2580
52	61.62	SAW & LUM PR	19631	2491	63979	102350	62620	2024869	48441	72820	1262
53	63	FURNITURE	370	126	865	954	105251	10518	2047	1376	0
54	64	OTHER WDWK	867	60	2176	11165	16078	20088	6814	6781	0
55	65	PAPER & PULP	15231	4392	37848	83807	185627	3494	2595	1675	29
56	66	WOOD CHEM	149	52	1156	11961	2163		1991	7072	0
57	67-73	CONST MAT	2427	15915	3029	5774	31365	6722320	50049	77497	840
58	74	GLASS	10323	283	726	88208	7134	455179	8334	12346	0
59	75-80	TEXTILS	6869	12304	15954	216593	240935	186693	86919	40378	0
60	81	SEWN GOODS	6376	4796	27889	14575	62669	343461	34329	64887	2956
61	82	OTH LT IND	1896	1305	3547	3061	26327	39226	25323	37866	0
62	83	FISH PROD	137	35	7500	41841	818	0	340	84860	0
63	84	MEAT PROD	1977	663	25936	211294	2552	0	1652	67691	0
64	85	DAIRY PROD	187	187	214453	53127	8977	0	0	160282	0
65	86	SUGAR	676407	934084	707728	579910	257164	0	0	109014	0
66	87-89	FLOUR&BREAD	148836	0	2337266	79011	25221	0	0	313337	0
67	90-94	OTHER FOOD	14416	1150	602056	5248754	59647	1270	6460	116341	0
68	95	IND NEC	15724	32864	57724	162885		139759	8713	617239	940
69	96-100	CONST	32043					570706			0
70	101	CROPS	3971	2270656	5793668	3789467	579127	22863	3403628	10923266	1405
71	102	ANIMAL HUSB	5941455	0	52504	5278	0	6049	291225	2005353	0
72	103	FOREST	0	83590	250129	351363	142263	3833754	453318	428920	12624
73	104-106	TRANS &COM	61999	107107	314708	302702	72470	314743	257597	581513	4776
74	107-109	TRADE & DIST	139204	13	1125	20914	53126	476723	36679	15719	1103
75	110	OTHER BRANCH	27	39949	2614929	1398612	32789	256288	335974	104530	3433
76		TAX ON PURCH	34361					0			
77		TOTAL PURCH	7263711	3621984	13262875	13143175	2800885	22374374	7811468	16879219	51444
78		DEPRECIATION	114744	130072	137617	230345	458384	1837900	2833510	1944575	2015
79		WAGES	303945	150749	796243	885250	1029115	15800000	19861322	18779304	409374
80		TURNOVER TAX	0	-612366	-911067	4580115	1886796	0	0	0	0
81		OTH NET INC	373432	-461617	-114824	5465365	2915911	3300033	9944248	1682003	-31907
82		NATIONAL INC	677377					19100033	29705570	20461307	377467
83		TOTAL OUTLAY	8055832	3290439	13285668	18838885	6175180	43312307	40350548	39285101	430926
84		EMPLOYMENT	308.7	154.9	808.7	899.1	970.0	9450.0	16183.1	17189.4	427.5
85		TOTL CAPITAL	1365997	1646475	2074742	3472682	6067904	11838000	34958600	32251400	21480
86		BLDGS&STRUCT	824158	680007	1358417	2040494	3455527	3779992	16227389	15013726	9011
87		POWER M&E	40843	140444	32869		196459	153065	286537	265107	154
88		GENERAL M&E	29803	82781	44353	87545	1091848	2329467	1105365	1022693	7466
89		SPECIAL M&E	418329	513606	605593	1190682	506095	4569350	1031922	2803488	2136
90		TRANS M&E	37565	15477	10493	25996	671495	696444	1137400	1052332	570
91		OTH CAPITAL	15299	14160	23017	44670	145630	309682	5269987	12094054	2143

SEQ NO.	110 ORDER NO.		TRANS &COM 73	TRADE & DIST 74	O-HER BRANCH 75	TURNOV ER TAX 76	INTIND USE 77	PRIVAT CONSUM 78	PUBLIC CONSUM 79	OTHER FD 80	TOTAL FD 81
1	1	FER ORES	0	0	0	0	766038	0	0	102147	102147
2	2	FER METALS	37217	6281	200	0	8828158	2293	206197	775651	984141
3	6	NONFER ORES	0	3189	0	0	1093505	0	0	-218298	-218298
4	7	NONFER METAL	-8701	0	145	0	5281321	0	234334	307129	541463
5	3	COKE PROD	0	0	0	0	1220389	0	0	113157	113157
6	4	REFRAC MAT	0	0	0	0	273300	0	0	22724	22724
7	5	INDMET PROD	37917	10857	1212	0	986624	4797	27291	41757	73845
8	8	COAL	170491	41750	889	0	4289337	109838	470125	158123	738086
9	9	OIL EXTRAC	0	0	0	0	787258	0	0	433319	433319
10	10	OIL REF	433550	38564	1861	0	2419678	57145	233430	597653	880228
11	11	GAS	416	9947	8	0	294034	17497	9063	30813	57373
12	12	PEAT	506	4291	0	0	314406	0	76753	-13503	63250
13	13	OIL SHALES	144	388	0	0	13069	0	0	4424	4424
14	14	ELEC POWER	390179	125443	7463	0	4850722	654710	542225	17124	1214059
15	15	EN&POW M&E	2008	31019	995	0	506841	0	0	934003	934003
16	16	ELTECH M&E	13779	12423	660	0	2629281	470293	178969	1650459	2299721
17	17	CABLE PROD	16663	0	0	0	1227484	5589	66233	-12895	58927
18	20	MACH TOOLS	984	0	1087	0	73580	0	22649	787525	810174
19	21	FORG- PR M&E	0	0	0	0	17341	0	0	179678	179678
20	22	CAST M&E	0	0	0	0	9131	0	0	27523	27523
21	23	TOOLS & DIES	19474	6227	553	0	345594	0	0	162892	162892
22	24	PRECIS INST	5887	7523	151	0	1304052	219235	98367	634090	951692
23	25,26,27	MI&MET M&E	0	0	0	0	473235	0	0	2088556	2088556
24	28,29	PUMPS&CHEM E	609	12867	0	0	310065	149327	50977	1049305	1249609
25	30	LOG&PA M&E	4889	0	0	0	38785	0	0	84434	84434
26	31	LT IND M&E	0	858	0	0	130758	40634	0	341879	382513
27	32	FD IND M&E	0	0	0	0	56913	0	0	331753	331753
28	33	PRINT M&E	0	0	0	0	9641	0	0	39556	39556
29	34	HOIST&TRAN E	15390	14391	235	0	143747	0	0	646048	646048
30	35	CONST M&E	1006	87	0	0	216378	0	0	728307	728307
31	36	CONMAT M&E	0	0	0	0	76121	0	0	153136	153136
32	37,38	TRANS M&E	126732	19388	2696	0	367273	0	40431	3327264	3367695
33	39	AUTOS	258263	1749	0	0	2359863	558542	187194	1261027	2006763
34	40	BEARNG M&E	9888	2290	0	0	2648979	0	0	1775857	1775857
35	41	AGRIC M&E	10086	16297	12	0	352235	0	7552	100183	107735
36	18,19,42,43	RADIO&OTH VB	57924	72674	57	0	7028104	1312561	372851	7494517	9179929
37	44	SANIT ENG PR	0	0	1075	0	877715	0	53993	50953	104946
38	45	OTHER METWRS	21107	0	0	0	1686430	731424	218062	404497	1353983
39	46	METAL STRUCT	0	0	0	0	616086	0	0	22703	22703
40	47	REPAIR	125650	0	0	0	1484473	0	27958	6701263	6729221
41	48	ABRASV	1097	218	21	0	390244	0	0	-44378	-44378
42	49	MINRL CHEM	0	0	0	0	280556	0	0	58490	58490
43	50	BASIC CHEM	15954	3087	7398	0	2404135	28133	70890	591280	690303
44	51	ANIL DYE PR	0	0	0	0	228413	4196	1918	36963	43077
45	52	SYN R& PLAS-	0	925	164	0	1301040	50646	17886	-289660	-221128

(Table 1.2 continued)

No.	Code	Sector									
46	53	SYN FIBERS	0	1864	8	1122008	0	97785	24147	-67565	-67565
47	55	ORGSYN PROD	7708	37776	258	1334026	0	4326	142295	108281	230213
48	56	PAINT & LAC	36402	49894	1113	1232334	0	18052	144295	-47196	101425
49	57	RUBBER PROD	438517	1266	2072	2497003	0		243948	498489	760489
50	54.58.59	OTHER CHEM	446		12614	1297265	0	399976	559073	-282067	676982
51	60	LOGG&G	59938	25113	249	3030602	0	86161	245729	120562	452452
52	61.62	SAW & LUM PR	59900	120390	1188	4627743	0	43261	110317	436174	589752
53	63	FURNITURE	5579	19570	2851	242224	0	1653016	21293	-26341	1647968
54	64	OTHER WDWK	0	7764	84	127711	0	65906	2748	5219	119873
55	65	PAPER & PULP	5990	153988	145300	1352685	0	0	62598	3821	66419
56	66	WOOD CHEM	1852	51	11	338673	0	0	3082	30882	30882
57	67-73	CONST MAT	24368	41743	722	8543374	0	46952	182989	169524	399465
58	74	GLASS	6811	60039	256	1076894	0	156542	22448	96287	275277
59	75-80	TEXTLS	50406	93280	21391	22453250	0	7052693	342869	-1494465	5901097
60	81	SEWN GOODS	76381	122855	2637	1346582	0	9138265	368229	-700069	8806425
61	82	OTH LT IND	24208	9401	25286	2945623	0	3284708	42008	-719771	2606945
62	83	FISH PROD	0	20169	0	2061311	0	1688050	213955	150711	205716
63	84	MEAT PROD	0	154849	27	4758642	0	7858407	523835	257710	8639952
64	85	DAIRY PROD	0	28557	0	1379342	0	5007481	873423	795586	6676490
65	86	SUGAR	0	12899	0	2523901	0	1161582	87671	-482715	766538
66	87-89	FLOUR&BREAD	53	39053	1	3074811	0	9969947	432547	-191637	10210857
67	90-94	OTHER FOOD	13170	65955	177	7021773	0	12597394	182922	-963204	1181112
68	95	IND NEC	0	213545	278359	3291075	0	2830867	468609	-415371	2884105
69	96-100	CONST	29802		0	0	0	0	0	43312307	43312307
70	101	CROPS	5790	75203	0	30113050	0	7056048	116668	3064782	10237498
71	102	ANIMAL HUSB	0	1438	0	2245136	0	13366764	361012	3122189	16849965
72	103	FOREST	431366	294303	15572	216632	0	0	0	214294	214294
73	104-106	TRANS &COM	109144	45133	23570	14158751	0	1911278	745716	2284255	4941249
74	107-109	TRADE & DIST		83710	15263	4185429	0	10322937	227634	994000	11544571
75	110	OTHER BRANCH	854463	91479	11361	1163102	0	2053421	192670	59218	2305309
76		TAX ON PURCH			3345	11439549	0	25351302	2345277	444772	28141351
77		TOTAL PURCH	4038205	2317801	590597	222521934	0	127639981	12359978	84514090	224514048
78		DEPRECIATION	2845900	1186000	35000	22310000	0	5560000	4440000	0	0
79		WAGES	6045359	6552046	1187424	105339696	39580900				
80		TURNOVER TAX	0	0	0	39580900	39580900				
81		OTH NET INC	6170536	5564153	1655390	57283453					
82		NATIONAL INC	12215895	12226199	2842814	202204048					
83		TOTAL OUTLAY	19100000	15730000	3468411	447035980	39580900				
84		EMPLOYMENT	4588.7	6896.6	977.5	84377.9	.0				
85		TOTL CAPITAL	41444000	19382000	537520	298080000	0	29808000			
86		BLDGS&STRUCT	26904173	14420569	248697	172529890					
87		POWER M&E	126017	120426	2456	8864747					
88		GENERAL M&E	4295903	1903568	90763	29976514					
89		SPECIAL M&E	715507	1482781	79472	46070390					
90		TRANS M&E	9115661	445417	87239	17254616					
91		OTH CAPITAL	286739	1009039	28893	20583843					

SEQ NO.	110 ORDER NO.		GVO 82
1	1	FER ORES	868185
2	2	FER METALS	9812299
3	6	NONFER ORES	875207
4	7	NONFER METAL	5822784
5	3	COKE PROD	1333546
6	4	REFRAC MAT	296024
7	5	INCMET PROD	1060469
8	8	COAL	5027423
9	9	OIL EXTRAC	1220577
10	10	OIL REF	3307906
11	11	GAS	351407
12	12	PEAT	377656
13	13	OIL SHALES	117493
14	14	ELEC POWER	6064781
15	15	EN&POW M&E	1440844
16	16	ELTECH M&E	4929002
17	17	CABLE PROD	1286411
18	20	MACH TOOLS	883754
19	21	FORG- PR M&E	197019
20	22	CAST M&E	36654
21	23	TOOLS & DIES	508486
22	24	PRECIS INST	2255744
23	25,26,27	MI&MET M&E	2561791
24	28,29	PUMPS&CHEM E	1559674
25	30	LCG&PA M&E	123319
26	31	LT IND M&E	513271
27	32	FD IND M&E	388666
28	33	PRINT M&E	49197
29	34	HOIST&TRAN E	789795
30	35	CONST M&E	944685
31	36	CONMAT M&E	229257
32	37,38	TRANS M&E	3734966
33	39	AUTOS	4366626
34	40	AGRIC M&E	4424836
35	41	BEAR&G	459971
36	18,19,42,43	RADIO&OTH MB	16208033
37	44	SANIT ENG PR	982661
38	45	OTHER METWRS	3040413
39	46	METAL STRUCT	638769
40	47	REPAIR	8213694
41	48	ABRASV	345866
42	49	MINRL CHEM	339046
43	50	BASIC CHEM	3094438
44	51	ANIL DYE PR	271490
45	52	SYN R& PLAST	1099012

(Table 1.2 continued)

46	53	SYN FIBERS	1054443
47	55	ORGSYN PROD	1564239
48	56	PAINT & LAC	1333759
49	57	RUBBER PROD	3257492
50	54,58,59	OTHER CHEM	1974247
51	60	LOGGNG	3483054
52	61,62	SAW & LUM PR	5217495
53	63	FURNITURE	1890192
54	64	OTHER WDWK	247584
55	65	PAPER & PULP	1419104
56	66	WOOD CHEM	369555
57	67-73	CONST MAT	8942839
58	74	GLASS	1352171
59	75-80	TEXTLS	28354347
60	81	SEWN GOODS	10153007
61	82	OTH LT IND	5552568
62	83	FISH PROD	4114027
63	84	MEAT PROD	13398594
64	85	DAIRY PROD	8055832
65	86	SUGAR	3290439
66	87-89	FLOUR&BREAD	13285668
67	90-94	OTHER FOOD	18838885
68	95	IND NEC	6175180
69	96-100	CONST	43312307
70	101	CROPS	40350548
71	102	ANIMAL HUSB	39285101
72	103	FOREST	430926
73	104-106	TRANS &COM	19100000
74	107-109	TRADE & DIST	15730000
75	110	OTHER BRANCH	3468411
76		TAX ON PURCH	39580900
77		TOTAL PURCH	447035980
78		DEPRECIATION	32310000
79		WAGES	
80		TURNOVER TAX	
81		OTH NET INC	
82		NATIONAL INC	
83		TOTAL OUTLAY	
84		EMPLOYMENT	
85		TOTL CAPITAL	
86		BLDGS&STRUCT	
87		POWER M&E	
88		GENERAL M&E	
89		SPECIAL M&E	
90		TRANS M&E	
91		OTH CAPITAL	

Source: B. Kostinsky, The Reconstructed 1966 Soviet Input-Output Table: Revised Purchasers' and Producers' Price Table, U.S. Department of Commerce, F.D.A.D., Foreign Economic Report No. 13, Washington, D.C.: Government Printing Office, 1976 (as revised by the authors).

final-demand quadrant of the producers' prices table because it is uncertain how these should be converted to producers' prices. Therefore, the other final-demand column includes the export-import balance as well as investment and miscellaneous elements of final demand.

As was indicated above, the original Soviet 1966 input-output table had 131 rows and columns but lack of data made it necessary to reduce by aggregation the number of original producing sectors from 110 to 75, the number of columns in final demand to five, and the number of rows in the value-added quadrant to four. The detailed breakdown of the final demand and value-added quadrants is characteristic of Soviet input-output tables which compare favorably in this respect with most Western tables,[5] and the loss of detail in the reconstructed table is therefore regrettable. It must be added that the detailed data for the final-demand and value-added categories are also absent from Soviet standard statistical sources such as the Narodnoe khoziaistvo annual handbooks and it would have been thus particularly interesting to present these statistics in the reconstructed input-output tables.

The process of estimating the missing statistics and of reconstructing the complete input-output table offers some trade-offs. Thus, it proved possible to expand the number of separate categories in the final-demand and value-added quadrants in the reconstructed table at the cost of reducing the number of producing sectors to 16.

Table 1.3 presents this version of the 1966 purchasers'-price Soviet input-output table. It will be noted that the single column labeled "public consumption" in Table 1.1 has been broken down into four separate categories.[6] The first three comprise public consumption proper, that is, the material expenditures of organizations and agencies directly serving the public. These three categories are public housing and communal services (including hotels, fire protection, public utilities, and such services as barbershops, public baths, and others), passenger transportation and communications serving the nonproductive sphere, and health, education, and cultural institutions and services. The category of state consumption consists of the material purchases of scientific and research organizations, banking and credit institutions, and various state administrative organizations including the courts.[7] The data on public and state consumption are extended into what can be called the fourth quadrant of the input-output table showing elements of value-added generated in the nonproductive sphere.[8] The value-added quadrant shows money wages, social security contributions, turnover taxes, profits, and other elements of national income.

TABLE 1.3

The Aggregated 1966 Soviet Input-Output Table in Purchasers' Prices (with Supplementary Data)

SEQ NO.	75-ORDER NO.		METAL-LURGY 1	FUELS 2	ELEC POWER &STEAM 3	MACH-BLDG & METWKG 4	CHEMI-CALS 5	WOOD-WORKNG &PAPER 6	CONST MATRLS &GLASS 7	TEXTILS & APPARL 8	FOOD 9
1	1-7	METALLURGY	8188.2	82.8	18.7	8107.3	579.0	188.3	744.0	46.4	238.8
2	8-13	FUELS	1908.1	3196.3	2656.2	656.0	519.7	356.2	712.0	110.8	622.1
3	14	ELEC POWER & STEAM	781.5	559.4	11.5	969.0	734.2	220.6	415.8	249.5	224.6
4	15-41	MACHBLDG&METALWKNG	611.8	266.0	79.8	17299.1	532.0	393.1	303.0	239.4	372.4
5	42-50	CHEMICALS	370.1	242.6	23.4	2630.0	4222.0	384.3	248.8	1452.1	180.5
6	51-56	WOODWORKING &PAPER	113.7	384.1	4.4	872.1	513.6	4559.4	234.1	171.9	627.5
7	57-58	CONST MATRLS&GLASS	43.2	34.6	4.5	343.8	93.9	128.8	2039.9	20.4	161.3
8	59-61	TEXTILES & APPAREL	172.6	74.3	4.4	775.2	589.4	387.1	106.2	26958.6	528.8
9	62-67	FOOD	46.3	19.8	5.4	161.5	661.9	56.8	62.4	701.4	22073.3
10	68	INDUSTRY NEC	318.1	60.8	29.7	405.5	149.0	50.3	122.2	118.9	301.7
11	69	CONSTRUCTION			.0	.0				.0	
12	70-72	AGRICULTURE&FOREST	2.0	1.0	.0	2.5	35.1	203.5	1.4	5441.5	31188.5
13	73	TRANSPORT&COMMUN	1880.1	4475.0	4.1	2223.1	1024.2	2262.6	3994.7	433.2	1454.8
14	74	TRADE&DISTRIBUTION	517.6	1007.1	.4	925.5	388.2	583.4	207.5	1679.5	6986.5
15	75	OTHER BRANCHES	319.7	.2	.8	77.9	7.9	46.6	25.0	25.4	36.2
16		TOTAL PURCHASES	15273.0	10404.0	2848.0	35448.6	10050.0	9821.0	9217.0	37649.0	64997.0
17		DEPRECIATION	1572.4	1687.0	1159.4	2909.1	740.6	862.0	837.2	440.4	958.7
18		WAGES	3039.1	3258.2	836.4	14249.7	1382.2	3553.0	2391.1	3860.4	3095.8
19		SOCIAL SEC PAYMNTS	240.1	290.0	51.9	1041.2	116.1	167.0	145.9	262.5	210.5
20		TURNOVER TAXES	155.0	3283.0	1458.0	1998.0	448.6	332.6	234.0	10869.4	20420.0
21		PROFITS	2428.0	-560.0	907.0	8711.0	2010.0	633.0	939.0	3822.0	4289.0
22		OTHER INCOME	-147.6	741.9	266.6	1843.4	1052.6	412.5	959.8	96.4	-4171.0
23		TOTAL NAT'L INCOME	5714.6	7013.1	3519.9	27842.3	5009.4	5098.0	4669.8	18910.6	23844.3
24		TOTAL OUTLAYS	22560.0	19104.1	7527.3	66200.0	15800.0	15781.0	14724.0	57000.0	89800.0
25		EMPLOYMENT	1803.0	1557.0	615.7	11150.0	1047.1	2838.2	1932.5	3968.6	2783.0
26		TOTL FIXED CAPITAL	21393.6	19391.1	23661.4	38278.0	10285.8	8288.2	10644.9	6603.7	13132.5
27		BUILDINGS&STRUCTRS	11765.8	14559.2	15408.3	23408.1	5981.5	4721.5	6650.0	3243.3	6733.2
28		POWER M&E	432.4	174.6	5203.9	1074.5	162.7	308.1	143.9	81.0	333.1
29		GENERAL M&E	1605.2	539.1	2428.1	10692.0	654.8	951.3	555.7	191.0	512.2
30		SPECIALIZED M&E	6991.8	3935.1	456.7	2375.3	3314.1	1766.0	3042.3	2929.8	3067.6
31		TRANSPORTATION M&E	433.1	89.8	119.3	359.4	103.8	435.6	118.0	39.0	2350.2
32		OTHER FIXED CAPITAL	165.3	93.4	45.2	568.8	69.0	105.7	134.9	119.3	136.2
33		TOTAL INVENTORIES	4826.0	997.0	648.0	19117.0	2223.0	2832.0	1580.0	7744.0	7701.0
34		OUTPUT ON HAND	2792.0	510.0	.0	8399.0	577.0	1277.0	523.0	1440.0	3033.0
35		OUTPUT IN TRANSIT	531.0	68.0	.0	2218.0	449.0	289.0	235.0	852.0	839.0
36		FUELS	92.0	6.0	258.0	101.0	14.0	64.0	39.0	28.0	69.0
37		SPARE PARTS	335.0	78.0	134.0	321.0	105.0	137.0	139.0	97.0	103.0
38		OTHER MATRL INPUTS	1076.0	336.0	256.0	8078.0	1078.0	1065.0	644.0	5327.0	3637.0

SEQ NO.	75-ORDER NO.		INDUSTRY NEC 10	CON-STRUCTION 11	AGRI-CULTRE &FORST 12	TRANS-PORT & COMMUN 13	TRADE& DISTRI BUTION 14	OTHER BRANCH 15	INTER IND USE 16	PRIVAT CONSUM 17	PUBLIC HOUSNG &SERV 18
1	1-7	METALLURGY	169.5	2039.0	51.0	102.7	22.2	1.7	20579.7	19.0	26.0
2	8-13	FUELS	122.1	678.6	1510.1	1766.0	214.8	6.1	15035.0	485.0	375.0
3	14	ELEC POWER & STEAM	113.9	297.6	186.8	457.7	154.0	9.2	5385.2	1162.0	244.0
4	15-41	MACHBLDG&METALWKNG	126.9	3663.9	1769.2	722.6	212.8	8.0	26600.0	5769.0	120.0
5	42-50	CHEMICALS	409.8	669.6	1265.3	522.5	99.8	27.1	12748.0	895.0	102.0
6	51-56	WOODWORKING &PAPER	425.0	2997.6	259.5	167.2	380.8	172.2	11883.0	2451.0	148.0
7	57.58	CONST MATRLS&GLASS	52.9	10157.2	207.2	42.5	126.1	1.3	13457.6	578.0	83.0
8	59-61	TEXTILES & APPAREL	333.2	575.4	295.7	152.6	227.8	49.9	31236.0	27749.0	94.0
9	62-67	FOOD	311.7	148.1	898.6	14.1	341.3	286.5	25503.0	61458.0	40.0
10	68	INDUSTRY NEC	67.4	587.3	645.1	30.7	219.0		3386.9	3525.0	84.0
11	69	CONSTRUCTION	.0								
12	70-72	AGRICULTURE&FCREST	615.0	30.5	17595.4	6.2	81.4	15.9	5220.3	21341.0	.0
13	73	TRANSPORT&COMMUN	131.0	47.7	924.7	53.6	144.1	47.1	19100.0	.0	.0
14	74	TRADE&DISTRIBUTION	352.8		2816.8	.0	93.0	264.7	15730.0	.0	.0
15	75	OTHER BRANCHES	59.0	529.5	58.2	.0		12.6	1291.9	2208.0	.0
16		TOTAL PURCHASES	3284.7	22422.1	28483.7	4038.2	2317.8	902.4	257156.6	127640.0	1316.0
17		DEPRECIATION	458.4	1837.9	4780.1	2845.9	1186.0	35.0	22310.0	5560.0	720.0
18		WAGES	1029.1	15600.0	39050.0	6045.4	6562.0	1187.4	105339.7	.0	2180.0
19		SOCIAL SEC PAYMNTS	74.1	784.0	720.7	320.4	295.3	59.0	4778.7	.0	102.0
20		TURNOVER TAXES	382.3					.0	39580.9	.0	.0
21		PROFITS	-910.0	1879.0	2463.0	5549.0	4319.0	1596.2	39998.0	.0	.0
22		OTHER INCOME	-100.0	637.0	8292.5	301.1	1049.8	2842.6	12831.1	.0	22.0
23		TOTAL NAT'L INCOME	3295.5	19000.0	50526.2	12215.9	12226.2		201828.4		2304.0
24		TOTAL OUTLAYS	7038.6	43360.0	83790.0	19100.0	15730.0	3780.0	481295.0	.0	4340.0
25		EMPLOYMENT	970.0	9450.0	33800.0	4588.7	6896.6	977.5	84377.9	.0	2489.0
26		TOTL FIXED CAPITAL	6057.9	11838.0	67131.5	41444.0	19382.0	537.5	298080.0	144000.0	19000.0
27		BUILDINGS&STRUCTFS	3445.5	3780.0	31250.1	26904.2	14420.6	248.7	172529.9		
28		POWER M&E	196.5	153.1	551.8	126.0	120.6	2.5	8864.5		
29		GENERAL M&E	1091.9	2329.5	2135.5	4295.9	1903.6	90.8	29976.5		
30		SPECIALIZED M&E	506.9	4569.3	13637.5	715.5	1482.8	79.5	48870.4		
31		TRANSPORTATION M&E	671.5	696.4	2190.3	9115.7	445.4	87.2	17254.6		
32		OTHER FIXED CEPTAL	145.6	309.7	17366.2	286.7	1009.0	28.9	20583.8		
33		TOTAL INVENTORIES	5309.0	5661.0	26392.0	1093.0	52520.0	4103.0	142746.0		860.0
34		OUTPUT ON HAND	594.0	739.0	4908.0		44615.0	2499.0	72386.0		
35		OUTPUT IN TRANSIT	552.0	420.0	276.0		4296.0	801.0	11836.0		
36		FUELS	16.0	167.0	470.00	115.00	61.00	29.00	1548.00		
37		SPARE PARTS	104.0	349.0	1019.0	224.0	9.0	5.0	3159.0		
38		OTHER MATRL INPUTS	3633.0	3966.0	19639.0	754.0	3539.0	769.0	53817.0		

(Table 1.3 continued)

SEQ NO.	75-ORDER NO.		NON-PROD T&C 19	HEALTH &EDUC &CULTR 20	SCIENC &BANKG &ADMIN 21	EXPORT 22	IMPORT 23	OTHER FINAL DEMAND 24	TOTAL FINAL DEMAND 25	GROSS VALUE OUTPUT 26
1	1-7	METALLURGY	27.0	9.0	596.0	2217.8	-738.7	-175.9	1980.3	22560.0
2	8-13	FUELS	588.0	379.0	273.0	1177.8	-228.7	1020.6	4069.1	19104.1
3	14	ELEC POWER & STEAM	175.0	350.0	194.0	16.5			2142.1	7527.3
4	15-41	MACHBLDG&METALWKNG	268.0	222.0	1141.0	1081.4	-1732.4	32731.0	39600.0	66200.0
5	42-50	CHEMICALS	150.0	614.0	605.0	394.5	-771.4	1062.9	3052.0	15800.0
6	51-56	WOODWORKING &PAPER	49.0	161.0	245.0	744.9	-352.0	451.1	3898.0	15781.0
7	57-58	CONST MATRLS&GLASS	28.0	91.0	130.0	35.0	-30.1	351.5	1266.4	14724.0
8	59-61	TEXTILES & APPAREL	46.0	653.0	164.0	730.4	-4882.9	1210.4	25764.0	57000.0
9	62-67	FOOD	20.0	2658.0		379.5	-1348.2	1043.7	64297.0	89800.0
10	68	INDUSTRY NEC	87.0	331.0	46.0	57.5	-140.2	-328.7	3651.7	7038.6
11	69	CONSTRUCTION						43360.0	43360.0	43360.0
12	70-72	AGRICULTURE&FOREST		494.0		340.0		7608.2	28569.7	83790.0
13	73	TRANSPORT&COMMUN					-1213.5			19100.0
14	74	TRADE&DISTRIBUTION								15730.0
15	75	OTHER BRANCHES		214.0		38.2	-16.7	44.6	2488.1	3780.0
16		TOTAL PURCHASES	1438.0	6176.0	3430.0	7213.6	-11454.6	88379.4	224138.4	481295.0
17		DEPRECIATION	1140.0	1430.0	1150.0	.0	.0	.0	10000.0	
18		WAGES	2660.0	13220.0	4782.0	.0	.0	.0	22842.0	
19		SOCIAL SEC PAYMNTS	138.0	767.0	277.0	.0	.0	.0	1284.0	
20		TURNOVER TAXES				.0	.0	.0	.0	
21		PROFITS	1900.0			.0	.0	.0	1900.0	
22		OTHER INCOME	104.0	577.0		.0	.0	.0	703.0	
23		TOTAL NAT'L INCOME	4802.0	14564.0	5059.0	.0	.0	.0	26729.0	
24		TOTAL OUTLAYS	7380.0	22150.0	9619.0			.0	43489.0	
25		EMPLOYMENT	2307.0	11702.0	3544.0			.0	20042.0	
26		TOTL FIXED CAPITAL	17856.0	27200.0	21800.0			.0	229856.0	
27		BUILDINGS&STRUCTRS								
28		POWER M&E								
29		GENERAL M&E								
30		SPECIALIZED M&E								
31		TRANSPORTATION M&E								
32		OTHER FIXED CAPTAL								
33		TOTAL INVENTORIES	535.0							
34		OUTPUT ON HAND								
35		OUTPUT IN TRANSIT								
36		FUELS								
37		SPARE PARTS								
38		OTHER MATRL INPUTS								

Sources: B. Kostinsky, The Reconstructed 1966 Soviet Input-Output Table: Revised Purchasers' and Producers' Price Table, U.S. Department of Commerce, F.D.A.D., Foreign Economic Report No. 13, Washington, D.C.: Government Printing Office, 1976, and Vladimir G. Treml, "Second and Fourth Quadrants in the 1966 Soviet Input-Output Table," Working paper, Duke University, Durham, 1977.

54

In addition to the fixed capital assets and employment statistics shown in the larger tables, the 16-sector table includes supplementary information on material working capital, that is, stocks and inventories, distributed among the producing sectors. These supplementary data record the value of stocks of finished goods on hand and in transit, as well as the value of inventories of material inputs broken down into fuels, spare parts for machinery and equipment, and other inputs. [9]

The picture of the Soviet economy presented in Table 1.3 is thus quite comprehensive and it is regrettable that the additional information provided here cannot be disaggregated to match the format of the 75-sector tables.

APPENDIX

Commodity Description of the 75-Sector Table

Sector No.	Commodity	Description
1	Ferrous ores	Mining of iron, manganese, chromite, and other ferrous ores; extraction of refractory clays and other nonmetallic materials for ferrous metallurgy
2	Ferrous metals	Pig iron, steel, and ferroalloys, rolled ferrous plate, sheet, bars, beams, rails, and pipe; galvanized and plated sheet metal
3	Nonferrous ores	Mining of bauxite and other nonferrous and rare-metal ores; precious stones, gold, and other precious metal ores
4	Nonferrous metals	All nonferrous and precious metals, alloys, and powders; semiconductor materials; carbon and graphite electrodes
5	Coke products	Coke, coke oven gas, coal oil, coal tar
6	Refractory products	Refractory brick, powder, and other refractory products

Sector No.	Commodity	Description
7	Industrial metal products	Steel wire, wire nails, metal cloth, welding electrodes, chains, springs, screws, bolts, rivets, and other industrial metal fasteners and hardware
8	Coal	Coal and lignite; briquets, raw liquid coal fuels
9	Oil extraction	Crude oil, by-product gas
10	Oil refining	Refined petroleum fuels, lubricants, and other products
11	Gas	Natural and manufactured gas; natural gasoline
12	Peat	Peat and peat briquets
13	Oil shales	Shale oil and products of shale processing
14	Electric power and steam	Generation and transmission of electric power and steam
15	Energy and power machinery and equipment*	Steam boilers; steam, gas, and hydraulic turbines; nuclear power reactors; diesel engines (except auto, tractor, combine, and aircraft engines)
16	Electrotechnical machinery and equipment	Electric motors and generators, transformers, rectifiers, and condensers; lighting equipment and fixtures, electric lamps, wet and dry batteries; electric insulating materials and products; electrical household appliances (except refrigerators); tape recorders, loudspeakers

---

*All machinery sectors (Nos. 15-39) also produce spare parts and components.

Sector No.	Commodity	Description
17	Cable products	Cable, including conducting wire and cord and cable sheathing
18	Machine tools	Metalcutting and woodworking machine tools, including automatic and semiautomatic lines; sawmill frames
19	Forging/pressing machinery and equipment	Power presses, hammers, shears, bending and riveting machines; automatic forging and stamping machinery
20	Casting machinery and equipment	Molding and casting equipment, including automatic and semi-automatic casting lines
21	Tools and dies	Cutting tools, dies, chucks, jigs, and other fixtures for metal and woodworking machinery; measuring tools (including scales); mechanics' hand tools, pneumatic and woodworking tools; chain saws
22	Precision instruments	Electronic computers and data processing equipment, calculators; cash registers, office equipment; control and measuring instruments; electrical and radio instruments; optical, astronomical, navigational, and medical instruments; cameras, film projectors; eyeglasses and other consumer optical devices; clocks and watches
23	Mining and metallurgical machinery and equipment	Iron and steel smelting and rolling equipment; oil and gas drilling, extraction, and refining equipment; ore and coal mining machinery

Sector No.	Commodity	Description
24	Pumps and chemical equipment	All types of pumps and compressors, fans and ventilators; refrigeration equipment (including household refrigerators); centrifuges, filter presses, vulcanizers, heat exchangers, and other chemical equipment
25	Logging and paper machinery and equipment	Log-handling equipment (except tractors); equipment for production of pulp, paper, and cardboard; equipment for match industry
26	Light industry machinery and equipment	Equipment for the knitting, sewing, footwear, leather, fur, textile, chemical fiber, cable, and glass industries; cotton-ginning equipment; household sewing machines
27	Food industry machinery and equipment	All kinds of food-processing equipment; equipment for flour mills, grain elevators
28	Printing machinery and equipment	Printing presses, typesetting and copying machines
29	Hoisting/transporting machinery and equipment	Cranes, conveyors, elevators, cable car equipment; power winches, jacks, hoists, and lifts; escalators
30	Construction machinery and equipment	Excavators, scrapers, graders, bulldozers, ditch diggers, pile drivers, and other machinery for construction and road building
31	Construction materials machinery and equipment	Equipment for cement and lime-making equipment for the production of prefabricated concrete, asbestos-cement products, insulating materials, brick; crushing and grinding equipment

Sector No.	Commodity	Description
32	Transportation machinery and equipment	Diesel, electric, and steam locomotives; railroad freight and passenger cars, subway and streetcars; railroad braking, coupling, switching and signaling equipment; ships, boats, and barges
33	Automobiles	Trucks, passenger cars, autobuses, auto tractors and trailers; motorcycles, scooters, and bicycles, automobile and motorcycle engines
34	Tractors and agricultural machinery and equipment	Tractors (including industrial and logging tractors) and engines, agricultural machinery and equipment
35	Bearings	All types of ball and roller bearings
36	Radio and other machinebuilding	Radio equipment, telephone and telegraph equipment, consumer radio and television receivers; electro-vacuum and semiconductor devices; equipment for retail trade (except scales), public dining, hospitals, pharmaceutical equipment; firefighting and sanitation equipment; commercial laundry and dry cleaning equipment; typewriters; castings, forging, and stampings
37	Sanitary engineering products	Heating and air-conditioning apparatus, plumbing fittings and fixtures, cast iron sewer pipe; wood, coal, and gas stoves
38	Other metal wares	Metal construction components (gratings, railings, stairways); metal containers, tools, metal furniture; baby carriages; chains, anchors, metal kitchen utensils, tableware, and cutlery; razors and blades;

Sector No.	Commodity	Description
		metal sporting goods (including guns and fishing tackle); knitting and sewing machine needles
39	Metal structures	Metal frames for buildings and structures, bridges, metal sheds and bridgework, utility poles and water towers
40	Repair of machinery and equipment	All repair of equipment, machinery, and instruments, including consumer appliances, performed in specialized enterprises, and capital repair of machinery and equipment performed by individual enterprises
41	Abrasives	Abrasive powders, pastes, and tools; synthetic diamonds, other abrasive materials, mica and graphite products (except pencils and electrodes)
42	Mineral chemistry products	Extraction and concentration of apatite and phosphorite, natural potassium salts, native sulphur and boron, mineral pigments, and other mineral materials for chemistry
43	Basic chemistry products	Inorganic acids, alkalies and compounds, synthetic ammonia, mineral fertilizers, caustic soda, nitric and sulfuric acid; chlorine, compressed gases, pesticides, herbicides, and disinfectants
44	Aniline dye products	All types of organic and synthetic aniline dyes and pigments for natural and synthetic textiles

Sector No.	Commodity	Description
45	Synthetic resins and plastics	A-1 types of synthetic resins and plastics, including fiberglass; products made from plastics, including plastic consumer goods; phonograph records
46	Synthetic fibers	Viscose, acetate, and synthetic staple fibers
47	Organic synthetic products	Synthetic organic acids, synthetic cleaning agents; acetone, phenols, synthetic alcohols, organic chlorine products; carbon black
48	Paints and lacquers	Paints, lacquers, varnishes; mineral pigments; wax compounds; brake fluid; household chemicals
49	Rubber and asbestos products	Rubber tires, hoses, belts, machine parts and fabrics, rubber toys, sporting goods, asbestos fiber, cord, and sheet
50	Other chemicals	Synthetic rubber of all types; synthetic pharmaceutical preparations, vitamins, antibiotics, vaccines, bacterial medications; rubber medical goods; photographic film, paper, and emulsions; magnetic tape
51	Logging	Felling and hauling of timber; firewood; railroad ties
52	Sawmills and lumber products	Lumber, prefabricated houses, wood products, wooden containers, wooden parts for industry, plywood and veneer
53	Furniture	Wood and woven furniture and parts; spring and soft mattresses; furniture repair

Sector No.	Commodity	Description
54	Other wood-working	Wooden dishes and household utensils, wooden sporting goods; matches
55	Paper and pulp	Wood pulp and cellulose; paper and cardboard
56	Wood chemistry products	Products of dry distillation of wood; turpentine
57	Construction materials	Cement; prefabricated concrete, block and brick, building stone; roofing tile; asbestos products; ceramic tile, crushed stone and and sand, lime, gypsum; insulation materials; linoleum and polymer products
58	Glass and porcelain products	Glass and products; fiberglass and glass wool; porcelain housewares, art goods, laboratory supplies, and plumbing fixtures
59	Textiles	Cotton, silk, wool, and linen yarn, thread, cloth, and fabrics; hosiery and knit goods; jute and hemp fiber, yarn, rope, and fabrics; felt products; umbrellas, and haberdashery
60	Sewn goods	Clothing and apparel; cloth headgear, underwear, bed linen; industrial sewn goods; clothing repair
61	Other light industry products	Natural and artificial leather and products; rubber, leather, and textile footwear; natural and synthetic furs; tanning agents; bristle and brush products; shoe repair
62	Fish products	Fishing and whaling; fresh and processed fish and seafood

Sector No.	Commodity	Description
63	Meat products	Meat and meat products; gelatin and glue; powdered eggs
64	Dairy products	Milk, butter, cheese, casein, and other milk products
65	Sugar	Refined and granulated sugar; refined molasses and syrup
66	Flour, bread, and confections	Flour and cereals, bread and bakery products; macaroni and related products; confectionery products
67	Other foods	Vegetable oils; margarine; laundry soap and candles; canned and frozen fruits and vegetables; tobacco products; cosmetics and perfumes; raw and refined alcohol; alcoholic and carbonated beverages; tea and coffee; table salt
68	Industry not elsewhere classified	Extraction of asbestos, graphite, asphalt, mica, and abrasives; industrial diamonds, clays for oil refining; plastic machine parts; printing and bookbinding; musical instruments; toys (except rubber); wallpaper; cardboard containers; pencils, pens, ink, notebooks, general office supplies; jewelry; buttons; art products; commercial laundering and dry cleaning; movie film and consumer film processing; water supply systems; processed animal feeds
69	Construction	Industrial, commercial, transportation, agricultural, and residential construction--new and maintenance; design and survey work; drilling for gas and oil

Sector No.	Commodity	Description
70	Crops	All grain, vegetable, fruit, berry, and technical (cotton, hemp, flax)
71	Animal husbandry	Livestock and poultry growing, apiculture, sericulture; unprocessed animal products (meat, raw milk, eggs, honey, raw wool, raw silk, raw hides, etc.)
72	Forestry	Planting and maintenance of forests
73	Transportation and communications	Freight transportation, including pipelines; communications serving production, including postal services
74	Trade and distribution	Wholesale and retail trade, including public dining; supply and distribution services; procurement of agricultural products
75	Other branches of material production	Collection of metal scrap; motion picture production; publishing; noncommercial hunting, fishing, and trapping; gathering of wild fruits, nuts, herbs, and so on

NOTES

1. For earlier versions see Treml, Gallik, Kostinsky, and Kruger 1972; Treml, Kostinsky, and Gallik 1973; Treml, Kostinsky, Kruger, and Gallik 1973; Kostinsky 1976; and Treml, Gallik, Kostinsky, Kurtzweg, and Tretyakova 1976. In addition to the tables and supplementary statistics these publications also include description and evaluation of the introduction and development of input-output techniques in the USSR. For the latter also see Levine 1962, Leontief 1960, Ellman 1973, and Tretyakova and Birman 1976. Treml 1975 offers a complete annotated bibliography of Soviet and Western sources on input-output analysis in the USSR.

2. The term "original" is used in this study to refer to the complete table as compiled by Soviet statisticians; this has never been published in full and is not available outside the Soviet Union.

The term "published table" refers to the incomplete and partially aggregated portion of the first quadrant published by the USSR Central Statistical Administration in its statistical yearbook (Narkhoz 67, pp. 63-111). "Reconstructed" pertains to the complete table as compiled by the authors of this study from the published table and other relevant data.

   3. The authors are indebted to Albina Tretyakova for the turnover tax estimates.

   4. For matrixes of direct and total input coefficients for Tables 1.1 and 1.2 see Kostinsky 1976.

   5. U.S. input-output tables prepared by the Department of Commerce show some eight separate columns in final demand and up to three separate rows in value-added.

   6. Estimation of various entries in the public and state consumption columns is based on data provided in Shneiderman 1974 and is documented and explained in Treml 1976.

   7. See the classification and definitions of nonproductive activities in Gosplan 1974, pp. 762-76.

   8. The few entries shown in Table 1.3 do not constitute a complete fourth quadrant arrangement of data which theoretically should show how the various income flows generated in the third quadrant support the activities of the second quadrant.

   9. Reconstruction of the matrix of working capital is based primarily on Belkin 1972, pp. 108-09 and on official Soviet data published in Narkhoz 1967, pp. 861-78 and described in Treml 1976.

REFERENCES

Becker, A. 1969. Soviet National Income 1958-1964. Berkeley: University of California Press.

Belkin, V. D. 1972. Ekonomicheskie izmereniia i planirovanie. Moscow: Mysl'.

Borovik, F. V., and N. A. Plashchinskii. 1972. Obrazovanie fonda proizvodstvennogo nakopleniia v promyshlennosti. Minsk: Nauka i tekhnika.

Buzunov, R. A. 1975. "Metod mezhotralevogo balansa v planirovanii razvitiia mashinostroeniia." In Ekonomicheskie problemy razvitiia mashinostroeniia, ed. D. S. L'vov, pp. 87-124. Moscow: Mashinostroenie.

Ellman, M. 1973. Planning Problems in the USSR. The Contribution of Mathematical Economics to Their Solutions. Cambridge: Cambridge University Press.

Gosplan SSSR. 1974. Metodicheskie ukazaniia k razrabotke gosudarstvennykh planov razvitiia narodnogo khoziaistva SSSR. Moscow: Ekonomika.

Granberg, A. G. 1975. Mezhotraslevye balansy v analize territorial'nykh proportsii SSSR. Moscow: Nauka.

Kostinsky, B. 1976. The Reconstructed 1966 Soviet Input-Output Table: Revised Purchasers' and Producers' Prices Tables. U.S. Department of Commerce, F.D.A.D., Foreign Economic Report No. 13. Washington, D.C.: Government Printing Office.

Leontief, W. 1960. "The Decline and Rise of Soviet Economic Science." Foreign Affairs (January): 261-72.

Levine, H. 1962. "Input-Output Analysis and Soviet Planning." American Economic Review 52, no. 2 (May): 127-37.

Mazanova, M. B. 1974. Territorial'nye proportsii narodnogo khoziaistva SSSR. Moscow: Nauka.

Narkhoz 19--. The abbreviation Narkhoz followed by the year refers to standard Soviet annual statistical handbooks published by the Tsentral'noe statisticheskoe upravlenie SSSR under the title of Narodnoe khoziaistvo SSSR v 19-- godu. Moscow: Statistika. The handbook is always published in the year following the year shown in the title.

Savinskii, E. S. 1972. Khimizatsiia narodnogo khoziaistva i proportsii razvitiia khimicheskoi promyshlennosti. Moscow: Khimiia.

Shatalin, S. S., and T. I. Serebrennikova. 1974. "Rol' mezhotraslevogo balansa v analize proportsii obshchestvennogo vosproizvodstva." In Mezhotraslevye issledovaniia, ed. E. I. Stepanov, pp. 3-21. Moscow: Statistika.

Shneiderman, I. M. 1974. Statistika uslug. Moscow: Statistika.

Slepov, V. 1976. "Mezhotraslevye sviazi lesopromyshlennogo kompleksa." Voprosy ekonomiki, no. 6: 36-48.

Treml, V. G. 1977. "Notes on Estimation of Various Entries in the Second, Third, and Fourth Quadrants of the 1966 Soviet Input-Output Table." Working paper, University of North Carolina Project on Input-Output Analysis in the USSR, Duke University.

_____, D. Gallik, B. Kostinsky, L. Kurtzweg, and A. Tretyakova. 1976. "The Soviet 1966 and 1972 Input-Output Tables." In U.S. Congress, Joint Economic Committee, Soviet Economy in a New Perspective, pp. 332-76. Washington, D.C.: Government Printing Office.

_____. 1975. Input-Output Analysis and the Soviet Economy. An Annotated Bibliography. New York: Praeger.

_____, B. Kostinsky, K. Kruger, and D. Gallik. 1973. Conversion of Soviet Input-Output Tables to Producers' Prices: the 1966 Reconstructed Table. U.S. Department of Commerce, F.D.A.D., Foreign Economic Report No. 1. Washington, D.C.: Government Printing Office.

_____, B. Kostinsky, and D. Gallik. 1973. "Interindustry Structure of the Soviet Economy: 1959 and 1966." In U.S. Congress, Joint Economic Committee, Soviet Economic Perspectives for the Seventies, pp. 246-69. Washington, D.C.: Government Printing Office.

_____, D. Gallik, B. Kostinsky, and K. Kruger. 1972. The Structure of the Soviet Economy. New York: Praeger.

Tretyakova, A. and I. Birman. 1976. "Input-Output Analysis in the USSR." Soviet Studies 28, no. 2 (April): 157-86.

TsSU (Tsentral'noe statisticheskoe upravlenie SSSR). 1971. Instruktsiia po zapolneniiu edinovremennogo ucheta zatrat na proizvodstvo produktsii za 1972 god (dlia promyshlennykh predpiiatii). Moscow: Statistika.

Volkov, A. M. 1976. Perspektivnoe planirovanie finansovykh resursov. Moscow: Finansy.

Volodarskii, L. M., and M. R. Eidel'man. 1969. "Osnovnye itogi razrabotki otchetnogo mezhotralevogo balansa proizvodstva i raspredeleniia produktsii v narodnom khoziaistve SSSR za 1966 god." Vestnik statistiki, no. 4: 19-30.

2

INDUSTRIAL INTERDEPENDENCE
AND PRODUCTION PLANNING
James W. Gillula

INPUT–OUTPUT MODELS OF PRODUCTION PLANNING

The extent of the technological interdependence of different producing sectors is an important characteristic of the structure of a Soviet–type economy, since this interdependence presents a major obstacle to the formulation of internally consistent production plans. The targets set in a plan for the total output of each sector must satisfy all final and intermediate demands without shortages or surpluses. But the use of intermediate inputs in production (directly or indirectly) links sectors together so that their levels of output are interdependent. In terms of the input–output model, this is the problem of determining values of gross output, X_i, for all sectors, $i = 1, \ldots, n$, such that

$$X_i = \sum_{j=1}^{n} a_{ij} X_j + Y_i \tag{1}$$

where Y_i is the planned value of output for final uses for sector i, and the a_{ij}, $i, j = 1, \ldots, n$, are the elements of the direct input coefficient matrix.[1]

The input–output solution for the consistent set of gross output targets which must be set in order for a given vector of final demands to be produced is found by computing the Leontief inverse matrix and solving the system:[2]

The author would like to thank Professor J. M. Montias for his comments on an earlier draft of this paper.

$$X = (I - A)^{-1} Y \tag{2}$$

For the large number of products centrally planned in the Soviet Union, the calculation of such an exact solution is infeasible. However, formulating the problem of planning interdependent output targets in terms of the input-output model suggests two iterative methods that could in theory be used to produce a nearly consistent plan.[3] Since the interdependence of sectors is systematically taken into account with these two iterative methods, they provide a basis for analyzing different aspects of the interdependence of sectors which must be taken into account with any approach to planning. In this paper, some simple measures of the extent of the interdependence of an individual sector with all other sectors in an input-output table are derived from these two iterative methods. The values of these measures are calculated for an 86-sector version of the 1966 input-output table for the Soviet Union,[4] and these values are used to identify major patterns of the interdependence of sectors in the Soviet table. This input-output analysis thus provides a quantitative indication of the potential effects of industrial interdependence on the consistency of alternative approaches to production planning in the Soviet Union.

The process of formulating an annual production plan in the Soviet Union starts with the setting, by the central planning agency, Gosplan, of tentative gross output targets (in terms of physical units) for the most important products. These control totals are disaggregated into production targets and supply quotas for different ministries, where they are then further disaggregated in the process of planning the production of specific commodities. At the ministry level, targets for the output of these and thousands of other less important commodities are matched against information received from enterprises about their tentative levels of production and input requirements. Revised production and supply targets are then reported back to Gosplan and Gossnab (the central committee for the planning of material supply) on a more detailed basis. A set of balances is then tabulated by both central planners and ministries to compare planned supplies and demands for all products.[5]

The effort to achieve consistency by the material-balances method is a complex process involving procedures that may introduce rather than eliminate imbalances in the final form of the plan. Reductions in the consumption of industrial materials in short supply may be ordered without a corresponding reduction in the output of the users of these products, thus forcing a change in input coefficients to achieve a balance. And often when an imbalance is corrected by changing the planned output of a particular product, only the output of the most important intermediate inputs used in its production can be adjusted to reflect this change; subsequent rounds of changes in the actual output required of many other intermediate goods may not be considered.[6]

While this paper focuses on the technological interdependence of different producing sectors, the consistency of planning in the Soviet Union is also greatly affected by other factors. Perhaps the most important is the limited proportion of the total value of production considered in the material balances. Balances are compiled for far fewer commodities than are produced, and the balances for many goods may include little more than 60 percent of the total production in the economy.[7] An additional problem is the loss of information during the process of aggregating the large number of specific commodities produced into the broader product groups used in compiling balances. Since the input coefficients for these product groups are averages of the coefficients for their individual products weighted by the gross outputs of the product mix of the previous period, any change in this product mix introduces a potential source of error in the planning of input requirements.[8]

Omitting these additional shortcomings of the material-balances method from consideration, the effects of the failure to consider secondary rounds of changes in intermediate goods requirements can be illustrated by an iterative input–output process that starts with a set of tentative output targets, X_0. Any imbalances that might result between these planned supplies and the total demand required to produce them (given a fixed vector of final demands) could be made progressively smaller by successive calculations of the total demand, X_i, as:

$$X_i = AX_{i-1} + Y \tag{3}$$

As the number of iterations increases, X_i converges to the solution which would be calculated using the Leontief inverse. By a series of substitutions for the X vectors on the right-hand side of this equation, the solution for X_i can be expressed as:

$$X_i = Y + AY + A^2Y + \ldots + A^{(i-1)}Y + A^iX_0 \tag{4}$$

Each successive iteration in equation (3) is a calculation of the value of intermediate goods required for the production of the total change in output of the previous round. With the material-balances method, when the planned supply of a particular product must be changed, this series of calculations is often stopped after only one or two such iterations. To provide an indication of the extent of the inconsistencies that might result if all secondary rounds of changes in inputs were not taken into account, the relative shares of direct and indirect rounds of inputs in the total change in input requirements that would be generated by a unit change in the output of each sector of the Soviet input-output table are calculated later in this chapter in the discussion on the indirect use of intermediate inputs. These calculations are based on the series of input coefficient matrixes in expression (4) produced by raising the A matrix to successively higher powers.

While this iterative input-output exercise illustrates the potential effects of interdependence on the consistency of planning by the material-balances method, the input-output formulation of the problem of planning interdependent production targets also suggests an alternative approach to planning, which greatly reduces the problems posed by industrial interdependence. A nearly consistent set of total output targets could be determined with fewer iterations (and perhaps with only a single iteration) by arranging sectors in the order of their importance as users of intermediate goods, and calculating their intermediate input requirements and total output targets recursively, beginning with final goods sectors. The ordering of sectors that would result in the most consistent set of output targets in a single iteration through the table can be identified by triangulating the matrix of interindustry transactions--that is, reordering the sectors so that the value of transactions on and below the main diagonal is at a maximum. Any imbalances between supply and demand could then be reduced much faster by calculating intermediate goods requirements for each sector on the basis of a total output target that includes interindustry demands for its output generated previously during the same iteration.

With the approach to planning based on the triangular ordering of sectors, most of the value of indirectly generated input requirements would be taken into account in a single iteration through the table. However, supply-demand imbalances would still remain for those sectors involved in interindustry transactions which are above the main diagonal of the triangular table. These elements represent feedback flows--deliveries from a sector higher in the triangular hierarchy to a sector lower, in the opposite direction to the primary pattern of interindustry flows identified by the triangular order. Such a transaction (x_{ij}, $i > j$) would be taken into account as an input required (for sector j) only after the total output of the supplying sector (i) had previously been determined. Later in this chapter a set of measures of the interdependence of sectors associated with these above-main-diagonal elements of the triangular form are defined and calculated for the 1966 Soviet input-output table. These measures of interdependence, which are defined both for the input-output table as a whole and for individual sectors, are derived from

the algorithm for triangulating an input–output table developed by
Helmstädter (1965; 1969), which suggests that the complex pattern of
interindustry production relations in an input–output table can be
summarized in terms of simple patterns of dependence and interdependence.

While the above–main–diagonal elements in the triangular
table can cause the output targets calculated by the recursive method
outlined above to be inconsistent, Montias (1962) has shown that if
the only sectors involved in such transactions are producing at the
limits of their capacity, a consistent set of output targets could be
determined in a single iteration by treating the final demands of these
capacity–limited sectors as a residual. Montias demonstrated the
usefulness of this "mixed model" with an input–output table for
Poland, identifying the major sources of inconsistencies by examining the ratios of the total input coefficient to the direct input coefficient for individual transactions. For the Soviet input–output table
used here, which has a much greater density,[9] summarizing the
interdependence of sectors that would produce inconsistencies in
plan targets is more difficult. But the measures of the interdependence of individual sectors provide a basis for systematically summarizing these interrelations. The major patterns of interdependence revealed by triangulating the Soviet input–output table will also
be described later in this chapter, and the results used to explain
the inconsistencies that arise in the calculations of gross output
targets based on the triangular form.

The analysis of different aspects of industrial interdependence
in this study provides an indication at an aggregate level of the potential effect of interdependence on various approaches to the planning of production in the Soviet Union. The calculations show that
if indirect input requirements were not considered in adjusting an
output target in the material–balances process, major inconsistencies
would be introduced. For many sectors, a large proportion of the
changes in intermediate input requirements thus generated would be
taken into account by considering only one or two rounds of changes
in inputs. But this proportion still varies widely among sectors.
The overall extent of interdependence associated with above–main–
diagonal elements of the triangular form of the table is not great,
but the measures of this aspect of interdependence also vary widely
among sectors. Furthermore, sectors other than the group of raw
materials and basic intermediate goods suppliers (which are most
likely to be capacity limited) are involved in feedback flows of goods.
However, given some realistic assumptions about the information
available to planners, the empirical results presented here suggest
that a set of gross output targets which are very nearly consistent
could be calculated in a single iteration when the recursive method
based on the triangular ordering of sectors is used.

INDIRECT USE OF INTERMEDIATE INPUTS

The state of the Soviet planning process in which the demands of all enterprises for intermediate inputs are determined on the basis of the tentative output targets they have been assigned is analogous to a single supply-demand iteration of the input-output expression (3) above. Since a full matrix of input coefficients for all centrally planned commodities is not known at the center, however, each such iteration may take months, and it may be impossible to repeat the entire process. The imbalances brought to light in the plan at this point may then be eliminated in any of several ways, including reducing planned deliveries for final uses, adjusting planned inventory levels or the foreign trade balance, or bargaining with producers to reduce their use of material inputs, as well as making changes in planned production. Ideally, all imbalances should thus be eliminated from the plan. But as the brief description of the Soviet planning process above pointed out, actual inconsistencies may remain (even though a balance may be achieved on paper), if secondary rounds of changes in supplies of intermediate inputs are not considered during the process of correcting imbalances.

Because of the many alternatives available for correcting imbalances in a plan, the material-balances method cannot strictly be represented as an iterative input-output process in which the output targets for all sectors are calculated simultaneously; and the relative sizes of the imbalances that may remain for individual sectors in the final form of a production plan cannot be determined with input-output data alone.[10] Neither can the imbalances inherent in a plan be identified by an ex post examination of plan fulfillment results, since plans may undergo many modifications as imbalances come to light, and the bottlenecks originally built into a plan may be overcome to varying degrees. However, the question of the effects of the interdependence of sectors in the Soviet economy on the planning of production by the material-balances method can be examined by focusing on known technological production relations to identify the potential sources of inconsistencies.[11]

The assumption implicit in using input-output data is that any small change in the output of a sector does indeed require a proportional change in its intermediate inputs, as given by its column vector of direct input coefficients. The bargaining among the various levels of the planning hierarchy in the Soviet Union about the output and input requirement targets set suggests that there is some flexibility in input norms, whether as a result of nonproportional inputs or the possibilities of economizing in the use of material inputs or substituting other inputs. However, given this assumption, if an imbalance is corrected by changing planned supplies of intermediate goods, a series of successive rounds of changes in the demand for intermediate goods inputs will be generated, which can be identified by expressing the Leontief inverse, $R = (I - A)^{-1}$, as the convergent series

$$R = I + A + A^2 + A^3 + \ldots \tag{5}$$

Since this series is to be used to compare the relative importance of the successive rounds of intermediate goods inputs only, the identity matrix is subtracted from both sides of this expression to make the main-diagonal elements of the matrix on the left-hand side comparable to all off-diagonal transactions.

$$(R - I) = A + A^2 + A^3 + \ldots \tag{6}$$

An element of this total intermediate input matrix, $R^* = (R - I)$, will be denoted r^*_{ij}, and an element of the direct input coefficient matrix raised to the kth power, A^k, will be denoted $_k a_{ij}$.

The relative importance of all the successive rounds of indirect deliveries between any pair of sectors, i and j, can be summarized by comparing the direct and the total input coefficients, $_1 a_{ij}$ and r^*_{ij}. The ratios of the corresponding elements in these two matrixes can give a misleading impression of the important indirect inputs, however, since a ratio of two very small coefficients (for example, $_1 a_{ij} = 0.00004$, $r^*_{ij} = 0.00012$) would indicate as important an indirect input as, for example, $_1 a_{ij} = 0.030$, $r^*_{ij} = 0.090$. The importance of all indirect inputs can be better identified by computing the difference between these two matrices, $R^* - A$, which gives, for each element, the total value of all indirect inputs required from one sector to produce a unit of the output of another.

The supplying sector for most of the largest differences, $r^*_{ij} - _1 a_{ij}$, calculated from the Soviet table are, as would be expected, primary products sectors--2-Ferrous metals, 4-Nonferrous metals, 8-Coal, 52-Logging, and 81-Crops, and sector 84-Transportation and communications. These six sectors are the suppliers involved in 129 of the 176 cases in which the value of $r^*_{ij} - _1 a_{ij}$ is greater than 0.05. While a large part of the output of these primary products sectors is embodied in the intermediate inputs used by sectors two, three, or more rounds removed, it is important to note that all 129 of these large indirect transactions (and 175 of the 176 greater than 0.05) would be on or below the main diagonal of the table in triangular form and thus would be largely taken into account in a single iteration through the triangular order.

Another characteristic of the indirect use of intermediate inputs apparent in examining the largest values of $r^*_{ij} - _1 a_{ij}$ is that some of the largest sources of indirect inputs are intra-industry flows. For sectors 66-Linen, 65-Wool, 63-Cotton, and 71-Fish products, the value of $r^*_{ii} - {}_1a_{ii}$ is greater than 0.25, and for seven other sectors this value is greater than 0.05.[12] However, for most of these sectors, this is because the method used to calculate the gross output produced by their individual enterprises differs from the standard practice of including only the value of output shipped out of the enterprise. For textiles, apparel, footwear, processed foods, coal, and possibly some other sectors, the value of some products produced and consumed within the same enterprise is included in the gross value of output of the sector and in the value of its intrasectoral deliveries.[13] This practice has been criticized by some Soviet specialists because of the inconsistencies it can produce if the large indirect input requirements that result are not taken into account. However, it is possible to alleviate this problem by extrapolating these intrasectoral transactions to approximate total direct plus indirect requirements, as shown below in the discussion of recursive plan calculations.

The relative size of each of the successive rounds of intermediate inputs for individual sectors in the Soviet table can be determined from the series of matrixes in expression (6) by computing, for each sector, the sums of its respective column in each matrix. The sum of any column, j, of the matrix R* gives the total value of direct plus indirect inputs from all sectors required to produce a unit of the output of sector j. Similarly, the sum of any column, j, of the A matrix gives the total value of direct inputs required to produce a unit of the output of sector j; and the sum of a column, j, of the A matrix raised to any power, k, gives the value of the kth round indirect inputs required to produce a unit of the output of sector j.

For the Soviet table, sums were calculated for each column of the R* matrix and the first three matrixes on the right-hand side of expression (6). These values were then used to calculate the proportions of the total (direct and indirect) input requirements that would be taken into account for each sector as each successive round of inputs generated is considered. The results of these calculations are given in Table 2.1. The sums of the columns of the direct input coefficient matrix, given in column 1 of this table, provide an indication of the relative importance of intermediate goods inputs for each sector. The sums of the columns of the R* matrix, given in column 2, are the denominators used in the calculation of the percentage ratios in the last three columns. Sectors have been listed here in the order of increasing share of direct inputs that would be generated by a unit change in the output of each sector.[14]

TABLE 2.1

Direct and Indirect Input Requirements for Each Sector
in the 1966 Soviet Input-Output Table

Sector Number and Name	(1)	(2)	(3)	(4)	(5)
66-Linen, flax materials	0.876	2.947	29.7	51.6	67.0
65-Wool materials	0.771	2.203	35.0	59.4	75.1
69-Sewn goods	0.722	1.866	38.7	63.6	78.7
70-Other light industry	0.596	1.418	42.0	68.6	83.9
67-Hosiery and knitwear	0.402	0.933	43.1	67.1	81.4
71-Fish products	0.681	1.559	43.7	69.5	83.8
50-Rubber products	0.605	1.381	43.8	71.7	86.3
40-Repair of machinery and equipment	0.421	0.948	44.5	70.9	85.2
17-Cable products	0.843	1.881	44.8	72.7	86.7
85-Trade and distribution	0.146	0.326	44.8	72.0	86.1
37-Sanitary engineering products	0.556	1.234	45.1	71.9	86.2
44-Aniline dye products	0.650	1.437	45.2	71.7	86.1
32-Transportation machinery and equipment	0.606	1.338	45.3	71.3	85.5
30-Construction machinery and equipment	0.594	1.311	45.3	70.9	85.1
80-Construction	0.526	1.160	45.4	73.7	87.3
68-Other textile products	0.663	1.459	45.5	69.9	83.2
36-Other machinebuilding	0.594	1.307	45.5	72.3	86.4
29-Hoisting/transporting machinery and equipment	0.586	1.278	45.9	71.4	85.5
34-Agricultural machinery and equipment	0.623	1.357	45.9	71.7	85.7
15-Energy and power machinery and equipment	0.520	1.132	45.9	72.0	86.1
39-Metal structures	0.652	1.417	46.0	72.5	86.6
25-Logging and paper machinery and equipment	0.484	1.050	46.0	71.9	85.9
16-Electrotechnical machinery and equipment	0.553	1.199	46.1	72.2	86.2
33-Automobiles	0.596	1.291	46.1	71.6	85.6
24-Pumps and compressors	0.648	1.402	46.2	71.8	85.9
7-Industrial metal products	0.663	1.425	46.6	72.9	86.7
27-Food industry machinery and equipment	0.544	1.166	46.6	72.2	86.1
49-Paints and lacquers	0.822	1.747	47.0	74.6	88.1
31-Construction materials machinery and equipment	0.462	0.974	47.4	72.8	86.5
54-Furniture	0.616	1.291	47.7	73.8	87.3
45-Synthetic resins and plastics	0.638	1.333	47.8	73.8	87.4
19-Forging/pressing machinery and equipment	0.412	0.861	47.9	73.0	86.6
28-Printing machinery and equipment	0.382	0.797	47.9	73.3	86.9
55-Other woodworking	0.520	1.085	47.9	75.3	88.3
38-Other metal wares	0.433	0.904	48.0	73.6	87.0
72-Meat products	1.205	2.509	48.0	76.9	89.9
46-Synthetic fibers	0.575	1.195	48.2	74.0	87.4
26-Light industry machinery and equipment	0.419	0.865	48.4	73.4	86.8
41-Abrasives	0.559	1.152	48.5	74.1	87.2
84-Freight transportation and communications	0.218	0.447	48.7	75.5	88.1
21-Tools and dies	0.465	0.954	48.8	74.0	87.3
5-Coke products	0.837	1.716	48.8	76.8	89.1
23-Mining/metallurgical machinery and equipment	0.302	0.617	49.0	74.2	87.3
48-Organic synthetic products	0.563	1.146	49.1	75.7	88.7
2-Ferrous metals	0.630	1.284	49.1	75.3	88.1
18-Machine tools	0.444	0.892	49.7	74.0	87.1
79-Industry unclassified	0.739	1.486	49.8	76.1	88.6
63-Cotton materials	0.655	1.302	50.3	75.9	88.3

Sector Number and Name	(1)	(2)	(3)	(4)	(5)
47-Synthetic rubber	0.779	1.544	50.5	76.6	89.3
20-Casting machinery and equipment	0.469	0.926	50.7	74.7	87.5
14-Electrical power	0.379	0.747	50.8	79.2	90.2
76-Bread and bakery products	0.814	1.597	51.0	84.9	93.7
64-Silk materials	0.477	0.933	51.1	75.9	88.2
35-Bearings	0.504	0.986	51.1	75.1	87.9
22-Precision instruments	0.318	0.619	51.4	75.2	87.7
59-Prefabricated concrete	0.678	1.319	51.4	77.6	89.3
86-Other branches	0.255	0.495	51.5	75.7	88.3
43-Basic chemistry products	0.523	1.010	51.8	76.6	89.0
57-Wood chemistry products	0.712	1.351	52.7	79.6	90.3
53-Sawmills and woodworking	0.726	1.371	53.0	79.1	90.1
56-Paper and pulp	0.688	1.297	53.0	78.3	89.5
13-Oil shales	0.347	0.649	53.5	77.1	88.9
4-Nonferrous metals	0.683	1.275	53.6	78.1	89.5
60-Roofing materials	0.762	1.400	54.4	78.5	90.0
83-Forestry	0.136	0.248	55.1	78.1	88.9
62-Glass and porcelain	0.350	0.634	55.1	78.3	89.5
51-Other chemistry products	0.579	1.048	55.2	78.5	89.7
3-Nonferrous ores	0.307	0.552	55.7	77.6	88.9
77-Confections	0.731	1.309	55.8	82.2	92.4
42-Mineral chemistry products	0.477	0.852	56.0	78.4	89.7
8-Coal	0.607	1.084	56.1	79.2	90.0
73-Dairy products	0.911	1.620	56.2	82.9	92.8
6-Refractory materials	0.480	0.852	56.3	79.5	90.1
58-Cement	0.557	0.972	57.3	80.3	90.6
1-Ferrous ores	0.480	0.833	57.6	78.7	89.7
12-Peat	0.410	0.708	58.0	80.0	90.2
61-Other construction materials	0.628	1.043	60.3	80.8	90.8
78-Other food products	0.480	0.794	60.4	83.2	92.4
81-Crops	0.235	0.383	61.4	81.9	91.1
52-Logging	0.485	0.783	62.0	81.3	90.8
10-Oil refining	0.500	0.854	63.7	84.0	92.3
82-Animal husbandry	0.467	0.733	63.8	84.9	92.9
74-Sugar	0.552	0.837	66.0	86.5	93.9
9-Oil extraction	0.438	0.660	66.4	83.0	91.9
11-Gas	0.495	0.735	67.3	89.8	92.3
75-Flour and cereals	0.748	1.039	72.0	88.8	94.7

Note: column (1): $\sum_i {}_1 a_{ij}$

(2): $\sum_i r^*_{ij}$

(3): $100 \sum_i {}_1 a_{ij} / \sum_i r^*_{ij}$

(4): $100(\sum_i {}_1 a_{ij} + \sum_i {}_2 a_{ij}) / \sum_i r^*_{ij}$

(5): $100(\sum_i {}_1 a_{ij} + \sum_i {}_2 a_{ij} + \sum_i {}_3 a_{ij}) / \sum_i r^*_{ij}$

Source: Compiled by the author.

77

As an example of the interpretation of the calculations given in Table 2.1, consider the sector listed in the first position, 66-Linen. An increase in the planned output of this sector would require an increase in the total value of its direct inputs from all sectors equal to 87.6 percent of the change in its output. But these direct inputs would represent only 29.7 percent of the total increase in direct plus indirect inputs needed to support the initial increase in output. If both direct inputs and the first round of indirect input requirements were considered, this proportion would increase to 51.6 percent, and if the second round of indirect inputs generated were considered, it would increase to 67.0 percent. Thus, 33.0 percent of the total value of inputs required are generated indirectly in all higher rounds.

Table 2.1 shows that several light industry sectors have the highest proportion of indirect inputs and converge to a full accounting of all input requirements most slowly, while the sectors with the lowest proportion of indirect inputs, near the bottom of the table, are for the most part primary products and processed foods sectors. Most of the machinery and equipment and other fabricated metal goods sectors are in the top half of the table, but the order of the remaining sectors presents no clear pattern. The ranking of sectors in Table 2.1 thus reflects to some extent the differences among sectors in the number of processing and fabricating stages the intermediate goods used by each have already undergone. But it shows also that the importance of indirect inputs for a sector does not depend either on its proportion of direct intermediate inputs (listed in column 1) or on whether it is primarily a final or intermediate goods producer. There are both final goods producers (69-Sewn goods, 67-Knitwear) and intermediate goods suppliers (66-Linen, 65-Wool, 50-Rubber products) near the top of the table, as at the bottom.

The calculations in Table 2.1 show that there is a rather wide range in the proportion of the total intermediate input requirements for a sector that direct inputs represent. And what is more important, this proportion is less than 60 percent for all but ten sectors. As successive rounds of intermediate inputs are considered, however, the proportion of total input requirements accounted for increases fairly rapidly for most sectors. With the exception of seven light industry sectors, more than 85 percent of the value of all changes in intermediate goods requirements would be taken into account for each sector if just the first two rounds of indirect inputs were considered in making any changes in output. The lower proportion of total input requirements included after any given round for these light industry sectors is due largely to the effects of the particular method of calculating the values of their gross outputs described above. Despite the fairly rapid convergence to a full accounting of intermediate input requirements for most other sectors, the difference in the proportion of their total requirements that would be taken into account with and without the consideration of these two rounds of indirect inputs is large.

If indirect inputs are not taken into account in the process of correcting the initial imbalances (generally shortages of supply) in a plan, the deficits in the output of the supplying sectors built into the plan will appear during its implementation. Unless the full impact then falls on final uses or is rapidly corrected through foreign trade or inventory adjustments, the effects of these shortfalls may spread through the economy, disrupting production in other sectors. However, the sectors thus affected may not be those that were the original sources of inconsistencies, since the distribution of available supplies of intermediate goods will ordinarily be greatly affected by the priority ranking of sectors. Thus, while the calculations presented in Table 2.1 may identify sectors that should be given greater consideration in accounting for indirect input requirements, they may provide little indication of where bottlenecks in plan fulfillment will ultimately result.

The identification above of the important suppliers of inputs used indirectly by many sectors showed that the indirect effects of an increase in planned output for most sectors would finally reach back to one of the primary products sectors. However, these sectors may be bottleneck sectors not because a large proportion of their output (which represents indirect requirements for other sectors) is not taken into account, but because their output is constrained by capacity limitations or subject to natural conditions. These supply-limiting factors must be taken into consideration in deciding how a supply-demand imbalance will be corrected for any sector that requires such indirect inputs from primary products sectors. This question of how the planning of interdependent output targets may be affected by considering information about capacity limitations is relevant for the recursive planning method based on the triangular form as well, and it will be examined below after the patterns of interdependence associated with the triangular table have been analyzed.

MEASURES OF INDUSTRIAL INTERDEPENDENCE

The extent of the interdependence of sectors in an input-output table has been measured in several different ways in input-output studies concerned with economic development and structural change. One approach is the measure of interrelatedness defined by Yan and

Ames (1965), which is based on the number of direct and indirect transactions between all sectors.[15] To calculate the Yan–Ames measure, an order matrix is first derived from the matrix expansion in equation (5) above. Each element of the order matrix, b_{ij}, has the integer value equal to the exponent of the first term in the series A, A^2, A^3, ..., for which the element in the ith row and jth column is positive. If there is no direct or indirect delivery from sector i to sector j, $b_{ij} = 0$. The interrelatedness measure for a technology matrix is then calculated:[16]

$$R[A] = \frac{1}{n^2} \sum_{i=1}^{n} \sum_{j=1}^{n} \frac{1}{b_{ij}} \tag{7}$$

Thus $0 \leq R \leq 1$, and the greater the value of R, the greater the interrelatedness of sectors. For the 86–sector 1966 Soviet input–output table, the value of this interrelatedness measure is a very high R = 0.896.

The Yan–Ames measure can be calculated for an individual sector as well, with separate calculations for input interrelatedness and output interrelatedness. For the Soviet table, these measures are nearly all, like the measure for the table as a whole, very high. The input interrelatedness measure is greater than 0.85 for all except 7 sectors, and 47 of these have values greater than 0.90. These high values of input interrelatedness suggest that an increase in the planned output of a single sector would require changes in inputs supplied by many other sectors. However, these uniformly high values are largely a result of the unusually large density of the Soviet input-output table, which includes many small transactions. For the purpose of evaluating the effects of interdependence on the consistency of planning, some new measures are defined here which reflect the value of interdependent transactions rather than their number. These measures are based on the triangular form of an interindustry transactions table and thus provide an indication of the inconsistencies that would result in a set of plan targets calculated recursively for sectors arranged in triangular order.

If an interindustry transactions matrix has a perfectly triangular form, no sector both buys from and sells to any other sector. (That is, for the two transactions between any pair of sectors, x_{ij} and x_{ji}, $i > j$, x_{ij} may be positive, but $x_{ji} = 0$).[17] There is only a one–way interdependence of sectors--deliveries from the lower to the higher sector, for any pair in the table. For a matrix that cannot be made perfectly triangular, however, two general patterns of the interdependence of sectors can be identified involving the elements

that remain above the main diagonal. The first is a situation in
which there is a mutual sale of goods between two sectors such as:[18]

   Electrical power $\leftrightarrow$ Coal

and the second, where there are circular interindustry production
relations such as:

   Ores $\to$ Metals $\to$ Mining machinery $\to$ Ores

   The first of these examples illustrates the direct interdependence of two sectors. Both $x_{ij} > 0$ and $x_{ji} > 0$, and one of these
positive transactions must appear above the main diagonal. The
second example illustrates a more indirect form of interdependence.
A transaction will appear above the main diagonal in this case even
where there are not flows of goods in both directions between any
pair of sectors. While the interrelations of input-output sectors
are a complex combination of these two aspects of interdependence,
the measures of interdependence defined below and the analysis in
the following section are based on this distinction.
   Since the triangulation of a matrix must at a minimum leave
each of the smallest transactions in all pairs, x_{ij}, x_{ji}, above the
main diagonal, only the direction and value of the difference in the
flow of goods between two sectors is considered in the triangulation
algorithm. A matrix composed of the differences between the two
transactions for each possible pair of sectors is calculated:[19]

$$d_{ij} = x_{ij} - x_{ji} \qquad\qquad i,j = 1,\dots,n \qquad\qquad (8)$$

In this difference matrix, elements on the main diagonal, which
have no effect on the triangular ordering of the table, are zero, and
$d_{ij} = -d_{ji}$ for all i,j. The value of an individual d_{ij} will be referred
to as the net flow of goods between two sectors, i and j.
   Using the difference matrix, an upper bound for the percentage
of the value of all transactions that can be shifted below the main
diagonal by triangulation can be calculated. The sum of the absolute
values of all elements below the main diagonal of the difference
matrix is included in this definition to reflect the assumption that
the largest element in each pair, x_{ij}, x_{ji}, is to appear below the
main diagonal of the transactions table.

$$\bar{\lambda} = 100 \,\frac{T + \overline{D}}{2T} \qquad\qquad (9)$$

where

$$T = \sum_{i,j=1}^{n} x_{ij} \qquad (i \ne j) \qquad (10)$$

and

$$\overline{D} = \sum_{i>j}^{n} |d_{ij}| \qquad (11)$$

$\overline{\lambda}$ represents a mathematical maximum for the degree of one-way interdependence of sectors in an input–output table. Since for most tables, however, there will be no possible sector ordering that places all of the smallest transactions in each pair, x_{ij}, x_{ji}, above the main diagonal, this absolute will not be reached. The actual degree of one-way interdependence can then be calculated (only after triangulating a table) as:

$$\lambda = 100 \frac{V_{max}}{T} \qquad (12)$$

where

$$V_{max} = \sum_{i>j}^{n} x_{ij} \qquad (13)$$

A measure of the direct interdependence of sectors as defined above can be calculated using the sum of the smallest of the two transactions, x_{ij}, x_{ji}, for all i, j. Expressing this sum as a percentage of the value of all interindustry flows (i ≠ j) produces a ratio that measures the minimum departure from a perfect one-way interdependence of sectors that must occur in the triangular table:

$$\gamma = 100 \frac{\sum_{i>j}^{n} \min (x_{ij}, x_{ji})}{T} \qquad (14)$$

or equivalently

$$\gamma = 100 - \overline{\lambda} = 100 \frac{T - \overline{D}}{2T} \qquad (14')$$

$\overline{\lambda}$ and γ can be calculated without putting the table in triangular form.

The percent of transactions above the main diagonal of the triangular table (equal to $100 - \lambda$) measures the total extent of the departure from the primary pattern of one-way interdependence of sectors. Where $\bar{\lambda} > \lambda$, the part of this $(100 - \lambda)$ total not accounted for by γ is identified as the ratio:

$$\delta = \bar{\lambda} - \lambda \tag{15}$$

so that

$$\gamma + \delta = 100 - \lambda \tag{16}$$

The difference, δ, results from all instances where $x_{ij} > x_{ji}$ but $i < j$. That is, a sector that is a net supplier for another appears above it in the table--a departure from the direction of the primary flow of goods dictated by the triangular hierarchy. $x_{ij} > x_{ji}$, $i < j$, implies $d_{ij} > 0$ where d_{ij} is an above-main-diagonal element of the difference matrix. Thus, δ can be calculated directly as the percentage ratio of the sum of all positive d_{ij}, $i < j$, to the total value of interindustry transactions, $(i \neq j)$.[20]

While $\bar{\lambda}$ and λ summarize the extent of one-way interdependence in the structure of production, γ and δ, from the opposite perspective, summarize the departure from this primary pattern. To analyze the relative importance, for individual sectors, of interdependence with all other sectors, ratios similar to the λ and $\bar{\lambda}$ measures for the entire table can be calculated for each sector.

A measure of the extent of one-way interdependence for an individual sector is defined as:

$$\lambda_i = 100 \, \frac{V_{i\,max}}{T_i} \tag{17}$$

where

$$V_{i\,max} = \sum_{k=1}^{(i-1)} x_{ik} + \sum_{k=i+1}^{n} x_{ki} \tag{18}$$

and

$$T_i = \sum_{k \neq i} x_{ik} + \sum_{k \neq i} x_{ki} \tag{19}$$

Similarly, an absolute measure, $\bar{\lambda}$, is calculated:

$$\bar{\lambda} = 100 \ \frac{\bar{V}_i}{T_i} \tag{20}$$

where

$$\bar{V}_i = \frac{T_i + \bar{D}_i}{2} \tag{21}$$

and

$$\bar{D}_i = \sum_{k=1}^{n} |x_{ik} - x_{ki}| \tag{22}$$

λ_i is the percentage ratio of the ith row and column elements below the main diagonal to all ith row and column elements for a sector in the triangular table. $\bar{\lambda}_i$, like $\bar{\lambda}$, takes into account the direct inter-dependence of sector i with all other sectors. Thus, measures similar to the γ and δ for the entire table can also be defined for individual sectors:

$$\gamma_i = 100 - \bar{\lambda}_i \tag{23}$$

$$\delta_i = \bar{\lambda}_i - \lambda_i \tag{24}$$

The γ_i ratio can also be calculated directly as the percentage ratio:

$$\gamma_i = 100 \ \frac{\sum_{k=1}^{n} \min(x_{ik}, x_{ki})}{T_i} \tag{23'}$$

While the values of the γ_i ratios (like the γ for the entire table) can be calculated without respect to a particular sector order-ing, the calculation of the values of δ_i is meaningless except for the triangular order of sectors, and they could change with any minor change in the sector ordering. However, both measures can be useful in summarizing the patterns of the interdependence of sectors in a table. The δ_i ratio for a sector can be calculated directly as the sum of all positive above-main-diagonal elements in the ith row and the ith column of the difference matrix for the triangular table as a percentage of T_i. A positive d_{ij}, $i < j$, identifies a transaction that departs from the primary direction of the flow of goods between sectors in the triangular hierarchy, and such a transaction represents one link in a set of circular interindustry production relations of the type illustrated above. Assume the sectors in that example appear in the triangular table in the following order (relative to each other):

		1	2	3
1	Mining machinery	$x_{1,1}$	$x_{1,2}$	$x_{1,3}$
2	Metals	$x_{2,1}$	$x_{2,2}$	$x_{2,3}$
3	Ores	$x_{3,1}$	$x_{3,2}$	$x_{3,3}$

Then $x_{3,1} = 0$ and $x_{1,3} > 0$ implies $d_{1,3} = x_{1,3} - x_{3,1} > 0$. Given this sector order, the contradictory flow of goods, $d_{1,3}$, will enter into the calculation of δ_1 and δ_3 but not δ_2, although all three sectors are involved in the circular production relation. The δ_i ratios thus provide a guide for identifying these circular flows of goods, but they are only indicators of the patterns of interdependence of sectors involved, and not comparable measures of their relative importance in the transactions of each sector.

The triangular form of the 86-sector 1966 Soviet input-output table has been identified in a previous paper (Gillula 1975). This sector ordering and the measures of interdependence for individual sectors defined above are given in Table 2.2. The measures of the extent of one-way interdependence of sectors for the table as a whole are $\bar{\lambda} = 94.47$ percent and $\lambda = 91.83$ percent. Thus, $\gamma = 5.53$ percent and $\delta = 2.64$ percent. These calculated values indicate a relatively strong one-way interdependence of sectors in the Soviet economy. But as the calculations in Table 2.2 show, there is considerable difference among individual sectors in the extent of interdependence. These values, and the special matrixes used in calculating them, are used in the following section to summarize the patterns of interdependence in the Soviet economy.

PATTERNS OF INTERDEPENDENCE

Examining the values of γ_i listed in Table 2.2 reveals a noticeable difference in the relative extent of direct interdependence for sectors in different broad product groups. In general, the values of γ_i for the agriculture-based sectors in the top third of

TABLE 2.2

Triangular Ordering of the 86-Sector Input-Output Table
of the Soviet Union for 1966

Position	Sector Name and Number	λ_i	γ_i	δ_i
1	80-Construction	100.0	0.0	0.0
2	77-Confections	98.8	1.2	0.0
3	71-Fish products	87.6	6.4	6.1
4	76-Bread and bakery products	99.7	0.3	0.0
5	59-Prefabricated concrete	99.6	0.3	0.1
6	32-Transportation machinery and equipment	88.6	3.4	8.0
7	25-Logging and paper	61.3	4.9	33.8
8	29-Hoisting/transporting machinery and equipment	89.3	7.1	3.6
9	54-Furniture	91.7	4.6	3.6
10	28-Printing machinery and equipment	97.6	1.4	1.0
11	37-Sanitary engineering products	95.8	2.8	1.4
12	69-Sewn goods	90.3	3.4	6.2
13	70-Other light industry	89.6	7.8	2.6
14	67-Hosiery and knitwear	99.3	0.6	0.1
15	72-Meat products	96.2	2.0	1.8
16	68-Other textile products	78.3	12.5	9.2
17	64-Silk materials	90.4	3.2	6.5
18	65-Wool materials	98.1	1.4	0.6
19	73-Dairy products	91.5	4.0	4.5
20	82-Animal husbandry	97.9	1.7	0.4
21	79-Industry unclassified	83.5	11.5	5.1
22	51-Other chemistry products	88.8	6.8	4.4
23	49-Paints and lacquers	77.3	6.7	15.9
24	78-Other food products	93.4	3.7	2.9
25	75-Flour and cereals	90.8	0.1	0.1
26	74-Sugar	99.2	0.5	0.3
27	66-Linen, flax materials	90.9	5.4	3.7
28	63-Cotton materials	90.6	3.9	5.5
29	26-Light industry machinery and equipment	83.4	6.2	10.4
30	81-Crops	98.4	1.4	0.2
31	61-Other construction materials	95.2	3.4	1.4
32	58-Cement	95.2	4.4	0.4
33	40-Repair of machinery and equipment	81.5	9.5	9.1
34	27-Food industry machinery and equipment	96.3	0.9	2.8
35	23-Mining/metallurgical machinery and equipment	72.9	13.4	13.7
36	30-Construction machinery and equipment	95.4	1.9	2.7
37	31-Construction materials machinery and equipment	94.2	3.6	2.2
38	34-Tractors/agricultural machinery and equipment	94.5	2.1	3.4
39	19-Forging/pressing machinery and equipment	85.4	9.4	5.2
40	15-Energy and power machinery and equipment	87.5	11.1	1.4
41	39-Metal structures	97.1	0.9	2.1

Position	Sector Name and Number	λ_i	γ_i	δ_i
42	18-Machine tools	89.5	6.2	4.3
43	24-Pumps and compressors	91.6	6.0	2.4
44	22-Precision instruments	81.9	13.5	4.6
45	33-Automobiles	81.9	13.5	4.6
46	20-Casting machinery and equipment	82.8	10.5	6.6
47	36-Other machinebuilding	84.3	13.9	1.8
48	16-Electrotechnical machinery and equipment	85.0	12.7	2.3
49	21-Tools and dies	85.3	11.4	3.2
50	35-Bearings	92.0	6.4	1.5
51	17-Cable products	87.0	13.1	2.0
52	38-Other metal wares	84.9	13.1	2.0
53	62-Glass and porcelain	87.7	10.6	1.7
54	55-Other woodworking	84.8	10.1	5.1
55	53-Sawmills and woodworking	92.2	6.2	1.6
56	7-Industrial metal products	84.9	9.5	5.6
57	2-Ferrous metals	94.2	5.1	0.6
58	6-Refractory materials	93.4	5.8	0.8
59	41-Abrasives	89.3	6.6	4.1
60	4-Nonferrous metals	95.5	3.6	0.8
61	3-Nonferrous ores	92.5	0.0	7.5
62	1-Ferrous ores	89.6	6.1	4.3
63	60-Roofing materials	94.7	3.7	1.6
64	86-Other branches	79.9	13.6	6.5
65	50-Rubber and asbestos products .	74.3	6.9	18.8
66	46-Synthetic fibers	95.7	2.4	1.9
67	47-Synthetic rubber	94.7	0.4	4.8
68	45-Synthetic resins/plastics	92.4	5.6	2.1
69	44-Aniline dye products	88.7	6.1	5.2
70	48-Organic synthetic products	85.8	11.1	3.1
71	43-Basic chemistry products	83.9	13.2	2.9
72	5-Coke products	97.6	1.9	0.5
73	56-Paper and pulp	83.4	11.5	5.0
74	42-Mineral chemistry products	88.3	7.1	4.6
75	57-Wood chemistry products	90.9	6.8	2.3
76	14-Electrical/thermal power	83.8	8.0	8.2
77	12-Peat	88.5	3.5	8.0
78	8-Coal	85.3	10.9	3.8
79	52-Logging	93.2	3.1	3.6
80	83-Forestry	89.3	1.4	9.3
81	10-Oil refining	78.8	20.7	0.5
82	9-Oil extraction	92.1	1.9	6.0
83	85-Trade and distribution	88.3	9.8	1.9
84	11-Gas	97.2	2.0	0.9
85	13-Oil shales	81.6	10.9	7.5
86	84-Transportation and communications	82.3	13.5	4.2

Source: Compiled by the author.

the triangular hierarchy--that is, crops, food products, textiles, and apparel--are below the $\gamma = 5.53$ percent for the table as a whole, while the values for basic industrial materials sectors in the bottom third of the triangular table are generally larger, with several more than twice this economywide average. Some of the sectors in the large group of fabricated metal goods and machinery and equipment manufacturing sectors also have relatively large values of γ_i, a result that has important implications for the applicability of a mixed model for production planning in the Soviet Union.

In order to summarize the major patterns of the direct interdependence of sectors in the Soviet input-output table, the 86 sectors have been grouped into the 12 broad categories of production shown in Table 2.3. The differences among these various groups in the relative extent of their direct interdependence with the rest of the economy are apparent in the average values of γ_i which have been calculated for each group. These $\bar{\gamma}$s are weighted averages of the γ_is for the sectors in each group, computed by using the values of T_i defined earlier in the discussion of the indirect use of intermediate inputs.

TABLE 2.3

Weighted Averages of γ_i for Selected Groups of Sectors

Sector Group	Sectors Included	$\bar{\gamma}$ (percent)
Construction*	80	0.0
Food products	71-78	2.1
Textiles and apparel	63-70	4.1
Agriculture	81, 82	1.6
Machinery and other manufacturing	15-40, 79, 86	10.1
Construction materials	58-62	3.0
Ores and metals	1-7	4.5
Chemical and rubber products	41-51	7.4
Wood and paper products	52-57, 83	5.6
Power	14	8.0
Fuel	8-13	13.4
Transportation and trade	84-85	11.9

*In the Soviet input-output table, sector 80-Construction has a zero row in the interindustry transactions matrix since by definition all of its output is recorded in the investment components of final output.

Source: Compiled by the author.

The sectors within each of the groups in Table 2.3 are in most cases near each other in the triangular hierarchy of the table, and the groups are listed in the order corresponding to the triangular form. Thus, the patterns of interdependence between these groups, summarized below, are useful for evaluating the effects of interdependence on the consistency of the recursive approach to planning based on the triangular table. To identify the most important interdependencies between these groups, a breakdown of the extent of the direct interdependence of individual sectors in each group with individual sectors in all other groups has been calculated. These percentage breakdowns of the interdependence of each group, given in Table 2.4, were calculated in the following way.

1. The interindustry transactions matrix was reordered to list together the sectors in each of the groups defined in Table 2.3.

2. An above-main-diagonal matrix was formed in which each element is $m_{ij} = min(x_{ij}, x_{ji})$. Main diagonal elements were set equal to zero.

3. This above-main-diagonal matrix was partitioned into the rectangular submatrixes formed by dividing the 86 sectors into the 12 sector groups by both row and column. (Those submatrixes formed along the main diagonal are triangular rather than rectangular.)

4. The values of m_{ij} within each submatrix were summed.

5. For each group, there was then a Σm_{ij} for its transactions with sectors in each other group and a similar sum for its intra-group transactions. These 12 sums were added together for each group, and the percentages of this overall sum which each Σm_{ij} represents for a group are the values given in Table 2.4.

Each row of Table 2.4 lists the groups that have the most extensive interdependence with the group of sectors shown on the left together with the proportion of that group's total direct interdependence in which each is involved. For each group of sectors on the left, all groups involved in more than 5 percent of this total are listed. These percentage values, together with the γ_i measures for individual sectors given in Table 2.2, provide a basis for identifying the major aspects of the direct interdependence of each group.

Transportation and trade. Transactions involving sectors 84-Freight transportation and communications ($\gamma_i = 13.5$), and 85-Trade and distribution ($\gamma_i = 9.8$) account for a large proportion of the direct interdependence of sectors in nine other groups in Table 2.4. For the food products and the textiles and apparel groups, this interdependence is largely a result of large two-way flows of goods

TABLE 2.4

Direct Interdependence of Selected Groups of Sectors
(in percent)

Food products	TrTr 29.6	Agri 20.5	Mach 18.8	Food 9.6	Chem 7.4			
Textiles and apparel	TrTr 27.5	Mach 27.1	Agri 11.7	Text 10.9	Chem 7.3			
Agriculture	Agri 36.6	Food 30.2	Text 18.2	Chem 10.7				
Machinery	Mach 27.0	TrTr 26.3	OrMt 12.1	Text 7.4	Chem 6.7	Wood 5.7		
Construction materials	Mach 29.3	TrTr 28.7	CoMa 11.4	Chem 7.8	Wood 6.6	Fuel 5.7		
Ores and metals	Mach 45.5	Chem 14.4	OrMt 12.4	TrTr 10.2				
Chemicals and rubber	Mach 22.4	TrTr 17.1	OrMt 12.7	Chem 11.2	Fuel 9.7	Wood 7.6	Text 6.6	Food 6.3
Wood and paper	TrTr 41.0	Mach 23.4	Chem 9.5	Text 5.6				
Power	Fuel 72.3	Mach 17.4						
Fuel	TrTr 65.8	Powr 16.8	Mach 5.7					
Trade and transportation	Fuel 39.0	Mach 24.7	Wood 9.3	Food 7.2	Text 7.1			

Source: Compiled by the author.

involving the trade and distribution sector, but for each of the other groups, there is extensive interdependence with both the trade and transportation sectors. As an example of the type of interindustry production relations involved, the largest single instance of direct interdependence in the table, which accounts for much of the interdependence of the fuel, transportation, and trade groups, is the following pair of transactions, expressed in thousands of rubles.

84-Freight transportation and communications →
    10-Oil refining   = 1,607,477
10-Oil refining → 84-Freight transportation
    and communications   = 1,516,114

While the oil refining industry is a large user of freight transportation services, it also supplies a large amount of the fuel needed by the freight-hauling sector. This basic pattern is repeated in the transactions of the trade and transportation sectors with each of their suppliers of material inputs.

Fuel. In addition to the interdependence with the transportation sector mentioned above, each of the fuel sectors is both a relatively large user of power inputs and a major supplier for sector 14-Electric power. Two of the fuel sectors—10-Oil refining ($\gamma_i = 20.7$) and 8-Coal ($\gamma_i = 10.9$)—also have a more extensive interdependence with the rest of the economy, including large two-way flows of goods with machinery and chemicals sectors such as 40-Repair of machinery and equipment, 22-Precision instruments, and 48-Organic synthetic products.

Power. In addition to its large direct interdependence with fuel sectors, 14-Electric power ($\gamma_i = 8.0$) makes large purchases from several machinery and equipment sectors for which it is a major supplier, such as 15-Energy and power machinery and equipment and 40-Repair of machinery and equipment. While both the power and fuel groups have relatively large measures of direct interdependence, most of their interdependence is a result of two-way transactions with very few sectors.

Wood and paper. Several sectors in this group are large suppliers for the transport and trade sectors, although most are net purchasers of the services of these two sectors. Much of the interdependence of the wood and paper group with the machinery group is a result of large purchases by 53-Sawmills and woodworking ($\gamma_i = 6.2$) from many machinery sectors for which it is an important supplier, while 56-Paper and pulp ($\gamma_i = 11.5$) has similar interindustry production relations with several chemical products sectors.

Chemical and rubber products. The chemical and rubber products
sectors have extensive interrelations with sectors in many other
groups. The two sectors in this group most significantly involved
in these two-way flows of goods with other sectors are 43-Basic
chemistry products (γ_i = 13. 2) and 48-Organic synthetic products
(γ_i = 11. 1). The most important of the sectors that supply large
inputs to (but are net purchasers from) the chemical and rubber
products sectors are 16-Electrotechnical machinery and equipment,
40-Repair of machinery and equipment, 24-Pumps and compressors,
2-Ferrous metals, and 63-Cotton materials. There are also large
two-way transactions between many of the sectors within this group,
in particular between 50-Rubber products (γ_i = 6. 9) and each of the
chemical products sectors.

Ores and metals. In addition to the interrelations mentioned above,
much of the direct interdependence of this group is accounted for by
large purchases from many machinery and equipment sectors by the
2-Ferrous metals and 4-Nonferrous metals sectors, which are their
major suppliers.

Construction materials. Of the sectors included in this group, only
62-Glass and porcelain (γ_i = 10. 6) has extensive interdependence
with sectors in several other groups, although several construction
materials sectors have two-way transactions with 40-Repair of
machinery and equipment.

Machinery and other manufacturing. The machinery and equipment
sectors are directly interdependent with each other group of sectors
in Table 2. 4 except agriculture. Several instances in which machinery group sectors supply large inputs to sectors (below them in
the triangular hierarchy) that are primarily their suppliers have
been mentioned above. The most important of these from the stand-
point of the machinery group are the transactions with 84-Freight
transportation and communications, 85-Trade and distribution,
43-Basic chemistry products, 2-Ferrous metals, 4-Nonferrous metals,
and 53-Sawmills and woodworking. The largest proportion of the interdependence of this group, however, is between sectors within the group;
16-Electrotechnical machinery and equipment (γ_i = 12. 7), 33-Automo-
biles (γ_i = 13. 5), and 40-Repair of machinery and equipment (γ_i = 9. 5)
all have large two-way transactions with several other machinery
group sectors.

Agriculture, textiles and apparel, food products. These three
groups of sectors, all of which have relatively low values of $\bar{\gamma}$,
are primarily interdependent with the trade and distribution sectors,
and with other sectors within this agriculture-based complex. The

direct interdependence of the food and textiles and apparel sectors
with the machinery group is largely a result of two-way transactions with the 40-Repair of machinery and equipment and 16-Elec-
trotechnical machinery and equipment sectors, while their interdependence with the chemical products group involves similar
transactions with 43-Basic chemistry products.

In addition to these patterns of the direct interdependence of
input-output sectors, the major aspects of the indirect interdependence of sectors can be summarized, as described earlier in this
chapter, by examining the transactions of sectors with large values
of δ_i. The position of an individual sector in the triangular table is
determined by its relations as a net supplier for all sectors in sum
above it and a net purchaser from all sectors in sum below it in the
table.[21] In satisfying these global criteria, however, the determination of the position of a sector may be dominated by its transactions with very few sectors, often with a single large supplier or
purchaser. As a result, a sector may be a net purchaser from some
sectors above it in the triangular table or a net supplier for some
below it. These interindustry transactions represent departures
from the primary direction of the flow of goods between sectors
dictated by the triangular hierarchy, and where they occur a circular flow of goods can be identified.

The position of sector 49-Paints and lacquers ($\delta_i = 15.9$) in
the triangular order is an example of this bounding effect. This
sector is a net supplier to all except two sectors in positions 25 to
59 in the triangular table but remains above them in position 25
because of a large net input from 78-Other food products--in position 24. To trace the chain of transactions back for just the largest
suppliers for each sector, the food products sector has a large input from 81-Crops, which in turn is positioned above the block of
machinery and equipment sectors because of large inputs from,
among others, 34-Agricultural machinery and equipment and
40-Repair of machinery and equipment.

Another complex chain of transactions can be traced involving
25-Logging and paper machinery and equipment which has the largest
δ_i ratio (33.8). This sector delivers most of its output for interindustry use to 52-Logging which is in position 79 of the triangular
order. Since its inputs from chemicals, metals, and machinery
and equipment sectors are larger in value, however, logging and
paper machinery and equipment appears above all these in position 7.
Logging is in turn a large supplier for several sectors in these
groups.

As a third example, circular production relations involving
50-Rubber products ($\delta_i = 18.8$) can be traced with sectors both
above and below it in the triangular table. It is a net supplier to

several fuel and services sectors but does not move lower in the
triangular order because of the large value of its inputs from
chemical products sectors. And it is a net purchaser from many
textiles sectors but does not appear higher in the table because of
larger net deliveries to machinery and equipment sectors.

As these examples show, the transactions that depart from the
primary one-way interdependence of sectors in the triangular table
are part of a complex interrelation of sectors. However, examining
the difference matrix reveals two general patterns of circular production relations between groups of sectors. The first of these is
indicated by the values of δ_i for several textile and light industry
sectors.   The general pattern of interdependence involved for
these sectors is similar to that described above for 49–Paints and
lacquers. Among others, 69–Sewn goods ($\delta_i = 6.2$), 68–Other textiles ($\delta_i = 9.2$), and 63–Cotton materials ($\delta_i = 5.5$) are also net
suppliers of many sectors below them in the triangular table, and
each is dependent on inputs from the agriculture sectors either
directly or at one stage of processing removed. This agriculture-
based block as a whole is above the block of machinery and equipment sectors in positions 33 to 52 because of the large machinery
inputs of 81–Crops and the net deliveries of most machinery and
equipment sectors to 40–Repair of machinery and equipment (primarily the supply of spare parts produced by each sector). The
feedback flows involved are largest to sectors such as 40–Repair of
machinery and equipment ($\delta_i = 9.1$), 22–Precision instruments
($\delta_i = 4.6$), and 33–Automobiles ($\delta_i = 4.6$).

A second major pattern of interdependence can be identified
involving the extractive sectors in the bottom half of the triangular
table. The position of each of these sectors is just below one of the
large users of its output. The extractive sector is in each case a
large net purchaser from several machinery and equipment sectors
and often from nonmetals sectors, while the major user of its output
is a net supplier for sectors in these groups. This pattern applies to

> 3–Nonferrous ores ($\delta_i = 7.5$) → 4–Nonferrous metals
> 1–Ferrous ores ($\delta_i = 4.3$) → 2–Ferrous metals
> 9–Oil extraction ($\delta_i = 6.0$) → 10–Oil refining
> 13–Oil shales ($\delta_i = 7.5$) → 14–Electric power and 11–Gas
> 83–Forestry ($\delta_i = 9.3$) → 52–Logging
> 8–Coal ($\delta_i = 3.8$) → 14–Electric power

The most important of the 13 machinery and metal goods sectors that
supply large net inputs to these extractive sectors are 23–Mining
and metallurgy machinery and equipment ($\delta_i = 13.7$) and 17–Cable
products ($\delta_i = 4.3$).

Various other instances of circular production relations can be identified in the Soviet input-output table, but these two general patterns account for most of the value of the positive above-main-diagonal elements of the difference matrix.

One of the results that stands out in this summary of patterns of the interdependence of sectors in the Soviet input-output table is the complex interrelation of machinery and fabricated metal goods sectors with the rest of the economy. In spite of the fact that many of these sectors deliver a large proportion of their output to final demand (investment) categories, the group as a whole still exhibits a strong direct and indirect interdependence with other sectors in terms of current interindustry transactions. Machinery and equipment sectors are among the most important nonservice sectors in the patterns of direct interdependence of each other group, and they are involved in each of the two major patterns of circular production relations identified above. This interdependence of machinery sectors is an important consideration in the evaluation of the potential gains from the use of a recursive method in plan calculations which follows.

SOME RECURSIVE PLAN CALCULATIONS

The fact that the Soviet interindustry transactions matrix can be put into a form that is very nearly triangular suggests that the process of formulating current production plans could be improved by taking advantage of the recursive method of calculating gross output targets described at the beginning of this chapter. Central planners in the Soviet Union do not have detailed information on the intermediate input requirements for the production of specific commodities, and thus the gross output targets set at the beginning of the planning process can only be approximate values. These control totals include estimates of intermediate goods production, which must be revised after the several-month process of disaggregating output targets, calculating input requirements, and relaying revised supply and demand figures back to the central planners. Much of this balancing of demand and supply for specific products is done by the various industrial ministries and their departments, which have information on the columns of the input coefficient matrix for their sectors of the economy on a much more disaggregated basis than that possessed by Gosplan. The need for further adjustments of output targets after this phase of the planning process is completed arises from the fact that many of the balances tabulated independently by these industrial branch planning bodies are in fact interdependent with each other. The significance of the recursive

approach to planning based on the triangular ordering of sectors is
that the interdependence of the plans worked out by the different
branch planning bodies can be more systematically taken into account.
Better estimates of the intermediate goods output for each sector
can be compiled with the efficient routing of information on interindustry input requirements this method provides.

The plan calculations carried out with this recursive method
here are made using the actual vector of final outputs recorded in
the 1966 Soviet input-output table. Thus, the gross outputs computed are estimates of the actual gross outputs produced in 1966,
and the effects of industrial interdependence on the consistency of
output targets calculated recursively with the triangular table can
be evaluated. The first series of calculations were made on the
assumption that the gross output target for each sector is the sum
of its final output target and the interindustry demands for its output
of sectors computed previously within the iteration. The calculation
of the gross output for each sector is followed by the calculation of
its intermediate input requirements. The value of X_1 was set equal
to $(Y_1 + a_{11}Y_1)$ and the gross output target for each successive
sector was computed in a single iteration through the triangular
table as:

$$X_i = (Y_i + \sum_{j=1}^{i-1} a_{ij}X_j)(1 + a_{ii}) \qquad (i = 2,\ldots,n) \qquad (25)$$

The percentages of the actual gross outputs that these estimated
values represent for each sector of the Soviet table are given in the
first column of Table 2.5. For more than one-half of the sectors
in the table, this approximation of gross output is found to be less
than 10 percent less than actual requirements. For 18 sectors this
shortfall is greater than 20 percent, and for another 28 it is between
10 and 20 percent.

The inconsistencies that result from this calculation reflect
the effects of each of the different aspects of interdependence distinguished above. Where there are above-main-diagonal elements
in the row of the triangular transactions matrix for a sector, the
calculated value of its interindustry deliveries (and thus its gross
output) will fall short of the actual demand. And since the input
requirements of these sectors will be calculated on the basis of an
understated gross output, the calculated outputs of their direct and
indirect suppliers will in turn be understated.

The large shortfalls in the gross output estimates for several
textiles and light industry sectors in the top third of the triangular
order can be traced to two of the characteristics of industrial

TABLE 2.5

Iterative Planning from Fixed Levels of Final Demand: Estimated Gross
Output Targets as a Percentage of Actual Gross Outputs Required
(percent)

Sector	Iteration Number		
	1	2	3
80-Construction	100.0	100.0	100.0
77-Confections	98.9	99.9	100.0
71-Fish products	78.8	91.3	96.5
76-Bread and bakery products	99.8	100.0	100.0
59-Prefabricated concrete	99.3	99.9	100.0
32-Transportation machinery and equipment	92.2	99.0	99.8
25-Logging and paper machinery and equipment	70.1	94.6	98.6
54-Furniture	94.4	99.3	99.8
28-Printing machinery and equipment	99.1	99.9	100.0
37-Sanitary engineering machinery and equipment	93.2	98.7	99.7
69-Sewn goods	91.8	99.0	99.7
70-Other light industry	87.5	96.2	98.8
67-Hosiery and knitwear	99.6	99.9	100.0
72-Meat products	88.2	96.5	99.0
68-Other textile products	73.3	92.2	97.5
64-Silk materials	81.0	93.0	97.6
65-Wool materials	62.2	77.9	87.2
73-Dairy products	91.0	98.4	99.7
82-Animal husbandry	91.4	97.2	98.9
79-Industry unclassified	87.7	98.1	99.4
51-Other chemistry products	93.6	98.6	99.6
49-Paints and lacquers	60.1	91.3	97.9
78-Other food products	93.9	98.4	99.6
75-Flour and cereals	99.2	99.8	99.9
74-Sugar	96.9	99.3	99.8
66-Linen, flax materials	46.5	63.3	75.2
63-Cotton materials	70.0	87.5	94.5
26-Light industry machinery and equipment	90.4	97.1	98.7
81-Crops	93.3	97.4	98.7
61-Other construction materials	94.9	99.2	99.8
58-Cement	96.0	99.4	99.8
40-Repair of machinery and equipment	92.8	98.7	99.6
27-Food industry machinery and equipment	98.7	99.7	99.9
23-Mining and metallurgical machinery and equipment	88.7	98.0	99.4
30-Construction machinery and equipment	97.7	99.6	99.9
31-Construction materials machinery and equipment	96.8	99.6	99.9
34-Tractors and agricultural machinery and equipment	91.1	97.4	99.2
19-Forging/pressing machinery and equipment	94.6	99.3	99.8
15-Energy and power machinery and equipment	88.6	98.5	99.7
39-Metal structures	97.2	99.6	99.9
18-Machine tools	96.7	99.5	99.9

(continued)

(Table 2.5 continued)

Sector	Iteration Number		
	1	2	3
24-Pumps and compressors	94.5	99.1	99.8
22-Precision instruments	94.1	99.1	99.8
33-Automobiles	84.2	95.7	98.8
20-Casting machinery and equipment	89.8	98.4	99.6
36-Other machinebuilding	89.3	97.6	99.4
16-Electrotechnical machinery and equipment	92.6	98.3	99.6
21-Tools and dies	83.3	97.1	99.2
35-Bearings	86.0	97.3	99.2
17-Cable products	87.1	97.5	99.3
38-Other metal wares	90.1	98.1	99.4
62-Glass and porcelain	89.0	98.0	99.5
55-Other woodworking	90.6	98.0	99.4
53-Sawmills and woodworking	85.9	96.1	98.9
7-Industrial metal products	76.5	95.6	98.8
2-Ferrous metals	87.9	96.5	99.0
6-Refractory materials	90.1	97.9	99.4
41-Abrasives	80.3	92.7	97.5
4-Nonferrous metals	84.6	94.7	98.3
3-Nonferrous ores	80.3	93.3	97.9
1-Ferrous ores	90.7	97.5	99.3
60-Roofing	94.5	99.1	99.7
86-Other branches	93.3	98.7	99.6
50-Rubber products	77.1	95.8	98.8
46-Synthetic fibers	77.2	91.0	95.7
47-Synthetic rubber	73.1	94.8	98.6
45-Synthetic resins and plastics	82.4	94.3	98.1
44-Aniline dye products	73.0	87.5	94.3
48-Organic synthetic products	74.9	92.8	97.9
43-Basic chemistry products	82.9	94.7	98.3
5-Coke products	85.4	95.4	98.6
56-Paper and pulp	77.0	94.0	98.2
42-Mineral chemistry products	85.2	95.8	98.7
57-Wood chemistry products	75.6	93.3	98.1
14-Electrical power	77.1	95.2	98.6
12-Peat	83.7	94.9	98.3
8-Coal	79.1	93.0	97.8
52-Logging	83.8	95.7	98.7
83-Forestry	92.3	97.8	99.4
10-Oil refining	72.5	94.2	98.4
9-Oil extraction	80.9	96.0	98.9
85-Trade and distribution	90.3	97.2	99.0
11-Gas	86.7	96.8	99.0
13-Oil shales	85.0	95.7	98.7
84-Freight transportation and communications	87.0	96.5	98.9

Source: Compiled by the author.

interdependence identified above: the circular production relations that link them with the agriculture sector on the input side and with many machinery and nonmetals sectors (lower in the table) on the output side; and the large intrasectoral transactions of several of these sectors, which generate large values of indirect input requirements. Two of the sectors for which actual interindustry demands are significantly understated are 49-Paint and lacquer and 68-Other textile products. The sectors most affected by large intrasectoral input coefficients are those identified earlier in the discussion on indirect use of intermediate inputs--66-Linen, 65-Wool, 63-Cotton, and 71-Fish products. The indirect input requirements of these four sectors pose a particular problem for achieving consistency with few iterations, but the extent of these inconsistencies can be reduced by extrapolating their internal requirements as shown below.

The 10-20 percent shortfalls in the estimated gross outputs for several of the machinery and metal products sectors result largely from their interdependence with the basic industrial materials suppliers below them in the triangular order. The understatement of the output of machinery sectors in turn has direct and indirect effects on the calculated gross outputs of both fabricated metal goods sectors and basic metals suppliers--for example, 35-Bearings, 21-Tools and dies, and 17-Cable products, as well as 2-Ferrous metals and 4-Nonferrous metals. Shortfalls in the output of other basic industrial materials sectors in the bottom third of the triangular order can similarly be traced to the cumulative effects of understatements in the estimated output of many sectors above them in the table, and to the patterns of interdependence between those sectors described above.

While many of the estimates of gross output calculated in a single iteration through the triangular table are unacceptably low, with further iterations these estimates converge rapidly to the actual values of gross output required for most sectors. Two additional iterations of the Soviet table were carried out using the revised estimates of total demand for the output of each sector that result when the above-main-diagonal transactions omitted in the gross output estimates of the first iteration are taken into account. The gross output of the ith sector in the tth iteration was computed according to the equation:

$$_tX_i = Y_i + \sum_{j=1}^{i-1} a_{ij} \cdot {}_tX_j + \sum_{j=i}^{n} a_{ij} \cdot {}_{t-1}X_j \quad (i = 1, \ldots, n) \quad (26)$$

The results of these calculations for the second and third iterations
are given in Table 2.5. Just one additional iteration is sufficient to
increase the percentage of actual requirements taken into account to
90 percent or more for all except four sectors, and three of these
are light industry sectors with large intrasectoral inputs. The estimates of gross output are within 5 percent of their actual values for
64 of the 86 sectors. With a third iteration, all except four sectors
are within 5 percent of their actual gross outputs, and 73 of these
are within 2 percent.

The major source of error in these plan calculations is the
large intrasectoral inputs for several light industry sectors. However, in practice this problem should not be great if the interpretation of this recursive process as a series of calculations made by
individual branch planning bodies is valid, since sectoral agencies
should have much more disaggregated information on these extensive
intrasectoral transactions. The estimates of the gross outputs of
these sectors can be improved by approximating their total direct
and indirect intrasectoral requirements, but the input-output calculations used to make this adjustment are primarily relevant for
instances in which only the aggregate intrasectoral input coefficient
is known. Montias (1959, pp. 969–70) has suggested that the output
of sectors that converge to their required total outputs slowly can be
better estimated by extrapolating from the estimates of their output
obtained in the first few iterations. If, as noted below, however,
it is important to limit the number of iterations, a more direct
method of considering these intrasectoral inputs is needed. For
most sectors, this can be accomplished quite well by multiplying
the initial gross output estimate by an approximation of the full
intrasectoral input coefficient rather than by the direct input coefficient. The full input coefficient for sector i can be approximated
by $(1/(1 - a_{ii}))$, and equation (25) would then be modified so that the
gross output for sectors with large intrasectoral transactions would
be calculated:

$$X_i = (Y_i + \sum_{j=1}^{i-1} a_{ij}X_j)(1/(1 - a_{ii})) \qquad (25')$$

Subsequent iterations would still be calculated using equation (26).

The three iterations described above were repeated with the
initial estimates of gross output for seven sectors--those with the
largest intrasectoral input coefficients--calculated according to
equation (25'). For each of these seven sectors, the direct input
coefficient, the full input coefficient, the value of $(1/(1 - a_{ii}))$, and
the new gross output estimate are given in Table 2.6.

TABLE 2.6

Sectors with Large Intrasectoral Inputs

Sector	a_{ii}	r_{ii}	$(1/(1 - a_{ii}))$	X_i
66–Linen	.6652	2.9890	2.9869	85.4
65–Wool	.5699	2.3289	2.3250	92.3
63–Cotton	.4025	1.6777	1.6376	87.4
71–Fish products	.3939	1.6504	1.6499	93.2
64–Silk	.2813	1.3921	1.3914	88.2
70–Other light industry	.2679	1.3671	1.3660	94.3
72–Meat products	.2512	1.3411	1.3355	94.5

Source: Compiled by the author.

These adjustments result in substantial improvements in the
estimates of gross output calculated for each sector in a single
iteration, and with additional iterations the estimates improve still
further. Only sector 66–Linen has a shortfall greater than 3 percent after the third iteration. However, making the adjustments in
the gross outputs of these sectors during the first iteration does not
have a significant effect on the calculated values of gross output for
other sectors. The largest increase in the proportion of actual
gross output taken into account for a sector after a single iteration
is 2.3 percent for sector 82–Animal husbandry.

The calculations just described suggest that a quite satisfactory degree of consistency can be attained with three or perhaps two
iterations through the triangular order. However, if each round of
this input-output exercise in practice represents a series of independent calculations, each carried out by a different industrial
ministry (or department of Gosplan), it may be important to limit
the plan calculation process to a single iteration. This may be
possible if the calculations made above are modified with two additional assumptions that are both more realistic and still consistent
with this interpretation of the planning process. The first of these
modifications involves the initial assumption that only final output
targets are known to each sector at the beginning of the planning
process. If the more realistic assumption is made that each sector
will plan to supply previous levels of interindustry demands, until
these tentative supply figures are replaced by current calculations,

a large proportion of above-main-diagonal transactions will be taken into account in the first iteration. The gross output of the ith sector in year t would then be calculated in a single iteration as:

$$_tX_i = \left[Y_i + \sum_{j=1}^{i-1} a_{ij} \cdot {_tX_j} + \sum_{j=i+1}^{n} a_{ij} \cdot {_{t-1}X_j} \right] (1 + a_{ii}) \quad (27)$$

To illustrate the effects of this assumption on the first approximation of the gross output for each sector, this series of calculations was carried out with the conservative assumption that the gross outputs of all sectors in 1966 represented a uniform 10 percent increase over those of previous years. The results of this computation are given in the first column of Table 2.7. This single iteration beginning with previous levels of gross output compares closely with the results of the second iteration in the previous set of calculations. Shortfalls in gross output are greater than 10 percent for only six sectors, and four of these are among the seven sectors listed in Table 2.6. For 66 sectors, the shortfall is already less than 5 percent. While this assumption alone seems sufficient to produce a nearly consistent set of gross output targets, another important consideration has been omitted in all of the calculations made thus far on the basis of actual values of final and gross outputs recorded in the Soviet input-output table. In practice, the planning process might begin with unrealistically high targets for final output, and the iterative process could then result in the calculation of gross output targets in excess of production capacity for some sectors. However, by taking capacity limitations directly into account, the consistency of plan calculations is improved still further, as Montias (1962) has shown.

Montias argued that for the purposes of plan calculations, the final output of capacity-limited sectors should be treated as a residual. Since the values of all intermediate input requirements of capacity-limited sectors can then be determined at the beginning of the planning process, this procedure has the benefit of eliminating the effects of all feedback flows in which these sectors are involved. In his study of the input-output table of Poland, Montias found that the occurrence of feedback flows was limited to transactions between the sectors producing raw materials and semifabricates-- ores, metals, basic chemicals, electricity, coal and petroleum products, lumber products, and so forth. And he argues that it is precisely these sectors that historically have been capacity-limited in the East European socialist countries. The summary of the patterns of interdependence in Table 2.4 showed that these basic industrial materials sectors also have the most extensive

TABLE 2.7

Modified Iterative Plan Calculations: Single Iteration Estimated Gross
Output Targets as a Percent of Actual Gross Output Required

Sector	(1)	(2)	(3)
80-Construction	100.0	100.0	100.0
77-Confections	99.7	99.4	99.8
71-Fish products	83.9	79.4	99.4
76-Bread and bakery products	100.0	99.9	100.0
59-Prefabricated concrete	99.9	99.7	100.0
32-Transportation machinery and equipment	99.2	96.1	99.6
25-Logging and paper machinery and equipment	97.0	98.8	99.8
29-Hoisting/transporting machinery and equipment	99.1	97.1	99.6
54-Furniture	99.4	96.3	99.6
28-Printing machinery and equipment	99.9	99.2	99.9
37-Sanitary engineering machinery and equipment	98.3	95.2	98.5
69-Sewn goods	99.1	96.0	99.6
70-Other light industry	92.3	89.3	99.6
67-Hosiery and knitwear	99.8	99.7	99.9
72-Meat products	92.8	89.9	99.6
68-Other textile products	94.0	80.9	96.0
64-Silk materials	90.6	86.8	99.3
65-Wool materials	66.8	64.8	99.5
73-Dairy products	98.6	92.4	98.7
82-Animal husbandry	95.4	92.4	99.2
79-Industry unclassified	98.3	95.2	99.5
51-Other chemistry products	97.5	95.8	98.0
49-Paints and lacquers	94.5	74.0	96.1
78-Other food products	96.0	95.3	96.2
75-Flour and cereals	99.7	99.6	99.9
74-Sugar	97.9	97.6	98.1
66-Linen, flax materials	53.7	51.2	99.2
63-Cotton materials	81.9	78.9	99.3
26-Light industry machinery and equipment	96.6	95.7	99.7
81-Crops	95.0	94.6	98.6
61-Other construction materials	99.2	97.5	99.5
58-Cement	99.4	98.5	99.8
40-Repair of machinery and equipment	98.9	98.6	99.8
27-Food industry machinery and equipment	99.4	99.1	99.8
23-Mining and metallurgical machinery and equipment	98.8	99.8	100.0
30-Construction machinery and equipment	99.7	99.7	99.9
31-Construction materials machinery and equipment	99.6	98.4	99.8
34-Tractors and agricultural machinery and equipment	95.2	94.6	96.1
19-Forging/pressing machinery and equipment	99.4	96.4	99.6
15-Energy and power machinery and equipment	98.7	91.2	99.1
39-Metal structures	99.7	99.4	99.9
18-Machine tools	99.6	98.0	99.8

(continued)

(Table 2.7 continued)

Sector	(1)	(2)	(3)
24–Pumps and compressors	99.4	98.3	99.8
22–Precision instruments	99.2	96.0	99.4
33–Automobiles	95.3	93.8	96.4
20–Casting machinery and equipment	98.6	96.0	99.3
36–Other machinebuilding	97.5	93.6	98.0
16–Electrotechnical machinery and equipment	98.0	96.9	98.6
21–Tools and dies	97.4	96.3	99.2
35–Bearings	97.3	96.6	98.7
17–Cable products	97.9	97.0	99.1
38–Other metal wares	98.2	98.3	99.6
62–Glass and porcelain	98.3	--	--
55–Other woodworking	98.0	--	--
53–Sawmills and woodworking	96.0	--	--
7–Industrial metal products	96.6	--	--
2–Ferrous metals	96.1	--	--
6–Refractory materials	98.0	--	--
41–Abrasives	90.2	--	--
4–Nonferrous metals	93.2	--	--
3–Nonferrous ores	91.3	--	--
1–Ferrous ores	97.3	--	--
60–Roofing	99.1	--	--
86–Other branches	98.7	--	--
50–Rubber products	96.5	--	--
46–Synthetic fibers	88.2	--	--
47–Synthetic rubber	95.2	--	--
45–Synthetic resins and plastics	94.4	--	--
44–Aniline dye products	85.2	--	--
48–Organic synthetic products	94.6	--	--
43–Basic chemistry products	95.3	--	--
5–Coke products	95.5	--	--
56–Paper and pulp	94.3	--	--
42–Mineral chemistry products	96.0	--	--
57–Wood chemistry products	94.8	--	--
14–Electrical power	96.0	--	--
12–Peat	94.8	--	--
8–Coal	93.0	--	--
52–Logging	96.1	--	--
83–Forestry	98.1	--	--
10–Oil refining	95.4	--	--
9–Oil extraction	96.9	--	--
85–Trade and distribution	95.9	--	--
11–Gas	97.0	--	--
13–Oil shales	96.1	--	--
84–Freight transportation and communications	96.3	--	--

Note: Calculated as described in the text.

Source: Compiled by the author.

interdependence with the rest of the economy in the Soviet Union. However, involvement in feedback flows is not limited solely to these sectors. A major exception is the extensive interdependence of the machinery and equipment sectors. To some extent this is due to the greater disaggregation of machinery and equipment production in the Soviet table.[22] But as Table 2.4 showed, the interdependence of the machinery and equipment group extends to many basic industrial materials sectors as well. Applying the method outlined by Montias for considering capacity limitations in the calculation of gross output targets should thus improve the estimates of gross output for machinery sectors as well as basic industrial materials suppliers.

The sectors in positions 53 to 86 of the triangular Soviet table correspond closely with the industries identified by Montias as most likely to be capacity-limited. If these sectors are assumed to be capacity-limited (with capacities equal to their actual levels of gross output produced) the plan targets for the gross outputs of all other sectors can be calculated in a single iteration according to the equation:

$$X_i = \left[Y_i + \sum_{j=1}^{i-1} a_{ij}X_j + \sum_{j=53}^{86} a_{ij}\overline{X}_j \right] (1 + a_{ii}) \quad (i = 1, \ldots, 52) \quad (28)$$

(The assumption that previous levels of gross output are employed in the initial iteration is dropped for the moment.)

The estimates of gross output for these 52 sectors are expressed as a percentage of their actual values in column 2 of Table 2.7. The shortfalls in these estimates are more than 10 percent for 9 sectors, between 5 percent and 10 percent for 7 others, and less than 5 percent for the remaining 36 sectors (in addition to the 34 assumed capacity-limited). Gross output estimates for the machinery and equipment sectors are all within 10 percent of their actual requirements in this single iteration. The 9 sectors with shortfalls greater than 10 percent include the 7 sectors listed in Table 2.6, for which gross output targets can be improved by using equation (25').

If the various methods of plan calculation described in this section are used together, a very nearly consistent set of gross output targets can be calculated in a single iteration, and this combination of input-output techniques can be interpreted as a simplified description of a production-planning process based on the efficient routing of information between independent sectoral planning bodies. At the beginning of the planning period, each planning body knows the level of its deliveries to all other sectors in the past year and its

input norms for purchases from all other sectors. The planning
process starts with the determination of feasible gross outputs for
the capacity-limited sectors during the planning period. Each
capacity-limited sector calculates its requirements for intermediate
inputs, and the values of these demands are communicated to all
other sectors. After targets for the final output of non-capacity-
limited sectors have been established, the iterative plan calculation
process begins with the first sector in the triangular order. Although no sectoral planning body knows the input coefficients of any
other sector, the calculation of the gross output target for each
sector (except the seven listed in Table 2.6) in year t can be represented in input–output terms as:

$$
{}_tX_i = {}_tY_i + \sum_{j=1}^{i-1} a_{ij} \cdot {}_tX_j + \sum_{j=i+1}^{52} a_{ij} \cdot {}_{t-1}X_j
$$

$$
+ \sum_{j=53}^{86} a_{ij} \cdot {}_t\overline{X}_j \, (1 + a_{ii}) \tag{29}
$$

For the seven sectors with large intrasectoral input coefficients,
equation (29) is modified by substituting the factor $(1/(1 + a_{ii}))$ for
$(1 + a_{ii})$. On the basis of this gross output target for each sector,
its intermediate input requirements are calculated and sent to all
other sectors.

Gross output targets were calculated for each of the 52 non-
capacity-limited sectors in the Soviet table with the assumption, as
above, that gross outputs in year t were 10 percent greater than in
year t – 1. The results of these calculations are given as percentages of actual gross outputs in column 3 of Table 2.7. With this
combination of assumptions about the planning process, the estimates of gross output for all except five sectors are within 2 percent
of their actual values. And for these five sectors the shortfalls are
all less than 4 percent. A sector-by-sector comparison shows that
these values calculated in a single iteration are, in general, equal
to or only slightly lower than comparable estimates calculated from
three full iterations in Table 2.5.

CONCLUSIONS

The input–output table of the Soviet Union has been used in
this paper to analyze several aspects of the technological interdependence of different producing sectors of the Soviet economy, which
have a direct effect on the consistency of production planning. The

relative importance of indirect inputs for each sector was first examined to provide an indication of the effects of ignoring secondary
rounds of changes in input requirements when a gross output target
is changed during the process of balancing the planned supply of and
demand for material inputs. The calculations showed that for most
sectors this failure to consider indirect inputs could result in large
proportional shortfalls in total input requirements. Imbalances between planned supplies and demands (and thus the need for extensive
corrections of initial plan targets) are to be expected with the Soviet
practice of transmitting control totals for gross output to all industries at the same time and requiring them to calculate their intermediate input requirements simultaneously but independently.
Alternatively, if gross output targets were calculated recursively
for each sector in the triangular hierarchy, such supply-demand
imbalances could be minimized. Other aspects of industrial interdependence could still cause inconsistencies in the gross outputs
calculated with this recursive approach, however, and the extent of
these particular aspects of interdependence in the Soviet economy
was examined.

While the degree of consistency that can be achieved by using
a recursive method of calculating gross output targets has been
contrasted here with that for a simple supply-demand iteration for
all sectors simultaneously, these input-output calculations are not
sufficient for evaluating the feasibility of adopting a recursive approach to planning. The input-output exercises described in the
discussion of recursive plan calculations were based on a very over-
simplified set of assumptions, and they ignored the major constraint
on the use of a recursive approach--the limited time available for
the formulation of an annual production plan. Breaking the planning
process down into 86 distinct steps corresponding to the number of
sectors identified in the Soviet input-output table used here (which is
more than twice the number of industrial ministries in the USSR)
would clearly be infeasible, and this is not the interpretation in-
tended. However, this study of industrial interdependence in the
Soviet economy at the greatest level of disaggregation possible with
available data suggests that the consistency of planning could be improved by taking advantage of the principle of recursive calculations
for the plans of larger divisions of the economy.

Previous calculations with the Soviet input-output table (Gillula
1975) have shown that even at a much greater (19-sector) level of
aggregation the proportion of the total value of interindustry transactions remaining above the main diagonal of the table in triangular
form is a very low 11.3 percent.[23] Furthermore, it was shown that
the sectors of the Soviet input-output table can be reordered and
grouped to produce a nearly block-angular form. Two of the three

blocks of sectors in this form are nearly independent of each other, and the third consists of sectors that supply intermediate inputs to sectors in these two blocks but purchase little of their output. This decomposibility suggests that the planning process could be broken down into two independent recursive processes carried out simultaneously, and good approximations of actual gross outputs required could still be calculated.

Descriptions of Soviet planning by Western economists have generally pointed to the lack of consideration given to the possibility of improving consistency with recursive plan calculations based on the triangular ordering of sectors. However, when the necessity of considering capacity limitations is taken into account, there is some evidence that Soviet planners in a very broad way do consider the structure of interindustry production relations, as evidenced by the way in which the sequence of calculations and information flows during the planning process is structured. A Soviet source (Gosplan SSSR 1969, p. 611) which gives guidelines for the compilation of the national economic plan points out the necessity of considering the interdependence of the plans for different branches, advising that deadlines for the elaboration of plans be established in the following sequence:[24] "raw material branches (agriculture, extractive industry) branches producing basic supplies and consumer goods machine building branches." Although this guideline is very general, the sequence suggests that consideration is given to the need for determining the output of capacity-limited sectors first, as in the last process of plan calculation described above. It also reflects the fact that balances for consumer goods can be completed simultaneously with those for other goods, since consumer goods production in the Soviet Union is based primarily on agricultural output (food, textiles, and other light industry) and this group of agriculture-based sectors represents a largely independent block. [25]

This general guideline establishing different deadlines for the final plans for different types of production allows for a recursive type of plan calculation. The results presented in this study suggest that the consistency of planning could be improved by extending it (where feasible, given the time constraints on the planning process) to provide a sequence of plan deadlines for branches within each of these major sectors of the economy as well. The major problem involved in formulating an annual production plan for a sector is one of calculating the changes in its input requirements that result from changes in its total output from the level of production of the previous year. Thus, planners in each sector need not wait to learn the total amount of their products required by all other sectors, but only the changes in these interindustry demands from previous levels. [26] With a recursive process, planning could then go on year-round as usual in each industrial ministry, but with a sequence of deadlines established for branches successively lower in the triangular hierarchy, each branch would have an accurate estimate of the total demands for its products and could in turn pass on accurate estimates of its intermediate input requirements.

NOTES

1. In practice this is only part of the much larger problem of planning the production of individual commodities in each sector as well as their distribution. See the mathematical formulation by Ellman (1972, pp. 64-66).

2. Throughout this paper, X and Y are (n x 1) column vectors, and A is the (n x n) matrix of input coefficients, where n is the number of sectors.

3. These uses of input-output analysis for a centrally planned economy were first described by J. M. Montias (1959).

4. This Soviet input-output table was reconstructed from the partially published version and other Soviet data sources (Treml et al. 1972).

5. The actual number of products for which balances were tabulated, as reported by Kalinin (1973) is as follows: 274 products prepared by Gosplan and approved by the Council of Ministers USSR; 1,669 prepared and approved by Gosplan; 17,484 prepared by Gossnab; and 40,000 prepared and approved by ministries.

6. The often quoted source that points out the difficulty of making changes in all of the balances that would be affected is Efimov (1957).

7. See Ellman (1972, pp. 72-73) and the sources cited there.

8. See the discussion of this problem by Treml (1967, pp. 87-90, 112).

9. In the Soviet table, 81 percent of the possible interindustry transactions are positive as compared to 3 percent for the Polish table used by Montias.

10. The question of the size of the imbalances that would remain in a plan under various assumptions about the approach to planning used has been examined by Manove (1971). He formulated a model of planning in a Soviet-type economy based on iterative input-output calculations, and showed with a series of simulation experiments using the 1959 Soviet table that the imbalances that would remain under any of a variety of sets of assumptions adopted would not be great.

11. The direct relevance of all the calculations in this study to current Soviet planning practice is limited, however, by the fact

that the correspondence between input-output sectors and the administrative units of the Soviet economy is imperfect. Input-output sectors are defined on a commodity basis to reflect technological relations.

12. These seven are 4-Nonferrous metals, 8-Coal, 41-Abrasives, 44-Aniline dye products, 64-Silk, 70-Other light industry, and 72-Meat products.

13. This difference in accounting practices is discussed in Treml et al. (1972, pp. 45-46).

14. In a Soviet input-output study (Efimov and Berri 1965, pp. 178-87), Iaremenko has used the sum $(\Sigma_i \; r_{ij} - 1)$ to compute the "material intensity" of the vectors of different components of final output. The ratio $(\Sigma_i \; r_{ij} - 1)/\Sigma_i \; a_{ij})$ was calculated for the sectors of an aggregated table as a measure of the extent of doublecounting—the extent to which previous stages of intermediate inputs are embodied in a sector's direct inputs.

15. The Yan-Ames measure is used in a study of the structure of the Soviet economy in 1923/24 by Dolan (1967) which is based on an input-output table constructed from published Soviet data. For other approaches to the measurement of industrial interdependence, see Santhanam and Patil (1972), and Ghosh and Sarkar (1970).

16. Yan and Ames give a more general definition of an interrelatedness function applicable to any nonnegative matrix or submatrix.

17. The measures of the interdependence of sectors defined in this section are based on the below-main-diagonal triangular form of an interindustry transactions matrix, and the subscripts of the elements of the matrix, x_{ij}, will refer to the positions of sectors in the triangular hierarchy.

18. In their comparative study of interdependence in the input-output tables of 18 countries, Lamel, Richter, and Teufelsbauer (1972) make a further distinction between the instances where $x_{ij} > x_{ji}$, $i > j$ and $x_{ij} > x_{ji}$, $i < j$ (both x_{ij}, $x_{ji} > 0$ in each case). This distinction is not considered here, however, since the x_{ji}s in the latter case—where the smaller of the two flows between a pair of sectors is below the main diagonal—account for less than 10 percent of the value of the sum in expression (14) below.

19. This difference matrix and the values of $\bar{\lambda}$ and λ in subsequent equations were defined by Helmstädter (1969, p. 234) in his work on triangulating input-output tables.

20. The calculation of the ratios defined above is described in greater detail by Helmstädter (1965, pp. 458-59).

21. See the description of the algorithm used in triangulating the Soviet table (Gillula 1975, Appendix).

22. In the Polish input–output table used by Montias (1962, p. 285) a similar interdependence may be concealed in the large intrasectoral transaction of the single machinery and equipment sector.

23. Values of λ_i (defined above) for each of the 19 sectors in this version of the Soviet table are also given (Gillula 1975, p. 29).

24. A sequence for the elaboration of plans which appears to start at both ends of the triangular hierarchy has also been noted by Montias (1959, pp. 970–71).

25. See the discussion of this agriculture-based group of sectors in Gillula (1975, pp. 31–32, 42–49).

26. This characteristic of the annual planning process is the explanation given by Manove (1971) for the small imbalances in the sectoral output targets that his model of Soviet planning produces.

REFERENCES

Dolan, E. G. 1972. "Structural Interdependence of the Soviet Economy Before the Industrialization Drive." Soviet Studies 19 (January): 66–73.

Efimov, A. N. 1957. Perestroika upravleniia promyshlennostiu i stroitel'stvom v SSSR. Moscow: Gos. Izd. Politicheskoi Literatury.

Efimov, A. N. and L. Ia. Berri. 1965. Metody planirovaniia mezhotraslevykh proportsii. Mooоow: Ekonomika.

Ellman, M. 1972. Soviet Planning Today. New York: Cambridge University Press.

Ghosh, A. and H. Sarkar. 1970. "An Input–Output Matrix as a Spatial Configuration." Economics of Planning 10, no. 1–2: 133–42.

Gillula, J. W. 1975. "The Structure of the 1966 Input–output Table of the Soviet Union in Basic Matrix Forms." in Jahrbuch der Wirtschaft Osteuropas, Vol. 6, pp. 21–56. Munich: Günter Olzog Verlag.

Gosplan SSSR. 1969. Metodicheskie ukazaniia k sostavleniiu gosudarstvennogo plana razvitiia narodnogo khoziaistva SSSR. Moscow: Ekonomika.

Helmstädter, E. 1965. "Ein Mass für das Ergebnis der Triangulation von Input–Output-Matrizen." Jahrbücher für Nationalökonomie und Statistik 177, no. 5: 456–63.

Iaremenko, Iu. V. 1963. "Izuchenie i planirovanie narodnokhoziaistvennykh proportsii metodom mezhotraslevogo balansa." Planovoe khoziaistvo 4: 34–41.

_____. 1969. "The Hierarchical Structure of Interindustrial Transactions." In International Comparisons of Interindustry Data. Industrial Planning and Programming Series, No. 2, pp. 231–43. New York: United Nations.

Kalinin, I. 1973. "Ulushshenie balansovoi raboty i voprosy sovershenstvovaniia planirovaniia." Planovoe khoziaistvo, no. 8: 15–29.

Lamel, J., J. Richter, and W. Teufelsbauer. 1972. "Patterns of Industrial Structure and Economic Development." European Economic Review 3: 47–63.

Manove, M. 1971. "A Model of Soviet-Type Economic Planning." American Economic Review 61, no. 3, part 1: 390–406.

Montias, J. M. 1959. "Planning with Material Balances in Soviet-Type Economies." American Economic Review 49, no. 6: 963–85.

_____. 1962. "On the Consistency and Efficiency of Central Plans." Review of Economic Studies 29, no. 4: 280–90.

Santhanam, K. V. and R. H. Patil. 1972. "A Study of the Production Structure of the Indian Economy: an International Comparison." Econometrica 40, no. 1: 159–75.

Treml, V. G. 1967. "Input–Output Analysis and Soviet Planning." In Mathematics and Computers in Soviet Economic Planning, ed. John P. Hardt et al., pp. 68–146. New Haven: Yale University Press.

Treml, V. G., D. M. Gallik, B. L. Kostinsky, and K. W. Kruger. 1972. The Structure of the Soviet Economy: Analysis and Reconstruction of the 1966 Input–Output Table. New York: Praeger.

Yan, C. and E. Ames. 1965. "Economic Interrelatedness." Review of Economic Studies 32, no. 4: 299–310.

3

ECONOMIES OF SCALE
IN SOVIET INDUSTRY:
INTERTEMPORAL, REGIONAL,
AND BRANCH ANALYSIS
Per O. Strangert

INTRODUCTION

The assumption of invariability of input-output coefficients with respect to output changes, which is so crucial in input-output analysis, is as restrictive as it is helpful. There are several reasons why the invariability assumption could be violated. One source of violation of the assumption is economies, or diseconomies, to scale. Economies to scale means that if all inputs to a production process change by the same factor $k > 1$, the output will change by a factor $> k$ (or, in the case of diseconomies, $< k$). If present, economies to scale make the aggregate input change due to an output change in an industry dependent on the size distribution of the firms involved. If the size distribution changes over time, the input-output coefficients will also change.

Soviet industry statistics indicate a strong trend toward the concentration of production in large plants in the Soviet Union--more so than can be explained by the production increase being spread out over existing firms. This makes worthwhile, as an adjunct to studies of Soviet input-output data, a study of economies of scale and related issues for Soviet industry.

In this paper is presented a study of labor and capital input functions for Soviet industry. These functions can serve as a means for assessing the existence of economies of scale. Input function here means the total amount of a particular input as a function of firm size. The concept of size is not unambiguous. Size as measured by output/year will be chosen as the most reasonable one in the present input-output context. The data available give in most cases the alternatives of labor and fixed capital value as size measures.[1]

The principal data sources for the present study are tables
found in Soviet and republican statistical handbooks giving the percentages of output and labor and capital used for each of a number
of intervals of firm sizes.[2] Table 3.1 is such a table for the Soviet
Union, covering all industry except electrical power for 1973. In
the following discussion such tables will be called size/share tables.
From the data contained in such tables it is possible to compute the
average labor and capital inputs for each size group at least up to a
factor common to all size groups of the table. The next step is to
fit some function to the data so obtained. In other words, the ex
post average input functions are to be estimated.

TABLE 3.1

Grouping of Industrial Firms by Gross Production in 1973
(percent of total)

Range of Firm Size (yearly output in thousands of rubles)	Number of Firms	Gross Production	Average Number of Employees	Average Value of Fixed Capital*
– 100	6.6	0.0	0.2	0.1
101 – 500	14.1	0.5	1.6	0.9
501 – 1000	12.7	1.1	2.7	1.4
1001 – 5000	37.8	10.8	17.8	11.4
5001 – 10000	12.6	10.3	13.4	10.6
10001 – 50000	13.0	31.7	32.4	28.2
50001 – 100000	1.8	14.5	12.2	13.6
100001 –	1.4	31.1	19.7	33.8

*The average value of fixed capital is not necessarily propor-
tional to the capital utilized during the same period.
Source: TsSU, Narodnoe khoziaistvo SSSR v 1973 godu
(Moscow: Statistika 1974), pp. 244-45.

In this study we use reported value of output in the estimation
of input or cost functions.[3] In his studies of economies of scale in
British manufacturing industry, Pratten (1971) used the so-called
engineering approach, which amounts to calculating production cost
for various volumes of output, rather than using accounting data. In
Pratten's opinion, the accounting cost approach is likely to yield

erroneous and not comparable results because of inconsistent capital cost accounting and market imperfections. The criticism of the comparability of results obtained by the ex post method may be not so serious in the Soviet case because there exist unionwide norms for capital valuation, and prices are fairly uniform among republics, and also over time.

Johnston (1960) gives several examples of mathematical forms for input functions. Not only linear and second degree polynomials, but also power functions have been used to measure total or average cost as a function of firm size. The Soviet data suggest a wide dispersion of firm sizes, and the grouping is made with the limits in an essentially geometrical progression, all of which is compatible with a loglinear cost model.[4] This type of model has been chosen for the present study. However, because of the severely limited number of size groups in each regression, there is hardly any possibility of testing for the correctness of this particular input function specification.

The results of the present study indicate that there are substantial labor savings per unit of output in large firms as compared to small ones in most branches of Soviet industry. It is also found that the average capital input often first decreases, then increases as the firm size increases. As a result, the sum of labor and capital average cost, as calculated from wages and depreciation, may vary little between firms of moderate and large sizes. In a crude calculation, this portion of total cost was actually found to be approximately constant in firms whose output was more than 10 million rubles per year.

The behavior of labor and capital input for varying firm sizes makes production more capital-intensive in the large firms of a particular branch. The expansion path, found by regressing total capital input K on total labor input L can be represented by a function:

$$K = aL^q$$

for some a, with q in the interval 1.0 to 1.4 in the majority of cases, and 1.2 as a typical value. This makes unrealistic the use of a Cobb-Douglas type of production function, or any other linearly homogeneous function, for modeling Soviet industry since such functions give a straight line expansion path if the firms are assumed to allocate labor and capital optimally for given prices.[5]

Input functions for fairly disaggregated branches, such as oil extraction, wall materials, or the meat industry, can reasonably be said to refer to fairly homogeneous outputs, with changes in technology possibly occurring along the curve, but not product change. The study indicates that the estimations made for such branches are in general reliable and consistent between regions in the cases where comparisons can be made.

When sectors are more aggregated, as in the case of the chemical industry, there is far less agreement. The explanation is that there is no longer a homogeneous output along the curve. The mix of industries constituting the sector is also a determining factor, and may vary over time as well as between regions. The problem of interpreting the regression results for aggregated branches is still more difficult when data for all industry aggregated--for example, in a republic--are processed. It is suggested that the results then tell something about the ability of the industrial sector to absorb and operate modern labor-saving technology. In any case, it has been considered worthwhile to process and interpret all the available Soviet data in some way, rather than to try to estimate economies to scale in the proper sense of the word, which would require unavailable data.

The input functions derived in this study pertain to conditions under which firms are free to choose their labor and capital inputs. Since this is a reasonable assumption in the long run, the results should be useful for the construction of dynamic input-output models (admitting at least a ten-sector breakdown of industry). In the short run, when capital capacity is fixed, it is the degree of utilization and volume of labor input that vary. Hopefully, the results obtained and estimation method developed may also provide a point of departure for deriving nonproportional short-run labor input functions.

The results presented in this paper do not represent all potential uses of the data base utilized. First, the available size/share tables also include size concepts other than output per year--namely, labor employed and fixed capital. The latter categories have not been used in obtaining the results presented here but can give an idea of the dispersion in the capital/labor ratios and possibly the marginal rates of substitution between these factors. Second, a very natural continuation of the work done here would be the estimation of gross output and fixed capital values in absolute ruble figures (labor is readily available in man-years), which would make possible comparisons of the same industry branch in different regions. An extension of the study using absolute GVO and fixed capital estimates is also desirable for the construction of rectangular input-output tables, consisting of input vectors for various scales of output in each sector of production. It should be possible to obtain by linear interpolation in the actual output vector a sufficiently good approximation of nonlinear input functions for labor and capital.

Finally, the investigation in this paper of labor and fixed capital should also be carried out with respect to the material inputs. With some obvious exceptions (such as electrical power input, which is conceivably more correlated to the amount of fixed capital than to the branch output), it is a reasonable guess that the intermediate material inputs behave more closely in accordance with the Leontief output proportionality assumption than do the primary inputs. However, this remains to be substantiated for Soviet industry, and there are almost no data available that are directly applicable for testing this assumption.

METHOD DESCRIPTION

The Use of Size/Share Tables for the Derivation of Input Functions for an Industry

Size/share tables, such as Table 3.1, were used to derive input functions for the Soviet industry and its branches. Assuming that output per year and (labor) input are known for each individual firm in a particular industry and that the firms are ordered in a sequence of increasing output, two series of numbers that illustrate the size/input relations can be uniquely defined: for each size of firm, the total value of output produced by firms up to and including this size; and for each output size, the total (labor) input to these firms.

Plotting the latter values against the format ones for varying firm size gives a sum polygon. Figure 3.1 shows a sum polygon for the wood and paper sector in Lithuania for 1968. The curvature of this sum polygon suggests that there are economies of scale in the sector. The 5.7 percent of total output value produced in the firms up to and including 50,000 rubles of output a year require 13.7 percent of the total manpower in the industry, while the largest firms, those producing more than 10 million rubles of output a year, contribute 23.5 percent of total output while using only 11.7 percent of the manpower. One also finds that the average labor input per unit of output produced by firms in the size range of 3-5 million rubles per year is 0.125 man-years per 1,000 rubles. The latter suggests a method of calculating the labor input function, to which we will return later.

The actual shape of the sum polygon is determined not only by the input function of the industry as defined earlier, but also by the size distribution of firms. The average slope at a point corresponding to a certain size is given by the input function, but the positions of such points along the sum polygon are determined by the size distribution. In Figure 3.2, the sum polygons a and b are derived from the same size/input relation and have the same totals for output and input, but polygon a corresponds to a size distribution with more firms in the medium-size range than does b.

FIGURE 3.1

Sum Polygon for the Wood and Paper Industry in Lithuania, 1968

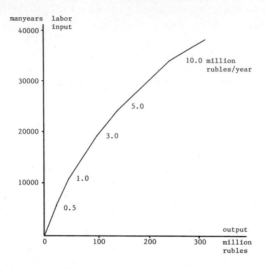

Source: Compiled by the author.

FIGURE 3.2

Sum Polygons for Industries with the Same Input Function but Different Size Distributions

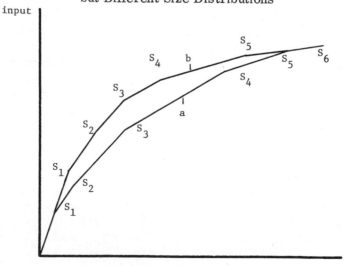

Source: Compiled by the author.

118

The sum polygon does not have a well-defined slope at every point. Even if the firms are ranked by output size, the corresponding inputs (labor or capital) are not necessarily in strictly ascending order, which causes the slope to oscillate. Considering this circumstance as a random disturbance, one may think instead of a smooth idealized sum curve. Now if a straight line is drawn connecting the points corresponding to output sizes S_1 and S_2, its slope is equal to

$$\frac{\sum_i \ell_i}{\sum_i o_i}$$

where the summations of individual firm inputs ℓ_i and outputs o_i extend over all firms with sizes in the interval between S_1 and S_2. The ratio can also be written

$$\frac{\frac{1}{n} \sum_i \ell_i}{\frac{1}{n} \sum_i o_i}$$

where the numerator can be interpreted as the arithmetic mean of the total inputs to the n firms in the sizes S_1 through S_2, and the denominator as the mean of their total outputs. In particular, if S_1 is near S_2, the line is almost a tangent to the sum curve and the denominator is almost equal to the size of either S_1 or S_2. Replacing the denominator by S, the (almost) common value of S_1 and S_2, the ratio can again be rewritten as

$$\frac{1}{n} \sum \frac{\ell_i}{S}$$

and the slope of the tangent to the sum curve can be interpreted as the arithmetic mean of the average inputs to firms in the size indicated by the point of tangency.

The size/share tables published do not yield sum polygons with actual output and input values but rather, cumulated percentages of the industry totals. This means that the sum polygons are contained in a 100 percent x 100 percent square and have to be transformed by the appropriate branch totals for output and labor or capital input to produce the input function. Even if this is not done, the output elasticity of (labor or capital) input can be computed because it is independent of the units of measurement.

The data available in general give between 3 and 12 points on the sum polygon. This makes it possible to get an idea of its shape.

However, an estimation of the input function requires knowledge of the slope of the sum curve, but the fact that a function is well approximated, for example, in a least squares sense, does not insure that its slope is accurately approximated by the derivative of the approximating function. The basic reason it is hard to estimate the slope econometrically is that there is no theory offering a functional form for the regression of the observed points on the sum polygon. As noted above, the shape of the latter is a combined consequence of the input function of the industry and the size distribution of firms in it, and there is no unifying framework for the two issues.

Size/share tables are published for different size concepts. So far, we have assumed a classification according to output size, but tables are also given for classification by labor and fixed capital, and in a few instances for energy input or by capital/labor ratio. Different classification modes in general are found to produce different sum polygons. If a ranking by output size of the firms in the industry at the same time were a ranking by, for example, labor input, there would be no difference. This is not likely to be the case, however, because fixed capital and labor may be employed in varying proportions in firms with about the same output. Therefore, the input function depends on the classification concept applied, and a choice has to be made. [6]

As was found above, if grouping is by output size, the labor input function derived from a size/share table gives the arithmetic mean of average labor inputs to firms of a given output size. Conversely, if grouping is by labor, the labor input curve would give the arithmetic mean of average output sizes of firms employing a given amount of labor. If ranking were by fixed capital, a labor input curve derived from it would give the mean of average labor inputs in firms with a certain amount of capital as a function of the mean of the output produced. The latter is clearly an artificial interpretation, and the most natural cost concept is undoubtedly that giving the mean of average inputs for firm outputs of a given size. With this concept only classifications according to output size will be used, which means that some 60 percent of the potentially available data material will be disregarded.

The Econometric Model

As a basic econometric functional relationship it is assumed that in an industry the total input y to a firm operating at output level x, is a power function of x for some exponent α plus an error term ϵ :

$$y = a \cdot x^{\alpha} + \epsilon \qquad \epsilon \sim (0, \sigma_x^2)$$

The rationale for choosing this particular specification was discussed earlier. If in this model α is equal to 1, input is proportional to output, so that the average input is constant. In the case $\alpha < 1$, the total input increases less, proportionally to output, and average input is a decreasing function of the output of a firm.

The relation above is assumed to hold for a single firm with its output considered a nonrandom parameter. If total input and output were known for a number of individual firms, the α value would be comparatively easy to estimate by loglinear regression (the error term being more conveniently applied to the model in its logarithmic form). The empirical data, however, give aggregated information about the firms over size groups. Aggregation by adding (over firms) variables with nonlinear relationships between them increases the difficulties of the estimation problem considerably. It is important to see how parameter α, which is of primary concern, can be estimated from the available data by an ad hoc method, and what error assumptions can be made about the grouped data.

Consider a particular size interval g ranging from a to b and let x_i and y_i be the outputs and the inputs (labor or capital) to the n individual firms in this group ($i = 1, 2, \ldots, n$). For each firm it is assumed that

$$y_i = c \cdot x_i^{\alpha} + \epsilon_i$$

where c and α are constants common to the whole industry, and

$$\epsilon_i \sim (0, \sigma_i^2).$$

A way is now sought to use the group totals given in the tables. The total input to the firms in the interval g is

$$Y_g = \sum_{i=1}^{n} (cx_i^{\alpha} + \epsilon_i)$$

and in a next step the aim is to eliminate the role of the individual x_i.

Dividing through by X_g, the total output from the firms in the size interval, the result is

$$\frac{Y_g}{X_g} = \frac{\Sigma cx_i^{\alpha} + \Sigma \epsilon_i}{\Sigma x_i} = c \cdot \frac{\frac{1}{n} \Sigma x_i^{\alpha}}{\bar{x}} + \frac{\Sigma \epsilon_i}{n\bar{x}}$$

where $\bar{x} = \frac{1}{n} \Sigma x_i$. This can also be written

$$\frac{Y_g}{X_g} = c \cdot \bar{x}^{\alpha-1} \cdot \frac{\frac{1}{n} \Sigma x_i^{\alpha}}{\bar{x}^{\alpha}} + \frac{\Sigma \epsilon_i}{n\bar{x}}$$

and this form is almost suitable for regression after taking the logarithms, provided the behavior of the ratio

$$R = \frac{\frac{1}{n} \Sigma x_i^{\alpha}}{\bar{x}^{\alpha}}$$

is known. Because $f(x) = x^{\alpha}$ is a strictly concave function for $x > 0$, $0 < \alpha < 1$, which is the most interesting region,

$$\Sigma x_i^{\alpha} < n\bar{x}^{\alpha}$$

will hold if there is more than one firm in g, so that $R < 1$.[7] The ratio will depend on the number of firms in the size group, the shape of the distribution of firms within the interval, the width of the interval (the ratio between its upper and lower limits), and the exponent α. The bias caused by having $R \neq 1$ is not very disturbing, however. First, the number of firms in the size group does not have a decisive influence over R. Provided other factors are kept constant, including the general shape of the size distribution within the size interval, R tends to a limit as the number of firms increases; it can therefore be expected to be fairly insensitive to this number. If there are two firms in a group, and the ratio between their outputs is 1.5, the R value is 0.9968 for $\alpha = 0.8$; this can be compared to the R values below for the case of a very large number of firms. Second, the influence of the shape of the size distribution may be investigated through the use of a few examples. Assuming a uniform size distribution over the interval (a,b), and a very large number of firms, the value of R can be found by integral estimation and is (when $\alpha = 0.8$) equal to 0.9997 for b/a = 1.2, to 0.9989 for b/a = 1.5, and reaches 0.9959 for b/a = 2.3, which also indicates the influence of the interval width in the relevant region. A uniform distribution may be a reasonable approximation in the closed intervals of medium firm sizes but at the lower and upper (open-ended) intervals of the size grouping, the situations might be better described by a triangular distribution. In that case an assumed b/a value of 1.85 gives R = 0.9988; the influence of the skewness is offset by the movement of the average $\bar{x}$. Finally the influence of varying α may be exemplified in a uniform size distribution. With b/a = 5/3, R is of course equal to 1 for $\alpha = 1$; for $\alpha = 0.75$,

$R = 0.9980$, and for $\alpha = 0.5$, indicating strong economies to scale, $R = 0.9974$. In summary, therefore, it does not seem necessary for practical purposes to investigate how $R \neq 1$ affects the input function and in particular the exponent α; the influence is a minor one.

We can therefore write, with good approximation

$$\frac{Y_g}{X_g} = c\, x^{-\alpha-1} + \frac{\Sigma \epsilon_i}{n\bar{x}} = c\, \bar{x}^{\alpha-1} \left(1 + \frac{\Sigma \epsilon_i}{nc} \cdot \bar{x}^{-\alpha}\right)$$

and have

$$^{10}\log \frac{Y_g}{X_g} = {}^{10}\log c + (\alpha - 1)\,{}^{10}\log \bar{x} + {}^{10}\log \left(1 + \frac{\Sigma \epsilon_i}{nc} \cdot \bar{x}^{-\alpha}\right)$$

Concentrating now on the error term, let it be replaced by the linear term of its Taylor expansion,

$$\frac{\Sigma \epsilon_i}{nc} \bar{x}^{-\alpha} \cdot {}^{10}\log e$$

This operation leads to some bias, because $\log (1 + x)$ is concave. This last step could have been avoided by starting with a suitable multiplicative form of the error ϵ, which, however, would have caused other difficulties. Essentially the error term is

$$\epsilon_g = \frac{\bar{x}^{-\alpha} \cdot \Sigma \epsilon_i}{n}$$

Assuming $\epsilon_i \sim (0, \bar{x}^{-\gamma} \sigma^2)$ for some γ, uncorrelated ϵ_i within the group is

$$\epsilon_g \sim (0, \bar{x}^{\gamma - 2\alpha} \cdot \frac{\sigma^2}{n})$$

Conventionally γ might be chosen somewhere in the interval $(1,2)$; because α is most often between 0.5 and 1, it is reasonable to assume that $\gamma - 2\alpha \approx 0$, and therefore a heteroscedastic model remains:

$$^{10}\log \frac{Y_g}{X_g} = \beta + (\alpha - 1)\,{}^{10}\log \frac{X_g}{N_g} + \epsilon_g$$

where Y_g, X_g, and N_g are the total input, output, and number of firms in group g, or alternatively the percentage shares of the possibly unknown industry totals. In the latter case, the constant coefficient cannot be interpreted directly. Further the ϵ_g can be assumed to be independently distributed with zero mean and variance = σ^2/N_g for some σ^2; the total number of firms in the branch is not important. This model is of a well-known type (see Kmenta 1971, section 9.2) and can be estimated with a generalized least squares estimator.

The Interpretation of Input Functions Obtained for Aggregated Industries

Soviet statistical sources provide not only branchwide data in size/share tables but also a large number of tables for the total industry in different regions and years. The concept of input function cannot be straightforwardly applied to the aggregate industry sector; there is not even a semblance of homogeneity in output. Among other things, even if the particular econometric model applies to the individual branches, it cannot be taken for granted that it applies to their aggregate. However, in order to make the best possible use of the data available, it is desirable to find a reasonable interpretation for the results obtained from the all-industry tables also.

The outcome from the regression method applied to an aggregation of two or more branches with given α values is indeterminate until the relative positions of input curves for the branches and the number of firms in different size groups is known. This is illustrated in Figure 3.3 where AA' and BB' are the average input functions for two "pure" branches with small and large economies to scale respectively. If the size distributions are such that most firms in branch AA' are small (grouped around size a), and those in BB' are large (grouped around size b), a regression run on an aggregate of the firms will yield a moderate downward slope--that is, moderate economies to scale (dotted line CC'). If the firm sizes in both branches are concentrated around a certain value (size b), a regression line fitted to the aggregated material will give a different fit (DD') and will tend to produce a smaller R^2 value and larger variance for the estimated parameters.

As will be seen below, the chemical industry is a sector in which the loglinear model shows particularly bad fit and unreliable estimates of the αs. This is not surprising in view of the explanation given above, considering the heterogeneity of the chemical industry. The branches in it, such as basic chemicals, analine dyes, and synthetic fibers are automated to different degrees, and should therefore have different shapes and positions for their input curves.

FIGURE 3.3

Regression of Average Input on Size for an Aggregation
of Two Industries

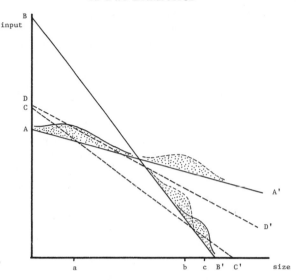

Source: Compiled by the author.

Going over to the case in which all industrial sectors are aggregated does not raise any fundamentally new issues, but the situation is, of course, more complicated. It is an important case because there are several time series, for the Soviet Union and the
republics, of tables for the aggregated industry. Some guidance in
the interpretation of the regression results is provided by the observation, empirically proved for the United States and the United King-
dom by Sargeant (1961, p. 68), that mechanized production tends to
be concentrated in large plants. There is, of course, reason to believe that the same holds for the Soviet Union. Mechanized production is by its very nature characterized by low average labor input
and high average fixed capital input. To the extent that there is a
significant amount of mechanized production in an economy and that
it takes place in large production units, the average labor-input
curve for the aggregated industry will slope steeply downward, but
the average fixed capital curve will not. Thus, as very crude indexes for the technological advancement for a region in a particular
year, one might use the labor α_L and the capital α_c.

Calculations and Presentation

The econometric method developed above was applied in the following way. Given a size/share table, the percentages of output values in the size intervals were multiplied by total output from the industry concerned, and the percentages of employment by the industry total. If percentages for workers only were given, instead of total employment, these figures were used. The two measures of labor generally run very close to each other.

The industry totals were available in absolute figures only in a few cases. For the time-series study (category A), index numbers for the totals were constructed using statistical handbook data. The application of these index numbers permits most of the intertemporal comparisons to be made. For the branchwide study (category B), the breakdown of output value by branches was not possible. The totals were all arbitrarily set equal to 1 and no comparisons between regions and years can be made for the input function values. Only comparisons of their slopes are possible.

For every size interval in which at least 1 percent of the industry output value was produced, its labor input was divided by its output value. Also, the output value was divided by the interval percentage of the total number of firms in the industry, giving a number proportional to the output mean $\bar{x}_g$ in the interval. The series of ratios for all size intervals meeting the 1 percent condition was then computed and printed out for manual inspection. If the series consisted of at least three values, their logarithms (base 10) were regressed on the logarithms of the X_gs as in Kmenta (1971, Ch. 9.1). The coefficient of determination R^2 was computed using the estimated error terms. Because the estimated errors do not necessarily add to zero, it may in extreme cases of bad fit happen that R^2, computed in this way, is negative. (R^2 is not corrected for the number of degrees of freedom.)

The linear coefficient found in the regression was increased by 1 to give an estimate of α_L. An analogous procedure to that outlined above for labor input was applied to fixed capital input.

The total fixed capital in each size interval was regressed (logarithmic linearly) on total labor employed. The linear coefficient, q, characterizes the capital/labor substitution taking place along the expansion path. [8] The fit was generally quite good, as measured by R^2, probably because totals instead of averages were regressed on each other.

RESULTS OF THE BRANCHWIDE STUDY

Below are reported the results of the branchwide study. First, a complete account of the regression results is given in table form.

Then, the results are commented upon and supplemented with observations from the manual inspection of the series of average inputs by sizes for the particular branches.

Table 3.2 gives first the $\widehat{\alpha}_L$, its estimated standard error, and the R^2 value, then the corresponding values for fixed capital, and finally the q value (slope of log K regressed on log L) and the number of size intervals used in the regression. Normally, some intervals of the smallest sizes were excluded, each with an insignificant contribution to the branch total output (often 0 percent or 0.1 percent). All values found, including the obvious cases of abnormal values and those for which the source statistics are of poor quality, are included in the table.

The error distribution is henceforth assumed to be normal. The discussion sometimes uses the expression "error limits"; these are not formally computed from t values but rather indicate a margin of about twice the estimated standard error.

The α values are sometimes identified with the output elasticities of (labor or capital) input. Also, the attribute "average" is sometimes omitted from (labor or capital) input function; no confusion should arise, however.

Discussion

The Energy Sector

The a priori expectations in this sector are for moderately decreasing average capital input, and considerable labor economies in large plants, and therefore substitution along the expansion path. Data for thermoelectrical power plants are given for the whole USSR for 1960 and for BSSR for 1963. The α values agree within the error limits: BSSR has $\alpha_L = 0.39$ (less than the USSR value) and $\alpha_c = 0.79$ (more); in both cases the a priori expectations are met.

Hydroelectrical plants are reported for USSR 1960. The scale economies in labor are even more pronounced than for thermoelectricity plants, which is not surprising, since manual work is almost completely reduced to monitoring functions and maintenance is less than for thermoelectrical plants. The labor α_L is 0.20. For capital input, $\alpha_c = 0.81$ which agrees with α_c for thermoelectricity within the error limits. The loglinear fit to the expansion path is too poor to justify any estimation.

The whole energy sector is published as an aggregate for Lithuania for 1968. According to production statistics, a decreasing share, about 7-8 percent, of the energy produced there came from hydroelectrical plants. Since the α_c value was about the same

TABLE 3.2

Regression Results from the Branchwide Study, by Branch and Region/Year

Branch	Labor			Fixed Capital			q (Capital Increase/ Labor Increase)	Number of Intervals Used in Regression
	$\hat{\alpha}_L$	Standard Error of $\hat{\alpha}_L$	R^2	$\hat{\alpha}_c$	Standard Error of $\hat{\alpha}_c$	R^2		
Electrical power								
Lithuania 1968	0.366	0.019	0.996	0.853	0.185	0.032	2.265	4
Thermoelectrical power								
USSR 1960	0.476	0.022	0.990	0.702	0.036	0.949	1.467	5
BSSR 1963	0.388	0.119	0.930	0.786	0.091	0.828	1.805	4
Hydroelectrical power								
USSR 1960	0.196	0.138	0.934	0.807	0.032	0.944	1.527	5
Fuel								
Lithuania 1968	0.764	0.114	0.762	1.052	0.167	0.173	1.257	4
BSSR 1968	0.384	0.128	0.961	0.665	0.080	0.950	1.533	4
BSSR 1968 (excluding largest size)	0.728	0.021	0.992	0.882	0.011	0.989	1.211	3
Coal								
USSR 1960	-0.233	0.160	0.965	0.005	0.141	0.967	0.374	4
RSFSR 1959	0.380	0.086	0.974	0.454	0.041	0.974	1.030	5
Peat								
BSSR 1963	0.705	0.022	0.982	1.028	0.080	-0.165	1.456	5
Oil extraction								
RSFSR 1959	0.377	0.044	0.987	0.503	0.188	0.879	1.360	4
USSR 1960	0.369	0.094	0.857	0.512	0.045	0.953	1.239	5
Oil refining								
RSFSR 1959	0.777	0.162	0.693	0.881	0.023	0.962	1.375	3
USSR 1960	0.684	0.130	0.649	0.966	0.147	-0.006	1.487	4
Metallurgy								
USSR 1960	0.829	0.093	0.617	1.142	0.037	0.920	1.344	4
RSFSR 1959	0.811	0.047	0.866	0.936	0.066	0.281	1.154	4
Chemical industry								
BSSR 1963	0.682	0.566	-0.092	-0.777	1.029	-0.366	0.484	4
BSSR 1968	0.987	0.243	-0.012	1.562	0.207	0.693	1.251	5
Lithuania 1968	0.794	0.171	0.328	1.538	0.273	0.600	1.874	5
USSR 1960	0.837	0.042	0.587	0.989	0.078	0.020	1.182	5
RSFSR 1959	0.804	0.026	0.971	0.789	0.037	0.951	0.982	4

Machinebuilding (and metalworking)								
Lithuania 1968	0.343	0.032	0.686	0.826	0.103	0.438	0.986	6
USSR 1968	0.339	0.011	0.978	0.859	0.048	0.532	1.061	6
BSSR 1963	0.354	0.038	0.834	0.979	0.041	0.250	1.142	4
USSR 1960	0.305	0.008	0.980	0.966	0.011	0.426	1.067	5
Construction materials								
RSFSR 1959	0.612	0.008	0.999	0.904	0.100	-0.007	1.412	5
BSSR 1968	0.380	0.067	0.969	0.916	0.096	-0.094	2.217	6
Lithuania 1968	0.754	0.098	0.661	1.078	0.089	0.229	1.364	6
Cement								
USSR 1960	0.769	0.038	0.933	0.804	0.070	0.777	1.045	4
Concrete elements								
USSR 1960	0.740	0.032	0.944	0.872	0.128	0.173	1.118	6
BSSR 1963	0.699	0.099	0.925	1.385	0.218	0.355	1.920	4
Wall materials								
USSR 1960	0.654	0.028	0.980	0.753	0.076	0.839	1.155	6
BSSR 1963	0.655	0.066	0.969	0.764	0.146	0.602	1.106	4
Wood and paper								
BSSR 1968	0.505	0.079	0.306	0.943	0.032	0.360	1.016	7
Lithuania 1968	0.535	0.049	0.957	1.048	0.045	0.235	1.884	6
Lumber								
RSFSR 1959	--	--	--	--	--	--	--	--
USSR 1960	0.905	0.044	0.505	1.229	0.036	0.823	1.353	5
BSSR 1963	1.074	0.045	0.533	1.221	0.043	0.925	1.136	4
Woodworking								
BSSR 1963	0.769	0.102	0.792	0.734	0.220	0.563	0.964	4
USSR 1960	0.743	0.029	0.871	0.968	0.059	-0.249	1.306	5
Paper								
RSFSR 1959	0.821	0.084	0.675	1.023	0.072	-0.001	1.237	4
Light industry								
Lithuania 1968	0.513	0.094	0.724	0.429	0.137	0.766	0.881	7
BSSR 1968	0.731	0.059	0.859	0.837	0.063	0.338	1.130	7
Cotton								
USSR 1960	0.347	0.018	0.902	0.953	0.027	0.301	1.125	5
Textile								
BSSR 1963	0.799	0.032	0.949	0.743	0.034	0.828	0.921	5
RSFSR 1959	0.363	0.041	0.714	0.759	0.071	0.803	0.851	6
USSR 1960	0.574	0.034	0.969	0.738	0.078	0.779	1.107	6

(continued)

(Table 3.2 continued)

Branch	Labor			Fixed Capital			q (Capital Increase/ Labor Increase)	Number of Intervals Used in Regression
	$\hat{\alpha}_L$	Standard Error of $\hat{\alpha}_L$	R^2	$\hat{\alpha}_c$	Standard Error of $\hat{\alpha}_c$	R^2		
Sewing and apparel								
BSSR 1963	0.646	0.042	0.981	0.648	0.126	0.771	1.005	5
RSFSR 1959	0.750	0.064	0.779	0.900	0.133	-0.291	1.212	4
USSR 1960	0.497	0.052	0.824	0.335	0.068	0.780	0.680	7
Hosiery								
USSR 1960	0.576	0.041	0.968	0.930	0.098	0.247	1.624	6
Fur and hides								
RSFSR 1959	0.737	0.054	0.882	0.818	0.034	0.939	1.080	4
Feed industry								
BSSR 1968	0.471	0.045	0.958	0.551	0.043	0.936	1.144	7
Lithuania 1968	0.584	0.056	0.794	0.808	0.066	0.296	1.305	8
Sugar								
USSR 1960	0.312	0.316	0.671	-0.236	0.350	0.893	0.634	5
RSFSR 1959	0.451	0.002	1.000	0.334	0.127	0.968	0.740	3
Meat industry								
RSFSR 1959	0.841	0.041	0.877	0.839	0.056	0.868	1.000	5
USSR 1960	0.823	0.058	0.476	0.790	0.034	0.865	0.954	5
BSSR 1963	0.765	0.054	0.766	0.724	0.060	0.748	0.946	4
Fish industry								
RSFSR 1959	0.687	0.047	0.949	0.879	0.080	0.473	1.276	5
BSSR 1963	-0.059	0.101	0.991	-0.550	0.934	0.792	9.238	3
USSR 1960	0.622	0.012	0.997	0.904	0.051	0.467	1.455	5
Dairy industry								
USSR 1960	0.827	0.051	0.339	0.774	0.068	0.336	0.942	6
BSSR 1963	0.871	0.108	0.440	0.644	0.163	0.645	0.728	5
Printing								
Lithuania 1968	0.904	0.038	0.558	1.067	0.055	0.297	1.173	5

Note: BSSR is Belorussia; RSFSR is Russian Soviet Federated Socialist Republic.
Source: Compiled by the author.

130

for thermo- and hydroelectrical plants, it may be expected to re-appear in the aggregated branch. In fact, the estimate is 0.85, but the error is wide, 0.19, and the linear fit poor for the four observed sizes. The labor exponent α_L is 0.37 which is between the values found for hydro- and thermoelectrical power.

The Fuel Sector (excluding oil extraction and refining)

Coal mining is carried out with different techniques in differ-ent scales of operations. Stripmining makes possible a huge produc-tion that can be achieved with about the same amount of capital and labor as in conventional shaft mining. Therefore, substantial econo-mies to scale, as they are defined here, may be expected. In fact, the data given for USSR 1960 are anomalous as processed by the re-gression method employed. Probably the approximation R ~ 1 does not hold well for αs that differ widely from 1. The estimated α_L turns out to be greater than zero which amounts to a "free lunch," and may possibly have a reasonable interpretation when the natural resources are brought into the picture. The output elasticity for capital input is estimated at 0.01, for which a similar criticism can be applied. The data for the coal industry in RSFSR 1959 are not as anomalous as those for USSR. The α_L is 0.38 and α_c is 0.45, still suggesting very considerable economies to scale.

The peat industry has some importance in Belorussia as well as in the Baltic republics. For BSSR for 1963, α_L is 0.71 but the α_c should not be used because of the bad fit (even if the standard error of α_c is moderate).

The fuel industry data are given for BSSR for 1968 and consist mostly of peat production, but to some extent of oil extraction which started in 1965. The series of average inputs of both labor and capi-tal show inverted shapes. In both cases, a good linear fit is obtained if the last interval (corresponding to the largest sizes) is excluded. The slopes in this restricted set of observations are α_L = 0.73 and α_c' = 0.88. The former value agrees with that for peat in BSSR for 1963 within the error limits. An interpretation might be that the oil production in 1968 occurred in large plants and that the output value per unit of labor was higher for oil than for peat.

The fuel industry data for Lithuania in 1968 also mostly refer to peat. The point estimate for α_L is 0.76, which checks with BSSR for 1963, and the fit of the average capital input observations is poor.

Oil Extraction and Refining

The capital-intensive oil extraction branch permits large economies to scale, especially in labor. The production is fairly homogeneous, and for this reason comparisons should be possible between the α values.

Data for oil extraction are given for RSFSR 1959 and for the whole USSR 1960. The share of national production coming from RSFSR was about 80 percent (in 1969). The labor cost behaves in a similar way in both cases, with α_L equal to 0.38 for RSFSR and 0.37 for USSR. The same is true for α_c--0.50 and 0.51, respectively. The capital/labor expansion is characterized by q = 1.36 (RSFSR) and 1.24 (USSR).

The same sources as above also give data for oil refining. For RSFSR α_L = 0.78 and α_c = 0.88 and for the USSR α_L = 0.68 with α_c equal to 1.03. The error margins are wide for labor so that the two α_L values do not contradict each other. The observation series for USSR indicate exceptional economies for production in the largest size range (more than 100 million rubles per year).

Metallurgy

Data are given for RSFSR 1959 and for USSR 1960, labeled ferrous metallurgy in RSFSR and metallurgy excluding electro-ferrous alloys in USSR. (The RSFSR share of national iron or steel production is about 50 percent.) The labor cost functions are quite similar, with α_L = 0.81 and 0.83, respectively. The capital cost functions differ, however, and the industry has increasing average capital input in USSR, α_c = 1.14 with α_c = 0.94 for RSFSR; in the latter case constant capital inputs are within the error limits.

The Chemicals Sector

There are several subsectors in the chemicals sector that are often distinguished in Soviet statistics, such as aniline dyes, plastic materials, synthetic fibers, rubber, paints and lacquers, rubber and asbestos products, and so on. These branches use different technologies with varying typical labor and capital utilization, and they operate on different scales of output volume. This makes the branch heterogeneous and the average inputs may be expected to behave irregularly. Moreover, comparisons between regions cannot be justified since the branch mix can vary considerably due to regional specialization. Both difficulties are encountered in this study, and although data for the chemicals sector are given in all the five possible instances, there are almost no reliable α values to report. The R^2 coefficients are often only about 0.2 - 0.4 and the standard error of the estimate for α lies in the 0.15 - 0.30 range. Only USSR 1960 data (α_L = 0.84 $\pm$ 0.04) and RSFSR 1959 data (α_L = 0.80 $\pm$ 0.03) offer accurate estimates; in the latter case

$\alpha_c = 0.79 \pm 0.04$ ($R^2 = 0.951$) seems to be reliable. In other cases the values give a diversified picture with α_L possibly in the same range as reported above, and α_c very variable, ranging between negative values and values for increasing average capital input. A clear conclusion is that the chemicals sector has to be further disaggregated before its cost behavior can be fruitfully analyzed.

The Machinebuilding and Metalworking Sector

This sector is represented for USSR 1968, USSR 1960, and Lithuania 1968 (as machinebuilding and metalworking), and for Belorussia 1963 (as machinebuilding). Although the branch is far from employing a uniform technology, the impression is that it fits the power function model of the behavior of the average input fairly well. It may also be noticed that capital and labor expansion occurs almost proportionally with $q = 1.0$ within the errors excepting for USSR (1.07 ± 0.01) and Belorussia 1963 (1.14 ± 0.08).

The R^2 values are generally high for labor input but not for capital (0.2 - 0.05). In the latter case, the estimated errors suggest that there is a tendency toward further increased productivity in the very largest firms. The moderate R^2 values for regression do not mean that the αs are inaccurately estimated; an alternative interpretation is that $\alpha_c = 1.0$--that is, constant average capital input is within the error limits in almost all cases.[9] The values are summarized for comparisons in the following table:

	α_L	α_c	q
USSR 1960	0.91 ± 0.01	0.97 ± 0.01	1.07
BSSR 1963	0.85 ± 0.04	0.98 ± 0.04	1.14
USSR 1968	0.87 ± 0.01	0.86 ± 0.05	1.06
Lithuania 1968	0.84 ± 0.03	0.83 ± 0.10	0.99

The Construction Materials Sector

Data for construction materials are given for the aggregated sector (RSFSR 1959, BSSR 1968, and Lithuania 1968) and for cement, concrete products, and wall materials separately.

For the whole sector, one might expect the aggregation disturbances to be mitigated because construction materials are as a rule produced locally, so that a fairly constant mix of subbranch output obtains (no regional specialization). However, the α_L values differ far more than the error margins can reconcile: RSFSR has 0.64, BSSR 0.38, and Lithuania 0.76. The α_c values come closer to each other (0.90, 0.92, and 1.08, respectively). The average capital input is in all cases U-shaped, indicating the beginning of diseconomies in the largest firms.

Among the branches, cement production is reported for USSR 1960 only, giving $\alpha_L = 0.76$ and $\alpha_c = 0.80$. The two average input curves are U-shaped for capital and inverted V-shaped (labor). This means that production in the largest plants takes place with particularly capital-intensive equipment. Although there are no regional data with which to check the values, it may be assumed that the results are representative because of the homogeneous output.

The technology employed in prefabricated concrete production should be expected to be fairly homogeneous, but only the labor α_Ls agree from the data given for USSR 1960 and BSSR 1963 (0.74 and 0.70, respectively). The behavior of average capital input is different in the two cases, with a U shape for the Soviet Union and $\alpha_c = 0.87$ (constant input within the error limits), and an inverted V shape for BSSR and a very high average α_c--1.39.

Wall materials (USSR 1960), or wall materials and brick (Belorussia 1963, with about 3 percent of the USSR production) agree extremely well: $\alpha_L = 0.65$ and 0.66, respectively; and $\alpha_c = 0.75$ and 0.76. The only notable difference is a slight U shape for BSSR due to rather capital-intensive and labor-saving production in the largest plants.

The Wood and Paper Sector

This sector is reported in aggregated form for Belorussia and Lithuania, both for 1968. In both cases, the fit as measured by R^2 is poor and the estimates differ considerably ($\alpha_L = 0.91$ and 0.54; $\alpha_c = 0.94$ and 1.05). For Belorussia, the average labor and capital input curves have an inverted V shape.

Lumber is reported for RSFSR for 1959 (labor only), USSR 1960, and BSSR 1963. In the latter two cases there is a typical increasing capital input industry ($\alpha_c = 1.23$ and 1.22) and at the same time an almost constant labor input ($\alpha_L = 0.91$ and 1.07).

Woodworking (USSR 1960, BSSR 1963) shows $\alpha_L = 0.74$ and 0.77, respectively, and these values agree within the error limits. The capital inputs are not reliably estimated (poor R^2 values).

The paper industry is a process industry with limited labor/capital substitutability in present technology, so that production volume is largely determined by, but not necessarily proportional to, the value of fixed capital equipment. The α_c value, 1.02, indicates in fact proportional output. Average labor input is moderately decreasing ($\alpha_L = 0.82$).

The Light Industry Sector

Light industry includes several branches: cotton, textile, sewing and apparel, hosiery, and fur and hides.

Data for the aggregated sector are given for Belorussia and Lithuania for 1968. As can be expected for aggregated branches, the elasticities do not agree. The Lithuania data suggest sharply decreasing average inputs ($\alpha_L = 0.51$, $\alpha_c = 0.43$), which are comparable within this sector only, to the USSR sewing and apparel industry.

The cotton industry is reported for USSR 1960. For labor, $\alpha_L = 0.85$ is fairly reliable, while average capital input is irregular; it is almost constant through the 50 million rubles/year sizes but then drops by almost 40 percent above this size. The mean size of firms in this latter, open-ended size interval is about 2.2 times that in the 30-50 million range--that is, about 100 million rubles/year.

Textile production (USSR 1960, RSFSR 1959, BSSR 1963) probably yields reliable α_c values (0.74, 0.76, and 0.74, respectively). For labor, USSR shows good linearity, $\alpha_L = 0.67$, but RSFSR (which produces roughly 70-80 percent of the Soviet Union output) exhibits a marked economy in the very largest firms (over 50 million rubles/year). With this point included, $\alpha_L = 0.86$; without it $\alpha_L = 0.91$ and a better R^2 value, 0.909. BSSR has an intermediate α_L, 0.80.

In the sewing and apparel industry there is falling average labor input throughout, but at different rates (USSR 1960, $\alpha_L = 0.50$, RSFSR 1959, 0.75, and BSSR 1963, 0.65). Only for the whole Soviet Union is capital input decreasing, and then sharply so ($\alpha_c = 0.34$). For RSFSR, capital input is instead U-shaped ($R^2 < 0$), and for BSSR it has an inverted V form. Probably a further subdivision of the branch could provide an explanation.

Hosiery (USSR 1960) data give $\alpha_L = 0.58$, indicating large-scale advantages by labor specialization but capital input does not fit the linear model (inverted V shape).

The fur and hides industry (for RSFSR 1959) behaves well with moderately decreasing average labor and capital inputs ($\alpha_L = 0.74$, $\alpha_c = 0.82$).

The Food Sector

The entire aggregated sector data are given for Lithuania 1968 only. They show strong labor economies to scale ($\alpha_L = 0.58$). The capital input is declining on the average, but the data show irregularities and the evidence is not conclusive ($R^2 = 0.3$).

The sugar industry branch (USSR 1960, RSFSR 1959; the latter region produced about 25 percent of the Soviet Union total) is a process-type industry with a homogeneous output, and one should expect consistent estimates from different sources. For USSR, $\alpha_L = 0.31$ with a wide error margin, and the capital input shows anomalously strong decrease with increasing size ($\alpha_c < 0$), so that the same comments made for the coal industry apply with regard to the validity of the estimation method. The RSFSR values are more realistic with $\alpha_L = 0.45$, $\alpha_c = 0.33$, again with very strong scale economies. Unfortunately there are only three usable size intervals, which makes the regression, and above all the error estimation, somewhat tenuous.

The meat industry data are reported for USSR 1960, RSFSR 1959, and BSSR 1963. The values agree within the error limits ($\alpha_L = 0.82$, 0.84, 0.77; $\alpha_c = 0.79$, 0.84, and 0.72). The near equality of α_L and α_c suggests that the industry is one with nearly fixed factor proportions. This is reflected by the q values, which are near 1. A closer examination of the estimated error term in most cases reveals that both input functions are slightly U-shaped, so that the scale economies are to some extent exhausted in the largest (30-50 million rubles) plants.

The fish industry may be expected to be localized on the coast and therefore subject to more concentrated production than the meat industry, which has a similar technology. For RSFSR 1959 and USSR 1960, the α_L values are 0.69 and 0.62, and the α_c values are 0.88 and 0.90. The similarities are to a considerable extent due to a substantial overlap (RSFSR has 70 percent of the USSR catch). The data given for BSSR for 1963 have three observations only, and they give seemingly wrong estimates.

The dairy industry is poorly estimated by the method employed. In both cases (USSR 1960, BSSR 1963) this is because of an irregularity in the 3-10 million rubles/year size interval; the average input drops steeply beyond this size. In spite of the bad fit, consistent estimates are obtained from the two sources: $\alpha_L = 0.83$ and 0.87; $\alpha_c = 0.77$ and 0.64, agreeing within the error limits.

Other Sectors

The printing industry (Lithuania 1968) has been estimated using the totals for industry not elsewhere covered which gives an error in the absolute input estimates. For capital, constant inputs cannot be rejected ($\alpha_c = 1.07 \pm 0.06$) and for labor, the average input remains about the same--0.08 to 0.09 man-years per 1,000 rubles of output, up to the size of 1 million rubles per year, and above that about 0.06 man-years per 1,000 rubles.

A Comparison with Soviet Results

In an article, Berri and Shilin (1965) give a descriptive treatment of economies of scale in a number of Soviet industry branches. The scale effects are observed in terms of production per employee, production per unit of fixed capital, amount of fixed capital per employee, and electrical effect installed per employee. The industries are classified according to three types of behavior: (1) all four indexes increase with firm size; (2) the amount of capital per employee decreases, the other indexes increase; and (3) production per unit of fixed capital decreases or behaves irregularly, the other indexes increase.

If the logarithmic linear model holds, the above classification can be expressed in α_L and α_c (see Note 8 at the end of this chapter).

1. $\alpha_L < \alpha_c < 1$
2. $\alpha_c < \alpha_L < 1$
3. $\alpha_L < 1 < \alpha_c$

In class (1), Berri and Shilin place oil extraction, machine-building, thermoelectricity and concrete elements. The results shown in this chapter agree if the translation to α_L and α_c is made. Deviations exist for separate republics. However, the data of Berri and Shilin refer to the national level.

In class (2), the article gives coal, sugar, and the dairy industry. Because of the irregularities in the results given in this chapter for these branches, only the dairy branch agrees.

Finally, (ferrous) metallurgy has $\alpha_L < 1 < \alpha_c$ for the whole USSR in 1960 which is in accordance with the class (3) location by Berri and Shilin. The authors also place woodworking and the fish industry into class (3) which cannot be confirmed conclusively from the results shown in this chapter.

Soviet Union data for 1960, 1963, 1964, 1968, 1971, 1972, and 1973 were processed with totals for output volume, labor, and capital estimated from statistical handbook data, so that a consistent time series was obtained with intertemporal comparisons possible in a relative sense.

Focusing on the labor input, one finds it to be decreasing throughout the size range in all years. The estimated regression error terms show that in 1960, 1963, and 1964 the input curve is concave. From 1968 on, the size interval of 100 million rubles and larger is reported separately, and labor inputs in these firms lie below the regression line.

TABLE 3.3

Regression Results of the All-Industry Study, by Region and Year

	$\hat{\alpha}_L$	Standard Deviation α_L	R^2	$\hat{\alpha}_c$	Standard Deviation $\hat{\alpha}_c$	R^2	Number of Intervals
USSR							
1960	0.665	0.017	0.990	0.850	0.061	0.824	4
1963	0.629	0.032	0.985	0.823	0.062	0.806	4
1964	0.725	0.029	0.973	0.864	0.042	0.680	6
1968	0.748	0.017	0.981	0.957	0.026	0.429	6
1971	0.750	0.017	0.984	0.962	0.032	0.312	6
1972	0.754	0.016	0.974	0.915	0.052	0.616	6
1973	0.756	0.017	0.972	0.928	0.024	0.771	6
RSFSR							
1960	0.659	0.007	0.999	0.843	0.044	0.920	4
1968	0.765	0.022	0.981	0.960	0.024	0.467	5
1972	0.775	0.017	0.952	0.952	0.037	0.401	6
1973	0.776	0.017	0.954	0.961	0.018	0.287	6
Ukraine							
1971	0.760	0.032	0.959	0.991	0.036	-0.039	6
1972	0.756	0.035	0.946	0.999	0.040	0.012	6
1973	0.756	0.024	0.971	0.993	0.027	0.101	6
Belorussia							
1963	0.732	0.037	0.893	0.723	0.097	0.728	6
1968	0.667	0.049	0.883	0.826	0.050	0.699	7
1972	0.665	0.066	0.798	0.746	0.037	0.865	7
Estonia							
1960	0.908	0.053	0.218	0.860	0.040	0.846	4
1967	0.559	0.049	0.980	1.013	0.232	0.048	3
Latvia							
1960	0.745	0.027	0.947	0.758	0.048	0.278	7
1964	0.660	0.031	0.232	0.640	0.064	0.814	6
1970	0.613	0.016	0.986	0.762	0.040	0.832	5
1971	0.634	0.024	0.974	0.775	0.029	0.879	5
Lithuania							
1960	0.379	0.168	0.457	0.369	0.136	0.100	9
1964	0.415	0.041	0.901	0.623	0.050	0.622	9
1966	0.431	0.029	0.808	0.524	0.047	0.222	9

1967	0.676	0.017	0.963	0.790	0.015	0.810	9
1968	0.519	0.068	0.834	0.726	0.048	0.773	8
1970	0.116	0.332	0.551	0.378	0.234	0.340	8
1972	0.768	0.310	0.227	0.984	0.214	0.020	8
Azerbaidzhan							
1970	0.697	0.284	0.685	0.537	0.222	-0.023	3
1972	0.592	0.032	0.949	1.082	0.107	-0.161	6
1973	0.599	0.040	0.965	1.056	0.130	-0.138	6
Uzbekistan							
1965	0.181	0.238	0.525	0.593	0.334	-0.164	5
1969	0.056	0.295	0.538	0.581	0.312	0.144	4
1972	0.563	0.047	0.926	0.728	0.086	0.251	7
Kirgistan							
1965	0.573	0.070	0.898	0.395	0.180	0.727	6
1966	0.453	0.087	0.922	0.185	0.156	0.838	6
Tadzhikistan							
1964	0.672	0.098	0.489	0.803	0.126	0.240	7
Kazakhstan							
1964	0.646	0.087	0.937	0.755	0.070	0.213	6
Pskov oblast							
1966	0.600	0.137	0.425	0.251	0.261	-0.335	8
Dnepropotrovsk oblast							
1965	0.823	0.025	0.969	1.136	0.089	0.143	3
Ivanovsk oblast							
1960	0.707	0.082	0.869	0.754	0.103	0.741	4
Gorkii oblast							
1965	0.838	0.021	0.841	0.967	0.027	0.002	8
Chelabinsk oblast							
1965	0.595	0.067	0.957	1.316	0.197	0.190	3
Chuvash ASSR							
1968	0.706	0.060	0.894	0.863	0.167	-0.054	5
Penza oblast							
1966	0.992	0.192	-0.012	1.001	0.186	-0.002	6
Riga gorod							
1962	0.660	0.048	0.738	0.850	0.110	0.319	6

Source: Compiled by the author.

139

The average capital input curves are U-shaped, except for
1960. The size interval in which capital productivity is highest is
for 1960--50 million rubles and larger; for 1963--5 to 50 million,
and for 1964 and later--10 to 15 million rubles of output per year.
Above the size for minimum average capital input, up to the largest
sizes (open-ended intervals), the labor input continues to decrease,
and that of fixed capital increases, by the following factors:

	Labor	Fixed Capital
1968	0.62	1.17
1971	0.63	1.23
1972	0.59	1.17
1973	0.62	1.23

On the average over these years, a difference in labor input
for the sizes concerned with a factor of 0.61 is accompanied by a
difference in fixed capital with a factor of 1.20. If only these two
components of cost are considered (a fairly well justified assumption
if material inputs increase proportionally to output), if the relative
cost of labor in terms of capital is p, and if the capital/labor ratio
in the size range concerned is a, there would be constant cost over
the range if

$$1 \cdot p + a \cdot 1 = 0.61 \, p + 1.20 \cdot a \cdot 1$$

If a = 40,000 rubles per employee, which is approximate for Lithuanian firms in this size range, by solving for p, one gets p approximately equal to 20,500 rubles per man-year. In other words, if the
use of 20,500 rubles of capital is calculated at the same cost as the
employment of one person, there would be approximately constant
cost in firms larger than 10 million rubles of output per year. Assuming capital cost equal to 7 percent of the capital value (an average depreciation rate in Soviet industry) the result would be:

1 man-year = 0.07 x 20,500 rubles = 1,435 rubles

which is of the same order of magnitude as the nominal wage-rate
cost in the Soviet Union and which supports the assumption of constant cost in fairly large firms in the aggregate of Soviet industry.
   Table 3.4 makes possible a comparison of average inputs over
time and across different sizes simultaneously. Here average inputs are referred to the right-end point of the corresponding interval
(no intervals, open-ended to the right, are included). The values
for 1 million rubles from 1968 on include the influence of firms
smaller than 0.5 million rubles (marked by arrows in the table),

which causes an upward bias. A corresponding remark applies to the 5-million- and the 50-million-ruble values for 1960 and 1963. Figure 3.4 is a graphic representation of the table.

TABLE 3.4

Development of Unit Labor and Capital Input, by Size,
USSR, All-Industry, Excluding Energy
(except for 1964) (millions of rubles)

	0.5	1	5	10	50	100
ALC (Average Labor Input)						
1960	1.28	→	1.07	→	0.89	--
1963	1.30	→	1.09	→	0.90	--
1964	1.26	1.14	1.00	0.89	0.81	--
1968	→	1.20	1.02	0.93	0.81	0.72
1971	→	1.12	0.95	0.86	0.74	0.65
1972	→	1.12	0.95	0.85	0.75	0.66
1973	→	1.10	0.93	0.83	0.72	0.64
ACC (Average Capital Input)						
1960	0.04	→	-0.13	→	-0.17	--
1963	0.11	→	-0.06	→	-0.16	--
1964	0.14	-0.02	-0.06	-0.14	-0.17	--
1968	→	0.00	-0.09	-0.08	-0.16	-0.12
1971	→	0.01	-0.09	-0.08	-0.15	-0.11
1972	→	0.08	-0.07	-0.07	-0.14	-0.10
1973	→	0.02	-0.06	0.07	-0.14	-0.11

Note: Values are in 10-base logarithms and are determined up to an additive constant for both ALC and ACC.
Source: Compiled by the author.

Data for RSFSR are available for 1960, 1968, 1972, and 1973. Indexes for the totals used were constructed from handbook data (excluding the energy sector in all cases). Because the RSFSR economy is roughly a 50 percent share of the Soviet Union total, it is not surprising that the conclusions drawn in the Soviet section are valid for RSFSR also. The focus here is on the changes in the capital/labor ratio over time.

FIGURE 3.4

Development of Average Inputs 1960-73, by Size of Firm, USSR, All-Industry, Excluding Energy (except for 1964)

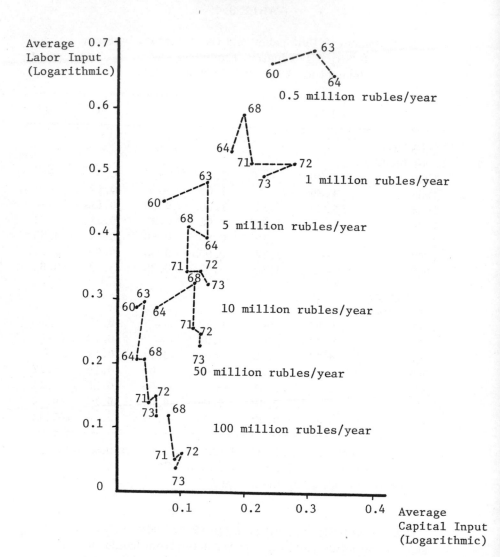

*Except in 1964

Source: Compiled by the author.

TABLE 3.5

Logarithms (Base 10) for Average Labor and Capital Inputs (up to a
Proportionality Constant) for RSFSR, by Size
(millions of rubles)

	1960		1968		1972		1973	
	Labor	Capital	Labor	Capital	Labor	Capital	Labor	Capital
0.1-0.5	0.36	0.04						
0.5-1			0.28	-0.03	0.21	+0.06	0.19	-0.01
1-5			0.12	-0.10	0.05	-0.09	0.03	-0.07
5-10			0.03	-0.11	-0.06	-0.12	-0.07	-0.11
10-50			-0.06	-0.14	-0.13	-0.13	-0.16	-0.13
50*	-0.16	-0.20	-0.24	-0.10	-0.22	-0.09	-0.24	-0.11

*For 1972 and 1973, the interval is 50-100 million rubles.
Source: Compiled by the author.

The size interval subdivision is not the same for 1960 as in the
later cases. Allowing for this, Table 3.5 shows how the average
labor input L and fixed capital input C have developed in a relative
sense in different size groups. The size with minimum average
fixed capital input is 10 to 50 million rubles per year, as it is for
the USSR. The U shape cannot be seen in the 1960 results. In the
sizes 5 million rubles and up, the fixed capital use seems to be
about stationary over time, while average labor input decreases
throughout. In the loglinear regression of total fixed capital on
total labor, we have the following coefficients:

Year	Constant	Linear Coefficient
1960	-0.438	1.278
1968	-0.214	1.255
1972	-0.067	1.229
1973	-0.042	1.236

The stability of the linear coefficients supports the impression that
the fixed capital buildup occurs uniformly across the firm sizes.
The movement of the constant term is steady and indicates an increase of the capital/labor ratio, for any firm size, of 7.9 percent
per year.

Data for the Ukraine for only three years--1971, 1972, and
1973--were available for the study, and they show the same general
pattern. Because the elasticities α for labor and fixed capital are

almost constant over these years, changes in the ratio between average labor and capital inputs are the same in all interval sizes and can be studied through the constant terms of the loglinear regression on firm output.

	Labor	Capital
1971	0.014	-0.736
1972	-0.003	-0.707
1973	-0.034	-0.701

As can be seen, the labor productivity rise, 4 percent per year, is bought at the expense of a decline in capital productivity of about the same size.

A closer study of the changes in the size distribution shows that the number of firms smaller than 1 million rubles per year is decreasing and that the increase instead takes place in the range of 10 to 50 million rubles and above. This is the range in which the lowest cost was found for the Ukraine, as well as for the Soviet Union and RSFSR, and the size distribution change is in accordance with the "survival" criterion for optimal plant size discussed by Stigler (1958) and applied also by Savings (1961).

The rest of the statistical material seems to be less rewarding to penetrate in great detail. The Belorussian series, from 1963, 1968, and 1972 is potentially interesting but only the latter two sets of data have the same size intervals. Moreover, the labor totals have changed a great deal over the decade covered, which is to a large extent due to the reclassification of employment in 1968, and it is difficult to establish the consistency of the totals.

The three Baltic republics show surprisingly little regularity, as assessed by the R^2 value, the coefficient movement over time, and manual plotting of the data. Since the quality of statistics from these regions is generally quite good,[10] an explanation may be the one provided by the discussion about the aggregations effects; considerable restructuring of the industry in the Baltic area may then be indicated.

The remaining time series, for Azerbaidzhan, Uzbek, and Kirgiz are likewise highly irregular. Here, poor quality of the statistical data given seems to be a likely interpretation. The regression results are merely reported without any further discussion. Also the isolated data available for a few additional republics, for some oblasts, and for one city are only reported in Table 3.3.

APPENDIX

Source Material

The following size/share tables were utilized for the study:

Category A: Tables for branches of industry in:

USSR	1960	21-sector classification
RSFSR	1959	14-sector classification
Belorussia	1963	13-sector classification
Belorussia	1968	7-sector classification
Lithuania	1968	9-sector classification

See Table 3A.1, which shows the branch breakdowns.

Category B: Tables for the whole industry by specific regions, forming time series with two or more observations:

	1960	1963	1964	1965	1966	1967	1968	1969	1970	1971	1972	1973
Soviet Union	1960	1963	1964*				1968			1971	1972	1973
RSFSR	1960						1968				1972	1973
Ukraine										1971	1972	1973
Belorussia		1963					1968				1972	
Estonia	1960					1967						
Latvia	1960		1964						1970	1971		
Lithuania	1960		1964		1966	1967	1968*		1970		1972	
Azerbaidzhan									1970		1972	1973
Uzbekistan				1965				1969			1972	
Kirgistan				1965*	1966*							

Category C: Isolated tables

Republics:

Kazakhstan	1964
Tadzhikistan	1964

ASSRs and oblasts:

Pskov oblast	1966†
Ivanovsk oblast	1960†
Gorkii oblast	1965†
Chuvash ASSR	1968†
Penza oblast	1966†
Cheliabinsk oblast	1965
Dnepropetrovsk oblast	1965

City:

Riga	1962†

---

*Whole industry in most cases excludes hydro- and thermo-electrical power plants and distribution systems. The items marked by an asterisk, however, include the sector mentioned.

†Including hydro- and thermoelectrical power plants and distribution systems.

TABLE 3A.1

Industry Branch Breakdown, by Regions

USSR 1960	RSFSR 1959	Belorussia 1963	Belorussia 1968	Lithuania 1968
Thermoelectrical power Hydroelectrical power		Thermoelectrical power		Electrical power
Coal	Coal		Fuel	Fuel
		Peat		
Oil extraction Oil refining	Oil extraction Oil refining			
Chemicals and rubber Metallurgy	Chemicals and rubber Ferrous metallurgy	Chemicals	Chemicals	Chemicals
Machinebuilding and metalworking		Machinebuilding	Machinebuilding and metalworking	Machinebuilding and metalworking
Lumber Woodworking	Lumber	Lumber Woodworking	Wood and paper	Wood and paper
Cement	Paper			
Precast concrete Wall materials	Construction materials	Precast concrete Wall materials	Construction materials	Construction materials
Cotton Textile Sewing Hosiery	Textile Sewing	Textile Sewing	Light industry	Light industry
	Fur and hides			
Sugar Meat Fish Dairy	Sugar Meat Fish	Meat Fish Dairy	Food industry	Food industry

Source: Compiled by the author.

The size/share tables were obtained from:

Region/year	Source

Category A: Branchwide data

USSR, 21 branches 1960 — Promyshlennost' SSSR. Moscow: Statistika, 1964, passim.

RSFSR, 14 branches 1959 — Promyshlennost' RSFSR. Moscow: Gosstatizdat TsSU SSSR, 1961, passim.

Belorussia, 13 branches 1963 — Promyshlennost' Belorusskoi SSR. Minsk: Statistika, Belorusskoe otdelenie, 1965, passim.

Belorussia, 7 branches 1968 — Belorusskaia SSR v Tsifrakh v 1969 godu. Minsk: Statistika, 1970, passim.

Lithuania, 9 branches 1968 — Promyshlennost' Litovskoi SSR. Vil'nius: Mintis, 1973, passim.

Category B: All-industry data, time series

USSR, all-industry
(excluding electrical power,
except in 1964):

1960 — Narodnoe khoziaistvo SSSR v 1962 godu. Moscow: Gosstatizdat TsSU SSSR, 1963, p. 137.

1963 — Narodnoe khoziaistvo SSSR v 1963 godu. Moscow: Statistika, 1965, p. 129.

1964 — Narodnoe khoziaistvo SSSR v 1965 godu. Moscow: Statistika, 1966, pp. 154-56.

1968 — Narodnoe khoziaistvo SSSR v 1969 godu. Moscow: Statistika, 1970, pp. 180-81.

1971 — Narodnoe khoziaistvo SSSR, 1922-1972 GG. Moscow: Statistika, 1972, pp. 154-55.

Region/Year	Source
1972	Narodnoe khoziaistvo SSSR v 1972 godu. Moscow: Statistika, 1973, pp. 192-93.
1973	Narodnoe khoziaistvo SSSR v 1973 godu. Moscow: Statistika, 1974, pp. 244-45.

RSFSR, all-industry
(excluding electrical power)

1960	Narodnoe khoziaistvo RSFSR v 1961 godu. Moscow: Gosstatizdat TsSU SSSR, 1962, p. 97.
1968	Narodnoe khoziaistvo RSFSR v 1969 godu. Moscow: Statistika, 1970, pp. 57-58.
1972	Narodnoe khoziaistvo RSFSR v 1972 godu. Moscow: Statistika, 1973, pp. 88-89.
1973	Narodnoe khoziaistvo RSFSR v 1973 godu. Moscow: Statistika, 1974, pp. 86-87.

Ukraine, all-industry
(excluding electrical power)

1971	Narodne hospodarstvo Ukrain'skoi RSR v 1971 rotsi. Kiev: Statystyka, 1972, pp. 84-85.
1972	Narodne hospodarstvo Ukrain'skoi RSR v 1972 rotsi. Kiev: Politvydav Ukrainy, 1974, pp. 118-19.
1973	Narodne hospodarstvo Ukrain'skoi RSR v 1973 rotsi. Kiev: Politvydav Ukrainy, 1974, pp. 108-09.

Belorussia, all-industry
(excluding electrical power)

| 1963 | Promyshlennost' Belorusskoi SSR. Minsk: Statistika, 1965, pp. 65-67. |

Region/Year	Source
1968	Belorusskaia SSR v tsifrakh v 1969 godu. Minsk: Statistika, 1970, p. 41.
1972	Statisticheskii ezhegodnik Belorusskoi SSR. Minsk: Belarus', 1973, pp. 30-31.
Estonia, all-industry	
1960 and 1967	Narodnoe khoziaistvo Estonskoi SSR v 1968 godu. Tallin: Statistika, Estonskoe otdelenie, 1969, pp. 56-57.
Latvia 1960 and 1964	Ekonomika i kul'tura Sovetskoi Latvii. Riga: Statistika, 1966, pp. 82-84.
Latvia 1971	Narodnoe khoziaistvo Latviiskoi SSR v 1971 godu. Riga: Statistika, Latviiskoe otdelenie, 1972, pp. 85-86.
Lithuania 1964 and 1966	Ekonomika i kul'tura Litovskoi SSR. Vil'nius: Statistika, Litovskoe otdelenie, 1967, pp. 99, 116, 120, 123.
Lithuania 1960 and 1970	Promyshlennost' Litovskoi SSR. Vil'nius: Mintis, 1973, pp. 75-77.
Lithuania 1967	Ekonomika i kul'tura Litovskoi SSR v 1967 godu. Vil'nius: Statistika, Litovskoe otdelenie, 1968, p. 43.
Lithuania 1968	Promyshlennost' Litovskoi SSR. Vil'nius: Mintis, 1973, pp. 78-79.
Azerbaidzhan 1970	Narodnoe khoziaistvo Azerbaidzhanskoi SSR v 1970 godu. Baku: Soiuzuchetizdat, 1972, p. 49.
Azerbaidzhan 1972	Narodnoe khoziaistvo Azerbaidzhanskoi SSR v 1972 godu. Baku: Soiuzuchetizdat, 1973, pp. 69-71.
Azerbaidzhan 1973	Narodnoe khoziaistvo Azerbaidzhanskoi SSR v 1973 godu. Baku: Soiuzuchetizdat, 1974, pp. 70-72.
Uzbek SSR 1965	Narodnoe khoziaistvo Uzbekskoi SSR v 1965 godu. Tashkent: Uzbekistan, 1966, p. 49.

Region/Year	Source
Uzbek SSR 1969	Narodnoe khoziaistvo Uzbekskoi SSR v 1969 godu. Tashkent: Uzbekistan, 1970, p. 52.
Uzbek SSR 1972	Narodnoe khoziaistvo Uzbekskoi SSR v 1971 godu. Tashkent: Uzbekistan, 1973, pp. 49-50.
Kirgiz SSR 1965	Sovetskii Kirgizstan za 40 let. (1926-1966). Frunze: Kyrgyzstan, 1966, pp. 45-48.
Kirgiz SSR 1966	Kirgizstan za 50 let Sovetskoi vlasti. Frunze: Kyrgyzstan, 1967, pp. 63-66.

Category C: all-industry, isolated tables

Kazakhstan 1964	Narodnoe khoziaistvo Kazakhstana. Alma-Ata: Kazakhstan, 1968, pp. 54-56.
Tadzhik SSR 1964	Narodnoe khoziaistvo Tadzhikskoi SSR v 1965 godu. Dushanbe: Statistika, 1966, pp. 56-57.
Pskov oblast 1966	Narodnoe khoziaistvo Pskovskoi oblasti. Pskov: Lenizdat, 1968. pp. 15-16.
Chel'abinsk oblast 1965	Narodnoe khoziaistvo Chel'iabinskoi oblasti. Chel'iabinsk: Statistika, Chel'iabinskoe otdelenie, 1967, p. 32.
Ivanovak oblast 1961	Narodnoe khoziaistvo Ivanovskoi oblasti. Moscow: Gosstatizdat TsSU SSSR, Ivanovskoe oblastnoe otdelenie, 1962, pp. 18-19.
Gorkii 1965	Narodnoe khoziaistvo Gor'kovskoi oblasti za 50 let. Gor'kii: Statistika, 1967, pp. 16, 19.
Chuvash ASSR 1968	Chuvashii za 50 let. Cheboksary: Chuvashkoe knizhnoe izdatel'stvo, 1970, pp. 35-36.

Region/Year	Source
Penza oblast 1966	Penzenskaia oblast' za 50 let Sovetskoi vlasti. Saratov-Penza: Privolzhskoe knizhnoe izdatel'stvo, 1967, pp. 34-35.
Dnepropetrovsk oblast 1965	Narodne hospodarstvo Dnipro-petrovs'koi oblasti. Donetsk: Statistika, 1966, pp. 70-71.
Riga 1962	Riga: Statisticheskii sbornik. Riga: Gosstatizdat, 1963, pp. 50-52.

NOTES

1. The latter cannot be used as a proxy for production capacity which is an often used size concept.

2. The Russian term used for the object classified in groups (predpriatie) should literally be translated as enterprise, which is not as well suited for the study of large scale economies as the concept of plant (the physical unit for production). However, the criterion for a unit to be distinguished in the tables is that it have an account of its own, which is usually the case for a "zavod," or plant. In this study, the word most often used will be "firm."

3. Since the data make it possible to treat labor and capital inputs separately, and since the two corresponding input functions play different roles in many input-output applications, the concept of cost function is avoided here as it normally refers to the total value of inputs.

4. A model with $y > 0$ as a function of $x > 0$ is loglinear if $\log y$ is a linear function of $\log x$; it is a power function model if y is proportional to a power x^{α} of x for some α. If one relation holds, so does the other, with the exponent α in the latter equal to the slope of the line in the former.

5. This is true even if the Cobb-Douglas function is modified so that the labor and fixed capital exponents do not sum to 1.

6. The problems associated with the choice of a size concept, and its impact on the estimations made, are discussed in Johnston (1960).

7. For $\alpha > 1$, which is relevant in some cases for capital input, an analogous reasoning can be carried out.

8. If $L = a_L x^{\alpha_L}$ and $K = a_c x^{\alpha_c}$, then $K = bL^{\alpha_c/\alpha_L}$ for some b. As can be verified from Tables 3.2 and 3.3, the relation $q = \alpha_c/\alpha_L$ holds fairly well in most cases.

9. The regression refers to $\alpha - 1$, which is near zero if α is near 1. In this case, an insignificant part of the variability of Y/X is explained by the influence of firm size.

10. The Lithuanian 1960 and 1970 data contain an obvious irregularity that distorts the results for these years.

REFERENCES

Berri, L. and I. Shilin. 1965. "Ekonomicheskaya effectivnost kontsentratsii proizvodstva v promyshlennosti." Voprosy ekonomiki, no. 9: 3-15.

Johnston, J. 1960. Statistical Cost Analysis. New York: McGraw-Hill.

Kmenta, J. 1971. Elements of Econometrics. New York: Macmillan.

Pratten, C. F. 1971. "Economies of Scale for Machine Tool Production." Journal of Indian Economics 19, no. 2: 148-65.

Savings, T. R. 1961. "Estimation of Optimum Size of Plant by the Survivor Technique." Quarterly Journal of Economics 75, no. 4 (November): 569-707.

Sargeant, F. P. 1961. The Logic of British and American Industry. London: Routledge and K. Paul.

Stigler, C. J. 1958. "Economics of Scale." Journal of Law and Economics 1 (October): 54-71.

4

ASPECTS OF SOVIET
TRANSPORTATION IN AN
INPUT-OUTPUT FRAMEWORK
Arthur L. Moses

INTRODUCTION

The analytical power of the input-output model lies in its potential for unraveling the intricate interdependencies among sectors in the processes of production and distribution. This approach is uniquely suited to the study of the transportation sector. Not only is the transport sector a significant user of economic resources; its services are a vital input of all other parts of the economy.

This analysis focuses upon several issues concerning transportation and interindustry relations in the Soviet Union. First, recent trends in Soviet transportation are briefly surveyed and the structural interdependence of transport in the Soviet economy is examined. Second, the distinction between productive and nonproductive transport is considered, and a method presented for separating passenger transportation from the final-demand column of a reconstructed Soviet input-output table. Third, statistical nuances and conventions pertaining to transport entries in Soviet input-output tables are set forth. More specifically, the fundamental reorientation of transport entries in the conversion of input-output tables from purchasers' to producers' prices is investigated. Finally, some early findings of transportation requirements within a regional input-output context are established, and some areas for further research are defined.

Since the late 1950s, Soviet economists and statisticians have been engaged in a large-scale effort devoted to constructing input-output accounts and models. Out of approximately 100 different tables already constructed, the ex post national tables for 1959, 1966, and 1972 are especially significant because of the amount of data and descriptive material available. These ex post national tables contain explicit consideration of transportation in which the Marxian distinction between productive and nonproductive usage is made. Accordingly, transport entries in the first quadrant of Soviet

input-output tables reflect productive freight transportation, while
passenger transportation is treated as a claimant on final demand.
For 1959, the Soviets aggregated all modes handling freight into a
single transport sector, while the 1966 table contained two sectors:
rail transportation and other transportation. Unfortunately, the
purity of the transport sector(s) is undermined in the published versions of these tables, where the area of communications serving the
productive sphere is combined with productive transportation into a
single sector. Explicit consideration of passenger transportation is
also lost because of the aggregation of all final-demand claimants
into a single broad final-demand column. Therefore, any attempt to
study Soviet transportation within an input-output framework must
recognize, and deal with, the limitations imposed by the published
tables.

Evidence of further complications is provided by a Soviet
specialist who has estimated the real national cost of Soviet transport for 1970 (Shafirkin 1972). The analysis reveals that of the total
real cost, 37 percent is composed of payments made for line haulage
of freight, while loading and unloading activities account for 22 percent of the total. Comparison of the estimated total real freight cost
of 49.9 billion rubles with the 1970 Gross Social Product figure of
25 billion rubles for transportation and communications combined
indicates that there is a substantial understatement of real costs in
the transport statistics of the national accounts (TsSU 1971, p. 60).
This discrepancy is largely explained by enterprise responsibility
for loading and unloading activities. The result is the inclusion of
transport-related costs in aggregate expenditure statistics recorded
for the other economic sectors, while transport entries exclude, for
the most part, the costs of loading and unloading operations. The
magnitude of these costs and the heavy commitment of industrial
workers to loading and unloading activities is revealed in information pertaining to 1965-66 (TsSU 1967, pp. 26, 83). Out of 7,364,000
workers employed in transport, 258,000 were engaged in loading and
unloading operations. However, in industry (as of August, 1965),
out of an employment of 19,695,000, fully 2,449,000, or 12 percent
of the total, were engaged in intraplant transport, loading and unloading operations, and warehouse services. Thus, to the extent
that transport flows in Soviet input-output tables reflect Gross Social
Product accounting procedures, the total real cost of operating the
transportation system is severely understated in the transport sec-
tor(s) of the ex post national tables.

Further difficulties arise in the acute measurement problems
of outputs as well as inputs. A transportation system produces
diverse outputs that are generally categorized into freight and passenger services. Within these broad categories such descriptive

variables as travel time, convenience, waiting time, and numerous other factors make the quest for a standard output unit quite elusive.[1] In the background analysis that follows, output measurement problems are sidestepped through the use of ton- and passenger-kilometers as the standard output units. As useful indicators of intermodal shifts in traffic flows, ton-kilometer and passenger-kilometer indexes provide insights into the transition that has taken place in Soviet transportation.

Input measurement difficulties, on the other hand, are compounded by the Soviet distinction between productive and nonproductive use, but Soviet statistical yearbooks circumvent the nonoperational nature of this distinction by reporting capital and labor figures for the transport sector as a whole. A detailed examination of the intractability of this problem is presented in a later section where the common usage of inputs and the importance of both freight and passenger transport are discussed.

Another dimension to transport's significance is revealed by its large requirements of capital stock. This stock which, for all intents and purposes, is nontransferable, presents the Soviets with several continuous and inflexible demands. Of primary importance is the steady drain on resources caused by maintenance of the existing system. These requirements ensure that the transport sector can never be overlooked in the planning process. Moreover, despite having developed transportation equipment industries of their own, the Soviets have relied heavily upon imports of transportation equipment. Consequently, the needs of the transport sector are also an important factor in the level and composition of Soviet foreign trade.

The overall impact of transport, therefore, is one that affects both foreign and domestic activity. As the integrating factor of an economic system, transport's importance should not be judged solely through its explicit contribution to national income. Rather, its position in infrastructure indicates that many of its benefits are indirect and hence, nonquantifiable. Measurement problems notwithstanding, the transport system has been an integral part of the Soviet growth pattern, and it is to an analysis of recent developments in Soviet transportation that attention is now directed.

SOVIET TRANSPORTATION--RECENT DEVELOPMENTS AND FUTURE PROSPECTS

The directives of the Tenth Five-Year Plan underscore a delicate resource allocation problem confronting Soviet planners. On the one hand, great importance is attached to increasing the living standards of the Soviet people. Alternatively, large capital require-

ments are projected for the intensified development of Soviet industry, with large proportions slated for infrastructure. While it is
not the purpose of this brief survey to investigate economywide implications of this trade-off, it should be pointed out that both objectives harbor significant implications for the transport sector and
the formulation of transport policy. Renewed emphasis on industrial
output, and in particular, heavy industry, suggests an intensified reliance on the railroads to satisfy the economy's expanding transport
requirements. In fact, the reemergence of the railroads as a primary growth mode tends to reverse a trend, evident since 1960,
that encompassed the relative expansion of nonrail forms of transport. During the 1960-74 period, the railroads continued to dominate the transport picture, although an analysis of traffic flows indicates that other modes accounted for an increasing share of traffic
conveyed. The basic functions of the railroads were supplemented
by expansion and integration of the nonrail transport modes where
innovation served to lessen the strain on the railroads, allowed them
to spin off inefficient operations, and permitted them to concentrate
on long-haul freight conveyance. The period with which this analysis
is concerned, 1960-74, should be viewed as one of maturation for the
transport sector, where principal modes came to operate in their
particular areas of comparative advantage.

    Both freight and passenger services have developed to a degree
sufficient to harbor signs of unification of the Soviet transportation
system.[2] Tables 4.1 and 4.2 provide evidence of this unification in
terms of freight and passenger traffic indexes. Growth in particular
sectors appears not to have infringed upon the functions of others.
Instead, recent developments reflect a rounding-out of the transport
system.

    In the freight sphere, virtual elimination of steam motive
power has allowed the railroads to satisfy the staggering freight
transport demands made upon them by the Soviet economy. Through
1971, electric and diesel traction accounted for 48.7 and 47.8 percent, respectively, of the share of rail ton-kilometer traffic. Their
performance capabilities, measured in terms of fuel efficiency,
speed, reduced maintenance time, and increased haulage capacity,
have combined to improve what were already considered excellent
operating ratios (Wilson 1962).

    Pipeline construction has come as a response to concentrated
demands for natural gas and petroleum-based products. The increased transportation of these products reflects technological development within Soviet industry and is a visible sign of the inter-
relationship between the energy and transport sectors.

    Maritime transport has experienced a rapid growth in terms
of ton-kilometer traffic. Coming as a result of expanded trade and

TABLE 4.1

Freight Transportation, by Different Modes of Public Use, by Year, 1960-74
(billions of ton-kilometers)

Year	Rail	River	Automotive	Pipeline	Maritime	Air	Total-- All Modes	Index
1960	1,504.3	99.6	98.5	51.2	131.5	.56	1,885.7	100
1961	1,566.6	106.0	105.7	60.0	159.1	.80	1,998.2	106
1962	1,646.3	109.9	111.9	74.5	173.4	.89	2,116.9	112
1963	1,749.4	114.5	119.7	90.9	226.3	.91	2,301.7	122
1964	1,854.1	124.5	132.1	112.1	297.6	1.14	2,521.5	134
1965	1,950.2	133.9	143.1	146.7	388.8	1.34	2,764.0	147
1966	2,016.0	137.7	155.3	165.0	442.8	1.45	2,918.3	155
1967	2,160.5	143.9	170.2	183.4	527.1	1.66	3,186.8	164
1968	2,274.8	155.4	187.1	215.9	586.8	1.80	3,421.8	181
1969	2,367.1	160.1	200.1	244.6	601.3	1.95	3,575.1	190
1970	2,494.7	174.0	220.8	281.7	656.1	1.88	3,829.2	203
1971	2,637.3	183.8	240.4	328.5	696.0	1.98	4,088.0	217
1972	2,760.8	180.3	258.1	375.9	698.4	2.19	4,275.7	227
1973	2,958.0	189.5	283.8	439.4	750.7	2.37	4,623.8	245
1974	3,097.7	212.3	312.3	533.4	778.1	2.49	4,936.3	262

Sources: TsSU, Transport i sviaz SSSR (Moscow: Statistika, 1972), p. 17; TsSU, Narodnoe khoziaistvo SSSR v 1974 godu (Moscow: Statistika, 1975), p. 472.

TABLE 4.2

Passenger Transportation, by Different Modes of Public Use, by Year, 1960-74
(billions of passenger-kilometers)

Year	Rail	River (IWT)	Maritime	Automotive Public Bus, Trolley	Air	Total-- All Modes	Index
1960	170.8	4.3	1.3	61.0	12.1	249.5	100
1961	176.3	4.4	1.4	69.3	16.4	267.8	107
1962	189.3	4.6	1.3	82.2	20.3	297.7	119
1963	192.0	4.7	1.4	95.2	25.3	318.6	128
1964	195.1	4.7	1.3	107.7	30.9	339.7	136
1965	201.6	4.9	1.5	120.5	38.1	366.6	147
1966	219.4	5.2	1.6	137.0	45.1	408.3	164
1967	234.4	5.3	1.7	153.0	53.3	447.9	180
1968	254.4	5.5	1.8	168.5	62.1	492.0	197
1969	261.3	5.5	1.7	183.0	71.5	523.0	210
1970	265.4	5.4	1.6	202.5	78.2	553.1	222
1971	274.6	5.7	1.7	215.8	88.8	586.6	235
1972	285.8	5.7	1.9	235.6	95.9	624.9	250
1973	296.6	5.9	1.9	253.9	98.8	657.1	263
1974	306.3	6.1	2.1	279.1	108.8	702.4	282

Sources: TsSU, Transport i sviaz SSSR (Moscow: Statistika, 1972), p. 19; TsSU, Narodnoe khoziaistvo SSSR v 1974 godu (Moscow: Statistika, 1975), p. 473.

aid, development of the merchant marine can be seen as an official
response to the heavy reliance on the charter market brought about
by increased Soviet commitments abroad. The effort to save hard
currency, as well as to fulfill military and economic obligations to
developing nations, has brought the Soviet Union from eleventh to
sixth place in world shipping (by tonnage) (Shadrin 1973).

Expanded air transportation has presented the Soviets with a
fundamentally different horizon. While other modes are dependent
upon and create centralized demands, air transport allows for the
decentralization of economic activity. Despite aviation's relative
insignificance in the freight transport picture, the conquest of time
and distance has provided ample opportunity for the conveyance of
perishable goods and vital supplies in times of emergency.

Development of the road sector in general and the automotive
industries in particular is serving, and will continue to serve, to
precipitate greater dispersion of economic activities. Accessibility
to outlying areas has been improved through a widespread road-
building campaign. Expansion has also aided the railroads, since
short-haul shipping has been shifted to the trucking fleets. During
the 1960-74 period, the automotive industry caught the attention of
the highest levels of Soviet authority, and investment decisions were
made to speed the Soviet Union toward a frenzied program of motori-
zation. Prospects for the industry have, therefore, been immeasur-
ably increased.

Trends within the passenger sphere, as in its freight counterpart, indicate that modes other than the railroads are increasing
their shares of traffic conveyed. Particularly noticeable in intercity transport has been the growth of air and bus traffic, while taxis
and buses have increased their intracity passenger-kilometer traffic
by factors of 4.0 and 3.5 respectively. Unlike any other industrialized
nation, however, the Soviet Union is in the enviable position of being
almost completely dependent upon public mass transportation. Despite official Soviet policies designed to expand the production of
passenger cars, it appears certain that no fundamental change in the
nation's method of passenger conveyance is likely to occur. This is
borne out on several fronts:

1. Foreign trade statistics for recent years indicate that auto
imports have all but stopped, while auto exports have risen markedly.
Entirely conceivable is the prospect that the automotive revolution
will bypass the Soviet citizenry and provide instead the impetus for
an important new source of foreign exchange.

2. The great push for production appears to be taking place
at the expense of facilities. Through its emphasis on final output
rather than ancillary support operations, the Soviet Union is casting

aside the advantage of being a latecomer to the automotive field.
Thus it seems that the chronic shortage of repair and fueling stations
will persist, and that the proliferation of new vehicles will make increasing demands on an already critical spare parts situation. In
short, once a Soviet citizen becomes the proud possessor of a new
car, he is likely to find that his troubles have just begun.

3. Not the least imposing of the impediments to mass public
ownership, however, is the price barrier. The price of a middle-
range Soviet auto is about three times the yearly wages of the average Soviet worker. In the absence of credit, cars must be fully paid
for by the date of delivery, and the inevitable outcome is that the
Soviet people will share unequally in the increased availability of the
passenger car (Edwards 1973). Given the current supply-demand
situation, the turnover tax accounts for about 60 percent of the price
of an automobile. Until such time as sufficient cars are forthcoming
from the production lines (and the turnover tax is correspondingly
lowered), only those members of the professional-managerial elite
who possess sufficient funds will be destined to participate in the
private-auto age.

Over the next five years, however, Soviet authorities envisage
increases of 30 and 23 percent in freight and passenger turnover, respectively. In order to fulfill this objective, they have once again
invoked the need for increased operating performances in all phases
of the transportation system, although substantial capital outlays are
being projected for the transport sector as well.[3] Nevertheless, the
emphasis on heavy industry and the further development of the fuel-
power complex, to a large extent in the eastern regions, will place
particularly large demands on the transport sector since fuels and
heavy industry already consume large proportions of transport services. Within an input-output framework, fuels and heavy industry
rank among the highest sectors in terms of transport intensity per
ruble of output.

As traffic demands across all sectors continue to grow, and
as the large investments in infrastructure are made to develop the
eastern portions of the country, it is expected that the transport
sector, already an important user of economic resources, will claim
an even larger share. An investigation of the transport sector within
an input-output context reveals some interesting insights into the
structure of transport requirements by sector, as well as transport's
own input requirements.[4] Thus, given the directives of the Tenth
Five-Year Plan, input-output analysis can help to enumerate potential sources of strain on the transport system as a whole.

The Structural Interdependence of Transport
in the Soviet Economy

Recent studies using the 71-sector reconstructed tables for 1959 and 1966 have examined changes in Soviet industrial structure and have identified several important trends that developed in the intervening years (Guill 1975; Moses 1975). More specifically, intermediate deliveries were found to comprise a large and growing share of the total value of goods and productive services in the Soviet economy. Also, structural changes in the 1959-66 time period permitted the production of a given set of final demands with a sharply reduced labor bill, but with larger requirements for capital and intermediate outputs.

Against this overall backdrop, an evaluation of the transportation sector was performed in order to obtain a more comprehensive view of its importance in the circulation process. The objective was to survey broad shifts in the input structure of transportation activity and then to gradually contract the focus until sector-by-sector shifts in the transport content of delivered final demand were considered.

TABLE 4.3

Intermediate Output, Labor, and Capital Requirements of the
Transportation (and Communications) Sector to Produce
1966 Final Demand with 1959 and 1966 Technologies

	1959	1966	Change in Requirements 1959-66	Percentage Change 1966/59
Intermediate requirements (thousands of rubles)	17,586,600	19,000,000	1,413,400	8.0
Labor requirements* (thousands of man-years)	8,265.4	4,565.0	-3,700.4	-44.8
Capital requirements* (thousands of rubles)	47,120,779	41,444,000	-5,676,779	-12.1

*Labor and capital requirements for producing 1966 final demand with 1959 technology are derived by multiplying the transportation (and communications) share in total labor and capital for 1959 by the total labor and capital requirements using 1959 technology.

Source: Compiled by the author.

As set forth in Table 4.3, intermediate output requirements of transportation (and communications)[5] to deliver the 1966 level and composition of final demand increased by 1,413,000 rubles, or 8 percent, with 1966 technology as opposed to 1959 technology. Labor requirements fell by almost 45 percent, perhaps reflecting the substitution of pipeline for rail transport, since pipelines are decidedly less labor-intensive than their railroad counterpart. A somewhat surprising result was the 12 percent decline in capital stock needed to produce 1966 final demand with 1966 technology. Conceivably, this development is due to more dense industrial concentration in 1966, thus causing lower transportation (and communications) capital requirements for this year.

Further investigation involved the analysis of transportation (and communications) requirements to deliver 14 subvectors of 1966 final demand using 1959 and 1966 technologies respectively (see Table 4.4.

TABLE 4.4

Change in Intermediate Output Requirements of Transport (and Communications) to Deliver 14 Subvectors of 1966 Final Demand with 1959 and 1966 Technologies

Sector	Percentage Change
Metallurgy	8
Fuel	13
Power	15
Machinebuilding and metalworking	16
Chemical products	-47
Woodworking and paper products	23
Construction materials and glass	16
Textile products	-2
Food industry	-10
Construction	23
Agriculture	-9
Transportation and communications	--
Other branches	-12
Unidentified	54

Source: Compiled by the author.

Transport needs jumped sizably for heavy industry, the energy-supplying sectors, and construction, while there was a marked decline in the requirements to deliver the final demands of chemicals, agriculture, and food. This measure was broadened by an analysis of changes in intermediate requirements expressed in rubles per ruble of final demand for each of the subvectors of 1966 final demand. As revealed in Figure 4.1, increases in transport intensity are shown for eight subvectors; five subvectors exhibit decreases. Especially noteworthy are the increasing transport intensities of construction materials and fuels. Consequently, expansion of final demands

FIGURE 4.1

Intermediate Requirements from Transportation (and Communications) to Deliver
14 Subvectors of 1966 Final Demand with 1959 and 1966 Technologies

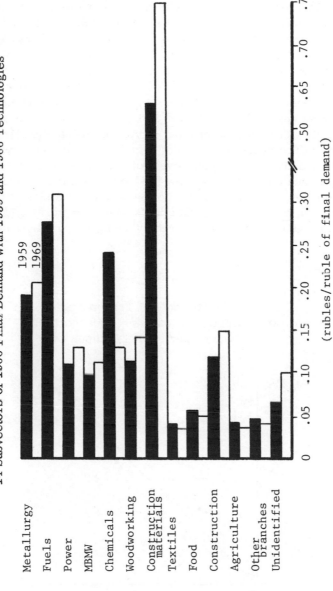

(rubles/ruble of final demand)

Source: Compiled by the author from available Soviet input-output tables.

encompassed by these subvectors can be expected to cause the most
severe squeeze on the Soviet transport system.

　　As a final inquiry into the transport sector, a scatter diagram
of transport requirements per ruble of output for each of the 71 sectors was constructed. [6] Figure 4.2 reveals that the majority of
input–output sectors have experienced an increase in transportation
(and communications) cost in the 1959–66 period. In particular, sectoral transport costs vary substantially, with oil extraction, coal,
and construction materials having large per ruble requirements; and
construction, trade and distribution, and electric and thermal power
having relatively low requirements. Gas, synthetic fibers, and casting machinery and equipment show large increases in transport requirements per ruble of output in 1966, while basic chemistry products, and printing machinery and equipment utilize sharply reduced
amounts of transport per ruble of output. Overall, energy suppliers
and heavy industry show high levels of transport intensity; transport
costs per ruble of output are low for food, and agricultural and textile products. Sectors falling into the broad categories of machinebuilding and metalworking, chemicals, and woodworking are in the
middle range of transportation requirements per ruble of output.

FIGURE 4.2

Direct Coefficients of Transportation
(and Communications) for 1959 and 1966
(rubles per ruble of output)

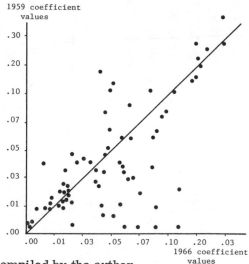

Source: Compiled by the author.

PASSENGER TRANSPORTATION IN SOVIET
INPUT-OUTPUT TABLES

Soviet adherence to Marxist economic philosophy necessitates differentiating between productive and nonproductive use of transportation services. In other words, there exists an explicit separation between the movement of goods and the movement of people. Such an approach is fundamentally at odds with the broad influence of transportation whose impact transcends the somewhat artificial boundaries of the material sphere. As a process encompassing the dimensions of space, time, and cost, transportation produces movement and communication, and permits the interaction of people, regions, goods, and ideas. While Soviet practice is, for the most part, workable in an output sense—all nations draw a distinction between passenger and freight traffic--it is in the area of input usage that the distinction presents particularly severe measurement problems. The ambiguity of the productive-nonproductive division and the nonoperationality of these concepts is clear from examination of Soviet statistics. Were the distinction significant in any aspect of planning, control, or administration, it appears certain that Soviet statistics would have recognized it. There are, in fact, national income accounts that incorporate only productive activities. However, such Soviet statistics as fixed capital stock, working capital, depreciation, average wages, employment, gross investment, and total profit are reported for the transport sector as a whole. In short, problems surrounding the divisibility of productive resources make the separation of these statistical aggregates empirically difficult. The Soviet practice of reporting capital and labor statistics for the transport sector in aggregated form avoids the difficulties of imputing to each form of service the appropriate proportion of input usage.

An important attempt to make operational the productive-nonproductive division of resources is revealed in Soviet input-output tables. These tables provide an expression of the separation of transport, where transportation entries in the interindustry matrix measure only that amount of productive service consumed in the functioning of the material sphere, that is, freight transportation. Nonproductive passenger transportation is omitted from the sector, and thus to the extent that freight shipment constitutes only a portion of transportation services provided, the importance of transportation is not completely reflected by considering only the first quadrant. The Soviets place passenger transportation in the final-demand quadrant of input-output tables, and unpublished tables contain explicit enumeration of material deliveries made to passenger transportation as well as the other categories of final demand. Unfortunately, the published versions of the 1959 and 1966 Soviet tables contain only one final-demand column, the material deliveries for all final-demand categories being aggregated into a single entry for each row of the matrix. Explicit consideration of nonproductive transportation is thus lost in the aggregation process, and any attempt to provide a more complete picture of transport's contribution to the economy must come to grips with this problem by separating out passenger transportation from the final-demand aggregate.

Having laid the groundwork for our exercise, a brief appraisal of passenger transport statistics is in order. The Soviet Union publishes on a regular basis accurate data for transport performance. [7] Statistics are collected for the major transport modes--rail, motor, river, maritime, air, and pipeline--and broken down into freight and passenger categories. It quickly becomes evident, however, that there is substantial emphasis upon freight statistics. Numerous series present information on operating performance, including the generation of ton- and passenger-kilometer traffic, average lengths of haul and carriage, the length of traffic networks, principal categories of freight shipment by different modes, and vehicle operating and turnaround times. In addition to the identification of interregional and interrepublic traffic patterns, the information also provides a measure of technological innovation in transport, as well as economy-wide shifts in energy consumption. Thus, the changeover from steam to diesel and electric rail traction is easily detected, and the growth of pipeline transport reflects the transition from a coal-consuming economy to one more intensive in oil and gas usage. Changes taking place within the passenger sphere are also easily detected, since the relative growth of motor and air carriage shows up in the disaggregated passenger-kilometer indexes.

Unfortunately, no information pertaining to material expenditures is provided in the official publications, thereby eliminating them as a source for freight/passenger disaggregations. Although reports of transport ministries provide separate listings of material expenditures made for passenger and freight transport, even Soviet specialists must undertake major data revisions to make the information operational. A highly placed input-output authority has presented a detailed description of the substantial efforts needed to fit the data into the appropriate input-output categories (Eidel'man 1966, pp. 174-82), and these efforts are treated in depth later in this chapter. Once the disaggregation process has been completed, Soviet input-output practice necessitates that the resulting transport entries that appear in the first quadrant of the official tables are those related to the productive sphere; passenger transport is relegated to the final-demand quadrant. Given the published Soviet tables with their single final-demand column, there is concern about the explicit understatement of transport services. Surely the 582 billion passenger-kilometers logged in 1966 should be considered in the transport sector which already reflects 2,918 billion ton-kilometers of freight shipments (TsSU 1972, pp. 17-19). The problem, however, is measurement. How, in fact, is the weighted distance measure of passenger-kilometer traffic translated into material expenditures?

The only recourse is to the spotty published information. While numerous monographs, essays, and technical papers extol the necessity of an efficiently functioning transport system, few sources allude to the statistical separation of productive and nonproductive transport. A review of the transport literature yields interesting insights into the relationship between freight and passenger traffic, but the problem is the lack of hard data regarding the separate use of productive resources.

Perhaps the best information on the cost structure of passenger transport appears in an input-output table constructed for the Latvian Republic (Shmulder et al. eds. 1971, pp. 138-43, 380-81). Table 4.5 presents a sectoral breakdown of material deliveries made to the transport sector compiled with data taken from this source. Also presented is the percentage distribution of deliveries made to freight and passenger transport, respectively. Materials allocated to freight transport comprise almost 72 percent of the total material allocation. Clearly eight of the ten industrial sectors distribute at least 70 percent of their transport deliveries to freight. The power sector alone deviates significantly from its industrial counterparts in delivering only 29 percent of its transport allocation to freight. For present purposes, however, the usefulness of this information is undermined somewhat because of the small geographical area and densely populated nature of the Latvian Republic.

Our pursuit of an analogue for an accurate economywide division leads to Eidel'man (1966, p. 177) whose calculations for the 1959 Soviet table reveal that 83.2 percent of all material expenditures made by railroads is allocated to freight transport and 16.8 percent to passenger transport. The geographical expanse of the Soviet Union as well as heightened industrial activities in the eastern regions suggest a greater significance of the freight sector than that reported for the Latvian Republic. However, additional information has become available which obviates the need to apply 1959 calculations to the 1966 Soviet table.

Shneiderman (1974) has provided data that allow estimates to be made for the cost structure of nonproductive transportation and communications for 1966. On the basis of the percent distribution of material costs in total public consumption, Treml (1975b) has derived estimates for broad aggregates of nonproductive transportation and communications corresponding to the sector classification

TABLE 4.5

Deliveries to Transportation Sectors in the Latvian SSR

	Material Deliveries			Passenger/ Freight Ratio
	Freight Transport (thousands of rubles)	Passenger Transport	Freight as Percentage of Total	
Metallurgy (all)	1,000	268.8	.789	.269
Fuels	27,200	8,589.8	.760	.316
Power	1,600	3,994.5	.291	2.496
Machinebuilding and metalworking	9,200	3,895.5	.703	.423
Chemical	4,800	1,930.1	.713	.402
Wood and paper	1,100	563.9	.661	.513
Construction materials	500	146.8	.773	.294
Light industry	2,300	825.4	.736	.359
Food industry	200	80.3	.714	.401
Industry not elsewhere classified	1,300	506.0	.720	.389
Agriculture	0	1.1	.000	--
Transportation and communication	3,300	0	1.000	.000
Trade and distribution	0	0	.000	.000
Other	200	118.3	.628	.591
Total	52,700	20,920.5	.716	.397

Source: M. Shmulder et al., eds., Dinamika mezhotraslevykh i mezhrespublikanskikh ekonomicheskikh sviazei Latviiskoi SSSR (Riga: Tsentral'noe statisticheskoe upravlenie Latviiskoi SSR, 1971), pp. 138–39, 280–81.

employed in the 1966 reconstructed Soviet input-output table.[8] The
data are presented in Table 4.6.

TABLE 4.6

Structure of Costs, Nonproductive Transportation and Communications, 1966

Sector Number*	Sector Designation	Millions of Rubles
5-10	Fuels	588
11	Electrical power	175
12-38	Machinebuilding and metalworking	268
39-48	Chemicals	150
49-58	Wood and construction materials	77
59-61	Light industry	46
62-68	Food industry	21
1-4, 69-76	Other costs	115
	Total material purchases	1,440
	Depreciation	1,140
	Wages	2,670
	Other elements of national income	2,140
	Total national income	4,810
	Total value of output	7,390

*Sector classification employed in Vladimir G. Treml, Dmitri M.
Gallik, Barry L. Kostinsky, and Kurt W. Kruger, The Structure of the
Soviet Economy (New York: Praeger, 1972), pp. 103-04.
    Source: Vladimir G. Treml, "Structure of Costs, Nonproductive
Transportation and Communications" (Unpublished manuscript, Duke
University, November 1975).

We rely on Treml's estimates as the basis for further disaggregation of nonproductive transportation and communications as well as
its separation from the final-demand aggregate. Thus, transportation and communications entries in the first quadrant of the 1966
Soviet table are complemented by material expenditures made for
nonproductive transportation and communications. The basis for
this procedure is presented below.
    Consider a standard three-quadrant input-output table with n
producing sectors--one of which, sector d, is freight transporta-
tion--one final-demand column, and one value-added row, where

x_{ij} = the value of input i purchased by sector j
x_{id} = the value of input i purchased by freight transport
x_{ip} = the value of input i purchased by passenger transport
x_{it} = the value of input i purchased by freight and passenger
        transport

x_{dj} = the value of freight transport services purchased by sector j

x_{pj} = the value of passenger transport services purchased by sector j

X_i = the gross value of output of sector i

Y_i = the value of deliveries to final demand made by sector i

V_i = the value-added attributable to sector i

a_{ij} = the input of sector i per ruble of output of sector j, that is, x_{ij}/X_j

According to Soviet input-output methodology, the following propositions are held to be true:

First, the value of produced and distributed output of each branch is balanced, that is,

$$\sum_{i=1}^{n} a_{ij}X_j + V_j = \sum_{i=1}^{n} a_{ji}X_i + Y_j \tag{1}$$

Second, the value of produced and distributed gross social product is balanced, that is

$$\sum_{j=1}^{n} \sum_{i=1}^{n} a_{ij}X_j + \sum_{j=1}^{n} V_j = \sum_{j=1}^{n} \sum_{i=1}^{n} a_{ji}X_i + \sum_{j=1}^{n} Y_j \tag{2}$$

Third, the value of produced net product and utilized final product is balanced, that is,

$$\sum_{j=1}^{n} V_j = \sum_{j=1}^{n} Y_j \tag{3}$$

Final demand may be viewed as a composite of several categories since Soviet practice requires the allocation of materials consumed by service activities to final demand. One of these categories is nonproductive transportation, which can be separated out to reflect a passenger transport row and column such that for any sector j,

$$\sum_{i=1}^{n} a_{ij}X_j + a_{pj}X_j + V_j' = \sum_{i=1}^{n} a_{ji}X_i + a_{jp}X_p + Y_j' \tag{4}$$

where $Y_j' = Y_j - a_{jp}X_p$ and $V_j' = V_j - a_{pj}X_j$

The complete system reflecting the inclusion of passenger transportation may then be expressed as:

$$\sum_{i=1}^{n} a_{ij} X_j + a_{pj} X_j + V'_j = \sum_{i}^{n} a_{ji} X_i + a_{jp} X_p + Y'_j \tag{1'}$$

$$\sum_{j=1}^{n} \sum_{i=1}^{n} a_{ij} X_j + \sum_{j=1}^{n} a_{pj} X_j + \sum_{j=1}^{n} V'_j + \sum_{i=1}^{n} a_{ip} X_p + a_{pp} X_p + V_p$$

$$= \sum_{j=1}^{n} \sum_{i=1}^{n} a_{ji} X_i + \sum_{j=1}^{n} a_{jp} X_p + \sum_{j=1}^{n} Y'_j + \sum_{i=1}^{n} a_{pi} X_i + a_{pp} X_p + Y'_p \tag{2'}$$

$$\sum_{j=1}^{n} V'_j + V_p = \sum_{j=1}^{n} Y'_j + Y'_p \tag{3'}$$

In a world of complete information, we would be able to apply the
above relations not only to establish the material purchases of the
passenger transport sector, but also to identify the consumption of
passenger transport by economic sector. The scarcity of Soviet
data, however, does not allow complete realization of this objective.
While rudimentary insights into passenger traffic uses are provided
in a discussion of intercity and suburban transportation (Shafirkin
1972, p. 134), the lack of supporting evidence regarding the consumption of passenger services makes any attempt at sectoral distribution
completely arbitrary. Shafirkin indicates that 15 percent of intercity
passenger traffic is attributable to productive purposes, that is,
changes in employment and business trips; fully 85 percent of this
intercity travel is undertaken for general living and vacation purposes. Analysis of suburban passenger travel, on the other hand,
reveals that 60 percent is undertaken for productive purposes, while
40 percent is devoted to the general needs of the urban population,
that is, shopping and recreation. Although this division of transportation services presents useful evidence as to the direction of the
productive-nonproductive separation of resources, it is insufficient
for disaggregation purposes. Accordingly, all entries along the
passenger transport row are left blank and the exercise is restricted
to a disaggregation of material purchases. However, in order to
maintain the balance of the passenger transport sector, it must be
true that

$$\sum_{i=1}^{n} a_{ip} X_p + a_{pp} X_p + V_p = Y_p \tag{5}$$

Therefore, the passenger-transport augmented system may be expressed as

TABLE 4.7

The Disaggregated Transportation Sector of the 76-Sector, Input-Output
Table of the Soviet Union for 1966
(in purchasers' prices, thousands of rubles)

Sector Number	Name	Freight (and Communications)	Passenger	Total Transport
1.	Ores and metals	61,715	36,760	98,475
2.	Coke products	--	--	--
3.	Refractory materials	--	--	--
4.	Industrial metal products	41,018	24,432	65,450
5.	Coal	246,966	82,232	329,198
6.	Oil extraction	--	--	--
7.	Oil refining	1,516,114	504,810	2,020,924
8.	Gas	2,123	706	2,829
9.	Peat	607	200	807
10.	Oil shales	152	47	199
11.	Electric, thermal power	457,683	175,000	632,683
12.	Energy and power machinery and equipment	2,060	716	2,776
13.	Electrotechnical machinery and equipment	14,423	5,014	19,437
14.	Cable products	17,863	6,210	24,073
15.	Machine tools	1,087	378	1,465
16.	Forging/pressing machinery and equipment	--	--	--
17.	Casting machinery and equipment	--	--	--
18.	Tools and dies	20,562	7,148	27,710
19.	Precision instruments	7,320	2,543	9,863
20.	Mining, metallurgical machinery and equipment	--	--	--
21.	Pumps and compressors	637	220	857
22.	Logging and paper machinery and equipment	4,993	1,734	6,727
23.	Light industry machinery and equipment	--	--	--
24.	Food industry machinery and equipment	--	--	--
25.	Printing machinery and equipment	--	--	--
26.	Hoisting/transporting machinery and equipment	16,154	5,615	21,769
27.	Construction machinery and equipment	1,061	367	1,428
28.	Construction materials machinery and equipment	--	--	--
29.	Transportation machinery and equipment	128,516	44,686	173,202
30.	Automobile	276,807	96,247	373,054
31.	Tractors, agricultural machinery and equipment	10,631	3,696	14,327
32.	Bearings	12,020	4,178	16,198
33.	Other products of machinebuilding	107,522	37,386	144,908
34.	Sanitary engineering products	--	--	--
35.	Other metal wares	22,069	7,673	29,742
36.	Metal structures	--	--	--
37.	Repair of machinery and equipment	125,839	43,754	169,593
38.	Abrasives	1,189	413	1,602
39.	Mineral chemistry products	--	--	--
40.	Basic chemistry products	17,555	5,039	22,594
41.	Aniline dye products	--	--	--
42.	Synthetic resins and plastics	--	--	--
43.	Synthetic fibers	--	--	--
44.	Synthetic rubber	--	--	--
45.	Organic synthetic products	8,096	2,324	10,420

Sector		Freight (and Communications)	Passenger	Total Transport
Number	Name			
46.	Paints and lacquers	38,367	11,015	49,382
47.	Rubber and asbestos products	457,943	131,468	589,411
48.	Other chemicals	535	153	688
49.	Logging	83,552	30,681	114,233
50.	Sawmills and woodworking	68,416	25,123	93,539
51.	Furniture	6,364	2,336	8,700
52.	Other woodworking	--	--	--
53.	Paper and pulp	6,890	2,529	9,419
54.	Wood chemistry products	1,965	721	2,686
55.	Cement	5,202	1,910	7,112
56.	Prefabricated concrete	570	209	779
57.	Other construction materials	29,232	10,734	39,966
58.	Glass and porcelain	7,499	2,754	10,253
59.	Textiles	50,891	15,344	66,235
60.	Sewn goods	77,164	23,265	100,429
61.	Other light industry products	24,512	7,390	31,902
62.	Fish products	--	--	--
63.	Meat products	--	--	--
64.	Dairy products	--	--	--
65.	Sugar	--	--	--
66.	Flour and cereals	55	82	137
67.	Bread, bakery products, and confections	--	--	--
68.	Other food	14,044	20,918	34,962
69.	Industry (not elsewhere classified)	84,178	50,140	134,318
70.	Construction	--	--	--
71.	Crops	6,154	3,665	9,819
72.	Animal husbandry	1	--	1
73.	Forestry	--	--	--
74.	Freight transportation and communications	53,577	--	53,577
74a.	Passenger transport	--	--	--
75.	Trade and distribution	--	--	--
76.	Other branches	--	--	--
77.	Material purchases	4,086,316	1,440,000*	5,526,316*
78.	Total purchases	4,139,893	1,440,000	5,579,893
79.	Depreciation	2,660,000	1,137,000	3,797,000
80.	Wages	6,014,188	2,670,000	8,684,188
81.	Other net income	6,185,919	2,140,000	8,325,919
82.	National income	12,200,107	4,810,000	17,010,107
83.	Total outlay	19,000,000	7,387,000	26,387,000
84.	Employment (thousands of man-years)	45,650	3,872	8,437
85.	Capital	41,444,000	17,856,000	59,300,000

*Figures do not coincide due to rounding.

Sources: V. Treml, D. Gallik, B. Kostinsky, and K. Kruger, The Structure of the Soviet Economy. Analysis and Reconstruction of the 1966 Input-Output Table (New York: Praeger, 1972), pp. 466-67; TsSU, Narodnoe khoziaistvo SSSR v 1967 godu (Moscow: Statistika, 1968), p. 883; V. Treml, Structure of Costs, Non-Productive Transportation and Communications (unpublished manuscript, Duke University, November 1975); TsSU, Narodnoe khoziaistvo SSSR v 1967 godu (Moscow: Statistika, 1968), p. 648; TsSU, Narodnoe khoziaistvo SSSR v 1968 godu (Moscow: Statistika, 1969), pp. 60-61.

$$\sum_{i=1}^{n} a_{ij} X_j + V_j = \sum_{i=1}^{n} a_{ji} X_i + a_{jp} X_p + Y_j' \tag{1''}$$

$$\sum_{j=1}^{n} \sum_{i=1}^{n} a_{ij} X_j + \sum_{j=1}^{n} V_j + \sum_{i=1}^{n} a_{ip} X_p + V_p$$

$$= \sum_{j=1}^{n} \sum_{i=1}^{n} a_{ji} X_i + \sum_{j=1}^{n} a_{jp} X_p + \sum_{j=1}^{n} Y_j' + Y_p \tag{2''}$$

$$\sum_{j=1}^{n} V_j + V_p = \sum_{j=1}^{n} Y_j' + Y_p \tag{3''}$$

The estimation of the nonproductive transport column was done for the reconstructed 1966 Soviet input-output table as published by Treml, Gallik, Kostinsky, and Kruger (1972). Information provided by Treml (1975b) served as the starting point for disaggregating the nonproductive transportation and communications sector. In order to arrive at a complete 76-sector column of entries for nonproductive transportation and communications, the value of each aggregated group of Treml's data was distributed to its component sectors by using the percentage distribution within the similar group in productive transportation and communications. When this amount is added to productive purchases already depicted in the first quadrant, a more complete picture of transport is revealed.

Table 4.7 presents the passenger transport column in purchasers' prices. Any application of these results, however, must be undertaken with a note of caution. The major deficiencies of the recorded transport entries in input-output tables are discussed elsewhere. Mention must also be made of the aggregation of communications together with transportation in the published, as well as reconstructed, Soviet input-output tables. Despite only minor distortions presented by this aggregation, the "purity" of the transport sector is undermined.[9] The imperfections of the resulting estimates are, it is believed, more than compensated for by the broadening of perspective, as a more detailed portrayal of passenger transport is obtained.

TRANSPORTATION ENTRIES IN THE CONVERSION OF INPUT-OUTPUT TABLES TO PRODUCERS' PRICES

This section evaluates the nature of transportation entries in input-output tables. In particular, it focuses upon the conversion from purchasers' to producers' prices of the reconstructed 1966 Soviet input-output table, although the results derived from the analysis are generally applicable elsewhere. The importance of transportation is established both explicitly and implicitly within the input-output framework. Transport's explicit significance may be seen through examination of its respective rows and columns in an input-output table. Application of standard input-output methodology will reveal the direct plus indirect effects of changes in the level and composition of final demand on transport as well as the full impact of changes within the transport sector itself upon the rest of the economic system. The importance of transportation is implicitly established through its function as an artery linking producers and consumers, the means by which one sector's output becomes another sector's input. In short, economic interdependence is meaningless in the absence of transport considerations.

The inclusion of transport statistics in input-output tables, however, is complicated by several price-valuation considerations. The compilation of input-output tables in value terms allows the computation of direct and full input coefficients of material inputs. An underlying assumption of the input-output model based on these data is that the distribution of a particular product in value terms as recorded in the table is proportional to the distribution of that output in physical form. Unfortunately, for spatially large economies such as the Soviet Union's, where the dispersion of fuel, mineral, and agricultural resources generates large transportation requirements, this assumption is not strictly applicable. Input-output tables are devoid of spatial considerations of the economic organization they represent, and this serves to create distortions that violate the correspondence assumption. Accordingly, considerations of accuracy warrant the deletion of distortive features from the various entries of the table. The first step that can be taken in this direction is the conversion of the value entries in the input-output table from purchasers' prices to producers' prices.

Entries in the first and second quadrant of Soviet input-output tables constructed in purchasers' prices include transportation charges for delivery of products to the point of input or consumption. These charges are again depicted as a separate entry in the transportation row of the interindustry matrix, resulting in a doublecounting of all transportation fees levied, as reflected in the overstatement of the gross value of output by that amount. For any industry j, the respective flow entry in the transportation cell of its input column represents the cost of shipping its output to the other sectors of the economy. In contrast, in a table valued at producers' prices, first- and second-quadrant entries cover only direct production costs and profits, while for each sector the flow entry in the transportation cell of its input column reflects the cost of shipping its inputs from the other sectors of the economy. The conversion from purchasers' to producers' prices thus brings with it a directional reorientation of transport costs. However, because the input-output relationships of

producers' prices are represented in value terms, albeit in prices
more attuned to technical-economic realities, the measure of transportation services provided might continue to represent inaccurately
the amount of transportation used in terms of volume shipped. This,
of course, depends crucially on the respective freight charges levied,
and hence requires an additional analysis of physical quantities trans-
ported. Here again the Soviet case is particularly troublesome
since Soviet administrators place considerable reliance on differentiated freight rates in order to control traffic flows.[10] Whereas
Western rate schedules are, for the most part, designed to reflect
cost conditions, Soviet rate-making practice appears to indicate the
inclusion of specific economic and regional objectives. Transport
rates, like price differentials, have been used to influence economic
behavior and to assure the attainment of certain priority goals. Perhaps the best example of this practice is the desire by the Soviets to
achieve nonduplication by alternative modes of transport, or more
succinctly, to encourage the growth of complementary rather than
competitive transport modes (Williams 1962; Moses 1974).

Because input-output tables in producers' prices correspond
more closely to the proportionality and homogeneity assumptions
basic to input-output methodology, and because they reflect more
accurately the pure input relations of a given sector--thereby pre-
senting a more reliable picture of intersectoral productive relation-
ships--considerations of analytical superiority warranted the construction of a table in producers' prices for the Soviet Union. Treml,
Kostinsky, Kruger, and Gallik (1972) (hereafter denoted by TKKG)
have performed this task using their reconstructed 1966 table in
purchasers' prices as their point of departure.[11] In separating out
transport and communications costs (hereafter referred to solely as
transport costs), TKKG devised an algorithm that removed these
costs proportionally from all entries in the conversion process
(Treml et al. 1973, pp. 7-8). The operation requires two steps:
(1) the removal of transportation costs from all deliveries; and (2)
the replacement of the transportation row with a row reflecting the
costs removed from each sector's purchases. A necessary assumption of the algorithm is the uniformity of transportation costs, or in
this case, because the absence of data so dictated, they are assumed
to be uniform. While such an assumption may appear to be extreme,
it seems that even the Soviets themselves are forced to revert to
this procedure in their own conversion operations. Two highly regarded Soviet economists, Efimov and Berri (1965), underscore the
problem with which Soviet input-output specialists are confronted:

> To obtain a more accurate picture of the produc-
> tive relations that exist among the sectors of the

national economy, the report input-output table
. . . was recomputed into producer prices and
conversion factors were derived to convert the
final demand prices into producer prices.

From the available statistical information
it was not possible to determine accurately the
cost of the . . . transportation services for the
production process in each sector. Therefore,
it was decided that the services which transport
. . . rendered in connection with the marketing
of the output already produced by a given sector
would be distributed proportionally with the output that this sector delivers for productive and
nonproductive consumption, accumulation and
export (Efimov and Berri 1965, pp. 178-98).

Additional use of this assumption may be seen in an analysis carried
out for the United States (Jack Faucett Associates 1968). Although
data availability was sufficient to allow disaggregation of transport
flows by sector to the different transport modes, the uniformity
assumption was employed in allocating a proportional amount of
each type of transport to each column entry. In other words, for
any sector j, the amount of transportation services could be broken
down by transport mode. For any input i, however, it was not possible to pinpoint the mode of transport used in bringing i to sector j.
Therefore, it was assumed that the overall distribution of transport
services purchased from the several modes by sector j was applicable to any input i.

In the interest of clarity and by way of example, the TKKG
algorithm is presented here (Treml et al. 1973, pp. 7-8), followed
by a discussion of the potential distortions of this approach. Four
examples are cited to underscore the costs and benefits of the uniformity assumption. In addition, an interesting calculation is performed for the coal industry in the United States, where the procedure of the TKKG algorithm is reversed. In the final analysis,
the conclusion is that the assumption is a necessary and not entirely
unwarranted one.

The system we are using is comprised of n producing sectors--
one of which, transportation, is identified as sector d--one final-
demand column and one value-added row. For any sector the transportation cost per ruble of gross output may be expressed as

$$o_{dj} = \frac{x_{dj}}{X_j + M_j} \tag{6}$$

where

x_{dj} = the purchases of transportation by sector j

X_j = the gross value of output of sector j

M_j = the value of imports transferred to sector j

This transportation cost, once estimated, is removed from each individual flow, including final demand. For any row i, then, each x_{ij} is reduced by the amount of transportation cost, that is,

$$x'_{ij} = x_{ij} - o_{di}x_{ij} \tag{7}$$

where x_{ij} = the purchases of input i by sector j.

The second step of the conversion procedure involves the creation of a new transportation row via the reallocation of transportation costs. The entries of this new row replace those of the original row (which also provided our initial transport flows). The transportation costs incurred by each sector in shipping its inputs are calculated as

$$x'_{dj} = \sum_{i=1}^{n} o_{di}x_{ij} \tag{8}$$

Thus, for any sector j, the new entry in the transportation row d becomes the sum of all transportation costs removed from each of the inputs in its column.

While the same procedure is applied to the conversion of the final-demand column--that is,

$$Y_d = \sum_{i=1}^{n} o_{di}Y_i \tag{9}$$

where Y_i = the value of final demand for the output of sector i-- the conversion into producers' prices results in the creation of a positive entry in the transportation cell of the final-demand column. In purchasers' prices, due to Soviet methodology, the final-demand transportation entry is zero. However, in order that the total value of transportation services supplied remain the same, it must be true that

$$\sum_{j=1}^{n} x'_{dj} + Y_d = \sum_{j=1}^{n} x_{dj} \tag{10}$$

The application of the TKKG algorithm results in a neat representation of economywide transportation costs, yet one that,
even under ideal circumstances, would seem to cause uneasiness.
It must be noted, however, that the situation is far from ideal, as
even the Soviets have been forced to admit. While there is no guar-
antee that transport flows in value terms agree with those flows in
physical terms, data restrictions appear to necessitate the standard
input-output spatial assumption. Moreover, an analysis of regional
imports and exports in physical terms indicates perhaps a better
justification for the uniform reallocation of transport costs. Using
a national input-output table that reflects regional aggregation as a
foundation, the following lines of thought are pursued.

Proposition 1: In the presence of ubiquitous strategic raw
materials and/or processed inputs, an economic region should be
relatively self-sufficient. Accordingly, the transportation cost element would tend to be minimized for industries within the economic
region and the transportation uniformity assumption could be applied
to all industrial sectors.

Proposition 2: In the extreme case in which the availability
of strategic raw materials and/or processed inputs is limited to a
single region, every other region would be relatively insufficient.
Accordingly, the transportation cost element would tend to be maximized for the industries within the deficit regions. Here, too, the
transportation uniformity assumption could be applied, since each
industrial sector is required to transport the inputs to its production center.

Proposition 3: In the presence of random availability of strategic raw materials and/or processed inputs, the relative degree of
self-sufficiency for any economic region would depend upon the location of the inputs. Accordingly, the transportation cost element
would tend to be high or low for industries within a particular region, depending upon locational circumstances. In this case, the
transportation uniformity assumption as applied to each industrial
sector is subject to the greatest potential distortions, although it is
possible that the standard deviations of transportation costs for industries in particular regions could be offsetting, thus yielding the
same average economywide transport costs.

Two statistical breakdowns of commodity haulage, by republic and by region, were compiled for four important material input
categories--oil and oil products, timber (including firewood), cement,
and coal and coke--in order to evaluate their geographical availability
within the Soviet Union. The data represent traffic flows for 1965,
and thus facilitate an evaluation of the transportation uniformity assumption in the light of the revealed geographical dispersions.

TABLE 4.8

Commodity Haulage, by Republic, 1965
(millions of tons)

Cement

Republic	Intrarepublic Haulage	Exports to Other Republics	Imports from Other Republics	Excess of Exports over Imports
RSFSR	35.31	1.59	--	1.59
Ukraine	10.21	.22	.41	-.19
Belorussia	1.39	.14	.40	-.26
Uzbekistan	1.54	.38	.42	-.04
Kazakhstan	3.39	.20	1.08	-.88
Georgia	.98	.06	.03	.03
Azerbaidzhan	.83	.17	.11	.06
Lithuania	.64	.05	.23	-.18
Moldavia	.45	.01	.26	-.25
Latvia	.37	.07	.15	-.08
Kirgizia	.13	.21	.26	-.05
Tadzhikistan	.02	.36	.13	.23
Armenia	.46	--	.28	-.28
Turkmenia	.20	.05	.18	-.13
Estonia	.37	.17	.11	.06

Timber (Including Firewood)

Republic	Intrarepublic Haulage	Exports to Other Republics	Imports from Other Republics	Excess of Exports over Imports
RSFSR	197.84	55.64	.18	55.46
Ukraine	8.50	.02	29.78	-29.76
Belorussia	3.44	.60	2.78	-2.18
Uzbekistan	.18	.02	3.32	-3.30
Kazakhstan	.95	.01	8.75	-8.74
Georgia	.62	.04	1.73	-1.69
Azerbaidzhan	.24	--	1.37	-1.37
Lithuania	.43	.11	1.50	-1.39
Moldavia	.09	--	1.84	-1.84
Latvia	1.67	.42	.96	-.54
Kirgizia	.04	--	1.18	-1.18
Tadzhikistan	.01	--	.87	-.87
Armenia	.04	--	.75	-.75
Turkmenia	.06	.03	.81	-.78
Estonia	.81	.14	1.16	-1.02

Oil and Oil Products

Republic	Intrarepublic Haulage	Exports to Other Republics	Imports from Other Republics	Excess of Exports over Imports
RSFSR	147.52	53.92	9.53	44.39
Ukraine	17.04	1.83	26.34	-24.51
Belorussia	1.60	2.20	6.56	-4.36
Uzbekistan	2.63	1.53	3.86	-2.33
Kazakhstan	3.58	1.68	8.09	-6.41
Georgia	.92	2.22	8.28	-6.06
Azerbaidzhan	11.29	14.32	0.16	14.16
Lithuania	.09	.09	5.80	-5.71
Moldavia	.06	--	1.83	-1.83
Latvia	.04	.06	9.11	-9.05
Kirgizia	.07	--	1.13	-1.13
Tadzhikistan	.01	--	1.17	-1.17
Armenia	.01	--	1.20	-1.20
Turkmenia	1.94	8.78	1.06	7.72
Estonia	.42	.18	1.19	-1.01

Coal and Coke

Republic	Intrarepublic Haulage	Exports to Other Republics	Imports from Other Republics	Excess of Exports over Imports
RSFSR	297.54	20.78	57.12	-36.34
Ukraine	177.26	50.32	7.53	42.79
Belorussia	.20	1.20	8.55	-7.35
Uzbekistan	2.40	.58	2.97	-2.39
Kazakhstan	19.97	23.28	7.82	15.46
Georgia	3.79	1.30	2.69	-1.39
Azerbaidzhan	.07	.03	.28	-.25
Lithuania	.01	--	3.38	-3.38
Moldavia	.04	--	2.37	-2.37
Latvia	.03	--	3.71	-3.71
Kirgizia	.65	1.65	1.65	0.00
Tadzhikistan	.33	1.28	.26	1.02
Armenia	.01	--	.71	-.71
Turkmenia	.01	--	.55	-.53
Estonia	.02	--	.52	-.52

Source: TsSU, Transport i sviaź SSSR (Moscow: Statistika, 1972), pp. 49, 53, 61, 65.

Disaggregation by republic (see Table 4. 8) shows that the wide-spread availability of cement and the relative uniformity of interregional haulage clearly conform to Proposition 1, reflecting not only the even distribution of lime and clay sources, but the self-sufficiency of regional production. Timber haulage is shown to conform with Proposition 2, and here one republic, the RSFSR, is seen to be completely dominant. Oil and oil products, and coke and coal fall within the realm of Proposition 3, and three republics are revealed to be resource-abundant in each of these input categories. Moreover, since these sources are sporadically distributed, it seems plausible to assume that wide variations in interrepublic transportation costs will tend to be offsetting.

A disaggregation by economic regions of the RSFSR is also presented (see Table 4. 9). This breakdown provides even more poignant evidence of the regional self-sufficiency in cement production and haulage, and the case for Proposition 1. Timber freight by economic region, however, is seen to conform more closely with Proposition 3, as four regions are revealed as important exporters and six regions are seen to be important importers. Similar interpretations apply for the haulage of oil and oil products, and coke and coal. Five regions are influential exporters of oil-related products while nine regions dominate imports. For coal and coke, there exist four large exporting regions and ten significant importing regions.

For these input categories, it would appear that the transportation uniformity assumption is warranted at least in a physical sense. Once freight rates are introduced, however, one is confronted with severe valuation problems and the nemesis of value and physical quantity relationships. Even if the uniformity assumption were completely valid, and freight rates were applied equally to all users, the presence of highly differentiated prices in the Soviet Union would serve to distort any transportation cost elements based upon non-physical relationships, that is, those similar to equation (6) (the TKKG algorithm). Given the insufficiency of information, however, there appears to be no viable alternative to the uniformity assumption; indeed, the analysis provides an additional justification based upon regional considerations.

As a final inquiry into the validity of the assumption of uniform distribution of transport costs, the TKKG algorithm was reversed. In using the coal industry vector for the 1963 U.S. Input-Output Table (National Economics Division 1969, pp. 16-47), the procedure began with a set of entries valued at producers' prices. The objective was to determine what transportation costs the coal industry would incur if it were responsible for the delivery of its output, and the operation required two steps: (1) the addition of transport costs to all deliveries; and (2) the replacement of the transportation entry with an

TABLE 4.9

Commodity Haulage, by Economic Region, 1965
(millions of tons)

Region	Cement				Timber (Including Firewood)			
	Intra-regional Haulage	Exports to Other Regions	Imports from Other Regions	Excess of Exports over Imports	Intra-regional Haulage	Exports to Other Regions	Imports from Other Regions	Excess of Exports over Imports
Northwestern	2.76	.57	.56	.01	43.29	31.85	2.24	29.61
Central	5.93	.32	1.82	-1.50	8.92	7.04	11.42	-4.38
Volga-Viatka	.43	.45	1.17	-.72	9.11	13.52	3.05	10.47
Central Blackearth	1.03	1.87	.42	1.45	.36	.01	5.30	-5.29
Volga Basin	3.91	3.45	1.00	2.45	11.48	5.72	15.50	-9.78
North Caucasian	1.40	.14	1.90	-1.76	3.16	1.61	10.02	-8.41
Ural	4.08	3.26	.12	3.14	20.48	24.07	1.88	22.19
West Siberian	2.47	.74	.92	-.18	17.01	5.82	4.01	1.81
East Siberian	1.71	.15	.96	-.81	16.61	22.02	.33	21.69
Far Eastern	2.14	.06	.37	-.31	9.94	1.15	.47	.68
Donets-Dnieper	4.43	2.25	.83	1.42	1.07	--	17.07	-17.07
Southeastern	2.34	1.13	1.14	-.01	6.12	.89	9.69	-8.80
Southern	.29	--	1.59	-1.59	.33	.12	4.00	-3.88
Baltic	1.57	.10	.47	-.37	3.39	.50	5.31	-4.81
Transcaucasian	2.42	.08	.26	-.18	.93	.01	3.83	-3.82
Central Asian	2.62	.27	.25	.02	.32	.02	6.15	-6.13
Kazakh SSR	3.39	.20	1.08	-.88	.95	.01	8.75	-8.74
Belorussian SSR	1.39	.14	.40	-.26	3.44	.60	2.78	-2.18
Moldavian SSR	.45	.01	.26	-.25	.09	--	1.84	-1.84

	Oil and Oil Products				Coal and Coke			
Northwestern	3.11	.12	9.19	-9.07	17.96	3.31	12.91	-9.60
Central	6.29	17.27	12.81	4.45	24.56	6.99	17.92	-10.93
Volga-Viatka	1.84	8.14	4.11	4.03	.10	1.03	9.19	-8.16
Central Blackearth	.77	.98	5.21	-4.23	.83	.04	14.69	-14.65
Volga Basin	21.95	69.01	7.12	61.89	6.27	3.30	19.44	-16.14
North Caucasian	12.99	14.00	27.65	-13.65	10.25	23.02	6.68	16.34
Ural	7.62	12.05	9.51	2.54	51.07	4.49	47.77	43.28
West Siberian	5.20	7.13	2.95	4.18	49.30	53.32	4.72	48.60
East Siberian	2.24	4.88	4.27	.61	28.81	5.90	.62	5.28
Far Eastern	5.34	.47	5.89	-5.42	26.00	.74	2.53	-1.79
Donets-Dnieper	1.75	2.66	8.31	-5.65	138.27	74.70	6.90	67.80
Southeastern	5.33	3.34	8.95	-5.61	8.71	4.16	17.72	-13.56
Southern	2.77	3.02	16.28	-13.26	1.19	.56	12.00	-11.44
Baltic	.64	.30	16.96	-16.66	.81	.26	9.90	-9.64
Transcaucasian	19.24	9.52	2.62	6.90	3.92	1.22	3.56	-2.34
Central Asian	9.93	5.02	1.94	3.08	6.62	.31	2.20	-1.89
Kazakh SSR	3.58	1.68	8.09	-6.41	19.97	23.28	7.82	15.46
Belorussian SSR	1.60	2.20	6.56	-4.36	.20	1.20	8.55	-7.35
Moldavian SSR	.06	--	1.83	-1.83	.04	--	2.37	-2.37

Source: TsSU, Transport i sviaź SSSR (Moscow: Statistika, 1972), pp. 70-85.

entry reflecting the costs added to each sector's purchases. An economywide application would necessitate the replacement of the transportation row with a row reflecting the costs added to each sector's purchases.

A general case of recalculating transportation costs in an input-output table in producers' prices can be described as follows. Transportation costs per dollar of gross output as defined in equation (1) above are calculated for all sectors. For any column j each x_{ij} is then inflated by the amount of transportation cost incurred in the shipping from producer i to buyer j, that is

$$x'_{ij} = x_{ij} + o_{di}x_{ij} \tag{11}$$

where x_{ij} = the purchases of input i by sector j.

The second step of the conversion procedure involves the creation of a new transportation row via the reallocation of transportation costs. The entries of this new row replace those of the original row (which also provided our initial transport flows). The transportation costs incurred by each sector in shipping its output are calculated as

$$x'_{dj} = \sum_{j=1}^{n} o_{di}x_{ij} \tag{12}$$

Thus, for any sector j, the new entry in the transportation row d becomes the sum of all transportation costs added to each of the outputs in its row.

The same procedure is also applied to the conversion of the final-demand column, that is,

$$Y_d = \sum_{j=1}^{n} o_{dj}Y_j \tag{13}$$

where Y_j = the value of final demand for the output of sector j, so that control figures for the exercise are established. In other words, it is ensured that the total value of transportation services supplied remains the same.

The results indicate that the procedure does not result in significant distortions. Instead, the derived output-shipment costs exceed the input-shipment costs by 23 percent. This is not unexpected since coal processing takes place at the resource sites, while the weight of the output dictates higher per unit transport costs to its consumption locations.

SOVIET TRANSPORTATION WITHIN A REGIONAL
CONTEXT: SOME EARLY FINDINGS AND
PROSPECTS FOR FURTHER RESEARCH

The inquiry into transportation entries in input-output tables stressed the implicit spatial assumptions underlying tables constructed in value terms, that is, that the distribution of a particular output is similar to the proportions of that output in physical form. This was considered particularly troublesome for a national input-output model of the Soviet Union where prices are widely differentiated by consumer and economic region and where the dispersion of fuel, mineral, and agricultural resources generates large transportation requirements. The spatial dimension problem can be circumvented by using regional input-output tables that provide a geographically disaggregated view of economic structure.

Soviet specialists have undertaken a large-scale effort in the field of regional input-output analysis, but until recently their initiatives had not been reflected in Western literature.[12] There are now available reconstructed tables for five republics--Latvia, Ukraine, Kazakhstan, Azerbaidzhan, and Estonia--which permit an analysis of regional differences in industrial production. Similar to their national counterparts, the republic tables contain transportation (and communications) entries that cover the productive portion of distributed services. Accordingly, they yield some insights into regional differentiation in input costs as well as sectoral transportation (and communications) requirements.

An additional source of information is provided by a recently published Soviet monograph on regional input-output analysis. Granborg (1975) presents a rather detailed discussion of transport within an input-output context which, together with the reconstructed republic tables, can be used to gain a preliminary impression of regional differences in transport costs and requirements, and form a background for further research in this field.[13]

The Soviet study pays close attention to the interplay between transport and production, noting that the share of transport in the gross value of output for each region ranges from 7 to 10 percent in the highest regions--for example, Far East, East Siberia, Northwest, North Caucasus, and Kazakh SSR, down to 1.8 percent in the Armenian SSR (Granberg 1975, p. 194). Although not strictly comparable to Granberg data, Table 4.10 presents a geographically disaggregated breakdown by republic of the GSP share of productive transportation (and communications). Granberg's (1975) evaluation of the relationship between transport flows and economic activity suggests that the increase in transport flows does not so much coincide with the interregional rise of production as with the increase in

TABLE 4.10

Shares of Transportation (and Communications)
in Gross Social Product and National Income
Produced, by Republic, 1966
(millions of current rubles)

Republic	Gross Social Product[a]	National Income Produced[a]	Transportation (and Communications)[b]	Percentage of GSP
RSFSR	267,054	120,735	12,284	4.60
Ukraine	84,332	38,892	3,120	3.70
Belorussia	15,150	6,465	424	2.80
Uzbekistan	12,860	5,846	373	2.90
Kazakhstan	19,562	9,231	1,369	7.00
Georgia	6,217	2,949	162	2.61
Azerbaidzhan	5,825	2,754	216	3.71
Lithuania	6,765	2,906	169	2.50
Moldavia	5,244	2,537	131	2.50
Latvia	6,280	2,746	207	3.30
Kirgizia	3,325	1,616	73	2.20
Tadzhikistan	3,016	1,369	75	2.49
Armenia	3,467	1,609	66	1.90
Turkmenia	2,719	1,246	125	4.60
Estonia	3,580	1,512	129	3.60
USSR total[c]	445,200	202,400	19,000	4.27

[a]Input-output definition without doublecounting of trade and distribution, and transportation and communications.

[b]Input-output and national income definition, that is, gross output of freight transportation and communications serving production.

[c]Individual entries do not add up due to different methods of estimation and rounding.

Source: Vladimir G. Treml, "Structure of Costs, Non-Productive Transportation and Communications" (Unpublished manuscript, Duke University, December 1975).

production within a single region. Furthermore, the structure of
production within a particular region is seen to have a more power-
ful impact on transport than transport has on production. Despite a
considerable time lag between the growth of economic activity and
the development of transport, there is evidence of an increasing
adaptation of transportation facilities to regional production requirements. In short, transportation has traditionally followed the growth
of regional economic activity, although economic activities have not
always benefited from the availability of the proper types of transport.[14] Not surprisingly, the study also determines that the greater
the economic specialization within a particular region, and therefore the greater the integration with other regions, the more important is the transport factor in that region.[15]

TABLE 4.11

Fourteen Subvectors of the 71-Sector
Reconstructed Comparable Format
Soviet Input-Output Tables

Subvector Number	Title	Sector Numbers*
1	Metallurgy	1-7
2	Fuels	8-13
3	Power	14
4	Machinebuilding and metalworking	15-38
5	Chemicals	30 16
6	Woodworking	47-52
7	Construction materials	53,54
8	Textiles	55-57
9	Food	58-63
10	Construction	64
11	Agriculture	65-67
12	Transport and communication	68
13	Other branches	69,70
14	Unidentified	71

*For sector titles corresponding to the 71-sector nomencla-
ture see Table 4.10, second column.
   Source: Compiled by the author.

TABLE 4.12

Transport Requirements per Ruble of Output, by Sector,
for the 71-Sector Reconstructed Comparable Format
Soviet Input-Output Tables

1966 Rank Order	Sector Name and Number	1966 Requirements	1959 Requirements
1	Gas (11)	.44331	.00082
2	Construction materials (53)	.30771	.23632
3	Oil extraction (9)	.28328	.35227
4	Logging (47)	.28197	.26767
5	Coal (8)	.22877	.23905
6	Ferrous ores (1)	.19898	.18735
7	Mineral chemistry products (39)	.19817	.19978
8	Oil refining (10)	.19456	.14732
9	Refractory materials (6)	.17422	.13993
10	Peat (12)	.14923	.13442
11	Bearings (34)	.13263	.01958
12	Casting machinery and equipment (20)	.12453	.00334
13	Nonferrous ores (3)	.10291	.09824
14	Sawmills and woodworking (48)	.09278	.07331
15	Basic chemistry products (40)	.08661	.39709
16	Ferrous metals (2)	.08540	.06185
17	Coke products (5)	.08302	.03279
18	Paper and pulp (51)	.08048	.05751
19	Synthetic fibers (43)	.08038	.00034
20	Abrasives (38)	.07678	.03583
21	Glass and porcelain (54)	.07604	.09805
22	Machine tools (18)	.07528	.05377
23	Synthetic rubber and plastics (42)	.07012	.01706
24	Tools and dies (21)	.06612	.00201
25	Food industry machinery and equipment (26)	.06407	.09029
26	Cable products (17)	.06364	.02887
27	Tractors and agricultural machinery and equipment (33)	.06351	.05424
28	Metal structures (37)	.06221	.02954
29	Wood chemistry products (52)	.05956	.00223
30	Furniture (49)	.05826	.03483
31	Industrial metal products (7)	.05555	.03383
32	Automobiles (32)	.05445	.03780
33	Light industry machinery and equipment (25)	.05416	.05477
34	Precision instruments (22)	.05352	.01087
35	Construction materials machinery and equipment (30)	.05191	.12458

1966 Rank Order	Sector Name and Number	1966 Requirements	1959 Requirements
36	Forging-pressing machinery and equipment (19)	.04998	.10384
37	Paints and lacquers (45)	.04987	.00568
38	Hoisting-transporting machinery and equipment (28)	.04806	.06138
39	Construction machinery and equipment (29)	.04783	.05037
40	Other woodworking (50)	.04692	.02644
41	Oil shales (13)	.04555	.07816
42	Mining and metallurgical machinery and equipment (23)	.04497	.00916
43	Nonferrous metals (4)	.04471	.03231
44	Organic-synthetic products (44)	.04452	.00645
45	Printing machinery and equipment (27)	.04110	.16590
46	Electrotechnical machinery and equipment (16)	.03855	.02464
47	Rubber products (46)	.03799	.02790
48	Aniline dye products (41)	.03720	.03350
49	Fish products (58)	.03066	.04531
50	Sugar (61)	.02332	.03942
51	Forestry (67)	.02079	.01566
52	Energy and power machinery and equipment (15)	.02040	.04410
53	Other food (63)	.01941	.02129
54	Unidentified (71)	.01866	.01804
55	Crops (65)	.01752	.01932
56	Other machinebuilding (35)	.01601	.03296
57	Logging and paper machinery and equipment (24)	.01597	.00262
58	Sanitary engineering products (36)	.01528	.01077
59	Other branches (70)	.01460	.02632
60	Transportation machinery and equipment (31)	.01353	.00874
61	Dairy products (60)	.01322	.01271
62	Flour and bread (62)	.01214	.01923
63	Trade and distribution (69)	.00893	.01040
64	Sewn goods (56)	.00886	.00882
65	Other light industry (57)	.00800	.01107
66	Meat products (59)	.00729	.00879
67	Textiles (55)	.00708	.01217
68	Animal husbandry (66)	.00305	.00897
69	Transportation and communication (68)	.00282	.00436
70	Construction (64)	.00110	.00133
71	Electric and thermal power (14)	.00055	.00134

Source: Compiled by the author.

Granberg (1975, p. 20) employs 16-sector input-output tables for 23 regions to investigate regional differences in the cost structure of transport. Depending upon the region, the share of fuels in transport is 1.4 to 8 times as high as in industrial production, while amortization ranges from 1.5 to 6 times as fast, and labor intensiveness is 1.2 to 2.5 times as high. Regions are grouped according to similar cost structures,[16] and an interesting result follows from an examination of material inputs where the Central European regions are seen to generate the largest requirements. This tends to suggest that the transport system of the oldest regions is aging, the higher material costs reflecting a lower technological level of transport.

Some preliminary research using the reconstructed republic tables confirms the disparate relationships between the input structures of transport and industrial production alluded to by Granberg. For example, although the fuel costs per unit of output for transportation (and communications) are quite similar for two groups of republics--Kazakhstan, Azerbaidzhan, Ukraine; and Estonia and Latvia--when compared to industrial production requirements in their respective regions, transportation (and communications) costs vary from 3.5 times (Estonia) to 1.1 times (Azerbaidzhan) those of industrial production. Similarly, a wide degree of disparity is presented in the consideration of depreciation costs where the level of depreciation per unit of output in transportation (and communications) in Estonia exceeds depreciation in industrial production by a factor of 5.3. In the Kazakh SSR, the figure is higher by 2.6 times. Finally, high labor intensity per unit of output is revealed for all republic transportation (and communications) sectors.

The reconstructed republic tables also provide some insights into the transport intensity of different economic sectors. Fuels, construction materials, and metals form the transport-intensive core of economic activities, while electric power, textiles, and food utilize low levels of transport services per unit of output. Although the ranking of sectors according to their transport intensities does not differ markedly across republics, there is a wide disparity in terms of absolute transportation (and communications) costs per ruble of output. Thus, transportation (and communications) costs for fuels in Kazakhstan exceed those in Azerbaidzhan and Estonia by factors of 5.5 and 2.6, respectively. For construction materials, Kazakhstan's transport intensity is 1.5 times that of Estonia and Azerbaidzhan, 1.3 times that of the Ukrainian SSR. For the low transport-intensive sectors, regional requirements are equally wide-ranging.

This evaluation of transport costs and flows within a regional perspective suggests the range and variation of regional economic

activity hidden in national input-output tables of the Soviet Union.
Reconstructed input-output tables for other republics and/or economic regions would undoubtedly add to the scope of this analysis.
Nevertheless, it is only partial in the sense that the focus has been
on the aspects of particular regions without examining their interrelatedness. A truly spatial dimension would be added by considering interregional transport flows within an input-output framework.
Further research in this field could result in an internally unified
model that would present a comprehensive picture of the interdependence between economic regions in the Soviet Union. To the extent that this model accurately reflected the importance of transportation, particularly in a general equilibrium sense, to the operations
of an economic system, it would be a major improvement over previous, and current, attempts.

NOTES

1. There has been much discussion in the literature on transportation economics about the substitutability of, say, rail for automotive transport. Each mode may be said to have certain operating
characteristics that are of fundamental importance to the user.
Therefore, rail may be used to transport low value, high density
items to centralized locations while trucking could be utilized for
high value, less bulky items whose distribution is more widespread.
Some transport specialists consider the services of each mode to be
inherently different, and thus consider the output of each mode as a
separate commodity. Others believe that the diverse services provided by each form of transport can be made comparable by the inclusion of certain factors in the measurement unit. For an informa-
tive discussion on this point, see Wilson (1962, Chs. 2 and 3).

2. This has been a long espoused goal in Soviet transportation
literature. For example, see Tverskoi (1935).

3. Experience has shown that the sector has been continually
subjected to overstrain, that it has been able to meet the growing
requirements of the Soviet economy, yet not without significant cost
to the nontransport sectors. Hunter (1968; 1957) and Williams (1962)
have examined, in great detail, the emphasis Soviet transport offi-
cials have placed upon efficient utilization of existing facilities. In
addition, after extensive testing, Williams concluded that the reported Soviet railway productivity gains were realizable.

4. Soviet input-output tables contain explicit consideration of
only productive transportation, thereby narrowing the focus of the
investigation to freight requirements. An attempt to gain a more
complete picture of nonproductive, that is, passenger transport, is

made later in this chapter. However, the scarcity of data restricts
the investigation to the input structure of passenger transport.

5. See the section of this chapter on passenger transportation
for discussion of the aggregation of transportation and communications into a single sector in Soviet input-output tables.

6. See Table 4.12 for transport requirements per ruble of
output, by sector.

7. Discussions of the accuracy and reliability of Soviet transport statistics are found in Hunter (1957) and Williams (1962).

8. The implied weights of the three components of public con-
sumption--housing and communal services, transport and communications, and health and education--in Shneiderman's data are 16.69
percent, 21.13 percent, and 62.18 percent, respectively. Using
this information and the total reported material cost of public consumption of 12,200 million rubles, Treml estimated the total material cost of nonproductive transportation and communications including depreciation as 2,580 million rubles. According to Shneiderman, depreciation in nonproductive transportation and communications comprised 44.1 percent of total material cost, or 1,140 million rubles. When added to the depreciation figure of 2,660 million
rubles for productive transportation and communications estimated
in Treml et al. (1972), total depreciation for transportation and
communications is then 3,800 million. This compares with the officially reported total of 3,797 million rubles (TsSU 1968, p. 883)
and serves as a verification of Treml's estimates.

9. Communications is estimated to account for at most 4 percent of the GVO of the combined sector. See Treml et al. (1972, p.
246; 1973, p. 41) for discussions on this point.

10. This discussion is based upon Williams (1962, pp. 68-69).

11. See also Rosefielde (1974).

12. Soviet efforts have come as a response to the importance
of regional economic planning in the overall planning system of the
Soviet Union. For reviews of the Soviet advances in this field, see
the chapter by Gillula and Bond in this volume.

13. A detailed examination of the accounting practices applied
to regional input-output tables appears in the chapter by Gillula and
Bond in this volume. More specifically, methodological problems
pertaining to transport flows can be found in the paper by Bond, also
included in this volume.

14. This trend is not inconsistent with the development of nonrail forms of transport described earlier in this chapter.

15. This coincides with Proposition 2.

16. See Granberg (1975, p. 202).

1. Estonia, Belorussia, Far East (including Tadzhik SSR)
2. Latvia, Moldavia, Ukraine
3. Kazakhstan, Lithuania (including Kaleningrad), West Siberia
4. Turkmen, Kirgiz, Azerbaidzhan
5. Georgia, Uzbekistan

Similar sectoral transport intensities for national sectors were reported and discussed earlier in this chapter.

REFERENCES

Bedenkova, M. F. 1973. "Osobennosti rascheta transportnoi otsenki v mezhotraslevom balanse soiuznoi respubliki." Economika i matematicheskie metody 9, no. 3: 458-66.

Bond, D. L. 1975. "A Comparison of the Soviet and U.S. Multi-regional Interindustry Accounts." In Duke University-University of North Carolina Occasional Papers on Soviet Input-Output Analysis, No. 9. Durham, N.C.

Edwards, I. U. 1973. "Automotive Trends in the U.S.S.R." In U.S. Congress, Joint Economic Committee, Soviet Economic Prospects for the Seventies. Washington, D.C.: Government Printing Office.

Efimov, A. N. and L. Ia. Berri, eds. 1965. Metody planirovaniia mezhotraslevykh proportsii. Moscow: Ekonomika.

Eidel'man, M. R. 1966. Mezhotraslevoi balans obshchestvennogo produkta. Moscow: Statistika.

Jack Faucett Associates, Inc. 1968. Input-Output Transactions by Transportation Mode, 1947 and 1958. Study Prepared for the Department of Transportation. Silver Spring , Md.: Jack Faucett Associates.

Gillula, J. W. 1976. "Input-Output Tables for Kazakh, Azerbaidzhan and Estonian Soviet Republics for 1966." In Duke University-University of North Carolina Occasional Papers on Soviet Input-Output Analysis, No. 15. Durham, N.C.

_____. 1975. "The 1966 Ukrainian Input-Output Table and an Analysis of the External Economic Relations of the Ukraine." Duke University-University of North Carolina Occasional Papers on Soviet Input-Output Analysis, No. 14. Durham, N.C.

Granberg, A., ed. 1975. Mezhotraslevye balansy v analize terri- torial'nykh proportsii SSSR. Moscow: Nauka.

Guill, G. 1975. "Intertemporal Comparison of the Structure of the Soviet Economy." Duke University-University of North Caro- lina Occasional Papers on Soviet Input-Output Analysis, No. 8. Durham, N.C.

Hunter, H. 1968. Soviet Transportation Experience: Its Lessons for Other Countries. Washington, D.C.: Brookings Institution.

_____. 1957. Soviet Transport Policy. Cambridge: Harvard Uni- versity Press.

Lefeber, L. 1958. Allocation in Space. Amsterdam: North Holland.

Marx, K. 1952. A History of Economic Theories. New York: Langland Press.

Moses, A. L. 1975. "Projections of the Energy Base of the Soviet Transport Sector." Ph.D. dissertation, Duke University.

_____. 1974. "Selected Topics on Transportation and Input-Output in the Soviet Union." Duke University-University of North Carolina Occasional Papers on Soviet Input-Output Analysis, No. 7. Durham, N.C.

National Economics Division, Office of Business Economics. 1969. "Input-Output Structure for 1963." Survey of Current Business 49, no. 11: 16-47.

Rosefielde, S. S. 1974. "The Complete Producers' Price Soviet Input-Output Table for 1966." Duke University-University of North Carolina Occasional Papers on Soviet Input-Output Analysis, No. 6. Durham, N.C.

Shadrin, N. G. 1973. "The Soviet Merchant Marine, A Late Devel- oping Economic Growth Sector." In U.S. Congress, Joint Eco- nomic Committee, Soviet Economic Prospects for the Seventies. Washington, D.C.: Government Printing Office.

Shafirkin, B. I. 1972. "Ratsionalizatsiia perevozok - vazhnyi faktor povysheniia effektivnosti obshchestvennogo proizvodstva." Zheleznodorozhnyi transport, no. 1 (January).

Shmulder, M., et al., eds. 1971. Dinamika mezhotraslevykh i mezhrespublikanskikh ekonomicheskikh sviazei Latviiskoi SSR. Riga: Tsentral'noe statisticheskoe upravlenie Latviiskoi SSR.

Shneiderman, I. M. 1974. Statistika uslug. Moscow: Statistika.

Treml, V. G. 1975a. Input-Output Analysis and the Soviet Economy: An Annotated Bibliography. New York: Praeger.

_____. 1975b. "Structure of Costs, Non-Productive Transportation and Communications." Unpublished manuscript, Duke University.

_____, B. L. Kostinsky, K. W. Kruger, and D. M. Gallik. 1973. Conversion of Soviet Input-Output Tables to Producers' Prices: the 1966 Reconstructed Table. U. S. Department of Commerce, F. D. A. D., Foreign Economic Report No. 1. Washington, D. C.: Government Printing Office.

_____, D. M. Gallik, B. L. Kostinsky, and K. W. Kruger. 1972. The Structure of the Soviet Economy: Analysis and Reconstruction of the 1966 Input-Output Table. New York: Praeger.

Tsentral'noe statisticheskoe upravlenie pri Sovete ministrov SSSR. 1972. Transport i sviaz' SSSR. Moscow: Statistika.

_____. 1971. Narodnoe khoziaistvo SSSR v 1970 godu. Moscow: Statistika.

_____. 1968. Narodnoe khoziaistvo SSSR v 1967 godu. Moscow: Statistika.

_____. 1968. Trud v SSSR. Moscow: Statistika.

TsSU. See Tsentral'noe statisticheskoe upravlenie.

Tverskoi, K. N. 1935. The Unified Transport System of the USSR. London: Victor Gollan.

U.S. Department of Commerce, Office of Business Economics.
     1969. "Input-Output Structure of the U.S. Economy." Survey
     of Current Business 49, no. 11 (November): 16-47.

Williams, E. W. 1962. Freight Transportation in the Soviet Union.
     Princeton, N.J.: NBER-Princeton University Press.

Wilson, G. W. 1962. Some Unsettled Questions in the Economics
     of Transportation. Bloomington, Ind.: University of Indiana
     Press.

5

CONVERSION OF THE 1966 PRODUCERS' PRICE INPUT-OUTPUT TABLE TO A NEW PRICE BASE

Vladimir G. Treml
Gene D. Guill

INTRODUCTION

The purpose of this study is to convert the 1966 input-output table to 1970 prices. The importance of this conversion for the analysis of input-output relations and, more broadly, for the analysis of the Soviet economy, cannot be overemphasized. To date, Soviet statisticians have constructed large-scale ex post input-output tables for 1959, 1966, and 1972, and a large number of republic and regional input-output tables for the latter two years.[1]

The overall behavior of Soviet prices was distinctly different in the 1959-66 and 1966-72 periods. Except for agricultural procurement prices there were only few decreed price changes between 1959 and 1966, although all the evidence suggests that prices of machinery and chemicals were creeping up during this period due to rapid introduction of new or modified products (see below). The 1966-72 period, on the other hand, was marked by a major price reform of 1967 affecting prices for most industrial products, construction, and services such as freight transportation, and trade and distribution, and by several rounds of subsequent price adjustments.[2] New "constant" 1967 prices replaced the "constant" 1955 prices in national income accounting and in measuring industrial output, while 1969 prices were introduced for calculations of investment in constant terms.

The conversion of the 1966 input-output table to post-1967 prices is thus important for any intertemporal comparison of input-output and related data and for analyses of various changes in the Soviet economy.

It must be added that the general issue of constant versus current prices in the framework of input-output analysis is a controversial one. Without going into a detailed discussion of different positions on this issue we may note that in one of his earlier books

pioneering input–output analysis, Professor Leontief (1951, pp. 33-
58) stressed the importance of constant prices for intertemporal
comparisons of input–output tables and for input–output coefficient
projections. Professor Klein (1974, pp. 342-46), analyzing input-
output tables as empirical tools which by necessity do not completely
agree with the theoretical framework of input–output analysis, challenged this view, suggesting that due to market forces and quantity-
price adjustments in input flows, input–output tables in current
prices were better for intertemporal comparisons. Numerous
empirical tests of the two hypotheses so far have not proved to be
conclusive. Thus, in some studies input–output coefficients display
greater stability over time when measured in constant prices, while
other studies show opposite results.[3]

It appears, however, that in the specific case of the 1966
Soviet input–output table the issue of preference of constant over
current prices does not arise. In the first place, the Soviet economy
is not a market one and price signals do not necessarily produce or
reflect the forces operating in a market economy, particularly in
input substitution. Probably an even more important argument concerns the magnitudes of price changes. In the 1967 Soviet price reform some prices were doubled and a great many other prices were
adjusted up or down by as much as 30 to 40 percent (see Appendix A),
while the physical relations between inputs and outputs determined
by the plan remained relatively stable. The need for constant prices
in this case is clear.

The exercise consisted in the construction of a set of 1966–70
price indexes and conversion by means of these indexes of the 1966
Soviet 75–sector producers' price table to 1970 prices. The process of conversion proved to be analytically interesting in itself as
it provided insights into several aspects of the Soviet price system
such as, for instance, the redefinition of profits and taxes in a producers' price table converted to a new price base.

The choice of the year and of the type of prices used was dictated essentially by the availability of the necessary data. Thus, it
is possible that for some analytical purposes a conversion of the
purchasers' price variant of the Soviet table would have been more
interesting. However, most of the data found in Soviet literature
refer to changes in producers' prices and there was no choice but
to select the producers' price table for the exercise.

The choice of 1970 as the target year was dictated by the fact
that the Central Statistical Administration of the Soviet Union converted the 1966 input–output table from 1966 to 1970 prices and a
fairly detailed methodological description with some numerical results is available in Eidel'man (1972). The use of the Soviet methodology of price conversion and of 1970 as the target year made it

possible to check the overall results of the exercise against the few
statistics available from the Soviet conversion. As will become
evident from the text below, the available data on price changes
found in the Soviet literature were ambiguous and poor and it was
necessary to resort to a number of simplifying assumptions and
approximations. Thus, without this test of the overall accuracy of
the 1966-70 price conversion it would have been difficult to claim
any acceptable level of confidence in the results of the study. The
test described in a later section of this chapter proved to be satisfactory in the sense that the results of the conversion agree with the
results obtained by Soviet specialists.

Since there is a Soviet national input-output table for 1972,[4] it
may be desirable for comparison purposes to convert the 1966 table
to 1972 rather than 1970 prices. In fact, a set of 1972 price indexes
was constructed but the reliability of most of them is questionable,
particularly since several official Soviet indexes had to be employed
in the absence of better data. Thus, this study is focused on a 1966-70
price conversion and the set of the estimated 1970-72 price indexes
has been assigned to an appendix (Appendix C).

Even if it seems clear that the 1966 input-output table recomputed in 1970 prices agrees with the Soviet conversion, the question
of its reliability may be legitimately raised because of the use of
notoriously poor Soviet price indexes.

Several Western and Soviet scholars have criticized the officially published Soviet price indexes on several grounds, particularly for the clearly evident downward bias (Becker 1974, Bornstein
1972, pp. 358-62; Kvasha and Krasovskii 1968, Krasovskii 1975).
Soviet price indexes published in official statistical publications such
as the annual Narodnoe khoziaistvo handbooks are constructed on the
basis of a fixed commodity sample.[5] The commodity composition of
the sample is changed infrequently and as a result, new products or
modified and redesigned products carrying higher "temporary" price
tags enter the market, bypassing the sample. As these products
appear, the prices of some of the old products included in the sample
may even be cut, reflecting lower costs of long production runs.
Thus, the price indexes based on fixed samples will display a high
degree of price stability or may even show a decline in prices, while
in fact the price level has been rising (Greenslade 1972, pp. 181-86).
Price indexes for the machinebuilding and chemical industries, where
the introduction of new or modified products is more rapid than in
other industries, are particularly poor.[6]

However, these defects do not affect, or affect very little, the
accuracy and the reliability of the 1966-70 price conversion undertaken in this study. Most of the price changes effected in the 1966-70
period resulted from the several stages of the 1967 price reform,

and the price changes decreed by the Price Office of Gosplan are, or should be, different from the official price indexes prepared by the Central Statistical Administration. This study made use of a variety of Soviet price data but a large share of these data consisted of announced price cuts or price increases where the magnitude of change was measured on the basis of new comprehensive price lists and the price levels existing at the time of the reform.

It is still possible that because of the introduction of new products, some creeping up of prices, particularly prices for machinery and chemicals, occurred in the 1966–70 period, and if it did it was not recorded in the price indexes prepared in this study. It appears, however, that if in fact this moderate rise did take place, the rates of increase were modest. Thus, Becker estimates the 1966–70 increases in prices of machinery at approximately less than 2 percent compared with a 23 percent increase in the 1958–66 period (Becker 1974, p. 378). One of the main reasons for the slowdown in the increase of prices was a much tighter control over pricing of new products exercised by the government after the 1967 price reform (Komin 1971, pp. 26–27).

CONVERSION EXERCISE

The conversion of the 1966 Soviet input–output table from 1966 to 1970 prices offered in this chapter can be briefly described as follows:

1. All available Soviet data on 1966–70 price changes were collected, interpreted, and organized to agree with the 110–sector commodity classification used in the 1966 input–output table. Since Soviet prices are differentiated by buyers, more than one index was prepared for the same sector in a number of instances. When the available price indexes referred to a more detailed commodity list than the 110–sector classification, these indexes were aggregated using input–output or other value or quantity weights. In some instances no direct price information was found in the literature. In such cases the indexes were estimated by a variety of means, or when it proved to be impossible, a price index of one was used. The derivation of 110–sector indexes is described in Appendix A.

2. The prepared set of 110–sector indexes was aggregated with the use of appropriate 1966 input–output value weights to agree with the 75–sector classification employed in the reconstructed 1966 input–output table in producers' prices (see Appendix A, Chapter 1). The prepared matrix of price indexes was thus rectangular, with 75 rows for the 75 producing sectors and 78 columns (that is, 75

producing sectors plus three columns for final demand: private consumption, public consumption, and gross investment and other uses).[7] Of course, in many instances prices were not differentiated by buyers and the same price index was used for the entire row.

3. As the next step, the 75 x 78 flow entries of the first and the second quadrants of the 1966 input-output table in producers' prices (Table 1.2 in this volume) were converted to new values by means of prepared 1966-70 price indexes. The various totals shown in the table, such as total interindustry deliveries (first quadrant row total), total final demand, total gross output, and total material cost, were obtained by summing the appropriate entries in the new 1970 prices.

4. Following the Soviet methodology of conversion, the depreciation on productive and nonproductive fixed capital and wage income were not converted to a new price base but taken unadjusted from the table in 1966 prices. The construction sector constitutes one exception: as noted by Eidel'man (1972, p. 5), wages in state construction rose so rapidly in the 1966-70 period that they had to be adjusted. According to the official data, construction wages rose by 32.5 percent (Narkhoz 67, p. 657, and Narkhoz 70, p. 520) and the total wage income in the construction sector was thus increased by this percentage.

The completion of the elements of value-added for the new 1970 price table was then made as follows: for any given sector, the row sum of all first- and second-quadrant entries converted to 1970 producers' prices, or the new values of gross output, was taken as given and entered as the new column sum for quadrants one and three. All material costs expressed now in 1970 prices and the unadjusted depreciation and wage income entries were subtracted from the new 1970 output total.[8] The resulting residual with a plus or a minus sign became then the new nonlabor component of the national income, or the balancing entry necessary to preserve the required row-column equality of input-output tables.

In algebraic terms the conversion of any sector k to a new price base can be described as follows:

$$\sum_j x_{kj} \cdot e_{kj} + Y_k \cdot e_{ky} = \sum_i x_{ik} \cdot e_{ik} + D_k + L_k + R_k \qquad (1)$$

where

x_{kj} = sales of sector k to sector j in 1966 producers' prices.

e_{kj} = 1970/1966 price index applicable to sales of sector k to sector j.

Y_k = final demand purchases of products of the k sector in 1966 prices

D_k = depreciation taken unchanged from the 1966 price table

L_k = labor wage income taken unchanged from the 1966 price table

R_k = the new national income component of sector k covering profits, taxes, and other expenditures

It will be recalled that in Soviet input–output tables in purchasers' prices, turnover taxes are shown as a separate row in the value-added quadrant. The entries in this row, T_j, record the value of turnover taxes levied on the output of sector j, and the row total corresponds to the total value of turnover taxes collected in the economy. In this respect the treatment of turnover taxes in the value-added quadrant of input–output tables agrees with the treatment of turnover taxes in Soviet national income accounts. In tables in purchasers' prices, turnover taxes are also included in flow entries, that is, any entry x_{ij} which stands for sales of output of sector i to sector j includes the payment received by sector i, as well as the cost of transporting and distributing the output and turnover tax on output of sector i if this output is taxed.

Conversion of an input–output table from purchasers' to producers' prices results in a different recording of turnover taxes (Treml et al. 1973, pp. 5–12; Kostinsky 1976, pp. 6–8). A new row of turnover taxes is computed in which each entry is defined as

$$T_j' = \sum_i t_{ij} \qquad (2)$$

where t_{ij} stands for turnover taxes that were included in the purchase price of input i purchased by sector j. The sum of the T_j' row now adds up not to total turnover taxes but to the value of turnover taxes levied on intermediate goods distributed in the first quadrant.

There are two methods of recording the T_j' row in Soviet input–output tables in producers' prices.[9] According to the first method the n x n transaction matrix (or the first quadrant) is expanded by one additional row and one additional column. The new (n + 1)th row in the first quadrant and in the final-demand quadrant shows turnover taxes paid on purchases of inputs and on final-demand purchases, respectively. The row labeled "turnover tax" is retained in the value-added quadrant but now it shows only zero entries, with the exception of the (n + 1)th entry, which records the total value of turnover taxes collected in the economy. The advantages of this method lie in the fact that the total value of interindustry transactions is identical in tables in producers' and in purchasers' prices. The disadvantage is in that a fictitious, purely fiscal row has been added to the first quadrant and must be removed before the inverse is calculated.

In the second method, the row of T_j entries is simply removed from the value-added quadrant and the row of T_j' entries is substituted for it. The disadvantage of this method is that the total national income is now different (that is, it is smaller than the national income recorded in a table in purchasers' prices by the value of taxes collected on products delivered to the final demand). The treatment of turnover taxes in the table in producers' prices shown in Chapter 1 of this volume follows the first method.

In the 1966 input-output table converted to 1970 producers' prices presented in this chapter, turnover taxes are not shown as a separate row but are included with the row labeled "other elements of national income." As was described above, the values in this row are the balancing entries necessary to insure the equality between the value of output in new prices (the row sum in quadrants one and two) with the cost of materials in new prices (column sums in quadrants one and three).

5. The various totals and subtotals, such as total material cost, total gross social product, and so forth, and the aggregate indexes derived in this study were then checked against independently available data to test the overall accuracy of the conversion. The results of these comparison tests are described in the next section.

The 1966 Soviet input-output table in 1970 producers' prices prepared in this study is shown in Table 5.1. As explained above, the treatment of turnover taxes in this table is different from the 1966 producers' price table (Table 1.2 in this volume). In all other aspects, such as the format, definition of various relations, and the sector-commodity classification, the two tables are identical.

The set of price indexes derived in the conversion exercise is shown in Table 5.2. As noted above, a matrix of price indexes containing 75 rows for the 75 producing sectors and 78 columns for the same producing sectors plus private and public consumption and investment was prepared first. Table 5.2 shows one additional row that records average price indexes applicable to material costs and three additional columns for aggregate price indexes for total interindustry deliveries (column 76), total final demand (column 80), and total gross output (column 81). The price indexes shown in these additional rows and columns were not derived from Soviet data but were calculated as ratios of the appropriate values in the 1966 producers' price table (Table 1.2) and in the 1970 producers' price table (Table 5.1).

TABLE 5.1

The Reconstructed Soviet 1966 Input–Output Table in 1970 Producers' Prices
(thousands of rubles; employment in thousands of man–years)

SEQ NO.	110 ORDER NO.		FER ORES 1	FER METALS 2	NONFER ORES 3	NONFER METAL 4	COKE PROD 5	REFRAC MAT 6	INDMET PROD 7	COAL 8	OIL EXTRAC 9
1	1	FER ORES	3186	1243509	31105	26468	0	57865	4496	508	81
2	2	FER METALS	15276	2036549	1310	91874	2234	0	653628	36176	3331
3	6	NONFER ORES	0	0	0	1431181	968	0	0	4886	0
4	7	NONFER METAL	9671	1156320	9389	239030	152723	10277	2380	840	168
5	3	COKE PROD	12591	1184116	0	3516	645	4286	1705	234	57
6	4	REFRAC MAT	6470	127135	0	0	1233	1156	24255	26973	1419
7	5	INDMET PROD	22803	65507	0	32427	0	8334	4336	0	90
8	8	COAL	0	526711	8196	0	1236479	0	5231	2289418	0
9	9	OIL EXTRAC	8189	72470	0	37696	1422	4771	0	7098	21643
10	10	OIL REF	0	0	5426	0	0	0	0	0	16771
11	11	GAS	0	153020	0	6969	9659	7321	3402	587	10558
12	12	PEAT	0	649	0	1677	958	0	0	408	0
13	13	OIL SHALES	325	2906	267	0	0	11	11	225	105
14	14	ELEC POWER	145357	333934	133306	627300	3645	15210	44041	242330	89767
15	15	EN&POW M&E	152	1724	390	261	37	27	13	407	278
16	16	ELTECH M&E	5151	17140	6560	6819	784	832	1451	11302	1440
17	17	CABLE PROD	2749	8251	2881	2071	253	320	543	26257	1120
18	20	MACH TOOLS	99	463	333	60	59	1	74	149	16
19	21	FORG-PR M&E	144	722	684	381	11	0	212	61	0
20	22	CAST M&E	313	0	399	414	3	2	4	6	0
21	23	TOOLS & DIES	2359	2387	3005	3124	108	134	702	4904	551
22	24	PRECIS INST	906	2737	719	1631	155	80	113	2069	362
23	25,26,27	MI&MET M&E	28284	95387	23570	23772	1317	963	2118	81734	8307
24	28,29	PUMP&CHEM E	530	1843	1159	326	498	36	10	365	1109
25	30	LOG&PA M&E	36	0	30	0	0	0	0	0	0
26	31	LT IND M&E	0	1	0	0	0	2	0	0	0
27	32	FD IND M&E	0	5	0	0	0	0	0	6	0
28	33	PRINT M&E	0	27	0	0	0	0	0	0	0
29	34	HOIST&TRAN E	242	1392	401	141	80	69	66	1185	22
30	35	CONST M&E	5405	915	2026	334	7	334	1	1376	3
31	36	CONMAT M&E	128	569	163	170	0	535	0	5	0
32	37,38	TRANS M&E	2558	1767	1513	1202	196	142	72	1067	5
33	39	AUTOS	5582	3854	3302	2623	67	205	206	839	680
34	40	AGRIC M&E	2225	644	2152	846	27	138	8	1496	586
35	41	BEARNG	1133	4854	755	1655	100	172	392	1095	152
36	18,19,42,43	RADIO&OTH MB	4345	14231	5180	6105	677	649	1108	6779	920
37	44	SANIT ENG PR	399	1623	384	852	158	70	159	819	52
38	45	OTHER METWRS	7037	16192	7169	8061	586	402	2848	13936	982
39	46	METAL STRUCT	501	1156	512	576	160	0	2	1223	13
40	47	REPAIR	22948	98185	15274	33491	11115	4214	3612	22466	3163
41	48	ABRASV	2606	11150	1734	3803	25	1475	845	392	213
42	49	MINRL CHEM	577	5312	476	2983	112	602	637	565	33
43	50	BASIC CHEM	13449	123218	11063	69201	15452	4106	12342	48709	3255
44	51	ANIL DYE PR	34	327	29	183	1	1	1	120	2
45	52	SYN R& PLAST	262	2410	215	1353	53	16	368	164	209

46	53	SYN FIBERS	45	420	37	235	0	0	74	0	0
47	55	ORGSYN PROD	751	6830	616	3864	148	592	83	3049	3373
48	56	PAINT & LAC	645	5917	530	3323	1116	210	500	2035	523
49	57	RUBBER PROD	4266	39092	3510	21954	1631	1162	914	32555	1575
50	54.58.59	OTHER CHEM	101	936	83	524	7	26	14	4459	88
51	60	LOGGNG	18694	0	15578	0	200	979	1336	250354	446
52	61.62	SAW & LUM PR	7159	16473	7294	8200	555	1003	15957	81057	1005
53	63	FURNITURE	396	1478	380	842	88	88	293	1144	147
54	64	OTHER WDWK	184	1693	151	951	38	54	325	822	87
55	65	PAPER & PULP	490	4501	403	2527	423	425	1880	432	150
56	66	WOOD CHEM	363	3329	299	1868	1133	582	13	35	155
57	67-73	CONST MAT	4138	9523	4216	4741	542	891	1210	22192	634
58	74	GLASS	776	3445	744	1646	151	74	391	564	127
59	75-80	TEXTLS	3440	15858	1752	9679	724	646	44966	5331	1304
60	81	SEWN GOODS	8167	37630	4157	22971	973	1685	4683	41693	2154
61	82	OTH LT IND	1763	8129	897	4963	383	251	441	7327	793
62	83	FISH PROD	2	12	2	7	2	0	0	0	0
63	84	MEAT PROD	77	354	38	216	2	24	2	0	1
64	85	DAIRY PROD	2937	13535	1493	8263	872	180	321	634	711
65	86	SUGAR	4	21	22	13	0	12	0	0	0
66	87-89	FLOUR&BREAD	43	208	619	127	0	0	0	2	0
67	90-94	OTHER FOOD	1219	5621	35170	3431	145	371	3225	3326	327
68	95	IND NEC	41751	140709	35170	61463	10485	5943	13602	44727	1954
69	96-100	CONST	0	0	0	0	0	0	0	0	0
70	101	CROPS	146	675	74	412	0	45	16	679	61
71	102	ANIMAL HUSB	76	351	38	213	0	0	0	0	0
72	103	FOREST	0	0	0	0	0	0	0	0	0
73	104-106	TRANS &COM	25511	709683	18472	259560	266642	20170	53187	117436	7650
74	107-109	TRADE & DIST	3711	134841	2950	89506	33521	2130	15388	9578	2631
75	110	OTHER BRANCH	0	372971	0	102841	45	9	2121	0	15
76		TOTAL PURCH	460877	8855198	380603	5374418	1794701	162312	958915	3468610	193371
77		DEPRECIATION	233825	674003	234551	293133	64636	30335	41837	877955	439227
78		WAGES	276163	1265419	179482	983016	77400	84521	172138	2786540	118292
79		OTH NET INC	884445	3627456	351885	453227	804972	172788	311766	1814987	1681944
80		NATIONAL INC	1160608	4893875	531367	1436243	882372	257309	483904	4601527	1800236
81		TOTAL OUTLAY	1855310	14424076	1146521	7103794	2741769	449956	1484656	8948092	2432834
82		EMPLOYMENT	178.4	818.1	91.2	499.5	50.0	54.6	111.2	1189.0	92.3
83		TOTL CAPITAL	3293316	943000	2960000	3710548	911211	427250	589258	9145370	5779301
84		BLDGS&STRUCT	2018579	457200	1978039	2270653	419941	220003	300580	6943256	5064324
85		POWER M&E	23954	267000	59704	41276	27427	4102	8603	79565	33520
86		GENERAL M&E	198680	689000	242332	258965	38726	56995	140536	308253	91780
87		SPECIAL M&E	813180	3863800	574209	1057368	414729	137146	131405	1753054	566027
88		TRANS M&E	154446	104800	87022	71470	7301	4059	3889	27527	10981
89		OTH CAPITAL	84477	30900	27694	10816	3007	4145	4243	33715	8669

(Table 5.1 continued)

SEQ NO.	110 ORDER NO.		OIL REF 10	GAS 11	PEAT 12	OIL SHALES 13	ELEC POWER 14	EN&POW M&E 15	ELTECH M&E 16	CABLE PROD 17	MACH TOOLS 18
1	1	FER ORES	814	10	47	6	1077	3979	10473	40	2190
2	2	FER METALS	11558	1134	1859	786	12556	315919	405958	12450	82687
3	6	NONFER ORES	0	0	0	0	0	0	0	0	0
4	7	NONFER METAL	0	0	0	198	0	57220	445619	621330	11874
5	3	COKE PROD	17994	0	86		94	2335	20124	180	6102
6	4	REFRAC MAT	373	21	51		2150	1357	4798	18	1035
7	5	INDMET PROD	1460	183	1456	3	8624	9969	41910	35175	8073
8	8	COAL	394	1321	820	662	1811212	3184	15129	2457	2026
9	9	OIL EXTRAC	1348172	31470	0	2937	16010				0
10	10	OIL REF	432374	7664	7025	797	262555	4827	13212	4134	1918
11	11	GAS	79994	56081	7	0	319770	5919	9285	444	1501
12	12	PEAT	0	2	72824	10669	17732	3	45	0	4
13	13	OIL SHALES	1016	8202	194	8161	36576	67	1337	689	181
14	14	ELEC POWER	280724	12051	8542	9	13136	44243	90568	20867	25037
15	15	EN&POW M&E	23	47	178	511	13375	23543	38081	5	39
16	16	ELTECH M&E	1499	240	482	769	7853	86726	502424	4215	69572
17	17	CABLE PROD	720	151	307	2	2413	4291	165915	8740	2373
18	20	MACH TOOLS	9	0	28	0	11	407	1924	96	13949
19	21	FORG- PR M&E	2	0	62	0	0	0	1241	101	19
20	22	CAST M&E	0	0	40		3	7	276		34
21	23	TOOLS & DIES	450	104	491	55	928	2907	11656	554	8851
22	24	PRECIS INST	1476	104	64	38	2765	9060	29030	153	4508
23	25,26,27	MI&MET M&E	11819	664	7338	1216	18	135	21	10	10
24	28,29	PUMPS&CHEM E	1280	202	12	34	893	6546	2940	53	5469
25	30	LOG&PA M&E	0	0	2	2	3	0	0	0	55
26	31	LT IND M&E	0	0	0	0	0	0	8	365	0
27	32	FD IND M&E	0	0	0	0	0	0	0	0	0
28	33	PRINT M&E	0	0	0	0	0	0	0	0	0
29	34	HOIST&TRAN E	18	8	188	13	266	65	453	97	1048
30	35	CONST M&E	1	0	260	89	19	0	15		0
31	36	CONMAT M&E	1	0	0	5	16	0	686	0	0
32	37,38	TRANS M&E	0	0	901	43	201	215	226		19
33	39	AUTOS	414	197	731	154	1104	8623	26235	183	310
34	40	AGRIC M&E	143	113	5638	25	555	1714	2050	31	212
35	41	BEARNG	147	33	526	60	595	3214	14950	150	8568
36	18,19,42,43	RADIO&OTH MB	1591	179	276	275	2839	114441	43335	5635	58911
37	44	SANIT ENG PR	79	13	120	20	296	797	999	56	118
38	45	OTHER METWRS	1730	293	1109	188	2413	6761	22620	3074	15293
39	46	METAL STRUCT	0	0	0	2	10	1449	1284		142
40	47	REPAIR	9695	600	979	393	43186	3308	8332	1403	1904
41	48	ABRASV CHEM	126	17	51	12	449	1778	73131	508	2908
42	49	MINRL CHEM	642	4	56	0	608	82	565	209	27
43	50	BASIC CHEM	74231	5752	1830	5185	13358	3276	38257	3947	1322
44	51	ANIL DYE PR	237	7	7	0	62	183	335	1421	24
45	52	SYN R& PLAST	189	12	8	3	2169	1038	105385	73522	1684

#	Code	Branch									
46	53	SYN FIBERS	0	2	0	0	0	0	7823	2720	0
47	55	ORGSYN PROD	39547	3227	27	6	627	655	8738	5978	1061
48	56	PAINT & LAC	1220	136	349	37	2122	4121	36969	12874	6120
49	57	RUBBER PROD	2664	450	762	1636	3185	3790	66629	13617	3818
50	54.58.59	OTHER CHEM	1422	87	51	5	165	270	5476	34793	79
51	60	LOGGING	495	35	1495	1293	681	1719	1489	325	1081
52	61.62	SAW & LUM PR	4880	142	1495	385	2097	9810	40617	23740	9354
53	63	FURNITURE	485	30	189	35	644	1585	2221	228	567
54	64	OTHER WDWK	74	32	45	34	421	150	2568	178	853
55	65	PAPER & PULP	1790	42	69	10	690	1172	39372	6292	127
56	66	WOOD CHEM	5542	1379	14	3	59	249	6101	1874	212
57	67-73	CONST MAT	1555	237	773	100	2517	1713	5653	305	1256
58	74	GLASS	1361	38	63	12	833	665	56854	2165	432
59	75-80	TEXTLS	2562	2164	887	177	3066	4151	42518	57564	2730
60	81	SEWN GOODS	4501	596	3516	568	4849	3757	17332	1252	2268
61	82	OTH LT IND	1134	132	692	186	1499	1342	5915	579	644
62	83	FISH PROD	15	0	0	0	16	11	2		1
63	84	MEAT PROD	90	0	0	0	0	11	187	7	42
64	85	DAIRY PROD	3938	422	36	57	2012	1147	7965	1587	1022
65	86	SUGAR	0	0	0	0	0	0	21	0	12
66	87-89	FLOUR&BREAD	6	0	0	0	2	0	49	0	2
67	90-94	OTHER FOOD	8853	62	158	63	2582	798	6187	2413	452
68	95	IND NEC	10424	690	756	356	28823	9517	89744	12017	11926
69	96-100	CONST	0	0	0	0	0	0	0	0	0
70	101	CROPS	23	14	134	0	0	0	72	0	10
71	102	ANIMAL HUSB	0	36	0	0	0	0	47	0	0
72	103	FOREST	0	0	0	0	0	0	0	0	0
73	104-106	TRANS &COM	490716	10379	4815	2193	740425	42328	145564	43829	20425
74	107-109	TRADE & DIST	176214	3335	1302	325	92375	10744	33162	21741	4859
75	110	OTHER BRANCH	45	61	0	35	711	1986	3128		1079
76		TOTAL PURCH	3041961	148908	132223	40839	3647892	831268	2783235	1048390	410429
77		DEPRECIATION	248442	57021	54935	9448	1159410	74224	140669	27552	56532
78		WAGES	148281	27170	144949	32937	836367	303908	643224	89843	250871
79		OTH NET INC	1473555	1056564	127877	51775	2603831	303406	866133	43441	201272
80		NATIONAL INC	1621836	1083734	272826	84712	3440198	607394	1709357	133284	452143
81		TOTAL OUTLAY	4912239	1289653	459984	134999	8247500	1512886	4633261	1209226	919104
82		EMPLOYMENT	115.7	21.2	113.1	25.7	615.7	237.8	659.8	70.3	196.3
83		TOTL CAPITAL	2823202	803118	716846	123290	23661429	976627	1850909	362521	743840
84		BLDGS&STRUCT	480174	625777	369965	71681	15406343	512730	1034473	171255	361728
85		POWER M&E	33878	18391	8674	542	5203058	27393	21876	6163	7066
86		GENERAL M&E	98047	16202	19282	5425	2428135	367114	651890	105893	319407
87		SPECIAL M&E	1196422	136142	240718	42758	456067	59046	97543	74932	39051
88		TRANS MSE	4517	4257	40501	2034	119253	4981	8884	761	3571
89		OTH CAPITAL	10164	2249	37706	850	45193	10840	30726	3517	13017

(Table 5.1 continued)

SEQ NO.	110 ORDER NO.		FORG-PR M&E 19	CAST M&E 20	TOOLS & DIES 21	PRECIS INST 22	MI&MET M&E 23	PUMPS& CHEM E 24	LOG&PA M&E 25	LT IND M&E 26	FD IND M&E 27
1	1	FER ORES	579	76	833	2038	9979	2679	179	1053	1602
2	2	FER METALS	25554	2556	157106	63117	313971	214839	16562	43586	58838
3	6	NONFER ORES	0	0	0	0	0	0	0	0	0
4	7	NONFER METAL	2931	1706	22340	86817	93314	59986	2142	15950	19949
5	3	COKE PROD	1241	271	259	988	5723	3916	503	3649	1297
6	4	REFRAC MAT	475	34	145	937	4594	1232	57	442	156
7	5	INDMET PROD	1400	330	2851	23431	17773	11657	1999	9986	4662
8	8	COAL	305	390	735	4713	7086	3361	252	1783	944
9	9	OIL EXTRAC	0	0	0	218	0	0	0	0	0
10	10	OIL REF	604	103	1250	3010	6000	3889	741	1144	778
11	11	GAS	411	51	297	2356	8283	2660	264	1078	245
12	12	PEAT	0	3		41	107	194	13	13	
13	13	OIL SHALES	6	0	21	148	68		8	125	109
14	14	ELEC POWER	7490	1187	14884	29497	47674	36468	3153	12276	6145
15	15	EN&POW M&E	2	10	12	2075	1493	1409	141		280
16	16	ELTECH M&E	8388	1557	4435	6410	11116	139949	5636	10260	19203
17	17	CABLE PROD	417	47	2619	18190	3918	13136	315	825	874
18	20	MACH TOOLS	149	38	601	1073	1061	624	65	198	93
19	21	FORG-PR M&E	1054		43	55	94	8	1	10	20
20	22	CAST M&E	6	568	279	11	182			37	15
21	23	TOOLS & DIES	918	274	2588	12603	5484	5096	343	2600	1552
22	24	PRECIS INST	795	134	129	104477	1928	16403	730	952	2150
23	25.26.27	MI&MET M&E	68	2		69	44306	7	0	2	3733
24	28.29	PUMPS&CHEM E	1155	349	132	483	9651	30429	823	1406	0
25	30	LOG&PA M&E	0	0	0	3	155	0	3298	1	0
26	31	LT IND M&E	0	0	0	0	0	0	0	18842	169
27	32	FD IND M&E	0	0	0	1	1	0	0	1	3519
28	33	PRINT M&E	6	0	20	5	0	43	0	65	0
29	34	HOIST&TRAN E	0	8	0	9	2213	228	193	130	329
30	35	CONST M&E	0	0	0	0	230		10		0
31	36	CONMAT M&E	0	0	0	0	17	2	3	0	7
32	37.38	TRANS M&E	8			10191	3903	26	549	4	0
33	39	AUTOS	93	9	77	136	25401	7211	5084	341	16305
34	40	AGRIC M&E	49	2	16	4501	14581	2814	1136	49	6240
35	41	BEARNG	683	146	2420		16986	3422	11098	2602	1862
36	18.19.42.43	RADIO&OTH MB	7334	1350	3611	149128	85229	66972	49	5107	9752
37	44	SANIT ENG PR	45	4	140	217	309	763	803	161	264
38	45	OTHER METWRS	1958	588	7723	3442	18993	14107	0	4011	3608
39	46	METAL STRUCT	878			0	969	69		696	4
40	47	REPAIR	549	5	1042	1998	5805	2029	224	697	383
41	48	ABRASV	305	72	4100	3428	2065	2339	223	1190	343
42	49	MINRL CHEM	69	156	11	159	70	38	0	146	3
43	50	BASIC CHEM	508	0	1192	10293	4496	7901	262	901	650
44	51	ANIL DYE PR	4	0	16	359	7	401	0	29	29
45	52	SYN R& PLAST	106	25	961	15499	1448	12206	97	3615	292

#	Name	Code	C1	C2	C3	C4	C5	C6	C7	C8	C9
46	SYN FIBERS	53	0	0	0	244	0	0	0	0	30
47	ORGSYN PROD	55	156	17	148	3492	819	2147	31	1191	189
48	PAINT & LAC	56	944	216	703	7058	4766	7319	509	4059	2522
49	RUBBER PROD	57	1109	270	850	6306	16867	10603	1032	3687	5986
50	OTHER CHEM	54.58.59	6	9	66	2933	807	196	88	372	236
51	LOGGNG	60	355	40	140	2295	2007	1819	303	608	444
52	SAW & LUM PR	61.62	1746	334	3253	20666	6391	11654	1704	12052	5623
53	FURNITURE	63	101	13	75	1373	451	266	61	175	104
54	OTHER WDWK	64	16	6	390	4632	218	2504	20	1037	51
55	PAPER & PULP	65	180	39	1037	6303	817	1829	105	225	228
56	WOOD CHEM	66	59	15	26	716	83	139	90	730	35
57	CONST MAT	67-73	251	61	480	2553	2075	2315	192	431	430
58	GLASS	74	127	15	88	11703	932	3442	67		85
59	TEXTLS	75-80	351	66	1318	15392	3323	3608	387	15208	1098
60	SEWN GOODS	81	761	96	1068	5734	3962	3635	427	1774	1090
61	OTH LT IND	82	182	20	934	8829	1128	879	120	1553	560
62	FISH PROD	83	0	0	0	5	1	1	0	5	8
63	MEAT PROD	84	11	2	43	352	35	36	5	98	26
64	DAIRY PROD	85	181	75	335	8772	3765	1800	89	869	167
65	SUGAR	86					19				2
66	FLOUR&BREAD	87-89			212	8	5			6	0
67	OTHER FOOD	90-94	93	21	2527	1623	659	725	65	602	143
68	IND NEC	95	1655	364		38052	13117	7656	692	3685	3262
69	CONST	96-100	0	0							0
70	CROPS	101	0	0	75	34	63			46	0
71	ANIMAL HUSB	102	0	0	0	73	0	0	0	0	0
72	FOREST	103	0	0	0						
73	TRANS &COM	104-106	4130	805	14230	39975	50716	39859	3435	11788	10549
74	TRADE & DIST	107-109	1061	205	4250	8634	12630	9310	841	3723	2653
75	OTHER BRANCH	110	1068	221	109	1640	3865	2432	187	1448	771
76	TOTAL PURCH		81086	14962	265265	815733	906143	782710	67393	224006	202674
77	DEPRECIATION		14420	2130	22084	76552	99661	61575	9575	22940	13247
78	WAGES		46647	11246	130739	642706	498292	259562	25432	135212	73996
79	OTH NET INC		62746	9732	110737	314718	1165290	471423	27226	90051	67655
80	NATIONAL INC		109393	20978	241476	957424	1663582	730985	52658	225263	141651
81	TOTAL OUTLAY		204899	38120	528825	1849709	2669386	1575270	129626	472209	357572
82	EMPLOYMENT		36.5	8.8	102.3	502.9	389.9	203.1	19.9	105.8	57.9
83	TOTL CAPITAL		189740	28680	290574	1007268	1311334	810191	125981	301843	174306
84	BLDGS&STRUCT		95647	16118	120153	542617	685500	465069	73767	154604	95851
85	POWER M&E		1803	384	3545	13699	16796	12424	1625	6067	3521
86	GENERAL M&E		78002	9029	153975	389007	475871	260575	39167	118745	62402
87	SPECIAL M&E		11499	2557	7206	30319	104063	5001	8668	17809	8610
88	TRANS M&E		702	173	668	6043	10807		655	875	1098
89	OTH CAPITAL		2087	419	5027	25383	18217	15469	2079	3743	2824

(Table 5.1 continued)

SEQ NO.	110 ORDER NO.		PRINT M&E 28	HOIST& TRAN E 29	CONST M&E 30	CONMAT M&E 31	TRANS M&E 32	AUTOS 33	AGRIC M&E 34	BEARNG 35	RADIO& OTH MB 36
1	1	FER ORES	70	2068	2226	1117	12520	7661	13768	760	107437
2	2	FER METALS	2926	106968	88829	45346	375755	592202	840266	140699	986115
3	6	NONFER ORES	1367	0	0	0	0	0	0	0	0
4	7	NONFER METAL	226	4260	7145	3387	123728	161903	91382	6566	330729
5	3	COKE PROD	51	1303	1644	931	3484	12745	23045	20	29300
6	4	REFRAC MAT	306	737	1342	667	5763	3103	7455	145	7555
7	5	INDMET PROD	181	10816	9700	1348	53610	66218	51013	13938	86979
8	8	COAL		1486	2022	738	7904	14206	10906	330	32381
9	9	OIL EXTRAC		0	0	0	0	0	0	0	570
10	10	OIL REF	262	1192	2153	807	10099	16401	13197	2417	41850
11	11	GAS	62	1779	1493	594	9630	12811	10353	565	26893
12	12	PEAT	0	0	58	0	460	9	0	0	66
13	13	OIL SHALES	5	116	184	35	211	1078	576	526	1135
14	14	ELEC POWER	1292	15413	17050	7459	90598	83202	121997	20996	311632
15	15	EN&POW M&E	1994	3842	7698	62	270048	1142	3141	8	21501
16	16	ELTECH M&E	216	66380	20441	10319	248755	68385	58082	999	262192
17	17	CABLE PROD	20	4744	2051	331	26392	13424	8842	396	218093
18	20	MACH TOOLS	0	498	962	188	3505	4784	6126	1607	7090
19	21	FORG- PR M&E		92	4	53	544	2094	2055	67	3068
20	22	CAST M&E		79	27	193	263	959	2162	0	683
21	23	TOOLS & DIES	313	2226	2691	382	13260	13624	25538	2704	57380
22	24	PRECIS INST	54	1578	1726	637	46632	3340	5428	71	723401
23	25,26,27	MI&MET M&E	83	8	0	0	948	36	19	7	89
24	28,29	PUMP&CHEM E	0	633	5353	326	108175	6369	5622	24	33398
25	30	LOG&PA M&E	0	0	0	0	137	2	0	0	128
26	31	LT IND M&E	0	0	0	0	3	4	0	0	494
27	32	FD IND M&E	18	1	0	0	1004	7	198	0	4453
28	33	PRINT M&E	0	0	0	0	0	0	0	0	0
29	34	HOIST&TRAN E		27949	1478	222	27782	2276	281	60	3357
30	35	CONST M&E		517	18946	613	122	69	3	0	0
31	36	CONMAT M&E	0	2089	2204	2554	21	6	3	0	1539
32	37,38	TRANS M&E	29	86476	46	9	82678	271	316	1	0
33	39	AUTOS	0	2551	34327	414	8243	879878	47348	110	138112
34	40	AGRIC M&E	130	8508	209405	31	1095	1370	891882	53	116225
35	41	BEARNG	0	44967	6746	1454	19839	37123	67400	4502	25491
36	18,19,42,43	RADIO&OTH MB	17	425	47242	20098	387756	121217	170748	0	3534551
37	44	SANIT ENG PR	622	5845	263	61	4581	1318	4381	44	17533
38	45	OTHER METWRS	563	3429	6559	1705	29053	31198	45914	3575	254017
39	46	METAL STRUCT		2339	87	58	2780	10	45	0	4193
40	47	REPAIR			1767	688	10038	5785	7803	1207	28416
41	48	ABRASV	85	584	714	167	11110	5623	9294	6634	96126
42	49	MINRL CHEM	0	0	43	80	69	304	74	74	1128
43	50	BASIC CHEM	56	1053	1768	695	13340	10494	8080	831	75352
44	51	ANIL DYE PR			0	0	397	187	3821	72	1077
45	52	SYN R& PLAST	198	982	723	24	8090	10831	2457	549	180025

Index	Code	Name									
46	53	SYN FIBERS	0	0	0	0	627	173	0	0	12523
47	55	ORGSYN PROD	42	772	463	53	2418	6242	4303	265	18984
48	56	PAINT & LAC	249	4781	3762	784	22647	37219	29392	236	68335
49	57	RUBBER PROD	434	22832	37569	1405	18463	485785	189501	2339	356075
50	54.58.59	OTHER CHEM	8	70	49	10	2641	320	488	35	5685
51	60	LOGGNG	108	534	518	118	4497	3284	2329	140	8462
52	61.62	SAW & LUM PR	799	6905	3661	1922	41805	39917	58119	3580	137435
53	63	FURNITURE	16	304	290	56	6889	1794	1557	457	8037
54	64	OTHER WDWK	1	218	100	10	266	1012	543	366	16098
55	65	PAPER & PULP	98	562	528	120	2124	9543	5283	2037	102098
56	66	WOOD CHEM	10	126	64	27	792	417	575	64	15242
57	67-73	CONST MAT	51	1073	1268	613	14185	5499	3082	346	50129
58	74	GLASS	84	581	525	67	7240	14930	2450	72	3153
59	75-80	TEXTLS	241	1726	1913	1228	21458	35298	15149	2511	143107
60	81	SEWN GOODS	100	1994	2053	672	22141	13580	13813	1652	57006
61	82	OTH LT IND	98	693	559	161	5104	18178	7456	602	36440
62	83	FISH PROD	0	0	0	0	3	5	0	16	12
63	84	MEAT PROD	3	30	36	18	172	217	59	16	805
64	85	DAIRY PROD	589	329	572	297	24894	2285	5905	105	24917
65	86	SUGAR	0	0	0	0	0	1	283	0	33
66	87-89	FLOUR&BREAD	0	0	0	15	30	11	9	1	88
67	90-94	OTHER FOOD	35	266	207	70	3067	2909	1529	349	9862
68	95	IND NEC	0	2776	4821	834	10592	23764	24456	0	38930
69	96-100	CONST	0	0	0	0	0	0	0	0	0
70	101	CROPS	0	0	0	0	44	73	99	0	0
71	102	ANIMAL HUSB	0	0	0	0	11	34	120	0	0
72	103	FOREST	0	0	0	0	0	0	0	0	0
73	104-106	TRANS &COM	825	25663	32521	6324	104848	169301	174345	13590	428473
74	107-109	TRADE & DIST	218	5000	5826	1562	23163	33082	37594	3986	84365
75	110	OTHER BRANCH	162	1443	3672	677	2659	6035	14897	0	5903
76		TOTAL PURCH	15317	492627	608094	120843	2363202	3104577	3151366	243241	9403751
77		DEPRECIATION	3029	26773	27338	15012	155838	146862	189025	30288	1049895
78		WAGES	13930	115787	132145	42557	534459	691142	833384	145692	4867007
79		OTH NET INC	15838	154097	177108	50845	868217	340528	514412	31550	-1949027
80		NATIONAL INC	29768	309884	309253	93402	1402676	1031670	1347796	177242	2917980
81		TOTAL OUTLAY	48114	829284	944685	229257	3921716	4283109	4688187	450771	13371626
82		EMPLOYMENT	10.9	90.6	103.4	33.3	418.2	540.8	652.1	114.0	3808.3
83		TOTL CAPITAL	39857	352273	359714	197530	2050497	1932390	2487177	398526	13814412
84		BLDGS&STRUCT	20135	194490	196368	114192	1300253	865615	1124204	142632	9033188
85		POWER M&E	654	3805	7986	1501	27680	44252	50738	2511	428864
86		GENERAL M&E	15133	119596	124209	63782	484208	870543	1109778	232979	2485855
87		SPECIAL M&E	3201	2604	24857	12642	186079	98937	163160	11837	792999
88		TRANS M&E	68	3029	2122	2035	11507	12367	15420	1633	90628
89		OTH CAPITAL	666	5249	4172	3378	39590	20676	23877	6934	182878

(Table 5.1 continued)

SEQ NO.	110 ORDER NO.		SANIT ENG PR 37	OTHER METWRS 38	METAL STRUCT 39	REPAIR 40	ABRASV 41	MINRL CHEM 42	BASIC CHEM 43	ANIL DYE PR 44	SYN R& PLAST 45
1	1	FER ORES	6039	2493	6919	16700	438	61	2521	179	10
2	2	FER METALS	266963	560149	422757	498751	6460	4412	72959	3037	3429
3	6	NONFER ORES	0	0	0	0	0	0	0	0	0
4	7	NONFER METAL	69089	244655	4860	103053	24392	571	48138	1166	4897
5	3	COKE PROD	25292	9373	1136	24092	267	56	167315	27480	15302
6	4	REFRAC MAT	2251	1147	115	8960	202	5289	1159	82	4
7	5	INDMET PROD	9319	65181	10528	53558	410	4042	6347	259	2013
8	8	COAL	5157	11497	1765	65157	1875	0	27215	1051	2758
9	9	OIL EXTRAC	0	0	0	0	0	0	1690	0	0
10	10	OIL REF	2475	4533	1585	45607	1773	8562	23635	1364	12383
11	11	GAS	3479	2051	1233	10360	708	2253	34336	1552	1310
12	12	PEAT	0	127	40	29	86	0	1	1	38
13	13	OIL SHALES	450	707	6	1699	6	0	975	782	72
14	14	ELEC POWER	26763	55370	17918	151404	16082	29670	442741	12639	47216
15	15	EN&POW M&E	433	1661	80	97220	4	22	218	0	2
16	16	ELTECH M&E	6911	18206	2823	143601	864	1456	5170	252	847
17	17	CABLE PROD	656	2311	1227	41742	154	1250	1856	111	236
18	20	MACH TOOLS	250	1014	143	11038	5	27	94	5	3
19	21	FORG- PR M&E	48	1056	80	1366	13	20	35	0	69
20	22	CAST M&E	964	133	0	326	0	7	10	0	5
21	23	TOOLS & DIES	1209	4717	952	19966	321	167	2055	130	341
22	24	PRECIS INST	1210	1609	60	27615	76	140	1485	95	398
23	25.26.27	MI&MET M&E	351	3133	24	35945	49	1951	319	0	0
24	28.29	PUMPS&CHEM E	755	445	0	24023	0	499	6949	584	1664
25	30	LOG&PA M&E	0	3	0	6	0	0	0	0	0
26	31	LT IND M&E	0	1697	0	643	0	0	4	0	0
27	32	FD IND M&E	0	82	0	5850	0	0	0	0	0
28	33	PRINT M&E	0	3	0	44	0	0	0	0	0
29	34	HOIST&TRAN E	12	115	229	5032	4	139	159	4	1
30	35	CONST M&E	0	13	6	73607	6	404	191	0	0
31	36	CONMAT M&E	2		4	313			13		0
32	37.38	TRANS M&E	3	420	2	1317794	0	52	143	0	1
33	39	AUTOS	492	6003	337	307995	0	251	1217	8	128
34	40	AGRIC M&E	314	6437	1323	683970	57	1491	199	54	4
35	41	BEAR&G	433	1629	528	50033	25	497	475	0	60
36	18.19.42.43	RADIO&OTH MB	19701	7666	4301	287189	152	181	214198	25	4935
37	44	SANIT ENG PR	128158	5437	3911	7597	0	108	423	36	86
38	45	OTHER METWRS	6856	77704	2553	60884	65	524	7040	419	1532
39	46	METAL STRUCT	13	129	5913	52233	1710	72	1	0	0
40	47	REPAIR	2442	6228	1614	39893	873	1635	16544	1792	4287
41	48	ABRASV	1300	5906	226	18047	101658	39	377	51	176
42	49	MINRL CHEM	350	1035	88	21142	551	6008	251005	761	236
43	50	BASIC CHEM	11446	9051	2350	286	2025	20640	292285	27023	34082
44	51	ANIL DYE PR	126	118	25			25	3503	64718	1745
45	52	SYN R& PLAST	2970	7744	109	10687	5399	212	3296	250	93387

Table of numeric data (row labels with sector codes and nine value columns):

#	Code	Label	1	2	3	4	5	6	7	8	9
46	53	SYN FIBERS	0	0	0	0	0	0	0	0	0
47	55	ORGSYN PROD	218	1796	341	6250	1374	7572	63594	24617	291707
48	56	PAINT & LAC	10903	14402	3422	55116	222	292	5338	322	2338
49	57	RUBBER PROD	6554	26356	1108	66620	290	2887	10877	491	3623
50	54,58,59	OTHER CHEM	46	1149	13	2047	33	142	160	106	98
51	60	LOGGNG	444	752	138	10248	50	1137	1908	87	218
52	61,62	SAW & LUM PR	10664	37766	992	115048	795	980	38362	2473	12057
53	63	FURNITURE	262	2004	178	1512	49	104	623	116	180
54	64	OTHER WDWK	62	5647	32	1640	302	73	805	58	380
55	65	PAPER & PULP	1888	24710	126	6487	1028	756	35146	255	13835
56	66	WOOD CHEM	115	278	34	2543	30	1004	9882	491	42608
57	67-73	CONST MAT	2087	3446	746	20893	964	657	7989	430	672
58	74	GLASS	3998	11324	177	7355	209	984	3487	105	10293
59	75-80	TEXTLS	4589	26529	418	59046	7491	1259	15882	2167	41223
60	81	SEWN GOODS	4203	15612	3084	22893	791	1574	11826	1473	2858
61	82	OTH LT IND	1390	21546	487	15564	158	505	1853	303	732
62	83	FISH PROD	0	4	0	41	6	2	316	395	550
63	84	MEAT PROD	39	243	0	396	894	304	5182	1447	521
64	85	DAIRY PROD	574	3427	375	11058	417	1763	10287	939	2574
65	86	SUGAR	0	0	0	24	0	0	29	0	0
66	87-89	FLOUR&BREAD	2	5	0	42	0	0	19	0	1
67	90-94	OTHER FOOD	818	2380	802	5640	707	576	10637	4118	6527
68	95	IND NEC	3196	26699	1588	62150		2620	79960	937	5326
69	96-100	CONST	0	0	35	509	0	13	181	0	0
70	101	CROPS	44	866			13				
71	102	ANIMAL HUSB	0	40	0	241	0	0	68	0	0
72	103	FOREST	33804	71816	31651	216609	12120	9374	135408	9568	37158
73	104-106	TRANS &COM	8682	22601	8919	42768	1236	1874	15885	1167	5790
74	107-109	TRADE & DIST	836	2621	0	13298	13	90	0	0	14
75	110	OTHER BRANCH									
76		TOTAL PURCH	700100	1453060	552436	3885573	195383	129295	2104000	197974	714943
77		DEPRECIATION	40425	79361	38421	470850	14301	67220	290522	18483	43383
78		WAGES	192339	618296	123199	2557789	70290	74976	420684	29832	85404
79		OTH NET INC	275808	1126347	215381	1940149	92869	274373	419111	57508	38108
80		NATIONAL INC	468147	1744643	338580	4497938	163159	349349	839795	87340	123512
81		TOTAL OUTLAY	1208672	3277554	929437	8854361	372843	545864	3234317	303797	881838
82		EMPLOYMENT	150.5	483.8	96.4	2001.4	55.0	56.8	318.7	22.6	64.7
83		TOTL CAPITAL	531902	1050798	505541	6195397	188172	884637	4046296	276176	551656
84		BLDGS&STRUCT	318024	567642	317783	3945440	118285	616503	2316908	178630	313451
85		POWER M&E	9096	19545	9302	142494	3462	12650	53816	7650	4579
86		GENERAL M&E	161006	378286	120471	1450130	44842	36000	330177	13919	42919
87		SPECIAL M&E	34893	59476	48330	381019	17989	181174	1284296	72690	182157
88		TRANS M&E	3245	9772	4296	157363	1600	34679	38844	1574	5681
89		OTH CAPITAL	5638	16077	5359	118951	1994	2831	22255	1713	2869

(Table 5.1 continued)

SEQ NO.	110 ORDER NO.		SYN FIBERS 46	ORGSYN PROD 47	PAINT & LAC 48	RUBBER PROD 49	OTHER CHEM 50	LOGGNG 51	SAW & LUM PR 52	FURNIT URE 53	OTHER WDWK 54
1	1	FER ORES	282	1683	1453	1773	185	0	0	0	4
2	2	FER METALS	4917	18041	4483	14532	6035	5278	35365	3916	1981
3	6	NONFER ORES	0	0		0		0	0	0	0
4	7	NONFER METAL	390	24019	97384	836	11977	1485	5180	896	498
5	3	COKE PROD	324	206640	41249	37	39152	95	127071	86	0
6	4	REFRAC MAT	130	775	668	34799	85		469	100	1
7	5	INDMET PROD	576	1300	628	4610	833	22100	23034	34581	882
8	8	COAL	5390	21926	2711	255	3461	5866	28252	13481	1497
9	9	OIL EXTRAC	0	13185						0	0
10	10	OIL REF	2423	70886	11100	10057	58088	89019	15911	3647	2347
11	11	GAS	888	26624	1409	2752	4018	0	3904	3207	271
12	12	PEAT	510	6	6	381	231	0	330	214	897
13	13	OIL SHALES	5	48			251	1029	4887	669	149
14	14	ELEC POWER	89793	134808	1169	87385	116743	19504	103359	32550	4576
15	15	ENSPOW M&E	0	73	9764	2050	40	1616	221	24	0
16	16	ELTECH M&E	1822	1683	348	802	2806	1903	5208	1693	372
17	17	CABLE PROD	308	476	113	50	225	2326	2625	709	78
18	20	MACH TOOLS	670	6		46	6	829	5835	1552	49
19	21	FORG- PR M&E	2	0		46	194	150	3	16	0
20	22	CAST M&E	0	0			2	11	0	0	0
21	23	TOOLS & DIES	220	179	187	1343	288	4749	2156	1447	100
22	24	PRECIS INST	415	704	82	476	612	290	305	109	0
23	25,26,27	MI&MET M&E	0	176		762				0	34
24	28,29	PUMPS&CHEM E	4013	1699	185	4817	1303	60	312	20	0
25	30	LOG&PA M&E	0	2		4		24780	2819	105	113
26	31	LT IND M&E	11582				4			14	0
27	32	FD IND M&E	0			328	20			0	0
28	33	PRINT M&E	0	8	17		0		0	21	0
29	34	HOIST&TRAN E	9	3	3	120	14	1679	764	37	0
30	35	CONST M&E	1	0			1	1191	27	0	0
31	36	CONMAT M&E	0	0	0	0	0	103	19	66	0
32	37,38	TRANS M&E	7	2	0	92	10	5973	4889	10	260
33	39	AUTOS	152	252	106	779	190	50335	2392	770	215
34	40	AGRIC M&E	28	70	12	143	442	44248	1680	206	42
35	41	BEARNG	296	152	63	300	79	2243	3249	195	218
36	18,19,42,43	RADIO&OTH MB	3582	8125	3890	14000	39543	1309	1729	1063	84
37	44	SANIT ENG PR	118	196	120	231	138	75		541	
38	45	OTHER METWRS	1818	5176	11721	11239	2064	11287	30461	76445	1825
39	46	METAL STRUCT	0	0	0	0	0	17	12665	1277	
40	47	REPAIR	2645	7547	2617	6491	3599	13152	13238	4835	1170
41	48	ABRASV CHEM	52	627	89	298	103	683	2259	12403	1329
42	49	MINRL CHEM	3368	3459	12454	4772	3760	12		9	164
43	50	BASIC CHEM	72879	95942	23553	28876	136391	744	12661	1727	6265
44	51	ANIL DYE PR	7551	3397	19607	3255	4717	50	396	3457	0
45	52	SYN R& PLAST	135712	4667	43427	8081	5326	6	39796	31555	859

Code	Sector	(1)	(2)	(3)	(4)	(5)	(6)	(7)	(8)	(9)
53	SYN FIBERS	0	0	0	218266	142459	0	1804801	0	18
55	ORGSYN PROD	10165	141114	126666	143512	32181	141	1011626	13034	693
56	PAINT & LAC	1641	10277	167999	14441	38427	1589	799	77309	4415
57	RUBBER PROD	2828	1894	722	74442	223202	36053	2988	8331	2358
54,58,59	OTHER CHEM	87	1965	215	680064	0	336	4446	2511	50
60	LOGGNG	67	1472	488	168	196447	109	5561	44781	36045
61,62	SAW & LUM PR	747	10445	8581	5822	22616	4105	9413	470044	60830
63	FURNITURE	230	452	153	408	1311	252	6759	25307	12
64	OTHER WDWK	112	578	247	366	2383	1881	17845	5245	12026
65	PAPER & PULP	145348	17847	5958	3304	291	15628	16248	4972	7645
66	WOOD CHEM	1137	20069	52722	9621	666	140007	0	1696	512
67-73	CONST MAT	608	1179	812	1073	4570	759	0	2073	176
74	GLASS	452	8891	7769	769	460	20308	0	62169	114
75-80	TEXTLS	20256	5047	1244	423139	8462	56345	0	246359	4360
81	SEWN GOODS	1787	5691	1538	7450	38540	5131	0	6076	871
82	OTH LT IND	579	1058	451	1313	720	10829	4731	8961	3207
83	FISH PROD	0	96	790	6	11220	0	0	41	0
84	MEAT PROD	271	2333	1700	567	9273	15	7334	5006	3553
85	DAIRY PROD	1928	2857	3317	3776	7849	186	12835	4236	181
86	SUGAR	256	8122	221	44	12477	4	0	18	0
87-89	FLOUR&BREAD	666	3793	350455	10655	4117	3	3238	1182	955
90-94	OTHER FOOD	1780	27188	11272	8195	89417	649	16800	24448	221
95	IND NEC	0	2910	0	0	31790	2487	1238	341	699
96-100	CONST	0	0	578	0	0	0	0	0	0
101	CROPS	0	504	0	0	24157	7285	0	0	0
102	ANIMAL HUSB	0	326	103	0	9912	152	120	0	0
103	FOREST	0	0	0	0	78598	395715	0	0	0
104-106	TRANS &COM	34255	81392	49173	106026	42025	113160	703291	83192	20533
107-109	TRADE & DIST	9014	16353	13673	105163	6522	17257	50437	19566	3160
110	OTHER BRANCH	12	0	0	430	0	0	0	367	34
	TOTAL PURCH	587104	1028817	1097485	2073847	1451813	1177811	4214560	1351682	188949
	DEPRECIATION	76904	89603	15559	62016	76888	419004	205812	79662	12418
	WAGES	141768	114312	61776	269148	184272	1649202	1129652	457331	88134
	OTH NET INC	172747	472288	212289	1178229	263372	933567	1655336	-24946	7599
	NATIONAL INC	314515	586600	274065	1447377	447644	2582849	2784988	432385	95733
	TOTAL OUTLAY	978523	1705020	1387109	3583240	1976345	4179664	7205360	1863729	297100
	EMPLOYMENT	107.4	86.6	46.8	203.9	139.6	1170.7	1003.3	406.3	78.3
	TOTL CAPITAL	1091004	1184659	217041	883048	1150383	2831109	2638615	813630	127070
	BLDGS&STRUCT	577469	669827	142075	462036	683778	1505300	1672870	550989	66941
	POWER M&E	8292	21561	1671	8486	49971	56339	118489	18958	1919
	GENERAL M&E	33712	74515	12849	52241	57677	90904	559690	197305	31375
	SPECIAL M&E	464440	385251	55345	346418	342308	774568	196543	26037	20940
	TRANS M&E	1309	7335	1883	3448	9040	344262	65971	7404	3265
	OTH CAPITAL	5782	6160	3213	10519	13609	59736	25052	12937	2630

(Table 5.1 continued)

SEQ NO.	110 ORDER NO.		PAPER & PULP 55	WOOD CHEM 56	CONST MAT 57	GLASS 58	TEXTILS 59	SEWN GOODS 60	OTH LT IND 61	FISH PROD 62	MEAT PROD 63
1	1	FER ORES	572	0	42825	22882	42	6	222	136	136
2	2	FER METALS	4204	958	638466	21619	9606	670	6179	61606	60183
3	6	NONFER ORES	7660	769	69686		0	0	0	0	0
4	7	NONFER METAL	215	256	40852	2781	3845	206	13803	2904	3785
5	3	COKE PROD	262	60	16508	12146	639	3	581	90	8
6	4	REFRAC MAT	3532	341	112358	5860	278	625	101	63	63
7	5	INDMET PROD	82496	15104	299506	9675	13792	5470	7681	12538	1513
8	8	COAL					31124		12408	12215	17452
9	9	OIL EXTRAC	0	0	0	0	0	0	0	0	0
10	10	OIL REF	7383	1750	131278	14497	12862	1404	9095	119478	4640
11	11	GAS	3831	1934	108554	18148	10305	579	4866	322	4958
12	12	PEAT	3530		8022	4584	4881	382	1252	104	209
13	13	OIL SHALES	997	376	17919	5458	1852	148	620	1435	382
14	14	ELEC POWER	81892	11064	443733	33157	92083	14959	19929	5231	15493
15	15	EN&POW M&E	226	133	1767	43	595	35	28	6795	86
16	16	ELTECH M&E	1769	264	18587	2361	12661	2580	2977	3291	1540
17	17	CABLE PROD	620	142	10099	683	3054	606	770	3704	744
18	20	MACH TOOLS	22	19	927	110	190	118	202	4	32
19	21	FORG- PR M&E	1		578	1	16	5	179	15	10
20	22	CAST M&E	12		68	63	28	0		0	2
21	23	TOOLS & DIES	610	76	8045	759	2797	1570	2619	4398	848
22	24	PRECIS INST	457	83	1878	1690	914	113	286	808	291
23	25,26,27	MI&MET M&E	26	233	6238	0	0			0	0
24	28,29	PUMPS&CHEM E	347	44	1205	618	202	12	1503	905	439
25	30	LOG&PA M&E	3400		57	22	5			5	5
26	31	LT IND M&E	2			535	72061	5306	7436	11	11
27	32	FD I&D M&E				19	0	35		7547	2449
28	33	PRINT M&E	18			0	0		3		
29	34	HOIST&TRAN E	145	19	3635	110	173	0	70	0	0
30	35	CONST M&E	8	2	12582	49	3	0	2	2203	83
31	36	CONMAT M&E	0	1	58246	280	25	0	1	0	0
32	37,38	TRANS M&E	70	16	1528	35	17		25	1296	5
33	39	AUTOS	511	166	15610	777	1505	912	522	2367	982
34	40	AGRIC M&E	110	51	8371	202	477		312	264	79
35	41	BEARNG	427	43	4344	311	1518	82	272	157	171
36	18,19,42,43	RADIO&OTH MB	1344	210	2913	231	2166	428	522	1955	868
37	44	SANIT ENG PR	201	36	11854	9366	1222	198	451	153	321
38	45	OTHER METWRS	1856	308	39972	3381	20018	14376	32360	42178	7063
39	46	METAL STRUCT	18	0	1693	64	119		29	0	58
40	47	REPAIR	5746	999	49785	13181	13756	4877	6699	64420	6107
41	48	ABRASV	336	20	1353	3462	818	123	2072	80	77
42	49	MINRL CHEM	18461	233	7608	11284	294		2621	8	82
43	50	BASIC CHEM	25413	8115	31130	45508	31713	166	24178	5213	3200
44	51	ANIL DYE PR	2028	3	1052	1174	94029	186	18799	13	29
45	52	SYN R& PLAST	917	247	19088	15987	7712	5400	24044	390	2326

Code	Code	Branch									
46	53	SYN FIBERS	0	0	0	0	782507	0	39	1473	0
47	55	ORGSYN PROD	2473	11447	42902	488	30129	183	79631	486	701
48	55	PAINT & LAC	997	176	7266	3623	5734	1300	10831	4108	1517
49	57	RUBBER PROD	1885	403	49186	2135	29382	12110	37098	5377	1445
50	54.58.59	OTHER CHEM	492	199	1519	504	2136	1121	82114	725	567
51	60	LOGGNG	279637	129694	16417	10202	4210	1032	30055	2358	3147
52	61.62	SAW & LUM PR	6583	16591	107646	36564	21406	3480	22561	179619	29967
53	63	FURNITURE	326	41	2849	524	2324	2264	1169	318	643
54	64	OTHER WDWK	186	86	3040	2974	9699	348	2289	3069	2245
55	65	PAPER & PULP	251220	290	64900	7606	28535	5914	27651	9934	9651
56	66	WOOD CHEM	21036	32492	4184	413	4284	47	11819	309	386
57	67-73	CONST MAT	3721	1301	1468790	12440	5668	1082	2570	2646	2577
58	74	GLASS	1656	359	32860	26789	3795	257	1692	3324	843
59	75-80	TEXTLS	35984	440	36522	8092	14201988	5686548	713002	155673	7758
60	81	SEWN GOODS	2360	697	42312	5635	17851	11828	8354	28811	7581
61	82	OTH LT IND	2316	305	14029	1117	21106	233471	2550470	12150	2334
62	83	FISH PROD	164	1035	177	3	1347	4	7627	1975676	1297
63	84	MEAT PROD	1466	200	193	42	1651	31	601210	1036	3544480
64	85	DAIRY PROD	7005	283	12461	1005	5162	54	8455	297	5480
65	86	SUGAR	5	371	2	2	23	1	1379	5086	2217
66	87-89	FLOUR&BREAD	2040	5	22	19	2103	592	187	2415	17525
67	90-94	OTHER FOOD	3310	678	44644	695	27875	4461	14660	98437	20770
68	95	IND NEC	95	1151	106797	11913	87488		23540	674	6977
69	96-100	CONST	0	0	0	0	0		0	0	0
70	101	CROPS	935	430	1067	223	4198344	312	1531	5308	10774
71	102	ANIMAL HUSB	0	63	83	0	2110087	0	597880	1129	16346495
72	103	FOREST	140904	52233	851719	50386	295868	54373	81698	135823	0
73	104-106	TRANS &COM	22151	2658	67377	6126	204484	8643	37244	39756	81886
74	107-109	TRADE & DIST	41488	24	20456	2028	496	275	22087	430	274915
75	110	OTHER BRANCH									10090
76		TOTAL PURCH	1092020	297794	5249340	454669	22555099	6091315	5184562	3040135	20531002
77		DEPRECIATION	120003	25070	781680	55515	274159	94881	71318	273435	72456
78		WAGES	191033	37529	2062637	328427	1796606	1390804	672767	620791	330831
79		OTH NET INC	401316	126680	2220697	243848	4461660	2312028	198056	385367	-7851864
80		NATIONAL INC	592349	164209	4283334	572275	6258466	3702832	870823	1006158	-7513033
81		TOTAL OUTLAY	1804372	487073	10314354	1082459	29087724	9889028	6126703	4319728	13090425
82		EMPLOYMENT	149.9	29.7	1648.0	284.5	1786.8	1523.0	658.8	285.5	326.1
83		TOTL CAPITAL	1621664	256071	9894681	750204	4153929	1416135	1033592	3255183	1317378
84		BLDGS&STRUCT	784723	140634	6224602	425441	1748866	942177	552243	614904	1015185
85		POWER M&E	88667	23559	132073	11853	59095	15401	15401	19531	16072
86		GENERAL M&E	55656	16337	412168	143514	116756	37103	37107	243246	24504
87		SPECIAL M&E	676093	71855	2889370	159966	2173796	351604	404448	112546	226840
88		TRANS M&E	-12325	2355	111567	6452	13777	20534	4651	2240217	20418
89		OTH CAPITAL	4000	1331	124901	9978	41639	57920	19742	24739	14359

(Table 5.1 continued)

SEQ NO.	110 ORDER NO.		DAIRY PROD 64	SUGAR 65	FLOUR& BREAD 66	OTHER FOOD 67	IND NEC 68	CONST 69	CROPS 70	ANIMAL HUSB 71	FOREST 72
1	1	FER ORES	211	3521	113	532	3658	0	0	0	0
2	2	FER METALS	39281	7326	6106	58176	131254	2111125	17321	14895	367
3	6	NONFER ORES	0	0	0	0	0	0	0	0	0
4	7	NONFER METAL	8743	0	4025	11492	51546	139591	4257	1656	131
5	3	COKE PROD	12	15204	154	133	15915	0	0	0	0
6	4	REFRAC MAT	97	1076	387	244	1706	174699	0	0	0
7	5	INDMET PROD	1531	1734	3739	6682	15575	219067	15516	11072	442
8	8	COAL	36161	43130	56537	51383	74840	87455	65166	9261	175
9	9	OIL EXTRAC	1	0	0	0	1738	1244	0	0	0
10	10	OIL REF	10595	40746	7364	37855	28219	341294	581735	168342	5942
11	11	GAS	2888	6844	11487	10756	4679	5967	0	0	0
12	12	PEAT	1131	2406	2274	1249	1239	5762	73987	11709	0
13	13	OIL SHALES	1072	996	473	3934	2666	7624	0	0	0
14	14	ELEC POWER	18361	10289	28018	36885	147814	333795	89015	102167	1259
15	15	ENSPOW M&E	203	103	83	464	5417	20994	0	0	0
16	16	ELTECH M&E	1582	1397	3230	4092	19192	406868	12973	11558	0
17	17	CABLE PROD	619	1002	1190	1797	4114	483945	5380	5208	0
18	20	MACH TOOLS	1	15	27	81	718	4726	0	0	0
19	21	FORG- PR M&E	1	23	0	116	132	0	0	0	0
20	22	CAST M&E	0	3	10	14	80	0	0	0	0
21	23	TOOLS & DIES	1056	689	1577	1365	1935	47747	14226	11973	353
22	24	PRECIS INST	402	473	516	564	3198	39380	2424	1651	0
23	25,26,27	MI&MET M&E	0	0	0	0	1121	110788	0	0	0
24	28,29	PUMPS&CHEM E	603	272	138	607	2836	10752	0	0	0
25	30	LOG&PA M&E	0	0	0	11	414	0	0	0	0
26	31	LT IND M&E	5	5	7	0	405	0	0	0	0
27	32	FD IND M&E	352	3752	8844	6264	126	0	0	0	0
28	33	PRINT M&E	7385	0	88	74	8979	0	0	0	0
29	34	HOIST&TRAN E	26	113	554	157	914	30549	0	0	0
30	35	CONST M&E	0	4	0	0	1288	94595	0	0	0
31	36	CONMAT M&E	218	0	0	2	770	7018	0	0	0
32	37,38	TRANS M&E	10	59	9	89	2725	8807	0	0	0
33	39	AUTOS	3796	1290	418	2207	18325	108701	138683	52137	6867
34	40	AGRIC M&E	161	2129	67	481	22396	62527	542721	119941	4534
35	41	BEARING	165	418	360	388	3202	5381	10315	2411	0
36	18,19,42,43	RADIO&OTH MB	947	900	1770	2194	4863	149969	10377	8856	0
37	44	SANIT ENG PR	276	97	549	512	2200	861899	0	0	0
38	45	OTHER METWRS	9270	1995	11836	66047	6930	385648	122249	93358	1227
39	46	METAL STRUCT	1085	7	66	87	1019	799569	0	0	0
40	47	REPAIR	8873	5845	11043	18517	3049	215076	375603	174989	0
41	48	ABRASV	86	89	77	204	3290	9987	4358	1527	0
42	49	MINRL CHEM	17	2043	127	487	18144	0	0	86919	0
43	50	BASIC CHEM	4620	3551	1484	45145	53124	42659	743657	19457	1145
44	51	ANIL DYE PR	104	145	89	635	6745	8193	0	0	0
45	52	SYN R& PLAST	478	188	563	4727	138265	12435	0	0	0

#	Code	Sector									
46	53	SYN FIBERS	0	0	0	0	12837	1112	0	0	0
47	55	ORGSYN PROD	283	274	405	53913	54735	43178	14094	2376	0
48	56	PAINT & LAC	1579	1387	2308	5836	33117	413489	7054	5829	0
49	57	RUBBER & LAC	2817	2159	5408	5655	27997	145905	161741	58016	0
50	54.58.59	OTHER CHEM	837	43	1059	3351	13339	0	7143	101381	0
51	60	LOGGNG	4339	926	2180	2840	144	550598	25179	45351	3096
52	61.62	SAW & LUM PR	27110	3440	88354	141345	86478	2796344	66897	100564	1742
53	63	FURNITURE	364	124	852	940	103777	10370	2018	1356	
54	64	OTHER WDWK	1040	72	2611	13398	19293		8176	8137	34
55	65	PAPER & PULP	18003	5191	44736	99059	252452	23744	3067	1979	0
56	66	WOOD CHEM	196	68	1523	15764	2850	4605	2624	9320	0
57	67-73	CONST MAT	2638	16903	3283	6282	34153	7890742	54923	84184	901
58	74	GLASS	8051	220	566	68802	5564	382805	6500	9629	0
59	75-80	TEXTLS	7529	13381	16400	243233	256234	194256	94637	43361	0
60	81	SEWN GOODS	6210	4671	27163	14196	61039	334531	33436	63199	2879
61	82	OTH LT IND	2092	1439	3913	3377	29049	43281	27941	41781	0
62	83	FISH PROD	143	36	7874	43933	858	0	356	89102	0
63	84	MEAT PROD	1931	647	25339	206434	2493	0	1614	66134	0
64	85	DAIRY PROD	660649	182	209520	51905	8770	0	0	155595	0
65	86	SUGAR	148836	934084	707728	579910	1235	0	0	109014	0
66	87-89	FLOUR&BREAD	-4084	0	2283508	77193	251249	1240	0	306130	0
67	90-94	OTHER FOOD	-5755	1152	603260	5259251	25271	140038	6472	116573	0
68	95	IND NEC	32043	32864	57724	162885	59647	570706	8713	617239	940
69	96-100	CONST	0	0	0	0	0	0	0	0	
70	101	CROPS	4006	2182100	5776287	3823572	584339	23068	3801852	12201288	1417
71	102	ANIMAL HUSB	7575355	0	67835	6819	0	7815	326463	2248000	0
72	103	FOREST	0	82336	0	0	140129	3776247	0	0	26510
73	104-106	TRANS &COM	31069	107107	246377	346092	72470	314743	446518	422486	4704
74	107-109	TRADE & DIST	139204	13	314708	302702	53126	476723	257597	581513	1103
75	110	OTHER BRANCH	27		1125	20914			36679	1519	0
76		TOTAL PURCH	8898859	3550698	10665445	11936250	3009410	25511376	8231657	18498703	65768
77		DEPRECIATION	114744	130072	137617	230345	458384	1837900	2833510	1944575	2015
78		WAGES	-303945	150749	796243	885250	1029115	17030000	19961322	18779304	409374
79		OTH NET INC	-1447001	-541080	1380792	5824717	1678271	5646438	12140287	11849427	427787
80		NATIONAL INC	-1143056	-390331	2177035	6709967	2707386	22676438	32001609	30628731	837161
81		TOTAL OUTLAY	7870547	3293433	12930097	18876562	6175180	50025714	43066776	51072009	904944
82		EMPLOYMENT	308.7	154.9	308.7	899.1	970.0	9450.0	16183.1	17189.4	427.5
83		TOTL CAPITAL	1365997	1646475	2074742	3472682	6067904	11838000	34858600	32251400	21480
84		BLDGS&STRUCT	824158	880007	1358417	2040494	3455527	3779992	16227389	15013726	9011
85		POWER M&E	40843	140444	32069	83295	196459	153065	286537	265107	154
86		GENERAL M&E	29803	82781	44353	87545	1091898	2329467	1105365	1022693	7466
87		SPECIAL M&E	418329	513606	605593	1190682	506895	4569350	10831922	2803488	2136
88		TRANS M&E	31565	15477	10493	25996	671495	696444	1137400	1052232	570
89		OTH CAPITAL	15299	14160	23017	44670	145630	309682	5269987	12094054	2143

(Table 5.1 continued)

SEQ NO.	110 ORDER NO.		TRANS &COM 73	TRADE & DIST 74	OTHER BRANCH 75	INT IND USE 76	PRIVAT CONSUM 77	PUBLIC CONSUM 78	OTHER FD 79	TOTAL FD 80	GVO 81
1	1	FER ORES	0	0	0	1636990	0	0	218320	218320	1855310
2	6	FER METALS	54708	9233	293	12977356	3370	303109	1140241	1446720	14424076
3	6	NONFER ORES	0	0	0	1432491	0	0	-285970	-285970	1146521
4	7	NONFER METAL	22815	3890	176	6443179	0	285887	374728	660615	7103794
5	3	COKE PROD	0	0	0	2509086	0	0	232683	232683	2741769
6	4	REFRAC MAT	0	0	0	415378	0	0	34578	34578	449956
7	5	INDMET PROD	53083	15171	1696	1381243	6715	38207	58491	103413	1484656
8	8	COAL	302792	74219	1578	7637215	195072	834941	280864	1310877	8940092
9	9	OIL EXTRAC	0	0	0	1436195	0	0	996639	996639	2432834
10	10	OIL REF	643821	57237	2763	3593182	84860	346643	887554	1319057	4912239
11	11	GAS	1526	36505	29	1079075	64213	33261	113114	210588	1289663
12	12	PEAT	616	5116	0	382924	0	93485	-16425	77060	459984
13	13	OIL SHALES	165	353	0	129881	0	0	5118	5118	134999
14	14	ELEC POWER	511134	172609	10269	6576923	900080	746101	24396	1670577	8247500
15	15	EN&POW M&E	2108	0	0	532152	0	0	980734	980734	1512886
16	16	ELTECH M&E	12952	29157	935	2471483	442075	168230	1551473	2161778	4633261
17	17	CABLE PROD	15663	11677	620	1153796	5253	62259	-12082	55430	1209226
18	20	MACH TOOLS	1023	0	0	76492	0	23554	819058	842612	919104
19	21	FORG- PR M&E	0	0	1130	18007	0	0	186892	186892	204899
20	22	CAST M&E	0	0	0	9480	0	0	28640	28640	38120
21	23	TOOLS & DIES	19212	6580	575	359383	0	0	169442	169442	528825
22	24	PRECIS INST	5647	6168	123	1069282	179772	80660	519995	780427	1849709
23	25,26,27	MI&MET M&E	0	0	0	493091	0	0	2176295	2176295	2669386
24	28,29	PUMPS&CHEM E	615	12995	0	313132	150820	51486	1059832	1262138	1575270
25	30	LOG&PA M&E	5143	0	0	40791	0	0	88835	88835	129626
26	31	LT IND M&E	0	0	0	120281	37383	0	314545	351928	472209
27	32	FD IND M&E	0	789	0	52343	0	0	305229	305229	357572
28	33	PRINT M&E	0	0	0	9414	0	0	36700	36700	46114
29	34	HOIST&TRAN E	16159	15110	246	150896	0	0	678388	678388	829284
30	35	CONST M&E	1006	87	0	216378	0	0	728307	728307	944685
31	36	CONMAT M&E	133068	0	0	76121	0	0	153136	153136	229257
32	37,38	TRANS M&E	253097	19000	2642	385610	0	42452	3493654	3536106	3921716
33	39	AUTOS	10580	1871	0	2316445	547371	183450	1235843	1966664	4283109
34	40	AGRIC M&E	9884	3224	11	2787989	0	0	1900198	1900198	4688187
35	41	BEARNG	47787	13445	0	345152	0	7400	98219	105619	450771
36	18,19,42,43	RADIO&OTH MB	0	3506	70	5791154	1082862	307602	6183008	7573422	13371626
37	44	SANIT ENG PR	22753	0	1158	1079553	0	66411	62708	129119	1208672
38	45	OTHER METWKS	0	78342	0	1817938	788475	235070	436081	1459626	3277564
39	46	METAL STRUCT	135450	0	0	896384	0	0	33053	33053	929437
40	47	REPAIR	0	0	0	1600223	0	30138	7224000	7254138	8854361
41	48	ABRASV	1182	235	22	420646	0	0	-47803	-47803	372843
42	49	MINRL CHEM	0	0	0	451664	0	0	94200	94200	545864
43	50	BASIC CHEM	16911	3272	7841	2502565	29820	75143	626789	731752	3234317
44	51	ANIL DYE PR	0	721	127	255565	4695	2146	41391	48232	303797
45	52	SYN R& PLAST	0	0	0	1054286	39503	13951	-225902	-172248	881838

220

No.	Code	Sector	(1)	(2)	(3)	(4)	(5)	(6)	(7)	(8)	(9)	(10)
46	53	SYN FIBERS	3401	0	0	7	1041212	0	0	-62689	-62689	978523
47	55	ORGSYN PROD	37858	2031		281	1454053	106585	26320	118062	250967	1705020
48	56	PAINT & LAC	482358	39287		1157	1281594	4499	150066	-49050	105515	1387109
49	57	RUBBER PROD	436	54383		2279	2746666	19857	268342	548375	836574	3583240
50	54,58,59	OTHER CHEM		1379		13749	1215111	449733	628621	-317120	761234	1976345
51	60	LOGGNG	71205	30135		298	3636695	103393	294874	144702	542969	4179664
52	61,62	SAW & LUM PR	82721	166258		-640	6390876	53743	152347	602394	814484	7205360
53	63	FURNITURE	5500	19296		2811	238792	1629873	20994	-25930	1624937	1863729
54	64	OTHER WDWK		9316		100	153226	79067	3297	61490	143874	297100
55	65	PAPER & PULP	7080	182013		197607	1725828	0	73990	4554	78544	1604372
56	66	WOOD CHEM	2440	67		14	446332	0	0	40741	40741	487073
57	67-73	CONST MAT	261137	45662		764	9883453	50642	197371	182888	430901	10314354
58	74	GLASS	5312	46830		199	8677709	122102	17509	75139	214750	1082459
59	75-80	TEXTLS	53163	95182		23868	23289863	6929270	336868	-1468277	5797861	29087724
60	81	SEWN GOODS	74395	115660		2568	1311532	8900670	358655	-681829	8577496	9889028
61	82	OTH LT IND	26711	10373		27900	3250164	3624346	46351	-794158	2876539	6126703
62	83	FISH PROD		21177		0	2164357	1772452	224652	158267	2155371	4319728
63	84	MEAT PROD		15287		26	4649155	7677663	511786	251821	8441270	13000425
64	85	DAIRY PROD		2900		0	1347581	489308	853334	777324	6522966	7870547
65	86	SUGAR		1899		0	2523901	1161582	87671	-482715	766538	3290439
66	87-89	FLOUR&BREAD	51	3154		0	3004055	9740638	422598	-187194	9976042	12980097
67	90-94	OTHER FOOD	13196	66086		177	7035787	12622588	183287	-965100	11840775	18877562
68	95	IND NEC	29802	213545		278359	3291075	2830867	468609	-415371	2884105	6175180
69	96-100	CONST				0	0	0	0	50025714	50025714	50025714
70	101	CROPS	5342	75879		0	32737120	7119952	117718	3092386	10329656	43066776
71	102	ANIMAL HUSB	0	1857		0	29301842	17269859	466427	4033881	21770167	51072009
72	103	FOREST	0	0		32701	454926	1882608	0	450018	450018	904944
73	104-106	TRANS &COM	424895	283888		23216	13946337	10322937	734530	2250022	4867160	18813497
74	107-109	TRADE & DIST	109144	45133		15263	4185429	2053421	227634	994000	11544571	15730000
75	110	OTHER BRANCH	0	83710		11361	1353244		192670	59218	230309	3658553
76		TOTAL PURCH	3767607	2430399		668649	241433728	105589414	11098107	93427952	210515472	451949200
77		DEPRECIATION	2845900	1186000		35000	22310000	5560000	4440000	0	10000000	32310000
78		WAGES	6045359	6582046		1187424	106569696					
79		OTH NET INC	6154631	5551555		1767480	81635777					
80		NATIONAL INC	12199590	12113601		2954904	188205472					
81		TOTAL OUTLAY	18613497	15720000		3658553	451949200					
82		EMPLOYMENT	4588.7	6696.6		977.5	84377.9					
83		TOTL CAPITAL	4144000	1932000		537520	296080000					
84		BLDG&STRUCT	26904173	1440569		248697	172529890					
85		POWER M&E	26017	120626		2456	8864747					
86		GENERAL M&E	4295903	1983560		90763	29976514					
87		SPECIAL M&E	715507	142781		79472	48870390					
88		TRANS M&E	9115561	435417		87239	17254616					
89		OTH CAPITAL	285739	1030039		28093	20560843					

TABLE 5.2

Matrix of Price Indexes Used to Convert the 1966 Producers' Prices Table to 1970 Prices

SEQ NO.	110 ORDER NO.		FER ORES 1	FER METALS 2	NONFER ORES 3	NONFER METAL 4	COKE PROD 5	REFRAC MAT 6	INDMET PROD 7	COAL 8	OIL EXTRAC 9
1	1	FER ORES	2.1370	2.1370	2.1370	2.1370	2.1370	2.1370	2.1370	2.1370	2.1370
2	2	FER METALS	1.4700	1.4700	1.4700	1.4700	1.4700	1.4700	1.4700	1.4700	1.4700
3	6	NONFER ORES	1.3100	1.3100	1.3100	1.3100	1.3100	1.3100	1.3100	1.3100	1.3100
4	7	NONFER METAL	1.2200	1.2200	1.2200	1.2200	1.2200	1.2200	1.2200	1.2200	1.2200
5	3	COKE PROD	2.0560	2.0560	2.0560	2.0560	2.0560	2.0560	2.0560	2.0560	2.0560
6	4	REFRAC MAT	1.5200	1.5200	1.5200	1.5200	1.5200	1.5200	1.5200	1.5200	1.5200
7	5	INDMET PROD	1.4000	1.4000	1.4000	1.4000	1.4000	1.4000	1.4000	1.4000	1.4000
8	8	COAL	1.7760	1.7760	1.7760	1.7760	1.9310	1.7760	1.7760	1.7760	1.7760
9	9	OIL EXTRAC	2.3000	2.3000	2.3000	2.3000	2.3000	2.3000	2.3000	2.3000	2.3000
10	10	OIL REF	1.4850	1.4850	1.4850	1.4850	1.4850	1.4850	1.4850	1.4850	1.4850
11	11	GAS	3.6700	3.6700	3.6700	3.6700	3.6700	3.6700	3.6700	3.6700	3.6700
12	12	PEAT	1.2180	1.2180	1.2180	1.2180	1.2180	1.2180	1.2180	1.2180	1.2180
13	13	OIL SHALES	1.1490	1.1490	1.1490	1.1490	1.1490	1.1490	1.1490	1.1490	1.1490
14	14	ELEC POWER	1.3760	1.3760	1.3760	1.3760	1.3760	1.3760	1.3760	1.3760	1.3760
15	15	EN&POW M&E	1.0500	1.0500	1.0500	1.0500	1.0500	1.0500	1.0500	1.0500	1.0500
16	16	ELTECH M&E	.9400	.9400	.9400	.9400	.9400	.9400	.9400	.9400	.9400
17	17	CABLE PROD	.9400	.9400	.9400	.9400	.9400	.9400	.9400	.9400	.9400
18	20	MACH TOOLS	1.0400	1.0400	1.0400	1.0400	1.0400	1.0400	1.0400	1.0400	1.0400
19	21	FORG- PR M&E	1.0400	1.0400	1.0400	1.0400	1.0400	1.0400	1.0400	1.0400	1.0400
20	22	CAST M&E	1.0400	1.0400	1.0400	1.0400	1.0400	1.0400	1.0400	1.0400	1.0400
21	23	TOOLS & DIES	1.0400	1.0400	1.0400	1.0400	1.0400	1.0400	1.0400	1.0400	1.0400
22	24	PRECIS INST	.8200	.8200	.8200	.8200	.8200	.8200	.8200	.8200	.8200
23	25,26,27	MI&MET M&E	1.0420	1.0420	1.0420	1.0420	1.0420	1.0420	1.0420	1.0420	1.0420
24	28,29	PUMPS&CHEM E	1.0100	1.0100	1.0100	1.0100	1.0100	1.0100	1.0100	1.0100	1.0100
25	30	LOG&PA M&E	1.0520	1.0520	1.0520	1.0520	1.0520	1.0520	1.0520	1.0520	1.0520
26	31	LT IND M&E	.9200	.9200	.9200	.9200	.9200	.9200	.9200	.9200	.9200
27	32	FD IND M&E	.9200	.9200	.9200	.9200	.9200	.9200	.9200	.9200	.9200
28	33	PRINT M&E	.9780	.9780	.9780	.9780	.9780	.9780	.9780	.9780	.9780
29	34	HOIST&TRAN E	1.0500	1.0500	1.0500	1.0500	1.0500	1.0500	1.0500	1.0500	1.0500
30	35	CONST M&E	1.0000	1.0000	1.0000	1.0000	1.0000	1.0000	1.0000	1.0000	1.0000
31	36	CONMAT M&E	1.0000	1.0000	1.0000	1.0000	1.0000	1.0000	1.0000	1.0000	1.0000
32	37,38	TRANS M&E	1.0500	1.0500	1.0500	1.0500	1.0500	1.0500	1.0500	1.0500	1.0500
33	39	AUTOS	.9800	.9800	.9800	.9800	.9800	.9800	.9800	.9800	.9800
34	40	AGRIC M&E	1.0700	1.0700	1.0700	1.0700	1.0700	1.0700	1.0700	1.0700	1.0700
35	41	BEARNG	.9800	.9800	.9800	.9800	.9800	.9800	.9800	.9800	.9800

SEQ NO.	110 ORDER NO.		FER ORES 1	FER METALS 2	NONFER ORES 3	NONFER METAL 4	COKE PROD 5	REFRAC MAT 6	INDMET PROD 7	COAL 8	OIL EXTRAC 9
36	18,19,42,43	RADIO&OTH MB	.8250	.8250	.8250	.8250	.8250	.8250	.8250	.8250	.8250
37	44	SANIT ENG PR	1.2300	1.2300	1.2300	1.2300	1.2300	1.2300	1.2300	1.2300	1.2300
38	45	OTHER METWRS	1.0780	1.0780	1.0780	1.0780	1.0780	1.0780	1.0780	1.0780	1.0780
39	46	METAL STRUCT	1.4550	1.4550	1.4550	1.4550	1.4550	1.4550	1.4550	1.4550	1.4550
40	47	REPAIR		1.0780	1.0780	1.0780	1.0780	1.0780	1.0780	1.0780	1.0780
41	48	ABRASV	1.0730	1.0780	1.0780	1.0780	1.0780	1.0780	1.0760	1.0780	1.0780
42	49	MINRL CHEM	1.5100	1.6100	1.6100	1.6100	1.6100	1.6100	1.6100	1.6100	1.6100
43	50	BASIC CHEM	1.0600	1.0600	1.0600	1.0600	1.0600	1.0600	1.0600	1.0600	1.0600
44	51	ANIL DYE PR	1.1190	1.1190	1.1190	1.1190	1.1190	1.1190	1.1190	1.1190	1.1190
45	52	SYN R& PLAST	.8000	.8000	.8000	.8000	.8000	.8000	.8000	.7800	.7800
46	53	SYN FIBERS	.9280	.9280	.9280	.9280	.9280	.9280	.9280	.9280	.9280
47	55	ORGSYN PROD	1.0500	1.0900	1.0900	1.0900	1.0900	1.0900	1.0900	1.0900	1.0900
48	56	PAINT & LAC	1.0400	1.0400	1.0400	1.0400	1.0400	1.0400	1.0400	1.0400	1.0400
49	57	RUBBER PROD	1.1000	1.0000	1.0000	1.0000	1.0000	1.0000	1.0000	1.1000	1.1000
50	54,58,59	OTHER CHEM	1.0664	1.0668	1.0667	1.0669	1.0900	1.0900	1.0900	1.0900	1.0900
51	60	LOGGNG	1.2000	1.2000	1.2000	1.2000	1.2000	1.2000	1.2000	1.2000	1.2000
52	61,62	SAW & LUM PR	1.3810	1.3810	1.3810	1.3810	1.3810	1.3810	1.3810	1.3810	1.3810
53	63	FURNITURE	.9860	.9860	.9860	.9860	.9860	.9860	.9860	.9860	.9860
54	64	OTHER WDWK	1.2000	1.2000	1.2000	1.2000	1.2000	1.2000	1.2000	1.2000	1.2000
55	65	PAPER & PULP	1.1320	1.1820	1.1820	1.1820	1.1820	1.1820	1.1820	1.1820	1.1820
56	66	WOOD CHEM	1.3180	1.3180	1.3180	1.3180	1.3180	1.3180	1.3180	1.3180	1.3180
57	67-73	CONST MAT	1.0665	1.0865	1.0865	1.0865	1.0763	1.0843	1.0798	1.1736	1.1352
58	74	GLASS	.7800	.7800	.7800	.7800	.7800	.7800	.7800	.7800	.7800
59	75-80	TEXTLS	1.0542	1.0542	1.0542	1.0542	1.0771	1.0653	1.0512	1.0747	1.0633
60	81	SEWN GOODS	.9740	.9740	.9740	.9740	.9740	.9740	.9740	.9740	.9740
61	82	OTH LT IND	1.0500	1.0340	1.0340	1.1034	1.1034	1.1034	1.1034	1.1034	1.1034
62	83	FISH PROD	1.0500	1.0500	1.0500	1.0500	1.0500	1.0500	1.0500	1.0500	1.0500
63	84	MEAT PROD	.9770	.9770	.9770	.9770	.9770	.9770	.9770	.9770	.9770
64	85	DAIRY PROD	.9770	.9770	.9770	.9770	.9770	.9770	.9770	.9770	.9770
65	86	SUGAR	1.0000	1.0000	1.0000	1.0000	1.0000	1.0000	1.0000	1.0000	1.0000
66	87-89	FLOUR&BREAD	.9770	.9770	.9770	.9770	.9770	.9770	.9770	.9770	.9770
67	90-94	OTHER FOOD	1.0020	1.0020	1.0020	1.0020	1.0020	1.0020	1.0020	1.0020	1.0020
68	95	IND NEC	1.0000	1.0000	1.0000	1.0000	1.0000	1.0000	1.0000	1.0000	1.0000
69	96-100	CONST	1.1550	1.1550	1.1550	1.1550	1.1550	1.1550	1.1550	1.1550	1.1550
70	101	CROPS	1.0090	1.0090	1.0090	1.0090	1.0090	1.0090	1.0090	1.0090	1.0090
71	102	ANIMAL HUSB	1.2920	1.2920	1.2920	1.2920	1.2920	1.2920	1.2920	1.2920	1.2920
72	103	FOREST	2.1000	2.1000	2.1000	2.1000	2.1000	2.1000	2.1000	2.1000	2.1000
73	104-106	TRANS &COM	.9850	.9850	.9850	.9850	.9850	.9850	.9850	.9850	.9850
74	107-109	TRADE & DIST	1.0000	1.0000	1.0000	1.0000	1.0000	1.0000	1.0000	1.0000	1.0000
75	110	OTHER BRANCH	2.0400	2.0400	1.0000	1.0000	1.0000	1.0000	1.0000	1.0000	1.0000
76		TOTAL PURCH	1.2067	1.4759	1.2025	1.2559	1.6276	1.4965	1.3536	1.5058	1.3766

(Table 5.2 continued)

SEQ NO.	110 ORDER NO.		OIL REF 10	GAS 11	PEAT 12	OIL SHALES 13	ELEC POWER 14	EN&POW M&E 15	ELTECH M&E 16	CABLE PROD 17	MACH TOOLS 18
1	1	FER ORES	2.1370	2.1370	2.1370	2.1370	2.1370	2.1370	2.1370	2.1370	2.1370
2	2	FER METALS	1.4700	1.4700	1.4700	1.4700	1.4700	1.4700	1.4700	1.4700	1.4700
3	6	NONFER ORES	1.3100	1.3100	1.3100	1.3100	1.3100	1.3100	1.3100	1.3100	1.3100
4	7	NONFER METAL	1.2200	1.2200	1.2200	1.2200	1.2200	1.2200	1.2200	1.2200	1.2200
5	3	COKE PROD	2.0560	2.0560	2.0560	2.0560	2.0560	2.0560	2.0560	2.0560	2.0560
6	4	REFRAC MAT	1.5200	1.5200	1.5200	1.5200	1.5200	1.5200	1.5200	1.5200	1.5200
7	5	INDMET PROD	1.4000	1.4000	1.4000	1.4000	1.4000	1.4000	1.4000	1.4000	1.4000
8	8	COAL	1.7760	1.7760	1.7760	1.7760	1.7010	1.7760	1.7760	1.7760	1.7760
9	9	OIL EXTRAC	1.8000	2.3000	2.3000	2.3000	2.3000	2.3000	2.3000	2.3000	2.3000
10	10	OIL REF	1.4850	1.4850	1.4850	1.4850	1.4850	1.4850	1.4850	1.4850	1.4850
11	11	GAS	3.6700	3.6700	3.6700	3.6700	3.6700	3.6700	3.6700	3.6700	3.6700
12	12	PEAT	1.2180	1.2180	1.2180	1.2180	1.2180	1.2180	1.2180	1.2180	1.2180
13	13	OIL SHALES	1.1490	1.1490	1.1490	1.1490	1.1490	1.1490	1.1490	1.1490	1.1490
14	14	ELEC POWER	1.3760	1.3760	1.3760	1.3760	1.3760	1.3760	1.3760	1.3760	1.3760
15	15	EN&POW M&E	1.0500	1.0500	1.0500	1.0500	1.0500	1.0500	1.0500	1.0500	1.0500
16	16	ELTECH M&E	.9400	.9400	.9400	.9400	.9400	.9400	.9400	.9400	.9400
17	17	CABLE PROD	.9400	.9400	.9400	.9400	.9400	.9400	.9400	.9400	.9400
18	20	MACH TOOLS	1.0400	1.0400	1.0400	1.0400	1.0400	1.0400	1.0400	1.0400	1.0400
19	21	FORG- PR M&E	1.0400	1.0400	1.0400	1.0400	1.0400	1.0400	1.0400	1.0400	1.0400
20	22	CAST M&E	1.0400	1.0400	1.0400	1.0400	1.0400	1.0400	1.0400	1.0400	1.0400
21	23	TOOLS & DIES	1.0400	1.0400	1.0400	1.0400	1.0400	1.0400	1.0400	1.0400	1.0400
22	24	PRECIS INST	.8200	.8200	.8200	.8200	.8200	.8200	.8200	.8200	.8200
23	25,26,27	MISMET M&E	1.0420	1.0420	1.0420	1.0420	1.0420	1.0420	1.0420	1.0420	1.0420
24	28,29	PUMPS&CHEM E	1.0100	1.0100	1.0100	1.0100	1.0100	1.0100	1.0100	1.0100	1.0100
25	30	LOG&PA M&E	1.0520	1.0520	1.0520	1.0520	1.0520	1.0520	1.0520	1.0520	1.0520
26	31	LT IND M&E	.9200	.9200	.9200	.9200	.9200	.9200	.9200	.9200	.9200
27	32	FD IND M&E	.9200	.9200	.9200	.9200	.9200	.9200	.9200	.9200	.9200
28	33	PRINT M&E	.9780	.9780	.9780	.9780	.9780	.9780	.9780	.9780	.9780
29	34	HOIST&TRAN E	1.0500	1.0500	1.0500	1.0500	1.0500	1.0500	1.0500	1.0500	1.0500
30	35	CONST M&E	1.0000	1.0000	1.0000	1.0000	1.0000	1.0000	1.0000	1.0000	1.0000
31	36	CONMAT M&E	1.0000	1.0000	1.0000	1.0000	1.0000	1.0000	1.0000	1.0000	1.0000
32	37,38	TRANS M&E	1.0500	1.0500	1.0500	1.0500	1.0500	1.0500	1.0500	1.0500	1.0500
33	39	AUTOS	.9800	.9800	.9800	.9800	.9800	.9800	.9800	.9800	.9800
34	40	AGRIC M&E	1.0700	1.0700	1.0700	1.0700	1.0700	1.0700	1.0700	1.0700	1.0700
35	41	BEARNG	.9800	.9800	.9800	.9800	.9800	.9800	.9800	.9800	.9800

SEQ NO.	110 ORDER NO.		OIL REF 10	GAS 11	PEAT 12	OIL SHALES 13	ELEC POWER 14	EN&POW M&E 15	ELTECH M&E 16	CABLE PROD 17	MACH TOOLS 18
36	18,19,42,43	RADIO&OTH MB	.8250	.8250	.8250	.8250	.8250	.8250	.8250	.8250	.8250
37	44	SANIT ENG PR	1.2300	1.2300	1.2300	1.2300	1.2300	1.2300	1.2300	1.2300	1.2300
38	45	OTHER METWRS	1.0780	1.0780	1.0780	1.0780	1.0780	1.0780	1.0780	1.0780	1.0780
39	46	METAL STRUCT	1.4550	1.4550	1.4550	1.4550	1.4550	1.4550	1.4550	1.4550	1.4550
40	47	REPAIR	1.0780	1.0780	1.0780	1.0780	1.0780	1.0780	1.0780	1.0780	1.0780
41	48	ABRASV	1.0780	1.0780	1.0780	1.0780	1.0780	1.0730	1.0780	1.0780	1.0780
42	49	MINRL CHEM	1.6100	1.6100	1.6100	1.6100	1.6100	1.6100	1.6100	1.6100	1.6100
43	50	BASIC CHEM	1.0600	1.0600	1.0600	1.0600	1.0600	1.0600	1.0600	1.0600	1.0600
44	51	ANIL DYE PR	1.1190	1.1190	1.1190	1.1190	1.1190	1.1190	1.1190	1.1190	1.1190
45	52	SYN R& PLAST	.7830	.7800	.7800	.7800	.7800	.7800	.8650	.7800	.7800
46	53	SYN FIBERS	.9280	.9280	.9280	.9280	.9280	.9280	.9280	.9280	.9280
47	55	ORGSYN PROD	1.0900	1.0900	1.0900	1.0900	1.0900	1.0900	1.0900	1.0900	1.0900
48	56	PAINT & LAC	1.0400	1.0400	1.0400	1.0400	1.0400	1.0400	1.0400	1.0400	1.0400
49	57	RUBBER PROD	1.1000	1.1000	1.1000	1.1000	1.1000	1.1000	1.1000	1.1000	1.1000
50	54,58,59	OTHER CHEM	1.0900	.9062	1.0900	1.0900	1.0900	1.0900	1.0900	.8754	1.0900
51	60	LOGGNG	1.2000	1.2000	1.2000	1.2000	1.2000	1.2000	1.2000	1.2000	1.2000
52	61,62	SAW & LUM PR	1.3810	1.3810	1.3810	1.3810	1.3810	1.3810	1.3810	1.3810	1.3810
53	63	FURNITURE	.9860	.9860	.9860	.9860	.9860	.9860	.9860	.9860	.9860
54	64	OTHER WDWK	1.2000	1.2000	1.2000	1.2000	1.2000	1.2000	1.2000	1.2000	1.2000
55	65	PAPER & PULP	1.1320	1.1820	1.1820	1.1820	1.1820	1.1820	1.1820	1.1820	1.1820
56	66	WOOD CHEM	1.3180	1.3180	1.3180	1.3180	1.3180	1.3180	1.3180	1.3180	1.3180
57	67-73	CONST MAT	1.0733	1.1214	1.1120	1.1258	1.0979	1.1075	1.0933	1.0878	1.1383
58	74	GLASS	.7800	.7800	.7800	.7800	.7800	.7800	.7800	.7800	.7800
59	75-80	TEXTLS	1.1035	1.0761	1.0655	1.0934	1.0896	1.0663	1.0761	1.0352	1.0848
60	81	SEWN GOODS	.9740	.9740	.9740	.9740	.9740	.9740	.9740	.9740	.9740
61	82	OTH LT IND	1.1034	1.1034	1.1034	1.1034	1.1034	1.1034	1.1034	1.1034	1.1034
62	83	FISH PROD	1.0500	1.0500	1.0500	1.0500	1.0500	1.0500	1.0500	1.0500	1.0500
63	84	MEAT PROD	.9770	.9770	.9770	.9770	.9770	.9770	.9770	.9770	.9770
64	85	DAIRY PROD	.9770	.9770	.9770	.9770	.9770	.9770	.9770	.9770	.9770
65	86	SUGAR	1.0000	1.0000	1.0000	1.0000	1.0000	1.0000	1.0000	1.0000	1.0000
66	87-89	FLOUR&BREAD	.9770	.9770	.9770	.9770	.9770	.9770	.9770	.9770	.9770
67	90-94	OTHER FOOD	1.0020	1.0020	1.0020	1.0020	1.0020	1.0020	1.0020	1.0020	1.0020
68	95	IND NEC	1.0000	1.0000	1.0000	1.0000	1.0000	1.0000	1.0000	1.0000	1.0000
69	96-100	CONST	1.1550	1.1550	1.1550	1.1550	1.1550	1.1550	1.1550	1.1550	1.1550
70	101	CROPS	1.0090	1.0090	1.0090	1.0090	1.0090	1.0090	1.0090	1.0090	1.0090
71	102	ANIMAL HUSB	1.2920	1.2920	1.2920	1.2920	1.2920	1.2920	1.2920	1.2920	1.2920
72	103	FOREST	2.1000	2.1000	2.1000	2.1000	2.1000	2.1000	2.1000	2.1000	2.1000
73	104-106	TRANS &COM	.9850	.9850	.9850	.9850	.9850	.9850	.9850	.9850	1.0000
74	107-109	TRADE & DIST	1.0000	1.0000	1.0000	1.0000	1.0000	1.0000	1.0000	1.0000	1.0000
75	110	OTHER BRANCH	1.0000	1.0300	1.0000	1.0000	1.0000	1.0000	1.0000	1.0000	1.0000
76		TOTAL PURCH	1.4161	1.8259	1.1872	1.1841	1.4400	1.1545	1.0911	1.1275	1.0858

225

(Table 5.2 continued)

SEQ NO.	110 ORDER NO.		FORG-PR M&E 19	CAST M&E 20	TOOLS & DIES 21	PRECIS INST 22	MI&MET M&E 23	PUMPS& CHEM E 24	LOG&PA M&E 25	LT IND M&E 26	FD IND M&E 27
1	1	FER ORES	2.1370	2.1370	2.1370	2.1370	2.1370	2.1370	2.1370	2.1370	2.1370
2	2	FER METALS	1.4700	1.4700	1.4700	1.4700	1.4700	1.4700	1.4700	1.4700	1.4700
3	6	NONFER ORES	1.3100	1.3100	1.3100	1.3100	1.3100	1.3100	1.3100	1.3100	1.3100
4	7	NONFER METAL	1.2200	1.2200	1.2200	1.2200	1.2200	1.2200	1.2200	1.2200	1.3100
5	3	COKE PROD	2.0560	2.0560	2.0560	2.0560	2.0560	2.0560	2.0560	2.0560	2.0560
6	4	REFRAC MAT	1.5200	1.5200	1.5200	1.5200	1.5200	1.5200	1.5200	1.5200	1.5200
7	5	INOMET PROD	1.4000	1.4000	1.4000	1.4000	1.4000	1.4000	1.4000	1.4000	1.4000
8	8	COAL	1.7760	1.7760	1.7760	1.7760	1.7760	1.7760	1.7760	1.7760	1.7760
9	9	OIL EXTRAC	2.3000	2.3000	2.3000	2.3000	2.3000	2.3000	2.3000	2.3000	2.3000
10	10	OIL REF	1.4850	1.4850	1.4850	1.4850	1.4850	1.4850	1.4850	1.4850	1.4850
11	11	GAS	3.6700	3.6700	3.6700	3.6700	3.6700	3.6700	3.6700	3.6700	3.6700
12	12	PEAT	1.2180	1.2180	1.2180	1.2180	1.2180	1.2180	1.2180	1.2180	1.2180
13	13	OIL SHALES	1.1490	1.1490	1.1490	1.1490	1.1490	1.1490	1.1490	1.1490	1.1490
14	14	ELEC POWER	1.3760	1.3760	1.3760	1.3760	1.3760	1.3760	1.3760	1.3760	1.3760
15	15	EN&POW M&E	1.0500	1.0500	1.0500	1.0500	1.0500	1.0500	1.0500	1.0500	1.0500
16	16	ELTECH M&E	.9400	.9400	.9400	.9400	.9400	.9400	.9400	.9400	.9400
17	17	CABLE PROD	.9400	.9400	.9400	.9400	.9400	.9400	.9400	.9400	.9400
18	20	MACH TOOLS	1.0400	1.0400	1.0400	1.0400	1.0400	1.0400	1.0400	1.0400	1.0400
19	21	FORG-PR M&E	1.0400	1.0400	1.0400	1.0400	1.0400	1.0400	1.0400	1.0400	1.0400
20	22	CAST M&E	1.0400	1.0400	1.0400	1.0400	1.0400	1.0400	1.0400	1.0400	1.0400
21	23	TOOLS & DIES	1.0400	1.0400	1.0400	1.0400	1.0400	1.0400	1.0400	1.0400	1.0400
22	24	PRECIS INST	.8200	.8200	.8200	.8200	.8200	.8200	.8200	.8200	.8200
23	25,26,27	MI&MET M&E	1.0420	1.0420	1.0420	1.0420	1.0420	1.0420	1.0420	1.0420	1.0420
24	28,29	PUMPS&CHEM E	1.0100	1.0100	1.0100	1.0100	1.0100	1.0100	1.0100	1.0100	1.0100
25	30	LOG&PA M&E	1.0520	1.0520	1.0520	1.0520	1.0520	1.0520	1.0100	1.0100	1.0520
26	31	LT IND M&E	.9200	.9200	.9200	.9200	.9200	.9200	.9200	.9200	.9200
27	32	FD IND M&E	.9200	.9200	.9200	.9200	.9200	.9200	.9200	.9200	.9200
28	33	PRINT M&E	.9780	.9780	.9780	.9780	.9780	.9780	.9780	.9780	.9780
29	34	HOIST&TRAN E	1.0500	1.0500	1.0500	1.0500	1.0500	1.0500	1.0500	1.0500	1.0500
30	35	CONST M&E	1.0000	1.0000	1.0000	1.0000	1.0000	1.0000	1.0000	1.0000	1.0000
31	36	CONMAT M&E	1.0000	1.0000	1.0000	1.0000	1.0000	1.0000	1.0000	1.0000	1.0000
32	37,38	TRANS M&E	1.0500	1.0500	1.0500	1.0500	1.0500	1.0500	1.0500	1.0500	1.0500
33	39	AUTOS	.9800	.9800	.9800	.9800	.9800	.9800	.9800	.9800	.9800
34	40	AGRIC M&E	1.0700	1.0700	1.0700	1.0700	1.0700	1.0700	1.0700	1.0700	1.0700
35	41	BEARNG	.9800	.9800	.9800	.9800	.9800	.9800	.9800	.9800	.9800

SEQ NO.	110 ORDER NO.		FORG-PR M&E 19	CAS- M&E 20	TOOLS & DIES 21	PRECIS INST 22	MI&MET M&E 23	PUMPS& CHEM E 24	LOG&PA M&E 25	LT IND M&E 26	FD IND M&E 27
36	18,19,42,43	RADIO&OTH MB	.8250	.8250	.8250	.8250	.8250	.8250	.8250	.8250	.8250
37	44	SANIT ENG PR	1.2300	1.2300	1.2300	1.2300	1.2300	1.2300	1.2300	1.2300	1.2300
38	45	OTHER METWRS	1.0780	1.0780	1.0780	1.0780	1.0780	1.0780	1.0780	1.0780	1.0780
39	46	METAL STRUCT	1.4550	1.4550	1.4550	1.4550	1.4550	1.4550	1.4550	1.4550	1.4550
40	47	REPAIR	1.0780	1.0780	1.0780	1.0780	1.0780	1.0780	1.0780	1.0780	1.0780
41	48	ABRASV	1.0780	1.0780	1.0780	1.0780	1.0780	1.0780	1.0780	1.0780	1.0780
42	49	MINRL CHEM	1.6100	1.6100	1.6100	1.6100	1.6100	1.6100	1.6100	1.6100	1.6100
43	50	BASIC CHEM	1.0600	1.0600	1.0600	1.0600	1.0600	1.0600	1.0600	1.0600	1.0600
44	51	ANIL DYE PR	1.1190	1.1190	1.1190	1.1190	1.1190	1.1190	1.1190	1.1190	1.1190
45	52	SYN R& PLAST	.7800	.7800	.7800	.8650	.7800	.7800	.7800	.7800	.7800
46	53	SYN FIBERS	.9280	.9280	.9280	.9280	.9280	.9280	.9280	.9280	.9280
47	55	ORGSYN PROD	1.0900	1.0900	1.0900	1.0900	1.0900	1.0900	1.0900	1.0900	1.0900
48	56	PAINT & LAC	1.0400	1.0400	1.0400	1.0400	1.0400	1.0400	1.0400	1.0400	1.0400
49	57	RUBBER PROD	1.1000	1.1000	1.1000	1.1000	1.1000	1.1000	1.1000	1.1000	1.1000
50	54,58,59	OTHER CHEM	1.0900	1.0900	1.0900	1.0900	1.0900	1.0900	1.0900	1.0900	1.0900
51	60	LOGGING	1.2000	1.2000	1.2000	1.2000	1.2000	1.2000	1.2000	1.2000	1.2000
52	61,62	SAW & LUM PR	1.3810	1.3810	1.3810	1.3810	1.3810	1.3810	1.3810	1.3810	1.3810
53	63	FURNITURE	.9860	.9860	.9860	.9860	.9860	.9860	.9860	.9860	.9860
54	64	OTHER WDWK	1.2000	1.2000	1.2000	1.2000	1.2000	1.2000	1.2000	1.2000	1.2000
55	65	PAPER & PULP	1.1820	1.1820	1.1820	1.1820	1.1820	1.1820	1.1820	1.1820	1.1820
56	66	WOOD CHEM	1.3180	1.3180	1.3180	1.3180	1.3180	1.3180	1.3180	1.3180	1.3180
57	67-73	CONST MAT	1.1297	1.1003	1.0855	1.0973	1.0903	1.0856	1.0937	1.1188	1.1173
58	74	GLASS	.7800	.7800	.7800	.7800	.7800	.7800	.7800	.7800	.7800
59	75-80	TEXTLS	1.0759	1.0484	1.0730	1.0645	1.0762	1.0819	1.0566	1.0413	1.0610
60	81	SEWN GOODS	.9740	.9740	.9740	.9740	.9740	.9740	.9740	.9740	.9740
61	82	OTH LT IND	1.1034	1.1034	1.1034	1.1034	1.1034	1.1034	1.1034	1.1034	1.1034
62	83	FISH PROD	1.0500	1.0500	1.0500	1.0500	1.0500	1.0500	1.0500	1.0500	1.0500
63	84	MEAT PROD	.9770	.9770	.9770	.9770	.9770	.9770	.9770	.9770	.9770
64	85	DAIRY PROD	.9770	.9770	.9770	.9770	.9770	.9770	.9770	.9770	.9770
65	86	SUGAR	1.0000	1.0000	1.0000	1.0000	1.0000	1.0000	1.0000	1.0000	1.0000
66	87-89	FLOUR&BREAD	.9770	.9770	.9770	.9770	.9770	.9770	.9770	.9770	.9770
67	90-94	OTHER FOOD	1.0020	1.0020	1.0020	1.0020	1.0020	1.0020	1.0020	1.0020	1.0020
68	95	IND NEC	1.0000	1.0000	1.0000	1.0000	1.0000	1.0000	1.0000	1.0000	1.0000
69	96-100	CONST	1.1550	1.1550	1.1550	1.1550	1.1550	1.1550	1.1550	1.1550	1.1550
70	101	CROPS	1.0090	1.0090	1.0090	1.0090	1.0090	1.0090	1.0090	1.0090	1.0090
71	102	ANIMAL HUSB	1.2920	1.2920	1.2920	1.2920	1.2920	1.2920	1.2920	1.2920	1.2920
72	103	FOREST	2.1000	2.1000	2.1000	2.1000	2.1000	2.1000	2.1000	2.1000	2.1000
73	104-106	TRANS &COM	.9850	.9850	.9850	.9850	.9850	.9850	.9850	.9850	.9850
74	107-109	TRADE & DIST	1.0000	1.0000	1.0000	1.0000	1.0000	1.0000	1.0000	1.0000	1.0000
75	110	OTHER BRANCH	1.0000	1.0000	1.0000	1.0000	1.0000	1.0000	1.0000	1.0000	1.0000
76		TOTAL PURCH	1.1715	1.1348	1.3020	1.0056	1.1905	1.1091	1.1045	1.1458	1.1504

(Table 5.2 continued)

SEQ NO.	110 ORDER NO.		PRINT M&E 28	HOIST& TRAN E 29	CONST M&E 30	CONMAT M&E 31	TRANS M&E 32	AUTOS 33	AGRIC M&E 34	BEARNG 35	RADIO& OTH MB 36
1	1	FER ORES	2.1370	2.1370	2.1370	2.1370	2.1370	2.1370	2.1370	2.1370	2.1370
2	2	FER METALS	1.4700	1.4700	1.4700	1.4700	1.4700	1.4700	1.4700	1.4700	1.4700
3	6	NONFER ORES	1.3100	1.3100	1.3100	1.3100	1.3100	1.3100	1.3100	1.3100	1.3100
4	7	NONFER METAL	1.2200	1.2200	1.2200	1.2200	1.2200	1.2200	1.2200	1.2200	1.2200
5	3	COKE PROD	2.0560	2.0560	2.0560	2.0560	2.0560	2.0560	2.0560	2.0560	2.0560
6	4	REFRAC MAT	1.5200	1.5200	1.5200	1.5200	1.5200	1.5200	1.5200	1.5200	1.5200
7	5	INDMET PROD	1.4000	1.4000	1.4000	1.4000	1.4000	1.4000	1.4000	1.4000	1.4000
8	8	COAL	1.7760	1.7760	1.7760	1.7760	1.7760	1.7760	1.7760	1.7760	1.7760
9	9	OIL EXTRAC	2.3000	2.3000	2.3000	2.3000	2.3000	2.3000	2.3000	2.3000	2.3000
10	10	OIL REF	1.4850	1.4850	1.4850	1.4850	1.4850	1.4850	1.4850	1.4850	1.4850
11	11	GAS	3.6700	3.6700	3.6700	3.6700	3.6700	3.6700	3.6700	3.6700	3.6700
12	12	PEAT	1.2180	1.2180	1.2180	1.2180	1.2180	1.2180	1.2180	1.2180	1.2180
13	13	OIL SHALES	1.1490	1.1490	1.1490	1.1490	1.1490	1.1490	1.1490	1.1490	1.1490
14	14	ELEC POWER	1.3760	1.3760	1.3760	1.3760	1.3760	1.3760	1.3760	1.3760	1.3760
15	15	ENSPOW M&E	1.0500	1.0500	1.0500	1.0500	1.0500	1.0500	1.0500	1.0500	1.0500
16	16	ELTECH M&E	.9400	.9400	.9400	.9400	.9400	.9400	.9400	.9400	.9400
17	17	CABLE PROD	.9400	.9400	.9400	.9400	.9400	.9400	.9400	.9400	.9400
18	20	MACH TOOLS	1.0400	1.0400	1.0400	1.0400	1.0400	1.0400	1.0400	1.0400	1.0400
19	21	FORG- PR M&E	1.0400	1.0400	1.0400	1.0400	1.0400	1.0400	1.0400	1.0400	1.0400
20	22	CAST M&E	1.0400	1.0400	1.0400	1.0400	1.0400	1.0400	1.0400	1.0400	1.0400
21	23	TOOLS & DIES	1.0400	1.0400	1.0400	1.0400	1.0400	1.0400	1.0400	1.0400	1.0400
22	24	PRECIS INST	.8200	.8200	.8200	.8200	.8200	.8200	.8200	.8200	.8200
23	25,26,27	MISMET M&E	1.0420	1.0420	1.0420	1.0420	1.0420	1.0420	1.0420	1.0420	1.0420
24	28,29	PUMPS&CHEM E	1.0100	1.0100	1.0100	1.0100	1.0100	1.0100	1.0100	1.0100	1.0100
25	30	LOG&PA M&E	1.0520	1.0520	1.0520	1.0520	1.0520	1.0520	1.0100	1.0100	1.0100
26	31	LT IND M&E	.9200	.9200	.9200	.9200	.9200	.9200	.9200	.9200	.9200
27	32	FD IND M&E	.9200	.9200	.9200	.9200	.9200	.9200	.9200	.9200	.9200
28	33	PRINT M&E	.9780	.9780	.9780	.9780	.9780	.9780	.9780	.9780	.9780
29	34	HOIST&TRAN E	1.0500	1.0500	1.0500	1.0500	1.0500	1.0500	1.0500	1.0500	1.0500
30	35	CONST M&E	1.0000	1.0000	1.0000	1.0000	1.0000	1.0000	1.0000	1.0000	1.0000
31	36	CONMAT M&E	1.0000	1.0000	1.0000	1.0000	1.0000	1.0000	1.0000	1.0000	1.0000
32	37,38	TRANS M&E	1.0500	1.0500	1.0500	1.0500	1.0500	1.0500	1.0500	1.0500	1.0500
33	39	AUTOS	.9800	.9800	.9800	.9800	.9800	.9800	.9800	.9800	.9800
34	40	AGRIC M&E	1.0700	1.0700	1.0700	1.0700	1.0700	1.0700	1.0700	1.0700	1.0700
35	41	BEARNG	.9800	.9800	.9800	.9800	.9800	.9800	.9800	.9800	.9800

SEQ NO.	110 ORDER NO.		PRINT M&E 28	HOIST& TRAN E 29	CONST M&E 30	CONMAT M&E 31	TRANS M&E 32	ALTOS 33	AGRIC M&E 34	BEARNG 35	RADIO& OTH MB 36
36	18,19,42,43	RADIO&OTH MB	.8250	.8250	.8250	.8250	.8250	.8250	.8250	.8250	.8250
37	44	SANIT ENG PR	1.2300	1.2300	1.2300	1.2300	1.2300	1.2300	1.2300	1.2300	1.2300
38	45	OTHER METWRS	1.0780	1.0780	1.0780	1.0780	1.0780	1.0780	1.0780	1.0780	1.0780
39	46	METAL STRUCT	1.4550	1.4550	1.4550	1.4550	1.4550	1.4550	1.4550	1.4550	1.4550
40	47	REPAIR	1.0780	1.0780	1.0780	1.0780	1.0780	1.0780	1.0780	1.0780	1.0780
41	48	ABRASV	1.0780	1.0780	1.0780	1.0780	1.0780	1.0780	1.0780	1.0780	1.0780
42	49	MINRL CHEM	1.6100	1.6100	1.5100	1.6100	1.6100	1.6100	1.6100	1.6100	1.6100
43	50	BASIC CHEM	1.0600	1.0600	1.0600	1.0600	1.0600	1.0600	1.0600	1.0600	1.0600
44	51	ANIL DYE PR	1.1190	1.1190	1.1190	1.1190	1.1190	1.1190	1.1190	1.1190	1.1190
45	52	SYN R& PLAST	.7800	.7800	.7800	.7800	.7800	.9080	.8650	.7800	.8300
46	53	SYN FIBERS	.9280	.9280	.9280	.9280	.9280	.9280	.9280	.9280	.9280
47	55	ORGSYN PROD	1.0900	1.0900	1.0900	1.0900	1.0900	1.0900	1.0900	1.0900	1.0900
48	56	PAINT & LAC	1.0400	1.0400	1.0400	1.0400	1.0400	1.2400	1.0400	1.0400	1.0400
49	57	RUBBER PROD	1.1000	1.0000	1.0000	1.0000	1.0000	1.0000	1.0000	1.0000	1.0000
50	54,58,59	OTHER CHEM	1.0900	1.0900	1.0900	1.0900	1.0900	1.0900	1.0900	1.0900	1.0900
51	60	LOGGNG	1.2000	1.2000	1.2000	1.2000	1.2000	1.2000	1.2000	1.2000	1.2000
52	61,62	SAW & LUM PR	1.3810	1.3810	1.3810	1.3810	1.3810	1.3810	1.3810	1.3810	1.3810
53	63	FURNITURE	.9860	.9860	.9860	.9860	.9860	.9860	.9860	.9860	.9860
54	64	OTHER WDWK	1.2000	1.2000	1.2000	1.2000	1.2000	1.2000	1.2000	1.2000	1.2000
55	65	PAPER & PULP	1.1820	1.1820	1.1820	1.1820	1.1820	1.1820	1.1820	1.1820	1.1820
56	66	WOOD CHEM	1.3180	1.3180	1.3180	1.3180	1.3180	1.3180	1.3180	1.3180	1.3180
57	67-73	CONST MAT	1.1421	1.1377	1.0980	1.0779	1.0662	1.0808	1.1056	1.0895	1.0946
58	74	GLASS	.7800	.7800	.7800	.7800	.7800	.7800	.7800	.7800	.7800
59	75-80	TEXTLS	1.0801	1.0513	1.0742	1.0381	1.0496	1.0713	1.0853	1.0973	1.0783
60	81	SEWN GOODS	.9740	.9740	.9740	.9740	.9740	.9740	.9740	.9740	.9740
61	82	OTH LT IND	1.1034	1.1034	1.1034	1.1034	1.1034	1.1034	1.1034	1.1034	1.1034
62	83	FISH PROD	1.0500	1.0500	1.0500	1.0500	1.0500	1.0500	1.0500	1.0500	1.0500
63	84	MEAT PROD	.9770	.9770	.9770	.9770	.9770	.9770	.9770	.9770	.9770
64	85	DAIRY PROD	.9770	.9770	.9770	.9770	.9770	.9770	.9770	.9770	.9770
65	86	SUGAR	.0000	1.0000	1.0000	1.0000	1.0000	1.0000	1.0000	1.0000	1.0000
66	87-89	FLOUR&BREAD	.9770	.9770	.9770	.9770	.9770	.9770	.9770	.9770	.9770
67	90-94	OTHER FOOD	.0020	1.0020	1.0020	1.0020	1.0020	1.0020	1.0020	1.0020	1.0020
68	95	IND NEC	.0000	1.0000	1.0000	1.0000	1.0000	1.0000	1.0000	1.0000	1.0000
69	96-100	CONST	1.1550	1.1550	1.1550	1.1550	1.1550	1.1550	1.1550	1.1550	1.1550
70	101	CROPS	1.0090	1.0090	1.0090	1.0090	1.0090	1.0090	1.0090	1.0090	1.0090
71	102	ANIMAL HUSB	1.2920	1.2920	1.2920	1.2920	1.2920	1.2920	1.2920	1.2920	1.2920
72	103	FOREST	2.1000	2.1000	2.1000	2.1000	2.1000	2.1000	2.1000	2.1000	2.1000
73	104-106	TRANS &COM	.9850	.9850	.9850	.9950	.9850	.9850	.9850	.9850	.9850
74	107-109	TRADE & DIST	1.0000	1.0000	1.0000	1.0000	1.0000	1.0000	1.0000	1.0000	1.0000
75	110	OTHER BRANCH	1.0000	1.0000	1.0000	1.0000	1.0000	1.0000	1.0000	1.0000	1.0000
76		TOTAL PURCH	1.1670	1.0833	1.0877	1.1500	1.0597	1.1083	1.1570	1.3286	.9774

229

(Table 5.2 continued)

SEQ NO.	110 ORDER NO.		SANIT ENG PR 37	OTHER METWRS 38	METAL STRUCT 39	REPAIR 40	ABRASV 41	MINRL CHEM 42	BASIC CHEM 43	ANIL DYE PR 44	SYN R& PLAST 45
1	1	FER ORES	2.1370	2.1370	2.1370	2.1370	2.1370	2.1370	2.1370	2.1370	2.1370
2	2	FER METALS	1.4700	1.4700	1.4700	1.4700	1.4700	1.4700	1.4700	1.4700	1.4700
3	6	NONFER ORES	1.3100	1.3100	1.3100	1.3100	1.3100	1.3100	1.3100	1.3100	1.3100
4	7	NONFER METAL	1.2200	1.2200	1.2200	1.2200	1.2200	1.2200	1.2200	1.2200	1.2200
5	3	COKE PROD	2.0560	2.0560	2.0560	2.0560	2.0560	2.0560	2.0560	2.0560	2.0560
6	4	REFRAC MAT	1.5200	1.5200	1.5200	1.5200	1.5200	1.5200	1.5200	1.5200	1.5200
7	5	INDMET PROD	1.4000	1.4000	1.4000	1.4000	1.4000	1.4000	1.4000	1.4000	1.4000
8	8	COAL	1.7760	1.7760	1.7760	1.7760	1.7760	1.7760	1.7760	1.7760	1.7760
9	9	OIL EXTRAC	2.3000	2.3000	2.3000	2.3000	2.3000	2.3000	2.3000	2.3000	2.3000
10	10	OIL REF	1.4850	1.4850	1.4850	1.4850	1.4850	1.4850	1.4850	1.4850	1.4850
11	11	GAS	3.6700	3.6700	3.6700	3.6700	3.6700	3.6700	3.6700	3.6700	3.6700
12	12	PEAT	1.2180	1.2180	1.2180	1.2180	1.2180	1.2180	1.2180	1.2180	1.2180
13	13	OIL SHALES	1.1490	1.1490	1.1490	1.1490	1.1490	1.1490	1.1490	1.1490	1.1490
14	14	ELEC POWER	1.3760	1.3760	1.3760	1.3760	1.3760	1.3760	1.3760	1.3760	1.3760
15	15	EN&POW M&E	1.0500	1.0500	1.0500	1.0500	1.0500	1.0500	1.0500	1.0500	1.0500
16	16	EL TECH M&E	.9400	.9400	.9400	.9400	.9400	.9400	.9400	.9400	.9400
17	17	CABLE PROD	.9400	.9400	.9400	.9400	.9400	.9400	.9400	.9400	.9400
18	20	MACH TOOLS	1.0400	1.0400	1.0400	1.0400	1.0400	1.0400	1.0400	1.0400	1.0400
19	21	FORG- PR M&E	1.0400	1.0400	1.0400	1.0400	1.0400	1.0400	1.0400	1.0400	1.0400
20	22	CAST M&E	1.0400	1.0400	1.0400	1.0400	1.0400	1.0400	1.0400	1.0400	1.0400
21	23	TOOLS & DIES	1.0400	1.0400	1.0400	1.0400	1.0400	1.0400	1.0400	1.0400	1.0400
22	24	PRECIS INST	.8200	.8200	.8200	.8200	.8200	.8200	.8200	.8200	.8200
23	25,26,27	MI&MET M&E	1.0420	1.0420	1.0420	1.0420	1.0420	1.0420	1.0420	1.0420	1.0420
24	28,29	PUMPS&CHEM E	1.0100	1.0100	1.0100	1.0100	1.0100	1.0100	1.0100	1.0100	1.0100
25	30	LOG&PA M&E	1.0520	1.0520	1.0520	1.0520	1.0520	1.0520	1.0520	1.0520	1.0520
26	31	LT IND M&E	.9200	.9200	.9200	.9200	.9200	.9200	.9200	.9200	.9200
27	32	FD IND M&E	.9200	.9200	.9200	.9200	.9200	.9200	.9200	.9200	.9200
28	33	PRINT M&E	.9780	.9780	.9780	.9780	.9780	.9780	.9780	.9780	.9780
29	34	HOIST&TRAN E	1.0500	1.0500	1.0500	1.0500	1.0500	1.0500	1.0500	1.0500	1.0500
30	35	CONST M&E	1.0000	1.0000	1.0000	1.0000	1.0000	1.0000	1.0000	1.0000	1.0000
31	36	CONMAT M&E	1.0000	1.0000	1.0000	1.0000	1.0000	1.0000	1.0000	1.0000	1.0000
32	37,38	TRANS M&E	1.0500	1.0500	1.0500	1.0500	1.0500	1.0500	1.0500	1.0500	1.0500
33	39	AUTOS	.9800	.9800	.9800	.9800	.9800	.9800	.9800	.9800	.9800
34	40	AGRIC M&E	1.0700	1.0700	1.0700	1.0700	1.0700	1.0700	1.0700	1.0700	1.0700
35	41	BEARNG	.9800	.9800	.9800	.9800	.9800	.9800	.9800	.9800	.9800

SEQ NO.	110 ORDER NO.		SANIT ENG PR 37	OTHER METWRS 38	METAL STRUCT 39	REPAIR 40	ABRASV 41	MINRL CHEM 42	BASIC CHEM 43	ANIL DYE PR 44	SYN R& PLAST 45
36	18.19.42.43	RADIO&OTH MB	.8250	.8250	.8250	.8250	.8250	.8250	.8250	.8250	.8250
37	44	SANIT ENG PR	1.2300	1.2300	1.2300	1.2300	1.2300	1.2300	1.2300	1.2300	1.2300
38	45	OTHER METWRS	1.0780	1.0780	1.0780	1.0780	1.0780	1.0780	1.0780	1.0780	1.0780
39	46	METAL STRUCT	1.4550	1.4550	1.4550	1.4550	1.4550	1.4550	1.4550	1.4550	1.4550
40	47	REPAIR	1.0780	1.0780	1.0780	1.0780	1.0780	1.0780	1.0780	1.0780	1.0780
41	48	ABRASV	1.0780	1.0780	1.0780	1.0780	1.0780	1.0780	1.0780	1.0780	1.0780
42	49	MINRL CHEM	1.6100	1.6100	1.6100	1.6100	1.6100	1.6100	1.6100	1.6100	1.6100
43	50	BASIC CHEM	1.0600	1.0600	1.0600	1.0600	1.0600	1.0600	1.0600	1.0600	1.0600
44	51	ANIL DYE PR	1.1190	1.1190	1.1190	1.1190	1.1190	1.1190	1.1190	1.1190	1.1190
45	52	SYN R& PLAST	.7800	.7800	.7800	.7800	.7800	.7800	.7800	.7800	.7800
46	53	SYN FIBERS	.9280	.9280	.9280	.9280	.9280	.9280	.9280	.9280	.9280
47	55	ORGSYN PROD	1.0900	1.0900	1.0900	1.0900	1.0900	1.0900	1.0900	1.0900	1.0900
48	56	PAINT & LAC	1.0400	1.0400	1.0400	1.0400	1.0400	1.0400	1.0400	1.0400	1.0400
49	57	RUBBER PROD	1.0000	1.0000	1.0000	1.0000	1.0000	1.0000	1.0000	1.0000	1.1000
50	54.58.59	OTHER CHEM	1.0900	.8829	1.0900	1.0900	1.0900	1.0900	1.0900	1.0900	1.0900
51	60	LOGGNG	1.2000	1.2000	1.2000	1.2000	1.2000	1.2000	1.2000	1.2000	1.2000
52	61.62	SAW & LUM PR	1.3810	1.3810	1.3810	1.3810	1.3810	1.3810	1.3810	1.3810	1.3810
53	63	FURNITURE	.9860	.9860	.9860	.9860	.9860	.9860	.9860	.9860	.9860
54	64	OTHER WDWK	1.2000	1.2000	1.2000	1.2000	1.2000	1.2000	1.2000	1.2000	1.2000
55	65	PAPER & PULP	1.1820	1.1820	1.1820	1.1820	1.1820	1.1820	1.1820	1.1820	1.1820
56	66	WOOD CHEM	1.3180	1.3180	1.3180	1.3180	1.3180	1.3180	1.3180	1.3180	1.3180
57	67-73	CONST MAT	1.1462	1.0892	1.0947	1.0752	1.0652	1.0883	1.0680	1.0980	1.0670
58	74	GLASS	.7800	.7800	.7800	.7800	.7800	.7800	.7800	.7800	.7800
59	75-80	TEXTLS	1.0545	.9979	1.0680	1.0680	1.1177	.9818	1.0729	1.0258	1.1214
60	81	SEWN GOODS	.9740	.9740	.9740	.9740	.9740	.9740	.9740	.9740	.9740
61	82	OTH LT IND	1.1034	1.1034	1.1034	1.1034	1.1034	1.1034	1.1034	1.1034	1.1034
62	83	FISH PROD	1.0500	1.0500	1.0500	1.0500	1.0500	1.0500	1.0500	1.0500	1.0500
63	84	MEAT PROD	.9770	.9770	.9770	.9770	.9770	.9770	.9770	.9770	.9770
64	85	DAIRY PROD	.9770	.9770	.9770	.9770	.9770	.9770	.9770	.9770	.9770
65	86	SUGAR	1.0000	.0000	1.0000	1.0000	1.0000	1.0000	1.0000	1.0000	1.0000
66	87-89	FLOUR&BREAD	.9770	.9770	.9770	.9770	.9770	.9770	.9770	.9770	.9770
67	90-94	OTHER FOOD	1.0020	1.0020	1.0020	1.0020	1.0020	1.0020	1.0020	1.0020	1.0020
68	95	IND NEC	1.0000	1.0000	1.0000	1.0000	1.0000	1.0000	1.0000	1.0000	1.0000
69	96-100	CONST	1.1550	1.1550	1.1550	1.1550	1.1550	1.1550	1.1550	1.1550	1.1550
70	101	CROPS	1.0090	1.0090	1.0090	1.0090	1.0090	1.0090	1.0090	1.0090	1.0090
71	102	ANIMAL HUSB	1.2920	1.2920	1.2920	1.2920	1.2920	1.2920	1.2920	1.2920	1.2920
72	103	FOREST	2.1000	2.1000	2.1000	2.1000	2.1000	2.1000	2.1000	2.1000	2.1000
73	104-106	TRANS &COM	.9850	.9850	.9850	.9850	.9850	.9850	.9850	.9850	.9850
74	107-109	TRACE & DIST	1.0000	1.0000	1.0000	1.0000	1.0000	1.0000	1.0000	1.0000	1.0000
75	110	OTHER BRANCH	1.0000	1.0000	1.0000	1.0000	1.0000	1.0000	1.0000	1.0000	1.0000
76		TOTAL PURCH	1.2810	1.2504	1.3814	1.0995	1.1178	1.2093	1.2193	1.1977	1.0688

(Table 5.2 continued)

SEQ NO.	110 ORDER NO.		SYN FIBERS 46	ORGSYN PROD 47	PAINT & LAC 48	RUBBER PROD 49	OTHER CHEM 50	LOGGNG 51	SAW & LUM PR 52	FURNIT URE 53	OTHER WDWK 54
1	1	FER ORES	2.1370	2.1370	2.1370	2.1370	2.1370	2.1370	2.1370	2.1370	2.1370
2	2	FER METALS	1.4700	1.4700	1.4700	1.4700	1.4700	1.4700	1.4700	1.4700	1.4700
3	6	NONFER ORES	1.3100	1.3100	1.3100	1.3100	1.3100	1.3100	1.3100	1.3100	1.3100
4	7	NONFER METAL	1.2200	1.2200	1.2200	1.2200	1.2200	1.2200	1.2200	1.2200	1.2200
5	3	COKE PROD	2.0560	2.0560	2.0560	2.0560	2.0560	2.0560	2.0560	2.0560	2.0560
6	4	REFRAC MAT	1.5200	1.5200	1.5200	1.5200	1.5200	1.5200	1.5200	1.5200	1.5200
7	5	INDMET PROD	1.4000	1.4000	1.4000	1.4000	1.4000	1.4000	1.4000	1.4000	1.4000
8	8	COAL	1.7760	1.7760	1.7760	1.7760	1.7760	1.7760	1.7760	1.7760	1.7760
9	9	OIL EXTRAC	2.3000	2.3000	2.3000	2.3000	2.3000	2.3000	2.3000	2.3000	2.3000
10	10	OIL REF	1.4850	1.4850	1.4850	1.4850	1.4850	1.4850	1.4850	1.4850	1.4850
11	11	GAS	3.6700	3.6700	3.6700	3.6700	3.6700	3.6700	3.6700	3.6700	3.6700
12	12	PEAT	1.2180	1.2180	1.2180	1.2180	1.2180	1.2180	1.2180	1.2180	1.2180
13	13	OIL SHALES	1.1490	1.1490	1.1490	1.1490	1.1490	1.1490	1.1490	1.1490	1.1490
14	14	ELEC POWER	1.3760	1.3760	1.3760	1.3760	1.3760	1.3760	1.3760	1.3760	1.3760
15	15	ENSPOW M&E	1.0500	1.0500	1.0500	1.0500	1.0500	1.0500	1.0500	1.0500	1.0500
16	16	ELTECH M&E	.9400	.9400	.9400	.9400	.9400	.9400	.9400	.9400	.9400
17	17	CABLE PROD	.9400	.9400	.9400	.9400	.9400	.9400	.9400	.9400	.9400
18	20	MACH TOOLS	1.0400	1.0400	1.0400	1.0400	1.0400	1.0400	1.0400	1.0400	1.0400
19	21	FORG- PR M&E	1.0400	1.0400	1.0400	1.0400	1.0400	1.0400	1.0400	1.0400	1.0400
20	22	CAST M&E	1.0400	1.0400	1.0400	1.0400	1.0400	1.0400	1.0400	1.0400	1.0400
21	23	TOOLS & DIES	1.0400	1.0400	1.0400	1.0400	1.0400	1.0400	1.0400	1.0400	1.0400
22	24	PRECIS INST	.8200	.8200	.8200	.8200	.8200	.8200	.8200	.8200	.8200
23	25,26,27	MI&MET M&E	1.0420	1.0420	1.0420	1.0420	1.0420	1.0420	1.0420	1.0420	1.0420
24	28,29	PUMPS&CHEM E	1.0100	1.0100	1.0100	1.0100	1.0100	1.0100	1.0100	1.0100	1.0100
25	30	LOG&PA M&E	1.0520	1.0520	1.0520	1.0520	1.0520	1.0520	1.0520	1.0520	1.0520
26	31	LT IND M&E	.9200	.9200	.9200	.9200	.9200	.9200	.9200	.9200	.9200
27	32	FD IND M&E	.9200	.9200	.9200	.9200	.9200	.9200	.9200	.9200	.9200
28	33	PRINT M&E	.9780	.9780	.9780	.9780	.9780	.9780	.9780	.9780	.9780
29	34	HOIST&TRAN E	1.0500	1.0500	1.0500	1.0500	1.0500	.9780	.9780	.9780	.9780
30	35	CONST M&E	1.0000	1.0000	1.0000	1.0000	1.0000	1.0000	1.0000	1.0000	1.0000
31	36	CONMAT M&E	1.0000	1.0000	1.0000	1.0000	1.0000	1.0000	1.0000	1.0000	1.0000
32	37,38	TRANS M&E	1.0500	1.0500	1.0500	1.0500	1.0500	1.0500	1.0500	1.0500	1.0500
33	39	AUTOS	.9800	.9800	.9800	.9800	.9800	.9800	.9800	.9800	.9800
34	40	AGRIC M&E	1.0700	1.0700	1.0700	1.0700	1.0700	1.0700	1.0700	1.0700	1.0700
35	41	BEARNG	.9800	.9800	.9800	.9800	.9800	.9800	.9800	.9800	.9800

SEQ NO.	110 ORDER NO.		SYN FIBERS 46	ORGSYN PROD 47	PAINT & LAC 48	RUBBER PROD 49	OTHER CHEM 50	LOGG'G 51	SAW & LUM PR 52	FURNITURE 53	OTHER WDWK 54
36	18,19,42,43	RADIO&OTH MB	.8250	.8250	.8250	.8250	.8250	.8250	.8250	.8250	.8250
37	44	SANIT ENG PR	1.2300	1.2300	1.2300	1.2300	1.2300	1.2300	1.2300	1.2300	1.2300
38	45	OTHER METWRS	1.0780	1.0780	1.0780	1.0780	1.0780	1.0780	1.0780	1.0730	1.0780
39	46	METAL STRUCT	1.4550	1.4550	1.4550	1.4550	1.4550	1.4550	1.4550	1.4550	1.4550
40	47	REPAIR	1.0780	1.0780	1.0780	1.0780	1.0780	1.0780	1.0780	1.0780	1.0780
41	48	ABRASV	1.0780	1.0780	1.0780	1.0780	1.0780	1.0780	1.0780	1.0780	1.0780
42	49	MINRL CHEM	1.6100	1.6100	1.6100	1.6100	1.6100	1.6100	1.6100	1.6100	1.6100
43	50	BASIC CHEM	1.0600	1.0600	1.0600	1.0600	1.0600	1.0600	1.0600	1.0600	1.0600
44	51	ANIL DYE PR	1.1190	1.1190	1.1190	1.1190	1.1190	1.1190	1.1190	1.1190	1.1190
45	52	SYN R& PLAST	.7800	.7800	.7800	.7800	.7800	.7800	.7800	.7800	.7800
46	53	SYN FIBERS	.9280	.9280	.9280	.9280	.9280	.9280	.9280	.9280	.9280
47	55	ORGSYN PROD	1.0900	1.0900	1.0900	1.0900	1.0900	1.0900	1.0900	1.0900	1.0900
48	56	PAINT & LAC	1.0400	1.0400	1.0400	1.0400	1.0400	1.0400	1.0400	1.0400	1.0400
49	57	RUBBER PROD	1.0000	1.0000	1.0000	1.0000	1.0000	1.0000	1.0000	1.0000	1.0000
50	54,58,59	OTHER CHEM	.0900	.0900	.8760	.8751	.0890	.0900	.0900	.8622	.0900
51	60	LOGG'NG	1.2000	1.2000	1.2000	1.2000	1.2000	1.2000	1.2000	1.2000	1.2000
52	61,62	SAW & LUM FR	1.3810	1.3810	1.3810	1.3810	1.3810	1.3810	1.3810	1.3810	1.3810
53	63	FURNITURE	.9860	.9860	.9860	.9860	.9860	.9860	.9860	.9860	.9860
54	64	OTHER WDWK	1.2000	1.2000	1.2000	1.2000	1.2000	1.2000	1.2000	1.2000	1.2000
55	65	PAPER & PULP	1.4270	1.1820	1.1820	1.1820	1.1820	1.1820	1.1820	1.1820	1.3180
56	66	WOOD CHEM	1.3180	1.3180	1.3180	1.3180	1.3180	1.3180	1.3180	1.3180	1.3180
57	67-73	CONST MAT	1.0759	1.0754	1.0699	1.0787	1.0810	1.0987	1.1152	1.0779	1.0923
58	74	GLASS	.7800	.7800	.7800	.7800	.7800	.7800	.7800	.7800	.7800
59	75-80	TEXTLS	1.1189	1.0965	1.0930	1.0398	1.1133	1.0433	1.0623	1.0932	1.0425
60	81	SEWN GOODS	.9740	.9740	.9740	.9740	.9740	.9740	.9740	.9740	.9740
61	82	OTH LT IND	1.1034	1.1034	1.1034	1.1034	1.1034	1.1034	1.1034	1.1034	1.1034
62	83	FISH PROD	1.0500	1.0500	1.0500	1.0500	1.0500	1.0500	1.0500	1.0500	1.0500
63	84	MEAT PROD	.9770	.9770	.9770	.9770	.9770	.9770	.9770	.9770	.9770
64	85	DAIRY PROD	.9770	.9770	.9770	.9770	.9770	.9770	.9770	.9770	.9770
65	86	SUGAR	1.0000	1.0000	1.0000	1.0000	1.0000	1.0000	1.0000	1.0000	1.0000
66	87-89	FLOUR&BREAD	.9770	.9770	.9770	.9770	.9770	.9770	.9770	.9770	.9770
67	90-94	OTHER FOOD	1.0020	1.0020	1.0020	1.0020	1.0020	1.0020	1.0020	1.0020	1.0020
68	95	IND NEC	1.0000	1.0000	1.0000	1.0000	1.0000	1.0000	1.0000	1.0000	1.0000
69	96-100	CONST	1.1550	1.1550	1.1550	1.1550	1.1550	1.1550	1.1550	1.1550	1.1550
70	101	CROPS	1.0090	1.0090	1.0090	1.0090	1.0090	1.0090	1.0090	1.0090	1.0090
71	102	ANIMAL HUSB	1.2920	1.2920	1.2920	1.2920	1.2920	1.2920	1.2920	1.2920	1.2920
72	103	FOREST	2.1000	2.1000	2.1000	2.1000	2.1000	2.1000	2.1000	2.1000	2.1000
73	104-106	TRANS &COM	.9850	.9850	.9850	.9850	.9850	.9850	.9850	.9850	.9850
74	107-109	TRADE & DIST	1.0000	1.0000	1.0000	1.0000	1.0000	1.0000	1.0000	1.0000	1.0000
75	110	OTHER BRANCH	1.0000	1.0000	1.0000	1.0000	1.0000	1.0000	1.0000	1.0000	1.0000
76		TOTAL PURCH	1.0802	1.3025	1.0755	.9857	1.1184	1.3414	1.2005	1.1482	1.1965

(Table 5.2 continued)

SEQ NO.	110 ORDER NO.		PAPER & PULP 55	WOOD CHEM 56	CONST MAT 57	GLASS 58	TEXTLS 59	SEWN GOODS 60	OTH LT IND 61	FISH PROD 62	MEAT PROD 63
1	1	FER ORES	2.1370	2.1370	2.1370	2.1370	2.1370	2.1370	2.1370	2.1370	2.1370
2	2	FER METALS	1.4700	1.4700	1.4700	1.4700	1.4700	1.4700	1.4700	1.4700	1.4700
3	6	NONFER ORES	1.3100	1.3100	1.3100	1.3100	1.3100	1.3100	1.3100	1.3100	1.3100
4	7	NONFER METAL	1.2200	1.2200	1.2200	1.2200	1.2200	1.2200	1.2200	1.2200	1.2200
5	3	COKE PROD	2.0560	2.0560	2.0560	2.0560	2.0560	2.0560	2.0560	2.0560	2.0560
6	4	REFRAC MAT	1.5200	1.5200	1.5200	1.5200	1.5200	1.5200	1.5200	1.5200	1.5200
7	5	INDMET PROD	1.4000	1.4000	1.4000	1.4000	1.4000	1.4000	1.4000	1.4000	1.4000
8	8	COAL	1.7760	1.7760	1.7760	1.7760	1.7760	1.7760	1.7760	1.7760	1.7760
9	9	OIL EXTRAC	2.3000	2.3000	2.3000	2.3000	2.3000	2.3000	2.3000	2.3000	2.3000
10	10	OIL REF	1.4850	1.4850	1.4850	1.4850	1.4850	1.4850	1.4850	1.4850	1.4850
11	11	GAS	3.6700	3.6700	3.6700	3.6700	3.6700	3.6700	3.6700	3.6700	3.6700
12	12	PEAT	1.2180	1.2180	1.2180	1.2180	1.2180	1.2180	1.2180	1.2180	1.2180
13	13	OIL SHALES	1.1490	1.1490	1.1490	1.1490	1.1490	1.1490	1.1490	1.1490	1.1490
14	14	ELEC POWER	1.3760	1.3760	1.3760	1.3760	1.3760	1.3760	1.3760	1.3760	1.3760
15	15	EN&POW M&E	1.0500	1.0500	.9400	.9400	1.0500	1.0500	1.0500	1.0500	1.0500
16	16	ELTECH M&E	.9400	.9400	.9400	.9400	.9400	.9400	.9400	.9400	.9400
17	17	CABLE PROD	.9400	.9400	.9400	.9400	.9400	.9400	.9400	.9400	.9400
18	18	MACH TOOLS	1.0400	1.0400	1.0400	1.0400	1.0400	1.0400	1.0400	1.0400	1.0400
19	20	FORG- PR M&E	1.0400	1.0400	1.0400	1.0400	1.0400	1.0400	1.0400	1.0400	1.0400
20	22	CAST M&E	1.0400	1.0400	1.0400	1.0400	1.0400	1.0400	1.0400	1.0400	1.0400
21	23	TOOLS & DIES	1.0400	1.0400	1.0400	1.0400	1.0400	1.0400	1.0400	1.0400	1.0400
22	24	PRECIS INST	.8200	.8200	.8200	.8200	.8200	.8200	.8200	.8200	.8200
23	25,26,27	MI&MET M&E	1.0420	1.0420	1.0420	1.0420	1.0420	1.0420	1.0420	1.0420	1.0420
24	28,29	PUMPS&CHEM E	1.0100	1.0100	1.0100	1.0100	1.0100	1.0100	1.0100	1.0100	1.0100
25	30	LOG&PA M&E	1.0520	1.0520	1.0520	1.0520	1.0520	1.0520	1.0520	1.0520	1.0520
26	31	LT IND M&E	.9200	.9200	.9200	.9200	.9200	.9200	.9200	.9200	.9200
27	32	FD IND M&E	.9200	.9200	.9200	.9200	.9200	.9200	.9200	.9200	.9200
28	33	PRINT M&E	.9780	.9780	.9780	.9780	.9780	.9780	.9780	.9780	.9780
29	34	HOIST&TRAN E	1.0500	1.0500	1.0500	1.0500	1.0500	1.0500	1.0500	1.0500	1.0500
30	35	CONST M&E	1.0000	1.0000	1.0000	1.0000	1.0000	1.0000	1.0000	1.0000	1.0000
31	36	CONMAT M&E	1.0000	1.0000	1.0000	1.0000	1.0000	1.0000	1.0000	1.0000	1.0000
32	37,38	TRANS M&E	1.0500	1.0500	1.0500	1.0500	1.0500	1.0500	1.0500	1.0500	1.0500
33	39	AUTOS	.9800	.9800	.9800	.9800	.9800	.9800	.9800	.9800	.9800
34	40	AGRIC M&E	1.0700	1.0700	1.0700	1.0700	1.0700	1.0700	1.0700	1.0700	1.0700
35	41	BEARNG	.9800	.9800	.9800	.9800	.9800	.9800	.9800	.9800	.9800

SEQ NO.	110 ORDER NO.		PAPER & PULP 55	WOOD CHEM 56	CONST MAT 57	GLASS 58	TEXTLS 59	SEWN GOODS 60	OTH LT IND 61	FISH PROD 62	MEAT PROD 63
36	18,19,42,43	RADIO&OTH M3	.8250	.8250	.8250	.8250	.8250	.8250	.8250	.8250	.8250
37	44	SANIT ENG PR	1.2300	1.2300	1.2300	1.2300	1.2300	1.2300	1.2300	1.2300	1.2300
38	45	OTHER METWRS	1.0780	1.0780	1.0780	1.0780	1.0780	1.0780	1.0780	1.0780	1.0780
39	46	METAL STRUCT	1.4550	1.4550	1.4550	1.4550	1.4550	1.4550	1.4550	1.4550	1.4550
40	47	REPAIR	1.0760	1.0780	1.0780	1.0780	1.0780	1.0780	1.0780	1.0780	1.0780
41	48	ABRASV	1.0780	1.0780	1.0780	1.0780	1.0780	1.0780	1.0780	1.0780	1.0780
42	49	MINRL CHEM	1.5100	1.6100	1.6100	1.6100	1.6100	1.6100	1.6100	1.6100	1.6100
43	50	BASIC CHEM	1.0600	1.0600	1.0600	1.0600	1.0600	1.0600	1.0600	1.0600	1.0600
44	51	ANIL DYE PR	1.1190	1.1190	1.1190	1.1190	1.1190	1.1190	1.1190	1.1190	1.1190
45	52	SYN R& PLAST	.7800	.7800	.7800	.7800	.7800	.7800	.7800	.7800	.7800
46	53	SYN FIBERS	.9280	.9230	.9280	.9280	.9280	.9280	.9280	.9280	.9280
47	55	ORGSYN PROD	1.0900	1.0930	1.0900	1.0900	1.0900	1.0900	1.0900	1.0900	1.0900
48	56	PAINT & LAC	1.0400	1.0400	1.0400	1.0400	1.0400	1.0400	1.0400	1.0400	1.0400
49	57	RUBBER PROC	1.1000	1.1000	1.1000	1.1000	1.1000	1.1000	1.1000	1.1000	1.1000
50	54,58,59	OTHER CHEM	1.0900	1.0900	1.0070	1.0900	1.0900	1.0900	.8760	1.0900	1.0900
51	60	LOGGING	1.2000	1.2000	1.2000	1.2000	1.2000	1.2000	1.2000	1.2000	1.2000
52	61,62	SAW & LUM FR	1.3810	1.3810	1.3810	1.3810	1.3810	1.3810	1.3810	1.3810	1.3810
53	63	FURNITURE	.9860	.9860	.9860	.9860	.9860	.9860	.9860	.9860	.9860
54	64	OTHER WDWK	1.2000	1.2000	1.2000	1.2000	1.2000	1.2000	1.2000	1.2000	1.2000
55	65	PAPER & PULP	1.4270	1.1820	1.1820	1.1820	1.1820	1.1820	1.1820	1.1820	1.1820
56	66	WOOD CHEM	1.3180	1.3180	1.3180	1.3180	1.3180	1.3180	1.3180	1.3180	1.3180
57	67-73	CONST MAT	1.0688	1.0636	1.0890	.9766	1.0900	1.0888	1.0811	1.1005	1.1028
58	74	GLASS	.7800	.7800	.7800	.7800	.7800	.7800	.7800	.7800	.7800
59	75-80	TEXTLS	1.0456	1.0777	1.0580	1.0626	1.0350	1.0273	1.0603	1.0343	1.0417
60	81	SEWN GOODS	.9740	.9740	.9740	.9740	.9740	.9740	.9740	.9740	.9740
61	82	OTH LT IND	1.1034	1.1034	1.1034	1.1034	1.1034	1.1034	1.1034	1.1034	1.1034
62	83	FISH PROD	1.0500	1.0500	1.0500	1.0500	1.0500	1.0500	1.0500	1.0500	1.3810
63	84	MEAT PROD	.9770	.9770	.9770	.9770	.9770	.9770	.9770	.9770	.9770
64	85	DAIRY PROD	.9770	.9770	.9770	.9770	.9770	.9770	.9770	.9770	.9770
65	86	SUGAR	1.0000	1.0000	1.0000	1.0000	1.0000	1.0000	1.0000	1.0000	1.0000
66	87-89	FLOUR&BREAD	.9770	.9770	.9770	.9770	1.0000	.9770	.9770	.9770	.9770
67	90-94	OTHER FOOD	1.0020	1.0020	1.0020	1.0020	1.0000	1.0020	1.0020	1.0020	1.0020
68	95	IND NEC	1.0000	1.0000	1.0000	1.0000	1.0000	1.0000	1.0000	1.0000	1.0000
69	96-100	CONST	1.1550	1.1550	1.1550	1.1550	1.1550	1.1550	1.1550	1.1550	1.1550
70	101	CROPS	1.0090	1.0090	1.0090	1.0090	1.3180	1.0090	1.0090	1.0090	1.0090
71	102	ANIMAL HUSB	1.2920	1.2920	1.2920	1.2920	1.3690	1.2920	1.2920	1.2920	1.3490
72	103	FOREST	2.1000	2.1000	2.1000	2.1000	2.1000	2.1000	2.1000	2.1000	2.1000
73	104-106	TRANS &COM	.9850	.9850	.9850	.9850	.9850	.9850	.9850	.9850	.9850
74	107-109	TRADE & DIST	1.0000	1.0000	1.0000	1.0000	1.0000	1.0000	1.0000	1.0000	1.0000
75	110	OTHER BRANCH	1.0000	1.0000	1.0000	1.0000	1.0000	1.0000	1.0000	1.0000	1.0000
76		TOTAL PURCH	1.2320	1.1365	1.1891	1.1817	1.1016	1.0309	1.0930	1.0807	1.2566

(Table 5.2 continued)

SEQ NO.	110 ORDER NO.		DAIRY PROD 64	SUGAR 65	FLOUR& BREAD 66	OTHER FOOD 67	IND NEC 68	CONST 69	CROPS 70	ANIMAL HUSB 71	FOREST 72
1	1	FER ORES	2.1370	2.1370	2.1370	2.1370	2.1370	2.1370	2.1370	2.1370	2.1370
2	2	FER METALS	1.4700	1.4700	1.4700	1.4700	1.4700	1.4700	1.4700	1.4700	1.4700
3	6	NONFER ORES	1.3100	1.3100	1.3100	1.3100	1.3100	1.3100	1.3100	1.3100	1.3100
4	7	NONFER METAL	1.2200	1.2200	1.2200	1.2200	1.2200	1.2200	1.2200	1.2200	1.2200
5	3	COKE PROD	2.0560	2.0560	2.0560	2.0560	2.0560	2.0560	2.0560	2.0560	2.0560
6	4	REFRAC MAT	1.5200	1.5200	1.5200	1.5200	1.5200	1.5200	1.5200	1.5200	1.5200
7	5	INDMET PROD	1.4000	1.4000	1.4000	1.4000	1.4000	1.4000	1.4000	1.4000	1.4000
8	8	COAL	1.7760	1.7760	1.7760	1.7760	1.7760	1.7760	1.7760	1.7760	1.7760
9	9	OIL EXTRAC	2.3000	2.3000	2.3000	2.3000	2.3000	2.3000	2.3000	2.3000	2.3000
10	10	OIL REF	1.4850	1.4850	1.4850	1.4850	1.4850	1.4850	1.4850	1.4850	1.4850
11	11	GAS	3.6700	3.6700	3.6700	3.6700	3.6700	3.6700	3.6700	3.6700	3.6700
12	12	PEAT	1.2180	1.2180	1.2180	1.2180	1.2180	1.2180	1.2180	1.2180	1.2180
13	13	OIL SHALES	1.1490	1.1490	1.1490	1.1490	1.1490	1.1490	1.1490	1.1490	1.1490
14	14	ELEC POWER	1.3760	1.3760	1.3760	1.3760	1.3760	1.3760	1.0000	1.0000	1.3760
15	15	EN&POW M&E	1.0500	1.0500	1.0500	1.0500	1.0500	1.0500	1.0500	1.0500	1.0500
16	16	ELTECH M&E	.9400	.9400	.9400	.9400	.9400	.9400	.9400	.9400	.9400
17	17	CABLE PROD	.9400	.9400	.9400	.9400	.9400	.9400	.9400	.9400	.9400
18	20	MACH TOOLS	1.0400	1.0400	1.0400	1.0400	1.0400	1.0400	1.0400	1.0400	1.0400
19	21	FORG- PR M&E	1.0400	1.0400	1.0400	1.0400	1.0400	1.0400	1.0400	1.0400	1.0400
20	22	CAST M&E	1.0400	1.0400	1.0400	1.0400	1.0400	1.0400	1.0400	1.0400	1.0400
21	23	TOOLS & DIES	1.0400	1.0400	1.0400	1.0400	1.0400	1.0400	1.0400	1.0400	1.0400
22	24	PRECIS INST	.8200	.8200	.8200	.8200	.8200	.8200	.8200	.8200	.8200
23	25,26,27	MI&MET M&E	1.0420	1.0420	1.0420	1.0420	1.0420	1.0420	1.0420	1.0420	1.0420
24	28,29	PUMPS&CHEM E	1.0100	1.0100	1.0100	1.0100	1.0100	1.0100	1.0100	1.0100	1.0100
25	30	LOG&PA M&E	1.0520	1.0520	1.0520	1.0520	1.0520	1.0520	1.0520	1.0520	1.0520
26	31	LT IND M&E	.9200	.9200	.9200	.9200	.9200	.9200	.9200	.9200	.9200
27	32	FD IND M&E	.9200	.9200	.9200	.9200	.9200	.9200	.9200	.9200	.9200
28	33	PRINT M&E	.9780	.9780	.9780	.9780	.9780	.9780	.9780	.9780	.9780
29	34	HOIST&TRAN E	1.0500	1.0500	1.0500	1.0500	1.0500	1.0500	1.0500	1.0500	1.0500
30	35	CONST M&E	1.0000	1.0000	1.0000	1.0000	1.0000	1.0000	1.0000	1.0000	1.0000
31	36	CONMAT M&E	1.0000	1.0000	1.0000	1.0000	1.0000	1.0000	1.0000	1.0000	1.0000
32	37,38	TRANS M&E	1.0500	1.0500	1.0500	1.0500	1.0500	1.0500	1.0500	1.0500	1.0500
33	39	AUTOS	.9800	.9800	.9800	.9800	.9800	.9800	1.0000	1.0000	.9800
34	40	AGRIC M&E	1.0700	1.0700	1.0700	1.0700	1.0700	1.0700	1.0000	1.0000	1.0700
35	41	BEARNG	.9800	.9800	.9800	.9800	.9800	.9800	.9800	.9800	.9800

236

SEQ NO.	110 ORDER NO.		DAIRY PROD 64	SUGAR 65	FLOUR& BREAD 66	OTHER FOOD 67	IND NEC 68	CONST 69	CROPS 70	ANIMAL HUSB 71	FOREST 72
36	18,19,42,43	RADIO&OTH MB	.8250	.8250	.8250	.8250	.8250	.8250	.8250	.8250	.8250
37	44	SANIT ENG PR	1.2300	1.2300	1.2300	1.2300	1.2300	1.2300	1.2300	1.2300	1.2300
38	45	OTHER METWRS	1.0780	1.0780	1.0780	1.0780	1.0780	1.0780	1.0780	1.0780	1.0780
39	46	METAL STRUCT	1.4550	1.4550	1.4550	1.4550	1.4550	1.4550	1.4550	1.4550	1.4550
40	47	REPAIR	1.0780	1.0780	1.0780	1.0780	1.0780	1.0780	1.0780	1.0780	1.0780
41	48	ABRASV	1.0780	1.0780	1.0780	1.0780	1.0780	1.0780	1.0780	1.0780	1.0780
42	49	MINRL CHEM	1.6100	1.6100	1.6100	1.6100	1.6100	1.6100	1.6100	1.6100	1.6100
43	50	BASIC CHEM	1.0600	1.0600	1.0600	1.0600	1.0600	1.0600	1.0000	1.0000	1.0600
44	51	ANIL DYE PR	1.1190	1.1190	1.1190	1.1190	1.1190	1.1190	1.1190	1.1190	1.1190
45	52	SYN R& PLAST	.7800	.7800	.7800	.7800	.7800	.7800	.7800	.7800	.7800
46	53	SYN FIBERS	.9280	.9280	.9280	.9280	.9280	.9280	.9280	.9280	.9280
47	55	ORGSYN PROD	1.0900	1.0900	1.0900	1.0900	1.0900	1.0900	1.0900	1.0900	1.0900
48	56	PAINT & LAC	1.0400	1.0400	1.0400	1.0400	1.0400	1.0400	1.0400	1.0400	1.0400
49	57	RUBBER PROD	1.1000	1.1000	1.1000	1.1000	1.1000	1.1000	1.1000	1.1000	1.1000
50	54,58,59	OTHER CHEM	1.0900	1.0900	1.0900	1.0850	1.0900	1.0000	1.0900	1.0000	1.0000
51	60	LOGGNG	1.2000	1.2000	1.2000	1.2000	1.2000	1.2000	1.2000	1.2000	1.2000
52	61,62	SAW & LUM PR	1.3810	1.3810	1.3810	1.3810	1.3810	1.3810	1.3810	1.3810	1.3810
53	63	FURNITURE	.9860	.9860	.9860	.9860	.9860	.9860	.9860	.9860	.9860
54	64	OTHER WDWK	1.2000	1.2000	1.2000	1.2000	1.2000	1.2000	1.2000	1.2000	1.2000
55	65	PAPER & PULP	1.1820	1.1820	1.1820	1.1820	1.3600	1.1820	1.1820	1.1820	1.1820
56	66	WOOD CHEM	1.3180	1.3180	1.3180	1.3180	1.3180	1.3180	1.3180	1.3180	1.3180
57	67-73	CONST MAT	1.0871	1.0621	1.0840	1.0800	1.0890	1.1753	1.0974	1.0863	1.0730
58	74	GLASS	.7800	.7800	.7800	.7800	.7800	.8410	.7800	.7800	.7800
59	75-80	TEXTLS	1.0960	1.0876	1.0280	1.1230	1.0635	1.0394	1.0888	1.0739	1.0000
60	81	SEWN GOODS	.9740	.9740	.9740	.9740	.9740	.9740	.9740	.9740	.9740
61	82	OTH LT IND	1.1034	1.1034	1.1034	1.1034	1.1034	1.1034	1.1034	1.034	1.1034
62	83	FISH PROD	1.0500	1.0500	1.0500	1.0500	1.0500	1.0500	1.0500	1.0500	1.0500
63	84	MEAT PROD	.9770	.9770	.9770	.9770	.9770	.9770	.9770	.9770	.9770
64	85	DAIRY PROD	.9770	.9770	.9770	.9770	.9770	.9770	.9770	.9770	.9770
65	86	SUGAR	1.0000	1.0030	1.0000	1.0000	1.0000	1.0000	1.0000	1.0000	1.0000
66	87-89	FLOUR&BREAD	.9770	.9770	.9770	.9770	.9770	.9770	.9770	.9770	.9770
67	90-94	OTHER FOOD	1.0020	1.0020	1.0000	1.0020	1.0000	1.0020	1.0020	1.0020	1.0020
68	95	IND NEC	1.0000	1.0000	1.0000	1.0000	1.0000	1.0000	1.0000	1.0000	1.0000
69	96-100	CONST	1.1550	1.1550	1.1550	1.1550	1.1550	1.1550	1.1550	1.1550	1.1550
70	101	CROPS	1.0090	.9610	.9970	1.0090	1.0090	1.0090	1.1170	1.1170	1.0090
71	102	ANIMAL HUSB	1.2750	1.2920	1.2920	1.2920	1.2920	1.2920	1.1210	1.1210	1.2920
72	103	FOREST	2.1000	2.1000	2.1000	2.1000	2.1000	2.1000	2.1000	2.1000	2.1000
73	104-106	TRANS &COM	.9850	.9850	.9850	.9850	.9850	.9850	.9850	.9850	.9850
74	107-109	TRADE & DIST	1.0000	1.0000	1.0000	1.0000	1.0000	1.0000	1.0000	1.0000	1.0000
75	110	OTHER BRANCH	1.0000	1.0000	1.0000	1.0000	1.0000	1.0000	1.0000	1.0000	1.0000
76		TOTAL PURCH	1.2309	.9913	1.0016	1.0163	1.0872	1.1534	1.1012	1.1028	1.3701

237

(Table 5.2 continued)

SEQ NO.	110 ORDER NO.		TRANS &COM 73	TRADE & DIST 74	OTHER BRANCH 75	INTIND USE 76	PRIVAT CONSUM 77	PUBLIC CONSUM 78	OTHER FD 79	TOTAL FD 80	GVO 81
1	1	FER ORES	2.1370	2.1370	2.1370	2.1370	2.1370	2.1370	2.1370	2.1370	2.1370
2	2	FER METALS	1.4700	1.4700	1.4700	1.4700	1.4700	1.4700	1.4700	1.4700	1.4700
3	6	NONFER ORES	1.3100	1.3100	1.3100	1.3100	1.3100	1.3100	1.3100	1.3100	1.3100
4	7	NONFER METAL	1.2200	1.2200	1.2200	1.2200	1.2200	1.2200	1.2200	1.2200	1.2200
5	3	COKE PROD	2.0560	2.0560	2.0560	2.0560	2.0560	2.0560	2.0560	2.0560	2.0560
6	4	REFRAC MAT	1.5200	1.5200	1.5200	1.5200	1.5200	1.5200	1.5200	1.5200	1.5200
7	5	INDMET PROD	1.4000	1.4000	1.4000	1.4000	1.4000	1.4000	1.4000	1.4000	1.4000
8	8	COAL	1.7760	1.7760	1.7760	1.7805	1.7760	1.7760	1.7760	1.7760	1.7799
9	9	OIL EXTRAC	2.3000	2.3000	2.3000	1.8243	2.3000	2.3000	2.3000	2.3000	1.9932
10	10	OIL REF	1.4850	1.4850	1.4850	1.4850	1.4850	1.4850	1.4850	1.4850	1.4850
11	11	GAS	3.6700	3.6700	3.6700	3.6700	3.6700	3.6700	3.6700	3.6700	3.6700
12	12	PEAT	1.2180	1.2180	1.2180	1.2180	1.2180	1.2180	1.2180	1.2180	1.2180
13	13	OIL SHALES	1.1490	1.1490	1.1490	1.1490	1.1490	1.1490	1.1490	1.1490	1.1490
14	14	ELEC POWER	1.3100	1.3760	1.3760	1.3559	1.3760	1.3760	1.3760	1.3760	1.3599
15	15	EN&POW M&E	1.0500	1.0500	1.0500	1.0500	.9400	1.0500	1.0500	1.0500	1.0500
16	16	ELTECH M&E	.9400	.9400	.9400	.9400	.9400	.9400	.9400	.9400	.9400
17	17	CABLE PROD	.9400	.9400	.9400	.9400	.9400	.9400	.9400	.9400	.9400
18	20	MACH TOOLS	1.0400	1.0400	1.0400	1.0400	1.0400	1.0400	1.0400	1.0400	1.0400
19	21	FORG- PR M&E	1.0400	1.0400	1.0400	1.0400	1.0400	1.0400	1.0400	1.0400	1.0400
20	22	CAST M&E	1.0400	1.0400	1.0400	1.0400	1.0400	1.0400	1.0400	1.0400	1.0400
21	23	TOOLS & DIES	1.0400	1.0400	1.0400	1.0400	1.0400	1.0400	1.0400	1.0400	1.0400
22	24	PRECIS INST	.8200	.8200	.8200	.8200	.8200	.8200	.8200	.8200	.8200
23	25,26,27	MI&MET M&E	1.0420	1.0420	1.0420	1.0420	1.0420	1.0420	1.0420	1.0420	1.0420
24	28,29	PUMPS&CHEM E	1.0100	1.0100	1.0100	1.0100	1.0100	1.0100	1.0100	1.0100	1.0100
25	30	LOG&PA M&E	1.0520	1.0520	1.0520	1.0520	1.0520	1.0520	1.0520	1.0520	1.0520
26	31	LT IND M&E	.9200	.9200	.9200	.9200	.9200	.9200	.9200	.9200	.9200
27	32	FD IND M&E	.9200	.9200	.9200	.9200	.9200	.9200	.9200	.9200	.9200
28	33	PRINT M&E	.9780	.9780	.9780	.9780	.9780	.9780	.9780	.9780	.9780
29	34	HOIST&TRAN E	1.0500	1.0500	1.0500	1.0500	1.0500	1.0500	1.0500	1.0500	1.0500
30	35	CONST M&E	1.0000	1.0000	1.0000	1.0000	1.0000	1.0000	1.0000	1.0000	1.0000
31	36	CONMAT M&E	1.0000	1.0000	1.0000	1.0000	1.0000	1.0000	1.0000	1.0000	1.0000
32	37,38	TRANS M&E	1.0500	1.0500	1.0500	1.0500	1.0500	1.0500	1.0500	1.0500	1.0500
33	39	AUTOS	.9800	.9800	.9800	.9816	.9800	.9800	.9800	.9800	.9809
34	40	AGRIC M&E	1.0700	1.0700	1.0700	1.0595	1.0700	1.0700	1.0700	1.0700	1.0595
35	41	BEARNG	.9800	.9800	.9800	.9800	.9800	.9800	.9800	.9800	.9800

SEQ NO.	110 ORDER NO.		TRANS &COM 73	TRADE & DIST 74	OTHER BRANCH 75	INTIND USE 76	PRIVAT CONSUM 77	PUBLIC CONSUM 78	OTHER FD 79	TOTAL FD 80	GVO 81
36	18,19,42,43	RADIO&OTH MB	.8250	.8250	.3250	.8250	.8250	.8250	.8250	.8250	.8250
37	44	SANIT ENG PR	1.2300	1.2300	1.2300	1.2300	1.2300	1.2300	1.2300	1.2300	1.2300
38	45	OTHER METWRS	1.0780	1.0780	1.0780	1.0780	1.0780	1.0780	1.0780	1.0780	1.0780
39	46	METAL STRUCT	1.4550	1.4550	1.4550	1.4550	1.4550	1.4550	1.4550	1.4550	1.4550
40	47	REPAIR	1.0780	1.0780	1.0780	1.0780	1.0780	1.0780	1.0780	1.0780	1.0780
41	48	ABRASV	1.0780	1.0780	1.0780	1.0780	1.0780	1.0780	1.0780	1.0780	1.0780
42	49	MINRL CHEM	1.6100	1.6100	1.6100	1.6100	1.6100	1.6100	1.6100	1.6100	1.6100
43	50	BASIC CHEM	1.0600	1.0600	1.0600	1.0410	1.0600	1.0600	1.0600	1.0600	1.0452
44	51	ANIL DYE PR	1.1190	1.1190	1.1190	1.1190	1.1190	1.1190	1.1190	1.1190	1.1190
45	52	SYN R&PLAST	.7800	.7830	.7280	.7986	.7800	.7800	.7800	.7800	.8024
46	53	SYN FIBERS	.9280	.9230	.9280	.9280	.9280	.9280	.9280	.9280	.9280
47	55	ORGSYN PROD	1.0900	1.0930	1.0900	1.0900	1.0900	1.0900	1.0900	1.0900	1.0900
48	56	PAINT & LAC	1.0400	1.0420	1.0400	1.0400	1.0400	1.0400	1.0400	1.0400	1.0400
49	57	RUBBER PROD	1.0000	1.0000	1.0000	1.0000	1.0000	1.0000	1.0000	1.0000	1.0400
50	54,58,59	OTHER CHEM	1.0900	1.0900	1.0900	.9367	1.1244	1.1244	1.1244	1.1244	1.0011
51	60	LOGGNG	1.2000	1.2000	1.2000	1.2000	1.2000	1.2000	1.2000	1.2000	1.2000
52	61,62	SAW & LUM PR	1.3810	1.3810	1.3810	1.3810	1.3810	1.3810	1.3810	1.3810	1.3810
53	63	FURNITURE	.9860	.9860	.9860	.9860	.9860	.9860	.9860	.9860	.9860
54	64	OTHER WDWK	1.2000	1.2000	1.2000	1.2000	1.2000	1.2000	1.2000	1.2000	1.2000
55	65	PAPER & PULP	1.1820	1.1820	1.3600	1.2759	1.1820	1.1820	1.1820	1.1820	1.2715
56	66	WOOD CHEM	1.3180	1.3160	1.3180	1.3180	1.3180	1.3180	1.3160	1.3180	1.3180
57	67-73	CONST MAT	1.0726	1.0959	1.0593	1.1569	1.0786	1.0786	1.0786	1.0786	1.1534
58	74	GLASS	.7800	.7800	.7800	.8058	.7800	.7800	.7800	.7800	.8005
59	75-80	TEXTLS	.0547	.0304	1.1158	1.0373	.9825	.9825	.9825	.9825	1.0259
60	81	SEWN GOODS	.9740	.9740	.9740	.9740	.9740	.9740	.9740	.9740	.9740
61	82	OTH LT IND	1.1034	1.1034	1.1034	1.034	1.1034	1.1034	1.1034	1.1034	1.1034
62	83	FISH PROD	1.0500	1.0500	1.0500	1.0500	1.0500	1.0500	1.0500	1.0500	1.0500
63	84	MEAT PROD	.9770	.9770	.9770	.9770	.9770	.9770	.9770	.9770	.9770
64	85	DAIRY PROD	.9770	.9770	1.0000	.9770	.9770	.9770	.9770	.9770	.9770
65	86	SUGAR	1.0000	1.0000	1.0000	1.0000	1.0000	1.0000	1.0000	1.0000	1.0000
66	87-89	FLOUR&BREAD	.9770	.9770	.9770	.9770	.9770	.9770	.9770	.9770	.9770
67	90-94	OTHER FOOD	1.0020	1.0020	1.0020	1.0020	1.0020	1.0020	1.0020	1.0020	1.0020
68	95	IND NEC	1.0000	1.0000	1.0000	1.0000	1.0000	1.0000	1.0000	1.0000	1.0000
69	96-100	CONST	1.1550	1.1550	1.1550	1.0000	1.1550	1.1550	1.1550	1.1550	1.1550
70	101	CROPS	1.0090	1.0090	1.0090	1.0871	1.0090	1.0090	1.0090	1.0090	1.0673
71	102	ANIMAL HUSB	1.2920	1.2920	1.2920	1.3061	1.2920	1.2920	1.2920	1.2920	1.3000
72	103	FOREST	2.1000	2.1000	2.1000	2.1000	2.1000	2.1000	2.1000	2.1000	2.1000
73	104-106	TRANS &COM	.9860	.9850	.9850	.9850	.9850	.9850	.9850	.9850	.9850
74	107-109	TRADE & DIST	1.0000	1.0000	1.0000	1.0000	1.0000	1.0000	1.0000	1.0000	1.0000
75	110	OTHER BRANCH	1.0000	1.0000	1.0000	1.1635	1.0000	1.0000	1.0000	1.0000	1.0548
76		TOTAL PURCH	1.1834	1.0917	1.1386	1.1438	1.0362	1.1082	1.1113	1.0720	1.1092

Source: Compiled by the authors.

239

While the overall accuracy of the 1966-70 price conversion appears to be acceptable, the scarcity of reliable data dictated the use of some simplifying assumptions and approximations, and some of the estimated price indexes probably contain significant error. It would be, therefore, instructive at this point to summarize and discuss these simplifying assumptions and other unavoidable shortcomings of the conversion exercise.

Probably the most serious shortcoming of the study is the relatively small number of price indexes used. Thus, compared with more than 1,000 indexes prepared in the 1966-70 conversion undertaken by the Central Statistical Administration (CSA) (Eidel'man 1972, p. 14), this present study is based on not more than one-third of this number. As can be seen from Table 5.2 many of the individual rows of the table have been adjusted by means of a single price index. Since prices of many Soviet commodities are differentiated by buyers, some cells in these rows should have been adjusted by different indexes, but lack of the necessary data made this impossible and single indexes were used. It must be stressed, however, that the comparison of the number of price indexes used by Soviet statisticians and in this conversion is somewhat misleading, as the Soviet exercise involved a purchasers' price table and here a table in producers' prices is used. Most of the price differentiation for the same commodity results from varying rates of turnover taxes, different transportation and distribution costs, and other factors affecting primarily purchasers' prices. Thus, in general, one should expect a higher degree of price differentiation in rows in a purchasers' price table.

There remains, however, the problem of the commodity mix in each sector or row of the input-output table. Since the entire output of the economy is shown in the input-output table in terms of only 75 commodity groups or producing sectors, most of these sectors represent virtually thousands of separate commodities. Thus, each of the row entries, x_{ij}, stands for a complex mix of different commodities comprising the producing sector i and purchased by the buying sector j, and this mix is probably different for each of the buying sectors. Thus, the price index applicable to each flow entry x_{ij} should ideally be a weighted average index corresponding to the mix of each of the commodities constituting the output of the producing sector. A good illustration of this is the matrix of price indexes used to convert the 1966 Soviet 15-sector Latvian input-output table to 1967 prices. In this matrix, which was published in complete form, each of the 225 indexes is different (Shmulder 1971, pp. 94-97).

Another shortcoming of the conversion exercise resulting from the absence of necessary data is that no attempt was made to modify the available price indexes to reflect commodity-establishment differentials. Soviet input-output tables use statistical data that have been adjusted to reflect production and distribution of pure commodities with all secondary outputs and by-products removed (Treml et al. 1972, pp. 123-46). In all probability some of the data used in the conversion exercise refer to the establishment basis such as price indexes for a given ministry or a firm, and should have been adjusted.

The simplified treatment of foreign trade vectors in the conversion of the input-output table to 1970 prices also probably resulted in some error. Both Soviet exports and imports are recorded in input-output tables in domestic prices: the exports are purchased by various foreign trade organizations from the manufacturers at domestic prices and the imports are sold through the distribution system at prices of similar products manufactured domestically. Thus, in theory, a price index for a particular commodity or a group of commodities would be applied to exports and imports of this commodity. Since the index is the same, it could be also applied to the export-import balance. In fact, Soviet prices of commodities produced for export and for imported goods differ from domestic prices for similar commodities. In the 1967 price reform, special foreign trade price catalogues were issued for at least some commodities (Turetskii 1969, p. 259). For instance, the new 1967 prices set for imported machinery were increased by a higher percentage than the prices for comparable domestically produced machines (Efremov, Maliugin, and Turianskii 1969, pp. 30-31). Thus, the proper procedure for conversion of any row would have required price adjustments separately for exports and imports. In the 1966 reconstructed table the exports and imports are not shown separately but are lumped together in the form of an export-import balance aggregated with the residual category covering gross investment, changes in inventories, losses, and other uses. A single price index for each row was employed to convert this column to 1970 prices, thus generating some error.

Another significant simplification employed in this study concerns the use of a single price index for the entire transportation and communications row. Rates for different modes of transportation were adjusted differently in the 1967 price reform, with the weighted average index reported as 0.985 (Planovoe khoziaistvo 1967, p. 17). However, adjustments in freight rates for specific commodities were much more significant than the economywide average change. Thus, for example, the rail rates for window glass were cut 50 percent and the rates for transporting construction bricks were increased by 35 percent (Turetskii 1969, p. 378). Unfortunately, lack of the necessary data made the use of separate indexes impossible and the economywide index of .985 was used.

It must be noted, however, that the failure to adjust the values in the transportation row should generate a significantly smaller error in a conversion of a producers' price table than in a conversion of a purchasers' price table. The transportation row of an input–output table in purchasers' prices records costs of delivery of output to various buyers. Thus, when freight rates on specific commodities are changed, these changes will directly affect the transportation entry. A producers' price input–output table, on the other hand, records in each cell of the transportation row the combined costs of having all material inputs delivered to the given sector. Thus, as long as the transportation rates for different modes and for different types of freight are adjusted up and down, some of these changes will cancel each other. One can still expect some errors but unless a given sector's bill of material purchases is dominated by a single input, it can be assumed that the average error introduced by a single index adjustment of the entire row of transportation costs will be rather small.

As mentioned above, this study essentially follows the methodology of price conversion employed by the CSA staff in their recalculation of the 1966 input–output table in 1970 prices.[10] It would be instructive at this time to point out several shortcomings of the Soviet method.

First of all, in the CSA conversion the depreciation row was left unadjusted, while the gross investment column of the final demand was recomputed in new prices. It seems that it would have been more accurate to adjust the depreciation row as well as the investment column. As stated by several Soviet authors, the actual depreciation accounts understate the real wear and tear of fixed capital stocks and hence an upward adjustment would have been only proper, particularly because the value of construction services was increased in 1970. Another case in point is the relationship between depreciation and gross investment. In an input–output framework, gross investment less depreciation equals net investment. By having increased the value of gross investment in new prices without an upward adjustment of the depreciation total, the table in new 1970 prices overstates the value of net investment.

The second aspect of the CSA conversion that can be challenged on methodological grounds is the treatment of the labor income row in the value-added quadrant. According to Eidel'man (1972, p. 5) only wages of construction workers were revised upward to reflect the 1970 wage increases. While, in fact, the increase in construction wages in 1970 was the highest among the producing sectors (32.5 percent over the 1966 level), wage increases in other sectors were not far behind. Thus, wages in the 1966–70 period in industry increased by 25 percent, in communications by

28 percent, and in sovkhozes by 27 percent. It seems that a better procedure would have been to adjust the entire wage income row to reflect correctly the pattern of distribution of national income in 1970 prices.

Needless to say, the necessary adjustments of the depreciation and wage income rows could have been effected without much difficulty in this exercise. However, this would have meant departing from the Soviet methodology and would have prevented tests of the accuracy of the 1966-70 conversion against Soviet data.

TESTS OF ACCURACY

The conversion of the 1966 input-output table into 1970 prices described in this study is based on separate conversion of each of the rows of the table by estimated price indexes. Some of these estimates are very rough and the whole exercise is based on several simplifying assumptions and approximations. Under these circumstances it would have been rather difficult, if not impossible, to evaluate the overall accuracy of the table in 1970 prices.

Fortunately we have several aggregative indexes obtained by the Central Statistical Administration in their conversion of the 1966 table to 1970 prices. Since these indexes were not employed in the exercise described above, they can now be used to test the accuracy of the 1970 price table.

According to a CSA report (Eidel'man 1972, pp. 13-14) the conversion of the 1966 table to 1970 prices resulted in the following changes which we can take as aggregative price indexes:

Gross social product	1.065
Material costs	1.090*
National income	1.040

*Approximately.

The conversion also resulted in changes in the distribution of shares in the national income used. Thus, before the price conversion consumption comprised 73 percent of the total, and investment and other uses comprised 27 percent; after the conversion the share of consumption decreased to 71 percent and the share of investment went up to 29 percent.

The problem with these data is that they are based on an input-output table in purchasers' prices, while this study is based on a table in producers' prices. Thus, before the accuracy of the price conversion can be tested by comparing the aggregative indexes with the Soviet measures, the key values of the table must be recalculated into 1970 purchasers' prices. Generally speaking, recalculation of an input–output table or of its several key totals from purchasers' to producers', or from producers' to purchasers' prices is relatively simple and straightforward (Treml et al. 1973, pp. 5-12).

However, this case is much more complex since it involves both conversion of an input–output table to a new price base and conversion from producers' to purchasers' prices. As explained above, the method of price conversion employed both by Soviet statisticians and in this study consists of converting each of the rows of the first and second quadrants to a new price base by appropriate price indexes. Since the depreciation and wage entries of the third quadrant remained unadjusted, this method will produce imbalances for most sectors, since revenues derived from sales of output in new prices would register different absolute changes (positive or negative) from changes affecting material purchases produced by price changes. Since the row sum/column sum equality (total sales equal total costs plus profits) of input–output tables must be preserved, these imbalances are corrected by necessary adjustments (positive or negative) of the free elements of value-added, that is, profits and turnover taxes. Strictly speaking, an input–output table converted to a new price base does not have separately identifiable profit and tax elements but simply new residual entries in the value–added quadrant.

In this case, the 1966 input–output table was first converted from purchasers' to producers' prices by removal and reimputation of distribution charges and turnover taxes and was then converted to the new 1970 producers' prices. In order to convert the 1970 price table to a purchasers' price table we need to know the relevant magnitudes of profits and turnover taxes, which are not available and which, in some sense, do not exist.

This problem could not have been resolved had an attempt been made to estimate these magnitudes for each of the 75 producing sectors of the table. However, since there are only five aggregate measures from the Soviet 1970 price table, all that is needed are the absolute ruble magnitudes of turnover taxes that would have been collected under the new price regimen.

It will be recalled that the introduction of new prices in 1967 and the subsequent price adjustments had two expressed goals: to reduce the variability in profitability among industrial branches, enterprises, and products, and to reduce or eliminate losses by bringing revenues more in line with costs. The 1965 reform of management and administration of the Soviet economy made profitability in relation to working and fixed capital one of the main success criteria of economic performance of enterprises. This newly defined profitability which was expected to be more or less uniform, at least within major industrial branches, was made the starting point in the computation of the new 1967 prices (Bornstein 1967, pp. 21-25; Schroeder 1969; Sitnin 1969). When necessary, the turn-over tax rates were adjusted to meet this goal. The 1967 price re-form thus resulted in a significant change in the relative shares of profits and turnover taxes in the value-added of industry, as can be seen from the fact that the ratio of taxes to profits in industry changed from 1.510 in 1966 to .901 in 1970 (Narkhoz 67, p. 229, and Narkhoz 73, p. 253). A prominent Soviet price specialist Iu. Iakovets (1974, p. 169) describes the change as follows: "As the result of the 1967 price reform, about one-half of turnover taxes levied on oil, gas and electricity was added to wholesale enterprise prices and assumed the form of profit (prinialo formu pribyli)."

The question is then as follows. Given the 1966 input-output table in 1970 prices and the total residual surplus in the industry's value-added (that is, total value-added less costs such as wages and social security payments), what absolute magnitudes of turnover taxes and profits would match the tax-profit relationship that ex-isted in 1970?

For the purposes of conversion of the 1970 price input-output table from producers' to purchasers' prices it is necessary to es-timate only two figures--the total turnover taxes and the turnover taxes collected in the first quadrant, which would be consistent with the 1970 profit-tax relationship. The very nature of the prob-lem makes the estimation method awkward and the results can be accepted only as approximations.

One can begin with a simple relationship for a producers' price table which can be described by the following equation:

$$P_t + T_i = R_t \tag{3}$$

where

P_t = total profit in industry

T_i = turnover taxes levied on material inputs purchased by industry

R_t = total residual surplus in industry, that is, the residual in the value-added, after all costs such as labor and social security payments have been subtracted.

The R_t value has been estimated for the 1966 input-output table in 1970 producers' prices as 35,222.2 million rubles (Appendix B).

The published Soviet data, giving the 1970 ratio of total profits to total turnover taxes in industry as .901, has already been referred to. Thus,

$$T_t^{1970} \div P_t^{1970} = .901 \tag{4}$$

Finally, it is estimated that in 1970, turnover taxes levied on inputs purchased by industry comprised 21.4 percent of the total collected, and taxes on inputs purchased by all sectors of the economy (T_e) comprised 25.0 percent of the total (Appendix B). Thus,

$$T_i^{1970} \div T_t^{1970} = .214 \tag{5}$$

and

$$T_e^{1970} \div T_t^{1970} = .225 \tag{6}$$

Substituting the estimated values in equation (3),

$$\frac{T_t^{1970}}{.901} + .214 \, T_t^{1970} = 35,222.2 \text{ million rubles}$$

and solving, the estimate of T_t as 26,605 million rubles is obtained, and of T_e as 5,694 million rubles. The exact meaning of these two estimates must be made clear. In 1966 the total turnover taxes collected on industrial products were equal to 39.6 billion rubles, and taxes included with the purchase price of intermediate goods were equal to 13.3 billion rubles (Table 1.2 above). The 1967 price reform resulted in a significant decrease of the share of turnover taxes and increased the share of profits in the national income generated in industry. Thus, having converted the 1966 table to 1970 prices, an estimate has been made of the value of the turnover taxes that would match the 1970 tax-profit relationship.

One can now proceed with the conversion of the totals and subtotals of the 1970 price input-output table from producers' to purchasers' prices in order to compare the resulting price changes with price indexes obtained by Soviet statisticians. The calculations for the major aggregates for which there are Soviet indexes are shown below. The 1970 price data (in millions of rubles) are from the input-output table in this chapter and the 1966 price data are from Chapter 1.

Gross Social Product

1966 GSP in 1970 producers' prices	451,949.2
Plus transportation and communications GVO in 1970 producers' prices	18,813.5
Plus trade and distribution GVO in 1970 producers' prices	15,730.0
Plus 1970-price determined total turnover taxes as estimated, incl. radio fees	27,000.0
Equals 1966 GSP in 1970 purchasers' prices	513,492.7

Value of Material Purchases

1966 material purchases in 1970 producers' prices	241,433.7
Plus transportation and communications GVO in 1970 producers' prices	18,813.5
Plus trade and distribution GVO in 1970 producers' prices	15,730.0
Plus 1970-price determined turnover taxes levied on material inputs in quadrant I, as estimated	5,694.0
Equals 1966 material purchases in 1970 purchasers' prices	281,671.2

National Income

1966 GSP in 1970 purchasers' prices	513,492.7
Less 1966 material purchases in 1970 purchasers' prices	281,671.2
Less 1966 productive depreciation	22,310.0
Equals 1966 national income in 1970 purchasers' prices	209,511.5

These values can now be compared with the corresponding values from the 1966 input-output table in 1966 purchasers' prices which are, respectively, 481,295.0, 257,156.6, and 201,828.4 million rubles (from Chapter 1). The implicit price indexes can then be calculated as

Gross social product	1.067
Material purchases	1.095
National income	1.038

which are identical with the price indexes reported by Soviet statisticians.

Lastly, a comparison can be made between the structure of the national income component of final demand in 1970 prices obtained in this study and the results of the conversion undertaken by the Central Statistical Administration. According to their report, after

the conversion of the 1966 national income to 1970 purchasers'
prices the share of consumption comprised 71 percent and investment 29 percent of the total (Eidel'man 1972, p. 14).

In the case of final demand in 1970 prices yet another difficulty
is encountered. This study is based on producers' prices, and most
if not all producers' prices changed between 1966 and 1970. The
Soviet conversion exercise was based on purchasers' prices and
with the exception of agricultural sales to consumption, purchasers'
prices of goods delivered to consumption did not change.[11] Thus,
as the various totals of the 1970 price table are transformed to
purchasers' prices, the unchanged 1966 consumption vector must be
substituted. The calculations, with the amounts shown in millions
of rubles, are as follows:

Total consumption in 1966 purchasers' prices	150,000.0
Less agricultural sales to consumption in 1966 purchasers' prices	21,835.0
Plus agricultural sales to consumption in 1970 producers' prices	24,973.6
Plus transportation and distribution cost of agricultural sales to consumption	993.0
Equals consumption in 1970 purchasers' prices	154,131.6
Gross investment, 1970 producers' prices	93,428.0
Less total depreciation	32,310.0
Equals net investment	61,118.0
Total national income (consumption plus investment)	215,249.6

Thus in the 1970 price table, consumption comprises 71.6
percent of national income and this agrees, within the rounding
range, with the results obtained by Soviet statisticians.

It can be concluded that despite the shortcomings and gaps in
the basic data and several simplifying assumptions used in the exercise, the overall accuracy of the conversion of the 1966 input-
output table to 1970 prices undertaken in this study is acceptable.

It must be stressed again that accuracy is used here only to
connote an agreement with the Soviet conversion. For some
analytical purposes it may be desirable to adjust upward prices of
machinery and chemicals to reflect the possible creeping up of
prices which was not reflected in the price indexes.[12]

APPENDIX A

Derivation of 1966–70 Price Indexes

The derivation of 1966–70 wholesale enterprise (or producers') price indexes on the basis of an input–output 110–commodity list is presented below. In cases where the available Soviet data are straightforward and clear, only the price index and the sources are given. In the absence of the necessary data on price changes, ambiguities in the description of the data, inconsistencies among different sources, and similar problems, the derivation of indexes is explained in detail.

1. Ferrous ores   2.137   (Komin 1971, p. 136)

2. Ferrous metals   1.47   (Eidel'man 1972, p. 4)

3. Coke products   2.056   (Komin 1971, p. 136)

4. Refractory materials. In the absence of any information on price changes in this sector, the price index is derived from physical and value data. It will be noted that the output in tons and the mix of products did not change significantly between 1966 and 1970 (Narkhoz 67, p. 284, and Narkhoz 73, p. 303).

	1966	1970
	(thousands of tons)	
Fireclay products	5,977	6,097
Silica products	641	597
Magnesiochromite products	1,401	1,423
Magnesium powder	1,362	1,344

However, the GVO in producers' prices (that is, net of transportation and communications charges) changed from 294,844,000 rubles in 1966 to 451,900,000 rubles in 1970. It can be concluded that with minimal output and mix changes, the increase in the value of output is explained by an increase in prices. Price index is then derived as a ratio of 1970/1966 GVO divided by the index of output in tons, or 1.52.

5. Industrial metal products. No information on price changes in this sector is available. Noting that the price of steel increased

by 48 percent and the price of pipes by 37.7 percent (Komin 1971, p. 136), the price index is arbitrarily estimated at 1.40.

6. Nonferrous ores   1.31   (Shkatov and Suponitskii
                                                    1969, p. 142)

7. Nonferrous metals   1.22   (Shkatov and Suponitskii
                                                    1969, p. 142)

8. Coal. The average price index for the whole economy was reported as 1.78 (Planovoe khoziaistvo 1967, p. 121; Komin 1971, p. 121) with the index for the coking coal (13.8 percent of deliveries in 1966) being 1.931, and the index for coal used for electrical power generation (22.9 percent of the total) being 1.701. Using these percentages as weights the price index applicable to coal sold to other users can be estimated as 1.776.

9. Oil extraction. The price index for the oil purchased by the oil processing sector was 1.8 (Eidel'man 1972, p. 3), while that for all other buyers was 2.3 (Planovoe khoziaistvo 1967, p. 15).

10. Oil processing   1.485   (Shkatov and Suponitskii
                                                    1969, p. 171)

11. Gas   3.67   (Belousov 1969, p. 89)

12. Peat. No information on price changes in the peat sector was found and the index was estimated in the following way. In the 1966–70 period the output of peat decreased from 65.4 million tons to 57.4 million (Narkhoz 67, p. 193 and Narkhoz 73, p. 217). The GVO as measured in input-output tables net of distribution costs increased in the same period from 377.7 million rubles to 403.5 million. Since we are dealing with a homogeneous product and there is no turnover tax, the price index was estimated by dividing the ratio of the two GVOs by the output index, or 1.218.

13. Oil shales. As with peat, the price index is estimated on the basis of output in physical units and output data in current prices as 1.149.

14. Electrical and thermal power. The Soviet system of prices or rates for electrical power is very complex with rates greatly differentiated by users and regions. On the average the 1966–67 price index for electrical power was reported as 1.36 (Stoliarov

1969, p. 69) and this index will be employed for all users with
two exceptions. Agriculture continued to pay the pre-1967
reform price (price index = 1.0) and the index for the price of
electrical power sold to the transportation sector for electrical
locomotion is estimated at 1.31 (Shkatov and Suponitskii 1969,
p. 9).

15-48. Machinebuilding and metalworking. Estimation of price indexes for the machinebuilding and metalworking industry was
made more difficult by the fact that in contrast to other products,
machinery prices underwent two major price revisions: the
general price reform of 1967 and the second round of price adjustments in the 1968-69 period. For the whole machinery industry the 1967 price reform resulted in a modest price increase
of 0.2 percent (Iakovets 1972, p. 57), while the 1968-69 price
changes amounted to an average 5 percent decrease (Komin
1971, pp. 185-86; Iakovets 1974, p. 95; Kuznetsov and Koshuta
1971, p. 73). The 1968-69 price changes are not discussed at
any length in the Soviet literature and it is therefore difficult to
incorporate these changes in this index. There are even some
well-grounded doubts as to the accuracy of Soviet statements
referring to an overall price cut of 5 percent (Becker 1974,
p. 378). The estimates of price indexes for machinery shown
below were made in several steps. First, all reported 1967
price changes were recorded and analyzed. Since no information was found on 1967 price changes for about one-fourth of the
total output, a residual price deflator of 1.078 was calculated
for all sectors for which no data are available. The residual
index was calculated on the basis of the total machinebuilding
and metalworking price index of 1.002, and available indexes
for specific sectors were weighted by 1966 GVO weights in producers' prices obtained from the 1966 Soviet input-output table
(Treml et al. 1972, pp. 470-71). Lastly, the 1967 price indexes
were adjusted to reflect the reported 1968-69 price changes.

    In the list of price indexes shown below, the final net 1966-70
price index is listed first, followed by a 1966-67 price index in
square brackets. For sectors for which only one price index is
shown, no information on the post-1967 prices was found.

15. Energy and power machinery   1.05 [1.076]   (Iakovets 1972,
     and equipment   p. 57; Iakovets
                                                     1974, p. 95)

16. Electrotechnical machinery and equipment	.94 [.9]	(Minnich 1968, p. 15; Kovaleva 1969, p. 57; Iakovets 1974, p. 95)
17. Cable products	.94 [.9]	(Minnich 1968, p. 15; Kovaleva 1969, p. 57; Iakovets 1974, p. 95)
18. Radio products	.81	(Minnich 1968, p. 15)
19. Electronics	.81	(Minnich 1968, p. 15)
20. Machine tools	1.04 [1.061]	(Iakovets 1972, p. 57; Iakovets 1974, p. 95)
21. Forging/pressing machinery and equipment	1.04 [1.061]	(Iakovets 1972, p. 57; Iakovets 1974, p. 95)
22. Casting machinery and equipment	1.04 [1.061]	(Iakovets 1972, p. 57; Iakovets 1974, p. 57)
23. Tools and dies	1.04 [1.061]	(Iakovets 1972, p. 57; Iakovets 1974, p. 95)
24. Precision instruments	.82 [.88]	(Planovoe khoziaistvo 1967, p. 17; Iakovets 1974, p. 95)
25. Oil industry machinery and equipment	1.01 [1.076]	(Iakovets 1972, p. 57; Iakovets 1974, p. 95)
26. Mining machinery and equipment	1.05 [1.076]	(Iakovets 1972, p. 57; Iakovets 1974, p. 95)
27. Metallurgical machinery and equipment	1.05 [1.076]	(Iakovets 1972, p. 57; Iakovets 1974, p. 95)
28. Pumps and compressors	1.01 [1.076]	(Iakovets 1972, p. 57; Iakovets 1974, p. 95)

29. Chemical industry ma- 1.01 [1.01] (Narkhoz 68,
    chinery and equipment   p. 260; Iakovets
                                         1974, p. 95)

30. Logging and paper ma- 1.052 (Narkhoz 68,
    chinery and equipment   p. 259)

31. Light industry machinery .92 [.88] (Minnich 1968,
    and equipment   p. 15; Iakovets
                                          1974, p. 95)

32. Food industry machinery .92 [.88] (Minnich 1968,
    and equipment   p. 15; Iakovets
                                         1974, p. 95)

33. Printing machinery and .978 (Narkhoz 68,
    equipment   p. 265)

34. Hoisting/transporting 1.05 [1.070] (Iakovets 1972,
    machinery and equipment   p. 57; Iakovets
                                           1974, p. 95)

35. Construction machinery 1.00 (Iakovets 1974,
    and equipment   p. 95)

36. Construction materials 1.00 (Iakovets 1974,
    machinery and equipment   p. 95)

37. Railroad rolling stock 1.05 [1.076] (Iakovets 1972,
                                           p. 57; Iakovets
                                           1974, p. 95)

38. Shipbuilding 1.05 [1.076] (Iakovets 1972,
                                p. 57; Iakovets
                                1974, p. 95)

39. Automobiles* .98 [1.05] (Minnich 1968,
                              p. 14; Iakovets
                              1974, p. 95)

40. Tractors and agricultural 1.07 [1.116] (Minnich 1968,
    machinery and equipment*   p. 14; Iakovets
                                             1972, p. 57;
                                             Iakovets 1974,
                                             p. 95)

41. Bearings .98 [1.078] (1967 residual
                           estimate;
                           Iakovets 1974,
                           p. 95)

---

*Except sales to agriculture where the index is 1.00.

42. Medical equipment	1.078	[residual estimate]
43. Other machinery	.92 [1.078]	(Iakovets 1974, p. 95)
44. Sanitary engineering	1.23	Based on an average price change for seven major products (Efremov et al. 1969, p. 28)
45. Metal ware	1.078	[residual estimate]
46. Metal structures	1.455	(Efremov et al. 1969, p. 28)
47. Repair	1.078	[residual estimate]
48. Abrasives	1.078	[residual estimate]

49-50. Chemical industry. Prices for chemical products were increased on the average by 5 percent in the 1967 price reform (Planovoe khoziaistvo 1967, p. 61; Sitnin 1967, p. 10). The price indexes shown below were derived as follows. First, all reported price changes were recorded. Using the 1966 input-output GVO's net of distribution charges (Table 1.1, Chapter 1) as weights, the index for sectors for which no data were found was estimated as a residual at 1.09.

| 49. Mineral chemistry | 1.61 | (Planovoe khoziaistvo 1967, p. 16) |

50. Basic chemicals. The estimation of the price index for this sector is rather difficult because of the complexity of the product mix. The following rates are known:

Mineral fertilizer	1.34	(Shkatov and Suponitskii 1969, p. 186; Planovoe khoziaistvo 1967, p. 16)
Sulphuric acid	1.539	(Shkatov and Suponitskii 1969, p. 183)
Most other products	1.057	(Shkatov and Suponitskii 1969, p. 175).

Fertilizer comprises about one-third of the value of output of the sector (Oznobin 1968, p. 152) but the price increase of 34 percent was somewhat artificial as the price of mineral fertilizer sold to agriculture remained unchanged. The fertilizer industry receives a state subsidy to cover the price increase, and the input-output table shows sales of basic chemicals to agriculture at unchanged prices. Under the circumstances an index of 1.0 will be used for fertilizer sales to agriculture and 1.06 for all other deliveries.

51. Aniline dyes   1.119   (Shkatov and
                                                          Suponitskii
                                                          1969, p. 175)

52. Synthetic resins and plastics. Prices of resins and plastics were adjusted selectively (Minnich 1968, p. 14 and p. 17). The price indexes are as follows (Shkatov and Suponitskii 1969, p. 175):

    On sales to all metallur-
      gical sectors   .80
    On sales to tractors and
      agricultural machinery
      and equipment sector,
      electrotechnical products
      sector, and instruments   .865
    On sales to radio industry   .93
    On sales to automobile
      industry   .908

For all other buyers the prices of plastics and resins were cut 18 percent and the prices on plastics were cut 25 percent. As the first approximation an index of .78 will be used for all other buyers.

53. Synthetic fibers   .928   (Planovoe
                                                          khoziaistvo
                                                          1967, p. 16;
                                                          Kul'bovskaia
                                                          1973, p. 90;
                                                          Shkatov and
                                                          Suponitskii 1969,
                                                          p. 175)

54. Synthetic rubber   .875   (Kovaleva 1969,
                                                          p. 58)

55. Organic synthetic products   1.09   [residual estimate]

56. Paints and lacquers   1.04   (Shkatov and
                                                 Suponitskii
                                                 1969, p. 175)

57. Rubber products   1.1
There have been selected price increases for rubber products.
Tires delivered for equipping new products (automobiles,
tractors, and construction machinery) were first increased by
16.2 percent (Shkatov and Suponitskii 1969, p. 175; Sitnin 1967,
p. 10) and subsequently cut. Prices on tires delivered as replacements were not changed (Komin 1971, p. 140). An index
of 1.1 applied to all deliveries will be used as a rough estimate.

58. Pharmaceuticals   1.09   [residual estimate]

59. Other chemicals   1.09   [residual estimate]

60. Logging and timber. The price index of cut timber was reported
as 1.256 (Planovoe khoziaistvo 1967, p. 16; Skvortsov 1972,
p. 44; Belousov 1969, p. 35), and the price of firewood remained
unchanged (Planovoe khoziaistvo 1967, p. 16). In physical units
firewood comprised about 27 percent of total output in 1966
(Narkhoz 67, p. 272) and about half of this was used in the first
quadrant (Krasovskii et al. 1970, p. 88). On the basis of these
data the overall price index for this sector will be estimated at
1.2.

61. Sawmills and woodworking   1.347   (Komin 1971,
                                                      p. 121; Belousov
                                                      1969, p. 35)

62. Plywood   1.969   (Efremov et al.
                                     1969, p. 28)

63. Furniture   .986   (Narkhoz 70,
                                      p. 252)

64. Other woodworking. In the absence of any information the price
index is arbitrarily set at 1.2 to be in line with price changes in
other sectors.

65. Paper and pulp. The price indexes for major products of the
paper sector were reported as follows:
          Sector average   1.268   (Shkatov and
                                                  Suponitskii
                                                  1969, p. 225)

Cellulose   1.427   (Minnich 1968,
                                         p. 14; Shkatov
                                         and Suponitskii
                                         1969, p. 225)

Paper and cardboard   1.063   (Shkatov and
                                         Suponitskii 1969,
                                         p. 225)

Newsprint   1.360   (Shkatov and
                                         Suponitskii 1969,
                                         p. 227)

These price indexes will be applied as follows:
    Sales within the paper
        sector   1.427
    Sales to synthetic fibers   1.427
    Sales to industry not
        elsewhere classified   1.360
    Sales to other branches
        of production   1.360
    Sales to all other buyers   1.182

The last index was estimated as a residual based on the average price index of 1.268 and weights determined by sales in the 1966 input–output table.

66. Wood chemistry   1.318   (Shkatov and
                                            Suponitskii
                                            1969, p. 175)

67. Cement   1.131   (Komin 1971,
                                            p. 121; Efremov
                                            et al. 1969, p. 25)

68. Prefab concrete   1.29   (Shkatov and
                                            Suponitskii 1969,
                                            p. 252; Efremov
                                            et al. 1969, p. 25)

69. Wall materials and tiles. Price indexes are available only for bricks--1.358 (Efremov et al. 1969, p. 27), and blocks--1.166 to 1.177 (Efremov et al. 1969, p. 27). An average index of 1.3 will be used.

70. Asbestos–cement materials and slate. Based on a few available indexes such as for cement pipes (1.25) and for slate (1.631), an average index of 1.4 will be used (Efremov et al. 1969, p. 28).

71. Roofing materials   1.264   (Shkatov and
                                                     Suponitskii
                                                     1969, p. 248)

72. Ceramics. Based on a few available indexes such as for ceramic
    pipes (.865) and for tiles (1.45), an average index of 1.0 will be
    used (Efremov et al. 1969, p. 28).

73. Other construction materials   .928   (Shkatov and
                                                     Suponitskii
                                                     1969, p. 238)

    Sales to the glass sector where the index is .789 are excepted
    (Shkatov and Suponitskii 1969, p. 238).

74. Glass and porcelain. The price index for window and other in-
    dustrial glass is .841 (Shkatov and Suponitskii 1969, p. 245) but
    no information is available for glass and porcelain wares. We
    can get an approximate index for the entire industry by compar-
    ing rates of growth in constant and in current prices. Input-
    output GVO data net of distribution cost for 1966 and 1972 are,
    respectively, 1,546.9 and 1,999.7 million rubles, while the
    output index is 1.793 (Narkhoz 73, p. 210 and Narkhoz 67,
    p. 189). The implicit price deflator is then .721. The latter
    measure is not too accurate because the GVO data contain an
    unknown turnover tax margin that cannot be adjusted for. The
    index of .841 will be used for sales of the glass sector to con-
    struction and an average of the two rates or .78 for all other
    buyers.

75. Cotton   1.129

    This estimate is based on a price index of 1.041 for cotton
    processing and 1.147 for cotton fabrics (Degtiar and Maslennikov
    1966, p. 10) weighted by 16.5 percent and 83.5 percent weights,
    respectively (Oznobin 1968, p. 183).

76. Silk   .818   (Degtiar and
                                                     Maslennikov
                                                     1966, p. 10)

77. Wool. As in the estimate for the cotton sector, the index is a
    weighted average of .947 for wool processing and 1.012 for wool
    fabrics with respective weights of 12.2 percent and 87.8 percent
    (Degtiar and Maslennikov 1966, p. 10).

78. Flax. As in the estimates above, the index is a weighted average of .94 for flax processing and .997 for flax fabrics with respective weights of 14 percent and 86 percent (Degtiar and Maslennikov 1966, p. 10).

79. Hosiery .909 (Degtiar and Maslennikov 1966, p. 10)

80. Other textiles. The price index for the entire textile industry was reported as 1.025 (Minnich 1968, p. 15). Using 1965 weights (Oznobin 1968, p. 183) for sectors 75-79, an index of 1.035 for other textiles is derived as a residual.

81. Sewn goods .974 (Narkhoz 69, p. 249)

82. Other light industry. A price index of 1.1034 for other light industry products is derived as a residual based on a price index of 1.037 reported (Belousov 1969, p. 35) for the whole textile and apparel branch (75-82) and gross value weights for 1965 of 56.3 percent for textiles, 26.8 percent for sewn goods, and 16.9 percent for other light industry (Oznobin 1968, p. 183).

83-94. Processed food industry. The 1967 price reform resulted in an overall decrease in processed food prices of 1.6 percent (Belousov 1969, p. 35). In terms of the 110-sector commodity classification employed in this study, price indexes are available or can be estimated for fish products, sugar, and the other-food-products group. For the remaining three sectors (meat, dairy, and bread) a residual index will be used.

83. Fish products. In the fish industry, wholesale prices increased at the expense of turnover taxes, which were completely eliminated (Skvortsov and Kabko 1968, pp. 8-9). According to the same source, the elimination of taxes and the corresponding increase in wholesale prices (retail prices remaining unchanged) doubled the rate of profitability. This is borne out by the reported profits for the fish industry which increased from 226 million rubles in 1966 to 460 million in 1967 (Narkhoz 67, p. 858). With the output in producers' prices equal to 4,548 million rubles in 1966, the pre-price-reform profitability was about 5 percent. In the absence of any additional data the wholesale price index for 1967 will thus be estimated as 1.05.

84. Meat products. No price indexes for this and several other
    food groups (see below) are available. A price index of .977
    was derived as an average weighted index based on the overall
    food industry index of .984 (Belousov 1969, p. 35) and appro-
    priate value weights from the 1966 input–output table.

85. Dairy products. See sector 84 above.

86. Sugar   1.0   (Skvortsov and
                                                    Kabko 1968, p. 8)

87. Flour. See sector 84 above.

88. Bread. See sector 84 above.

89. Confections. See sector 84 above.

90–94. Other food products. Below is the available price index
    information on products comprising the other-food group:

Vegetable oil	1.0	(Skvortsov and Kabko 1968, p. 8)
Tobacco products	1.0	(Skvortsov and Kabko 1968, p. 8)
Cosmetics	.967	(Kudriavtseva 1972, p. 8)
Salt	.937	(Kudriavtseva 1972, p. 28)
Beer	1.10	(Kudriavtseva 1972, p. 28)
Tea	1.0	(Skvortsov and Kabko 1968, p. 8)
Vodka	1.0	(Skvortsov and Kabko 1968, p. 8)
Non-alcoholic beverages	1.1	(Kudriavtseva 1972, p. 62)
Mineral water	.936	(Kudriavtseva 1972, p. 62)
Wine and wine products, 1967	.993	(Kudriavtseva 1972, p. 28)
Wine and wine products, 1969	1.117	(Kudriavtseva 1972, p. 64)

Using value weights from the 1966 input-output tables and additional weights from Vinogradov (1968, p. 57), the 1966-70 price index can be estimated as 1.002.

95. Industry not elsewhere classified. In the absence of any data a price index of 1.0 will be used.

96-100. Construction   1.155   (Efremov et al.
                                                                      1969, p. 33)

The index shown above is for the average cost of construction-assembly work (stroitel'no-montazhnye raboty), and its use as a price deflator for the value of construction output can be legitimately questioned. However, this index was checked against a variety of other data and it appears to be relatively accurate. Thus, for instance, the implicit price index used to convert the data on basic fixed capital introduced (vvod v deistvie osnovnykh fondov) from early 1960s prices to constant 1969 prices is 1.167 (Narkhoz 73, p. 537 and Narkhoz 67, p. 605). A similar index is obtained from capital investment data (Narkhoz 73, p. 544, and Narkhoz 67, p. 613). Available regional data yield similar results. For instance, an implicit price deflator for the 1965-70 period for construction in the Lithuanian republic is 1.147 (Ekonomika i kul'tura Litovskoi SSR 1972, p. 125); and for 1966-70 for the Kazakh republic is 1.134 (Narkhoz Kasakh SSR 1971, pp. 27-28).

101-02. Agriculture. The derivation and use of price indexes for Soviet agriculture are complex and are explained in Appendix 5A.2 below. The following indexes will be used:

101. Crops--a price index applicable to the use of crops within agriculture (sales to sectors 101-02) of 1.117, and for all other sales, 1.040.

102. Animal husbandry--a price index applicable to the use of products of animal husbandry within agriculture (sales to sectors 101-02) of 1.121, and for all other sales, 1.311.

103. Forestry   2.1   (Shkatov and
                                                                    Suponitskii 1969,
                                                                    pp. 204-05)

104-06. Transportation and communications. Average freight transportation charges were changed in 1967 as follows (Planovoe
khoziaistvo 1967, p. 17; Belousov 1971, p. 378; Shafirkin
1971, p. 579):

Railroads	.98
River transport	1.086
Sea and ocean transport	1.044
Trucking	1.000
Pipelines and air	No information
Average	.985

However, while the economywide average changed only
slightly, the price reform resulted in significant changes in
freight rates for specific commodities. For example, rail
rates for window glass were cut 50 percent, and the rates for
construction bricks were increased 35 percent (Turetskii
1969, p. 378). Unfortunately, attempts to prepare a set of
price indexes for all sectors failed because of the absence of
sufficient data. Accordingly, the average rate of .985 will be
used for the entire row.

107-109. Trade and distribution. Some trade and supply mark-ups
were also adjusted by the 1967 price reform (Eidel'man 1972,
p. 4; Gofman 1968, p. 20; Skvortsov and Kabko 1968, p. 8)
but apparently the changes were relatively small. The available mark-up rates for urban retail trade show a small increase of 1 to 3 percent (Petrov 1973, p. 80). The overall
rate of earnings of the trade and distribution sectors was
hardly affected by the reform. Thus the trade mark-up as
percent of total retail trade turnover was 7.55 in 1965, 7.88
in 1966, and 8.19 in 1967 (Narkhoz 68, p. 638). The growth
of the relative level of the trade mark-up probably reflects
first of all the changing mix of commodities and there is no
significant departure from this trend between 1966 and 1967.

In the absence of any additional information a price index of 1.0 will be used for the entire row. It will be noted
that the same price index of 1.0 is shown in the table of price
deflators used in converting the 1966 input-output table for the
Latvian republic from 1966 to 1967 prices (Shmulder 1971,
pp. 94-97).

110. Other branches of material production. In the absence of any
data on price changes an index of 1.0 will be used for the entire row with the exception of sales to ferrous metals repre-
senting scrap iron, where a price index of 2.04 will be used
(Shkatov and Suponitskii 1969, pp. 114-15).

Derivation of 1966-70 Price Indexes for Agriculture

According to standard Soviet statistical practice, gross output in current prices is derived by pricing different output components as follows (Gaabe et al. 1971, pp. 227-28; Tresorukova 1974, pp. 4-5):

1. Agricultural commodities produced by sovkhozes and other state enterprises and delivered to the state are measured in delivery prices set by the state.
2. Agricultural commodities produced by kolkhozes and on private plots and sold to the state are measured in procurement prices set by the state.
3. Agricultural commodities produced by kolkhozes and on private plots and sold to cooperative trade organizations are measured in prices agreed upon by buyers and sellers, as are prices of commodities sold by peasants on urban markets.
4. Agricultural commodities produced by kolkhozes and distributed to kolkhoz members as a part of their income from the kolkhoz are valued at state procurement prices. [Until 1969 these commodities were priced in state retail prices.]

These four measures comprise the so-called marketed output of agriculture. Gross output of agriculture is obtained as the sum of marketed output and the following additional elements:

5. Agricultural commodities produced and used within the sovkhoz for productive purposes are valued at sovkhoz cost.
6. Agricultural commodities produced and used within the kolkhoz for productive purposes are valued at kolkhoz cost.
7. Agricultural commodities produced on private plots and used either for productive purposes or for human consumption within households are valued at average prices of marketed output.

The principle of differentiated component pricing does not apply, however, to measurements of either marketed or gross output of agriculture in constant prices. For constant price output valuation all agricultural commodities--regardless of the production origin or disposition--are measured in uniform constant prices set by the Central Statistical Administration of the USSR (Tresorukova 1974, p. 232).

Reflecting the Soviet practice of pricing of output, two sets of price indexes will be constructed for the purposes of this study. The price indexes for marketed output will be constructed on the basis of published ruble data for all deliveries and sales to the state by kolkhozes, sovkhozes, and private producers. That is, due to the

absence of data the possible price changes occurring in urban markets and cooperative trade will be disregarded (element 3 above).
The derivation of separate price indexes for crops and products of
animal husbandry is shown in Tables 5A.1 through 5A.4.

It is then necessary to adjust the values calculated in these
tables to reflect the faster 1965–66 growth of state delivery prices
paid to sovkhozes. According to Stoliarov (1969, p. 122) average
delivery prices for crops increased in 1965–66 by 1.51 and for
animal husbandry by 1.051, compared with 1.012 and 1.038 for
procurement prices, respectively. In 1965 the breakdown of total
deliveries to the state was as follows.

> Crops: sovkhoz––25.98 percent; kolkhoz and private––74.02
> percent.
> Animal husbandry: sovkhoz––41.40 percent; kolkhoz and pri-
> vate––58.60 percent.

Using these percentages as weights and the price indexes given
above, a correction coefficient is derived that reflects different
movements of sovkhoz delivery prices as 1.036 for crops and 1.005
for animal husbandry. Thus, 1966 deliveries to the state in average
procurement-delivery prices are estimated as follows:

> For crops: 16,316.2 million rubles x 1.036 = 16,903.6
> million rubles.
> For animal husbandry: 19,163.6 million rubles x 1.005
> = 19,259.4 million rubles.

As the last step, the value of 1966 state procurements is calculated
in 1970 prices, using the quantities given in Table 5A.4 and the
prices estimated in Table 5A.2. The value of crops is calculated
as 17,575.5 million rubles and the value of animal husbandry products
as 25,244.7 million rubles. The price indexes are:

$$\text{Crops: } \frac{17,575.5}{16,903.6} = 1.040$$

$$\text{Animal husbandry: } \frac{25,244.7}{19,259.4} = 1.311$$

Since the value of output used within agriculture for productive
purposes is estimated at cost, cost indexes must now be constructed.
This is done in Tables 5A.5 through 5A.7.

TABLE 5A.1

Derivation of Average Procurement-Delivery Prices Paid by the State
to Kolkhozes, Sovkhozes, and Private Producers, 1965

	Value (millions of rubles)	Quantity (millions of tons)	Average Price (rubles/ton)
Grains	3,256	36.300	89.70
Cotton	2,504	5.660	442.40
Sugar beets	1,925	67.500	28.52
Sunflower seeds	837	3.890	215.17
Flax	621	.430	1,444.19
Potatoes and vegetables	1,638	17.600	93.07
Fruits	1,328	4.480	296.43
Total crops	12,109		
Cattle and poultry	9,220	5.800	1,589.66
Milk	5,747	38.700	148.50
Eggs*	826	10.500	78.67
Wool	1,209	.368	3,285.33
Total animal husbandry	17,002		

*Output in billions; price in rubles per thousand.
Source: TsSU, Narkhoz 73 (Moscow: Statistika, 1974), pp. 357, 359.

TABLE 5A.2

Derivation of Average Procurement-Delivery Prices Paid by the State
to Kolkhozes, Sovkhozes, and Private Producers, 1970

	Value (millions of rubles)	Quantity (millions of tons)	Average Price (rubles/ton)
Grains	7,126	73.300	97.22
Cotton	3,824	6.890	555.01
Sugar beets	2,028	71.400	28.40
Sunflower seeds	893	4.610	193.71
Flax	786	.431	1,827.91
Potatoes and vegetables	2,487	22.100	112.53
Fruits	1,874	6.180	303.24
Total crops	19,018		
Cattle and poultry	18,452	8.100	2,278.02
Milk	8,772	45.700	191.95
Eggs*	1,634	18.100	90.44
Wool	1,967	.441	4,460.32
Total animal husbandry	30,825		

*Output in billions; price in rubles per thousand.
Source: TsSU, Narkhoz 73 (Moscow: Statistika, 1974), p. 372.

TABLE 5A.3

Adjustment of Average Procurement-Delivery, 1965-66
(rubles per ton)

	1965 Price	1966/65 Index[a]	1966 Price
Grains	89.70	1.087	97.50
Cotton	442.40	.952	421.24
Sugar beets	28.52	1.036	29.54
Sunflower seeds	215.17	1.070	230.23
Flax	1,444.19	.925	1,335.88
Potatoes and vegetables[b]	93.07	.945	87.95
Fruits	296.43	.952	282.20
Average for crops[c]	--	1.012	--
Cattle and poultry	1,589.66	1.062	1,688.41
Milk	148.50	1.014	150.58
Eggs[d]	78.67	1.003	78.91
Wool	3,285.33	.992	3,259.05
Average for animal husbandry	--	1.038	--

[a]The price index is applicable only to procurement prices paid to kolkhozes and private producers. Price indexes for sovkhoz deliveries to the state are available only for aggregate crops (1.151) and animal husbandry (1.051).

[b]Potatoes only.

[c]Averaged using 1965 quantities as weights.

[d]Rubles per thousand.

Sources: TsSU, Narkhoz 73 (Moscow: Statistika, 1974), pp. 357, 359; S. G. Stoliarov, O tsenakh i tsenoobrazovanii v SSSR, 3d ed. (Moscow: Statistika, 1969), pp. 119-22.

TABLE 5A.4

Estimation of the Value of State Procurements, 1966 Prices

	Quantity (millions of tons)	Price (rubles per ton)	Value (millions of rubles)
Grain	75.000	97.50	7,312.5
Cotton	5.980	421.24	2,519.0
Sugar beets	69.700	29.54	2,058.9
Sunflower seeds	4.660	230.23	1,072.9
Flax	.426	1,335.88	569.1
Potatoes and vegetables	17.300	87.95	1,521.5
Fruits	4.473	282.20	1,262.3
Total crops			16,316.2
Cattle and poultry	6.500	1,688.41	10.974.7
Milk	40.100	150.58	6,038.3
Eggs*	11.560	78.91	912.2
Wool	.380	3,259.05	1,238.4
Total animal husbandry			19,163.6

*Output in billions; price in rubles per thousand.

Sources: TsSU, Narkhoz 73 (Moscow: Statistika, 1974), pp. 357, 359, and Narkhoz 76, p. 337; S. G. Stoliarov, O tsenakh i tsenoobrazovanii v SSSR, 3d ed. (Moscow: Statistika, 1969), pp. 119-22.

TABLE 5A.5

Estimation of Average Kolkhoz-Sovkhoz Costs, 1966

| | Kolkhoz | | Sovkhoz | | Average |
	Cost	Weight	Cost[a]	Weight	Cost
Grains	45	.52	60.5	.48	52.4
Cotton	332	.80	298	.20	352.2
Sugar beets	22	.90	25.5	.10	22.4
Sunflower seeds	45	.84	no data	.16	45.0
Potatoes	47	.64	62.5	.36	52.6
Vegetables	88	.43	71.5	.57	78.6
Fruits	no data		no data		
Meat[b]	1,065.1	.52	1,015.1	.48	1,041.1
Milk	160	.57	164.5	.43	161.9
Eggs[c]	75	.38	71	.62	72.5
Wool	3,346	.51	2,978	.49	3,165.7

[a]1966 cost data for sovkhozes are not available, and average 1965-67 costs are used.

[b]Cost data are reported separately for beef, pork, and mutton. Averages are derived using physical output weights as follows: beef 44 percent, pork 45 percent, mutton 11 percent.

[c]Rubles per thousand.

Note: Costs are in rubles per ton.

Sources: TsSU, Narkhoz 67 (Moscow: Statistika, 1968), pp. 484-85; Narkhoz 65, pp. 428-29; Narkhoz 67, p. 333; TsSU, Strana sovetov za 50 let 1967, p. 126.

TABLE 5A.6

Estimation of Average Kolkhoz-Sovkhoz Costs, 1970

| | Kolkhoz | | Sovkhoz | | Average |
	Cost	Weight	Cost	Weight	Cost
Grains	50	.54	53	.46	51.4
Cotton	404	.73	362	.23	378.2
Sugar beets	22	.92	29	.08	22.6
Sunflower seeds	56	.80	n.a.[a]	.20	56.0
Potatoes	62	.60	76	.40	67.6
Vegetables	94	.42	84	.58	88.2
Fruits	n.a.		n.a.		
Meat[b]	1,141	.51	1,155	.49	1,236.1
Milk	177	.56	189	.44	182.3
Eggs[c]	73	.30	64	.70	66.7
Wool	3,862	.48	3,585	.52	3,718.0

[a]Data not available.

[b]Cost data are reported separately for beef, pork, and mutton. Averages are derived using physical output weights as follows: beef 49 percent, pork 41 percent, mutton 10 percent.

[c]Rubles per thousand.

Note: Costs are in rubles per ton.

Sources: TsSU, Narkhoz 73 (Moscow: Statistika, 1974), p. 353; TsSU, Sel'skoe khoziaistvo SSSR (Moscow: Statistika, 1971), pp. 504, 593.

Physical quantities are needed in order to derive the average weighted cost of agricultural commodities produced and used within kolkhozes and sovkhozes for productive purposes. In the absence of better data the differences between gross and marketed output will be used. A certain error is introduced here as the ratio of marketed output to gross output for private plots is probably different from the sovkhoz–kolkhoz ratio. It is, however, believed that the distortion in the constructed cost indexes will be relatively small. The derivation of the weights is shown in Table 5A.7.

TABLE 5A.7

Agricultural Commodities Used within Agriculture
(millions of tons)

	Gross Output	Marketed Output	Used within Agriculture[a]
Grains	171.200	80.600	90.600
Cotton	5.980	5.980	0
Sugar beets	74.000	69.700	4.300
Sunflower seeds	6.150	5.020	1.130
Potatoes	87.900	15.000	72.900
Vegetables	17.900	10.600	7.300
Cattle	10.700	7.700	3.000
Milk	76.000	42.200	33.800
Eggs[b]	31.700	15.300	16.400
Wool	.371	.346	.025

[a]Gross output minus marketed output.
[b]In billions.
Sources: TsSU, Narkhoz 67 (Moscow: Statistika, 1968), pp. 330, 332; Narkhoz 67, p. 334.

As the last step calculations are made of the total cost of production of agricultural commodities used within agriculture in 1966, in 1966 and 1970 values, using cost data estimated in Tables 5A.5 and 5A.6, and quantities from Table 5A.7. The totals for crops are as follows: in 1966 values, 9,302.9 million rubles; and in 1970 values, 10,389.2 million rubles. The totals for products of animal husbandry are, in 1966 values, 9,863.7 million rubles; and in 1970 values, 11,056.9 million rubles. The cost index for crops is 1.117 and for animal husbandry, 1.121. In the absence of better data on

the distribution of output, the 1966-70 price indexes will be applied
to all input-output flows with the exception of flows within agriculture, and the cost indexes will be applied to flows within agriculture.

APPENDIX B

Estimating the Value of Total Residual Surplus in the 1966
Input-Output Table in 1970, in Producers' Prices

The "other elements of national income" total for industry in
the 1966 Soviet input-output table in 1970 producers' prices is shown
as 38,098.2 million rubles. In order to estimate the value of the
residual surplus, that is, profits and turnover taxes, two categories
of costs must be removed: social security payments and miscellaneous costs. The average weighted rate of social security payments
in industry was estimated at 7.2 percent. Applying this rate to total
industrial wages of 36,694.9 million rubles, the value of social
security contributions is calculated at 2,642 million rubles.

Soviet national income produced in industry has in addition to
such major elements as wages, social security payments, profits,
and turnover taxes, a variety of smaller expenditures such as costs
of business travel, cost of on-the-job training of workers, court
penalties and fines, expenditures on work clothing, subsidized food
in plant cafeterias, and the like. The sum of these miscellaneous
costs can be estimated as a residual, after subtracting all major
national income elements in the following tabulation, expressed in
millions of rubles:

National income in industry	104,600	(Narkhoz 67, p. 672)
Less total wages	- 36,901	(Vestnik statistiki, No. 4, 1971, p. 88)
Less social security payments	- 2,657	
Less profits	- 25,088	(Narkhoz 67, p. 857)
Less turnover taxes	- 39,581	(See Chapter 1)
Plus subsidies	+ 3,600	(Treml 1976)
Equals residual costs	3,973	

It will be noted that some of the values shown above differ from
the values recorded in the 1966 input-output table. These discrepancies stem from the fact that input-output values have been adjusted
for commodity-establishment differences. In the tabulation above,
only national non-input-output statistics are used for the sake of
consistency of definitions. It is believed, however, that the estimate of miscellaneous costs included in national income is not

significantly affected by these differences. The residual surplus consisting of profits and turnover taxes is then estimated as follows (in millions of rubles):

Total residual	38,098.2
Less social security payments	-2,642.0
Less miscellaneous costs	-3,973.0
Plus profit–wage adjustment	+3,739.0
Equals residual surplus	35,222.0

Estimating the Share of Turnover Taxes in the First Quadrant of the 1970 Input–Output Table

As was explained in Chapter 1 of this volume, the conversion of the 1966 input–output table from purchasers' to producers' prices showed that 29.1 percent of the total turnover taxes are collected within the first quadrant, that is, levied on intermediate goods. The task now is to estimate this ratio for the 1966 table in 1970 prices.

The 1967 price reform resulted in a shift of turnover taxes from the first to the second quadrant, primarily because tax rates were lowered (and profits increased) on such inputs as electrical power, gas, and refined petroleum products (Iakovets 1974, pp. 168–70). It must also be noted that in 1970 the share of turnover taxes collected in the first quadrant was lower because of a rapid growth in final consumption of such taxed commodities as electrical appliances and automobiles. The share of taxes in the first quadrant of the 1966 input–output table in 1970 prices is estimated by assuming that the distribution of taxes between the first and the second quadrants for each given sector did not change between 1966 and 1970; that is, it will be assumed that while specific product tax rates have changed, these changes have been uniform along any given row. The calculations are shown below in Table 5B.1.

Thus, if a 1970 Soviet input–output table were to be constructed in producers' prices, the turnover taxes collected on intermediate products (that is, first-quadrant transactions) would amount to 12,449 million rubles, or 25.0 percent of total taxes of 49,400 million rubles (Narkhoz 70, p. 703).

Finally, it must be noted that of the taxes collected within the first quadrant of the 1966 table in producers' prices, 85.6 percent fell on products purchased by industry. Under the same set of assumptions this percentage is applicable to the 1966 table in 1970 prices. Thus, in the 1970 table, 25.0 percent of total taxes are collected in the first quadrant and 21.4 percent (.250 x .856) are collected on industrial purchases.

TABLE 5B.1

Calculations of Turnover Taxes in Quadrant I, 1970

Products Taxed In Quadrant I in 1966 Table	Percent of Total Taxes Collected in Quadrant I (percent)	1970 Total Tax on Output of the Sector (millions of rubles)	Estimated Tax on Output in 1970* (millions of rubles)
Oil refining	82.8	3,900	3,229
Gas	78.8	160	126
Electrical power	36.4	477	174
Light industry	31.7	13,832	4,385
Food industry	18.0	25,184	4,535
Total	--	--	12,449

*Column 1 times column 2.

Sources: Chapter 1 of this volume; B. Kostinsky, The Reconstructed 1966 Soviet Input-Output Table: Revised Purchasers' and Producers' Prices Tables. U.S. Department of Commerce, F.D.A.D., Foreign Economic Report No. 13 (Washington, D.C.: Government Printing Office, 1976); P. E. Kuchkin and N. N. Morozov, Chistyi dokhod sotsialisticheskogo obshchestva (Moscow: Finansy, 1974), p. 33; TsSU, Narkhoz 70 (Moscow: Statistika, 1971), p. 705.

APPENDIX C

Derivation of 1970-72 Price Indexes

The derivation of producers' price indexes for the 1970-72 period was handicapped by the absence of necessary data, forcing the use in a number of instances of the official Soviet price indexes, which are notoriously poor. It was still deemed desirable to include this set of price indexes, imperfect as it is, in this study to enable analysts to convert the 1966 table to 1972 prices for purposes of comparison with the 1972 Soviet input-output table. The estimated price indexes for individual sectors or groups of sectors are shown in Table 5C.1. The sector number classification is that of the 75-sector table used throughout this volume (see Appendix A, Chapter 1). Unless otherwise noted, the indexes were calculated on the basis of data provided in Narkhoz 73, p. 250. Indexes obtained from different sources or estimated are described below.

TABLE 5C.1

Derivation of 1970–72 Producers' Price Indexes

Sector Number	Sector Designation	Index
1–2	Ferrous metallurgy	.99
3–4	Nonferrous metallurgy	1.00
5–7	Coke, refractory materials and hardware	1.00
8	Coal	1.00
9	Oil extraction	1.00
10	Oil refining	0.98
11–13	Other fuels, including gas	1.00
14	Electrical power	1.00
15–41	Machinebuilding and metalworking	1.03
42–50	Chemicals	1.01
51–54	Timber and woodworking	0.99
55	Paper products	0.98
56	Wood chemistry	1.00
57–58	Construction materials and glass	1.00
59–61	Textiles and apparel	1.00
62–64	Fish, meat, dairy products	1.00
65	Sugar	1.148
66	Flour and bread	1.024
67	Other food products	1.00
68	Industry not elsewhere classified	1.00
69	Construction	0.98
70	Crops (applicable to flows outside agriculture)	1.052
	(applicable to flows within agriculture)	1.230
71	Animal husbandry (outside agriculture)	1.022
	(within agriculture)	1.088
72–75	Forestry, other branches of material production, Transportation and communication, and Trade and distribution	1.00

Source: TsSU, Narkhoz 72 (Moscow: Statistika, 1973), pp. 353, 391.

1. The general problem of price inflation caused by the introduction of new products at "temporary" high prices which particularly affects machinebuilding and chemical industries was discussed
above. In the construction of 1966-70 price indexes offered in this
study, this phenomenon was disregarded because of (a) the absence
of any quantitative information on price trends, (b) the fact that the
1966-70 period was marked by several rounds of across-the-board
price revisions, and (c) strengthened state control over temporary
prices introduced after the 1967 price reform. The last two of
these factors were clearly becoming less important with time and it
was felt that the 1970-72 price index must reflect the increase of
prices of machinery and chemicals. The fact that in 1973 the State
Committee on Prices decreed price cuts averaging some 12 percent
for a large share of machinery output suggests that in fact the upward
movement of prices, which was arrested or at least slowed down in
the late 1970s, accelerated and had to be corrected (Iakovets 1974,
p. 67). Unfortunately, there are almost no data on the magnitudes
of 1970-72 price changes. Almost arbitrarily we will use a price
index of 1.03 for machinery, basing it on the trends discussed by
Becker for the late 1960s and the evidence of post-1970 price increases (Becker 1974, p. 373 and p. 378). An arbitrary index of
1.01 will be used for the chemical industry.

2. The processed foods group of sectors. The officially published price index for the food industry is 1.03 (Narkhoz 73, p. 250).
Within the food industry the price of refined sugar increased by 12
percent and the price of lump sugar by 26 percent (Iakovets 1974,
p. 101). Lump sugar comprised about 20 percent of total sugar
output and using weights of .8 and .2, an average price increase of
14.8 percent is derived for the sugar sector. Prices of flour and
cereals increased by 12 percent. As the first approximation,
weights obtained from retail trade data are used which show that
flour and cereals comprised about 20 percent of sales of the sector.
Thus, the price index applicable to the entire flour and cereals sector is estimated as 1.024. Using weights from the table in producers' prices it was possible to establish that the increases in the
prices of sugar, flour, and cereals would have resulted in an average price increase for the entire food sector of approximately the
magnitude shown by the official price index. Thus, in the absence
of any other data, price indexes of 1.0 were entered for the rest of
the food industry.

3. Construction. Soviet statistical sources do not indicate
overall price levels for construction. In the absence of any other
data the price changes in construction are estimated as the ratio of
quantity indexes of construction in current and constant prices.
Using the published gross social product statistics it is calculated

that the output of construction measured in current prices increased
in the 1970–72 period by 14.5 percent (Narkhoz 73, p. 57). The
output in constant prices is not available but can be approximated
as the sum of the following components, all in 1969 constant prices,
expressed in billions of rubles (Narkhoz 73, pp. 556, 560, 565).

	1970	1972
Output of construction-assembly work done internally	6.500	6.800
Output of construction-assembly work done by contract	47.000	55.800
Investment in new private housing	1.636	1.643
Value of output of construction design organizations	1.548	1.952
Total	56.684	66.195

Thus, we can calculate the 1970–72 output index in constant prices
as 1.168. The ratio of the two indexes is then

$$1.145 \div 1.168 = .98$$

which can be accepted as the price index for the entire construction
sector. The price decrease is not unexpected, as a reduction in
construction prices of 3 to 5 percent was announced by the government in July of 1972 (Iakovets 1974, p. 94).

4. Agriculture. Derivation of 1970–72 indexes for agriculture follows the methodology described in Appendix A, and the actual
calculations will not be shown here. Separate price indexes for
deliveries of agricultural commodities outside of agriculture were
estimated for crops and animal husbandry on the basis of state
deliveries in 1970, measured in 1972 and 1970 prices (Narkhoz 73,
pp. 357–59). The estimated price indexes are 1.0519 for crops and
1.0218 for animal husbandry. Price indexes applicable to the use
of agricultural commodities within agriculture were estimated on
the basis of average kolkhoz-sovkhoz cost data in 1972 and 1970
(Narkhoz 72, pp. 353, 391, and 401). The estimated indexes are
1.230 and 1.088 for crops and animal husbandry, respectively.

NOTES

1. For a summary description of the development of input-
output analysis in the Soviet Union see Treml et al. 1976, pp. 332–38
and Treml 1975. The development of regional input-output techniques
is discussed in Chapter 6 of this volume.

2. Bornstein 1972, Schroeder 1969, Minnich 1968. The 1967 price reform in its various stages did not affect the prices of agricultural commodities. However, the program of increases and adjustments of agricultural prices launched at the March 1965 session of the Central Committee of the CPSU continued throughout the period under discussion (Bush 1976).

3. For an excellent summary of the controversy and related empirical studies, see Bezdek and Wendling 1976, pp. 543-51. The authors' analysis of the accuracy of forecasts in current and constant prices on the basis of U.S. input-output tables for five different years showed that constant price projections were more accurate in the long run (six years and longer). In the short run the results appear to be inconclusive.

4. Large segments of the first quadrant and some additional data on the 1972 Soviet input-output table were published in Narkhoz 1973, pp. 67-123. A preliminary reconstruction, that is, preparation of a complete three-quadrant table with estimated missing flows, was published in Treml et al. 1976. A more elaborate and a larger 1972 table for the Soviet Union, including some additional vectors, is in preparation at the Foreign Demographic Analysis Division, U.S. Department of Commerce, and should be ready in 1978.

5. See, for instance, the price indexes published in Narkhoz 1973, pp. 250-53. The available information on these price indexes is at best scarce. All we know is that the indexes reflect end-of-the-year prices and, since 1961, are constructed on the basis of a sample of 961 commodities that comprised some 56 percent of the marketed output of industry in 1961 (Freimundt and Eidel'man 1970, pp. 205-07). The difficulties facing a user of these indexes are compounded by the fact that they are available only for some 11 industrial branches, omitting some key ones such as nonferrous metallurgy and gas. The indexes are published in terms of two digits only (1949 = 100), affecting the statistical significance of any computed year-by-year index.

6. Becker (1974) analyzed the phenomenon of declining machinery price indexes and rising machinery prices in a well-documented comprehensive study. Thus, he estimated that in the 1960-70 period machinery prices rose 15 percent (p. 378) while the official price index for the same period shows a decline of some 11 percent.

7. See Chapter 1. "Gross Investment and Other Uses" column of final demand is an aggregation of new investment, replacements of capital stock, capital repair, change in inventories, export-import balance, and losses out of national income.

8. Strictly speaking, there are other elements of the value-added quadrant that must remain unchanged, such as social security contributions and miscellaneous expenditures such as free food and clothing provided to the workers in some industries, business travel, court-imposed fines and penalties, short-term interest payments and the like. These expenditures have not been separately identified in the input-output table used in this study and hence they are not shown in the equation.

9. It must be stressed that with the exception of a few of the smaller republics, all Soviet input-output tables to date have been prepared in purchasers' prices. Some pilot aggregated tables prepared in producers' prices utilize the first method of recording turnover taxes (Efimov and Berri 1965, pp. 168-71; Eidel'man 1966, pp. 220-29).

10. The Soviet methodology of converting an input-output table to a new price base does not differ significantly from standard Western statistical procedures. For example, the Bureau of Economic Analysis of the U.S. Department of Commerce which is responsible for construction of U.S. input-output tables is using the same procedure of converting the tables, row by row, and then treating value-added components as residuals. The only difference is that unlike a single value-added row of U.S. tables, the Soviet tables show several different rows in the third quadrant, some of which are kept unchanged in a price conversion.

11. Eidel'man (1972 , p. 4) reports that prices of gasoline used for private consumption were also adjusted in the 1967 price reform. This increase, however, was relatively small and is not significant statistically, as gasoline is lumped together with other consumer purchases of refined petroleum products such as fuel oils. Accordingly, this adjustment is disregarded in this study.

12. Unfortunately, there is absolutely no data on this possible price increase caused by the introduction of new products. Becker suggests that the 1966-70 machinery price increase was approximately 2 percent (Becker 1974, p. 378). One could apply an index of 1.02 to all machinery rows, but while for the whole machinery branch the change would probably be in the right direction, the accuracy of individual sectors' adjustment can be seriously questioned.

REFERENCES

Becker, A. 1974. "The Price Level of Soviet Machinery in the 1960s." Soviet Studies 26, no. 3 (July): 363-79.

Belousov, R. A., ed. 1971. Planirovanie perspektivnykh optovykh tsen. Moscow: Ekonomika.

_____. 1969. Tsena i tsenoobrazovanie v promyshlennosti. Moscow: Znanie.

Bezdek, R. H. and R. M. Wendling. 1976. "Current- and Constant-Dollar Input-Output Forecasts for the U.S. Economy." Journal of the American Statistical Association 71, no. 355 (September): 543-51.

Bornstein, M. 1976. "Soviet Price Policy in the 1970s." In U.S. Congress, Joint Economic Committee, Soviet Economy in a New Perspective, pp. 17-66. Washington, D.C.: Government Printing Office.

_____. 1972. "Soviet Price Statistics." In Soviet Economic Statistics, ed. V. Treml and J. P. Hardt, pp. 355-96. Durham, N.C.: Duke University Press.

Bush, K. 1976. "Soviet Agriculture: Ten Years Under New Management." In Economic Development in the Soviet Union and Eastern Europe, ed. Z. Fallenbuch. Vol. 2, pp. 157-204. New York: Praeger.

Degtiar, L. and V. Maslennikov. 1966. "Novye optovye tseny v legkoi promyshlennosti." Finansy SSSR, no. 12: 7-14.

Eidel'man, M. 1972. "Opyt pereotsenki otchetnogo mezhotraslevogo balansa za 1966 god v novykh tsenakh." Vestnik statistiki, no. 2: 3-14.

_____. 1966. Mezhotraslevoi balans obshchestvennogo produkta. Moscow: Statistika.

Efimov, A. N. and L. Ia. Berri, eds. 1965. Metody planirovaniia mezhotraslevykh proportsii. Moscow: Ekonomika.

Efremov, S., V. Maliugin, and M. Turianskii. 1969. Novye smetnye normy i tseny v stroitel'stve. Moscow: Stroitel'stvo.

Freimundt, E. and M. Eidel'man, eds. 1970. Ekonomicheskaia statistika. Moscow: Statistika.

Gaabe, Iu. E., I. I. Levitin, and A. N. Pavlov. 1971. Statistika sel'skogo khoziaistva. 2d ed. Moscow: Statistika.

Gofman, G. 1968. "Reforma i rentabel'nost'." Sovetskaia torgovlia, no. 5: 20-27.

Greenslade, R. V. 1972. "Industrial Production Statistics in the USSR." In Soviet Economic Statistics, ed. V. G. Treml and J. P. Hardt, pp. 155-94. Durham, N.C.: Duke University Press.

Guill, G. 1975. "Intertemporal Comparison of the Structure of the Soviet Economy." Duke University--University of North Carolina Occasional Papers on Soviet Input-Output Analysis, No. 8. Durham, N.C.

Iakovets, Iu. 1974. Tseny v planovom khoziaistve. Moscow: Ekonomika.

_____. 1972. "Effektivnost' nauchno-tekhnicheskogo progressa i dinamika tsen." Voprosy ekonomiki, no. 6: 52-64.

Klein, L. R. 1974. A Textbook of Econometrics. 2d ed. Englewood Cliffs, N.J.: Prentice-Hall.

Komin, A. N. 1971. Problemy planovogo tsenoobrazovaniia. Moscow: Ekonomika.

_____. 1968. Ekonomicheskaia reforma i optovye tseny v promyshlennosti. Moscow: Finansy.

Kostinsky, B. 1976. The Reconstructed 1966 Soviet Input-Output Table: Revised Purchasers' and Producers' Prices Tables. U.S. Department of Commerce, F.D.A.D., Foreign Economic Report No. 13. Washington, D.C.: Government Printing Office.

Kovaleva, A. M. 1969. Finansy khimicheskoi promyshlennosti. Moscow: Khimicheskaia promyshlennost.

Krasovskii, V. 1975. "Obshchestvennyi produkt i konechnyi effekt." Voprosy ekonomiki, no. 6: 101-11.

Krasovskii, V. P. et al., eds. 1970. Intensifikatsiia i rezervy ekonomiki. Moscow: Nauka.

Kuchkin, P. E. and N. N. Morozov. 1974. Chistyi dokhod sotsialisticheskogo obshchestva. Moscow: Finansy.

Kudriavtseva, I. G. 1972. Tsenoobrazovanie v pishchevoi promyshlennosti. Moscow: Pishchevaia promyshlennost'.

Kul'bovskaia, N. K. 1973. Ekonomicheskie problemy formirovaniia balansa tekstil'nogo syr'ia. Moscow: Legkaia industriia.

Kuznetsov, A. and A. Koshuta. 1971. "Novyi etap sovershenstvovaniia sistemy tsen na produktsiiu mashinostroeniia." Voprosy ekonomiki, no. 5: 71-81.

Kvasha, Ia. and V. Krasovskii. 1968. "Perspektivnoe planirovanie i khoziaistvennye izmereniia." Voprosy ekonomiki, no. 4: 71-80.

Leontief, W. 1951. The Structure of the American Economy. 2d ed. New York: Oxford University Press.

Minnich, B. 1968. "Materials on the Soviet Price Reform of July 1967." ASTE Bulletin 10, no. 2: 12-19.

Narkhoz Kazakh SSR 1971. 1972. Published by the Tsentral'noe statisticheskoe upravlenie Kazakhskoi SSR under the title of Narodnoe khoziaistvo Kazakhskoi SSR v 1971, godu. Alma-Ata: Statistika.

Narkhoz 19--. The abbreviation Narkhoz followed by the year refers to standard Soviet annual statistical handbooks published by the Tsentral'noe statisticheskoe upravlenie SSSR under the title of Narodnoe khoziaistvo SSSR v 19-- godu. Moscow: Statistika. The handbook is always published in the year following the year shown in the title.

Oznobin, N. M. et al., eds. 1968. Sovershenstvovanie struktury promyshlennogo proizvodstva. Moscow: Ekonomika.

Petrov, G. K. 1973. Tovarooborot i pribyl'. Leningrad: Lenizdat.

Planovoe khoziaistvo 1967. "Novye tseny--etap khoziaistvennoi reformy." (Unsigned.) Planovoe khoziaistvo, no. 7: 13-18.

Schroeder, G. 1969. "The 1966-67 Soviet Industrial Price Reform: A Study in Complications." Soviet Studies 20, no. 4 (April): 462-77.

Shafirkin, B., ed. 1971. Ekonomicheskii spravochnik zheleznodorozhnika. Moscow: Transport.

Shkatov, V. and B. Suponitskii. 1969. Optovye tseny na produktsiiu tiazheloi promyshlennosti. Moscow: Ekonomika.

Shmulder, M. et al., eds. 1971. Dinamika mezhotraslevykh i mezhrespublikanskikh sviazei Latviiskoi SSR. Riga: Tsentral'noe statisticheskoe upravlenie Latviiskoi SSR.

Sitnin, V. 1969. "Nekotorye voprosy politiki tsen." Kommunist, no. 1: 85-94.

_____. 1967. "Reforma tsen zavershena." Ekonomicheskaia gazeta, no. 25 (June): 10-11.

Skvortsov, L. 1972. Tseny i tsenoobrazovanie v SSSR. Moscow: Vysshaia shkola.

_____ and G. Kabko. 1968. "Reforma optovykh tsen na pishchevye produkty." Sovetskaia torgovlia, no. 10: 8-10.

Stoliarov, S. G. 1969. O tsenakh i tsenoobrazovanii v SSSR. 3rd ed. Moscow: Statistika.

Treml, V. 1976. "Agricultural Subsidies in the Soviet Union." Working Paper, F.D.A.D. (December): Washington, D.C.: Department of Commerce.

_____. 1975. Input-Output Analysis and the Soviet Economy: An Annotated Bibliography. New York: Praeger.

_____, D. Gallik, B. Kostinsky, L. Kurtzweg, and A. Tretyakova. 1976. "The Soviet 1966 and 1972 Input-Output Tables." In U.S. Congress, Joint Economic Committee, Soviet Economy in a New Perspective, pp. 332-76. Washington, D.C.: Government Printing Office.

_____, B. Kostinsky, K. Kruger, and D. Gallik. 1973. Conversion of Soviet Input-Output Tables to Producers' Prices: the 1966 Reconstructed Table. U.S. Department of Commerce, F.D.A.D., Foreign Economic Report no. 1. Washington, D.C.: Government Printing Office.

_____, D. Gallik, B. Kostinsky, and K. Kruger. 1972. The Structure of the Soviet Economy. New York: Praeger.

Tresorukova, Z. G. 1974. Tovarnaia produktsiia sel'skogo khoziaistva. Moscow: Statistika.

Tsentral'noe statisticheskoe upravlenie Litovskoi SSR. 1972. Ekonomika i kul'tura Litovskoi SSR. Vil'nius: Statistika.

Tsentral'noe statisticheskoe upravlenie SSSR. 1971. Sel'skoe khoziaistvo SSSR. Moscow: Statistika.

_____. Strana sovetov za 50 let 1967. Moscow: Statistika.

Turetskii, Sh. Ia., ed. 1969. Tseny i tarify. Moscow: Vysshaia shkola.

Vinogradov, N. V., ed. 1968. Ekonomika pishchevoi promyshlennosti. Moscow: Pishchevaia promyshlennost'.

CHAPTER

6

DEVELOPMENT OF REGIONAL
INPUT-OUTPUT ANALYSIS.
IN THE SOVIET UNION
James W. Gillula
Daniel L. Bond

INTRODUCTION

In several recent surveys of regional input-output analysis published in the West (Richardson 1972; Miernyk 1973; Riefler 1973),
there is scarcely any mention of the Soviet achievements in this field.
This omission is understandable in the light of the limited contacts
between Soviet and Western scholars and the language difficulties involved. However, it is unfortunate for Western scholars since major
advances are being made in the Soviet Union in the theoretical study
of regional input-output models and in the gathering of data for regional input-output accounts. In fact, this Soviet research is probably the most advanced of its type in the world. More than 100 regional tables have been produced and a flood of books and articles
have appeared in the Soviet Union during the past 15 years.[1] In at-
taining this high level of achievement Soviet scholars have paid close
attention to input-output studies carried out in the West. Now Soviet
specialists are making original and significant contributions that
merit the attention of their Western counterparts.

The scale of the Soviet involvement in the application of regional input-output models is largely the result of the commitment
on the part of the Soviet government to collect the necessary data
for input-output accounts. The national and republic Central Statistical Administrations (TsSU) now periodically (about every six years)
undertake extensive statistical surveys to compile both national and
regional input-output tables for the same year using a standard
methodology and classification system. In addition, several Union
republics are attempting to compile ex post tables on a more frequent
basis. This wealth of data provides the indispensable basis for empirically implementing a wide range of input-output models that are

merely suggested in theoretical studies. In the West it is primarily
the contrasting lack of an adequate data-gathering system that fetters
further advances in regional input-output research.[2]

The regions of the USSR for which ex post input-output tables
have been compiled include each of the 15 Soviet Union republics
(hereafter designated as Union republics), many of the 18 large economic regions into which the country is divided,[3] and a number of
smaller administrative subdivisions such as oblasts, krai, and
autonomous republics. The construction of these ex post input-output
tables has provided a valuable new source of statistical information
on the economies of individual regions at all levels, and this in itself
has been an important factor contributing to the widespread interest
in regional input-output analysis in the Soviet Union. For Union republics, these input-output tables represented the most disaggregated
and complete set of national income and product accounts that had yet
been compiled, including previously uncollected data on the imports
and exports of all sectors. The national income and product accounts
calculated annually by republic TsSUs are compiled identifying only
the major sectors of the economy, and external relations are included
only as a balancing entry--the overall export-import balance. For
the large economic regions and the various administrative subdivisions of Union republics, even these aggregate income and product
accounts are not calculated, and the construction of ex post input-
output tables for these regions in most cases involved the first calculation of national income and gross product by sector for each region (Semenov 1973a). Thus, many of the initial input-output studies
for each region of the Soviet Union have been devoted to a basic analysis of the structural economic relations revealed by these ex post
tables.

Beyond this basic analysis of the structure of the economics of
individual regions, the use of regional input-output analysis in the
Soviet Union has centered around the construction of planning input-
output models. Most of this work has been done at the Union republic level. In at least a dozen republics the construction of one or
more ex post input-output tables has been followed by the compilation
of a static planning input-output table for some future year (involving
associated studies of changes in input coefficients over time and forecasts of the level and structure of final demand), and experimental
calculations with some form of dynamic input-output model for the
republic. In addition a number of modifications of the basic input-
output model have been introduced to increase its compatibility with
traditional planning techniques. The most recent development in the
use of regional mathematical-economic models in the Soviet Union
has been the construction of input-output-based simulation models
that include submodels for forecasting such factors as demographic

trends and the balance of labor supply with projected needs, the balance of income and consumption of the population, and projected import needs and export potential for the republic. At the present stage of its development, regional input-output analysis remains somewhat apart from the formal planning process. However, since much of the work on constructing planning input-output models has been done in institutes associated with republic Gosplans, there is reason to believe that the results of such models are examined during the process of formulating the republics' five-year plans.

The aim of this paper is to provide a short survey of the development of regional input-output analysis in the Soviet Union through the mid-1970s. Many topics deserving of more detailed discussion in a more extensive paper (such as the methodology of constructing ex post tables, the many variants of dynamic models, and the path-breaking new work on input-output-based systems of models) are treated only briefly here. An account of ex post regional tables that have been compiled is given below, followed by a discussion of the type of interregional trade data that have been collected and of attempts to implement interregional input-output models. The construction and use of various types of planning input-output models for regions is summarized in the final section.

EX POST TABLES

Experimental work on the construction of regional input-output tables in the Soviet Union was begun in the late 1950s at the Laboratory of Economic-Mathematical Methods of the Academy of Sciences under the direction of V. S. Nemchinov.[4] Nemchinov, who for 15 years until his death in 1964 was a member of the Council for the Study of Productive Forces (SOPS), involved in the study of industrial location and regional development, was instrumental in emphasizing the need for applying input-output analysis and other mathematical-economic techniques at the regional level. The Laboratory, which he directed, grew and was merged into the newly created Central Economic-Mathematical Institute, TsEMI, in 1963. Many of the young economists who joined Nemchinov in this early work now hold important positions in both planning and research organizations (for example, V. V. Kossov who is deputy director of an important department of the national Gosplan, and E. F. Baranov and V. S. Dadaian who direct research projects within TsEMI).

During the period 1958-62 ex post tables were compiled for four small regions within the Russian republic. (See Table 6.1.) The construction and analysis of input-output tables for one of these regions--the Mordovian autonomous republic--was the basis for the

TABLE 6.1

Ex Post Regional Input-Output Tables in the Soviet Union

Ex post tables for years other than 1966 or 1972

Region	Year	Number of Sectors	Units of Measurement
Mordovian ASSR	1958	14	purchasers' prices
Mordovian ASSR	1959	86	purchasers' prices
Tatar ASSR	1959	165	purchasers' prices
Tatar Sovnarkhoz	1960	150	purchasers' prices
Tatar Sovnarkhoz	1961	150	purchasers' prices
Kaliningrad Oblast'	1960	15	purchasers' prices
Karelian ASSR	1961	75	purchasers' prices
Latvian SSR	1961	239	producers' prices
Latvian SSR	1969	22	purchasers' prices
Latvian SSR	1970	22	purchasers' prices
Lithuanian SSR	1961	239	producers' prices
Estonian SSR	1961	239	producers' prices
Three Baltic republics	1961	239	producers' prices
Armenian SSR	1963	91	purchasers' prices
Azerbaidzhan SSR	1964	215	physical units
Belorussian SSR	1965	135	purchasers' prices

Ex Post Tables for 1966

Region	Number of Sectors	Region
Ukrainian SSR	110	Russian SFSR (103 sectors)
Donbass	61	Northwest economic region
Latvian SSR,		Komi ASSR
value terms	185	Karelian ASSR
Latvian SSR,		Central economic region
physical units	236	Volgo-Viatskii economic region
Estonian SSR	152	Central-Blackearth economic region
Lithuanian SSR	n.a.	Volga economic region
Belorussian SSR	n.a.	Saratov oblast'
Moldavian SSR	n.a.	Bashkir ASSR
Armenian SSR,		Tatar ASSR
value terms	112	North Caucasus economic region
Armenian SSR,		Krasnodarskii Krai
physical units	252	Ural economic region
Azerbaidzhan SSR,		West Siberian economic region
value terms	103	Novosibirsk oblast'
Azerbaidzhan SSR,		East Siberian economic region
physical units	251	Krasnoiarskii Krai
Georgian SSR	111	Irkutskaia oblast'
Kazakh SSR	105	Tuvinskaia ASSR
Kirgiz SSR	105	Buriatskaia ASSR
Tadzhik SSR	109	Chitinskaia oblast'
Uzbek SSR	n.a.	Far East economic region
Turkmen SSR	n.a.	Amurskaia oblast'
		Khabarovskii Krai
		Primorskii Krai
		Sakhalinskaia oblast'
		Kamchatskaia oblast'
		Iakutskaia ASSR
		Magadanskaia ASSR

Ex Post Tables for 1972

Ex post tables for all Union republics and for each of the ten large economic regions within the RSFSR were again to be compiled, but the number of smaller administrative subdivisions of Union republics for which 1972 ex post tables have been compiled is unknown.

Note: n.a. = data not available.
Source: Compiled by the authors.

first extensive regional input-output studies to be published in the
Soviet Union (Dadaian and Kossov 1962; Kossov 1964a). The next
regional input-output project undertaken was the construction of the
1961 ex post tables for each of the Baltic republics (Mints 1967a).
This project was also initiated and directed by the Laboratory of
Economic-Mathematical Methods and was carried out in connection
with the Economic Institutes of the Academy of Sciences in each republic. It produced the first detailed set of methodological guidelines for constructing regional input-output tables (Mints, Kossov,
and Baranov 1967).

During the 1962-65 period initial attempts at constructing
input-output tables were also undertaken in the Belorussian, Armenian, Georgian, and Azerbaidzhan republics. The work carried
out in these republics involved two new innovations in the construction of regional input-output tables. First, a 1962 table for Belorussia (Ippa 1965) and a 1964 table for Georgia (Kekelidze 1968) were
compiled on the basis of data from the plans of individual enterprises,
rather than from ex post data on production and the use of material
inputs.[5] The use of data from these enterprise "tekhpromfinplans"
assembled in matrix form--an idea developed by Modin (1964)--was
praised at the time as a means of using existing statistical materials
to construct input-output tables, but it has not been employed again
since TsSU began undertaking periodic statistical surveys for the
construction of regional tables in 1966. Secondly, the 1964 tables
for Georgia and Azerbaidzhan represented the first experiments with
constructing regional input-output tables in terms of physical units.
(The characteristics of tables in physical units are described in the
section on planning applications.)

Through 1965 work on the construction and analysis of regional
input-output tables was carried out primarily by various economic institutes. In 1966 data were collected by the Central Statistical Administration for the second ex post input-output table for the Soviet
Union as a whole, and the national and republic TsSUs assumed the
task of constructing tables for all Union republics for this year as
well.[6] These 1966 input-output tables for republics were compiled
using the information from enterprises in each republic which had
been included in the survey for the national table, but work on many
was begun only after the table for the Soviet Union as a whole had
been completed. In several republics the data from this national
survey were insufficient for compiling the republic table, and additional surveys of the enterprises of some branches of the economy
(particularly those of local specialization) were necessary. Thus,
the tables for some republics were not completed until 1970.

The completion of this comprehensive set of survey-based regional input-output tables for 1966 was a major accomplishment.

However, due to the vast differences in the sizes of the 15 Soviet republics, this set of tables did not fully meet the needs of modeling interregional economic relations. In particular, a need was recognized for a breakdown of the large Russian republic, which occupies over three-fourths of the land area of the Soviet Union and accounts for about 60 percent of the country's gross social product. Some work on the construction of 1966 input-output tables for various regions of the RSFSR was begun as early as 1968, including the East Siberian and Far East economic regions and their component administrative subdivisions (Shniper and Denisova 1974), the Saratov oblast' (Anfinogentova 1973), and the Bashkir autonomous republic (Bashkirskii filial AN SSSR 1973). Then in 1970 a major effort was undertaken to compile 1966 input-output tables for each of the ten economic regions into which the RSFSR is divided. This work was carried out by economic institutes and universities located in the various regions under the general direction of TsEMI economists (Semenov 1973b).

In 1972 data were again collected by the national and republic TsSUs to construct input-output tables for the Soviet Union and all Union republics. In addition the TsSU of the Russian republic was given the task of compiling tables for each of its large economic regions (Guzhvin and Luk'ianov 1976). Some basic changes in the organization of the statistical survey for these 1972 tables should lead to improvements in the quality of the regional tables compiled for this year. The number of sectors for which complete surveys of all enterprises were undertaken was greatly increased in 1972, and the collection of data was decentralized. Enterprises submitted their completed survey forms to republic TsSUs (either directly or indirectly through local TsSU offices), which in turn forwarded them to the national TsSU. In addition, enterprises received the survey forms earlier and supplied a wider range of information than in previous years (Eidel'man 1972). Since the 1966 input-output tables for republics were compiled after the national table, often on the basis of additional surveys, there were some basic inconsistencies between the republic and national tables. For example, there were 41 individual interindustry flow entries in the published data for the RSFSR input-output table which exceeded the corresponding entries for the USSR table. Since republic TsSUs supervised the statistical survey for the 1972 input-output tables, the agreement among republic and national tables should be improved.

The list of ex post regional input-output tables given in Table 6.1 includes all survey-based tables known to have been compiled in the Soviet Union, but it is incomplete in one respect. Several input-output tables were compiled in various republics for years between 1966 and 1972 in connection with work on the construction of planning

input-output tables for 1975. In some cases limited surveys of enterprises were undertaken in order to construct ex post input-output
tables for years during this period on an aggregated basis. For example, in the Latvian republic ex post input-output tables distinguishing 22 sectors are apparently now being constructed on an annual
basis (Shmulder et al. 1974). However, in other cases ex post tables
for these interim years were constructed without additional surveys
of enterprises using existing statistical sources and adjusted 1966
input coefficients. Such tables were constructed by economic institutes in the RSFSR, the Ukraine, and perhaps other republics, but
these nonsurvey tables have not been included in Table 6.1 since
little about these tables has been published.

A final aspect of work on ex post input-output tables that should
be mentioned is the collection of supplementary data on labor and
capital for these tables. One of the most important considerations in
developing plans for regional development in the Soviet Union is the
spatial distribution of labor supply. In a book on the territorial planning of labor, Mints (1967b) discussed ways in which input-output
planning models could be expanded to incorporate considerations of
aggregate and regional labor supply constraints by using data on manpower requirements by industry and occupation, and by also taking
into consideration interoccupational and interregional labor mobility.
In a more recent study, a pilot input-output table of population movements and labor resources was compiled by TsEMI economists for a
single region (Breev and Kriukov 1974). However, the information
necessary for more extensive studies of this type has not been systematically collected. For example, in constructing the 1966 input-
output tables for all republics, data on labor requirements (and capital stock) by sector in the input-output classification scheme were
compiled for less than one-half of the tables. This is a primary
shortcoming of these regional input-output accounts, limiting their
usefulness for some of the planning applications discussed below.

INTERREGIONAL TRADE DATA AND
INTERREGIONAL MODELS

Most of the ex post input-output tables for regions of the Soviet
Union have been constructed under the general direction of two organizations: TsEMI, which organized work on the construction of
several of the first experimental tables and the 1966 tables for sub-
regions of the RSFSR; and the national and republic TsSUs, which
constructed the 1966 tables for Union republics and the 1972 tables
for Union republics and large economic regions within the RSFSR.
While many aspects of the methodology used in compiling all of these

tables were identical, some of the tables compiled under the direction of TsEMI have differed in basic respects from the standard methodology adopted by TsSU. The most important of these differences involves the way in which imports are recorded in a regional input-output table and the way in which trade and transport costs in interregional trade are handled.

For any entry in the first or second quadrant of a regional table, denoted as x_{ij} (the purchase of output of sector i by production or final-demand sector j), three components can be distinguished: (1) purchases of products produced within the region, denoted here by x'_{ij}; (2) purchases of imported products of a type also produced in the region, that is, competitive imports, denoted by x''_{ij}; and (3) purchases of imported products of a type not produced in the region, that is, noncompetitive imports, denoted by x'''_{ij}. In most recent Soviet regional input-output tables (and in all those compiled under the direction of TsSU) each first- and second-quadrant entry represents the total deliveries of the products of one sector to another productive sector or final user, regardless of whether they were produced within the region or imported. (That is, each of these entries is equal to $x'_{ij} + x''_{ij} + x'''_{ij}$.) The import entry for each productive sector is defined as the value of the products of that sector which are imported, with no distinction of competitive imports, that is, the import entry for sector i is defined as $\Sigma_j (x''_{ij} + x'''_{ij})$. Thus, when imports are recorded in a column (as negative entries) in the final-demand quadrant, the row sum of all first- and second-quadrant deliveries (including exports) for a given sector is equal to the gross value of output of that sector produced within the region. [7]

A few regional input-output tables have deviated from or expanded on this standard treatment of imports. One of the first experimental Soviet regional input-output tables (Kossov 1964a) distinguished noncompetitive imports. Each entry in the first and second quadrants was defined as $x'_{ij} + x''_{ij}$, and a separate row of the noncompetitive imports purchased by each sector was introduced between the first and third quadrants. Each entry in this row was defined as $\Sigma_i x'''_{ij}$. In this table the difference between exports and competitive imports for each productive sector was entered as a trade balance in the final-demand quadrant. While this table was constructed on an entirely different basis, attempts have also been made to collect additional information on the uses of imports as a supplement to the standard regional input-output table described above. For example, a special table showing the distribution of the imports of each sector for all first- and second-quadrant uses--that is, a matrix with entries defined as $x''_{ij} + x'''_{ij}$--was compiled in connection with work on input-output tables for Georgia (Kekelidze 1968, pp. 38-43) and Latvia (Shmulder 1971). By subtracting the elements

of this matrix from the corresponding entries in the first and second
quadrants of the input-output table in standard form, a matrix showing only intraregional flows, $x_{ijs}^!$, could be calculated. For other
regional tables, supplementary information on the use of imports
has been collected, but in a less detailed form, such as the shares
of the imported products of each sector delivered for all intermediate
and all final uses.

A related aspect of regional input-output accounting is the valuation of imports and exports. With the exception of some of the first
regional tables, all ex post regional input-output tables in the Soviet
Union have been constructed in purchasers' prices--the prices paid
by the ultimate users and consumers which include the value of trade,
distribution, and transportation costs incurred in delivering the output of each sector. [8] However, two different methods of valuing imports and exports have been used in these tables. In most tables
constructed under the direction of TsEMI, import and export entries
include the full value of interregional transportation and distribution
costs. These costs are charged to the producing region. Thus, the
costs of transporting imported goods within the region are recorded
as exports of the transportation sector, and the transportation costs
incurred outside the region on its exports are recorded as imports
of the transportation sector. In the republic tables constructed by
TsSU, however, both imports and exports are valued F.O.B. at the
border of the republic, and there are no exports or imports of transportation and distribution services. [9]

The extent to which the source and destination of imports and
exports have been identified geographically has also differed among
regional input-output tables compiled in the Soviet Union. Data on
interregional flows which are sector-specific and region-specific
for both the source and destination have not been compiled for any
Soviet regional input-output table. However, for a number of tables
information has been collected for supplementary matrixes of the
geographical distribution of the imports and exports of each sector.
Such matrixes were compiled for the 1961 input-output tables for
each Baltic republic showing the interregional trade flows of each
of these republics with the other 14 Union republics and with the ten
economic regions of the RSFSR.

A general methodology for collecting data on regional exports
and imports with a similar breakdown of interregional flows was
drawn up to be used in constructing the 1966 input-output tables for
all republics (Bedenkova 1967). However, collecting these data was
the most time-consuming part of the work on these tables, and while
in several republics a complete survey of all enterprises and organizations involved in external trade was undertaken, a geographical breakdown of exports and imports was not compiled for all

republics.[10] Furthermore, since each republic collecting such data
carried out an independent survey, the data on interregional flows in
the input-output tables of different republics were frequently inconsistent with each other (Granberg 1975, p. 81). A number of Soviet
economists have called for centralized control over the collection of
data on interregional flows for the 1972 input-output tables, but no
reports on the collection of these data have yet been published.

The construction of input-output tables for all republics and
the ten economic regions of the RSFSR for 1966 provided a basis for
work on several multiregional input-output models, even though the
interregional trade data collected for these tables were not uniform
for all regions. However, two of the most ambitious attempts at
constructing multiregional models in the Soviet Union to date were
begun even before this data base was complete. The most extensive
of these models was a 16-sector, 10-region, optimizing multiregional input-output model constructed at the Institute of Economics
and the Organization of Industrial Production (IEOPP) in Novosibirsk
under the direction of A. G. Granberg (1973). The first variant of
this model was constructed in 1967 using existing statistical sources
and projections made for the period 1965-75 with a dynamic input-
output model of the Soviet Union. It was a linear programming model
with 700 variables and 162 constraints. The first stage in the solution process involved the estimation of regional production and consumption and interregional trade for the last year of the 1965-75
planning period. Consumption in the final year was maximized. On
obtaining the solution for the last year, the pattern of economic
growth of the regions over the intervening years was computed.
Since these initial experiments, which were viewed primarily as an
attempt to develop the model with approximate data, additional calculations have been made regularly as improved data have become
available.[11]

A different type of multiregional model has been developed by
the Soviet Council for the Study of Productive Forces (Nikolaev 1971).
This model is a static, purely locational one designed to determine
the optimal distribution of production in a number of branches of the
economy, given national totals for production and final consumption
in these branches. Total national production and transportation costs
(including capital, labor, and natural resource charges) are minimized. While this model incorporates alternative production functions for certain branches, it does not include all output of the economy. Experimental calculations with the model were carried out
with a subdivision into 5 regions and 25 branches.

In addition to the two models mentioned above,[12] at least
three static interregional models have been developed on the basis
of 1966 regional input-output tables: (1) a two-region model with the

large Russian republic comprising one region and the rest of the USSR as the second region; (2) a three-region model for the Transcaucasian region linking the input-output tables for each of the three Transcaucasian republics and treating the rest of the Soviet Union as exogenous;[13] and (3) an interregional model for Central Asian republics for which no information has been published (Granberg 1975, pp. 251-71). Each of the first two models was formulated on the basis of the multiregional model originally developed by L. N. Moses (1955). The available data on interregional trade was used to calculate matrixes of trade coefficients reflecting the share of the total output of each sector consumed in a given region that was produced domestically, and the shares supplied by each other region. With these matrixes of trade coefficients and the matrixes of direct input coefficients for each individual region, a complete interregional matrix of full input coefficients was calculated. Each model was then used to analyze the direct and indirect linkages among regions including the labor and capital embodied in the exports and imports of each region. A 16-sector model of this type was constructed for the Transcaucasian republics, and two variants of the RSFSR-"rest of the USSR" model (distinguishing 16 and 50 sectors) were analyzed.

In addition to the empirically implemented models described above, extensive theoretical work on the formulation of various multiregional input-output models has been done in the Soviet Union.[14] The fact that complete sets of regional input-output tables encompassing the entire Soviet Union will soon be available for two accounting years should provide increased opportunities for implementing some of the models that have been developed. The idea of a system of models for optimal planning that would include regional as well as sectoral models to be coordinated and solved iteratively has been developed at both TsEMI (Baranov, Danilov-Danil'ian, and Zavel'skii 1970) and at IEOPP (Aganbegian, Bagrinovskii, and Granberg 1972). However, it seems safe to conclude that this and other work with multiregional models is even further away from incorporation into the existing planning system than the single-region models to be discussed in the following section. While in recent years increased emphasis has been placed on the need for long-term planning in the Soviet Union, the framework set up for elaborating these plans--the General Scheme for the Distribution of Production Forces or "Genskhema"[15]-- has not included the use of such mathematical-economic techniques.

PLANNING APPLICATIONS

Regional economic planning occupies a secondary place in the Soviet planning system.[16] The most significant regional planning is

that done at the Union republic level, since plans approved by the
republic councils of ministers carry the force of law. The national
Gosplan also engaged in some regional planning, compiling basic
economic indicators for the 18 economic regions into which the Soviet
Union is divided. However, the planning commissions that previously existed in these regions were abolished in 1969. Some regional
planning is also done at the level of the administrative subdivisions
of Union republics (oblasts, autonomous republics, and so forth),
but this is largely limited to problems of local industry, local labor
supply, and the nonproductive sphere.

While each Union republic has a planning commission (republic
Gosplan), the ability of these planning organs to formulate consistent
and comprehensive plans for the development of each republic is constrained by the fact that they are often bypassed in the vertical flow
of information between enterprises and ministries of certain branches
of the economy. The Soviet system of economic administration includes three types of ministries: (1) all-Union ministries which ad-
minister enterprises of a given branch located throughout the country
directly from Moscow, (2) Union-republic ministries which combine
central administration from Moscow with subordinate administrative
organs in each republic where enterprises of each branch organized
on this two-level principle are located, and (3) republic ministries
for branches administered directly by the councils of ministers of
Union republics only.[17] During the process of formulating national
plans, enterprises of all-Union subordination report directly to their
corresponding ministries in Moscow. Regional (that is, republic)
breakdowns of the plans of these all-Union branches are not compiled. In practice, republic Gosplans usually receive information on
the plans of enterprises of all-Union subordination located on their
territory only after these plans have been approved by Gosplan USSR
and the USSR Council of Ministries.

Republic planning organs thus have only limited input into the
planning of what can be a significant share of their local economies.
In 1970, the share of industrial output subordinated to republic councils of ministers was 52 percent for the country as a whole, ranging
from 87-88 percent in Kazakhstan, Tadzhikistan, and Moldavia to
40 percent in the RSFSR (Granberg 1973, p. 24; Pavlenko 1971,
p. 46). Since 1970 these shares have decreased as a result of re-
organization in the fuel and chemical industries. In effect, the plans
compiled by republic Gosplans are only an after-the-fact summation
of branch plans.

Given these limitations on planning by Union republics, many
Soviet economists have viewed the construction of regional input-
output tables as a valuable new tool for regional planning. The ex
post regional tables that have been constructed include all production

in a given region, regardless of the form of administrative subordination, and thus provide comprehensive accounts of the structure
of the economies of individual regions which were never available
before. The input-output model has been characterized as an integrated set of material balances that can be used to ensure consistency of the plans for individual sectors of the economy. It has introduced the concept of starting the planning process from a desired
final output rather than from initial gross output targets that may
require continuous revisions to approach consistency. And, no less
importantly, the fact that input-output models can be solved with the
aid of electronic computers has provided the possibility of calculating a number of alternative variants of a given plan based on different assumptions about the level and structure of final demand.[18]

Many of the planning applications of input-output models discussed below were used first at the national level and adapted for
use at the regional level. However, no attempt is made here to
trace the original development of these models.

The leading republics in the development of regional planning
input-output models have been the three Baltic republics--Latvia,
Lithuania, and Estonia. Following the completion of the first ex
post input-output tables (for 1961) for these republics, work was begun on static planning input-output tables for 1970 for each. This
project produced the first extensive studies of methods of projecting
direct input coefficients and vectors of final consumption which are
the basic components of the static planning model (Baranov 1968).
During the first half of the 1960s, static planning models for 1970
were also constructed for Belorussia (Gurvich 1967) and Georgia
(Kekelidze 1964), but work on similar models for other republics
was begun only after the completion of the 1966 ex post input-output
tables. During the 1968-72 period, static planning models for 1970
were constructed for at least six other republics--Armenia, Azerbaidzhan, Kazakhstan, Tadzhikistan, Kirgizstan, and Moldavia. In
most cases, while these tables were constructed on the basis of
plan data for 1970, they were not in fact completed until after this
year.[19] These 1970 planning tables were compiled primarily as a
basis for subsequent work on static tables for 1975 (the final year of
the Ninth Five-Year Plan) and for the development of dynamic input-
output models. With the initial experience of constructing these
planning input-output models, it has become a regular part of the
work of research groups in several republics. For example, in
Armenia static planning tables on a 21-sector basis have been compiled for 1970, 1975, 1980, 1985, and 1990 (Gevorkian, 1974).

The usefulness of these static planning tables depends to a
large extent on the accuracy with which the direct input coefficients
for the planning year can be estimated. Soviet economists have in

general rejected mechanistic techniques of modifying the coefficients
from some base-year table to correspond to planning-year row and
column totals such as the RAS method.[20] The Soviet approach, particularly for highly disaggregated tables, has been to identify the
most important coefficients in an ex post table and systematically
analyze the factors underlying changes in these coefficients over
time. The importance of an individual coefficient has been defined
in terms of the effect of any change in it on the values of gross output calculated with the model (Sedova 1968). For example, in the
1970 planning table for Estonia, which distinguished 152 sectors of
material production, only 4.3 percent of all direct input coefficients
accounting for 80 percent of the total value of material inputs were
considered for adjustment. All other coefficients were taken as calculated in the base-year ex post table (Kukke 1968). A rule of thumb
was also established for identifying the most important coefficients
in the 1970 planning table for Latvia (all those larger than 0.01 for
industry). However, very rapid growth over the planning period
anticipated for certain coefficients resulted in some deviation from
this guideline (Tsipe 1971, p. 85). Coefficients selected for adjustment were carefully analyzed to correct for factors such as changes
in product mix of sectors, changes of technology, substitution of
new materials, and price changes, on the basis of consultation with
experts on the technology of various branches of the economy.

The second major phase of work on these static planning tables
is projection of the various components of final demand for the planning year. Much of this information is ordinarily drawn from the
planning data normally compiled by republic Gosplans. For example,
capital formation data for the 1970 Latvian table was taken largely
from the investment plans of ministries for the purchases of various
types of machinery. Deliveries for social consumption were estimated from Gosplan data and projected trends in the use of material
inputs in different categories of public and government consumption
(Tsipe 1971, pp. 86-95). The largest share of final product is accounted for by personal consumption of the population, and forecasts
of this component have involved the use of additional mathematical
models. For example, the estimation of personal consumption for
the 1970 Estonian table involved the calculation of income elasticities of demand for individual products, distinguishing urban from
rural consumers and taking into account family size (Strazh 1966;
Valdsoo 1967).

Soviet regional input-output specialists feel that the use of
these static planning models can be usefully incorporated into the
existing planning process at two stages--in the preliminary stage
of plan formation for calculating several variants of a given plan
based on alternative vectors of final demand, and at the final stage

for evaluating the overall consistency of the plan.[21] While, as noted in the introduction to this paper, these models have not become a part of the formal planning process, a number of experiments of both types have been carried out, and much of the work with such models has been done by economic institutes associated with republic Gosplans. For example, 15 variants of the 1970 planning table for Estonia (Linnaks and Ennuste 1966), and 21 variants of a 16-sector planning table for 1975 for Azerbaidzhan, were calculated to analyze the effects of varying proportions of consumption and capital accumulation in total final demand (Akhundov et al. 1972). An interesting experiment was carried out with the 1970 planning table for Latvia to evaluate the consistency of the planned values of gross output for all sectors established by Gosplan for the republic (Rokpelne and Tsipe 1968). This study showed that after allowing for intermediate uses, an unrealistically small value of output remained for final uses in many sectors, given reasonable estimates for possible imports of the products of these sectors.

In many republics the construction of the first static planning tables was followed immediately by the beginning of work on various forms of dynamic input-output models. The Baltic republics were again in the forefront of the development of these new planning models. For the Latvian and Estonian republics, dynamic input-output models, distinguishing 29 and 30 sectors respectively, were constructed in the late 1960s for the period 1971-80. Each of these models incorporated coefficients for lagged capital formation (Baranov 1972). In the Lithuanian republic experimental calculations were carried out for the period 1965-70 with a much more aggregated (four-sector) model developed by Satunovskii (1973). This model first determined gross output by sector for the entire period, and additional relations were then used to determine gross output and capital formation by sector for each year of the planning period.

During the early 1970s work was begun on dynamic input-output models in at least eight other republics.[22] In five of these republics--the RSFSR, Azerbaidzhan, Armenia, Kirgizstan, and Kazakhstan--the model used was a dynamic input-output model originally developed at the Economic Institute of Gosplan (Klotsvog and Novichkov 1971).[23] In this model, given values of capital stock by sector in the first year of the planning period and values of final product by sector (consumption plus accumulation of nonproductive capital) for each year of the planning period, gross output and capital formation by sector were determined year by year. In most republics a model distinguishing 16 to 21 sectors of material production (with only two sectors involved in capital formation--machine-building and construction) was used for experimental calculations

for a period extending to 1990. The primary use of these models
has been to generate initial estimates of basic economic indicators
for the construction of more disaggregated static planning models
for selected future years. In at least one republic, Armenia, material from the long-term development plan for the republic was incorporated into calculations with a dynamic input-output model
(Adonts and Gevorkian 1974).

All of the planning models described above (both static and
dynamic) have been constructed using the sector classification system employed in compiling ex post Soviet input-output tables. These
input-output accounts are based on a system of sectors defined on a
commodity basis (that is, each sector is composed of a group of related products), which differs from the sector classification systems
defined on an establishment or administrative basis used in standard
Soviet national income and product accounts, and in economic planning. This basic methodological difference is one of the factors
that have limited the introduction of input-output models into the
planning process, since a basic requirement of plan targets is that
they be "addressed." One method of dealing with this problem,
which has been employed in using the static planning tables of several republics to calculate the consistency of plans formulated by
republic Gosplans, has been to convert Gosplan gross output targets
to an input-output basis using ex post coefficients of the shares of
each input-output sector in the total output of each planning branch
(that is, ministry).[24] In a few cases experimental input-output
models with sectors defined on an establishment basis have been
developed (Bondarenko 1974, pp. 183-91).

An additional limitation on the use of input-output models in
economic planning is that much of the planning by Gosplan is done
in physical units. This problem has led to the development of separate input-output accounts in physical units, that is, tables in
which intersectoral flows are measured in physical units rather
than value terms. The number of separate commodities distinguished in a physical balance is considerably greater than for a
value table; however, all output of the economy is not included.
Such tables are considered necessary by Soviet specialists for use
in detailed planning, and are also an intermediate stage in the construction of more aggregated value tables. By treating a large number of separate intersectoral flows in physical units, the establish-
ment/commodity problem is kept under better control than is possible with purely value accounts. Ex post and planning tables in
physical units have been compiled for the Azerbaidzhan, Armenian,
and Latvian republics.

The advantages of both variations of the basic input-output
model described above have been incorporated in the combined

physical-value tables compiled for the Latvian republic (Dagovich 1971). Entries in value terms are included for activities that cannot be entered in physical units, to ensure complete coverage of the economy in the table.

On another important frontier Soviet economists are now trying to integrate input-output and flow-of-funds analysis into a single planning framework (such as was proposed by Ragnar Frisch as early as 1957). In order to be an effective tool for planning, Soviet specialists realize that in addition to the real physical flows that characterize production relations, financial sectors and financial flows must be included in input-output models. This type of accounting framework was developed by Isaev (1969; 1973) and has been applied using ex post data for the Estonian and Georgian republics.

While these innovations introduced in work with planning input-output models have increased their compatibility with traditional planning techniques, a number of Soviet economists are of the opinion that for the type of regional planning done by republic Gosplans, much more consideration must be given to factors outside the basic input-output model. Given the constraints on planning at the Union republic level noted at the beginning of this section, although republic Gosplans are responsible for the annual planning of production and material supply for enterprises of republic subordination, they are primarily concerned with medium-term and long-term planning. In this longer time framework greater consideration must be given to such factors as demographic developments and labor supply, changes in the structure of consumption with rising income levels, and the development of the services sector of the economy. During the past five years research groups in two republics have developed input-output-based systems of models that are composed of submodels for forecasting changes in the type of factors listed above, linked to an input-output model. These systems are solved iteratively to simulate the development of the republic. The Baltic republics have again been the leaders in developing these new regional models. Such a system of models was first elaborated by a Lithuanian research group under the direction of Raiatskas (1972), and similar work has been done in the Latvian SSR (Adirim, Ianov, and Pochs 1975). If the previous pattern of the development of Soviet regional input-output research is repeated, similar work on systems of models may be anticipated soon in other republics.

NOTES

1. For a comprehensive bibliography on Soviet input-output analysis see Treml (1975). Approximately one-fifth of the more

than 800 entries from the Soviet literature listed here deal with regional analyses, and many additional items on this topic have been
added to this bibliography since its publication. Previous surveys
of Soviet regional input-output work are Kossov (1964b) and Ellman
(1968). Tretyakova and Birman (1976) provide a recent overview of
the contribution of input-output models to economic analysis and
planning in the Soviet Union.

     2. Nonsurvey methods of deriving regional coefficients such
as those widely used in U.S. regional analyses are criticized in the
Soviet Union as being inaccurate and allowing insufficient treatment
of distinctive regional characteristics (Kossov 1973, p. 281).

     3. A large economic region may include more than one repub-
lic, or, in the case of the largest republics (the Ukraine and the
Russian republic), one republic can contain several large economic
regions. The Moldavian republic is not included in any large economic region and in effect constitutes a nineteenth region in this
scheme.

     4. Intersectoral regional accounts for the Ukraine for 1923/24
and 1924/25 were prepared in 1927 under the direction of V. S.
Myshkis of the Ukrainian Gosplan, but this work had no effect on the
later development of Soviet input-output statistics.

     5. Similar work was also carried out in the Tatar autonomous
republic. While these regional tables have been called planning tables
in the Soviet literature, each was in fact not completed until after the
year for which it was compiled. Thus, they should be distinguished
from the planning tables compiled for future years which are discussed in the section on planning applications.

     6. While the republic TsSUs were responsible for construct-
ing these 1966 tables, in nearly every republic this work was carried
out with the help of local economic institutes.

     7. Soviet regional input-output tables are often presented in a
format that lists imports in a row at the bottom of the table. In this
form, both the column and the row for each productive sector sum to
the total value of domestic output plus imports for that sector.

     8. The only ex post regional input-output tables compiled in
producers' prices were the 1961 tables for the three Baltic republics.

     9. The treatment of transportation and distribution services
for goods shipped through a region is also different with these two
methods. For a full discussion see Chapter 7 of this volume.

     10. Among the republics for which such a geographical break-
down of exports and imports by sector in 1966 was compiled are the
RSFSR, the Baltic republics, the Transcaucasus republics, and
Kirgizstan. Similar data were also collected for some economic
regions of the RSFSR.

11. An interesting study carried out with the data base for the IEOPP optimizing multiregional input-output model is the "West-East" model which was constructed to simulate a decentralized two-level planning process. The purpose of this study was to examine the functioning of national and regional planning bodies in the search for a solution giving maximal growth of national consumption consistent with equal distribution of per capita income among the regions (Granberg and Chernyshev 1971).

12. A third model has apparently been developed at TsEMI (Kiselev 1971). However, while reference has been made to experimental calculations carried out with this model, no results have been published.

13. The export-import balance of each sector in each of the three republics with the rest of the Soviet Union and with other countries was entered as a column in the final-demand quadrant of the input-output table for each republic. Similarly, in the two-region RSFSR-"rest of the Soviet Union" model, the export-import balance with other countries of each sector in each of the two regions was recorded as a column in the final-demand quadrant.

14. Two survey articles by Achelashvili (1971a, 1971b) provide an overview of some Soviet multiregional models and modifications of Western multiregional models.

15. A Genskhema plan outlining the distribution of production and the development of the economies of individual regions for the period 1971-80 was developed under the direction of the Council for the Study of Productive Forces (SOPS) with the participation of more than 500 scientific organizations throughout the country (SOPS Gosplan SSSR 1966).

16. This summary of regional economic planning in the Soviet Union refers to the system of planning and administration as it has existed since the abolition of the "Sovnarkhozy" in 1965.

17. The system is even more complex in practice, since in some cases a single enterprise may be subordinated to more than one ministry.

18. For a more complete discussion of the applicability of input-output models in the context of Soviet economic planning, see Treml (1967) and Ellman (1972, Ch. 6).

19. In this respect these tables were similar to those constructed earlier for Belorussia (1962) and Georgia (1964). See the section on ex post tables in this chapter.

20. See Bacharach (1970) for a description of this technique, which has been widely experimented with by Western input-output specialists.

21. See, for example, Belov (1968).

22. The experience with these models and many other recent developments in Soviet input-output research was discussed at a national conference of input-output specialists from throughout the country in Erevan in 1974 (Baranov and Gevorkian 1974).

23. Somewhat different models have been employed in Tadzhikistan, Georgia, and Belorussia. No published reports of any work with dynamic input-output models are available for Turkmenistan, Uzbekistan, Moldavia, or the Ukraine. However, economists in the Ukraine have developed the first econometric model for a republic (Emel'ianov and Kushnirskii 1974).

24. Semenov (1974) has developed a scheme for regional input-output accounting that relates input-output sectors to both establishment-based sectors and the branches (ministries) employed in economic planning.

REFERENCES

Achelashvili, K. V. 1971a. "Balansovye mezhraionnye modeli i ikh ispol'zovanie v ekonomiko-matematicheskom analize pazmeshcheniia proizvoditel'nykh sil." In Metody i modeli territorial'nogo planirovaniia, vypusk I, ed. A. G. Granberg, pp. 181-242. Novosibirsk: IEOPP AN SSSR, Sibirskoe otdelenie.

_____. 1971b. "Ekonomiko-matematicheskii analiz nckotorykh optimizatsionnykh mezhraionnykh modelei." In Metody i modeli territorial'nogo planirovaniia, vypusk II, ed. A. G. Granberg, pp. 72-99. Novosibirsk: IEOPP AN SSSR, Sibirskoe otdelenie.

Adirim, I. G., Ia. A. Ianov, and R. Ia. Pochs. 1975. Sistema modelei prognozirovaniia rosta narodnogo khoziaistva respubliki. Riga: Zinatne.

Adonts, M. A. and M. A. Gevorkian. 1974. "Osnovnye napravleniia razvitiia narodnogo khoziaistva Armianskoi SSR po rezul'tatam resheniia dinamicheskoi modeli mezhotraslevogo balansa." In Voprosy primeneniia mezhotraslevykh balansov v praktike planirovaniia, ed. E. F. Baranov and M. A. Gevorkian, pp. 49-55. Erevan: NIIEP Gosplan Armianskoi SSR.

Aganbegian, A. G., K. A. Bagrinovskii, and A. G. Granberg. 1972. Sistema modelei narodnokhoziaistvennogo planirovaniia. Moscow: Mysl'.

Akhundov, V. D., M. S. Ragimov, and E. E. Rasul-zade. 1972. "Ekonomicheskaia effektivnost' variantov raspredeleniia konechnogo obshchestvennogo produkta Azerbaidzhanskoi SSR (makroekonomicheskii aspekt)." Trudy 5. NIIE Gosplan Azerbaidzhanskoi SSR, Baku.

Anfinogentova, A. A. 1973. Planirovanie mezhotraslevykh sviazei oblasti. Saratov: Saratov University.

Bacharach, M. 1970. Biproportional Matrices and Input-Output Change. Cambridge: Cambridge University Press.

Baranov, E. F., ed. 1972. Dinamicheskie modeli territorial'nogo planirovaniia. Moscow: Nauka.

_____, ed. 1968. Planovyi mezhotraslevoi balans soiuznoi respubliki. Moscow: Nauka.

_____ and M. A. Gevorkian, eds. 1974. Voprosy primeneniia mezhotraslevykh balansov v praktike planirovaniia. Erevan: NIIEP Gosplan Armianskoi SSR.

_____, V. I. Danilov-Danil'ian, and M. G. Zavel'skii. 1970. Problemy razrabotki sistemy optimal'nogo planirovaniia narodnogo khoziaistva. Moscow: TsEMI AN SSSR.

Belov, M. I. 1968. "Voprosy ispol'zovaniia mezhotraslevogo balansa v praktike planirovaniia narodnogo khoziaistva soiuznoi respubliki." In Planovyi mezhotraslevoi balans soiuznoi respubliki, ed. E. F. Baranov, pp. 5-15. Moscow: Nauka.

Bashkirskii filial AN SSSR. 1973. Opyt razrabotki i analiza mezhotraslevogo balansa obshchestvennogo produkta Bashkirskoi ASSR. Ufa.

Bedenkova, M. F. 1967. Metodicheskie ukazaniia po sostavleniiu mezhraionnykh balansov vvoza i vyvoza produktsii proizvodstvennotekhnicheskogo naznacheniia za 1966 god. Moscow: Gosplan SSSR and TsEMI AN SSSR.

Bondarenko, V. V., ed. 1974. Balansovyi metod vyvchennia rozvytku narodnogo hospodarstva. Kiev: Naukova Dumka.

Breev, B. D. and V. P. Kriukov. 1974. Mezhotraslevye balansy
    dvizheniia naseleniia i trudvoykh resursov (metodologicheskie
    voprosy). Moscow: Nauka.

Dadaian, V. S. and V. V. Kossov. 1962. Balans ekonomicheskogo
    raiona kak sredstvo planovykh raschetov. Moscow: AN SSSR.

Dagovich, B. A. 1971. Analiz i planirovanie ekonomiki soiuznoi
    respubliki metodom mezhotraslevogo balansa. Riga: Liesma.

Eidel'man, M. 1972. "Novyi otchetnyi mezhotraslevoi balans
    proizvodstva i raspredeleniia produktsii v narodnom
    khoziaistve SSSR." Vestnik statistiki, no. 6: 3-15.

Ellman, Michael. 1972. Soviet Planning Today: Proposals for an
    Optimally Functioning Economic System. Cambridge: Cam-
    bridge University Press.

_____. 1968. "The Use of Input-Output in Regional Economic Plan-
    ning: The Soviet Experience." Economic Journal 78 (Decem-
    ber): 855-67.

Emel'ianov, A. S. and F. I. Kushnirskii. 1974. Modelirovanie
    pokazatelei razvitiia ekonomiki soiuznoi respubliki. Moscow:
    Ekonomika.

Gevorkian, M. A. 1974. "Opyt razrabotki mezhotraslevykh balansov
    Armianskoi SSR." NIIEP Gosplan Armianskoi SSR. Erevan:
    Aiastan.

Granberg, A. G., ed. 1975. Mezhotraslevye balansy v analize
    territorial'nykh proportsii SSSR. Novosibirsk: Nauka,
    Sibirskoe otdelenie.

_____. 1973. Optimizatsiia territorial'nykh proportsii narodnogo
    khoziaistva. Moscow: Ekonomika.

_____ and A. A. Chernyshev. 1971. "Eksperimental'nye raschety
    zadachi 'Zapad-Vostok'." In Metody i modeli territorial'nogo
    planirovaniia, ed. A. G. Granberg, pp. 100-37. Novosibirsk:
    IEOPP AN SSSR.

Gurvich, G. Ts. 1967. Voprosy metodiki i praktiki rascheta
    planovogo mezhotraslevogo balansa Belorusskoi SSR. Minsk:
    Gosplan Belorusskoi SSR.

Guzhvin, P. and V. Luk'ianov. 1976. "Balans proizvodstva i raspredeleniia produktsii RSFSR." Vestnik statistiki, no. 5: 16-22.

Ippa, M. M. 1965. Analiz i planirovanie mezhraionnykh ekono-micheskikh sviazei i spetsializatsii ekonomicheskogo raiona. Minsk: Gosplan Belorusskoi SSR.

Isaev, B. L. 1973. Balansy mezhotraslevykh finansovykh sviazei. Moscow: Nauka.

_____. 1969. Integrirovannye balansovye sistemy v analize i planirovanii ekonomiki. Moscow: Nauka.

Kekelidze, M. V. 1968. Analiz mezhotraslevykh sviazei respubliki. Moscow: Nauka.

Kiselev, V. I. 1971. "Nekotorye voprosy formirovaniia i realizatsii mngootraslevoi mezhregional'noi modeli perspektivnogo planirovaniia." In Pervaia konferentsiia po optimal'nomu planirovaniiu narodnym khoziaistvom, seksiia I, vypusk II, pp. 102-10. Moscow: TsEMI AN SSSR.

Klotsvog, F. N. and V. A. Novichkov. 1971. "Primenenie dinamicheskoi modeli mezhotraslevogo balansa dlia narodnokhoziaistvennykh raschetov na dlitel'nuiu perspektivu." In Metodologiia prognozirovaniia ekonomicheskogo razvitiia SSSR, ed. L. M. Gatovskii and S. A. Kheinman, pp. 102-14. Moscow: Ekonomika.

Kossov, V. V. 1973. Mezhotraslevye modeli. Moscow: Ekonomika.

_____, ed. 1964a. Mezhotraslevoi balans proizvodstva i raspredeleniia produktsii ekonomicheskogo raiona. Moscow: Nauka.

_____. 1964b. "Regional Input-Output Analysis in the U.S.S.R." Regional Science Association: Papers 14: 175-81.

Kukke, L. A. 1968. "Analiz ustoichivosti koeffitsientov priamykh zatrat." In Planovyi mezhotraslevoi balans soiuznoi respubliki, ed. E. F. Baranov, pp. 70-78. Moscow: Nauka.

Linnaks, E.. and Iu. Ennuste. 1966. Metody sostavleniia i analiza variantov planovogo mezhotraslevogo balansa respubliki. Tallin: Institut Ekonomiki AN Estonskoi SSR.

Miernyk, W. H. 1973. "Regional and Interregional Input-Output Models: A Reappraisal." In Spatial, Regional, and Population Economics, ed. Mark Perlman, Charles Levin, and Benjamin Chinitz, pp. 263-92. New York: Gordon and Breach.

Mints, L. E., ed. 1967a. Mezhotraslevye issledovaniia v ekonomicheskikh raionakh: opyt raboty po Pribaltiiskomu raionu. Moscow: Nauka.

_____. 1967b. Problemy balansa truda i ispol'zovaniia trudovykh resursov v SSSR. Moscow: Statistika.

_____, V. V. Kossov, and E. F. Baranov. 1967. Mezhotraslevoi balans ekonomicheskogo raiona. Moscow: Nauka.

Modin, A. A. 1964. "Mezhotraslevoi balans i sistema matrichnykh modelei." Voprosy ekonomiki, no. 1: 112-23.

Moses, I. N. 1955. "The Stability of Interregional Trading Patterns and Input-Output Analysis." American Economic Review 45 (December): 803-32.

Nikolaov, S. A. 1971. Mezhraionnyi i vnutriraionnyi analiz razmeshcheniia proizvoditel'nykh sil. Moscow: Nauka.

Pavlenko, V. F. 1971. Territorial'noe i otraslevoe planirovanie. Moscow: Ekonomika.

Raiatskas, R. L. 1972. Integrirovannaia sistema planirovaniia narodnogo khoziaistva soiuznoi respubliki. Vil'nius: Mintis.

Richardson, H. W. 1972. Input-Output and Regional Economics. New York: Wiley.

Riefler, R. F. 1973. "Interregional Input-Output: A State of the Arts Survey." In Studies in Economic Planning over Space and Time, ed. George C. Judge and Takashi Takayama, pp. 133-62. New York: North Holland.

Rokpelne, E. Ia. and K. A. Tsipe. 1968. "Sopostavlenie balansovykh variantov, iskhodiashchikh iz raznykh otpravnykh pokazatelei (valovyi vypusk i konechnyi produkt)." In Planovyi mezhotraslevoi balans soiuznoi respubliki, ed. E. F. Baranov, pp. 29-37. Moscow: Nauka.

Satunovskii, L. M. 1973. Mezhotraslevye modeli territorial'nogo planirovaniia. Vil'nius: Mintis.

Sedova, A. A. 1968. "Matematicheskie metody otbora naibolee vazhnykh koeffitsientov v mezhotraslevykh modeliakh." In Planovyi mezhotraslevoi balans soiuznoi respubliki, ed. E. F. Baranov, pp. 56-69. Moscow: Nauka.

Semenov, A. K. 1974. Metody sistemnogo analiza struktury narodnogo khoziaistva. Moscow: Nauka.

_____. 1973a. "Metodologicheskie i organizatisionnye voprosy razrabotki otchetnykh mezhotraslevykh balansov ekono-micheskikh raionov RSFSR." In Voprosy izucheniia i analiza mezhotraslevykh sviazei ekonomicheskikh raionov, ed. A. K. Semenov, pp. 16-25. Moscow: TsEMI AN SSSR.

_____, ed. 1973b. Voprosy izucheniia i analiza mezhotraslevykh sviazei ekonomicheskikh rainov. Moscow: TsEMI AN SSSR.

Shmulder, M. V. et al. , eds. 1971. Dinamika mezhotraslevykh i mezhrespublikanskikh economicheskikh sviazei Latviiskoi SSR. Riga: TsSU Latviiskoi SSR.

_____, A. Zh. Orlovskaia, O. E. Bauer, O. Ia. Berzkaln, and M. Iu. Rimsha. 1974. "Metodicheskie voprosy ezhegodnogo sostavleniia otchetnykh mezhotraslevykh balansov soiuznoi respubliki (na primere Latviiskoi SSR)." In Voprosy primeneniia mezhotraslevykh balansov v praktike planirovaniia, ed. E. F. Baranov and M. A. Gevorkian, pp. 226-34. Erevan: NIIEP Gosplan Armianskoi SSR.

Shniper, R. I. and L. P. Denisova. 1974. Mezhotraslevye sviazi i narodnokhoziaistvennye proportsii Vostochnoi Sibiri i Dal'nego Vostoka. Novosibirsk: Nauka, Sibirskoe otdelenie.

SOPS Gosplan SSSR. 1966. Obshchaia metodika razrabotki general'noi skhemy razmeshcheniia proizvoditel'nykh sil SSSR na 1971-1980 gg. Moscow: Ekonomika.

Strazh, S. 1966. "O nekotorykh metodakh planirovaniia lichnogo potrebleniia pri sostavlenii eksperimental'nogo planovogo mezhotraslevogo balansa Estonskoi SSR." Izvestiia AN Estonskoi SSR, seriia obshchestvennykh nauk XV, no. 2: 176-87.

Treml, V. G. 1975. Input-Output Analysis and the Soviet Economy: An Annotated Bibliography. New York: Praeger.

_____. 1967. "Input-Output Analysis and Soviet Planning." In Mathematics and Computers in Soviet Economic Planning, ed. John P. Hardt, Marvin Hoffenberg, Norman Kaplan, and Herbert S. Levine, pp. 68-120. New Haven: Yale University Press.

Tretyakova, A. and I. Birman. 1976. "Input-Output Analysis in the USSR." Soviet Studies 28 (April): 157-86.

Tsipe, K. A. 1971. Sistema mezhotraslevykh balansov soiuznoi respubliki. Moscow: Ekonomika.

Valdsoo, M. K. 1967. "O planirovanni lichnogo potrebleniia." In Mezhotraslevye issledovaniia v ekonomicheskikh raionakh, ed. L. E. Mints, pp. 94-109. Moscow: Nauka.

7

A CASE STUDY IN
REGIONAL INPUT-OUTPUT
ANALYSIS: THE LATVIAN
REPUBLIC
Daniel L. Bond

INPUT-OUTPUT STUDIES OF THE LATVIAN SSR

The nature of regional input-output data being collected at the republic level in the Soviet Union is well illustrated by the example of the Latvian SSR. Many "firsts" in republic input-output research --the use of producers' prices in compiling a republic input-output table, the construction of an interregional account, the development of planning input-output tables and of combined physical and value balances, research on dynamic input-output models--have been based on studies of the Latvian economy. Although this Latvian experience should not be considered typical of Soviet regional input-output research in the past, it does represent the type of work being undertaken currently in several other republics.

The Latvian SSR is one of the three Baltic republics located in the northwestern portion of the Soviet Union. It is the third smallest republic in the Soviet Union in size of population, approximately 2.4 million in 1970 (roughly 1 percent of total national population), and fourth smallest in territory (less than three-tenths of a percent of the land area of the Soviet Union). During this century the region has undergone rapid industrialization which has changed the previously agriculture-centered economy into one with an emphasis on heavy and light industries. Concomitant with this change has been the urbanization of the population. In 1967 63 percent of the population in Latvia lived in towns (with almost half of

The author wishes to thank Per Strangert for his help in preparing an earlier version of part of this paper which was presented at the Southern Regional Science Association Meeting in Atlanta, Georgia, April 4, 1975.

these residing in the capital city of Riga). This figure was exceeded among the Union republics only by the neighboring republic, Estonia. Labor force participation in Latvia is very high. In 1966 41 percent of the Latvian population was in the work force, compared with 31 percent for the Soviet Union as a whole. The Latvian people have achieved one of the highest levels of per capita income among the republics. National income per capita in 1970, according to Soviet statistics, was 1,574 rubles in Latvia compared to a national average of 1,194. Only Estonia, with 1,587 rubles per capita had a higher reported figure among republics.

There are no significant mineral deposits in Latvia, and the republic depends to a large extent on electricity transmitted from Estonia and Lithuania. Agricultural production remains important, but the growth of agricultural output has been significantly less than that for the nation as a whole. It is the rapid rate of industrial growth that distinguishes the Latvian economy, which produces and supplies the other republics with significant quantities of steel, electrotechnical machinery and equipment (especially telephone exchanges, radio receivers, and home appliances), railroad passenger cars, motorcycles, furniture, linoleum, knitted wear, ready-made garments, and fish and milk products. (The commodity structure of economic relations in Latvia for 1966 can be seen in the data presented in Table 7.1, which are taken from the aggregated physical input-output table found in TsSu Latvia [1971, Appendix 6].) Latvia has retained trading ties with foreign countries also, exporting food products (fish, meat, and milk products in particular), radio receivers, and paper and wood products.

There is a rich experience in compiling and using regional input-output tables for the republic. The first Latvian table was constructed on the basis of data for 1961 and was part of a major study of the Baltic region that resulted in the preparation of the first interregional input-output table compiled in the Soviet Union--a combined account for Latvia, Lithuania, and Estonia. The research on these detailed (239 sectors) tables was directed by the Laboratory on Economic-Mathematical Methods of the National Academy of Sciences (which later became a part of the Central Economic-Mathematical Institute--TsEMI). This work served as a proving ground for early Soviet input-output techniques.[1]

By 1968 work had been completed on another set of data for 1966. This work began at the start of 1966, and involved 20-25 researchers from the Latvian branch of the Scientific Research Institute of the TsSU USSR, the Latvian TsSU, and the Bureau of Economic-Mathematic Methods of the Latvian Gosplan. In addition to the compilation of data for 1966, the 1961 table was converted from 1961 producers' prices to 1966 purchasers' prices for

TABLE 7.1

Commodity Structure of the 1966 Latvian Economy

		Imports	Exports	Total Distributed*
1.	Iron ore (tons)	155,848	15	178,619
2.	Steel (tons)	15	107,896	332,960
3.	Rolled ferrous metal products (tons)	601,521	182,170	888,021
4.	Steel pipe (tons)	58,000	190	58,317
5.	Coal, coal concentrate, briquets (tons)	1,727,000	--	1,729,156
6.	Natural gas (thousands of cubic meters)	655,600	--	665,600
7.	Peat and peat briquets (tons)	--	--	6,559,000
8.	Electric power (thousands of kilowatt hours)	1,830,000	688,002	3,988,170
9.	Thermal power (hecto-calories)	--	--	7,596,913
10.	Diesel engines and generators (horse power)	15,450	169,815	200,250
11.	Electric apparatus (thousands of rubles)	12,122	4,277	26,707
12.	Household refrigerators (units)	17,970	47,807	69,451
13.	Household washing machines (units)	19,653	440,259	500,575
14.	Radio receivers and televisions (units)	133,259	1,358,606	1,542,906
15.	Automation equipment (thousands of rubles)	9,505	9,944	22,610
16.	Refrigeration equipment (units)	1,034	20,179	21,600
17.	Railroad passenger cars (units)	27	554	608
18.	Tram cars (units)	--	227	243
19.	Buses (units)	354	1,994	2,410
20.	Iron molds (tons)	1,713	4,786	57,867
21.	Steel molds (tons)	218	1,456	16,116
22.	Phosphate fertilizer (tons)	63,169	165,321	410,164
23.	Synthetic fibers (tons)	3,060	9,138	15,609
24.	Paints and lacquers (tons)	17,485	45,065	72,318
25.	Rubberized flat belts (thousands of square meters)	5	678	1,808
26.	Timber (cubic meters)	667,000	140,000	3,365,142
27.	Sawn timber (cubic meters)	159,987	106,944	1,357,165
28.	Composition boards (cubic meters)	1,195	--	30,951
29.	Glued plywood (cubic meters)	495	83,751	122,862
30.	Planed plywood (square meters)	1,499,000	144	8,940,000
31.	Furniture (thousands of rubles)	1,683	20,573	61,514
32.	Paper (tons)	27,359	80,363	139,140
33.	Cardboard (tons)	10,483	11,424	35,144
34.	Cement (tons)	192,709	183,466	972,298

	Imports	Exports	Total Distributed*
35. Prefabricated concrete products (thousands of cubic meters)	7	37	912
36. Wall materials (thousands of standard pieces)	307	--	424,481
37. Asbestos-cement and slate (thousands of standard pieces)	740	48,431	100,290
38. Linoleum (square meters)	71,000	3,736,000	4,490,000
39. Window glass (thousands of square meters)	84	127	2,388
40. Cotton yarn (tons)	1,496	--	16,472
41. Finished cotton fabrics (thousands of square meters)	31,523	23,333	82,870
42. Finished silk fabrics (thousands of square meters)	8,683	2,182	18,413
43. Washed wool (tons)	2,351	204	5,645
44. Wool yarn (tons)	497	105	6,612
45. Finished wool fabrics (thousands of linear meters)	2,609	4,332	14,682
46. Finished linen fabrics (thousands of square meters)	4,141	9,317	16,316
47. Hosiery (thousands of pairs)	1,255	25,770	41,488
48. Knitted underwear (thousands of pieces)	3,960	20,881	31,195
49. Outer knitwear (thousands of pieces)	2,036	3,535	10,325
50. Sewn goods (thousands of rubles)	42,000	64,427	217,006
51. Leather shoes (thousands of pairs)	1,527	4,421	11,689
52. Rubber shoes (thousands of pairs)	287	6,190	6,000
53. Hard leather goods (tons)	--	635	2,494
54. Outer leather goods (thousands of square decimeters)	34	8,365	169,783
55. Fresh fish (tons)	1,881	--	35,232
56. Fish products (tons)	3,307	20,712	23,674
57. Meat and meat products (tons)	3,605	25,056	104,643
58. Sausage products (tons)	--	1,228	33,346
59. Whole milk (tons)	--	--	1,847,125
60. Whole milk products (tons)	--	36,011	169,654
61. Animal butter (tons)	3,100	22,165	37,824
62. Granulated sugar (tons)	9,115	45,190	167,061
63. Bread and bakery products (tons)	--	--	353,045
64. Potatoes (tons)	4,000	15	1,962,049
65. Livestock and poultry (live) (tons)	55	9,107	282,955

*Total distributed is the sum of the quantities of the commodity imported and produced in Latvia.

Source: M. Shmulder et al., eds., Dinamika mezhotraslevylkh i mezhrespublikanskikh ekonomicheskikh sviazei Latviiskoi SSR. Riga: Tsentral'noe statisticheskoe upravlenie Latviiskoi SSR. 1971, Appendix 6.

comparison with the new table, a price coefficient conversion matrix was prepared for evaluation of current prices by prices of July 1, 1967, [2] and various sets of data were compiled for 1967 and 1969 for use in examining trends in the economy.

Two 1966 tables were compiled--one in physical units, the other in value units--and two versions of the material-flows table were prepared: an aggregated table with 65 major products and a detailed 236-product table. The value-flows table covers 185 sectors of material production, plus 25 sectors of final consumption and 9 types of value-added. [3] (The coverage and details of classification of this matrix are presented in Table 7.2.) Matrixes detailing certain economic relations, included in the traditional four-quadrant table only in summary form, were also prepared. The most important of these concern the sectoral location and type of outlay involved in depreciation payments, investment, and other forms of current accumulation, plus the structure of the fixed capital stock in Latvia. [4] These data are essential for the construction of dynamic regional models. Another important group of data provides the details of interrepublic and interregional trade. Latvian foreign exports and imports, and interregional inflows and outflows are distinguished, and the latter further disaggregated as to region of origin and destination.

In recent years aggregated ex post tables were prepared for 1969 and 1970 (very little has yet been published on the methods used to compile these tables), and Latvia was the first republic to publish (in TsSU Latvia 1974, pp. 64-65) an ex post table produced as part of the 1972 national-regional data-gathering effort. [5]

In addition to these ex post input-output tables based on accounting data, several planning tables have been completed. The first such tables were done in 1964-65 for the year 1970 by the Institute of Economics of the Latvian Academy of Sciences. The basis of these tables was the 1961 ex post table for Latvia. Two variants were calculated--one on the basis of projected final demand and technical coefficients, and the other on the basis of projected gross outputs and technical coefficients. This research was conducted jointly with the other two Baltic republics (Tsipe 1971, Ch. 3). Later, in 1968-69, researchers at the Bureau of Economic-Mathematic Methods of the Latvian Gosplan produced two variants of planning tables for 1970 and for 1975 on the basis of planning data (Dagovich 1971). An experimental dynamic planning table has been prepared covering the period 1971-80. Part of the data for this table was taken from the 1961, 1966, and 1970 Latvian tables, while part was supplied by various planning agencies (Tsipe 1971, p. 127). Finally, Latvian researchers have prepared an experimental planning table combining data in both value and physical units for 1975. This was the first table of its kind in the Soviet Union (Molodtsov 1973).

TABLE 7.2

Classification Scheme of the 1966 Latvian
Input–Output Table in Value Terms

Interindustry Transactions Quadrant (Row Titles)		Final-Demand Quadrant (Column Titles)	
Sectors		Sectors	
1–7	Ferrous and nonferrous metals and ores	187	Private consumption
8–14	Fuels	188–206	Public and state consumption including:
15–16	Electric and thermal power		Public health
17–55	Machinebuilding and metal-work and repair		Physical training and sports
			Scientific research
56–68	Chemicals		Cultural activities
69–83	Woodworking and paper		Public transportation
84–95	Construction materials and glass		Housing
			Municipal services
96–121	Textiles and apparel		Passenger transportation
122–140	Food industry		Nonproductive communications
141–143	Industry not elsewhere classified	207	Net accumulation of fixed capital
144–156	Construction	208	Replacement of fixed capital written off and capital repair
157–169	Agriculture		
170	Forestry	209	Net accumulation of working capital
171–178	Freight transport		
179	Communications	210	Replacement of losses of fixed capital and working capital
180–184	Trade and distribution		
185	Other branches of material production		
		211	Exports
186	Total material purchases	212	Total final demand
187	Depreciation	213	Gross value of output plus imports
188	Total material purchases plus depreciation		

Value-Added Quadrant
(Row Titles)

Sectors	
189	Wages and salaries
190–192	Other labor income and social security payments
193	Profits of state enterprises
194	Turnover tax
195–197	Other elements of net product
198	Net income of the population
199	Gross value of output (GVO)
200	Imports
201	GVO plus imports

Source: Compiled by the author.

313

The regional input–output work carried out on the Latvian economy has been extensively documented, with several books and numerous articles available to Western analysts (Mints 1967; Baranov 1968; Raman et al. 1973; Dagovich 1971; Shmulder 1970 and 1971; Boiarskii 1971; Orlovskaia 1973; Molodtsov 1973). Of particular interest, and the basis of much of the data presented here, is a special statistical handbook describing the methods and results of the compilation of data for the 1966 Latvian tables (TsSU Latvia 1971). The material presented in this book is of value not only for the data it provides, but for the description of methods used in compiling these data. Although a general methodology and classification system were supplied by the TsSU USSR to serve as a standard for the republics, there were unanticipated difficulties and gaps of coverage that made for substantial variation in details of table construction for 1966. For this reason the example available in the description of the Latvian table provides a guide for Western analysts examining work in other republics and regions for which only limited documentation is available.

RECONSTRUCTION OF THE LATVIAN
INPUT–OUTPUT TABLES

Soviet input–output tables in full detail are rarely published in sources available to Western researchers. The most common form of published data is an aggregated and/or incomplete version of the intersectoral transactions matrix. By itself this data is not very useful. However, it is sometimes possible, by using the available input–output data together with various related input–output indexes and percentage breakdowns found in the Soviet literature, to reconstruct a table. This reconstruction process involves fitting together all the available input–output data, estimating essential missing elements, and compiling a condensed three–quadrant version of the original table. (The table is condensed since the second and third quadrants are often reduced to one or two columns or rows due to the lack of data necessary for a more detailed breakdown.)

It is possible to reconstruct portions of the Latvian ex post input–output tables for 1961, 1966, 1969, and 1972 in an aggregated format using published sources. For 1961, data on both the purchasers' price and producers' price tables are available.[6] In addition, the 1961 and 1966 purchasers' price tables can be revalued in 1967 prices. Thus a total of seven tables can be reconstructed (Tables 7.3 through 7.9).

TABLE 7.3

The 1961 Latvian Input-Output Table in 1961 Producers' Prices
(millions of rubles)

SEQ NO.	75-ORDER NO.		METLGY 1	FUELS 2	POWER 3	MB&W 4	CHEM 5	WD&PAP 6	CM&GL 7	TX&APP 8	FOOD 9	INDNEC 10
1	1-7	METALLURGY	11.1		13.4	50.1	.3	1.6	4.9	.6	6.2	2.4
2	8-13	FUELS	1.3	3.5	3.3	2.9	.3	1.9	6.6	.1	7.5	2.4
3	14	ELEC POWER&STEAM	.7	.5		7.5	1.2	7.0	4.2	4.1	4.8	1.4
4	15-41	MACHBLDGS&METALWKNG	.8	.7		89.2		5.0	2.1	4.3	4.8	1.6
5	42-50	CHEMICALS	.1	.3	.1	14.2	21.2	5.7	2.0	9.1	2.6	1.7
6	51-56	WOODWORKNG&PAPER	.1	.3	.7	13.6	2.0	66.6	2.8	5.4	11.1	6.1
7	57-58	CONST MATLS&GLASS	.1	.0	.0	3.2	.7	1.5	9.4	.4	2.4	.4
8	59-61	TEXTILES & APPAREL	.1	.1	.1	5.6	2.4	4.6	4.0	516.2	14.6	2.4
9	62-67	FOOD	.0	.0	.1		3.0	3.5	1.6	2.7	256.7	3.8
10	68	INDUSTRY NEC	.2	.0	.2	3.5	.3	.6	.2	2.6	2.2	8.6
11	69	CONSTRUCTION	.0	.0	.0	.0	.0	.0	.0	.0	.0	.0
12	70-72	AGRICULTURE&FOREST	.0	.0	.0	.0	1.3	3.0	.0	69.6	248.3	.0
13	73	TRANSPORT&COMM	.6	.4	5.7	9.0	.0	11.4	6.7	3.0	13.9	1.1
14	74	TRADE&DISTRIBUTION		.1	.1	2.8	.0	1.5	.1	2.2	15.4	4.6
15	75	OTHER BRANCHES	1.6	.1		.1	.0	3.0	.1	2.1	.3	.0
16		TOTAL PURCHASES	16.7	6.1	24.4	203.7	33.0	116.8	44.5	623.5	590.8	31.3
17		NAT'L INC&DEPREC	17.1	14.0	25.5	258.7	14.2	106.4	48.6	353.9	364.8	43.1
18		TOTAL OUTLAYS	17.8	20.1	49.9	462.0	47.2	223.2	93.1	977.4	955.6	74.4
19		IMPORTS	70.4	71.7	2.7	184.6	80.4	37.0	8.2	195.1	128.9	18.7
20		TOTAL SUPPLY	88.2	91.8	52.6	646.6	127.6	260.2	101.3	1172.5	1084.5	93.1

SEQ NO.	75-ORDER NO.		CONST 11	AG&FOR 12	T&C 13	T&D 14	OTH BR 15	II USE 16	CONSAC 17	EXPORT 18	TOT FD 19	TOT SP 20
1	1-7	METALLURGY	11.9	1.0	1.0	.0	.0	91.1	-8.5	5.6	-2.9	88.2
2	8-13	FUELS	4.2	9.6	25.0	1.9	.0	79.6	9.8	2.4	12.3	91.8
3	14	ELEC POWER&STEAM	.8	2.8	7.3	1.0	.1	42.3	9.8	.5	10.3	52.6
4	15-41	MACHBLDGS&METALWKNG	26.3	10.4	7.3	1.0	.0	153.0	223.5	270.1	493.6	646.6
5	42-50	CHEMICALS	5.1	10.1	1.4	5.9	1.7	81.0	21.1	25.5	46.6	127.6
6	51-56	WOODWORKNG&PAPER	29.0	4.1	.6	1.7	.1	151.4	47.6	61.2	108.8	260.2
7	57-58	CONST MATLS&GLASS	57.2	.4	1.3	2.0		81.5	1.4	18.4	19.8	101.3
8	59-61	TEXTILES & APPAREL	2.1	2.1		2.9	.2	556.1	317.5	298.9	616.4	1172.5
9	62-67	FOOD	.1	31.6		.8	.1	366.9	559.2	218.4	777.6	1084.5
10	68	INDUSTRY NEC	4.0	16.3	.5		2.6	42.7	26.4	24.0	50.4	93.1
11	69	CONSTRUCTION	.0	.0	.0	.0	.0	.0	303.8	.0	303.8	303.8
12	70-72	AGRICULTURE&FOREST	.0	220.5	2.0	1.1	1.4	542.6	334.0	28.5	362.5	905.1
13	73	TRANSPORT&COMM	21.1	2.0	.0	22.3	.1	101.8	78.1	33.1	111.2	213.0
14	74	TRADE&DISTRIBUTION	2.8	4.6	1.4	.2	.1	36.4	103.2	52.2	155.4	191.8
15	75	OTHER BRANCHES	1.0	.5	.5	.1		10.4	18.6	6.3	24.9	35.3
16		TOTAL PURCHASES	171.3	320.1	51.1	43.0	6.9	2283.4	2039.0	1045.2	3084.2	5367.6
17		NAT'L INC&DEPREC	132.5	498.5	161.9	123.6	24.7	2171.7				
18		TOTAL OUTLAYS	303.8	819.3	213.0	166.6	31.6	4455.1				
19		IMPORTS	.0	85.8	.0	25.2	3.7	912.5				
20		TOTAL SUPPLY	303.3	905.1	213.0	191.8	35.3	5367.6				

Source: Compiled by the author.

TABLE 7.4

The 1961 Latvian Input-Output Table in 1966 Purchasers' Prices
(millions of rubles)

SEQ NO	75-ORDER NO		METLGY 1	FUELS 2	POWER 3	MBMW 4	CHEM 5	WD&PAP 6	CM&GL 7	TX&APP 8	FOOD 9	INDNEC 10
1	1-7	METALLURGY	10.0	4.1	.1	52.6	.2	1.5	4.6	.5	5.6	2.7
2	8-13	FUELS	1.5	4.2	13.8	6.0	.7	3.6	8.8	2.2	7.9	.5
3	14	ELEC POWER&STEAM	.7	.3	.0	.8	.7	2.9	2.5	2.9	1.9	1.0
4	15-41	MACHBLDG&METALWKNG	.1	.7	.5	82.4	.3	5.1	2.0	3.9	4.2	2.6
5	42-50	CHEMICALS	.1	.3	.1	16.5	22.5	6.3	2.5	10.2	2.6	7.1
6	51-56	WOODWORKING&PAPER	.1	.0	.0	12.8	1.9	63.9	9.5	5.7	10.5	.6
7	57,58	CONST MATLS&GLASS	.1	.1	.1	3.1	.6	1.3	3.2	.3	1.7	.6
8	59-61	TEXTILES & APPAREL	.0	.1	.1	.6	2.5	4.5	1.6	481.0	12.2	4.8
9	62-67	FOOD	.1	.0	.0		3.0	.3	.2	2.6	237.6	7.7
10	68	INDUSTRY NEC				1.8	.3			2.5	.9	
11	69	CONSTRUCTION	.0	.0	.0	.0	.0	.0	.0	.0	.0	.0
12	70-72	AGRICULTURE&FOREST	.0	4.0	.0	3.8	.7	3.1	24.7	91.0	381.3	1.7
13	73	TRANSPORT&COMM	.9	1.6		13.4	2.1	9.5	3.0	3.0	19.7	3.8
14	74	TRADE&DISTRIBUTION	.8		.0			12.7		51.3	82.5	
15	75	OTHER BRANCHES	1.5				2.8	2.8	1.8	1.8	2.3	
16		TOTAL PURCHASES	16.3	11.7	14.8	201.5	35.1	121.3	65.9	658.9	769.8	32.7
17		NAT'L INC&DEPREC	2.4	21.1	18.0	266.5	16.4	108.0	46.4	323.9	161.5	46.9
18		TOTAL OUTLAYS	18.7	32.8	32.8	468.0	51.5	229.3	112.3	982.8	931.4	79.6
19		IMPORTS	78.9	80.0	2.8	179.6	92.3	45.6	9.6	198.7	137.7	19.5
20		TOTAL SUPPLY	97.6	112.8	35.6	647.6	143.8	274.9	121.9	1181.5	1069.1	99.1

SEQ NO	75-ORDER NO		CONST 11	AG&FOR 12	T&C 13	T&D 14	OTH BR 15	II USE 16	CON&AC 17	EXPORT 18	TOT FD 19	TOT SP 20
1	1-7	METALLURGY	13.0	.7	.8		.0	92.4	-.6	5.8	5.2	97.6
2	8-13	FUELS	5.8	9.7	19.7	2.0	.0	86.4	23.0	3.4	26.4	112.8
3	14	ELEC POWER&STEAM	1.5	1.3	.5	1.7	.1	23.7	11.4		11.9	35.6
4	15-41	MACHBLDG&METALWKNG	27.3	7.1	4.6	.8	.0	140.2	252.2	255.2	507.4	647.6
5	42-50	CHEMICALS	6.0	8.8	6.0	1.3	.2	85.4	27.5	30.9	58.4	143.8
6	51-56	WOODWORKING&PAPER	34.2	4.7	1.3	6.9	.2	155.3	53.4	66.1	119.6	274.9
7	57,58	CONST MATLS&GLASS	67.7	3.6	.5	1.7	.0	90.3	13.3	18.3	31.6	121.9
8	59-61	TEXTILES & APPAREL	2.2	2.3	.9	1.7	.1	512.3	359.3	309.9	669.2	1181.5
9	62-67	FOOD		31.5	.1	3.1	.1	289.3	532.5	247.3	779.8	1069.1
10	68	INDUSTRY NEC	4.1	16.3	.4	.8	3.3	39.7	33.2	26.2	59.4	99.1
11	69	CONSTRUCTION	.0	.0	.0	.0	.0	.0	304.2		304.2	304.2
12	70-72	AGRICULTURE&FOREST	.0	272.7	.1	1.4	.0	749.6	409.7	40.6	450.3	1199.9
13	73	TRANSPORT&COMM	3.8	6.2	2.0	1.1	2.4	82.2	53.5		53.5	135.7
14	74	TRADE&DISTRIBUTION	.0	22.2				195.8	-22.6		-22.6	173.2
15	75	OTHER BRANCHES	.9	.4	.4			9.7	29.8	6.8	36.6	46.3
16		TOTAL PURCHASES	166.6	387.5	37.4	22.8	9.9	2552.3	2051.7	1132.8	3184.5	5736.8
17		NAT'L INC&DEPREC	137.6	698.3	98.3	150.4	32.2	2127.9				
18		TOTAL OUTLAYS	304.2	1085.8	135.7	173.2	42.1	4680.2				
19		IMPORTS	.0	114.1	.0	.0	4.2	1056.6				
20		TOTAL SUPPLY	304.2	1199.9	135.7	173.2	46.3	5736.8				

Source: Compiled by the author.

316

TABLE 7.5

The 1961 Latvian Input-Output Table in 1967 Purchasers' Prices
(millions of rubles)

SEQ NO.	75-ORDER NO.		METLGY 1	FUELS 2	POWER 3	MB&MW 4	CHEM 5	WD&PAP 6	CM&GL 7	TX&APP 8	FOOD 9	INDNEC 10
1	1-7	METALLURGY	14.6	4.3		71.4	.3	2.3	6.7	.7	6.9	3.2
2	8-13	FUELS	1.6		21.6	8.8	.9	4.1	13.2	3.1	10.0	3.7
3	14	ELEC POWER&STEAM	.5	.4		9.0	.4	3.8	3.3	4.0	2.6	1.4
4	15-41	MACHBLDG&METALWKNG	.8	.7	.5	77.7		5.0	2.1	3.9	4.0	1.6
5	42-50	CHEMICALS	.1	.3	.1	16.0	21.5	6.1	2.6	9.3	2.6	1.7
6	51-56	WOODWORKING&PAPER	.1	.3	.1	14.7	2.3	65.8	2.6	6.6	11.4	8.8
7	57-58	CONST MATLS&GLASS	.1	.0	.0	3.2	.6	1.3	10.4	.3	1.7	.6
8	59-61	TEXTILES & APPAREL	.1	.1	.0	.6	2.5	4.8	3.1	484.4	12.5	8.2
9	62-67	FOOD	.0	.1	.0	.9	3.0	3.7	.6	2.5	235.2	4.8
10	68	INDUSTRY NEC	.1	.0	.0	1.7	.3	.3	.2	2.2	1.8	7.2
11	69	CONSTRUCTION	.0	.0	.0	.0	.0			.0	.0	.0
12	70-72	AGRICULTURE&FOREST	.0	4.0	.0	.0	.0	3.1	.0	91.0	381.3	.0
13	73	TRANSPORT&COMM	.9	.0	.1	3.8	.7	9.5	24.5	3.0	19.8	1.7
14	74	TRADE&DISTRIBUTION	.8	1.6	.0	13.4	2.1	12.7	3.5	51.3	82.5	3.8
15	75	OTHER BRANCHES	1.5			1.2	.0	2.8	.1	1.8	2.3	3.0
16		TOTAL PURCHASES	20.8	12.1	22.1	212.4	35.5	129.9	73.9	660.9	772.2	33.5
17		NAT'L INC&DEPREC	-2.1	20.7	10.7	255.6	16.0	99.4	38.4	321.9	159.2	46.1
18		TOTAL OUTLAYS	18.7	32.8	32.3	468.0	51.5	229.3	112.3	982.8	931.4	79.6
19		IMPORTS	108.6	102.1	3.2	179.0	87.5	55.3	10.1	198.6	136.3	79.9
20		TOTAL SUPPLY	127.3	134.9	36.0	647.0	139.0	284.6	122.4	1181.4	1067.7	99.5

SEQ NO.	75-ORDER NO.		CONST 11	AG&FOR 12	T&C 13	T&D 14	OTH BR 15	II USE 16	CON&AC 17	EXPORT 18	TOT FD 19	TOT SP 20
1	1-7	METALLURGY	19.2	1.0	1.1	.0	.0	128.0	-9.6	8.9	-.7	127.3
2	8-13	FUELS	6.5	10.7	21.5	2.8	.0	107.6	22.8	4.5	27.3	134.9
3	14	ELEC POWER&STEAM	1.3	1.3	.7	1.7	.1	31.0	4.4		5.0	36.0
4	15-41	MACHBLDG&METALWKNG	28.3	7.3	4.5	.8	.8	135.0	268.6	243.4	512.0	647.0
5	42-50	CHEMICALS	6.2	9.2	6.2	1.3	.2	81.9	29.9	27.2	57.1	139.0
6	51-56	WOODWORKING&PAPER	38.6	5.1	1.4	7.6	3.3	173.3	36.5	74.8	111.3	284.6
7	57-58	CONST MATLS&GLASS	73.1	4.0	.6	1.8		97.1	6.3	19.0	25.3	122.4
8	59-61	TEXTILES & APPAREL	2.3	2.4	.9	2.0	.1	517.9	348.1	315.4	663.5	1181.4
9	62-67	FOOD		31.4	.4	3.1	.8	286.4	533.4	247.9	781.3	1067.7
10	68	INDUSTRY NEC	3.9	16.3		.4	3.2	38.4	35.4	25.7	61.1	99.5
11	69	CONSTRUCTION	.0	.0	.0	.0	.0	.0	304.2	.0	304.2	304.2
12	70-72	AGRICULTURE&FOREST	.0	272.7	.1	1.4	1.0	749.6	409.7	40.6	450.3	1199.9
13	73	TRANSPORT&COMM	3.8	6.2	2.0	1.1	1.0	81.8	53.9		53.9	135.7
14	74	TRADE&DISTRIBUTION		22.2			2.4	195.8	-22.6	.0	-22.6	173.2
15	75	OTHER BRANCHES	.9	.4	.5	.1	.1	9.7	29.8	6.8	36.6	46.3
16		TOTAL PURCHASES	183.9	390.6	40.0	23.7	10.4	2626.3	2029.9	1136.5	3166.4	5792.7
17		NAT'L INC&DEPREC	120.3	695.2	95.7	149.5	31.7	2053.9				
18		TOTAL OUTLAYS	304.2	1085.8	135.7	173.2	42.1	4680.2				
19		IMPORTS	.0	114.1		.0	4.2	1112.5				
20		TOTAL SUPPLY	304.2	1199.9	135.7	173.2	46.3	5792.7				

Source: Compiled by the author.

TABLE 7.6

The 1966 Latvian Input-Output Table in 1966 Purchasers' Prices
(millions of rubles)

SEQ NO.	75-ORDER NO.	Branch	1 METLGY	2 FUELS	3 POWER	4 MB&W	5 CHEM	6 WD&PAP	7 CM&GL	8 TX&APP	9 FOOD	10 INDNEC	11 CONST	12 AG&FOR	13 T&C	14 T&D	15 OTH BR	16 II USE	17 CONSAC	18 EXPORT	19 TOT FD	20 TOT SP
1	1-7	METALLURGY	17.7	.3	.2	78.2	5.5	2.3	9.5	.6	4.2	.0	17.7	.4	1.0	.1	.0	142.8	3.8	23.3	27.1	169.9
2	8-13	FUELS	2.5	4.6	12.5	9.9	1.9	8.1	9.9	2.4	13.7	5.6	7.8	16.9	27.6	1.5	.1	119.6	31.2	4.5	35.7	155.3
3	14	ELEC POWER&STEAM	.8	.3	.0	12.5	2.7	4.9	4.6	5.1	4.1	1.4	2.7	1.8	1.6	2.8	.1	45.4	28.7	18.0	46.7	92.1
4	15-41	MACHBLDG&METALWKNG	1.3	.4	.1	254.8	4.1	7.1	3.9	6.3	16.3	2.1	40.9	17.1	9.2	3.8	.2	368.6	508.0	600.6	1108.6	1477.2
5	42-50	CHEMICALS	.3	.7	.1	38.6	51.0	10.5	3.5	50.2	16.9	8.4	8.7	21.2	4.8	.2	.5	203.4	49.6	109.5	159.1	362.5
6	51-56	WOODWORKING&PAPER	.2	.1	.1	25.8	1.3	92.7	2.4	4.6	5.1	7.7	31.6	4.9	1.1	6.5		200.5	57.2	87.4	144.6	345.1
7	57-58	CONST MATLS&GLASS	.	.1	.1	4.8	6.4	2.9	16.8			.2	105.7	1.9	.1	1.2	3.0	141.1	19.2	43.1	62.3	203.4
8	59-61	TEXTILES & APPAREL	.3	.1	.1	11.5	10.8	11.7	2.4	561.7	13.8	1.9	3.2	2.7	2.3	2.1	.3	623.5	422.0	481.9	903.9	1527.4
9	62-67	FOOD	.1	.1	.0	1.8	2.0	1.1	2.2	5.9	384.1	11.6	.3	15.1	.2	4.1		437.6	821.2	470.9	1292.1	1729.7
10	68	INDUSTRY NEC	.0	.0	.0	8.7		1.0	2.2	4.5	9.6	5.7	4.1	36.7	1.3	3.1	3.2	82.1	48.4	40.1	88.5	170.6
11	69	CONSTRUCTION	.0	.0	.0	.0	.0	.9	.0	.0	.0	.0	.0	.0	.0	.0	.0	.0	425.2	.0	425.2	425.2
12	70-72	AGRICULTURE&FOREST	.0	.0	.0	.0	2.2	2.9	.0	64.0	538.6	20.1	.0	314.9	.0	1.2	1.0	941.8	341.7	32.0	373.7	1315.5
13	73	TRANSPORT&COMM	1.9	3.0	.1	8.7	2.2	12.2	41.1	3.7	27.2	2.8	4.7	6.7	3.3	1.6	1.0	120.2		117.1	117.1	237.3
14	74	TRADE&DISTRIBUTION	1.8	1.3	.0	32.9	6.8	16.4	4.8	63.8	114.1	6.9	.0	24.6	.0	.0	3.6	277.0		45.3	45.3	322.3
15	75	OTHER BRANCHES	4.5	.0	.3	1.4	.1	1.6	.0	.4	1.0	.3	.0	.0	.2	.2		10.4	43.2	4.9	48.1	58.5
16		TOTAL PURCHASES	31.5	11.0	14.3	489.6	97.1	175.4	106.5	773.6	1153.0	74.8	228.1	465.0	52.7	28.7	12.1	3714.0	2799.4	2078.5	4877.9	8591.9
17		NAT'L INC&DEPREC	6.2	13.6	36.3	534.5	68.5	118.8	74.6	436.2	327.6	69.4	197.1	708.9	160.6	189.9	36.5	2978.7				
18		TOTAL OUTLAYS	37.7	24.6	50.6	1024.1	166.2	294.2	181.1	1209.8	1480.6	144.2	425.2	1173.9	213.3	218.6	48.6	6692.7				
19		IMPORTS	132.2	130.7	41.5	453.1	196.3	50.9	22.3	317.6	249.1	26.4	.0	141.6	24.0	103.7	9.9	1899.2				
20		TOTAL SUPPLY	169.9	155.3	92.1	1477.2	362.5	345.1	203.4	1527.4	1729.7	170.6	425.2	1315.5	237.3	322.3	58.5	8591.9				

Source: Compiled by the author.

TABLE 7.7

The 1966 Latvian Input-Output Table in 1967 Purchasers' Prices
(millions of rubles)

SEQ NO.	75-ORDER NO.		METLGY 1	FUELS 2	POWER 3	MBMW 4	CHEM 5	WD&PAP 6	CM&GL 7	TX&APP 8	FOOD 9	INDNEC 10
1	1-7	METALLURGY	25.8	.4	.3	106.3	7.2	3.6	13.9	.8	5.2	6.0
2	8-13	FUELS	2.8	4.8	19.5	14.5	2.4	9.2	14.8	3.5	17.4	.8
3	14	ELEC POWER&STEAM	1.1	.4	.0	17.6	3.5	6.3	6.0	7.0	5.5	1.9
4	15-41	MACHBLDG&METALWKNG	1.4	.8	1.2	240.3	48.7	7.1	4.1	6.4	15.4	2.0
5	42-50	CHEMICALS	.3	.3	.1	37.4	3.6	10.1	3.5	45.5	4.3	7.2
6	51-56	WOODWORKING&PAPER	.2	.1	.1	29.5	1.3	101.3	2.5	5.4	18.4	9.5
7	57-58	CONST MATLS&GLASS	.1	.0	.1	5.0	6.5	2.9	18.6		5.1	
8	59-61	TEXTILES & APPAREL	.3			12.0	10.8	12.3	5.8	565.7	14.1	2.0
9	62-67	FOOD	.1	.0	.0	1.8	1.8	1.8	2.3	5.7	380.3	11.5
10	68	INDUSTRY NEC	.0			8.3			2.1	4.1	9.2	5.3
11	69	CONSTRUCTION	.0	.0	.0		.0	.0	.0			
12	70-72	AGRICULTURE&FOREST	2.0	3.0	.1	8.6	2.2	2.9	40.8	64.0	538.6	20.1
13	73	TRANSPORT&COMM	1.8	1.3	.0	32.9	6.8	12.2	4.8	3.6	27.3	2.8
14	74	TRADE&DISTRIBUTION	4.5	.0		2.4	.0	16.4	.0	63.8	114.1	7.0
15	75	OTHER BRANCHES					1.6	1.6		1.0	1.0	1.0
16		TOTAL PURCHASES	40.4	11.4	21.5	515.6	98.8	187.8	119.2	776.3	1155.9	76.6
17		NAT'L INC&DEPREC	16.7	15.7	40.5	453.2	58.9	129.4	74.0	449.2	318.8	63.1
18		TOTAL OUTLAYS	57.1	27.1	62.0	968.8	157.7	317.2	193.2	1225.5	1474.7	139.7
19		IMPORTS	182.0	166.8	47.8	451.5	186.0	61.7	23.4	317.5	246.6	26.9
20		TOTAL SUPPLY	239.1	193.9	109.8	1420.3	343.7	378.9	216.6	1543.0	1721.3	166.6

SEQ NO.	75-ORDER NO.		CONST 11	AG&FOR 12	T&C 13	T&D 14	OTH BR 15	II USE 16	CON&AC 17	EXPORT 18	TOT FD 19	TOT SP 20
1	1-7	METALLURGY	26.2	.5	1.4	2.1	.1	197.8	5.4	35.9	41.3	239.1
2	8-13	FUELS	8.8	18.6	29.7	2.8	.2	149.0	38.9	6.0	44.9	193.9
3	14	ELEC POWER&STEAM	3.0	1.3	9.1	3.6	.2	59.3	29.9	20.6	50.5	109.8
4	15-41	MACHBLDG&METALWKNG	42.4	7.6	5.0	7.2	.2	355.2	492.3	572.8	1065.1	1420.3
5	42-50	CHEMICALS	9.0	22.2	1.6	1.2	.2	195.2	52.0	96.5	148.5	343.7
6	51-56	WOODWORKING&PAPER	35.7	5.3		2.2		223.8	56.3	98.8	155.1	378.9
7	57-58	CONST MATLS&GLASS	114.2	2.1	2.4	4.1	3.8	151.8	20.0	44.8	64.8	216.6
8	59-61	TEXTILES & APPAREL	3.4	2.8				630.0	422.5	490.5	913.0	1543.0
9	62-67	FOOD	.3	15.0	1.2	2.9	.3	433.3	815.9	472.1	1288.0	1721.3
10	68	INDUSTRY NEC	3.9	36.7			3.1	79.4	47.9	39.3	87.2	166.6
11	69	CONSTRUCTION							449.9		449.9	449.9
12	70-72	AGRICULTURE&FOREST	.0	314.9				941.8	341.7	32.0	373.7	1315.5
13	73	TRANSPORT&COMM	4.6	6.7				119.9	.3	117.1	117.4	237.3
14	74	TRADE&DISTRIBUTION		24.6				277.1	-.1	45.3	45.2	322.3
15	75	OTHER BRANCHES	.7	.2				10.4	43.2	4.9	48.1	58.5
16		TOTAL PURCHASES	252.2	468.9	56.6	29.8	13.0	3824.0	2816.1	2076.6	4892.7	8716.7
17		NAT'L INC&DEPREC	197.7	705.0	156.7	188.8	35.6	2903.3				
18		TOTAL OUTLAYS	449.9	1173.9	213.3	218.6	48.6	6727.3				
19		IMPORTS		141.5	24.0	103.7	9.9	1989.4				
20		TOTAL SUPPLY	449.9	1315.5	237.3	322.3	58.5	8716.7				

319

TABLE 7.8

The 1969 Latvian Input-Output Table in 1969 Purchasers' Prices (Interindustry Flows)
(millions of rubles)

SEQ NO.	75-ORDER NO.		METLGY 1	FUELS 2	POWER 3	MBMW 4	CHEM 5	WD&PAP 6	CM&GL 7	TX&APP 8	FOOD 9	INDNEC 10	CONST 11	AG&FOR 12	T&C 13	T&D 14	OTH BR 15	II USE 16
1	1-7	METALLURGY	28.9	.3	.5	132.4	6.0	4.3	13.9	1.8	6.1	8.3	13.1	.8	2.5	.2	.0	219.1
2	8-13	FUELS	3.3	5.1	16.8	10.9	4.4	9.1	16.1	7.6	19.8	.7	12.6	24.1	28.4	2.8	.1	161.8
3	14	ELEC POWER&STEAM	1.9	.3	.0	18.5	5.9	6.3	7.5	6.0	4.5	1.1	2.8	2.6	2.5	3.3	.2	63.4
4	15-41	MACHBLDG&METALWKNG	1.3	2.1	2.3	291.2	7.2	6.3	6.4	6.6	15.5	1.9	64.5	23.4	14.2	4.9	.2	445.4
5	42-50	CHEMICALS	.4	.5	.4	51.6	78.7	16.7	6.2	82.0	8.0	5.7	14.6	29.8	7.2	.7	.6	304.7
6	51-56	WOODWORKING&PAPER	.3	.5	.1	28.1	5.7	134.6	6.5	11.4	27.4	14.9	19.0	7.4	1.7	9.6	5.4	272.9
7	57-58	CONST MATLS&GLASS	.3	1.0	.1	10.0	4.8	6.5	33.1	1.8	8.1	3.1	131.9	5.0	1.0	2.1	.0	206.5
8	59-61	TEXTILES & APPAREL	.2	.2	.1	9.7	9.5	10.5	5.7	673.0	8.4	.8	4.5	3.8	4.2	2.1	.4	733.9
9	62-67	FOOD	.1	.3	.1	2.9	16.7	2.2	4.1	13.2	476.1	15.5	.5	16.5	.3	5.4	.0	553.9
10	68	INDUSTRY NEC	.0	.0	.0	5.9	1.2	.5	.6	2.0	5.4	11.3	6.6	45.3	4.5	4.0	4.4	91.7
11	69	CONSTRUCTION	.0	.0	.0	.0	.0	.0	.0	.0	.0	.0	.0	.0	.0	.0	.0	.0
12	70-72	AGRICULTURE&FOREST	2.3	4.1	.0	10.2	3.4	4.3	59.3	80.1	603.5	43.9	.0	395.0	.1	1.5	.0	1128.5
13	73	TRANSPORT&COMM	2.1	1.7	.2	39.2	10.7	15.3	5.2	4.7	34.5	4.3	8.6	8.5	6.3	2.1	.3	164.1
14	74	TRADE&DISTRIBUTION	6.7	.0	.0	4.9	.5	19.9	5.1	79.6	127.6	10.7	.0	32.8	.0	.1	4.4	333.9
15	75	OTHER BRANCHES	.0	.0	.0	5.5		.5	.8	.8	.0	.2	1.2	.1	.3	.1	.1	16.2
16		TOTAL PURCHASES	47.8	16.1	20.9	615.5	154.4	233.7	164.7	970.6	1345.9	122.4	279.9	595.1	73.2	39.6	16.2	4696.0

Source: Compiled by the author.

TABLE 7.9

The 1972 Latvian Input-Output Table in 1972 Purchasers' Prices (Incomplete)
(millions of rubles)

SEQ NO.	75-ORDER NO.		METLGY 1	FUELS 2	POWER 3	MB&W 4	CHEM 5	WD&PAP 6	CM&GL 7	TX&APP 8	FOOD 9	INDNEC 10
1	1-7	METALLURGY	30.7	.1	.4	165.4	12.1	3.6	22.0	1.9	6.2	19.4
2	8-13	FUELS	3.5	9.1	21.9	11.5	3.4	9.2	15.9	4.0	25.7	1.5
3	14	ELEC POWER&STEAM	2.7	.3	.2	25.9	8.0	7.6	10.2	10.6	7.4	1.6
4	15-41	MACHBLDG&METALWKNG	1.7	1.0	2.0	389.4	6.0	11.1	6.4	7.7	23.7	3.5
5	42-50	CHEMICALS	.6	.5	.3	68.0	103.7	13.9	9.5	77.2	7.3	6.3
6	51-56	WOODWORKING&PAPER	.4	.1	.1	27.0	5.9	148.3	6.0	8.2	27.6	13.9
7	57.58	CONST MATLS&GLASS	.2	.1	.1	5.2	2.0	3.7	42.4	.7	27.4	.7
8	59-61	TEXTILES & APPAREL	.2	.7	.1	15.9	5.1	16.1	6.3	891.3	12.7	3.4
9	62-67	FOOD	.1	.7	.1	2.3	14.6	3.1	2.0	16.0	530.6	22.7
10	68	INDUSTRY NEC	.1	1.0	.5	3.2	1.9	1.8	.4	3.0	5.4	11.9
11	69	CONSTRUCTION	.0	.0	.0	.0	.0	.0	.0	.0	.0	.0
12	70-72	AGRICULTURE&FOREST	.0	.0	.0	.0	.0	9.0	.0	75.4	942.7	55.0
13	73	TRANSPORT&COMM	2.6	3.7	.5	25.9	5.5	28.5	47.7	7.9	47.0	6.7
14	74	TRADE&DISTRIBUTION	2.2	1.5	.0	51.5	14.8	14.7	8.3	95.3	145.2	12.8
15	75	OTHER BRANCHES	10.1	.0	.0	.5	.0	.0	.0	.0	2.9	.0
16		TOTAL PURCHASES	55.1	17.2	26.4	792.6	183.0	271.2	177.2	1199.1	1791.8	159.8
17		NAT'L INC&DEPREC	20.5	19.3	48.4	730.5	155.0	142.1	118.6	804.7	319.6	47.9
18		TOTAL OUTLAYS	75.6	36.5	74.8	1523.1	338.0	413.3	295.8	2003.8	2111.4	207.7
19		IMPORTS	274.6	236.7	85.2	795.3	385.0	85.2	37.9	631.2	356.6	34.7
20		TOTAL SUPPLY	350.2	273.2	160.0	2318.4	723.0	498.5	333.7	2635.0	2468.0	242.4

SEQ NO.	75-ORDER NO.		CONST 11	AG&FOR 12	T&C 13	T&D 14	OTH BR 15	II USE 16	CON&AC 17	EXPORT 18	TOT FD 19	TOT SP 20
1	1-7	METALLURGY	31.1	1.9	1.6	.2	.0	296.6	5.2	48.4	53.6	350.2
2	8-13	FUELS	12.5	29.2	51.9	4.4	.4	203.8	59.2	10.2	69.4	273.2
3	14	ELEC POWER&STEAM	4.1	8.7	3.3	5.0	.1	95.7	53.8	10.5	64.3	160.0
4	15-41	MACHBLDG&METALWKNG	70.9	36.3	12.6	3.6	.7	576.0	706.7	1035.7	1742.4	2318.4
5	42-50	CHEMICALS	13.0	45.3	8.7	1.6	.7	357.5	112.0	253.5	365.5	723.0
6	51-56	WOODWORKING&PAPER	47.1	6.6	2.4	1.9		302.7	67.7	128.1	195.8	498.5
7	57.58	CONST MATLS&GLASS	188.2	1.5	.8	2.9	3.1	255.3	34.2	44.2	78.4	333.7
8	59-61	TEXTILES & APPAREL	5.0	5.7	3.9	2.3		969.4	783.9	881.2	1665.6	2635.0
9	62-67	FOOD	.4	79.7	.2	3.9	.6	676.4	1200.4	591.2	1791.6	2466.0
10	68	INDUSTRY NEC	1.4	70.1	1.1	3.8	5.4	110.0	91.5	40.9	132.4	242.4
11	69	CONSTRUCTION	.0	.0	.0	.0	.0	1515.4	272.9	65.6	338.5	1853.9
12	70-72	AGRICULTURE&FOREST	.0	429.9	1.9	2.7	.6	209.9				
13	73	TRANSPORT&COMM	18.5	9.9		3.3	.9	386.2				
14	74	TRADE&DISTRIBUTION	.0	39.0		.0	.9	16.3				
15	75	OTHER BRANCHES	.9	.1		.7	11.9					
16		TOTAL PURCHASES	393.2	763.9	88.5	40.3	18.9	5971.2				
17		NAT'L INC&DEPREC		875.4								
18		TOTAL OUTLAYS		1639.3								
19		IMPORTS		214.6								
20		TOTAL SUPPLY		1853.9								

Source: Compiled by the author.

The critical data base for reconstruction of each table was the availability of an aggregated version of the first quadrant (the intersectoral transactions matrix). A 24–sector version of the first quadrant of the 1961 producers' price table is included in a paper by Baranov (Mints 1967, pp. 150–53). The first quadrants from the 1961 and 1966 purchasers' price tables are given in Shmulder (1971), along with price conversion coefficients necessary for revaluing the matrixes from 1966 prices to 1967 prices. The 1966 matrix is also available in TsSU Latvia (1968, pp. 56–59), in an early and uncorrected form. The first–quadrant data for both the 1969 and 1972 tables are published in Latvia statistical handbooks (TsSU Latvia 1972, pp. 56–57; TsSU Latvia 1974, pp. 64–65). Except for the 1961 matrix given by Baranov, these matrixes are given in an aggregated 15–sector version with figures rounded to the nearest 100,000 rubles.

To reconstruct the second and third quadrants (the final–demand and value–added quadrants) for these tables it is necessary to make a number of estimates. In no case are absolute value figures on gross value of output (GVO) available for all sectors in these tables. These figures are estimated by using various percentage breakdowns and relative size or growth figures usually given in conjunction with the published intersectoral flows table, or by using first–quadrant coefficients together with flow data when both are available for the same entries. Good estimates of GVOs can be obtained for the 1961 and 1966 tables due to the abundance of data available in these tables, which allows cross–checking. For the 1961 producers' price table, GVOs were estimated using data given in Kossov and Mints (1964); Mints (1967); and Tsipe (1971). GVOs for the 1966 purchasers' price table (in 1966 prices) were estimated using various coefficients and flow data given in Shmulder (1971), including interindustry data from Table 24 and Appendix 3, capital data from Tables 39 and 40, trade data from Tables 42 and 48, and depreciation data from Tables 23 and 34. Due to the small number of significant digits given in these tables, an average of alternative estimates was used in arriving at the final estimates of GVOs. Using the rate of growth of total GVO and percentage breakdown of GVO figures given in Shmulder (1971, Table 1, pp. 15–16), estimates were made of 1961 purchasers' price GVOs (in 1966 prices). GVOs for the 1961 and 1966 tables in 1967 prices were obtained by applying the price conversion coefficients given in TsSU Latvia (1971, Table 19, pp. 94–97) to the previously estimated GVOs in 1966 prices.[7] A separate estimate was made for the 1966 GVOs in 1967 prices using the first quadrant technical coefficient matrix in Dagovich (1973) together with the same matrix in absolute flows given in Shmulder (1971, Appendix 4). These

estimated GVOs were very close to the previous estimates.   No
input–output data are available that would allow estimation of GVOs
for the 1969 table.   For the 1972 table, it was possible to estimate
GVOs for the ten industrial branches and for agriculture using the
input–output data reported in TsSU Latvia (1974, pp. 62–67).

Values of exports and imports were derived from basically the
same sources as the GVOs.   A percentage breakdown of imports and
exports by sector is given in Kossov and Mints (1964, pp. 22–23),
for the 1961 producers' price table.   Together with the total values
of these external trade flows (estimated from information in Mints
(1967, pp. 150–53, 217–21), this breakdown allows an easy calculation of sectoral imports and exports.   Export and import values for
the 1961 and 1966 purchasers' price tables (given in 1966 prices)
and the 1966 purchasers' price table in 1967 prices are given in
Shmulder (1971, Table 42, pp. 193–95; Table 44, pp. 204–06; and
Table 47, p. 216).   Only a crude estimate of 1961 imports and exports in 1967 prices could be made.   This was done by calculating
price conversion coefficients from the ratio of the 1966 and 1967
price variants of 1966 exports and imports by sector, and applying
these coefficients to the 1961 export and import values given in
1966 prices.   The assumption implicit in such a conversion is that
the product composition of each sector's imports and exports remained constant from 1961 to 1966.   Since it cannot be determined
how appropriate this assumption is, these estimates can be considered only approximate.

No data on exports and imports are available for the 1969
table.   For the 1972 table, exports and imports were estimated for
most sectors from the data given in Shmulder (1974, pp. 62–67).

Given the first quadrant and estimates of sectoral GVOs, exports, and imports, accounts such as those presented in the fore-
going tables can be constructed.   For the 1966 table there is sufficient information in Shmulder (1971) to give a more detailed breakdown of the second and third quadrants.   Since these data are not
usually available for Soviet tables, they are presented in Table
7.10. [8]

In addition to these accounts, additional economic indicators
based on input–output data can be collected for the various years.
At the aggregate level, the cost structure of gross social product
(see Table 7.11) indicates an increase in the share of total outlays
going for material inputs, with a corresponding decline in value-
added, over the period covered by the tables.   The tables showing
the structure of exports and imports (Table 7.12) and the role of
imports and exports--that is, the ratio of a sector's imports to
the total consumption of products of that sector in the region, and
the ratio of a sector's exports to its total GVO (see Table 7.13)--

TABLE 7.10

Disaggregation of Second and Third Quadrants of 1966 Latvian Input–Output Table

Sector	Components of Third Quadrant				Components of Second Quadrant (millions of rubles)		
	(1) Depreciation	(2) Variable Capital	(3) Surplus Product	(4)* Turnover Tax	(5) Personal Consumption	(6) Public Consumption	(7) Accumulation
1. Metals	2.1	.5	3.6	.9	.2	1.0	2.6
2. Fuels	3.4	4.4	5.8	1.4	5.4	17.8	7.9
3. Power	11.3	3.9	21.1	8.8	12.7	15.8	.1
4. Machinebuilding and metalworking	25.1	193.0	316.4	66.1	89.6	13.8	402.9
5. Chemicals	5.0	15.1	48.4	4.3	25.1	11.8	12.4
6. Wood and paper	13.8	63.3	41.7	10.5	39.2	7.0	10.4
7. Construction materials	10.1	34.1	30.4	7.5	5.9	6.9	6.0
8. Textiles and apparel	8.7	79.1	348.4	243.7	384.6	11.2	35.0
9. Food industry	23.0	71.6	233.0	156.4	772.2	30.4	16.1
10. Industry not elsewhere classified	3.8	21.3	44.3	21.0	36.4	6.8	5.0
Total industry	106.3	486.3	1,093.1	520.7	1,371.3	122.5	498.3
11. Construction	13.6	143.9	39.6	0	0	0	424.5
12. Agriculture	58.7	532.5	117.7	.7	305.9	7.0	26.7
13. Transportation and communication	37.2	61.9	61.5	.9	0	0	0
14. Trade and distribution	13.4	69.3	107.2	0	0	0	0
15. Other branches	.5	30.4	5.5	0	40.6	3.3	-.8
Total	229.6	1,324.3	1,424.6	522.3	1,717.8	132.8	948.6

*Turnover taxes are a component of surplus product.

Sources: M. Shmulder et al., eds., Dinamika mezhotraslevykh i mezhrespublikanskikh ekonomicheskikh sviazei Latviiskoi SSR (Riga: Tsentral'noe statisticheskoe upravlenie Latviiskoi SSR, 1971): column (1), Tables 23 and 34, pp. 111, 155; column (4), Table 6, p. 39; column (5), Table 27, p. 126; column (6), Table 31, p. 138. See note 7 for columns (2) and (3). Column (7) was calculated as a residual.

TABLE 7.11

Cost Structure of Total Social Product of 1966
Latvian Input-Output Table
(percent)

	(1) 1961 (1961 prices)	(2) 1961 (1966 prices)	(3) 1966 (1966 prices)	(4) 1966 (1967 prices)	(5) 1969	(6) 1972
Material inputs	51.2	54.5	55.5	56.8	--	--
Depreciation	2.3	2.3	3.4	3.5	--	--
Material inputs and depreciation	53.5	56.8	58.9	60.2	60.1	61.6
Wages and labor payments	--	22.2	19.8	19.7	19.0	18.2
Surplus product*	--	21.0	21.3	20.1	20.9	20.2
Total value-added	46.5	43.2	41.1	39.8	39.9	38.4
Total social product	100.0	100.0	100.0	100.0	100.0	100.0

*Surplus product includes profits and losses, turnover tax, subsidies, and so on.

Sources: Column (1): K. A. Tsipe and R. I. Meerovich, "Otchetnyi mezhotras levoi balans proizvodstva i raspredeleniia produktsii Latviiskoi SSR za 1961 god," in Mezhotraslevye issledovaniia v ekonomicheskikh raionakh, ed. L. E. Mints (Moscow: Nauka, 1967), pp. 212-42. Columns (2) and (3): TsSU Latvia, Narodnoe khoziaistvo Latviiskoi SSR v 1970 godu. Statisticheskii sbornik (Riga: Statistika, 1972), p. 55; TsSU Latvia, Narodnoe khoziaistvo Sovetskoi Latvii. Statisticheskii sbornik (Riga: Statistika, 1968), p. 54; TsSU Latvia, Narodnoe khoziaistvo Latviiskoi SSR v 1973 godu. Statisticheskii sbornik (Riga: Riesma, 1974), p. 62. Column (4): B. A. Dagovich, "Planirovanie i analiz ekonomiki soiuznoi respubliki metodom mezhotraslevogo balansa (na primere Latviskoi SSR)," Ph.D. dissertation, 1973, Ch. 3. Column (5): TsSU Latvia, 1972, op. cit., p. 55. Column (6): TsSU Latvia, 1974, op. cit., p. 62.

TABLE 7.12

Structure of Imports and Exports: Latvia, 1966
(percent of total)

Sector	(1) 1961 (1961 prices)	(2) 1961 (1966 prices)	(3) 1966 (1966 prices)	(4) 1966 (1967 prices)	(5) 1970	(6) 1972
Imports						
1. Metals	7.8	8.2	7.5	9.8	8.6	8.7
2. Fuels	8.0	8.3	7.4	9.0	7.8	7.5
3. Power	.3	.3	2.3	2.6	1.7	2.7
4. Machinebuilding and metalworking	20.8	18.7	25.6	24.3	23.4	25.2
5. Chemicals	9.4	9.6	11.1	10.0	10.2	12.2
6. Wood and paper	4.0	4.7	2.9	3.3	1.9	2.7
7. Construction materials	.9	1.0	1.3	1.3	.9	1.2
8. Textiles and apparel	22.4	20.6	17.9	17.1	21.0	20.0
9. Food industry	14.1	14.3	14.1	13.2	16.4	11.3
10. Industry not elsewhere classified	2.6	2.0	1.5	1.4	1.5	1.1
Total industry	90.3	87.7	91.5	91.9	93.4	92.6
12. Agriculture	9.7	11.8	8.0	7.6	6.1	6.8
15. Other branches	0	.4	.6	.5	.5	.6

326

Exports

	(1)	(2)	(3)	(4)	(5)	(6)
1. Metals	.9	.6	1.2	1.9	1.7	1.6
2. Fuels	.2	.3	.2	.3	.3	.3
3. Power	.1	0	.9	1.1	.4	.3
4. Machinebuilding and metalworking	27.4	25.2	31.3	29.9	31.1	32.6
5. Chemicals	4.5	3.1	5.7	5.0	8.7	8.2
6. Wood and paper	6.0	6.5	4.6	5.2	4.9	4.3
7. Construction materials	1.8	1.8	2.3	2.3	2.2	1.4
8. Textiles and apparel	29.1	30.6	25.1	25.6	25.9	27.8
9. Food industry	24.2	24.5	24.6	24.7	20.1	18.8
10. Industry not elsewhere classified	2.4	2.6	2.1	2.1	3.5	2.6
Total industry	96.7	95.3	98.1	98.1	98.8	97.9
12. Agriculture	2.8	4.0	1.7	1.7	.9	1.9
15. Other branches	.5	.7	.3	.3	.3	.2

Sources: Column (1): K. A. Tsipe, Sistema mezhotraslevykh balansov soiuznoi respubliki (Moscow: Ekonomika, 1971), p. 35; columns (2), (3), and (4): M. Shmulder et al., eds., Dinamika mezhotraslevykh i mezhrespublikanskikh ekonomicheskikh sviazei Latviiskoi SSR (Riga: Tsentral'noe statisticheskoe upravlenie Latviiskoi SSR, 1971), pp. 193–95, 204–06, 216; column (5): TsSU Latvia, Narodnoe khoziaistvo Latviiskoi SSR v 1970 godu. Statisticheskii sbornik (Riga: Statistika, 1972), p. 50; column (6) TsSU Latvia, Narodnoe khoziaistvo Latviiskoi SSR v 1973 godu. Statisticheskii sbornik (Riga: Riesma, 1974), p. 67.

TABLE 7.13

Role of Imports and Exports: Latvia, 1966
(percent of total republic consumption)

Sector	(1) 1961 (1961 prices)	(2) 1961 (1966 prices)	(3) 1966 (1966 prices)	(4) 1966 (1967 prices)	(5) 1970	(6) 1972
Imports						
1. Metals	85.2	86.2	90.2	89.6	93.0	91.0
2. Fuels	80.7	74.6	86.7	88.8	87.0	90.0
3. Power	4.9	8.0	56.0	53.6	39.0	57.0
4. Machinebuilding and metalworking	49.0	46.4	51.7	53.3	53.0	62.0
5. Chemicals	81.5	82.9	77.6	75.2	69.0	82.0
6. Wood and paper	18.7	22.2	19.8	22.0	14.0	23.0
7. Construction materials	9.9	9.1	13.9	13.6	n.a.	13.1
8. Textiles and apparel	21.9	23.5	30.4	30.2	36.0	36.0
9. Food industry	14.7	16.0	19.8	19.7	25.0	19.0
10. Industry not elsewhere classified	25.5	26.4	20.2	21.1	n.a.	17.2
Total industry	28.0	29.9	37.2	38.4	40.0	42.0
12. Agriculture	10.6	9.9	11.0	11.0	9.0	12.0
15. Other branches	12.8	10.7	18.5	18.5	n.a.	n.a.
Total	22.2	23.0	28.4	22.8	n.a.	n.a.

Exports

	(1)	(2)	(3)	(4)	(5)	(6)
1. Metals	31.5	31.5	61.8	62.9	72.0	64.0
2. Fuels	12.2	11.1	18.3	22.1	21.0	28.0
3. Power	.9	1.5	35.6	33.2	12.0	14.0
4. Machinebuilding and metalworking	58.5	55.1	58.6	59.1	59.0	68.0
5. Chemicals	54.1	61.8	65.9	61.2	64.0	75.0
6. Wood and paper	27.5	29.3	29.7	31.1	29.0	31.0
7. Construction materials	19.8	16.1	23.8	23.2	n.a.	14.9
8. Textiles and apparel	31.6	32.4	39.8	40.0	40.0	44.0
9. Food industry	22.9	25.6	31.8	32.0	28.0	28.0
10. Industry not elsewhere classified	31.4	32.5	27.8	28.1	n.a.	19.7
Total industry	31.7	32.8	40.7	40.6	40.0	43.0
12. Agriculture	3.5	3.8	2.7	2.7	1.0	4.0
15. Other branches	19.9	16.3	10.1	10.1	n.a.	n.a.
Total	23.6	24.2	31.1	30.4	n.a.	n.a.

Note: n.a. = data not available.

Sources: Column (1): K. A. Tsipe, Sistema mezhotraslevykh balansov soiuznoi respubliki (Moscow: Ekonomika, 1971), p. 38, and reconstructed table; columns (2) and (3): M. Shmulder et al., eds., Dinamika mezhotraslevykh i mezhrespublikanskikh ekonomicheskikh i mezhrespublikanskikh sviazei Latviiskoi SSR (Riga: Tsentral'noe statisticheskoe upravlenie Latviiskoi SSR, 1971), p. 217; column (4): calculated from reconstructed table; column (5): TsSU Latvia, Narodnoe khoziaistvo Latviiskoi SSR v 1971 godu. Statisticheskii ezhegodnik (Riga: Statistika, 1972), pp. 49-50; column (6) TsSU Latvia, Narodnoe khoziaistvo Latviiskoi SSR v 1973 godu. Statisticheskii sbornik (Riga: Riesma, 1974), p. 66, and reconstructed table.

329

reveal a substantial increase in trade (both export and import) for
almost all sectors, with the shares of trade in machinebuilding and
metalworking, chemicals, and metal products increasing while the
shares of textiles and apparel, food, and agricultural products decrease.

Since the Latvian economy is a highly developed and specialized part of the Soviet economy, a comparison of input-output data
from the 1966 Latvian and Soviet Union tables gives an indication of
the degree of regional variation that may be expected in Soviet input-
output statistics. Here such comparisons are presented for share
of total intermediate inputs in gross value of output, labor output/
capital output ratios, and fixed capital/working capital ratios.

In Table 7.14 are shown total intermediate input coefficients
as calculated from the 1966 Latvian and Soviet Union input-output
table. (Here, and in the following comparisons, the Latvian input-
output data comes from a version of the 1966 table in purchasers'
prices adjusted to conform to the method used in compiling the 1966
national table. See the following section of this paper for details on
the conversion technique used.) These coefficients were calculated
in each sector by dividing total purchases of material inputs by
gross value of output minus value of material services (that is,
transport, communications, trade and distribution inputs) as recorded
in the purchasers' price tables. (The value of material service inputs is already included in the value of material inputs in purchasers'
prices. The row entry for material services in a purchasers' price
table reflects distribution costs of outputs, and not inputs, and thus
must be deducted from GVO in our calculation of total input coefficients.)

These ratios thus reflect the share of gross value of output
required for intermediate production and, implicitly in the residual
share, for depreciation payments plus wages and salaries, social
security payments, profits, taxes, subsidies, and other elements of
national income. As is obvious from the percent differences given
in the third column of the table, the Latvian figures in many cases
vary greatly from the national average. No effort was made to determine the cause of these differences. However, it can be reasonably assumed that they reflect variations in product mix, technology,
production efficiency, and the like occurring among the regions of
the Soviet Union.

The analytical usefulness of input-output data is greatly enhanced by the availability of capital stock data and labor force data
in a comparable format suitable for the calculation of capital and
labor requirements coefficients. Such data are available for the
1966 Soviet table (Treml et al. 1973, Ch. 11). Estimates of capital
stock and labor force were prepared for the 1966 Latvian table and

coefficients for these primary inputs calculated and compared with national coefficients.

TABLE 7.14

Comparison of Latvian and National Total
Intermediate Input Coefficients

Sector	(1) Latvian Input Coefficients[a]	(2) National Input Coefficients[a]	(3) Percent Differences[b]
1. Metals	.818	.592	38.2
2. Fuels	.329	.362	−9.1
3. Power	.282	.379	−25.6
4. Machinebuilding and metalworking	.456	.507	−10.1
5. Chemicals	.569	.569	0.0
6. Wood and paper	.553	.542	2.0
7. Construction materials	.447	.458	−2.4
8. Textiles and apparel	.618	.647	−4.5
9. Food industry	.755	.695	8.6
10. Industry not elsewhere classified	.484	.676	−28.4
11. Construction	.531	.526	1.0
12. Agriculture	.379	.308	23.1
13. Transport and communications	.236	.216	9.3
14. Trade and distribution	.125	.138	−9.4
15. Other branches	.171	.176	−2.8

[a]Rubles of total intermediate inputs per ruble of gross output.
[b]$\frac{[\text{Column (1)} - \text{Column (2)}]}{\text{Column (2)}} \times 100$

Source: Compiled by the author.

In Shmulder (1971, Table 30, pp. 172-73) is given a matrix of values of fixed capital for all sectors of the aggregated 1966 table except for machinebuilding and metalworking, chemicals, industry not elsewhere classified, and other branches of material production. Estimates of fixed capital stock for these excluded branches were made by dividing depreciation payments in Latvia for 1966 by the national depreciation rates (Treml et al. 1973, pp. 191, 322, and

325), and then adjusting the estimated values to equal the unallocated residual in the Latvian capital stock table.

No labor data have been published with the Latvian input–output tables. It was therefore necessary to use labor force statistics from standard statistical sources, and to adjust these to conform to the classification system and commodity basis of the input–output data. For a discussion of the differences between the "establishment" basis of statistical data in non–input–output sources and the "commodity" basis used in input–output accounting, see Treml et al. (1972, Ch. 6). Two sources were used to determine an initial 18–sector breakdown of Latvian labor in industry: a table on p. 73 of TsSU Latvia (1968) which gives the percent distribution of workers in Latvia by industrial sector; and a table on p. 109 of TsSU (1968) which gives in absolute figures the number of all employees and of workers by sector and for all industry.[9] In each of these sources there were omissions in the data. Therefore it was necessary to make a number of rough estimates to complete the tables. (Such estimates were necessary for metals, power, machinebuilding and metalworking, chemicals, and other branches. The final estimates of number of employees (by the establishment classification) were converted to a commodity classification using the matrix of commodity–establishment distributions published in Shmulder (1971, Table 4, pp. 25–27). The percentage distribution across the input–output sectors (defined on the establishment basis) is given by this matrix. This adjustment is only approximate since the redistribution of labor inputs may not correspond to the redistribution of output.

By dividing these estimates of capital stock and labor force by the appropriate values of GVO, primary input coefficients were calculated for the 1966 Latvia table. These are given in Tables 7.15 and 7.16 along with similar coefficients for the 1966 national table. (The national data are from Treml et al. (1972, Chs. 9 and 11, Table 13–14, pp. 402–04.) These figures indicate a rather wide range of variation between national and Latvian primary input requirements at this level of sectoral disaggregation.

Such variations in primary input coefficients arise not only because of differences in regional production processes, but also because of regional differences in the assortment of products produced in these major branches. An indication of the degree of actual differences in regional production processes (those not due to assortment differences) is provided by a discussion in Granberg (1973, pp. 121–22), concerning the choice of labor and capital coefficients for a multiregional model of the Soviet economy.[10] In this work it was considered essential that regional accounting data be used for determining labor coefficients for electrical energy, metals, fuels, and wood products, and for agriculture. For these sectors it was

TABLE 7.15

Comparison of Latvian and National Capital Coefficients

Sector	Estimated Latvian Capital Coefficients[a]	National Capital Coefficients[a]	Percent Differences[b]
1. Metals	.723	.899	-19.0
2. Fuels	1.005	1.016	- 1.1
3. Power	4.241	3.143	34.9
4. Machinebuilding and metalworking	.339	.510	-33.5
5. Chemicals	.425	.382	11.3
6. Wood and paper	.407	.526	-22.6
7. Construction materials	.673	.698	- 3.6
8. Textiles and apparel	.104	.115	- 9.6
9. Food industry	.219	.146	50.0
10. Industry not elsewhere classified	.411	1.183	-65.3
11. Construction	.312	.273	14.3
12. Agriculture	.974	.801	21.6
13. Transport and communications	2.465	2.181	13.0
14. Trade and distribution	.954	1.200	-20.5
15. Other branches	.161	.165	- 2.4

[a]Rubles of fixed capital stock per ruble of gross output.

[b]$\frac{[\text{Column (1)} - \text{Column (2)}]}{\text{Column (2)}}$ x 100.

Source: Compiled by the author.

TABLE 7.16

Comparison of Latvian and National Labor Coefficients

Sector	(1) Estimated Latvian Labor Coefficients[a]	(2) National Labor Coefficients[a]	(3) Percent Differences[b]
1. Metals	.154	.080	92.5
2. Fuels	.133	.082	62.2
3. Power	.094	.082	14.6
4. Machinebuilding and metalworking	.120	.148	-18.9
5. Chemicals	.117	.068	72.1
6. Wood and paper	.158	.180	-12.2
7. Construction materials	.134	.132	1.5
8. Textiles and apparel	.067	.070	-4.3
9. Food industry	.032	.030	6.7
10. Industry not elsewhere classified	.074	.065	13.8
11. Construction	.155	.267	-41.9
12. Agriculture	.086	.368	-76.6
13. Transport and communications	.488	.240	103.3
14. Trade and distribution	.348	.439	-20.7
15. Other branches	.657	.264	148.9

[a]Man-years of labor per thousand rubles of gross output.

[b]$\frac{[\text{Column (1)} - \text{Column (2)}]}{\text{Column (2)}}$ x 100.

Source: Compiled by the author.

accepted that regional variations in the productivity of labor were significant. For the remaining manufacturing branches, labor coefficients were based on national average coefficients. Apparent differences here were said to be almost fully accounted for by differences in the composition of the branches. As for capital coefficients, national average coefficients were used as regional coefficients for all branches of material production. (The sectors serving production, that is, the transportation and trade sectors, were not included in these comparisons.) The data presented here for Latvia do not seem to cast doubt upon this procedure. In the comparison of Latvian and national labor coefficients, metals, fuels, wood products, and agriculture do stand out in their differences, as suggested. The apparent large differences in machinebuilding and metalworking may be explained, as also suggested, by differences in the composition of products included in these especially complex, multiproduct sectors. In general, the Latvian and national capital coefficients are more comparable than are the labor coefficients, which again supports the approach taken by the Soviet researchers.

Another comparison of Latvian and national capital input structure is possible, using the data on fixed and working capital stock presented in Belkin (1972, Tables 8 and 9, pp. 104–05 and 108–09).[11] Because of differences in the classification systems used, comparisons can be made for only some sectors, with the remaining sectors grouped into a residual. In the case of agriculture, it is thought that the effect of the inclusion of forestry in the Latvian table would not create any great distortion, so an additional comparison of figures for this sector was added, giving two different residual classifications--the first with agriculture included and the second without agriculture. Here again there are rather large differences in the capital coefficients between the republic and the national table (see Table 7.17). However, it is very interesting to note that in the ratio of working capital to fixed capital (given in the last section of the table) the two areas show remarkable similarity. The exception to this--in the construction sector--may be due to the uncompleted construction of large hydroelectric plants in Latvia at that time (1966).

These comparisons of Latvian and national coefficients of various types generally indicate substantial differences in the structures of regional economies in the Soviet Union. Other studies of a multiregional nature, such as Granberg (1975), give even stronger proof of this condition. Since the types of coefficients examined here are often used as parameters in econometric models, it would seem that regionally specific as well as sectorally specific disaggregation of such models, especially at the level of sectoral aggregation used here, could improve their portrayal of the Soviet economy.

TABLE 7.17

Comparison of Latvian and National Fixed and Working Capital Coefficients

Sector	Fixed Capital Coefficients		Working Capital Coefficients		Ratios of Working Capital to Fixed Capital	
	Soviet Union	Latvia	Soviet Union	Latvia	Soviet Union	Latvia
1 Metals	0.8935	0.7401	0.2027	0.1459	0.2256	0.1971
3 Power	3.2767	4.2411	0.1119	0.1166	0.0341	0.0275
6 Wood and paper	0.5263	0.4035	0.1799	0.1230	0.3417	0.3050
8 Textiles and apparel	0.1152	0.1024	0.1351	0.1160	1.1728	1.1324
9 Food	0.1464	0.2153	0.0858	0.0962	0.5864	0.4468
11 Construction	0.2730	0.3116	0.1306	0.9043	0.4782	2.9019
13 Transportation and communications	2.1813	2.4651	0.0656	0.0684	0.0301	0.0278
Residual 1	0.7438	0.6672	0.5103	0.3776	0.6861	0.5659
Total	0.6121	0.5157	0.3026	0.2772	0.4943	0.5375
12 Agriculture	0.7452	0.9775	0.3166	0.3838	0.4249	0.3927
Residual 2	0.7430	0.4657	0.6243	0.3735	0.8403	0.8021

Sources: Soviet Union data from V. D. Belkir, Ekonomicheskie izmereniia i planirovanie (Moscow: Mysl', 1972), Tables 8 and 9, pp. 104-05, 108-09; Latvian capital stock data from M. Shmulder et al., eds., Dinamika mezhotraslevykh i mezhrespublikanskikh ekonomicheskikh sviazei Latviiskoi SSR (Riga: Tsentral'noe statisticheskoe upravlenie Latviiskoi SSR, 1971), Table 39, pp. 172-73.

THE TREATMENT OF TRADE AND TRANSPORT
COSTS IN THE 1966 LATVIAN TABLE

Examination of the Latvian input-output studies provides information on the methods used in Soviet regional research for handling a troublesome aspect of input-output analysis--the treatment of trade and transport costs in regional tables. The basic issue involved can be reduced to the question of the relation between quantity and price variables in the expression of intersectoral relations. In the case of Soviet national input-output statistics, this issue is addressed in other studies. (See Treml et al. 1973 and the chapter by A. Moses in this volume.) But additional consideration is called for in the case of regional data because of the extreme openness to trade of these economies in comparison with the country as a whole. The substantial role played by exports and imports in each republic, plus the different regional effects of distance on prices, have required the development of special accounting practices to properly reflect trade and transport costs in republic and regional input-output accounts.[12]

The problems presented by trade and transport costs have been widely discussed in the Soviet literature. Especially for the compilation of multiregional accounts, attempts have been made to develop a standard method of gathering regional data with consistent accounting for trade and transport markups in order to facilitate the linking of separately produced regional tables. Three distinct methods can be identified in Soviet regional analysis for dealing with these problems. In the accompanying tables (Tables 7.18, 7.19, and 7.20) the various entries of a republic or regional table are defined according to each of these approaches.

Table 7.18 presents an input-output table in which the entries are given in (one form of) producers' prices. In this case, the values of intersectoral flows do not include intraregional transport and trade expenditures needed to deliver products to the consumer. Tables 7.19 and 7.20 present two forms of purchasers' price tables. The valuations of flows in these tables reflect the prices at which products are actually consumed (either by other producers or by the population).[13]

Input-output tables--based on the Latvian 1966 data--for each of these three methods are presented below (Tables 7.21, 7.22, and 7.23).[14] As can be seen by examining both the definitions and values of the various entries in the two sets of tables, there are substantial differences in the pattern of flows resulting from differences in the treatment of trade and transport services. All three methods have been utilized in the construction of republic and regional tables. During the initial period of regional input-output study

TABLE 7.18

Producers' Prices Table, Modified Form

		Sectors of Material Production 1 2...	Trade and Transport m	Final Demand m+1...n-1	Exports n	GVO and Imports n+1
Sectors of material production	1 2 · · · m-1	$a_{ij}^* = p_i^m q_{ij}^m + p_i^r q_{ij}^r + g\,d_{ij}^m$ for i=1,...,m-1; j=1,...,n-1			$a_{in}^* = p_i^r q_{in}^r$ for i=1,...,m-1	$(GVO + M)_i^* = \sum_{j=1}^{n} a_{ij}^*$ for i=1,...,m-1
Trade and transport sector	m	$a_{mj}^* = \sum_{i=1}^{m-1} (b\,d_{ij}^m + b\,d_{ij}^r)$ for j=1,...,r-1			$a_{mn}^* = \sum_{i=1}^{m-1} b\,d_{in}^m + \sum_{i=1}^{m-1} b\,d_{in}^r$	$(GVO + M)_m^* = \sum_{j=1}^{n-1} a_{mj}^* + a_{mn}^*$
Value-added	m+1 · · · n-1	v_{kj} for k=m+1,...,n-1; j=1,...,n-1			0	$\sum_{j=1}^{n-1} v_{kj}$ for k = m+1, ...,n-1
Gross value of output	n	$GVO_j^* = (\sum_{i=1}^{m-1} a_{ij}^*) + a_{mj}^* + (\sum_{k=m+1}^{n-1} v_{kj})$ for j = 1,...,n				$\sum_{j=1}^{n} GVO_j^*$
Imports	n+1	$m_j^* = \sum_{k=1}^{n-1} (p_j^m q_{jk}^m + g\,d_{jk}^m)$ for j=1,...,m-1	0	0	0	$\sum_{j=1}^{m-1} m_j^*$
GVO and imports	n+2	$(GVO + M)_j^* = GVO_j^* + m_j^*$ for j=1,...,n				$\sum_{j=1}^{n} (GVO + M)_j$

Source: Compiled by the author.

TABLE 7.19

Purchasers' Prices Table, TsEMI Method

	Sectors of Material Production (1 2 ... m-1)	Trade and Transport (m)	Final Demand (m+1...n-1)	Exports (n)	GVO and Imports (n+1)
Sectors of material production (1, 2, ..., m-1)	$a_{ij} = p_i^m q_{ij}^m + p_i^r q_{ij}^r + g_{ij}^m + b d_{ij}^m + b d_{ij}^r$ for $i = 1,\ldots,m-1$ $j = 1,\ldots,n-1$			$a_{in} = p_i^r q_{in}^r + g_{in}^r + b d_{in}^r$ for $i = 1,\ldots,m-1$	$(GVO + M)_i = \sum_{j=1}^{n} a_{ij}$ for $i = 1,\ldots,m-1$
Trade and transport sector (m)	$a_{mj} = (\sum_{k=1}^{n-1} b d_{jk}^r) + (b d_{jn}^r + g_{jn}^r)$ for $j = 1,\ldots,m-1$	0	0	$a_{mn} = \sum_{i=1}^{m-1}\sum_{j=1}^{n-1} b d_{ij}^m$ $+ \sum_{i=1}^{m-1} b d_{in}$	$(GVO + M)_m =$ $\sum_{j=1}^{m-1} a_{mj} + a_{mn}$
Value-added (m+1, ..., n-1)	v_{kj} for $k = m+1,\ldots,n-1$ $j = 1,\ldots,n-1$			0	$\sum_{j=1}^{n-1} v_{kj}$ for $k = m+1,$ $\ldots,n-1$
Gross value of output (n)	$GVO_j = (\sum_{i=1}^{m} a_{ij}) + (\sum_{k=m+1}^{n-1} v_{kj})$ for $j = 1,\ldots,n$				$\sum_{j=1}^{n} GVO_j$
Imports (n+1)	$m_j = \sum_{k=1}^{n-1} (p_j^m q_{jk}^m + g_{jk}^m + b d_{jk}^m)$ for $j = 1,\ldots,m-1$	$m_m = \sum_{i=1}^{m-1} g_{in}^r$	0	0	$\sum_{j=1}^{m} m_j$
GVO and imports (n+2)	$(GVO + M)_j = GVO_j + m_j$ for $j = 1,\ldots,n$				$\sum_{j=1}^{n} (GVO + M)_j$

Source: Compiled by the author.

TABLE 7.20

Purchasers' Prices Table, TsSU Method

	Sectors of Material Production 1 2...	Trade and Transport m-1	Final Demand m	Final Demand m+1...n-1	Exports n	GVO and Imports n+1
Sectors of material production 1, 2, ⋮, m-1	$a_{ij} = p_i^m q_{ij}^m + p_i^r q_{ij}^r + g d_{ij}^m + b d_{ij}^m + b d_{ij}^r$ for $i = 1,...,m-1$; $j = 1,...,n-1$				$a_{in}' = p_i^r q_{in}^r + b d_{in}^r + b d_{in}^m$ for $i = 1,...,m-1$	$(GVO + M)_i' = \left(\sum_{j=1}^{n-1} a_{ij}\right) + a_{in}'$ for $i = 1,...,m-1$
Trade and transport sector m	$a_{mj}' = \left(\sum_{k=1}^{n-1} b d_{jk}^r + b d_{jk}^m\right) + b d_{jn}^r + b d_{jn}^m$ for $j = 1,...,m-1$		0	0	0	$(GVO + M)_m' = \sum_{j=1}^{m-1} a_{mj}'$
Value-added m+1, ⋮, n-1	v_{kj} for $k = m+1,...,n-1$; $j = 1,...,n-1$				0	$\sum_{j=1}^{n-1} v_{kj}$ for $k = m+1, ...,n-1$
Gross value of output n	$GVO_j' = \left(\sum_{i=1}^{m-1} a_{ij}\right) + a_{mj}' + \left(\sum_{k=m-1}^{n-1} v_{kj}\right)$ for $j = 1,...,n$					$\sum_{j=1}^{n} GVO_j'$
Imports n+1	$m_j' = \sum_{k=1}^{n-1} (p_j^m q_{jk}^m + g d_{jk}^m)$ for $j = 1,...,m-1$		0	0	0	$\sum_{j=1}^{m-1} m_j'$
GVO and imports n+2	$(GVO + M)_j' = GVO_j' + m_j'$ for $j = 1,...,n$					$\sum_{j=1}^{n} (GVO + M)_j'$

Source: Compiled by the author.

Key for Tables 7.18, 7.19, and 7.20

a_{ij} purchases of product i by sector j in value terms

q_{ij} purchases of product i by sector j in physical terms

p_i enterprise wholesale price of product i

d_{ij} transport and trade margin on the flow of product i to sector j

v_{kj} value-added entry of type k for sector j

m_j import of product of sector j

GVO_j gross value of output of sector j

$_b d_{in}^m$ transport and trade margin on products in transit across the region

Right-hand superscripts: ^{m} indicates the entry refers to a product imported from another region or country.

     ^{r} indicates the entry refers to a product produced in the region.

     * indicates that the entry in the producers' prices table is defined differently than in the TsEMI table.

     $^\prime$ indicates that the entry in the TsSU table is defined differently than in the TsEMI table.

Left-hand subscripts: $_g$ indicates that the transport and trade margin is the result of services rendered outside of the region.

     $_b$ indicates that the transport and trade margin is the result of services rendered within the region.

TABLE 7.21

1966 Latvian SSR Input-Output Table: Producers' Prices, Modified Form

(millions of rubles)

	1 Heavy Industry	2 Light Industry	3 Total Industry	4 Construction	5 Agriculture	6 Transportation and Trade
1 Heavy industry	729.98	141.51	871.49	191.64	95.90	62.53
2 Light industry	62.47	924.00	986.47	3.39	16.70	8.28
3 Total industry	792.45	1,065.51	1,857.96	195.03	112.60	70.81
4 Construction	0.00	0.00	0.00	0.00	0.00	0.00
5 Agriculture	22.31	585.91	608.22	0.00	306.80	1.16
6 Transportation and trade	35.79	68.43	104.22	32.43	15.19	9.16
7 Other branches	7.28	1.30	8.58	0.65	0.09	0.28
8 Total	857.80	1,721.20	2,579.00	228.10	434.70	81.40
9 Depreciation and value-added	921.90	763.80	1,685.70	197.10	708.90	350.50
10 Gross value of output	1,779.70	2,485.00	4,264.70	425.20	1,143.60	431.90
11 Imports	1,017.90	545.20	1,563.10	0.00	135.80	0.00
12 GVO plus imports	2,797.60	3,030.20	5,827.80	425.20	1,279.40	431.90

	7 Other Branches	8 Total	9 Consumption	10 Accumulation	11 Exports	12 GVO plus Imports
1 Heavy industry	6.68	1,228.23	282.19	441.51	845.83	2,797.76
2 Light industry	0.29	1,015.16	1,133.71	42.82	838.50	3,030.19
3 Total industry	6.97	2,243.39	1,415.90	484.33	1,684.33	5,827.95
4 Construction	0.00	0.00	0.00	425.20	0.00	425.20
5 Agriculture	0.10	916.27	304.70	28.11	30.32	1,279.40
6 Transportation and trade	0.84	162.03	89.30	11.79	168.78	431.90
7 Other branches	0.00	3.71	40.67	-0.74	4.06	53.70
8 Total	7.90	3,331.40	1,850.60	943.70	1,887.50	8,018.20
9 Depreciation and value-added	36.40	2,978.40				
10 Gross value of output	44.30	6,309.80				
11 Imports	9.20	1,708.10				
12 GVO plus imports	53.50	8,017.89				

Source: Compiled by the author.

341

TABLE 7.22

1966 Latvian SSR Input-Output Table: Purchasers' Prices, TsEMI Method
(millions of rubles)

	1 Heavy Industry	2 Light Industry	3 Total Industry	4 Construction	5 Agriculture	6 Transportation and Trade
1 Heavy industry	761.70	148.30	910.00	219.20	100.90	66.30
2 Light industry	65.30	965.50	1,030.80	3.50	17.80	8.70
3 Total industry	827.00	1,113.80	1,940.80	222.70	118.70	75.00
4 Construction	0.00	0.00	0.00	0.00	0.00	0.00
5 Agriculture	23.00	602.60	625.60	0.00	314.90	1.20
6 Transportation and trade	142.90	208.80	351.70	4.70	31.30	4.90
7 Other branches	7.90	1.40	9.30	0.70	0.10	0.30
8 Total	1,000.80	1,926.60	2,927.40	228.10	465.00	81.40
9 Depreciation and value-added	921.90	763.80	1,685.70	197.10	708.90	350.50
10 Gross value of output	1,922.70	2,690.40	4,613.10	425.20	1,173.90	431.90
11 Imports	1,053.40	566.70	1,620.10	0.00	141.60	127.70
12 GVO plus imports	2,976.10	3,257.10	6,233.20	425.20	1,315.50	559.60

	7 Other Branches	8 Total	9 Consumption	10 Accumulation	11 Exports	12 GVO plus Imports
1 Heavy industry	7.10	1,303.50	295.40	450.70	926.50	2,976.10
2 Light industry	0.30	1,061.10	1,198.40	44.80	952.80	3,257.10
3 Total industry	7.40	2,364.60	1,493.80	495.50	1,879.30	6,233.20
4 Construction	0.00	0.00	0.00	425.20	0.00	425.20
5 Agriculture	0.10	941.80	312.90	28.80	32.00	1,315.50
6 Transportation and trade	4.60	397.20	0.00	0.00	162.40	559.60
7 Other branches	0.00	10.40	43.90	-0.80	4.90	58.40
8 Total	12.10	3,714.00	1,850.60	948.60	2,078.60	8,591.80
9 Depreciation and value-added	36.40	2,978.50				
10 Gross value of output	48.50	6,692.50				
11 Imports	9.90	1,899.30				
12 GVO plus imports	58.40	8,591.80				

Source: Compiled by the author.

TABLE 7.23

1966 Latvian SSR Input-Output Table: Purchasers' Prices, TsSU Method
(millions of rubles)

	1 Heavy Industry	2 Light Industry	3 Total Industry	4 Construction	5 Agriculture	6 Transportation and Trade	7 Other Branches	8 Total	9 Consumption	10 Accumulation	11 Exports	12 GVO plus imports
1 Heavy industry	761.70	148.30	910.00	219.20	100.90	66.30	7.10	1,303.50	295.40	450.60	948.10	2,997.60
2 Light industry	65.30	965.50	1,030.80	3.50	17.80	8.70	0.30	1,061.10	1,198.40	44.80	890.60	3,194.90
3 Total industry	827.00	1,113.80	1,940.80	222.70	118.70	75.00	7.40	2,364.60	1,493.80	495.40	1,838.70	6,192.50
4 Construction	0.00	0.00	0.00	0.00	0.00	0.00	0.00	0.00	0.00	425.20	0.00	425.20
5 Agriculture	23.00	602.60	625.60	0.00	314.90	1.20	0.10	941.80	312.90	28.80	37.20	1,320.70
6 Transportation and trade	199.90	168.10	368.00	4.70	42.30	4.90	5.60	425.50	0.00	6.40	431.90	431.90
7 Other branches	7.90	1.40	9.30	0.70	0.10	0.30	0.00	10.40	43.90	-0.80	5.20	58.70
8 Total	1,057.80	1,885.90	2,943.70	228.10	476.00	81.40	13.10	3,742.30	1,850.60	948.50	1,887.50	8,428.90
9 Depreciation and value-added	921.90	763.80	1,685.70	197.10	708.90	350.50	36.40	2,978.50				
10 Gross value of output	1,979.70	2,649.70	4,629.40	425.20	1,184.90	431.90	49.50	6,720.80				
11 Imports	1,017.90	545.20	1,563.10	0.00	135.80	0.00	9.20	1,708.10				
12 GVO plus imports	2,997.60	3,194.90	6,192.50	425.20	1,320.70	431.90	58.70	8,428.90				

Source: Compiled by the author.

several republic tables were prepared using producers' price valuation, since the resulting tables were considered a more accurate reflection of technical relations than were tables compiled in purchasers' prices. This preference was well-founded. In purchasers' price tables the costs of trade and transportation are counted twice --once as a component of each intersectoral flow expressed in final purchasers' prices, and then again as separate entries in the trade and transportation sector rows. Thus the structure of an input-output table in purchasers' prices reflects a composite of production functions and distribution patterns. This doublecounting distorts the distribution of sectoral gross social product; thus these input-output indicators are not equivalent to corresponding measures given in standard statistical sources. This distortion also makes it more difficult to relate the value tables to physical tables. An additional distortive impact in regional input-output tables can occur because the role of trade costs can vary depending upon the spatial pattern of regional purchases and sales. In interregional studies this distortion will be even more adverse, since these components of product costs can vary sharply among regions (Bedenkova 1973, pp. 458-59). In theory, with a producers' prices table these difficulties are prevented by valuing all intersectoral flows in enterprise wholesale prices--which do not include trade and transport markups --plus turnover taxes, if any.[15] The trade and transport margins on all products consumed by each sector (including the nonproductive sectors) are instead recorded in the trade and transport row of the table. The trade and transport costs involved in the handling of exports up to the border of the region, plus charges placed on the handling of products in transit across the region are recorded as an export of the trade and transport sector. The column entries for trade and transport reflect the gross product of these sectors in the region.

Given the data available for Latvia in 1966 it was not possible to reconstruct a producers' prices table along these lines, since there was no way to determine the trade and transport margin on imports incurred outside the republic. However, a modified producers' prices table was prepared in which imports are valued f.o.b. at the border of the republic (that is, including cost of transport up to the republic's border). A summary of the entries for the trade and transport sector was also prepared (see Table 7.24). In such a table, of course, the impact of the distribution pattern of imports from other regions is obscured. However, intraregional distribution markups are clearly delimited. In some instances the republic input-output tables classified by the Soviets as producers' prices tables correspond to the method used here (Belov 1970). In any case, tables defined in this modified version of producers'

TABLE 7.24

Components of the Row Entries of Transportation and Communications,
and Trade and Distribution, in the 1966 Latvian
Input-Output Table
(millions of rubles)

	Producers' Prices	Purchasers' Prices	
		TsEMI Method	TsSU Method
(1) Sectors of material production and final uses, total	263.1	397.2	425.5
Shipping goods produced and consumed within the region	191.0	191.0	191.0
Shipping exported goods to the border of the region	--	71.3	71.3
Shipping exported goods from border to purchaser	--	127.7	--
Shipping imported goods to the border of the region	--	--	--
Shipping imported goods from border to purchaser	64.9	--	64.9
Shipping goods in transit through the region	--	--	91.1
Communications services	6.2	6.2	6.2
(2) Exports of transportation, trade and distribution, total	168.8	162.4	6.4
Exports of transportation (unallocated residual)	6.4	6.4	6.4
Shipping exported goods to the border of the region	71.3	--	--
Shipping imported goods from border to purchaser	--	64.9	--
Shipping goods in transit through the region	91.1	91.1	--
(3) Imports of transportation, trade and distribution, total (shipping exported goods from border to purchaser)	--	-127.7	--
Gross value of output of transportation and communications, and trade and distribution (sum of lines 1, 2, and 3)	431.9	431.9	431.9

Source: Compiled by the author.

prices are well suited to many types of regional analysis in which competitive imports should be evaluated as if they were produced at the border of the region.

In the Soviet Union, with the existing accounting system at the enterprise level, it is very difficult to calculate trade and transport expenditures necessary for producing national and regional input-output tables in producers' prices.[16] For this reason most regional tables (and all national tables) have been, and continue to be, compiled in some form of purchasers' prices. In preparing their 1966 accounts, various forms of purchasers' prices were used by the republic statistical agencies. The lack of a standard method resulted in serious obstacles to a comparison of data from the resulting republic tables. In response to this situation the Central Mathematical Economics Institute of the Academy of Sciences (TsEMI) developed a method that was used in the construction of tables for certain economic regions of the RSFSR. (This method is the same as that actually used in Latvia in the compilation of its 1966 table.) In keeping with the valuation of all flows in the table in purchasers' prices, the entries in the transport and trade sector give the expenditures on transporting and selling regionally produced goods. It should be noted that these transport and trade costs are included regardless of the region in which these expenditures occur. The column entries for trade and transport, on the other hand, reflect only the domestic (Latvian) gross product of these sectors. In order to bring into balance the row and column sums of this sector it is necessary to treat as an import the value of services of trade and transport of other regions in delivering products produced in Latvia, and to treat as an export the value of service of Latvia's trade and transport sector in handling imports into Latvia and goods in transit across Latvia. Again using Latvian data, the effects of this method of trade and transport services balancing is illustrated in Table 7.24.

This TsEMI method allows a consistent system of valuation of entries in a purchasers' prices table. However, the existing statistics on republic and regional production, trade, and transport do not include the measures necessary for directly obtaining indicators on the separate components of regionally produced, imported, and exported values called for by the TsEMI method. Numerous estimates and rough approximations are necessary in the compilation of tables along these lines (Bedenkova 1973). The method later developed by the Central Statistical Administration (TsSU) for the 1966 and 1972 system of input-output accounts recognizes this constraint imposed by existing statistics. In addition the new method reflects the TsSU's interest in developing a system of integrated national/multiregional input-output and interregional flow accounts--an interest that supersedes the development of strictly regional accounts.

There are two major modifications of the purchasers' prices table brought about by the TsSU method: the region's imports are given in prices f.o.b. at the border of the region, while exports are given in the same prices, with income from transit shipments added on; and in the trade and transport rows the entries reflect the transport expenditures on the handling of all products within the borders of the region itself, including products regionally produced, imported, and in transit through the region. As critics of this method have pointed out, this approach results in a table having certain undesirable features (Bedenkova 1973; Granberg 1975, pp. 104-09). First, the output of a sector in the region is inflated by the amount of transport expenditures on imported products of that sector and on products of that sector in transit through the republic. Thus, the output of a sector can appear to increase when, in reality, only regional consumption of products of that sector has increased. Second, the valuation system is not consistent for all entries since the values of gross output, imports, and exports are not in purchasers' prices, whereas all other entries are.

A breakdown of the row entries of the services sectors in the Latvian input–output table compiled according to the TsSU method is presented in Table 7.24. The conversion of these row entries from the TsEMI to the TsSU method involves subtracting the value of trade and transport expenditures on Latvian exports incurred outside the republic, and adding the value of expenditures incurred within the republic on both imported goods and goods in transit through the republic. Thus, the row entries do not reflect trade and transport margins consistent with either a purchasers' prices or a producers' prices valuation of flows.

The rationale for the TsSU method lies in the fact that in 1972 data was collected in a manner permitting the simultaneous construction of national, republic, and regional input-output accounts. This is an important advance in improving the collection of regional and national input-output data. The data gathering was organized on a nationwide basis by the TsSU USSR which provided the instructions and supervised the sampling. However, most of the actual collection of data was decentralized--carried out by the republic TsSUs, or at their behest by the statistical administrations of regions, territories, and ASSRs (Autonomous Soviet Social Republics) (Eidel'man 1972). One exception to this plan was that for the trade and transport sectors data obtained centrally from the corresponding national ministries and agencies by the TsSU USSR, where it was to be disaggregated on a regional basis and then communicated to the statistical agencies of the republics and regions. Given the type of trade and transport data regularly collected by these national trade and transport ministries, it is only possible for the

TsSU USSR to disaggregate the transactions of these sectors by region and product type on the basis of regional expenditures--that is, without regard to the region of production of the products. This corresponds to the type of entry required in the TsSU approach.

Similarly, the valuation of interregional trade flows in f.o.b. border prices, and the inclusion in exports of trade and transport markups for transit shipments, minimize the number of estimations involved in preparing the regional accounts. This helps to ensure that the final multiregional account will be balanced for the nation.

Thus, the TsSU method, although not corresponding to the dictates of a conceptually unified account at the regional level, does seem to fulfill the need for an approach that will result in a consistent set of interregional data, and that makes maximum use of existing sources of data.

As is pointed out in Granberg (1975, pp. 104-09), the preferability of any method of valuation in regional tables depends on the goal of analysis. Interregional models have been developed utilizing input coefficients based on both producers' and purchasers' (TsEMI type) price accounts. However, the mixed approach followed by the TsSU results in data that are not directly utilizable in any current form of multiregional model. For the study of different aspects of regional economics it is necessary to be able to convert balances from one type of prices to another. This is possible if the transport and trade component of the value of each entry in the table can be separately identified.

THE COMPARABILITY OF INCOME AND PRODUCT
AND INPUT-OUTPUT STATISTICS

The uniqueness of input-output accounts arises from their portrayal of the economic interdependencies of many subdivisions of the economy, and especially, the relations among separate branches of production. However, these data do not constitute a separate system of accounting apart from the more traditional income and product accounts. The input-output system consists of a disaggregated accounting of the formation and distribution of income and product. Thus the components of the two systems should, with appropriate aggregation, be in agreement.

In the case of Soviet input-output accounts, both national and regional, such correspondence with income and product accounts is achieved. However, this correspondence is often not directly perceivable. First, there are differences in accounting definitions between the two systems which result in seemingly different values for similarly labeled indicators. Second, since data gathering for the input–output accounts is based largely on special surveys supplementing the normal reporting for income and product accounts, there arises on occasion the necessity of correcting figures in the standard accounts. (In general, however, the income and product accounts provide control totals for input–output accounting.) Third, the accounting consistencies required in an input–output balance have required some changes in the valuation of its entries from those usually used in other accounts. For the reconstruction and utilization of Soviet statistics it is often necessary to combine data from both sources, that is, national income accounts and input–output tables. In such cases an understanding of these differences is essential.

The availability of an excellent set of data from the 1966 Latvian SSR input–output study has made it possible to illustrate various relationships between income and product accounting data and input–output data at the republic level. Here only a quantitative picture of these relations will be presented since detailed discussions of these differences, on a general level, are available in other sources (Becker 1972 and Treml 1969). Three aspects of accounting differences will be covered here, involving measures of gross social product and national income, branch statistics for industry, and the redistribution of income in the economy.

The two main aggregates of Soviet income and product accounting are gross social product (valovoi obshchestvennyi produkt) and national income, or net material product, (natsional'nyi dokhod). These are succinctly described in Becker (1972, pp. 73–74) as follows.

> GSP [gross social product] is defined as the total of material values produced in the economy during the accounting period. . . . In terms of "value" (stoimost'), GSP is the sum of transferred value—means of production consumed in the process of production (material inputs plus depreciation)—and newly created value ("national income"). The first component, identified with Marx's c (constant capital), is called the fund of replacement of material production expenditures. "National income" [NMP] is the sum of labor earnings (v) and surplus value (m). Thus NMP, as newly created value, is the difference between GSP and transferred value or the national-production replacement fund.

The values of GSP and NMP can usually be obtained from republic statistical handbooks, along with breakdowns of the total value into branch values for industry, construction, agriculture, transportation and communication, and trade, distribution, and other branches of material production. Table 7.25 gives these figures for the Latvian SSR in 1966.

Corresponding values for GSP and NMP can be obtained from an input-output table. The third quadrant of an input-output table consists of NMP entries for the branches of material production. The first quadrant and the row of depreciation payments--usually placed in the table between the first and third quadrants--yield values of material production expenditures. GSP is the combined value of these two components--the column sums of the first and third quadrants. These values as they are contained in the 1966 Latvian input-output table are also given in Table 7.25.

The differences in the two sets of figures in Table 7.25 can be explained as follows. First, the prices used in traditional income and product accounts are current wholesale industry prices, while those used in input-output accounts are (usually) purchasers' prices. The difference between these prices is the markup for transportation and distribution costs incurred in getting products from producers to consumers. Since these costs of distribution for each branch's output are given in the transportation and trade row entry for that branch, this adjustment between the income and product figures and the input-output figures is easily made. It applies specifically to material production expenditures (and thus in turn to GSP). The results of this adjustment for the 1966 Latvian data are shown in Table 7.26 where the transport and trade margins taken from the input-output table are added to material production expenditure figures obtained from handbook data.

After this adjustment on material production expenditures is made, several discrepancies in the totals for the two accounts still exist. The major of these is in industry where the value of material purchases is 44 million rubles higher in the input-output account than the adjusted product account figure. This difference can be explained by the practice in input-output accounting of valuing agricultural products (livestock, grain, cotton, and so on), at the prices realized by the agricultural producers in sales to intermediary procurement agencies, rather than in the lower prices that industrial enterprises pay the procurement agencies for these products. The necessity of balancing income and expenditures for each sector of the input-output account forces this change in valuation. As a result of this adjustment the value of material expenditures (and thus GSP) both in industry and in the total are increased in the input-output account (Shmulder 1971, p. 12, and Eidel'man 1968).

The remaining discrepancies seen in this portion of Table 7.26 are not as well accounted for in the available literature. The only

TABLE 7.25

Aggregate Indicators in National Income and Input-Output Accounts: Latvia, 1966

(millions of rubles)

	Industry	Construction	Agriculture	Transportation and Communications	Trade, Distribution, and Other Branches	Total
Income and Product Account Data						
GSP (c + v + m)	4,194	410	1,142	214	347	6,307
	(66.5)*	(6.5)	(18.1)	(3.4)	(5.5)	
NMP (v + m)	1,555	172	669	121	295	2,812
	(55.3)	(6.1)	(23.8)	(4.3)	(10.5)	
Means of Production (c)	2,639	238	473	93	52	3,495
	(75.5)	(6.8)	(13.5)	(2.7)	(1.5)	
Input-Output Account Data						
GSP (c + v + m)	4,613	425	1,174	213	267	6,692
	(68.9)	(6.4)	(17.5)	(3.2)	(4.0)	
NMP (v + m)	1,578	184	652	124	212	2,750
	(57.4)	(6.7)	(23.7)	(4.5)	(7.7)	
Means of production (c)	3,035	241	522	89	55	3,942
	(77.0)	(6.1)	(13.2)	(2.3)	(1.4)	

*Figures in parentheses are percentages of totals.

Sources: TsSU Latvia, Latviiskaia SSR v tsifrakh v 1968 godu. Statisticheskii sbornik (Riga: Statistika, 1969), p. 50; M. Shmulder et al., eds., Dinamika mezhotraslevykh i mezhrespublikanskikh ekonomicheskikh sviazei Latviiskoi SSR (Riga: Statistika, 1971), pp. 15-16, 23, and Appendix 5.

TABLE 7.26

Reconciliation of National Income and Input–Output Account
Aggregate Indicators: Latvia, 1966
(millions of rubles)

	Industry	Construction	Agriculture	Transportation and Communications	Trade, Distribution, and Other Branches	Total
Adjustment to means of production payments (c)						
Income and product data	2,639	238	473	93	52	3,495
Adjustments[a]	352	5	31	0	5	393
Adjustments[b]	2,991	243	504	93	57	3,888
Input-output data	3,035	241	522	89	55	3,942
Residual[c]	-44	2	-18	4	2	-54
Adjustments to NMP (v + m)						
Income and product data	1,555	172	669	121	295	2,812
Adjustments[a]	24d	0	0	0	-86e	-62
Adjustments[b]	1,579	172	669	121	209	2,750
Input-output data	1,578	184	652	124	212	2,750
Residual[c]	1	-12	17	-3	-3	0

[a] Trade and transportation margins taken from the 1966 Latvian input-output table.

[b] Income and product data plus adjustments[a].

[c] Adjustments[b] minus input-output data.

[d] Subsidy to milk industry.

[e] Foreign trade adjustment (residual undistributed value of trade).

Source: M. Shmulder et al., eds., Dinamika mezhotraslevykh i mezhrespublikanskikh ekonomicheskikh sviazei Latviiskoi SSR
(Riga: Tsentral'noe statisticheskoe upravelnie Latviiskoi SSR, 1971), Tables 23 and 34, pp. 111, 155; and pp. 13, 220-21.

explanation found is a statement in Shmulder (1971, p. 13) to the
effect that in the process of compiling the input-output table for
Latvia several omissions or errors were found in the national income
accounts that were corrected in the table. An example is given, in
this source, of the omission from the accounts for the construction
sector of the costs of completed land-improvement work. Corrections were also noted as being made for the values of material purchases and national income in the agriculture and transportation
sectors. These discrepancies between the two sets of accounts are
probably reflected in the residual figures seen in column (5) of
Table 7.26, both for the material purchases and the NMP portions
of the table.

The remaining values of NMP, there are two major adjustments necessary to make the handbook data correspond to the input-
output data. First, there is a direct subsidy (dotatsiia) to the milk
industry which, by accounting practices in force in 1966, was not
included in NMP of this sector in the standard income accounts.
Again, in order to achieve balancing of income and expenditures in
the input-output account, it was necessary to add this value to NMP
of industry. Thus it can be seen from this example, and the case
of agricultural product pricing mentioned above, that the location of
corrections for a subsidy in the input-output accounts is determined
by the means through which the subsidy is realized. When the subsidy is realized through a differentiated pricing system, the correction is made in the first quadrant of the table. When the subsidy is a
direct payment from the budget, it is reflected in the third quadrant
(in the row "turnover-tax payments and balance of interrelationships
with the union budget").

The second adjustment to NMP is the deduction, from the
handbook value for the trade and distribution sector, of an adjustment for foreign trade transactions. This is a credit made to the
republic, arising from the differences in domestic and foreign trade
prices for import and export operations with other countries. Since
the input-output table is compiled in domestic prices, it is necessary to subtract this portion of income, credited to Latvia but arising
from the national foreign trade operations of the Soviet Union (TsSU
Latvia 1971, p. 13).

The remaining discrepancies in NMP figures are quite small,
and their possible origin in corrections made to the income accounts
was mentioned above. Overall then, it can be seen (in Table 7.26)
that the correspondence between the income and product account and
the input-output account for the Latvian republic is quite good at the
level of major aggregates.

At the next more detailed level of disaggregation of income and
product accounts--the subdivision of industry into its major branches

(usually nine such branches are specified in handbook tables)--the correspondence of entries with those in the input–output account is not as close due to differences in the definition of branch composition. In the input–output account production activities are classified by groups of commodities. (In Soviet terminology these are <u>chistyi</u> branches.) In contrast, handbook statistics are based on the classification of branches by firm, or enterprise, identification (see Treml et al. 1972, Ch. 6). The degree of difference resulting from these two approaches can be seen in the case of 1966 Latvian data in the following figures from TsSU Latvia (1971, p. 29):

Industrial Branches of Non–Input–Output Statistics	Share of Branch Output not Classified in Same Sector when Data Adjusted to Commodity Basis
	(percent)
Ferrous metals	3.9
Fuels	14.6
Energy	0.7
Machinebuilding	3.0
Metalwork	17.3
Chemicals	15.5
Wood products	4.2
Paper products	24.4
Construction materials	10.4
Glass and pottery	5.2
Textiles	1.1
Sewn goods	4.7
Other light industry	9.1
Fish products	1.9
Meat products	0.8
Milk products	0.8
Other food industry	2.7
Other branches	14.4

As a result of such differences the data available in handbooks on the structure of outlays of industrial branches cannot be expected to conform exactly to similar values calculated from input–output data. In Table 7.27 data on this structure from the two sources are compared.[17] Surprisingly, for several branches (machinebuilding and metalworking, chemicals, wood and paper, textiles and apparel) the structures of outlays correspond very closely. The input pattern for industry in total is almost a perfect match, indicating that the commodity–establishment adjustments cancel out in the aggregate.[18]

TABLE 7.27

Structure of Outlays of Industrial Branches: (1) from
Handbook Data; (2) from Input–Output Data[a]
(in percent)

		Material Inputs	Labor Payments	Depreciation
Metals[b]	(1)	75.5	19.6	4.9
	(2)	91.4	1.6	6.9
Fuels	(1)	40.5	34.4	25.1
	(2)	46.2	30.3	23.4
Energy	(1)	42.3	24.3	33.4
	(2)	48.2	13.3	38.4
Machinebuilding	(1)	67.7	28.8	3.5
and metalworking	(2)	67.2	29.0	3.8
Chemicals	(1)	80.8	14.3	4.9
	(2)	81.5	13.9	4.6
Wood and paper	(1)	66.0	28.4	5.6
	(2)	65.6	28.3	6.2
Construction	(1)	66.3	24.8	8.9
materials	(2)	57.8	32.5	9.6
Textiles and	(1)	88.6	10.5	.9
apparel	(2)	88.9	10.0	1.1
Food industry	(1)	91.0	6.9	2.1
	(2)	91.4	6.5	2.1
All–industry	(1)	81.2	15.6	3.2
	(2)	81.3	15.4	3.4

[a]The doublecounting of trade and distribution costs in the input–
output data was corrected for before calculating these input figures.
[b]Only ferrous metals are covered in handbook statistics.
Sources: (1) TsSU Latvia, Latvia za gody Sovetskoi vlasti.
Statisticheskii sbornik (Riga: Statistika, 1967), pp. 104–51; (2) reconstructed 1966 Latvian input–output table.

Returning to the aggregate level, in addition to data on the
(branch) formation of NMP, standard statistical sources usually
give a breakdown of national income according to its utilization.
Here a distinction between two definitions of NMP is introduced.
Two aggregate measures are given in income accounts: produced
(proizvedennyi) and utilized (ispol'zovannyi) national income. See
TsSU Latvia (1969, p. 51), for these values for Latvia in 1966. In

the discussion above the produced value of NMP was dealt with.
Utilized NMP differs from this by the amount of losses in the economy (accidental damage, abandoned construction, and the like) and
certain transactions between the local economy and the rest of the
world that results in transfers of income between the two. For
Latvia in 1966 these differences were as follows, expressed in
millions of rubles:

National income produced	2,812
Minus interregional trade balance	− 179
Minus foreign trade adjustment	− 87
Minus losses	− 18
Plus turnover tax balance	+ 7
Equals national income utilized	2,535

The turnover tax balance noted here is the difference between
the value of taxes realized (paid to trade organizations) in the republic and the value of taxes produced (applied to products produced)
in the republic. In Latvia during 1966 the former was 529.1 million
rubles and the latter 522.3 million rubles, resulting in a net increase
of utilized regional income in Latvia of 6.8 million rubles (Shmulder
1971, pp. 38–40). In the input–output account this turnover tax
adjustment is not made. Otherwise utilized NMP as represented
in the second quadrant is consistent with that found in the handbook.
Several components of utilized income are given in standard
statistical sources. However, a more detailed and complete depiction of the utilization of income is provided in the input–output
account. Unfortunately, only rarely is this input–output information
available in any complete and detailed form in publications available outside the Soviet Union. However, in the case of the 1966
Latvian account a detailed depiction of these flows is made possible
by the information provided in TsSU Latvia (1971). This redistribution of income is presented here in two forms. First, a portion of
the 1966 Latvian input–output table is given in Table 7.28. This is
the fourth quadrant of the table together with the boundary sums of
the first, second, and third quadrants. This table gives a static
depiction of accounting relations during the year. In Table 7.29
this data is presented again, but with added detail and in a form that
represents the flow of income from its generation in the sphere of
material production, through secondary income receivers in the
nonproductive (service) sphere, and finally to material consumption
and accumulation.
Only a scattering of the indicators presented in these tables
is available in non–input–output statistical sources. The most useful of those available is the breakdown of utilized national income,

TABLE 7.28

Fourth Quadrant of the 1966 Latvian Input–Output Table
(millions of rubles)

	(186) Inter-industry Total	(187) Personal Consumption	(188–206) Public Consumption	(207) Net Accumulation of Fixed Capital
(186) Total material inputs	3,714.3	1,717.8	132.8	285.5
(187) Depreciation	229.6	64.0	87.3*	--
(188) Total transferred value (c)	3,943.9	1,781.8	220.1	285.5
(189) Wages of state employees	804.5	--		--
(190) Other labor income of state employees	19.4	--		--
(191) Labor income of kolkhoz members	152.4	--	604.2	--
(192) Other labor income	348.0	--		--
(193) Profits of state enterprises	666.9	--		--
(194) Turnover taxes and balances of budget payments	522.3	--		--
(195) Social security payments	55.6	--	112.0	--
(196) Net income of kolkhoz and cooperatives	70.9	--		--
(197) Other surplus product	108.9	--		--
(198) Total national income (v + m)	2,748.8	--	716.2	--
(199) Total production	6,692.7	1,781.8	936.3	285.5
(200) Imports	1,899.2	--	--	--
(201) Total production plus imports	8,591.9	1,781.8	936.3	285.5

(208) Replacement of Capital Written Off	Capital Repair	(209) Net Accumulation of Working Capital	(210) Losses	(211) Exports	(212) Total Final Consumption	(213) Total Production Plus Imports
213.3	167.6	264.3	17.8	2,078.5	4,877.6	8,592.0
--	--	--	--	--	151.3	380.9
213.3	167.6	264.3	17.8	2,078.5	5,028.9	8,972.9
--	--	--	--	--		
--	--	--	--	--		
--	--	--	--	--	604.2	1,928.5
--	--	--	--	--		
--	--	--	--	--		
--	--	--	--	--		
--	--	--	--	--	112.0	1,536.6
--	--	--	--	--		
--	--	--	--	--		
--	--	--	--	--	716.2	3,465.0
213.3	167.6	264.3	17.8	2,078.5	5,745.1	12,437.9
--	--	--	--	--	--	1,899.2
213.3	167.6	264.3	17.8	2,078.5	5,745.1	14,337.1

*76.0 (depreciation) + 11.3 (nonamortized capital deductions).

Note: Sector numbering as in original Latvian table.

Source: M. Shmulder et al., eds., Dinamika mezhotraslevykh i mezhrespublikanskikh ekonomicheskikh sviazei Latviiskoi SSR. Sbornik statisticheskikh materialov (Riga: Statistika, 1971), Appendix 5 and passim.

TABLE 7.29

System of Income Redistribution in Latvia in 1966

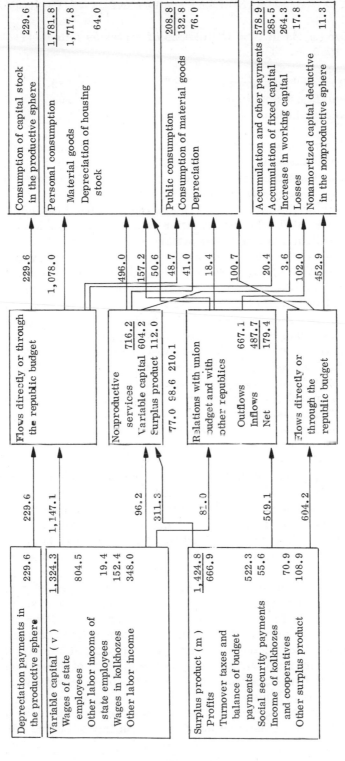

Note: All values in millions of rubles.

Source: M. Shmulder et al., eds., Dinamika mezhotraslevykh i mezhrespublikanskikh ekonomicheskikh sviazei Latviiskoi SSR. Sbornik statisticheskikh materialov (Riga: Statistika, 1971), Scheme I and passim.

given for Latvia in 1966 in millions of rubles as follows (TsSU
Latvia 1969, p. 51):

Personal consumption	1,782
Public consumption	204
Accumulation	549

These figures match very well those found in the input–output data.
(The accumulation figure in the handbook covers only the increase
in fixed and working capital stock, given in the input–output table
as 285.5 + 264.3 = 549.8 million rubles.)

Data on capital investment--increase in fixed capital stock,
replacement of fixed capital written off, and increase in uncompleted construction (the latter is part of the increase in working
capital stock)--is also available in the handbooks, classified by
branch and type of expenditure. For Latvia in 1966 the total value
of investment was given as 540 million rubles (in 1955 prices) in
both the TsSU Latvia handbook (1968, p. 278) and as based on input-
output statistics in Shmulder (1971, p. 149). This correspondence
is rarely evident in such sources, however, since capital investment is not identified as an independent column in the input–output
tables, and the data given there is seldom disaggregated sufficiently
to be usable in figuring this measure.

Other isolated data are given in standard sources (such as the
666.9-million-ruble figure for profits given in TsSU Latvia (1969,
p. 460), but these are of little help in obtaining a comprehensive
view of the generation and redistribution of income. It is also often
the case with handbook data that the coverage of a given indicator is
incomplete, being limited to those enterprises under Union ministry
control only, or otherwise restricted.

One data source in addition to the republic yearbooks that
would seem to be of value in studying these flows is the budget for
the republic. In it are contained figures on turnover tax collections,
deductions from profits, social security payments, and so forth, in
the income balance; and in the expenditures balance are given figures by sector and type of expenditure such as wages, stipends,
investments, and the like. (The 1966 Latvian budget is summarized
in Ministerstvo Finansov SSSR [1972, pp. 180-86].) However, only a
part of Latvian income (721.7 million rubles in 1966) passes through
the republic budget, the remaining portion going either directly or
through the national budget from source to point of utilization. Thus
the republic budget figures can be used to obtain only partial values
of income components.

Only in the input–output data is provided a fairly complete
portrayal of the redistribution of income in Latvia during 1966.

Various accounting relations take concrete form in these accounts. For example, it can be seen in these figures that total consumption plus accumulation is equal to income generated in material production, since the expenditures on services of income generated in material production are matched by expenditures on material goods of income received in the nonproductive sphere (Spulber 1969, Ch. 8). When the data on relations between the Latvian economy and the rest of the world in the two tables are compared it can be seen that the monetary balance of these transactions (given in Table 7.29 as 667.1 - 487.7 = 179.4 million rubles) and the real balance between the export and import of goods and services (given in Table 7.28 as 2,078.5 - 1,899.2 = 179.3 million rubles) have the same value. Also the data shown here on income in the nonproductive service sectors allow a calculation of Latvian output akin to the Western concepts of net national product: NMP plus nonproductive services (2,749.1 + 716.2 = 3,465.3 million rubles), and gross national product--net national product plus depreciation in both the productive and nonproductive spheres (3,465.3 + 229.6 + 140.0 = 3,834.9 million rubles). [19]

NOTES

1. A distinctive feature of Soviet regional research has been the very active role of national planning and research organizations in this work. The most active of these has been TsEMI. Under the direction of academician V. S. Nemchinov, this group worked in cooperation with local statistical and planning agencies during the early 1960s in the production of most of the early regional input-output tables. The methods developed by researchers in TsEMI were widely published, discussed, and used as a basis for most subsequent regional work. From 1962 another group of researchers, located in Novosibirsk and associated with the Laboratory for Economic-Mathematic Research at the State University and the Institute of Economics and Organization of Industrial Production of the Siberian branch of the Academy of Sciences (IEOPP), became actively involved in regional research. The IEOPP has been especially important as a center of research on Siberian development. Finally, the Council for the Study of Productive Forces (SOPS) must be mentioned. Attached to Gosplan USSR, this organization performs methodological research in regional planning and advises Gosplan concerning the development of regional objectives for long-range national planning.

At first these organizations were primarily involved with individual regions, helping to establish the necessary methods for compiling regional data. Today, as the republics have developed self-sufficiency in this work, the efforts of the TsEMI, IEOPP, and SOPS economists have been turned to theoretical and experimental research concerned with the development of multiregional models for national planning.

2. This revaluation was necessary because of a major reform of industrial wholesale prices in 1967, which resulted in substantially higher prices for the metals, fuels, and energy sectors. In order for the 1966 data to be used in the construction of the 1970 and 1975 planning tables this price adjustment was necessary.

There are admitted shortcomings in the data and methods used by the Latvian specialists in revaluing the 1966 Latvian data with 1967 prices. This pioneering effort was completed before the national 1966 table was revalued, and thus could not draw from this source of information which has served as an aid to the other republics making similar revaluations (Shmulder 1970, pp. 135-36).

3. In most of the discussions of the table and in many cases where actual figures from the table are presented, an aggregated 15-sector classification is used in TsSU Latvia (1971). (The tables presented in this paper use this classification.)

4. Here, and throughout this paper, Soviet accounting terminology is used. Treml and Hardt (1972) is recommended as a reference on Soviet usage.

5. See Bond (1975) for a discussion of Soviet plans for compiling the 1972 input-output accounts on a multiregional basis.

6. The 1961 producers' price table was recompiled by Latvian researchers in 1966 purchasers' prices and in such a manner as to make the 1961 and 1966 tables comparable. This involved such adjustments as the recalculation of intrasectoral flows to conform to the accounting methods used in 1966 (Shmulder 1970, pp. 135-36).

7. Although the price conversion coefficients given in TsSU Latvia (1971, Table 19), were obtained by converting the 1966 input-output data to 1967 prices, they were used to revalue the 1961 table (given in 1966 prices) in the estimates given here. These price conversion coefficients would not be the same for the 1961 table if the product composition of the flow values had changed between 1961 and 1966. One check on the degree of distortion produced in using these price coefficients with 1961 data was obtained by comparing the estimates of subtotals of estimates in 1967 prices obtained by converting individual flows and summing the results, with estimates obtained by converting the subtotals directly. This is possible since price conversion coefficients are given both for all 15 sectors and for industry and all production totals. The differences were quite insignificant, indicating that this estimation procedure was acceptable.

8. But for minor exceptions depreciation, turnover tax, and the components of final demand are taken directly from the sources indicated. The calculation of the major components of value-added was more indirect. The total of value-added for each of the sectors of the table was obtained by subtracting the total of material inputs including depreciation from the gross value of output of each sector. The next step involved the breaking down of these value-added figures into two components: variable capital (wages), and surplus product (profits, taxes, and other nonlabor elements of value-added). Several sources of information were used in this process. First, the total value of variable capital and surplus product for the productive sectors was given in Orlovskaia (1973, p. 199) as 1,324.3 million rubles, and 1,424.6 million rubles, respectively. The ratios of surplus product to variable capital for the five major branches are given on page 38 of Shmulder (1971). Using these together with the estimates of total value-added by branch allowed estimates of the two components to be made for these major branches.

The calculations of components of value-added for the ten industrial sectors were based on the 1966–67 price conversion coefficients for total value-added, surplus product, and variable capital given in Table 19 of Shmulder (1971), pages 94–96. Since the variable capital component of value-added remained constant when the 1966 table was revalued in 1967 prices, the value of surplus product in 1966 prices can be estimated by dividing the increase in value of total value-added by the rate of increase in surplus value. The corresponding values for variable capital are then determined simply by subtraction.

9. As a result of a reclassification of industrial activities made in August 1967 (Feshbach 1972, pp. 208–09), the reported annual average numbers of workers and employees in industry, construction, and agriculture in Latvia during 1966 is not the same in more recent statistical sources as in those used here (TsSU 1968; TsSU Latvia 1968).

10. Development of a 16-sector, 10-region optimizing multiregional input–output of the Soviet Union (Optimizatsionnaia mezhotraslevaia mezhregional'aia model'--OMMM)began at the Institute of Economics and Organization of Industrial Production (IEOPP) in 1967.

11. Working capital consists primarily of stocks of various material and supplies (simple tools, instruments, implements, equipment, and furnishings not exceeding 50 rubles in value and/or having a durability of less than one year), and inventories of finished and unfinished products of the producing sectors. For a complete definition and description of Soviet working capital accounting see F.D.A.D., U.S. Department of Commerce (1972).

12. The Soviet practice of compiling tables in physical units
--including interregional trade tables in physical units--has allowed
some circumvention of these problems. The computational problems created by the necessarily large number of sectors of these
tables, the difficulty of constructing models based on physical relations, and the necessity in planning of using value relations preclude
sole use of physical tables in input–output analysis.

13. The definitions as presented are still greatly simplified
since the fact is ignored that each entry is an aggregation of the
flows of many different products, and that the prices of imported
goods may vary by region of origin.

14. Table 7.22 is a direct reconstruction of the 1966 Latvian
table and is based on information presented in Shmulder (1971) and
Dagovich (1971). Table 7.21 entries were calculated by modifying
the data in Table 7.22 by the application of data on the various components of the trade and transport margins provided in the former
reference. The primary assumption used was that distribution
costs were not differentiated by buyer (see Treml et al. 1973,
pp. 7-8). Table 7.23 is also based on Table 7.22, but with changes
in the trade and transport and imports rows and the export column.
Data from TsSU Latvian SSR (1971, pp. 250-56) were used to obtain
these entries.

In these tables light industry comprises textiles and apparel
and food industry, while heavy industry is the aggregation of the remaining industrial sectors. The two sectors transportation and
communications and trade and distribution have also been combined.

15. The term producers' prices can mean prices without not
only the trade and transport margin, but also without the turnover
tax. This would normally be the case when using Western terms.
However, Soviet usage more often indicates the absence of the
former component only (Eidel'man 1966, Ch. 10).

16. The basic source of data for compiling input–output statistics in the Soviet Union comes from special reports prepared by
enterprises which provide information on production expenditures
only. The nature of the Soviet supply system is such that the enterprises have little knowledge of the final purchasers of their products.
Without this information it is not possible for them accurately to
determine trade and transport costs.

17. In the handbook purchases are broken down into (1) raw
materials and basic materials, (2) auxiliary materials, (3) fuel and
energy, (4) wages and social security payments, (5) depreciation,
and (6) other costs not specifically allocated. Entries (1), (2), (3),
and (6) are combined in Table 7.27 to give the total value of material inputs.

18. An argument as to why such a balance may not be expected for total industry, arising from the method used for estimating input requirements for branches classified on a commodity basis, is given in Treml et al. (1972), pp. 125-32).

19. The relating of these values to concepts used in Western statistics on the basis of just these redefinitions is somewhat superficial. Various other readjustments and revaluations are necessary before an adequate correspondence in accounting terms can be achieved. An example of such adjustments for republic statistics is provided by Koropeckyj (1975).

REFERENCES

Baranov, E. F., ed. 1972. Dinamicheskie modeli territorial'nogo planirovaniia. Moscow: Nauka.

Becker, A. S. 1972. "National Income Accounting in the USSR." In Soviet Economic Statistics, ed. V. G. Treml and J. P. Hardt, pp. 69-119. Durham, N.C.: Duke University Press.

Bedenkova, M. F. 1973. "Osobennosti rascheta transportnoi otsenki v mezhotraslevom balanse soiuznoi respubliki." Ekonomika i matematicheskie metody 9, no. 3: 458-66.

Belkin, V. D. 1972. Ekonomicheskie izmereniia i planirovanie. Moscow: Mysl'.

Belov, M. I. 1970. "Voprosy sovershenstvovaniia balansovykh raschetov." Planovoe khoziaistvo, no. 8: 33-37.

Boiarskii, A. Ia., ed. 1971. Problemy mezhotraslevogo balansa. Moscow: Statistika.

Bond, D. L. 1975. "A Comparison of the Soviet and U.S. Multi-regional Interindustry Accounts." Duke University-University of North Carolina Occasional Papers on Soviet Input-Output Analysis, No. 9, Durham, N.C.

Breev, B. D., and V. P. Krykov. 1974. Mezhotraslevoi balans dvizheniia naseleniia i trudovykh resursov. Moscow: Nauka.

Dagovich, B. A. 1973. "Planirovanie i analiz ekonomiki soiuznoi respubliki metodom mezhotraslevogo balansa (na primere Latviskoi SSR)." Ph.D. dissertation, Moscow: Gosplan SSSR.

_____. 1971. Analiz i planirovanie ekonomiki soiuznoi respubliki metodom mezhotraslevogo balansa. Na opyte Latviiskoi SSR. Riga: Liesma.

Eidel'man, M. R. 1972. "Novyi otchetnyi mezhotraslevoi balans proizvodstva i raspredeleniia produktsii v narodnom khoziaistve SSSR." Vestnik statistiki, no. 6: 3-15.

_____. 1968. "Kak otrazhaetsia v mezhotraslevom balanse nalog s oborota." Vestnik statistiki, no. 8: 55-61.

_____. 1966. Mezhotraslevoi balans obshchestvennogo produkta. Moscow: Statistika.

Feshbach, M. 1972. "Soviet Industrial Labor and Productivity Statistics." In Soviet Economic Statistics, ed. V. G. Treml and J. P. Hardt, pp. 195-228. Durham, N.C.: Duke University Press.

Foreign Demographic Analysis Division (F.D.A.D.), U.S. Department of Commerce. 1972. Structure and Accounting of Working Capital in the U.S.S.R., International Population Reports Series, P95, No. 70. Washington, D.C.

Granberg, A. G. 1973. Optimizatsiia territorial'nykh proportsii norodnogo khoziaistva. Moscow: Ekonomika.

_____, ed. 1975. Mezhotraslevye balansy v analize territorial'-nykh proportsii SSSR. Novosibirsk: Nauka, Sibirskoe otdelenie.

Koropeckyj, I. S. 1975. "National Income of the Soviet Union Republics in 1970: Revision and Some Applications." In Economic Efficiency in the Soviet Union and Eastern Europe, ed. Z. Fallenbuchl. New York: Praeger.

Kossov, V. Y., and L. E. Mints. 1964. "Nekotorye itogi razrabotki mezhotraslevykh balansov po pribaltiiskomu ekonomicheskomu raionu." Vestnik statistiki, no. 6: 16-25.

Ministerstvo Finansov SSSR, Biudzhetnoe upravlenie. 1972. Gosudarstvennyi biudzhet SSSR i biudzhety soiuznykh respublik 1966-1970 gg. Moscow: Finansy.

Mints, L. E., ed. 1967. Mezhotraslevye issledovaniia v ekonomicheskikh raionakh. Moscow: Nauka.

Molodtsov, V. 1973. "Natural'no stoimostnyi mezhotraslevoi balans soiuznoi respubliki." Planovoe khoziaistvo, no. 12: 76-83.

Orlovskaia, A. Zh. 1973. "Analiz mezhotraslevykh proportsii v Latviiskoi SSR." In Statistika i elektronno-vychislitel'naia tehknika v ekonomike, ed. A. Ia. Boiarskii et al., pp. 199-207. Moscow: Statistika.

Raman, M., Z. Osis, K. Tsipe, and M. Shmulder. 1970. "Opyt razrabotki otchetnykh mezhotraslevykh balansov v Latviiskoi SSR i ikh znachenie dlia planirovaniia." Vestnik statistiki, no. 10: 12-18.

Shmulder, M., ed. 1970. Metodologicheskie problemy postroeniia mezhotraslevogo balansa soiuznoi respubliki (na primere Latviiskoi SSR). Riga: TsSU Latvian SSR.

_____ et al., eds. 1971. Dinamika mezhotraslevykh i mezh-respublikanskikh ekonomicheskikh sviazei Latviiskoi SSR. Riga: Tsentral'noe statisticheskoe upravlenie Latviiskoi SSR.

Spulber, N. 1969. The Soviet Economy. New York: Norton.

Treml, V. G. 1969. "A Note on Soviet Input-Output Tables." Soviet Studies 21, no. 1 (July): 21-34.

_____, B. Kostinsky, K. Kruger, and D. Gallik. 1973. Conversion of Soviet Input-Output Tables to Producers' Prices: the 1966 Reconstructed Table. U.S. Department of Commerce, F.D.A.D., Foreign Economic Report No. 1. Washington, D.C.: Government Printing Office.

_____, D. Gallik, B. Kostinsky, and K. Kruger. 1972. The Structure of the Soviet Economy. New York: Praeger.

Treml, V. G. and J. P. Hardt, eds. 1972. Soviet Economic Statistics. Durham, N.C.: Duke University Press.

Tsipe, K. A. 1971. Sistema mezhotraslevykh balansov soiuznoi respubliki. Moscow: Ekonomika.

_____, and R. I. Meerovich. 1967. "Otchetnyi mezhotraslevoi balans proizvodstva i raspredeleniia produktsii Latviiskoi SSR za 1961 god." In Mezhotraslevye issledovaniia v ekonomicheskikh raionakh, ed. L. E. Mints, pp. 212-42. Moscow: Nauka.

TsSU (Tsentral'noe statisticheskoe upravlenie pri Sovete ministrov SSSR). 1968. Trud v SSSR. Statisticheskii sbornik. Moscow: Statistika.

TsSU Latvia (Tsentral'noe statisticheskoe upravlenie pri Sovete ministrov Latviiskoi SSR). 1967. Latvia za gody Sovetskoi vlasti. Statisticheskii sbornik. Riga: Statistika.

TsSU Latvia. 1968. Narodnoe khoziaistvo Sovetskoi Latvii. Statisticheskii sbornik. Riga: Statistika.

TsSU Latvia. 1969. Latviiskaia SSR v tsifrakh v 1968 godu. Statisticheskii sbornik. Riga: Statistika.

TsSU Latvia. 1972. Narodnoe khoziaistvo Latviiskoi SSR v 1970 godu. Statisticheskii sbornik. Riga: Statistika.

TsSU Latvia. 1972a. Narodnoe khoziaistvo Latviiskoi SSR v 1971 godu. Statisticheskii sbornik. Riga: Statistika.

TsSU Latvia. 1973. Narodnoe khoziaistvo Latviiskoi SSR v 1973 godu. Statisticheskii ezhegodnik. Riga: Liesma.

CHAPTER

8

A STRUCTURAL COMPARISON
OF THE U.S. AND USSR
ECONOMIES BASED ON
INPUT-OUTPUT DATA
Laurie R. Kurtzweg

INTRODUCTION

The purpose of this study is to use input-output tables for the
United States and the Soviet Union to compare structural characteristics of their respective economies. In connection with this general
purpose, the specific focus of attention is on obtaining comparative

The present study is a condensed version of the author's unpublished Ph. D. dissertation, in connection with which assistance
was received from a number of individuals and organizations. The
author's dissertation committee made many helpful suggestions. The
author is especially grateful to her supervisor, Vladimir G. Treml,
for advice, constructive criticism, patience, and encouragement. In
addition to the committee members, Judith A. Thornton made valuable comments on early drafts and gave other generous assistance.
The USSR/East Europe Branch, Foreign Demographic Analysis Division of the Bureau of Economic Analysis, Department of Commerce,
provided data on computer cards. The author is grateful to Murray
Feshbach, chief of the branch, for this help and for general encouragement. Dimitri M. Gallik and Barry L. Kostinsky, both of the
same branch, answered numerous questions concerning interpretation of the data. The Interindustry Economics Division of the Bureau
of Economic Analysis, Department of Commerce, provided a number
of mimeographed documents about the U.S. input-output table. The
author is also grateful to Philip M. Ritz, chief of the division, for
furnishing data from the unpublished, 478-sector version of the table.
The author, of course, retains responsibility for errors and omissions.

369

information about corresponding processes of production in the two economies.

The use of input-output data to compare productive processes in the two economies can be placed in perspective by observing that this lies between two others in the range of approaches to such comparison. At one end of the range, an aggregate production function can be estimated for each economy. In this approach attention focuses on the relationship between total output of final goods and services, and inputs of primary factors such as labor and capital. At the other end of the range, a detailed study of a particular industry or group of industries can be made for each economy. In this approach attention focuses on technological relationships in a fairly narrow area of the economy.

Within the range, the input-output approach combines relatively detailed data for many industries with a consistent method for recording the relationships between detailed data and aggregative measures for the economy as a whole. It should be pointed out, however, that input-output data do not provide as much technological information about production in a particular industry as would a detailed study of that industry. Moreover, when input-output data are used to compare corresponding processes of production, certain assumptions must be made. For most of the comparisons in this study, it is assumed that both the U.S. and Soviet economies have optimal allocation of resources and prices that reflect relative scarcities. Although these assumptions are not strictly applicable to either economy, they are especially tenuous in the case of the Soviet economy.

This study is organized as follows. First, the input-output tables that are the sources of data are described: a 1963 table for the United States and a 1966 table for the Soviet Union. Problems of adjusting the data to achieve an acceptable degree of comparability with respect to classification of sectors and to accounting conventions are also discussed.

Next, an overview of the assumptions and methods on which comparisons of the tables are based is presented. The comparisons apply to pairs of corresponding columns of direct input coefficients. Subject to qualifications discussed in this section, they can be interpreted as comparisons of corresponding production functions.

The methods used in comparisons and the results are described next. Six statistical tests are conducted, two classical and four distribution-free. In the context of this study the results of the latter tests are considered more reliable than the results of the classical tests.

Finally, the conclusions drawn from the results of the comparisons are presented. In general, it is judged that the results show important structural similarities between the U.S. and Soviet economies.

PROBLEMS OF COMPARING THE U.S.
AND USSR TABLES

The U.S. input-output table for 1963 is valued in current (1963) producers' prices. It has been compiled in three different sizes by the Office of Business Economics, U.S. Department of Commerce (henceforth, OBE).[1] The largest table (which has not been published but has been available on computer tape, for sale) has 478 sectors in the interindustry quadrant, 10 columns in the final-demand quadrant, and one row in the value-added quadrant. The next largest table (OBE 1969b) has 367 sectors in the inter-industry quadrant, 10 columns in the final-demand quadrant, and one row in the value-added quadrant. The smallest table (OBE 1969a) has 85 sectors in the interindustry quadrant, six columns in the final-demand quadrant, and one row in the value-added quadrant.[2] The methods and concepts used in constructing the U.S. table are described in OBE (1970).

The USSR input-output table for 1966 has been reconstructed from a table originally prepared by the Central Statistical Adminis- tration of the USSR and has subsequently been converted from valua- tion in purchasers' prices to valuation in producers' prices. The original table has 110 sectors in the interindustry quadrant, 21 sec- tors in the final-demand quadrant, and 21 sectors in the value- added quadrant. It is valued in current (1966) purchasers' prices and has never been published in full. This table has been recon- structed from Soviet sources by V. G. Treml, D. M. Gallik, B. L. Kostinsky, and K. W. Kruger (1972). The reconstructed table has 76 sectors in the interindustry quadrant, three sectors in the final- demand quadrant, and three sectors in the value-added quadrant. It is valued in current purchasers' prices. This table has been con- verted to valuation in current producers' prices by Treml, Kostinsky, Kruger, and Gallik (1973). The reconstructed table in producers' prices has 71 sectors in the interindustry quadrant, three sectors in the final-demand quadrant, and four sectors in the value-added quad- rant. It is this table that is analyzed in the present study.[3]

Any empirical input-output table is of course subject to errors in data. It is important to note, however, that the USSR table studied here involves two stages of error to which the U.S. table is not sub- ject: reconstruction from data not published in full, and conversion from purchasers' to producers' prices. Errors at these stages can- not be assessed quantitatively, but their presence should be kept in mind.

Problems of adjusting the data to achieve an acceptable degree of comparability between the U.S. and USSR tables are discussed below. At the outset, it should be noted that fundamental political and organizational differences between the U.S. and Soviet economic systems cause some problems of comparability. An important problem in this regard stems from the different roles played by prices in the two systems. In the Soviet economy prices do not, in general, reflect relative scarcities. A single commodity, moreover, can be sold at different prices to different purchasers. Consequently, the Soviet price system poses special difficulties (see the discussion of methods of comparison below) for the interpretation of an input-output table in value terms. The rest of the data problems discussed here concern incomparabilities in classification of sectors and in accounting conventions.

Classification of Sectors

The major adjustment required for comparability is reconciliation of the different schemes according to which sectors are classified in the two tables. A reconciliation worked out by D. M. Gallik (1971) is used in this study. It is reproduced in Table 8.9. For the reconciliation, sectors from the 478-order U.S. table have been selected and, when appropriate, aggregated in such a way that the product list of a new sector in the reconciled U.S. table corresponds as closely as possible to that of a given sector in the 71-order Soviet table.[4]

In reconciling the sector classification schemes, the objective is to find pairs of comparable sectors so that the only intercountry differences remaining between sectors in the same pair are differences in methods of producing the same products. The method of reconciliation attempts to match as closely as possible lists of products produced by sectors in the same pair. Even if product lists can be matched perfectly, however, it is likely that intercountry differences will remain between products produced, as well as production methods used, by sectors in the same pair. For example, the share of a given single product in the output of one sector is likely to differ from the share of the same product in the output of the paired sector. Moreover, a given product that is essentially the same in both sectors of a pair may have somewhat different specifications between sectors. It is not possible to adjust for differences of the kind just described, but their presence should be kept in mind.

The results of the reconciliation are presented in Table 8.1, which shows that there are 63 pairs of comparable sectors in the reconciled tables. In addition to the comparable sectors, groups of uncomparable leftover sectors remain in both tables after reconciliation. Nevertheless, transactions among only comparable sectors account for a large share of all interindustry transactions: 94 percent in the U.S. table and 97 percent in the USSR table.

It should be pointed out that some of the pairs of sectors in Table 8.1 show a lesser degree of comparability than others. The comparability of sectors in a pair could be improved in a number of cases by appropriate aggregation of selected pairs. The comparisons in this study, however, are conducted at as disaggregated a level as possible. They are all based on the 63-sector reconciled tables.

Accounting Conventions

Problems of comparability of accounting conventions used in the U.S. and USSR tables are discussed below. A number of the problems arise because of deficiencies in the conventions of one or both tables. Since data that can be used to correct the deficiencies are often unavailable, it is not feasible to adjust for most of the problems. In fact, the only adjustment made for purposes of this study is one for different treatment of imports in the two tables, and that adjustment is incomplete.

In the USSR table the interindustry quadrant shows only trans-actions among sectors considered productive, and most services are considered nonproductive.[5] For nonproductive services, pur-chases from productive sectors are recorded in the final-demand quadrant, and sales to productive sectors are recorded in the value-added quadrant. In the U.S. table all transactions among service and other interindustry sectors are recorded in the interindustry quadrant. Thus the boundaries between the interindustry and final-demand quadrants on the one hand, and between the interindustry and value-added quadrants on the other, differ for the two tables.

Data for the comparisons in this study apply only to reconciled sectors in the interindustry quadrants of both tables. The difference in treatment of services therefore limits the number of sectors that can be compared. The difference in boundaries between quadrants, however, poses no problems, and no adjustment is made for it.[6]

In the reconstruction of the USSR table, uncertainties about methods of recording three important kinds of data could not be re-solved: foreign trade, military expenditures, and private economic activities. The treatment of foreign trade is discussed later in this section. Methods of recording military expenditures in general are not clear in Soviet sources, and expenditures for military hardware are a particularly important problem. It does seem that expendi-tures for hardware are not included in gross investment. Private economic activities include two activities that receive appreciable

TABLE 8.1

Reconciled Scheme for Classification of Sectors: Comparable Sectors in the U.S. Input-Output Table for 1963 and the USSR Input-Output Table for 1966

Number of Sector (63-Order)	Name of Sector in 71-Order USSR Table	Number of Sector in 71-Order USSR Table
1	Ferrous ores	1
2	Ferrous metals and coke products	2, 5
3	Nonferrous ores	3
4	Nonferrous metals	4
5	Refractory materials	6
6	Industrial metal products	7
7	Coal	8
8	Oil extraction, gas, and oil shales	9, 11, 13
9	Oil refining	10
10	Electric and thermal power	14
11	Energy and power machinery and equipment	15
12	Electrotechnical machinery and equipment	16
13	Cable products	17
14	Machine tools	18
15	Forging/pressing machinery and equipment	19
16	Tools and dies	21
17	Precision instruments	22
18	Mining and metallurgical machinery and equipment	23
19	Pumps and compressors	24
20	Logging and paper machinery and equipment	25
21	Light industry machinery and equipment	26
22	Food industry machinery and equipment	27
23	Printing machinery and equipment	28
24	Hoisting/transporting machinery and equipment	29
25	Construction machinery and equipment	30
26	Transportation machinery and equipment	32
27	Automobiles	33

Number of Sector (63-Order)	Name of Sector in 71-Order USSR Table	Number of Sector in 71-Order USSR Table
28	Tractors and agricultural machinery and equipment	34
29	Bearings	35
30	Other machinebuilding	36
31	Sanitary engineering products	37
32	Other metal wares	38
33	Metal structures	39
34	Abrasives	41
35	Mineral chemistry products	42
36	All other chemicals	43
37	Logging	44
38	Sawmills and woodworking	45
39	Furniture	46
40	Other woodworking	47
41	Paper and pulp	48
42	Wood chemistry products	49
43	Cement	50
44	Prefab concrete	51
45	Other construction materials	52
46	Glass and porcelain	53
47	Textiles	54
48	Sewn goods	55
49	Other light industry	56
50	Fish products	57
51	Meat products	58
52	Dairy products	59
53	Sugar	60
54	Flour and cereals	61
55	Bread and confections	62
56	Other foods	63
57	Industry, not elsewhere classified	64
58	Construction	65
59	Crops	66
60	Animal husbandry	67
61	Transportation and communications	69
62	Trade and distribution	70
63	Other branches of material production	71

Source: D. M. Gallik, "Sector Correlation, USSR 1966-US 1963," Working Paper SIP-33 (McLean, Va.: Research Analysis Corporation, 1971).

inputs of labor: construction of residences by prospective owners, and sales of farm products by private growers. Methods of recording these activities are not known (Treml et al. 1972, pp. 50-51, 53).

Diagonal entries are recorded in the USSR table by methods that are inconsistent from sector to sector. For most sectors diagonal entries exclude inputs produced and used inside a single plant, but for some sectors, especially in agriculture and in the light and food industries, diagonal entries include such intraplant turnover (Treml et al. 1972, p. 46).

Interindustry transactions in the USSR table apparently include flows of some capital goods with flows of current goods (Treml et al. 1972, p. 45). The inclusion of flows of capital goods in the interindustry quadrant can be expected to distort the apparent distribution of products to interindustry uses, as opposed to final uses, and also to add an element of instability to the apparent uses of inputs by producing sectors.

In the interindustry quadrant of the USSR table, the construction row consists entirely of zero entries. Like the construction sector in the U.S. table, the USSR sector includes both new construction and maintenance and repair construction; unlike the U.S. sector, the USSR sector has its entire output defined as part of gross investment (Treml et al. 1972, p. 48). It would be possible to adjust for the difference in treatment of construction by redistributing the entire output of the U.S. row to gross investment, but this procedure has not been followed.

The producers' prices at which transactions are valued in the U.S. table are defined so as to include "Federal and State and local excise taxes collected and paid by the producer" (OBE 1970, p. 8, fn. 1). Such taxes should be removed from producers' prices, as turnover taxes have been removed from producers' prices in the USSR table.

Because of imperfections in the reconciliation of sector classification schemes of the U.S. and USSR tables, a given product may belong to a reconciled sector in one table, but a leftover sector in the other table. When this happens, leftover and comparable sectors overlap. Since leftover sectors are more important in the U.S. than in the USSR table, moreover, interindustry transactions among comparable sectors are likely to be biased downward in the U.S. table relative to the USSR table. Leftover sectors are involved in 6 percent and 3 percent of all interindustry transactions in the U.S. and USSR tables, respectively.

Data for input-output tables are first reported by establishments that produce goods and services. A single establishment, however, can produce a variety of goods and services. In national income and product accounts an establishment is classified in a sector according to its primary product. Other, secondary products of the establishment are classified in the same sector as the primary product. For input-output accounts, in which attention is focused on products instead of establishments, such treatment of secondary products is not desirable. Secondary products are reclassified, at least partially, by means of a commodity-establishment adjustment.

Data for the U.S. table are collected on an establishment basis, then adjusted so that they are recorded on a transfer basis. The gross output of sector i is adjusted by letting the secondary commodities produced by sector i remain counted in the gross output of sector i but also transferring them to the gross outputs of the sectors where they are primary. A transfer from sector i to sector k is recorded as if it were a sale from sector i to sector k. Transfers like this let all sales of commodity k to using sectors be recorded as if the sales were made by sector k (OBE 1970, pp. 10-11).

Use of the transfer basis in the U.S. table makes it possible to create dummy sectors that do not engage in production. The row entries of a dummy sector show the distribution to various users of the output of a group of related products; the column entries show transfers of the products from the sectors where they are produced to the dummy sector. The table uses dummy sectors to record business travel, entertainment, and gifts; office supplies; and scrap, used and secondhand goods.

Data for the USSR table are collected on a modified establishment basis. Purchases of inputs are reported by establishments that produce both primary and secondary products, but the inputs purchased are identified by product rather than by producing sector. The data collected are then adjusted so that they are recorded on an approximately commodity basis. The gross output of sector i is adjusted by subtracting from it the outputs of secondary commodities produced by sector i. The outputs of secondary commodities are then added to the gross outputs of the sectors to which the commodities are primary. The inputs used by sector i to produce secondary commodities are subtracted from the inputs purchased by sector i, and additions to purchases by sector i are estimated in order to account for inputs used by other sectors to produce commodity i. An addition is calculated by assuming that the input coefficient that shows use of commodity k to produce commodity i in sector i also applies to use of commodity k to produce commodity i in any other sector (Treml et al. 1972, pp. 126-27).

Data in the interindustry quadrants of the two tables are thus not comparable with respect to treatment of secondary products. Moreover, it is not feasible to adjust the data to make them comparable.[7] In terms of its effect on comparability of the tables,

treatment of secondary products is probably the most serious instance of incomparability of accounting conventions.

The U.S. and USSR tables differ in a number of ways with respect to treatment of foreign trade. Two special features of foreign
trade data in the USSR table should be noted immediately. First,
only trade in material commodities is recorded in the table. This
convention is in accord with the general Soviet distinction between
productive and nonproductive economic activities (Treml et al. 1972,
pp. 147–48). Second, the USSR table has two balances of foreign
trade. Soviet domestic prices are kept separate, as a matter of
policy, from world market prices, and Soviet foreign trade transactions are carried out at world market prices. The balance in foreign trade prices is calculated as the difference between "foreign
exchange earnings from the sale of exports and the foreign exchange
paid for imports," where the difference is converted to rubles at
the official exchange rate (Treml et al. 1972, p. 149). This balance
is then converted from foreign trade prices to domestic prices by
means of a conversion coefficient, and the resulting converted balance is included both in losses, in the final–demand quadrant, and
in the value-added entry for the trade sector.[8] The balance of foreign trade in domestic prices is calculated as "the difference between revenues from the sale of imports to domestic users and payments to domestic producers of exports made by the state trade
agencies" (Treml et al. 1972, p. 149). Exports minus imports
then makes up part of final demand.

Except for the special features of foreign trade data just described, the two tables record exports in comparable ways. The
tables differ further, however, with regard to treatment of imports.
Imports can be conceptually separated into two groups. Those that
can be considered substitutes for domestically produced products
are called competitive imports, and those that cannot are called
noncompetitive imports.

In the U.S. table imports are shown in two sectors, both of
which have row entries but no column entries: directly allocated
imports and transferred imports. Competitive imports of product i
are included with domestic production of product i in row i of the
interindustry quadrant, except as noted below. They are also recorded in the transferred imports row of column i. Noncompetitive
imports of various products purchased by sector i are shown in the
directly allocated imports row of column i. All imports, competitive and noncompetitive, that are sold to final demand "in substantially the same form in which they were imported" are recorded in
the directly allocated imports row of the appropriate final-demand
column (OBE 1970, p. 12).

In the USSR table, imports in domestic prices are entered with a minus sign in the final-demand quadrant. Both competitive imports of product i and noncompetitive imports that are classified with sector i are included with domestic production of product i in row i of the interindustry quadrant (Treml et al. 1972, pp. 43, 147).

An adjustment is made for only one of the differences in treatment of foreign trade data between the two tables. Gross output includes imports in the U.S. table but excludes imports (in domestic prices) in the USSR table. Therefore, the gross output of sector i in the U.S. table is adjusted by subtracting from it total imports (competitive and noncompetitive) recorded in column i.

METHODS OF COMPARISON

This section provides background material for the comparisons described in the sections on column tests. First, some brief remarks are made about methods of comparison employed in previous international and intertemporal studies of input-output tables. Next, a review appears of the model on which an input-output table in value terms is based. The notation used in the discussion of the column tests is introduced. Finally, the methods of comparison employed in the tests are outlined.

A review of the large volume of literature concerning international and intertemporal comparisons of input-output tables is not made here. Two major approaches, however, can be identified in the literature. The first approach, attributable to W. W. Leontief (1951, pp. 152-59, 214-18) involves estimating the vector of gross outputs for one table on the basis of the vector of final demands for that table and the matrix of direct-plus-indirect input coefficients for another table. The second approach, also attributable to Leontief (1953), involves analyzing the differences between the matrixes of direct input coefficients for two tables.[9] All of the comparisons in this study take the second approach.

Previous international comparisons of U.S. and USSR tables have been made by N. B. Long (1970) and by V. G. Treml (1968). Long deals with a U.S. table for 1947 and a USSR table for 1959; Treml, with U.S. tables for 1947 and 1958 and a USSR table for 1959.

Before the present comparisons are described, the open, static model that serves as a basis for input-output tables in value terms will be reviewed. At the same time, the notation used in the rest of this study will be established. Consider the input-output table in value terms for an economy in which resources are allocated optimally and prices reflect relative scarcities. Denote a typical element of the interindustry quadrant by $x_{ij} = p_i q_{ij}$, which shows the value of inputs from sector i used to produce the current value of output of sector j. Let the final-demand quadrant be represented by a single column with typical element $Y_i = p_i F_i$, and let the value-added quadrant be represented by a single row with typical element $V_j = p_L L_j$. The gross output in value terms of sector i is equal to the sum of all entries in row i of the interindustry quadrant plus the entry in row i of the final-demand quadrant or, equivalently, to the sum of all entries in column i of the interindustry quadrant plus the entry in column i of the value-added quadrant. Denote the gross output of sector i by $X_i = p_i Q_i$.

The transactions table just discussed can be converted to a table of direct input coefficients. Divide each element in the inter-industry quadrant and each element in the value-added quadrant of the transactions matrix by the gross output of the sector in whose column the element is located, as follows:

$$a_{ij} = x_{ij} / X_j \qquad\qquad \begin{aligned} &(i = 1,\ldots,n) \\ &(j = 1,\ldots,n) \end{aligned}$$

$$v_j = V_j / X_j \qquad\qquad (j = 1,\ldots,n)$$

Since optimal allocation of resources and scarcity prices have been assumed, column j of direct coefficients in value terms can be interpreted as a Cobb-Douglas production function for sector j. Column j, it should be noted, includes coefficients for inputs of both intermediate products and primary factors. The production function can be written as follows:

$$Q_j = k_j \, q_{1j}^{a_{1j}} \, q_{2j}^{a_{2j}} \, \cdots \, q_{nj}^{a_{nj}} \, L_j^{v_j}$$

where k_j is a constant for sector j.[10]

The assumption of optimal resource allocation amounts to an assumption of perfect competition for a market economy, or to an assumption of optimal allocation by plan for a centrally planned economy. If the assumption cannot be made, column j must be considered to reflect other economic information besides the technical information conveyed by a production function. Along with the assumption of optimal resource allocation, the further assumption is made that the prices at which the input-output table is valued are scarcity prices that are identical for all purchasers of the same output. While the assumptions of optimal resource allocation and scarcity prices are not strictly applicable to either the U.S. or the Soviet economy, they are especially tenuous in the case of the Soviet

economy. A particularly important problem is that Soviet prices
are differentiated by purchaser, rather than being identical for all
purchasers of the same output.

Even if optimal resource allocation and scarcity prices could
be assumed, however, there are further problems with regard to
the interpretation of column j as a production function. The data
for the present comparisons do not include all input coefficients in
column j. Rather, coefficients that show inputs to column j from
uncomparable leftover sectors and from primary factors are excluded. Thus the data for column j can at most be considered to
represent the interindustry portion of the production function for
sector j. Moreover, the data problems discussed earlier in this
chapter complicate the interpretation of input coefficients in column j.
This is especially true of problems associated with the treatment of
secondary products.

In many of the present comparisons, reference is made to
corresponding entries in the U.S. and USSR tables. Superscripts
are therefore used to avoid confusion between entries in different
tables: superscript "US" designates the U.S. table, and superscript
"SU" designates the USSR table.

Comparisons of pairs of corresponding columns of direct input
coefficients in the two tables are described below.[11] The comparisons are considered important because of the economic interpretation of columns as production functions. This interpretation, of
course, is subject to the qualifications discussed above. The methods
of comparison selected are ones for which results can be evaluated
statistically. First, three tests of the null hypothesis that a pair of
corresponding columns are identical in the U.S. and USSR tables are
presented, followed by three tests of the null hypothesis that a pair
of corresponding columns are independent.

COLUMN TESTS FOR IDENTITY

In this section and in the following one, pairs of corresponding
columns from the input-output tables for the United States and the
USSR are compared, one pair at a time. Observations on a pair of
columns consist of pairs of direct input coefficients from the two
tables, which are reconciled and adjusted as described in the discussion of problems of comparison, above. Because the reconciled
tables have 63 pairs of comparable sectors, the number of observations on a pair of columns is 63. When both of the paired input coefficients for an observation are zero, however, that observation is
disregarded for purposes of the tests. That is, the number of observations is taken as the number of pairs of coefficients such that at
least one member of each pair is not zero.[12]

Description of the Tests

In the tests of identity described below, differences between corresponding input coefficients in a given pair of columns are used to evaluate whether there is a significant difference between the columns taken as entireties. Z. S. Wurtele (1959) has developed in detail a rationale for using the Student matched pair t test to assess the significance of the difference between two columns of direct coefficients from input-output tables in physical terms. In this section, an extension of Wurtele's rationale serves as a basis for using the Student test to assess the significance of the difference between columns of direct coefficients from tables in value terms.[13]

The differences between pairs of corresponding coefficients in columns j of the U.S. and USSR tables can be denoted by e_{ij}:

$$a_{ij}^{US} = a_{ij}^{SU} + e_{ij} \qquad\qquad (i = 1, \ldots, n)$$

If the e_{ij} observed for the pair of columns j can be regarded as random fluctuations about a mean of zero, it can be concluded that the difference between columns j is insignificant. Because input coefficients are estimated with zero degrees of freedom, observations on columns j provide only one estimate of each e_{ij}. If certain assumptions are made, however, all the e_{ij} can be treated as independent observations from a single normal distribution. The null hypothesis that the mean of the distribution is zero can then be tested by the Student test.

Three assumptions are necessary for such a procedure: (1) The e_{ij} are independent of each other. (2) The e_{ij} are all normally distributed. (3) The e_{ij} all have equal variance. Each e_{ij} can be considered to be composed of three error terms: the difference between the unobserved, true coefficients that are the counterparts of a_{ij}^{US} and a_{ij}^{SU}, plus the difference between a_{ij}^{US} and its true counterpart, minus the difference between a_{ij}^{SU} and its true counterpart. The first assumption is then justified if the size of the difference between the observed and true values of a given coefficient in column j of either table does not affect the size of the difference between the observed and true values of any other coefficient in column j. The second assumption is justified if the number of observations is large and the Central Limit Theorem applies. The third assumption is justified if the differences between the observed and true values of coefficients in column j of each table reflect producer behavior in which more expensive inputs are used more carefully than less expensive inputs, so that the variance of the cost of an input is the same for all inputs.

Let $E(e_{ij})$ denote the mean of the observed e_{ij}, and let var(e_{ij}) denote their variance. The t statistic for the Student test is then calculated by the following formula:

$$ST_j = \frac{E(e_{ij})}{\sqrt{var(e_{ij})/(n-1)}}.$$

where n is the number of observations on which the test is based. The significance of the test statistic ST_j is evaluated by comparing ST_j with a table of the t distribution, where the number of degrees of freedom is taken as (n - 1).

Two distribution-free statistical tests are described below. Both are based on a rationale similar to that for the classical test just described, but the former tests differ from the latter in two important ways. First, the distribution-free tests have null hypotheses that differ somewhat from the null hypothesis for the classical test. Second, the distribution-free tests require different, less restrictive assumptions than the classical test.[14]

Consider again corresponding columns j in the input-output tables for the United States and the USSR, and let e_{ij} be defined as before. Like the Student test, the Wilcoxon signed rank test assesses the significance of the difference between columns j in terms of the e_{ij}. While the Student test is based on the actual values, or signed magnitudes, of the e_{ij}, however, the Wilcoxon test is based on the ranks of the absolute values of the e_{ij} taken in combination with the signs of the e_{ij}. If the e_{ij} can be regarded as symmetrically distributed about a median of zero, it can be concluded that differences between the columns are insignificant.

More precisely, the null hypothesis of the Wilcoxon test is that each of the e_{ij} (i = 1,...,n) is symmetrically distributed about a median of zero. Depending on the distributions of the a_{ij}^{US} and the a_{ij}^{SU}, the null hypothesis can be interpreted in two somewhat different ways. If each a_{ij}^{US} and each a_{ij}^{SU} is distributed symmetrically and the null hypothesis is true, then columns j have the same median. If each a_{ij}^{US} and each a_{ij}^{SU} is distributed asymmetrically and the null hypothesis is true, then columns j are identical. Generally, the test requires three assumptions about the e_{ij}: (1) The e_{ij} are independent of each other. (2) None of the e_{ij} are equal to zero. (3) None of the e_{ij} are tied in absolute value.[15]

In order to calculate the test statistic for the Wilcoxon test, let the following notation be introduced:

$$s_{ij}^{+} = \begin{cases} 1 \text{ if } e_{ij} > 0 \\ 0 \text{ if } e_{ij} < 0 \end{cases}$$

$$s_{ij}^{-} = \begin{cases} 1 \text{ if } e_{ij} < 0 \\ 0 \text{ if } e_{ij} > 0 \end{cases}$$

$$R_{ij} = \text{Rank of } |e_{ij}| \text{ over } i = 1, \ldots, n$$

Then two complementary test statistics can be calculated for columns j:

$$WT_j^{+} = \sum_i s_{ij}^{+} R_{ij}^{e}$$

$$WT_j^{-} = \sum_i s_{ij}^{-} R_{ij}^{e}$$

and the significance of the test can be evaluated by comparing the smaller of WT_j^{+} and WT_j^{-} with a table of critical values for the Wilcoxon test.[16]

Again consider corresponding columns j in the input-output tables for the United States and the USSR, and let e_{ij} be defined as before. Like the Student and Wilcoxon tests, the Sign test for the median difference assesses the significance of the difference between columns j in terms of the e_{ij}. Unlike the other two tests, however, the Sign test is based only on the signs of the e_{ij}. If the e_{ij} can be regarded as distributed about a median of zero, it can be concluded that differences between the columns are insignificant.

More precisely, the null hypothesis of the Sign test is that each of the e_{ij} ($i = 1, \ldots, n$) is distributed about a median of zero.[17] This test requires two assumptions about the e_{ij}: (1) The e_{ij} are independent of each other. (2) None of the e_{ij} are equal to zero.

In order to calculate the test statistic for the Sign test, let s_{ij}^{+} and s_{ij}^{-} be defined as before. Then two complementary test statistics can be calculated for columns j:

$$ZT_j^{+} = \sum_i s_{ij}^{+}$$

$$ZT_j^{-} = \sum_i s_{ij}^{-}$$

and the significance of the test can be evaluated by comparing the smaller of ZT_j^{+} and ZT_j^{-} with a table of critical values for the Sign test.[18]

Three caveats on the present applications of these tests should be noted.[19] First, if the procedure for estimating transactions data in a table requires that the entries in column j add up to a previously fixed total, the assumption that the e_{ij} are independent of each other will be violated. Second, if data are unavailable for certain pairs of corresponding coefficients in columns j, those pairs may be omitted from the tests, provided that sizes of the differences between coefficients in the pairs are not related to the availability of data. Third, even if the tests show no significant difference between columns j taken as entireties, it is possible that a reapplication of the tests to a smaller group of selected pairs of coefficients in columns j would show a significant difference. This situation may arise if the coefficients for inputs of products of one group are significantly larger in column j of the U.S. table, while the coefficients for inputs of products of another group are significantly larger in column j of the USSR table.

Two of the three tests have been employed in previous empirical studies comparing direct input coefficients from different input-output tables. Watanabe (1961, pp. 348-49) has used the Wilcoxon test according to the method described here. C. A. K. Lovell (1967, p. 3) has used the Student test, but apparently not according to the method described here.

Results of the Tests

Each of the three column tests of identity is conducted on all pairs of corresponding columns from the reconciled input-output tables for the United States and the USSR. The results of the tests are presented below, but first a caveat on their interpretation is in order. Any statistical test is designed in such a way that the probability of committing a Type I error (rejecting a true null hypothesis) can be set at a level considered reasonable by the tester. The probability of committing a Type II error (accepting a false null hypothesis), however, is unknown to the tester. A test that results in acceptance of the null hypothesis thus does not have as straightforward an interpretation as a test that results in rejection of the null hypothesis. Therefore, when a test discussed below indicates that differences for a pair of columns are not significant, it should be kept in mind that the result of the test is subject, to an unknown extent, to Type II error.

For each test, the value of the test statistic for any pair of columns is evaluated for significance by means of a two-tailed test of the appropriate null hypothesis at the .10 significance level. Table 8.2 shows whether the null hypothesis is accepted or rejected

TABLE 8.2

Evaluation of the Significance of the Results of Three
Statistical Tests of Identity, by Sector

Sector[a]	Sign Test[b]	Wilcoxon Test[b]	Student Test[b]
1	REJ (USSR)	REJ (USSR)	ACC
2	REJ (USSR)	ACC	ACC
3	REJ (USSR)	ACC	ACC
4	ACC	ACC	ACC
5	REJ (USSR)	ACC	ACC
6	ACC	ACC	ACC
7	REJ (USSR)	REJ (USSR)	ACC
8	REJ (USSR)	REJ (USSR)	ACC
9	REJ (USSR)	REJ (USSR)	ACC
10	REJ (USSR)	REJ (USSR)	ACC
11	ACC	ACC	ACC
12	ACC	ACC	ACC
13	REJ (USSR)	ACC	ACC
14	ACC	ACC	ACC
15	ACC	ACC	REJ (U.S.)
16	ACC	ACC	ACC
17	ACC	ACC	ACC
18	ACC	ACC	REJ (U.S.)
19	ACC	ACC	ACC
20	REJ (USSR)	ACC	ACC
21	ACC	ACC	ACC
22	REJ (USSR)	ACC	ACC
23	ACC	ACC	ACC
24	ACC	ACC	ACC
25	REJ (USSR)	ACC	ACC
26	REJ (USSR)	REJ (USSR)	ACC
27	REJ (USSR)	ACC	ACC
28	ACC	ACC	ACC
29	REJ (USSR)	REJ (USSR)	ACC
30	ACC	ACC	ACC
31	ACC	ACC	ACC
32	ACC	ACC	REJ (U.S.)
33	ACC	ACC	ACC
34	REJ (USSR)	REJ (USSR)	ACC
35	REJ (USSR)	ACC	ACC

Sector[a]	Sign Test[b]	Wilcoxon Test[b]	Student Test[b]
36	REJ (USSR)	REJ (USSR)	ACC
37	REJ (USSR)	REJ (USSR)	ACC
38	ACC	ACC	ACC
39	ACC	ACC	ACC
40	REJ (USSR)	REJ (USSR)	ACC
41	REJ (USSR)	REJ (USSR)	ACC
42	REJ (USSR)	REJ (USSR)	ACC
43	REJ (USSR)	REJ (USSR)	REJ (USSR)
44	REJ (USSR)	REJ (USSR)	REJ (USSR)
45	REJ (USSR)	ACC	ACC
46	REJ (USSR)	REJ (USSR)	ACC
47	ACC	ACC	ACC
48	REJ (USSR)	ACC	ACC
49	REJ (USSR)	ACC	ACC
50	REJ (USSR)	REJ (USSR)	ACC
51	REJ (USSR)	ACC	ACC
52	REJ (USSR)	ACC	ACC
53	REJ (USSR)	REJ (USSR)	ACC
54	ACC	REJ (U.S.)	ACC
55	REJ (USSR)	ACC	ACC
56	REJ (USSR)	ACC	ACC
57	REJ (USSR)	REJ (USSR)	ACC
58	ACC	ACC	ACC
59	ACC	ACC	ACC
60	ACC	ACC	ACC
61	ACC	ACC	ACC
62	ACC	REJ (USSR)	ACC
63	REJ (U.S.)	REJ (U.S.)	REJ (U.S.)

[a]For sector names corresponding to the numbers given, see Table 8.1.

[b]Significance is evaluated by means of a two-tailed test of the null hypothesis at the .10 significance level. The symbol "ACC" indicates that the null hypothesis is accepted, the symbol "REJ" that the null hypothesis is rejected. For each sector where the null hypothesis is rejected, the letters in parentheses following "REJ" show the table, U.S. or USSR, in which the coefficients for that sector's column are larger.

Source: Compiled by the author.

in each case. When the significance of the Sign test is evaluated, the null hypothesis is rejected for 36 and accepted for 27 of the 63 sectors. Of the 36 sectors where the null hypothesis is rejected, 35 tend to have larger coefficients for the sector's column in the USSR table than for the sector's column in the U.S. table. When the significance of the Wilcoxon test is evaluated, the null hypothesis is rejected for 22 and accepted for 41 of the sectors. Of the 22 sectors where the null hypothesis is rejected, 20 tend to have larger coefficients for the sector's column in the USSR table. When the significance of the Student test is evaluated, the null hypothesis is rejected for six and accepted for 57 of the 63 sectors.[20] Of the six sectors where the null hypothesis is rejected, four tend to have a larger average value of coefficients for the sector's column in the U.S. table.

In general, the results of the three tests of identity are more in conflict than in agreement. Because of the simplicity of its assumptions, the Sign test is considered most reliable when conflicting results arise. The results of the Sign test are therefore discussed in further detail below.

For each of the 36 sectors where the null hypothesis of the Sign test is rejected, it can be concluded that the median difference between corresponding coefficients in the sector's columns in the U.S. and USSR tables is significantly different from zero. Thus for just under 60 percent of the 63 sectors tested, the Sign test supports the hypothesis that the columns by which a sector is represented in the U.S. and USSR tables are not identical. For all but one of the 36 sectors where the null hypothesis of the Sign test is rejected, the differences between corresponding coefficients for a sector show that the sector's column in the USSR table tends to have larger coefficients than the sector's column in the U.S. table.

It must be noted that conclusions about the comparative efficiency of input use by a pair of sectors in the two tables cannot be drawn from these findings. First, rejection of the null hypothesis of the Sign test does not necessarily imply that the sector with a greater number of larger coefficients has a larger average value of coefficients (Bradley 1968, pp. 172-73).[21] Second, conclusions about comparative efficiency would require that direct input coefficients in value terms for the two tables be adjusted for differences in prices and qualities of corresponding inputs. Such conclusions would also require information about inputs not only of intermediate products, but also of labor and capital.

For each of the 27 sectors where the null hypothesis of the Sign test is accepted, it can be concluded that the median difference between corresponding coefficients in the sector's columns in the U.S. and USSR tables has not been shown to be significantly different from zero. Thus for just over 40 percent of the 63 sectors tested, the Sign test does not discredit the hypothesis that the columns by which a sector is represented in the U.S. and USSR tables are identical.

Table 8.3 shows the distribution of the 27 sectors where the null hypothesis of the Sign test is accepted among major groups of sectors. Consider the major groups that include four or more sectors. There are three groups where the null hypothesis is accepted for an especially small proportion of sectors--fuel and power, construction materials and glass, and food--and two groups where the null hypothesis is accepted for an especially large proportion of sectors--machinebuilding and metalworking. The finding that sectors in the machinebuilding and metalworking groups tend to show significant differences between their U.S. and USSR columns less often than sectors in other industrial groups is of some interest. Roughly, sectors in the former groups can be expected to purchase intermediate inputs that have undergone some processing and to sell outputs (on current or capital account) to other producing sectors. That is, such sectors are likely to be relatively insulated from intercountry differences in patterns of consumption and in availability of natural resources.

The relationship between the results of the Sign test and the results of the other tests for identity is discussed below. While the null hypothesis of the Sign test is rejected for 36 sectors, the (somewhat different) null hypothesis of the Wilcoxon test is rejected for 22 sectors. Table 8.2 shows that for 20 of the 22 sectors where the null hypothesis of the Wilcoxon test is rejected, the null hypothesis of the Sign test is also rejected, and that for the 20 sectors the two tests agree as to which table has larger coefficients. The (still different) null hypothesis of the Student test is rejected for only six sectors. Table 8.2 shows that for three of the six sectors where the null hypothesis of the Student test is rejected, the null hypotheses of the Sign and Wilcoxon tests are also rejected; for the other three sectors, neither the null hypothesis of the Sign test nor the null hypothesis of the Wilcoxon test is rejected. Thus results differ among all three tests, but the results of the Sign and Wilcoxon tests are more similar than the results of the Sign and Student tests.

The results of the Sign test, then, are that for slightly more than 40 percent of the sectors tested, the hypothesis that the two columns by which a sector is represented in the U.S. and USSR tables are identical cannot be rejected. The degree to which these results show important similarities between the tables is a question that must be decided subjectively. In the light of special problems of this study, however, the results can be considered to show important similarities. First, it could hardly have been expected that all of the sectors tested would turn out to be identical. Second, there are unresolved data problems that can be expected to cause at least some similar sectors to appear dissimilar.[22] Third, the results of the Sign test tend to indicate fewer similarities than the results of other tests conducted in this study. Thus the Sign test can be considered the most stringent criterion, among the present tests, of similarity.

TABLE 8.3

Sectors in which the Null Hypothesis of the Sign Test
Is Accepted, by Major Group of Sectors

Major Group of Sectors*	Number of Sectors in Group	Number of Sectors where H_0 of Sign Test Is Accepted
Metallurgy	6	2
Fuels and power	4	0
Machinebuilding	20	13
Metalworking	4	3
Chemicals	2	0
Wood and paper	6	2
Construction materials and glass	4	0
Textiles and apparel	3	1
Food	7	1
Industry not elsewhere classified	1	0
Construction	1	1
Agriculture	2	2
Transportation and communications	1	1
Trade and distribution	1	1
Other branches	1	0
Total	63	27

*Sectors that belong to the major groups are listed in Table 8.10.

<u>Source</u>: Compiled by the author.

COLUMN TESTS FOR INDEPENDENCE

In this section pairs of corresponding columns from the input-output tables for the United States and the USSR are again compared, one pair at a time. As before, observations on a pair of columns consist of pairs of direct input coefficients from the two tables, and the number of observations is taken as the number of pairs of co-efficients such that at least one member of each pair is not zero.

Description of the Tests

Three tests are described below that evaluate whether a pair of columns are statistically independent of each other or there is a significant functional relationship between the columns. The test described first is classical, and the two tests described subsequently are distribution-free.

The classical test evaluates whether one column of a pair can be expressed as a linear function of the other. First, an equation is presented that specifies the linear relationship to be tested for the columns. The calculation of a Pearson product moment coefficient of correlation on the basis of the equation and several assumptions is then described. Finally, a test of whether the coefficient of correlation differs significantly from zero is used to evaluate whether there is a linear relationship between the columns.[23]

If there is a linear relationship between columns j in the U.S. and USSR tables, a given coefficient in column j of the USSR table can be expressed as a function of the corresponding coefficient in column j of the U.S. table, as follows:

$$a_{1j}^{SU} = m_0 + m_1 a_{ij}^{US} + u_{ij} \qquad (i = 1, \ldots, n)$$

where m_0 and m_1 are constants, and where u_{ij} is a disturbance term. In order to evaluate whether a set of n equations like the one above gives a satisfactory explanation of the relationship between columns j, it is necessary to make several assumptions about the u_{ij}. Because input coefficients are estimated with zero degrees of freedom, the data in columns j provide only one estimate of each u_{ij}. If the assumptions are made, however, the u_{ij} can be treated as independent observations from a single normal distribution, observations that have no systematic effect on a linear relationship between the a_{ij}^{SU} and the a_{ij}^{US}. The null hypothesis that columns j are independent of each other can then be tested by evaluating whether the correlation coefficient for the columns differs significantly from zero.

Four assumptions are necessary for such a procedure: (1) The u_{ij} are independent of each other. (2) The u_{ij} are all normally distributed. (3) The u_{ij} all have equal variance. (4) The u_{ij} all have a mean of zero. The first three assumptions are the same as the three assumptions made earlier about the e_{ij} of the Student test. Three assumptions here can thus be justified on the same grounds as the earlier assumptions. The fourth assumption is justified if m_0 adequately represents any nonzero constant in the relationship between the a_{ij}^{SU} and the a_{ij}^{US}.

Let $E(a_{ij})$ denote the mean of the observed coefficients in a given column j, and let $var(a_{ij})$ denote their variance. The Pearson coefficient of correlation between columns j in the U.S. and USSR tables is then calculated by the following formula:

$$(r_p)_j = \frac{\sum\limits_i \left[a_{ij}^{US} - E(a_{ij}^{US})\right]\left[a_{ij}^{SU} - E(a_{ij}^{SU})\right]}{n\sqrt{var(a_{ij}^{US})\ var(a_{ij}^{SU})}}$$

where n is the number of observations on which the test is based. In order to test the null hypothesis that $(r_p)_j$ is equal to zero, the following formula is used:

$$crt(r_p) = r_p\ \sqrt{n-2}\ /\sqrt{1 - r_p^2}$$

where the subscript j is omitted for convenience. The significance of the test statistic $crt(r_p)$ can then be evaluated by comparing $crt(r_p)$ with a table of the t distribution, where the degrees of freedom are taken as (n - 2).

Two distribution-free statistical tests are described below. Both are based on a rationale similar to that for the classical test just described. The null hypothesis and assumptions of the distribution-free tests, however, differ from those of the classical test.[24] Both distribution-free tests evaluate whether one of a pair of columns can be expressed as a monotonic function of the other. An equation specifying the relationship between the columns and assumptions made in connection with the equation are discussed first. On the basis of the equation and assumptions, which are the same for both tests, Kendall and Spearman coefficients of rank correlation can be calculated. The Kendall coefficient is presented first, then the Spearman coefficient. Finally, tests of whether the coefficients of rank correlation differ significantly from zero are used to evaluate whether there is a monotonic functional relationship between the columns.

If there is a monotonic relationship between corresponding columns j, a given coefficient in column j of the USSR table can be expressed as a function of the corresponding coefficient in column j of the U.S. table, as follows:

$$a_{ij}^{SU} = f(a_{ij}^{US}, w_{ij}) \qquad\qquad (i = 1, \ldots, n)$$

where f is a monotonic function of a_{ij}^{US}, and where w_{ij} is a disturbance term. In order to evaluate whether a set of n equations like the one above gives a satisfactory explanation of the relationship between columns j, it is necessary to make two assumptions: (1) The w_{ij} are independent of each other. (2) None of the a_{ij}^{US} are tied with each other, and none of the a_{ij}^{SU} are tied with each other. The null hypothesis that columns j are independent can then be tested either by evaluating whether the Kendall coefficient of rank correlation for the columns differs significantly from zero, or by evaluating whether the Spearman coefficient of rank correlation for the columns differs significantly from zero.

In this study the data are such that assumption (2) is violated, to a greater or lesser extent, for every pair of columns j in the U.S. and USSR tables. Ties that occur in violation of assumption (2) are treated according to procedures recommended by Kendall (1962, pp. 34-41).[25] The procedures, to be described presently, involve the calculation of two versions of each Kendall or Spearman coefficient of rank correlation. Version (a) can be interpreted as a measure of accuracy, that is, of the correspondence between two sets of ranks when one set is taken as accurate. Alternatively, version (a) can be interpreted as an average of the various coefficients that could be calculated by assigning ranks to tied observations in all possible ways. Version (b) can be interpreted as a measure of agreement, that is, of the correspondence between two sets of ranks when there is no basis for selecting one set as accurate. Both versions are calculated in this study.

To calculate either the Kendall or the Spearman coefficient of rank correlation, first replace each value of a_{ij}^{US} by its rank R_{ij}^{US}, in order of increasing size, within column j of the U.S. table; similarly, replace each value of a_{ij}^{SU} by its rank R_{ij}^{SU}. If several values of the a_{ij}^{US}, or of the a_{ij}^{SU}, are tied, replace each such value by the average of the ranks for which the several values are tied.

The Kendall coefficient for columns j can then be calculated as follows. Arrange the ranks R_{ij}^{US} in their natural order $(1,2,3,\ldots,n)$, and arrange the ranks R_{ij}^{SU} so that each R_{ij}^{SU} has the same position among the USSR ranks as its corresponding rank R_{ij}^{US} has among the U.S. ranks. For each R_{ij}^{SU} arranged in this new order, count the number of times that it is followed by a larger rank and the number of times that it is followed by a smaller rank. If some R_{ij}^{SU} is followed by a rank with which it is tied, do not count the tied rank. Furthermore, if some R_{ij}^{SU} has a corresponding R_{ij}^{US} that is involved in a tie, do not count any following rank R_{kj}^{SU} whose corresponding R_{kj}^{US} is involved in the same tie as R_{ij}^{US}. For each R_{ij}^{SU}, take the difference between the count of the times that it is followed by a larger rank and the count of the times that it is followed by a smaller rank. Then sum the differences calculated for all the R_{ij}^{SU} and call the sum S. The numerator for both versions of the Kendall coefficient is 2S.

Information about ties is needed to calculate the denominator for version (b) of the Kendall coefficient. For each set of ties among the ranks R_{ij}^{US}, count the number of ranks involved in the tie, call that number t, and calculate the product t(t - 1). Then sum the products calculated for all sets of ties and call the sum T. For each set of ties among the ranks R_{ij}^{SU}, follow the same procedure and find the sum U.

The formulas for versions (a) and (b) of the Kendall coefficient for columns j are as follows:

$$r_{ka} = \frac{2S}{n(n - 1)}$$

$$r_{kb} = \frac{2S}{\sqrt{[n(n - 1) - T]\ [n(n - 1) - U]}}$$

where n is the number of observations on which the coefficients are based, and where the subscript j is omitted for convenience. In order to test the null hypothesis that r_{ka} and r_{kb} do not differ significantly from zero, the following formula can be used:

$$crn(r_k) = \frac{S - k}{\sqrt{var(S)}}$$

where k is a correction for continuity here set equal to its maximum possible value $\frac{1}{2}n$, and where the variance of S is calculated by the following formula:[26]

$$var(S) = \frac{1}{9n(n - 1)(n - 2)}(n^3 - 3n^2 + 2n + 3T - T') $$
$$(n^3 - 3n^2 + 2n + 3U - U') + \frac{1}{2n(n - 1)}$$
$$(n^2 - n - T)(n^2 - n - U)$$

where T′ and U′ are defined below, in connection with the Spearman coefficient. The significance of the test statistic $crn(r_k)$ can then be evaluated by comparing $crn(r_k)$ with a table of the normal distribution.[27]

The Spearman coefficient for columns j can be calculated as follows. The sum of the squares of the differences between the ranks of corresponding coefficients in the two columns,

$$S' = \sum_i (R_{ij}^{US} - R_{ij}^{SU})^2$$

forms part of the numerator for both versions of the Spearman coefficient.

Information about ties is needed to calculate both versions. For each set of ties among the ranks R_{ij}^{US}, count the number of ranks involved in the tie, call that number t, and calculate the product $t(t-1)(t+1)$. Then sum the products so calculated for all sets of ties and call the sum T′. For each set of ties among the ranks R_{ij}^{SU}, follow the same procedure and find the sum U′.

The formulas for versions (a) and (b) of the Spearman coefficient for columns j are as follows:

$$r_{sa} = \frac{n^3 - n - \frac{1}{2}(T' + U') - 6S'}{n^3 - n}$$

$$r_{sb} = \frac{n^3 - n - \frac{1}{2}(T' + U') - 6S'}{\sqrt{(n^3 - n - T')(n^3 - n - U')}}$$

where n is the number of observations on which the coefficients are based, and where the subscript j is omitted for convenience. In order to test the null hypothesis that r_{sa} and r_{sb} do not differ significantly from zero, the following formula can be used:

$$crn(r_s) = \frac{n^3 - n - \frac{1}{2}(T' + U') - 6S' - 6k'}{(n^3 - n - T')(n^3 - n - U')} \sqrt{n-1}$$

where k′ is a correction for continuity here set equal to its maximum possible value $\frac{1}{4}n^2$. The significance of the test statistic $crn(r_s)$ can then be evaluated by comparing $crn(r_s)$ with a table of the normal distribution.[28]

Two of the three tests described above have been employed in previous studies comparing direct input coefficients from different input-output tables. Usui and Miyamoto (1968, pp. 7-9) have used the test based on the Pearson correlation coefficient, according to the method described here. Treml (1968) has used the test based on the Spearman coefficient, but not according to the column approach described here.

Results of the Tests

Each of the three column tests of independence is conducted on all pairs of corresponding columns from the reconciled input-output tables for the United States and the USSR. Tables 8.4 through 8.6 present the resulting coefficients of correlation. Values of the Pearson coefficient are shown in Table 8.4, values of version (b) of the Kendall coefficient in Table 8.5, and values of version (b) of the Spearman coefficient in Table 8.6. Values of version (b) of the Kendall and Spearman coefficients are shown instead of values of version (a) because, as noted above, version (b) can be interpreted as a measure of agreement between two sets of ranks when there is no basis for selecting one set as accurate.[29] For the Pearson coefficient, values range from .17 to .99. The median value of the coefficient is .76, and the middle third of the values lie in the range from .63 to .85. For the Kendall coefficient, values range from .29 to .61. The median value of the coefficient is .46, and the middle third of the values lie in the range from .43 to .50. For the Spearman coefficient, values range from .40 to .77. The median value of the coefficient is .60, and approximately the middle third of the values lie in the range from .57 to .65.

For each of the three column tests of independence, the value of the coefficient of correlation for any pair of columns has been evaluated for significance by conducting a one-tailed positive test of the appropriate null hypothesis at the .05 significance level. The results of the evaluations of significance are that the null hypothesis of independence is rejected for all 63 pairs of columns by all three tests, except that for one pair of columns, the null hypothesis is not rejected by the classical test.[30] Thus the Kendall and Spearman coefficients are significantly positive for all 63 sectors for which pairs of columns are tested. All 63 sectors can therefore be considered similar in the U.S. and USSR tables, if the criterion of similarity for a sector is taken as a significantly positive rank correlation coefficient for the sector's columns in the two tables. The finding that all 63 sectors are similar on this basis, even though almost 60 percent of the sectors can be shown not to be identical on the basis of the Sign test, is an important one.

TABLE 8.4

Results for the Pearson Product Moment Coefficient of Correlation, by Sector

Value of r_p	Sector(s) in which Value Is Found[a]	Value of r_p	Sector(s) in which Value Is Found[a]
.17	3[b]	.59	
.18		.60	
.19		.61	
.20		.62	14, 16, 19
.21		.63	61, 63
.22		.64	
.23		.65	24
.24		.66	45
.25	10	.67	
.26		.68	41
.27		.69	22
.28		.70	62
.29		.71	
.30		.72	21
.31		.73	
.32		.74	
.33	5	.75	23, 53
.34		.76	4
.35	1	.77	15, 26, 29, 31
.36		.78	
.37	57	.79	
.38		.80	
.39	25	.81	
.40		.82	30, 55
.41		.83	
.42		.84	17, 39
.43		.85	9, 43
.44	35	.86	38
.45	42, 50	.87	
.46	59	.88	
.47	8	.89	2, 27, 40, 44
.48		.90	60
.49	58	.91	49, 52, 54
.50	20	.92	12, 13
.51		.93	
.52		.94	48
.53		.95	56
.54	37	.96	7, 32, 34, 47
.55	28	.97	33, 36
.56		.98	
.57	11, 18	.99	6, 51
.58	46		

[a]For sector names corresponding to the numbers given see Table 8.1.

[b]This is the only value of r_p that is not significant. Significance is evaluated by means of a one-tailed positive test of the null hypothesis at the .05 significance level.

Source: Compiled by the author.

TABLE 8.5

Results for the Kendall Coefficient of Rank Correlation (Version b), by Sector

Value of r_{kb}[a]	Sector(s) in which Value Is Found[b]	Value of r_{kb}[a]	Sector(s) in which Value Is Found[b]
.28		.45	21, 22, 31, 45, 60, 62
.29	20	.46	8, 18, 29, 30, 46, 59
.30	63	.47	4
.31	61	.48	13
.32	1, 9, 23	.49	19, 39
.33	3, 7, 33	.50	17
.34		.51	24, 28, 41, 48, 53, 57
.35	35	.52	44
.36		.53	51, 58
.37	6, 10, 54	.54	36
.38	5, 40	.55	12, 25
.39	16, 43	.56	47
.40	15, 34	.57	32, 49
.41		.58	2, 27
.42	14, 37	.59	56
.43	11, 38, 42	.60	
.44	50	.61	26, 52, 55

[a]All values of r_{kb} are significant. Significance is evaluated by means of a one-tailed positive test of the null hypothesis at the .05 significance level.

[b]For sector names corresponding to the numbers given, see Table 8.1.

Source: Compiled by the author.

TABLE 8.6

Results for the Spearman Coefficient of Rank Correlation (Version b), by Sector

Value of r_{sb}[a]	Sector(s) in which Value Is Found[b]	Value of r_{sb}[a]	Sector(s) in which Value Is Found
.40	20	.59	15
.41		.60	11, 21
.42	1	.61	31, 62
.43	7, 9, 23, 63	.62	
.44	61	.63	29, 39
.45	3	.64	4, 18, 30, 53
.46		.65	13
.47	35	.66	17, 19, 44, 48
.48	10, 33, 54	.67	41
.49		.68	24, 28, 51, 57
.50	6	.69	
.51	43	.70	47
.52		.71	36, 49
.53	34, 40	.72	25
.54	5	.73	12, 58
.55	16, 37, 42	.74	2, 32
.56	60	.75	55, 56
.57	8, 14, 38, 50	.76	26, 27
.58	22, 45, 46, 59	.77	52

[a]All values of r_{sb} are significant. Significance is evaluated by means of a one-tailed positive test of the null hypothesis at the .05 significance level.

[b]For sector names corresponding to the numbers given, see Table 8.1.

Source: Compiled by the author.

The extent to which the results of the three column tests of independence agree can be viewed in two ways. All three tests agree quite closely as to whether the null hypothesis should be accepted or rejected for a given pair of columns. The two distribution-free tests agree quite closely as to the relative magnitude of the correlation coefficient for a given pair of columns. Because of the simplicity of the assumptions required by the distribution-free tests, their results are considered more reliable than the results of the classical test when conflicts arise.

In order to assess the extent to which the three correlation coefficients show the same ordering of sectors with respect to the relative magnitude of the coefficient for a pair of columns, Spearman coefficients of rank correlation have been calculated between the values of the three correlation coefficients by sector. That is, the ranks of the Spearman coefficients (version b) calculated for the 63 sectors under study here are correlated, by means of the Spearman coefficient of rank correlation, first with the ranks of the Pearson coefficients calculated for the 63 sectors, and second, with the ranks of the Kendall coefficients (version b) calculated for the 63 sectors. The results of this exercise are (1) that the Spearman coefficient of rank correlation between the values by sector of the Spearman and Pearson coefficients is .28, and (2) that the Spearman coefficient of rank correlation between the values by sector of the Spearman and Kendall coefficients is .98.

Values by sector of the Kendall coefficient of rank correlation are discussed in some detail below. The Kendall coefficient is selected for further analysis instead of the Spearman coefficient for two reasons. First, the Kendall coefficient, unlike the Spearman coefficient, does not give more weight to large differences in rank order than to small differences. Second, it is possible to test the Kendall coefficient, but not the Spearman coefficient, for the significance of its divergence from a nonzero value when the coefficient is calculated from observations that contain ties (Kendall 1962, pp. 62-63). The discussion below is based on Table 8.5. A rough evaluation of the significance of the differences between obtained values of the Kendall coefficient is made first. Then the distribution of values of the Kendall coefficient among major groups of sectors is considered.

The significance of the differences between the obtained values of the Kendall coefficient is evaluated by finding confidence intervals for the lowest and highest values of the coefficient. These confidence intervals are calculated from a formula given by Kendall (1962, p. 64).[31] The lowest value of the Kendall coefficient is .28. It has a 95 percent confidence interval of -.09 to .59, or a 90 percent confidence interval of -.03 to .55. The highest value of the

Kendall coefficient is .61. It has a 95 percent confidence interval of .26 to .82, or a 90 percent confidence interval of .33 to .79. Because the two 95 percent confidence intervals and the two 90 percent confidence intervals overlap, it is concluded that there is no statistically significant difference between the lowest and highest values of the Kendall coefficient.

Table 8.7 shows the distribution of three size groups of values of the Kendall coefficient among major groups of sectors. Because the values do not significantly differ from each other, they are roughly classified as belonging to the lower, middle, or upper third of all values obtained. Consider the major groups that include four or more sectors. There are two groups where values of the Kendall coefficient tend to be low--metallurgy, and fuels and power; there is one group where values of the Kendall coefficient tend to be high--food. For the machinebuilding group, values of the Kendall coefficient tend to lie in the middle range.

TABLE 8.7

Three Size Groups of the Kendall Coefficient of Rank
Correlation (Version b), by Major Group of Sectors

Major Group of Sectors*	Number of Sectors in Group	Number of Sectors in which Value of r_{kb} Lies in		
		Lower Third	Middle Third	Upper Third
Metallurgy	6	4	1	1
Fuels and power	4	3	1	--
Machinebuilding	20	5	9	6
Metalworking	4	2	1	1
Chemicals	2	1	--	1
Wood and paper	6	2	3	1
Construction materials and glass	4	1	2	1
Textiles and apparel	3	--	--	3
Food	7	1	1	5
Industry not elsewhere classified	1	--	--	1
Construction	1	--	--	1
Agriculture	2	--	2	--
Transportation and communications	1	1	--	--
Trade and distribution	1	--	1	--
Other branches	1	1	--	--
Total	63	21	21	21

*Sectors that belong to the major groups are listed in Table 8.10.

Source: Compiled by the author.

As pointed out earlier in this section, ties occur among the a_{ij}^{US} or among the a_{ij}^{SU}, or among both, for every pair of columns in the two tables. The variables T and U are used by the Kendall coefficient to measure the extent of ties in the U.S. and USSR columns, respectively.[32] Analysis of obtained values of T and U shows that the value of T for a given pair of columns is likely to be larger than the corresponding value of U. For most sectors, the value of T is so large that it reflects a set of at least 15 of the a_{ij}^{US} all tied with each other.[33]

It turns out that large values of T are observed because the following situation arises. When a coefficient of rank correlation is calculated for a pair of columns, any pair of observations on the columns must have at least one member greater than zero. The other member, however, may be zero. If nonzero observations in one of the columns are frequently paired with zero observations in the other, a number of observations in the latter column will be tied at the same value, zero. Large values of T thus occur when zero values of a_{ij}^{US} tend to be paired with nonzero values of a_{ij}^{SU}.

There are several possible explanations of the tendency for a pair of columns j to include more pairs of coefficients where a_{ij}^{US} is zero and a_{ij}^{SU} is nonzero than vice versa. According to Leontief (1966, p. 49), a larger, more highly developed economy will tend to have fewer zero entries in its input-output table. If this explanation were adopted, it would lead to the conclusion that the U.S. economy is less highly developed than the Soviet economy. Such a conclusion is rejected here because it conflicts with the general results of previous research comparing the two economies.

It has also been suggested that an input-output table tends to have fewer zero entries, the better the system of collecting data for the table. If this explanation were adopted, it would lead to the conclusion that the U.S. system for collecting input-output data is inferior to the USSR system. Such a conclusion is rejected here for two reasons. First, the most detailed version in which the U.S. table has been compiled has more than four times as many sectors as the most detailed version in which the USSR table has been compiled. Second, data for the U.S. table are usually derived from complete censuses, while data for the USSR table are based on surveys, some of which are complete but most of which cover only samples.[34]

Another possible explanation is that a number of accounting conventions are not comparable between the two tables. Of the incomparabilities discussed earlier, one seems particularly relevant here. In the USSR table, purchases on capital account may be recorded in some cases as purchases on current account.

Finally, it is possible that imperfections in the reconciliation of sector classification schemes of the two tables cause more a_{ij}^{US}

than a_{ij}^{SU} to be zero. Such imperfections can be expected to cause some a_{ij}^{SU} as well as some a_{ij}^{US} to be zero. After reconciliation according to the scheme used in this study, however, more unreconciled leftover sectors remain in the U.S. table. Thus inputs similar to those that are included in an a_{ij}^{SU} that shows purchases by sector j from a reconciled sector i in the USSR table may be included in an a_{kj}^{US} that shows purchases by sector j from an unreconciled sector k in the U.S. table.

Relationships between the Tests for Identity and Independence

It is of interest to see whether there is some association between the results of the Sign test and values of the Kendall coefficient of rank correlation. Table 8.8 shows how often the null hypothesis of the Sign test is accepted or rejected for sectors that belong to three groups: groups in which the value of the Kendall coefficient for a sector is in the lower third, middle third, or upper third of all obtained values. A tendency for the null hypothesis of the Sign test to be rejected more often for sectors where the Kendall coefficient has a low value than for sectors where the Kendall coefficient has a high value might be expected. Such a tendency does not appear in Table 8.8. The absence of such a tendency, however, does not mean that the results of the Sign test and the Kendall test are contradictory. A sector's corresponding columns in the U.S. and USSR tables can be found similar according to the Kendall test and either identical or not identical according to the Sign test.

TABLE 8.8

Association between the Results of the Sign Test and Values of the Kendall Coefficient of Rank Correlation

Value of r_{kb}	Null Hypothesis of Sign Test		
	Accepted	Rejected	All
Low	8	13	21
Middle	13	8	21
High	6	15	21
All	27	36	63

Source: Compiled by the author.

The ties brought to light in connection with the Kendall test have an important relationship with the results of the Sign test. The Sign test leads to rejection of the null hypothesis that columns j in the two tables are identical if the a_{ij}^{US} exceed their corresponding observations a_{ij}^{SU} significantly more often than the reverse occurs, or vice versa. In this study the a_{ij}^{SU} exceed the a_{ij}^{US} more often than the reverse occurs for all but one of the cases where the null hypothesis of the Sign test is rejected. When extensive ties occur in column j of the US table, the ties mean that positive values of a_{ij}^{SU} often exceed corresponding zero values of a_{ij}^{US}. Such ties can thus be expected to contribute to rejection of the null hypothesis of the Sign test for columns j. There are 23 sectors for which the pair of columns j includes at least 20 zero values of a_{ij}^{US} that correspond to positive values of a_{ij}^{SU}. For 21 of these 23 sectors, the null hypothesis of the Sign test is rejected.

If extensive ties occur in the U.S. member of a pair of columns and if the ties do not occur because of incomparabilities in the data, then the ties properly contribute to rejection of the null hypothesis of the Sign test for that pair of columns. If the ties do occur because of incomparabilities in the data, however, they may contribute to rejection of a null hypothesis that should be accepted. Therefore, it may be that improvements in the data for the present study would cause the null hypothesis of the Sign test to be rejected for fewer pairs of columns.

CONCLUSIONS

In this study a U.S. input-output table for 1963 and a USSR table for 1966 are compared. Data are taken from the interindustry quadrants of the two tables, which are reconciled and adjusted. The interindustry quadrants of the reconciled tables include 94 percent and 97 percent of all interindustry transactions in the U.S. and USSR tables, respectively. The data are kept disaggregated as much as possible.

Comparisons of pairs of corresponding columns of direct input coefficients are made. Subject to qualifications discussed in the section on methods of comparison, they can be interpreted as comparisons of corresponding production functions. The methods of comparison selected are statistical. The results of the comparisons are summarized below, and conclusions are drawn.

Three tests of the null hypothesis that a pair of columns of direct input coefficients are identical in the two tables are presented. In general, the results of the three tests do not agree among themselves. The results of the Sign test for the median difference are

TABLE 8.9

Correspondence of Sectors in USSR 1966 Table (71-Order) and U.S. 1963 Table (478-Order)

USSR Sector (71-Order)	U.S. Sectors (478-Order)
1 Ferrous ores	0500
2 Ferrous metals	3312, 3313, 3316, 3317, 3399
3 Nonferrous ores	0601, 0602
4 Nonferrous metals	3331, 3332, 3333, 3334, 3339, 3341, 3351, 3352, 3356, 3361, 3362, 3369, 3392, 3496, 3497
5 Coke products	Included with ferrous metals
6 Refractory materials	3255, 3297
7 Industrial metal products	3315, 3493, 4101
8 Coal	700
9 Oil extraction	800
10 Oil refining	2951, 3101
11 Gas	Included with oil extraction
12 Peat	No comparable sector
13 Oil shales	Included with oil extraction
14 Electric and thermal power	6801, 7802, 7902
15 Energy and power machinery and equipment	3511, 3519
16 Electrotechnical machinery and equipment	3264, 3564, 3612, 3613, 3621, 3622, 3623, 3624, 3629, 3633, 3634, 3635, 3639, 3641, 3642, 3691, 3692, 3699, 5503
17 Cable products	3357
18 Machine tools	3541, 3553
19 Forging/pressing machinery and equipment	3542
20 Casting machinery and equipment	No comparable sector
21 Tools and dies	3423, 3425, 3565, 4703
22 Precision instruments	3571, 3576, 3579, 3611, 3693, 3811, 3821, 3822, 3831, 3851, 3871, 3872
23 Mining and metallurgical machinery and equipment	3532, 3533, 3548
24 Pumps and compressors	3561, 3567, 3585, 3586, 3632
25 Logging and paper machinery and equipment	3554
26 Light industry machinery and equipment	3552, 3636
27 Food industry machinery and equipment	3551
28 Printing machinery and equipment	3555
29 Hoisting/transporting machinery and equipment	3534, 3535, 3536, 3537
30 Construction machinery and equipment	3531
31 Construction materials machinery and equipment	No comparable sector
32 Transportation machinery and equipment	3731, 3732, 3741, 3742
33 Automobiles	3694, 3713, 3715, 3717, 3751, 3791, 3799
34 Tractors and agricultural machinery and equipment	3522
35 Bearings	3562
36 Other machinebuilding	3391, 3461, 3566, 3569, 3572, 3581, 3582, 3589, 3599, 3651, 3661, 3662, 3674, 3679, 3702, 3841, 3843, 5701
37 Sanitary engineering products	3431, 3432, 3433, 3631, 4208
38 Other metal wares	2514, 2522, 2542, 3411, 3421, 3429, 3442, 3444, 3446, 3471, 3479, 3481, 3491, 3492, 3499, 3914, 3964
39 Metal structures	3441, 3443, 3449
40 Repair of machinery and equipment	Not comparable

USSR Sector (71-Order)	U.S. Sectors (478-Order)
41 Abrasives	3291
42 Mineral chemistry products	1000
43 All other chemicals	2701, 2821, 2822, 2823, 2824, 2842, 2843, 2851, 2871, 2872, 2879, 2895, 2899, 2901, 3011, 3031, 3069, 3293, 3652
44 Logging	2411
45 Sawmills and woodworking	2100, 2421, 2426, 2429, 2431, 2432, 2433, 2491, 2541
46 Furniture	2511, 2512, 2515, 2519, 2521, 2531, 2591, 2599, 3987
47 Other woodworking	2499, 3983
48 Paper and pulp	2611, 2621, 2631, 2641, 2642, 2643, 2645, 2646, 2647, 2661
49 Wood chemistry products	2861
50 Cement	3241
51 Prefab concrete	3272
52 Other construction materials	2952, 3251, 3253, 3259, 3271, 3273, 3274, 3275, 3281, 3292, 3296, 3982
53 Glass and porcelain	3221, 3261, 3262, 3263, 3269, 3501
54 Textiles	1701, 2201, 2241, 2251, 2252, 2253, 2254, 2256, 2259, 2280, 2284, 2291, 2292, 2293, 2294, 2296, 2297, 2298, 2299, 2393, 2394, 2396, 3995
55 Sewn goods	1804, 2391, 2392, 2395, 2397, 2399
56 Other light industry	2295, 3021, 3111, 3121, 3131, 3141, 3142, 3151, 3161, 3171, 3172, 3199, 3981
57 Fish products	2031, 2036
58 Meat products	2011, 2013, 2015, 2094
59 Dairy products	2021, 2022, 2023, 2024, 2026
60 Sugar	1419
61 Flour and cereals	2041, 2043, 2044, 2045
62 Bread and confections	2051, 2052, 2071, 2072, 2098
63 Other foods	2032, 2033, 2034, 2035, 2037, 2046, 2073, 2082, 2083, 2084, 2085, 2086, 2087, 2091, 2092, 2093, 2095, 2096, 2099, 2111, 2121, 2131, 2141, 2841, 2844, 3984
64 Industry not elsewhere classified	2042, 2097, 2500, 2605, 2644, 2649, 2753, 2761, 2771, 2782, 2789, 2791, 2793, 2794, 2890, 3079, 3295, 3299, 3842, 3911, 3912, 3913, 3931, 3941, 3942, 3943, 3949, 3951, 3952, 3953, 3955, 3961, 3962, 3963, 3988, 3993, 3999, 6803, 8200
65 Construction	1503-1519, 1601-1627, 1710-1737
66 Crops	201-207
67 Animal husbandry	101, 102, 103
68 Forestry	No comparable sector
69 Transportation and communications	6501, 6503-6507, 6600, 7801
70 Trade and distribution	6901, 6902
71 Other branches of material production	2711, 2721, 2731, 2732, 2741, 7601, 8300

Source: Compiled by Dimitri M. Gallik.

taken as the most reliable. When the Sign test is conducted for 63 pairs of columns, the null hypothesis of identity is rejected for about 60 percent and accepted for about 40 percent of the pairs.[35] The results of other tests indicate that in some instances, rejection of the null hypothesis may be caused by unresolved data problems. Thus the results of the Sign test, although they do not show an overwhelming degree of similarity between the U.S. and USSR tables, do show that similarities between the tables are quite important.

TABLE 8.10

Major Groups of Sectors

Major Group of Sectors	Numbers of Component Sectors in 63-Order Reconciled Sector Classification Scheme
Metallurgy	1 through 6
Fuels and power	7 through 10
Machinebuilding	11 through 30
Metalworking	31 through 34
Chemicals	35, 36
Wood and paper	37 through 42
Construction materials and glass	43 through 46
Textiles and apparel	47 through 49
Food	50 through 56
Industry not elsewhere classified	57
Construction	58
Agriculture	59, 60
Transportation and communications	61
Trade and distribution	62
Other branches	63

Note: For sector names corresponding to the numbers given, see Table 8.1.

Source: Compiled by the author.

Three tests of the null hypothesis that a pair of columns of direct input coefficients are independent in the two tables are also presented. The results of the three tests agree closely as to whether the null hypothesis should be accepted or rejected for a given pair of columns. The Spearman and Kendall rank correlation tests agree closely with each other, but not with the Pearson correlation test,

as to the relative magnitude of the correlation coefficient for a given
pair of columns. When Spearman and Kendall rank correlation tests
are conducted for 63 pairs of columns, the null hypothesis of independence is rejected in favor of the alternative hypothesis of positive
correlation for all of the pairs.[36] Thus the results of the Spearman
and Kendall tests indicate strong similarity between the U.S. and
USSR tables.

The results of the comparisons show some tendency for sectors
to be similar more often between the U.S. and USSR tables if the sectors belong to major groups that are relatively insulated from intercountry differences in patterns of consumption and in availability of
natural resources, and for sectors to be dissimilar more often between the two tables if the sectors belong to major groups that are
influenced relatively strongly by such differences. Thus the null
hypothesis of the Sign test is accepted especially frequently for sectors that belong to the machinebuilding and metalworking groups,
where sectors may be expected to purchase intermediate inputs that
have undergone some processing and to sell outputs (on current or
capital account) to other producing sectors. Moreover, the null
hypothesis is rejected especially frequently for sectors that belong
to the fuel and power, construction materials and glass, and food
groups. Sectors in the fuel and power and construction materials
and glass groups may be expected to be influenced strongly by availability of natural resources; sectors in the food group, by patterns
of consumption.

There is no observed tendency for sectors in which the null
hypothesis of the Sign test is accepted to have high Kendall coeffi
cients of rank correlation and sectors where the null hypothesis is
rejected to have low Kendall coefficients. All Kendall coefficients
are significantly positive, however, and differences between high
and low coefficients are not significant. Thus the results of the
Sign and Kendall tests are not contradictory, and the results of the
Sign test give a better indication of differences in the extent to which
similarities are likely to occur for certain groups of sectors.

The results of all the comparisons taken together indicate important similarities between the U.S. input-output table for 1963 and
the USSR table for 1966. Especially in the light of many unresolved
data problems, which tend to decrease the apparent similarity of the
tables, the results of the present study in general provide good support for the view that there are important structural similarities between the U.S. and Soviet economies.

The results of this study also have implications about methods
that appear especially promising for future research involving comparison of input-output tables. Several statistical tests have been
applied, and results have varied substantially, depending on the test.

Three distribution-free tests are considered the most reliable: the Sign test for the median difference, and the Kendall and Spearman tests for rank correlation.

The present study could be improved and extended in several ways. Some improvements could be made by repeating the comparisons conducted here after some rather simple adjustments of the data. It was pointed out that diagonal entries and entries in the construction row are treated according to diffcrent accounting conventions in the two tables. The comparisons could be repeated after excluding such entries from the data for both tables. The comparisons could also be repeated after further aggregation of the data in order to increase the degree of agreement of sector classification schemes in the tables. Another improvement could be made by further investigating the reasons why many pairs of corresponding input coefficients have zero values in the U.S. table but positive values in the USSR table.

This study could be extended by applying the present methods of comparison to further data. It would be interesting to obtain two kinds of data that are not now available for the tables compared here: more detailed data for the components of value-added in the U.S. table, and information for conversion of the U.S. and USSR tables to valuation in the same prices. Data are now available that make it possible to consider comparisons of four input-output tables for the United States, for the years 1947, 1958, 1963, and 1967, and three tables for the USSR, for the years 1959, 1966, and 1972. Comparisons involving at least two tables for each country would allow differences between tables for a given country and differences between tables for the two countries to be evaluated on a consistent basis. Furthermore, such comparisons would allow an assessment to be made as to whether economic structures in the two countries are becoming more or less similar over time.

NOTES

1. The Office of Business Economics is now the Bureau of Economic Analysis of the Department of Commerce.

2. For the 85-sector table, A. J. Walderhaug (1973) has expanded the value-added quadrant to three rows. A similar expansion of value-added data is not available, however, for the two larger tables.

3. A 75-sector revised version of the reconstructed table in producers' prices appears in Chapter 1 of this volume.

4. Two new sectors in the reconciled Soviet table are formed by aggregating sectors in the 71-order table. The rest of the sectors in the reconciled table consist of single sectors in the 71-order table.

5. In Soviet economic accounting, productive activities are considered to be those that participate directly in the production of material goods. Services are considered nonproductive, except for three kinds: freight transportation, communications serving production, and trade and distribution (Treml et al. 1972, p. 42).

6. There is an exception to this statement. The transportation and communications sector in the reconciled U.S. table includes some services, such as passenger transportation, that would be considered nonproductive in the USSR table. No adjustment is made for this problem.

7. Value-added, final-demand, and gross output data from the two tables also are not comparable in this respect. Final-demand and gross output data can be made comparable by means of a rather simple adjustment, but value-added data cannot. Methods of treating secondary products are discussed in more detail in Kurtzweg (1975, pp. 44-69).

8. See Treml et al. (1972, pp. 149, 152-55, 158-59). There is some uncertainty over whether the balance in foreign trade prices is included in the original input-output table. The table has been reconstructed on the assumption that the balance is included.

The conversion coefficient is an export conversion coefficient if exports in foreign trade prices exceed imports; it is an import conversion coefficient if imports in foreign trade prices exceed exports.

9. The second approach has been modified and expanded in a number of subsequent studies, of which one of the most widely applied is H. B. Chenery and T. Watanabe (1958) An interesting assortment of international and intertemporal comparisons can be found in published volumes of the proceedings of six international conferences on input-output analysis: Netherlands Economic Institute (1953), T. Barna (1956 and 1963), A. P. Carter and A. Brody (1970), A. Brody and A. P. Carter (1972), and K. R. Polenske and J. V. Skolka (1976).

10. The model for an input-output table in value terms is discussed further in L. R. Klein (1953b, pp. 201-10) and in an exchange between Klein (1953a and 1956) and M. Morishima (1956 and 1957). If assumptions in addition to that of optimal resource allocation are made, a column of direct coefficients in an input-output table in physical terms can be interpreted as a Leontief production function. See R. Dorfman, P. A. Samuelson, and R. M. Solow (1958, pp. 204-64).

11. In this study no attempt is made to include a comprehensive selection of the kinds of comparisons used in previous international and intertemporal studies of input-output tables. Some additional comparisons of the present tables appear in Kurtzweg (1975).

12. The reason behind this procedure for counting observations is that a pair of zero coefficients causes complications if it is included in a distribution-free test. See Kurtzweg (1975, pp. 76-78, 85-88, 108) for a more detailed discussion. For the Student matched pair t test in this section and for the Pearson product moment correlation test in the next section, the number of observations is counted in two alternative ways: first as described above, then as 63.

13. See Kurtzweg (1975, pp. 80-84, 158-60) for an explanation of how Wurtele's rationale for a test on columns in physical terms can be extended to serve as a rationale for a test on columns in value terms.

14. For more information about the distribution-free tests, see J. V. Bradley (1968, pp. 96-103, 170-74).

15. Assumptions (2) and (3) are sufficient rather than necessary. Bradley (1968, p. 99) explains ways in which these assumptions can be modified.

16. See Bradley (1968, p. 101) for a normal approximation that can be used when n is too large for exact tables to apply. In this study exact tables are used.

17. See Bradley (1968, pp. 172-74) for some caveats concerning the interpretation of this null hypothesis.

18. See Bradley (1968, p. 166) for a normal approximation that can be used when n is too large for exact tables to apply. In this study exact tables are used.

19. The first two caveats are pointed out by Wurtele (1959, pp. 150-51) in connection with the Student test. The third caveat is pointed out by Bradley (1968, pp. 173-74) in connection with the Sign test.

20. This result is not changed by taking the number of observations for the test as 63.

21. A similar caveat applies to the interpretation of rejection of the null hypothesis of the Wilcoxon test (Bradley 1968, pp. 103-04).

22. An indication that data problems do appear to cause some of the dissimilarities is discussed in the section below.

23. For more information about this test, See J. Johnston (1963, pp. 5-34).

24. For more information about the distribution-free tests, see M. G. Kendall (1962, pp. 1-93) and Bradley (1968, pp. 91-96, 284-87).

25. Bradley (1968, pp. 49-50, 93) favors a different procedure for treating ties, but he does acknowledge (1968, p. 287) Kendall's procedure, at least as applied to the Kendall coefficient.

26. Kendall (1962, p. 72) gives a different but equivalent formula for the variance of S.

27. Kurtzweg (1975, pp. 106, 161-75) gives a more detailed description of the procedure for testing the significance of r_{ka} and r_{kb}. A shortcut procedure used for this study is also described.

28. A more detailed description of the procedure for testing the significance of r_{sa} and r_{sb} appears in Kurtzweg (1975, pp. 107, 175-87). A shortcut procedure used for this study is also described.

29. It should be noted that the value of version (b) of a given coefficient will exceed the value of version (a). The maximum amount by which a value of r_{kb} in Table 8.5 exceeds the corresponding value of r_{ka} is .07, and the maximum amount by which a value of r_{sb} in Table 8.6 exceeds the corresponding value of r_{sa} is .04.

30. The null hypothesis is not rejected by the classical test for sector 3. The results just stated for the classical test are not changed by taking the number of observations for the test as 63.

31. The formula expresses the upper and lower limits of the population value of a Kendall coefficient as a function of the value of the coefficient obtained for a sample:

$$\text{Interval} = \frac{r_{kb} \overset{+}{\underset{-}{}} z \sqrt{\frac{2}{n}} \sqrt{1 + \frac{2z^2}{n} - r_{kb}^2}}{1 + \frac{2z^2}{n}}$$

where z is a normal deviate that depends on the confidence interval (1.96 for a 95 percent interval, 1.645 for a 90 percent interval). See Kendall (1962, pp. 62-65) for further discussion of this formula and related topics. It should be noted here that an interval calculated by means of the formula may err by being too large, but not by being too small.

32. The values of T′ and U′, the variables used by the Spearman coefficient to measure the extent of ties in the U.S. and USSR columns, are monotonic functions of the values of T and U, respectively.

33. The evidence supporting these statements appears in Kurtzweg (1975, pp. 118-19).

34. The most detailed U.S. table has 478 sectors in the interindustry quadrant, while the most detailed USSR table has 110 sectors in the interindustry quadrant. OBE (1970, Appendix 3) describes the data on which the U.S. table is based. Sample surveys for the USSR table are discussed in Treml et al. (1972, pp. 63-66).

35. A two-tailed test of the null hypothesis is made at the .10 significance level.

36. A one-tailed positive test of the null hypothesis is made at the .05 significance level.

REFERENCES

Barna, T., ed. 1963. Structural Interdependence and Economic Development. New York: St. Martin's Press.

_____, ed. 1956. The Structural Interdependence of the Economy. New York: Wiley.

Bradley, J. V. 1968. Distribution-Free Statistical Tests. Englewood Cliffs, N.J.: Prentice-Hall.

Brody, A. and A. P. Carter, eds. 1972. Input-Output Techniques. Amsterdam: North Holland.

Carter, A. P. and A. Brody, eds. 1970. Applications of Input-Output Analysis. Amsterdam: North Holland.

Chenery, H. B. and T. Watanabe. 1958. "International Comparisons of the Structure of Production." Econometrica 26 (October): 487-521.

Dorfman, R., P. A. Samuelson, and R. M. Solow. 1958. Linear Programming and Economic Analysis. New York: McGraw-Hill.

Gallik, D. M. 1971. "Sector Correlation, USSR 1966--US 1963." Working Paper SIP-33. McLean, Va.: Research Analysis Corporation.

Johnston, J. 1963. Econometric Methods. New York: McGraw-Hill.

Kendall, M. G. 1962. Rank Correlation Methods. London: Charles Griffin.

Klein, L. R. 1956. "The Interpretation of Leontief's System-- A Reply." Review of Economic Studies 24 (October): 69-70.

_____. 1953a. "On the Interpretation of Professor Leontief's System." Review of Economic Studies 20 (January): 131-36.

_____. 1953b. A Textbook of Econometrics. Evanston, Ill.: Row, Peterson.

Kurtzweg, L. R. 1975. "A Comparison of Economic Structures in the US and the USSR, Using Input-Output Data." Ph.D. dissertation, Duke University.

Leontief, W. W. 1966. Input-Output Economics. New York: Oxford University Press.

_____. 1953. "Structural Change." In Studies in the Structure of the American Economy, W. W. Leontief et al., pp. 17-52. New York: Oxford University Press.

_____. 1951. The Structure of American Economy, 1919-1939. 2d ed. New York: Oxford University Press.

Long, N. B., Jr. 1970. "An Input-Output Comparison of the Economic Structures of the U.S. and the U.S.S.R." Review of Economics and Statistics 52 (November): 434-41.

Lovell, C. A. K. 1967. "Comments" on Treml (1968). Paper read at Southern Economic Association meeting, November, New Orleans.

Morishama, M. 1957. "Dr. Klein's Interpretation of Leontief's System--A Rejoinder." Review of Economic Studies 25 (October): 59-61.

_____. 1956. "A Comment on Dr. Klein's Interpretation of Leontief's System." Review of Economic Studies 24 (October): 65-68.

Netherlands Economic Institute. 1953. Input-Output Relations. Leiden: H. E. Stenfert Kroese.

OBE. See U.S. Department of Commerce, Office of Business Economics.

Polenske, K. R. and J. V. Skolka, eds. 1976. Advances in Input-Output Analysis. Cambridge, Mass.: Ballinger.

Treml, V. G. 1968. "Structural Similarities in the US and Soviet Economies, Based on Comparisons of Input-Output Data." In Selected Studies in Soviet Economic Trends, Structure, and Institutions, J. P. Hardt, S. H. Cohn, D. M. Gallik, and V. G. Treml, Report RAC-R-30, pp. 169-221. McLean, Va.: Research Analysis Corporation.

_____, D. M. Gallik, B. L. Kostinsky, and K. W. Kruger. 1972. The Structure of the Soviet Economy: Analysis and Reconstruction of the 1966 Input-Output Table. New York: Praeger.

_____, B. L. Kostinsky, K. W. Kruger, and D. M. Gallik. 1973. Conversion of Soviet Input-Output Tables to Producers' Prices: The 1966 Reconstructed Table. U.S. Department of Commerce, F.D.A.D., Foreign Economic Report No. 1. Washington, D.C.: Government Printing Office.

U.S. Department of Commerce, Office of Business Economics. 1970. "Definitions and Conventions of the 1963 Input-Output Tables." Washington, D.C. Mimeographed.

_____. 1969a. "Input-Output Structure of the U.S. Economy: 1963." Survey of Current Business (November), pp. 16-47.

_____. 1969b. Input-Output Structure of the U.S. Economy: 1963. Supplement to Survey of Current Business, 3 vols. Washington, D.C.: Government Printing Office.

Usui, M. and K. Miyamoto. 1968. "Intercountry Comparisons of Technical Coefficients in Large Tables." Paper read at Fourth International Conference on Input-Output Techniques, January, Geneva. Mimeographed.

Walderhaug, A. J. 1973. "The Composition of Value Added in the 1963 Input-Output Study." Survey of Current Business (April), pp. 34-44.

Watanabe, T. 1961. "A Test of the Constancy of Input-Output Coefficients among Countries." International Economic Review 2 (September): 340-50.

Wurtele, Z. S. 1959. "A Problem Encountered in the Comparison of Technical Coefficients." Review of Economic Studies 26 (February): 148-52.

INPUT-OUTPUT WITHIN THE CONTEXT OF THE SRI-WEFA SOVIET ECONOMETRIC MODEL
Gene D. Guill

INTRODUCTION

Macroeconometric models of market economies have traditionally emphasized the determinants of demand and income while
allowing aggregate production to be determined as the sum of expenditures or effective demand. Within these models aggregate demand performs the crucial role of stimulating industrial activity
which in turn determines labor requirements and influences the levels
of investment. When the production side of these models is disaggregated, it becomes necessary to translate final expenditures into effective demand for the outputs of the individual producing sectors.

The research presented in this paper is part of a larger effort
by the Stanford Research Institute (SRI) and Wharton Econometric
Forecasting Associates (WEFA) to construct an econometric model
of the Soviet Union. Since many of the problems treated here were
discussed at considerable length in project conferences, a number
of people made valuable contributions. Although it would be impossible to pinpoint the contributions of specific individuals, the author
wishes to acknowledge the advice and encouragement of Donald W.
Green, Lawrence R. Klein, Herbert S. Levine, Peter Miovic, Ross
S. Preston, Per O. Strangert, and Vladimir G. Treml. In addition,
the author is grateful to the Foreign Demographic Analysis Division
of the U.S. Department of Commerce for providing copies of the
1959, 1966, and preliminary version of the 1972 Soviet input-output
tables. Of course, the responsibility for all errors and omissions
is assumed by the author.

415

The first attempts in providing this link between final expenditure categories and sectoral production were made with regression equations relating sectoral output directly to the categories of final expenditure (Fisher, Klein, and Shinkai 1965 and Kresge 1969). More recent efforts have sought to take advantage of nonstochastic estimates of the elements of this conversion matrix provided by input-output data (Preston 1972 and 1975a).

Although our work in developing the input-output component of the SRI-WEFA Soviet Econometric Model (SOVMOD) has benefited from earlier work in the use of input-output data in macroeconometric models, the role of the input-output component in this model is quite different from that of the input-output component in macroeconometric models of market economies. This difference is due principally to the emphasis that the SRI-WEFA Soviet Econometric Model places upon the determinants of production and supply rather than demand and income. Within SOVMOD the primary causal flow runs from input supplies to output and finally to end use. In this framework, production functions perform the crucial role of transforming inputs into outputs which are then distributed among final spending categories. Given the supply orientation of the SRI-WEFA Soviet Econometric Model, the input-output component of this model was designed to interact with the production functions in the determination of sectoral outputs. This interaction is carried out by introducing material inputs as a third factor, along with labor and capital, in the production functions and utilizing the input-output component in the endogenous determination of the vector of material input flows. The calculation of material inputs in this manner enables the model to account for the structural interdependencies among the producing sectors. In this paper the development of the input-output component of the SRI-WEFA Soviet Econometric Model will be discussed and the interaction between the input-output component and the macromodel described in detail.

THE DETERMINATION OF A SEQUENCE OF INPUT-OUTPUT COEFFICIENT MATRIXES, 1959-72

The construction of an input-output table for an economy as large and complex as that of the Soviet Union is of necessity a very costly, time-consuming activity. As a consequence--and in spite of the fact that the number of tables constructed for the Soviet economy compares quite favorably with the construction of input-output tables for other economies--there have been only three ex post national input-output tables of the Soviet economy constructed in the last 18 years, namely, for the years 1959, 1966, and 1972. As is generally

known, these Soviet input-output tables have never been released in
their complete three-quadrant formats, and it has been necessary
for Western analysts to reconstruct the missing entries in these
tables before they can be used in Western studies of the Soviet economy (Treml, Gallik, Kostinsky, and Kruger 1972). At the present
time the 1959 and 1966 reconstructions have been completed, and
these tables are available for use (Treml, Gallik, and Kostinsky
1973 and 1975). The 1972 table, however, was only released in
1975, but the author is grateful to Professor Treml and analysts at
the Foreign Demographic Analysis Division of the U.S. Department
of Commerce for providing a preliminary version of this reconstructed table in time for these data to be included in the present
study.[1]

The scarcity of input-output data in comparison to national income and product statistics, which have been published annually in
the Soviet Union since the late 1950s, makes it necessary to begin
by estimating input-output coefficient matrixes for those years in the
sample period, 1959-72, for which input-output data are not available. The technique used in determining this sequence of matrixes
is a combination of linear interpolation and weighted RAS balancing.
In the following sections the development of the weighted RAS algorithm will first be described and then its use in estimating the changes
in Soviet input-output coefficients over the period 1959 to 1972 explained.

The Development of the Weighted RAS Method

Although there exists a variety of techniques for estimating
the changes in input-output coefficients over time, the algorithm
used is based inherently upon the RAS method. This method of approximating coefficient change was originally formulated by Leontief
and later developed by Stone (Stone and Brown 1965 and 1972) in conjunction with the Cambridge Growth Project. The chief merits of
this method are two: its minimal data requirements, and the support of recent studies that have found the accuracy of the RAS method
to be superior to other nonsurvey coefficient adjustment techniques
(Morrison and Smith 1974).

In its standard form the RAS method requires three sets of
data: (1) the direct coefficient matrix of an input-output table for an
initial year t, denoted by A^t; (2) a column vector of sectoral gross
outputs in year t+1; and (3) vectors of intermediate inputs and outputs in year t+1. Given these sets of data, an iterative adjustment
procedure is then applied to the direct coefficient matrix A^t which
yields an adjusted coefficient matrix for year t+1 that is consistent

with the intermediate input and output vectors of that year. This adjustment procedure postulates that it is possible to analyze factors affecting the stability of input-output coefficients over time in terms of two general effects: the effect of absorption, measured by the extent to which a given commodity has been substituted for, or replaced by, other commodities as an intermediate input in industrial processes; and the effect of fabrication, measured by changes in the relationship of intermediate to primary inputs. The first of these effects operates across rows; the second works along columns.

In the original statement of the RAS method it was furthermore assumed that the absorption and fabrication effects operate uniformly across each row and along each column. In other words, it was assumed that the coefficients in row i of A^t are related to the coefficients of row i of A^{t+1} by the same absorption multiplier, called r_i, and the coefficients of column j of A^t are related to the coefficients of column j of A^{t+1} by the same fabrication multiplier s_j. This assumption is commonly known as the assumption of biproportional coefficient adjustment and is stated mathematically as:

$$A^{t+1} = \tilde{r} \; A^t \; \tilde{s} \tag{1}$$
$$\text{(nxn)} \quad \text{(nxn)} \quad \text{(nxn)} \quad \text{(nxn)}$$

where A^t and A^{t+1} are matrixes of direct input coefficients for years t and t+1 respectively, and $\tilde{r}$ and $\tilde{s}$ are diagonal matrixes formed from the vectors of r and s multipliers.

A detailed explanation of the estimation of A^{t+1} and the $\tilde{r}$ and $\tilde{s}$ multipliers in equation (1) must begin by noting two properties of input-output tables. First, the product of the gross output vector, X^t, and the direct coefficient matrix A^t yields the vector of intermediate output, or

$$A^t \; X^t = z^t \tag{2}$$
$$\text{(nxn)} \quad \text{(nx1)} \quad \text{(nx1)}$$

where z^t is the (nx1) vector of intermediate output for year t. Second, the sum of direct input coefficients along each column of the A matrix must equal the ratio of intermediate inputs to total inputs (which equals gross output) in that column or sector. Denoting the ratio of intermediate inputs to gross output by sector in year t by the row vector w^t, this second property is represented by the equation

$$\sum_{i=1}^{n} a_{ij}^t = w_j^t \qquad (j = 1, \ldots, n) \tag{3}$$

These two properties serve as row and column constraints in the estimation procedure which follows.

By hypothesis the elements of A^{t+1} are not known. In order to estimate these coefficients from A^t, an initial estimate of z^{t+1} must first be made. This estimate is made by multiplying A^t times the vector of gross output for year $t+1$, or

$$A^t_{(n \times n)} \; X^{t+1}_{(n \times 1)} \; = \; \hat{z}^{t+1}_{(n \times 1)} \tag{4}$$

In general $\hat{z}^{t+1}$ will not be equal to z^{t+1}. If $\hat{z}_i^{t+1}$ is less than z_i^{t+1}, this means that the coefficients in the ith row of A^t are on average too small. Thus, some or all of the coefficients in this row must be increased. In accordance with the assumption of proportional adjustment of each element along a given row, this equality is forced by multiplying all elements of the ith row by the ratio $z_i^{t+1}/\hat{z}_i^{t+1}$.

These row adjustments in the A matrix now insure that the row constraints of equation (2) hold exactly. But as a result of these adjustments, it will no longer be true in general that the column constraints of equation (3) are still valid. Therefore, it is necessary for similar adjustments to be made along each of the columns of the A matrix in order to insure that the sum of direct input coefficients along each column equals the ratio of intermediate inputs to gross output in each respective column. This is done by multiplying each of the j columns of the A matrix by the ratio $w_j^{t+1}/\hat{w}_j^{t+1}$, where $\hat{w}_j^{t+1}$ is the sum of the coefficients in the jth column of A after the first round of row adjustments.

Following these column adjustments, it will not necessarily be true that the product of the adjusted coefficient matrix A and the vector of gross output in year $t+1$ will equal z^{t+1}, the intermediate output vector for year $t+1$. Hence, the adjustment process must continue, first adjusting the rows and then the columns of the coefficient matrix, and each time bringing the matrix more and more into balance with its marginal totals. The coefficient matrix to emerge from this balancing process is recorded as the coefficient matrix for year $t+1$.[2]

Of the many desirable properties of the RAS method, the following are especially attractive to input-output analysts. First, this procedure preserves the nonnegative characteristics of input-output coefficients. Second, it preserves zero entries in the coefficient matrix. (This property is desirable even in input-output matrixes of relatively small size, and consequently with few zero entries, since quite often accounting conventions restrict certain entries to be zero--for example, the construction row of the interindustry matrix in Soviet input-output tables.) Finally, work by

Bacharach has shown that the adjustment process described above is convergent for any coefficient matrix with nonnegative elements, and furthermore, this solution is unique (Bacharach 1970, pp. 47-55).

Subsequent studies have attempted to modify the original RAS method to reduce its requirements of data and alter the relative adjustment of coefficients in the balancing process. First, it has been shown that by attaching a vector of final-demand coefficients (defined as F_i/GNP, where F_i is the delivery of sector i to final demand) to the matrix of direct input coefficients and allowing these final-demand coefficients to change in the adjustment process just as interindustry coefficients, it is possible to use the RAS method to estimate changes in input-output coefficients without requiring data on intermediate outputs in year t+1. This reduction in the data required by the RAS method greatly increases the applicability of this estimation procedure since annual observations on intermediate outputs are seldom available.

The inclusion of the final-demand vector in the adjustment process results in a slight change in the row and column constraints of equations (2) and (3). In this algorithm the row constraints of equation (2) are expressed as

$$\overline{A}^t_{(n \times n+1)} \ \overline{X}^t_{(n+1 \times 1)} = X^t_{(n \times 1)} \tag{5}$$

where the (n+1)th column of $\overline{A}$ is a column of final demand coefficients and the (n+1)th element of the $\overline{X}$ vector is GNP.[3] The column constraints of equation (3) remain unchanged for the first n columns of $\overline{A}$, but the (n+1)th column must sum to unity.

A second modification of the original RAS procedure involved replacing the assumption of biproportional coefficient adjustment with a constraint that minimizes the sum of squared percentage changes in the coefficients along any row or column and at the same time satisfies the row and column constraints. To illustrate how this minimization constraint affects the adjustment procedure described above, consider first the rows of the matrix $\overline{A}^t$. According to this algorithm we are interested in calculating a set of d_{ij}s in the (k+1)th iteration such that, for any row i, $\Sigma_j (d_{ij})^2$ is a minimum and the product of the adjusted coefficients times the vector of gross output for year t+1 equals gross output in t+1. Stated as a Lagrangian function (all a_{ij}s refer to elements of $\overline{A}$, X_js refer to elements of $\overline{X}^{t+1}$ and X_is refer to elements of X^{t+1}, unless otherwise specified),

$$M = \sum_j (d_{ij})^2 + \lambda \left(\sum_j (1 + d_{ij}) \ a_{ij}^k \ X_j - X_i \right) \tag{6}$$
$$(j = 1, \ldots, n+1)$$

and solving for d_{ij} by minimizing $\Sigma_j (d_{ij})^2$ yields

$$d_{ij} = (X_i - \hat{X}_i)\, a_{ij}^k\, X_j\, \{\sum_j a_{ij}^{k\,2} X_j^2\}^{-1} \qquad (7)$$

$$(j = 1, \ldots, n+1)$$

where

$$a_{ij}^k\, X_j \quad = \quad x_{ij}, \text{ the flow or deliveries from sector } i \text{ to}$$
sector j in the kth iteration,

$$\sum_j a_{ij}^{k\,2} x_j^2 \quad = \quad \text{the sum of the squares of the flows across any}$$
row i, and

$$\hat{X}_i^{t+1} \quad = \quad \sum_j a_{ij}^k\, X_j, \text{ an estimate of the gross output of}$$

sector i, derived from the product of the coefficients of row i in the kth iteration and the
gross output vector of period t+1.

Similarly for any column j, the algorithm calculates a set of d_{ij}s in
the (k+1)th iteration such that $\Sigma_i (d_{ij})^2$ is a minimum, while at the
same time insuring that the sum of the coefficients in column j is
equal to the ratio of intermediate inputs to total inputs for the first
n columns of A and is equal to 1.0 for the (n+1)th column. Stating
these conditions as a Lagrangian (w_js refer to elements of w^{t+1},
unless otherwise specified),

$$M = \sum_i (d_{ij})^2 + \lambda(\sum_i (1 + d_{ij})\, a_{ij}^k - w_j) \qquad (i = 1, \ldots, n) \qquad (8)$$

and solving for d_{ij} by minimizing $\Sigma_i (d_{ij})^2$ yields

$$d_{ij} = (w_j - \hat{w}_j)\, a_{ij}^k \{\sum_i a_{ij}^{k\,2}\}^{-1} \qquad (i = 1, \ldots, n) \qquad (9)$$

where

$$\hat{w}_j = \sum_i a_{ij}^k, \text{ an estimate of the ratio of material inputs to total}$$

inputs in sector j, derived by summing the direct input
coefficients of column j after the kth iteration.

This procedure attempts to constrain the movement of coefficients
through time by minimizing the change in coefficients at each step
in the adjustment procedure. This property is attractive since evidence indicates that structural relationships within an economy
change slowly over time.

In spite of the attractive features of this modified RAS method,
it remains the case that the relative adjustment of coefficients in the
A matrix is determined by relationships incorporated into the balancing algorithm; that is, by implicit properties of the objective
functions. Furthermore, investigation has revealed that the nature
of these relationships within the algorithm is such that the major impact of adjustment is forced onto the larger flows of the transactions
matrix. Since large flows are usually associated with large coefficients, it can be argued that the modified RAS algorithm operates
counter to the results of numerous studies which have found that
large coefficients tend to be more stable through time than small
coefficients.

These findings led to the interesting task of designing a matrix
balancing procedure in which the relative adjustments of coefficients
are not determined by assumption, but are carried out in accordance
with information on the relative stability of individual coefficients in
the A matrix.[4] The construction of this algorithm required the introduction of a set of weights, c_{ij}s, which serve as indexes of stability of coefficients in the A matrix. The manner in which these
weights are formulated is determined by the availability of relevant
information. For example, when only a single input-output table is
available, such weights might be derived from the absolute size of
the coefficients in the A matrix. The availability of two or more
input-output tables, however, provides the necessary information
for the direct measurement of stability of each coefficient within the
period spanned by these observations. Given these weights, the task
then became one of calculating a set of d_{ij}s such that for any row or
column, the weighted sum of squares of the d_{ij}s is a minimum. The
introduction of these weights into the calculation of the row adjustments yields the following Lagrangian for any row i in the (k+1)th
iteration,

$$M = \sum_j c_{ij} d_{ij}^2 + \lambda \left(\sum_j (1 + d_{ij}) a_{ij}^k X_j - X_i \right) \qquad (10)$$
$$(j = 1, \ldots, n+1)$$

and solving for d_{ij} by minimizing $\Sigma_j c_{ij} d_{ij}^2$ gives

$$d_{ij} = (X_i - \hat{X}_i) \frac{a_{ij}^k X_j}{c_{ij}} \left[\sum_j \frac{a_{ij}^{k 2} X_j^2}{c_{ij}} \right]^{-1} \qquad (j = 1, \ldots, n+1) \qquad (11)$$

Similarly, for any column j in the (k+1)th iteration,

$$M = \sum_i c_{ij} d_{ij}^2 + \lambda \left(\sum_i (1 + d_{ij}) a_{ij}^k - w_j \right) \qquad (i = 1, \ldots, n) \qquad (12)$$

and

$$d_{ij} = (w_j - \hat{w}_j) \frac{a_{ij}^k}{c_{ij}} \left[\sum_i \frac{a_{ij}^{k 2}}{c_{ij}} \right]^{-1} \qquad (i = 1, \ldots, n) \qquad (13)$$

Comparing the row and column adjustments for this weighted RAS procedure, as shown in equations (11) and (13), with the row and column adjustments for the modified RAS method [equations (7) and (9)], it is immediately obvious that if $c_{ij} = 1.0$ for all i and j, the weighted RAS method is reduced to the modified RAS procedure. In other words, the modified RAS procedure implicitly assumes a set of weights, all of which are equal to one.

To investigate the relationship between the weighted RAS method and the standard RAS procedure, we choose an alternative weighting scheme. According to this scheme, the weights for the row adjustments are set equal to the flows, while the weights for the column adjustments are set equal to the coefficients. In this case the row adjustments of equation (11) become

$$d_{ij} = (X_i - \hat{X}_i) \left\{ \sum_j a_{ij}^k X_j \right\}^{-1} \qquad (j = 1, \ldots, n+1)$$

$$d_{ij} = \frac{X_i - \hat{X}_i}{\hat{X}_i} \qquad (j = 1, \ldots, n+1) \qquad (14)$$

Since

$$(1 + d_{ij}) = r_{ij} \qquad (j = 1, \ldots, n+1)$$

substituting for d_{ij} in equation (14) yields

$$r_{ij} = \frac{X_i}{\hat{X}_i} \qquad (j = 1, \ldots, n+1)$$

which is the row multiplier for the standard RAS or biproportional method of coefficient adjustment. Similarly, if we set $c_{ij} = a_{ij}$ for the column adjustments, equation (13) becomes

$$d_{ij} = (w_j - \hat{w}_j) \{\sum_i a_{ij}^k\}^{-1} \qquad (i = 1, \ldots, n)$$

$$d_{ij} = \frac{w_j - \hat{w}_j}{\hat{w}_j} \qquad (i = 1, \ldots, n)$$

And substituting for s_{ij} from the equation

$$(1 + d_{ij}) = s_{ij} \qquad (i = 1, \ldots, n)$$

yields

$$s_{ij} = \frac{w_j}{\hat{w}_j} \qquad (i = 1, \ldots, n)$$

which is the column multiplier for the standard RAS method. Thus, the standard RAS procedure and the modified RAS procedure are specific cases of the weighted RAS procedure.

In summary, the inclusion of a vector of final-demand coefficients, the assumption of minimum coefficient change at each step in the balancing process, and the introduction of a set of weights into the objective functions of the balancing algorithm represent modifications of the original RAS procedure designed to increase the flexibility of the algorithm and accommodate constraints imposed by the data. As shown above, these modifications yield a more general RAS algorithm and, in addition, provide the analyst a means of affecting the relative adjustment of coefficients in the balancing process. The control that the weighted RAS method provides the analyst is an important means of offsetting the relatively weak theoretical basis of these RAS methods.[5]

The Estimation of the Changes in the Soviet Input-Output Coefficients, 1959-72

Before estimating the changes in the Soviet input-output coefficients between 1959 and 1972, it was first necessary to decide on an appropriate level of aggregation for the interindustry matrix of

the input-output component. This decision was influenced by the
feedbacks specified between the input-output component and the
macromodel and the availability of data required for the estimation
procedure described below. Since the input-output component of
this model was designed to interact with the production functions in
the determination of sectoral outputs, it was decided to aggregate
the reconstructed Soviet input-output tables to a level consistent
with the classifications used on the production side of the macromodel. This aggregation resulted in the following sectoral breakdown:

1.	Metallurgy[6]	11.	Processed foods
2.	Coal products	12.	Industry not elsewhere
3.	Petroleum and gas		classified
4.	Electric power	13.	Construction
5.	Machinebuilding	14.	Agriculture
6.	Chemicals	15.	Transportation and
7.	Forest products		communications
8.	Paper	16.	Trade and distribution
9.	Construction materials	17.	Other branches of
10.	Soft goods		material production

In addition to the reconstructed input-output tables for 1959,
1966, and 1972, the procedure used in estimating the sequence of
balanced input-output tables for the Soviet economy also required a
set of indexes to move the vector of sectoral gross outputs in current prices from 1959 to 1972 and a set of indexes to move the row
vector of material inputs also in current prices and over the same
time period. Since Soviet national income and gross social product
statistics are not disaggregated beyond the level of five sectors (industry, construction, agriculture, transportation and communications, and trade and other) it was necessary to construct series of
current price indexes to move these aggregates between the bench-
mark input-output observations. The procedure followed involved
the reconstruction of the Soviet financial accounts for each industrial sector beginning in 1959. In this exercise data on employment,
average wages, fixed capital stock amortization, and profits were
applied to the Soviet official distribution of costs in percentage terms
to yield estimates of the gross value of output and value-added by industrial sectors. The difference between the vectors of gross output
and value-added provided estimates of material inputs by industrial
sector.[7]

The algorithm used in estimating Soviet input-output coefficients
for those years in the sample period for which input-output data are
not available is a combination of linear interpolation and weighted RAS

balancing. [8] This algorithm can be described as follows. Considering first the interval 1959 to 1966 and beginning with the matrix of
direct input coefficients for 1966, the algorithm begins by linearly
interpolating this matrix to derive a "first" estimate of the coefficient
matrix for 1965. In the next step, information on current production
and material input levels is introduced by balancing this "first" estimate of the 1965 matrix with the marginal totals for 1965 using the
weighted RAS procedure. [9] The matrix to emerge from this balancing
procedure is then accepted as a "best" estimate of the 1965 matrix
of direct input coefficients. This 1965 matrix is then used with the
1959 matrix of direct input coefficients to derive a linearly interpo-
lated estimate of the 1960 matrix which is next balanced with 1960
gross output and material input statistics. This procedure continues,
first linearly interpolating and then balancing coefficient matrixes at
alternative ends of the estimation period until a complete set of
matrixes for the period 1959 to 1966 is determined.

The estimation of matrixes of direct input coefficients for the
years 1967-71 was carried out in the same manner as described for
the period 1959-66 with one exception. This exception was made in
regard to the 1967 price reform. Since this price reform instituted
major revisions in the structure of Soviet prices, it was felt that the
use of the 1966 matrix of direct input coefficients, constructed from
current price 1966 flow data, would be inappropriate for the estimation of the 1967 matrix of direct input coefficients, since this matrix
does not reflect the price structure that existed in 1967. For this
reason the choice was made to rebase the 1966 flow table into post-
reform (1970) prices and use the coefficient matrix from this table
for the estimation of the direct coefficient matrix for 1967. [10]
Matrixes of direct input coefficients for the years 1968-71 were then
estimated according to the procedure described above.

This exercise generates a set of current price input-output coefficient matrixes for the years 1960-65 and 1967-71. Using the
annual observations on sectoral gross outputs and gross national
product, these coefficient matrixes were converted into standard
input-output flow matrixes in current prices. The introduction of
these data into the macroeconometric model is discussed in the following section.

THE EXOGENOUS INPUT-OUTPUT COMPONENT OF THE
SRI-WEFA SOVIET ECONOMETRIC MODEL

As an intermediate step in the development of the input-output
component of the SRI-WEFA Soviet Econometric Model, the sequence
of balanced input-output tables was introduced into the macromodel

as exogenous data. The purpose of this exercise was to develop the linkages between the input-output component and the macromodel, and investigate the overall performance of the model under these conditions. The results of this study are discussed below.

As mentioned in the introduction to this paper, the primary function of the input-output component in the SRI-WEFA Soviet Econometric Model is to account for the structural interdependencies among the producing sectors of the model. This function was carried out by introducing material input flows among the sectors. First, total material inputs into each producing sector were included as a third factor, along with labor and capital, in the estimated production functions. The set of balanced input-output tables was next transformed into allocation matrixes (referred to as B matrixes) by dividing each flow by its row total,[11]

$$b_{ij} = \frac{x_{ij}}{X_i} \qquad \begin{array}{l} (i = 1, \ldots, 17; \\ j = 1, \ldots, 18) \end{array} \tag{15}$$

where

x_{ij} = the current price delivery of the output of sector i to producing sector j,

X_i = the current price gross value of output of sector i.

These matrixes were then introduced into the macromodel as exogenous matrixes which remained unchanged for a given year. Since the sequence of input-output tables pertain to the years 1959-72, it was necessary to record input-output data for years beyond 1972 in order that this exogenous input-output system could be used in forecasting exercises. For these exercises the B matrix constructed from the 1972 input-output table was usually recorded for each year in the forecast period. This practice imposed the assumption that the structural relationships reflected in the 1972 input-output table did not change in future years.

In the solution to this version of the model, the vector of constant price gross output estimates obtained from the production functions was first transformed into a vector of gross outputs in current prices using exogenous price deflators. These current price estimates of gross outputs were next multiplied by the exogenous allocation matrix for the given year, converting this allocation matrix into a standard input-output flow matrix in current prices,

$$\underset{(n \times n+1)}{[X]} = \underset{(n \times n)}{\tilde{X}} \quad \underset{(n \times n+1)}{B^t} \tag{16}$$

where

$[X]$ = (nxn+1)   input-output flow matrix where the (n+1)th
column is a column of final demand,

$\tilde{X}$ = (nxn)   diagonal matrix with current price estimates
of sectoral GVOs entered along the main
diagonal and all off-diagonal elements equal
to zero, and

B^t = (nxn+1)   exogenous allocation matrix for year t.

The elements along the columns of this flow matrix were next summed
to yield current price estimates of material inputs into each producing
sector. This vector of current price material input flows was then
deflated to 1970 prices and entered into the production functions in the
next iteration. This procedure was repeated in each iteration until
the estimates of gross outputs and material inputs converged to their
solution values. These solution values were consistent with the
underlying structural relationships among the producing sectors reflected in the allocation matrix for that year.

Forecasts with this system, and comparisons between these
forecasts and the forecasts obtained using the two-factor (labor and
capital) production functions of SOVMOD revealed that the exogenous
input-output component imposed a "leveling" effect on sectoral growth
rates that rendered unbalanced or disproportional development difficult to maintain (Green, Guill, Levine, and Miovic 1976). Although
the constraints imposed by this input-output system are partially
valid, it was not possible to separate the effects of the introduction
of sectoral interdependencies into the model from the assumption of
unchanging structural relationships among the sectors in the forecast period. Consequently, the primary objective in the further development of the input-output component became the direct endogenization of the input-output relationships.

THE ENDOGENIZATION OF THE INPUT-OUTPUT COMPONENT

An important advance in the development of the SRI-WEFA
Soviet Econometric Model was the endogenization of the input-output
component. This feature allows structural relationships among sectors to change in response to information generated within the macromodel. As a result of this development, the input-output component
of the model can be used in scenario analysis and forecasting exercises without imposing an exogenous input-output structure on the
producing sectors of the model.

The techniques used to endogenize the input–output relationships within the SRI-WEFA Soviet Econometric Model were derived from earlier results of Hickman and Lau (1973) and Preston (1975). The first of these writers (Hickman and Lau) were concerned with the problem of changing coefficients in international trade share matrixes and sought to explain these changes on the basis of relative prices, a time trend, and a partial adjustment variable. Recognizing the applicability of this work to the problem of price induced material input substitution in an input-output framework, Preston used the techniques developed by Hickman and Lau to provide a means of directly endogenizing input–output relationships within the Wharton Annual Model. The typical equation estimated by Preston is of the form

$$x_{ij} - \overset{o}{\ell}_{ij} x_{\cdot j} = -\sigma_j \overset{o}{x}_{ij} \beta_{ij} - \sigma_j \overset{o}{x}_{ij} \alpha_{ij} t - \sigma_j (1 - \delta_j) \overset{o}{x}_{ij} (P_i - P_j)$$

$$+ \delta_j (x_{ij} - \overset{o}{\ell}_{ij} x_{\cdot j})_{-1} \qquad (i = 1, \ldots, n; \qquad (17)$$
$$j = 1, \ldots, n+m)$$

where

x_{ij} = constant dollar delivery of material inputs from sector i to sector j

$x_{\cdot j}$ = constant dollar value of total material inputs into the jth producing sector

$\overset{o}{\ell}_{ij}$ = $\overset{o}{x}_{ij}/\overset{o}{x}_{\cdot j}$, ith product's share in the jth producing sector's total material inputs (superscript o refers to base-year data

σ_j = elasticity of substitution between any two material inputs in jth production process

P_i = price index associated with the output of the ith producing sector

P_j = $\Sigma_i \overset{o}{\ell}_{ij} P_i$ price index associated with the material inputs into the jth producing sector

δ_j = partial adjustment coefficient entering the function through a partial adjustment hypothesis

β_{ij} = constant term

t = time trend

α_{ij} = time-trend coefficient

In estimating these equations, all observations on the deliveries of
material inputs to the jth producing sector were pooled, and it was
assumed that the α_{ij} are invariant with respect to the delivering sector. Linear restrictions were added to these pooled regressions to
insure that the sum of the intercepts and trend coefficients for each
producing sector are respectively equal to zero. When estimated in
this way, the regression equations for the jth producing sector possess the feature that adding across the delivering sectors results in
a value of zero, that is,

$$\sum_i (x_{ij} - \ell^o_{ij} x_{\cdot j}) = 0 \qquad\qquad (j = 1, \ldots, n+m) \qquad (18)$$

This property insures that the distribution of total material inputs
among delivering sectors maintains the column identity of the input-
output matrix.

The problem of endogenizing the input-output component of the
SRI-WEFA Soviet Econometric Model is very similar in concept to
the problem faced by Preston with the Wharton Annual Model. However, since the Soviet economy is a planned economy in which prices
are fixed by the state and do not reflect conditions of scarcity or demand, it was not reasonable to expect changes in relative input
prices to be a primary factor in explaining shifts in material input
use within a producing sector. It was decided, therefore, to modify
the Hickman-Lau specification shown in equation (17) to include more
appropriate measures of supply and demand conditions among material
inputs in the Soviet economy. Since more research is necessary in the
attempt to derive meaningful shadow prices that could be used in place
of observed prices in equation (17), it was decided in the meantime to
introduce average wage rates in producing sectors as the explanatory
variables in this expression.[12] Equation (17) then becomes

$$x_{ij} - \ell^o x_{\cdot j} = - \sigma_j x^o_{ij} \beta_{ij} - \sigma_j x^o_{ij} \alpha_{ij} t - \sigma_j (1 - \delta_j) x^o_{ij} (\omega^P_i - \omega^R_j)$$

$$+ \delta_j (x_{ij} - \ell^o_{ij} x_{\cdot j})_{-1} \qquad (i = 1, \ldots, 17; \qquad (19)$$

$$j = 1, \ldots, 18)$$

where

ω^P_i = average wage rate in the ith producing sector

$\omega^R_j = \sum_i \ell^o_{ij} \omega^P_i$, an index of average rates weighted by ma-

terial input shares in the jth producing sector.

Since wage rates in the Soviet economy are determined by the average productivity of labor, priority campaigns to attract labor inputs to a particular industrial branch, and locational circumstances that merit compensation for various disadvantages, a significant co-efficient on the relative wage term in equation (19) is subject to several interpretations. First, it may reflect a general priority of the producing sector. In this case, higher wage rates would probably be accompanied by higher allocations of investment funds and material inputs in order to increase the output of this sector. Commodities produced by this sector would then become more available in the overall economy, and it is likely that there would be a shift in favor of the use of these commodities as inputs among other producing sectors. If this interpretation is of primary relevance in explaining the relative wage rates among producing sectors in the Soviet economy, we would expect the σ_js estimated with this specification to have a positive sign. There is also the possibility, however, that planners might attach a high priority to a given sector and successfully attract unskilled labor to that sector--thereby lowering the average wage rate within the industry. In this case it is no longer true that one should expect a positive sign on the estimated σ_js.

An alternative explanation of a significant coefficient on the relative wage term in equation (19) suggests a recognition by planners of the relative scarcity of labor within the Soviet economy. According to this interpretation planners might raise wages, and subsequently output prices, in an effort to induce industries to substitute in favor of those material inputs with lower unit labor costs. Although this interpretation is less likely to explain the overall wage structure in the Soviet economy, it would be consistent with a negative sign on the estimated σ_js.

The data required for the estimation of the coefficients in equation (19) are in part available from published sources, either official Soviet releases or Western reconstructions of Soviet data, and in part must be constructed. Fortunately, estimates of ℓ_{ij}^{o} for the base year 1970[13] and time series data on x_{ij} are available from the sequence of balanced input-output tables in current prices. Although the equations derived by Hickman and Lau are specified in terms of constant price data, it was necessary to use current price data in this exercise, since only crude deflators are available for the Soviet economy with the exception of the 1967 price reform. Given ℓ_{ij}^{o} and the average wage rates in producing sectors, the ω_j^{R}s were computed as

$$\sum_i \ell_{ij}^{o} \, \omega_i^{P} = \omega_j^{R} \qquad\qquad (j = 1, \ldots, 18)$$

Selected results obtained using this pooled time-series/cross-section constrained regression technique are presented in Table 9.1. This table shows the estimated values of the short-run elasticity of substitution $\sigma_j(1 - \delta_j)$ and the speed-of-adjustment coefficient δ_j for 15 producing sectors and a single aggregate final-demand category. In all cases but one, the speed-of-adjustment coefficients are highly significant and fall within the stable range of zero and one. The short-run elasticity of substitution is positive in 11 of the 16 categories presented. Among the remaining five categories in which the elasticity of substitution is negative, its value is statistically significant in only two.

The results of this exercise suggest that most producing sectors in the Soviet economy substitute in favor of material inputs produced by sectors with increasing relative wage rates. This finding is in agreement with the hypothesis that changes in relative wage rates reflect the relative availability of products within the Soviet economy. Although the sign on the estimated short-run elasticity of substitution for the construction industry is not in agreement with this hypothesis, it can be explained if expansion in that sector is usually associated with increasing the number of unskilled workers, thereby lowering the average wage.

Finally, the positive sign on the estimated short-run elasticity of substitution for the aggregate final demand sector is most likely an indication of the dominance of investment and public consumption within this aggregate sector, rather than an indication of the behavior of Soviet consumers. The sign on this estimated coefficient therefore suggests that there is substitution through time among those goods delivered for end-use purposes in favor of goods produced by sectors in which the relative wage rates are increasing, that is, priority sectors.

THE ENDOGENOUS INPUT-OUTPUT COMPONENT OF THE SRI-WEFA SOVIET ECONOMETRIC MODEL

As mentioned above, the primary function of the input-output component in this model is to account for the structural interdependencies among the producing sectors. This function is carried out by enabling the input-output component to interact with the three-factor production functions in the endogenous determination of a vector of material inputs. These estimates of sectoral material inputs are then entered into the production functions to derive new estimates of gross output. As this system iterates in the solution process, the estimates of sectoral outputs converge to solution values that are consistent with the material input requirements of each

TABLE 9.1

Estimates of $\sigma_j(1 - \delta_j)$ and δ_j for 15 Producing Sectors and Final Demand

	$\sigma_j(1 - \delta_j)$	δ_j
Metallurgy	-0.0766	0.0631
	(0.4)	(9.1)
Coal	-0.1404	0.8547
	(-0.4)	(11.4)
Petroleum and gas	1.4957	-0.1272
	(6.2)	(-1.5)
Electrical power	-0.0593	0.9136
	(-0.6)	(23.4)
Machinebuilding and metalworking	0.3557	0.5070
	(1.8)	(7.5)
Chemicals	0.1744	0.9466
	(1.1)	(17.5)
Forest products	0.2030	0.7204
	(1.8)	(13.3)
Paper	-0.1851	0.8622
	(-2.0)	(16.0)
Construction materials	0.1525	0.7588
	(1.4)	(15.3)
Soft goods	0.0204	0.6605
	(0.3)	(10.6)
Processed foods	0.0304	0.3949
	(0.2)	(5.7)
Construction	-0.6243	0.4042
	(-4.4)	(7.8)
Agriculture	1.2589	0.7397
	(5.7)	(16.0)
Transportation and communication	0.5060	0.9193
	(22.0)	(19.0)
Trade and distribution	0.1092	0.9722
	(0.5)	(24.9)
Final demand	0.3162	0.3983
	(2.3)	(6.1)

Note: Values in parentheses are t-statistics.
Source: Compiled by the author.

producing sector as determined by the structural relationships within
the input-output component. It was shown earlier how exogenous
input-output data could be introduced into the model and used in the
determination of sectoral material input flows consistent with given
output levels. In this section the functioning of the endogenous input-
output component within the context of the complete system will be
described. Since this system is yet to be used in forecasting exercises, the following discussion will concentrate upon the structure
and linkages in this version of the model.

The estimation and inclusion of the constrained-regression
equations, equation (19), within the model enable the input-output relationships among the producing sectors to change in response to information generated within the macromodel. In the solution to this
version of the model, the vector of current-price gross outputs derived from the gross output estimates of the production functions is
first multiplied by an allocation matrix determined in the previous
iteration. This multiplication yields a standard input-output flow
matrix in current prices,

$$[X] \quad = \quad \tilde{X} \quad B^{i-1}$$
$$(n \times n+1) \quad (n \times n) \quad (n \times n+1) \tag{20}$$

where

$$B^{i-1} \quad = \quad (n \times n+1) \text{ allocation matrix determined in the previous iteration.}$$

Summation down the columns of this flow matrix provides estimates
of current price material input flows into each producing sector.
Before these current price estimates of sectoral material inputs are
deflated and returned to the macromodel, they are used in the determination of a current iteration allocation matrix which will then
be used in the following iteration in the determination of material
inputs. This current period allocation matrix is constructed from
a flow matrix estimated using the constrained regression equations
described in the previous section. In addition to information on sectoral material inputs, these equations require data on average wage
rates in producing sectors, which are generated in the macromodel,
and coefficients estimated for these functions using sample period
data from 1959 to 1972. The current iteration allocation matrix is
then constructed from this flow matrix by summing the flows along
each row and then dividing each flow by its row total.

At this point the vector of current value material input flows
is deflated, using exogenous material input price deflators, and returned to the macromodel to enter the production functions in the

next iteration. In the next iteration, this procedure is repeated and a new vector of material inputs and a new allocation matrix are calculated. In the final iteration, the values of material inputs and gross outputs converge to their respective solution values. These values are consistent with the structural relationships reflected in the allocation matrix used in the last iteration.

CONCLUSION

In concluding this paper, several areas in which further research is needed in the future development of this input-output component are worth noting. The first of these areas concerns the basic data. At the present time the input-output component is constructed in current prices while the macromodel is based upon constant price statistics. Conceptually, these different price bases present a problem only in estimating the constrained regression equations using current price statistics. However, since price indexes are required to move between the input-output component and the macromodel, the further refinement of the indexes should make it possible to deflate the entire input-output component to constant prices, and then reestimate the modified Hickman-Lau functions using constant price data.

The second area of future research regards the specification of the constrained regression equations. At the present time average wage rates are used in place of observed sectoral prices to explain material input substitution in the different production processes. It is hoped that further research will yield a set of shadow prices that will be more effective in explaining these changes in material input use over time. Also, in regard to those equations, it might be interesting to try alternative specifications. One possibility concerns the use of an investment variable in place of the time trend. This change would attach a more solid economic explanation to the changes in structural relationships over time, and is also likely to improve the performance of the system in long-term projections.

NOTES

1. Since this preliminary version of the 1972 Soviet input-output table was in purchasers' prices, and the author has chosen to work with the input-output tables in producers' prices, it was necessary to convert this 1972 table into producers' prices. This conversion was carried out by the author according to the methodology described in Treml, Gallik, and Kostinsky (1973).

2. In this solution the r and s multipliers relating A^t and A^{t+1} can be calculated as follows. For any row i, r_i is equal to the product of the scalar adjustments for this row in each iteration of the adjustment process. The column multipliers are calculated in the same manner.

3. Equation (5) can be written in an alternative form

$$\begin{array}{ccccc} A & X & + & H & g & = & X \\ \text{(nxn)} & \text{(nx1)} & & \text{(nx1)} & \text{(1x1)} & & \text{(nx1)} \end{array}$$

where H is the column vector of final-demand coefficients and g is a scalar equal to GNP. Written in this form, the adjustment algorithm would affect both the A and H matrixes.

4. This algorithm was developed in collaboration with Per O. Strangert and originally appeared in Bond (1975).

5. Attempts at incorporating more sophisticated theories of coefficient change into the RAS methods of adjustment are complicated by the iterative adjustment procedure of these algorithms. As discussed above, these adjustment procedures operate upon the rows and the columns of the coefficient matrix separately and thereby divide the adjustment process into discrete steps which are implemented in an iterative fashion until the new matrix is brought into balance with its marginal totals. Because of this step-by-step implementation of the adjustment process, the RAS methods of coefficient adjustment fail to take into account the interdependencies among the rows and the columns in the complete balancing process, and it is for this reason that the constraints designed to affect the relative adjustment of coefficients in a prescribed manner in each step in the balancing procedure may fail to have the desired effect in the overall balancing process. For discussions of an alternative means of estimating the changes in input-output data which does take into account the interdependencies of the row and column constraints see Matuszewski, Pitts, and Sawyer (1964), and Guill and Preston (1975).

6. Although metallurgy is treated as a single producing sector in the input-output component, it is disaggregated into ferrous and nonferrous metallurgy in the macromodel. Since material inputs are determined within the input-output component, there is only a single variable for material inputs into the metallurgy sector. This variable enters into the production functions for both ferrous and nonferrous metallurgy.

7. For a detailed discussion of this exercise see Thornton (1965 and 1970), and Desai (1973).

8. This estimation of procedure was carried out using current price data. The use of these data reflects theoretical considerations (see Klein 1952-53, Haldi 1959, Tilanus and Rey 1964, and Sarma

1972) and the scarcity of price indexes that can be used to convert current price Soviet statistics to a constant price base.

9. As a choice of weights for balancing the 1965 table, let

$$c_{ij} = \frac{1.0}{1.0 + (\log \frac{a_{ij}^{59}}{a_{ij}^{66}})^2}$$

This particular set of weights provides a direct measure of the relative stability of each coefficient in the A matrix between the 1959 and 1966 observations, without distinguishing the direction of change for individual coefficients. Inspection will reveal that these weights are bounded between zero and positive one, and they have been constructed so as to assign a relatively larger weight to the more stable coefficients since these weights appear in the denominators of equations (11) and (13). Weights used in balancing coefficient matrixes for other years in the sample period were calculated according to the above expression with the exception that previously estimated coefficients were substituted for the observed 1959 and 1966 data in constructing these indexes of stability.

10. See Chapter 5 of this volume.

11. It should be noted that these allocation matrixes are based upon the assumption that the delivery of a particular commodity to a sector is a function only of the level of output or availability of that commodity. According to this assumption, the total inputs purchased by a sector are not determined by the level of output of that sector, but instead by the availability of each of the products in its input listing. This relationship causes the material inputs delivered to a sector to be affected by the output levels of other sectors in the economy.

12. Since the specification of equation (17) was derived under the assumption of cost-minimizing behavior on the part of producers in purchasing material inputs to deliver a specific quantity of output, the modification suggested here weakens the theoretical basis of this specification. See Armington (1969).

13. Since 1970 is the base year for the macromodel, the same year was chosen as the base year for the input-output component.

REFERENCES

Armstrong, P. S. 1969. "Theory of Demand for Products Distinguished by Place of Production." International Monetary Fund Staff Papers 16 (March): 159-76.

Bacharach, M. 1970. Biproportional Matrices and Input-Output Change. Cambridge: Cambridge University Press.

_____. 1965. "Estimating Non-Negative Matrices from Marginal Data." International Economic Review 6 (September): 294-310.

Bond, D. L. 1975. "Input-Output Structure of a Soviet Republic: The Latvian SSR," with an Appendix on Matrix Balancing Techniques by Gene D. Guill and Per O. Strangert. Duke University-University of North Carolina Occasional Papers on Soviet Input-Output Analysis, No. 10. Durham, N.C.

Carter, A. P. 1970. Structural Change in the American Economy. Cambridge: Harvard University Press.

Desai, P. 1973. "Soviet Industrial Production Estimates of Gross Output by Branches and Groups." Oxford Bulletin of Economics and Statistics 35, no. 2 (May): 153-71.

Fisher, R. M., L. R. Klein, and V. Shinkai. 1965. "Prices and Output Aggregation in the Brookings Econometric Model." In The Brookings Quarterly Econometric Model of the United States, ed. J. S. Duesenberry, G. Fromm, L. R. Klein, and E. Kuh, pp. 653-59. Chicago: Rand McNally.

Green, D. W., G. D. Guill, H. S. Levine, and P. Miovic. 1976. "An Evaluation of the Tenth Five-Year Plan Using the SRI-WEFA Econometric Model of the Soviet Union." In U.S. Congress, Joint Economic Committee, Soviet Economy in a New Perspective. Washington, D.C.: Government Printing Office.

Guill, G. D. 1975. "The RAS Method of Coefficient Adjustment and Soviet Input-Output Data." WEFA-SRI Soviet Econometric Model, Working Paper No. 34 (September).

_____ and R. S. Preston. 1975. "The Use of Linear Programming in Estimating the Changes in Soviet Input-Output Data." WEFA-SRI Soviet Econometric Model, Working Paper No. 34 (September).

_____. 1974. "Intertemporal Comparison of the Structure of the Soviet Economy." Duke University-University of North Carolina Occasional Papers on Soviet Input-Output Analysis, No. 8. Durham, N.C.

Haldi, J. 1959. "A Test of Two Hypotheses Concerning Interpretation of Input-Output Coefficients." Weltwirtschaftliches Archiv 83: 1-14.

Hickman, B. G. and L. J. Lau. 1973. "Elasticities of Substitution and Export Demands in a World Trade Model." European Economic Review 4: 347-80.

Klein, L. R. 1953. A Textbook of Econometrics. Evanston, Ill.: Row, Peterson.

_____. 1952-53. "On the Interpretation of Professor Leontief's System." Review of Economic Studies 20: 131-36.

Kresge, D. T. 1969. "Price and Output Conversion: A Modified Approach." In The Brookings Model: Some Further Results, ed. J. S. Duesenberry, G. Fromm, L. R. Klein, and E. Kuh, pp. 85-108. Chicago: Rand McNally.

Leontief, W. W. 1951. The Structure of the American Economy, 2d Ed. New York: Oxford University Press.

Matuszewski, T. I., P. R. Pitts, and J. A. Sawyer. 1964. "Linear Programming Estimates of Changes in Input Coefficients." Canadian Journal of Economics and Political Science 30, no. 2 (May): 203-10.

Morrison, W. I. and P. Smith. 1975. "Nonsurvey Input-Output Techniques at the Small Area Level: An Evaluation." Journal of Regional Sciences 14, no. 1 (April): 1-14.

Narkhoz 19—. The abbreviation Narkhoz followed by the year refers to standard Soviet annual statistical handbooks published by the Tsentral'noe statisticheskoe upravlenie SSSR under the title of Narodnoe khoziaistvo SSSR v 19— godu. Moscow: Statistika. The handbook is always published in the year following the year shown in the title.

Preston, R. S. 1975. "The Input-Output Sector of the Wharton Annual and Industry Forecasting Model." In The Brookings Model: Perspective and Recent Developments, ed. G. Fromm and L. R. Klein. New York: American Elsevier.

_____. 1975. "The Wharton Long-Term Model: Input-Output Within the Context of a Macro Forecasting Model." International Economic Review 16, no. 1 (February): 3-19.

_____. 1972. The Wharton Annual and Industry Forecasting Model. Philadelphia: Economic Research Unit, Department of Economics, University of Pennsylvania.

Sarma, K. S. 1974. "Comparison of Alternative Methods of Improving Input-Output Forecasts: A Simulation Study." Presented at the Sixth International Conference on Input-Output Techniques (April), Vienna, Austria.

_____. "Comparative Performance of Input-Output Models with Alternative Production Functions." Ph.D. dissertation, University of Pennsylvania.

Stone, R. and A. Brown. 1972. "A Computable Model of Economic Growth." In A Programme for Growth, vol. 1, ed. R. Stone. London: Chapman and Hall.

_____ and A. Brown. 1965. "Behavioral and Technical Change in Economic Models." In Problems in Economic Development, ed. E. A. G. Robinson. New York: Macmillan.

Thornton, J. 1970. "Value-Added and Factor Productivity in Soviet Industry." American Economic Review 60, no. 5 (December): 863-71.

_____. 1965. "Estimation of Value-Added and Average Return to Capital in Soviet Industry from Cross Section Data." Journal of Political Economy 73, no. 6 (December): 620-35.

Tilanus, C. B. 1966. Input-Output Experiments: The Netherlands, 1948-1961. Rotterdam: Rotterdam University Press.

_____ and G. Rey. 1964. "Input-Output Volume and Value Predictions for the Netherlands, 1948-1958." International Economic Review 5, no. 1 (January): 34-45.

Treml, V. G., D. M. Gallik, and B. L. Kostinsky. 1975. The Conversion of Soviet Input-Output Tables to Producers' Prices: the 1959 Reconstructed Table. U.S. Department of Commerce, F.D.A.D., Foreign Economic Report No. 6. Washington, D.C.: Government Printing Office.

_____, D. M. Gallik, and B. L. Kostinsky. 1973. Conversion of Soviet Input-Output Tables to Producers' Prices: the 1966 Reconstructed Table. U.S. Department of Commerce, F.D.A.D., Foreign Economic Report No. 1. Washington, D.C.: Government Printing Office.

_____, D. M. Gallik, B. L. Kostinsky, and K. W. Kruger. 1972. The Structure of the Soviet Economy. New York: Praeger.

Tsentral'noe statisticheskoe upravlenie SSSR. 1965. Promyshlennost' SSSR. Moscow: Statistika.

_____. 1968. Trud v SSSR. Moscow: Statistika.

Note: Entries in parentheses indicate coauthorship of works cited in the text by first author only.

ABOUT THE EDITOR AND CONTRIBUTORS

VLADIMIR G. TREML is Professor of Economics at Duke University where for the last five years he has been directing a research project on input-output analysis in the USSR, funded first by the Ford Foundation and then by the Advanced Research Projects Agency. He received his doctorate in economics from the University of North Carolina. Dr. Treml is the author and editor of several books and monographs dealing with various aspects of the Soviet economy and a frequent contributor to scholarly journals. He has served as a consultant to various U.S. government agencies, the United Nations, and private organizations.

DANIEL L. BOND is an analyst for Stanford Research Institute working at the University of Pennsylvania on the SRI-WEFA Econometric Model of the Soviet Union. He is a Ph.D. candidate in city planning at the University of North Carolina at Chapel Hill, and did research at Leningrad State University for ten months during 1975-76 under the auspices of the International Research and Exchanges Board. Mr. Bond has worked in the area of U.S. and Soviet regional input-output analysis for several years and is the author of a number of monographs on this topic.

DIMITRI M. GALLIK is the head of the Soviet input-output section of the Foreign Demographic Analysis Division, BEA, U.S. Department of Commerce. He has an M.A. degree in economics from the University of California at Berkeley and has taught economics at the University of Maryland. Mr. Gallik is the author of several monographs on various aspects of the Soviet economy and has contributed to compendiums on the Soviet economy published by the Joint Economic Committee of Congress.

JAMES W. GILLULA is a Research Associate with the research project on Soviet input-output analysis at Duke University where he is completing his doctorate in economics. Mr. Gillula has spent one year at the Moscow Institute of the National Economy doing research under the auspices of International Research and Exchange Board. He has written several papers and monographs on economic planning and regional input-output analysis.

GENE D. GUILL is an economist on the staff at Wharton Econometric Forecasting Associates, Inc., in Philadelphia, Pennsylvania. He is a Ph.D. candidate in economics at Duke University and has served there as an instructor of economics. Mr. Guill has also served as a research analyst for the Stanford Research Institute and an instructor in economics at Franklin and Marshall College. He is the author of several monographs on the Soviet economy and a contributor to the 1976 compendium on the Soviet economy published by the Joint Economic Committee of Congress. Mr. Guill's current research interests concern the integration of input-output tables with macroeconometric models for both the U.S. and the Soviet economies.

BARRY L. KOSTINSKY is an economist on the staff of the Foreign Demographic Analysis Division, BEA, U.S. Department of Commerce. He has a degree in economics from Franklin and Marshall College and has done additional graduate work. Mr. Kostinsky is the author of several monographs on input-output analysis in the USSR, including a detailed study of Soviet foreign trade. He has also contributed to compendiums on the Soviet economy published by the Joint Economic Committee of Congress.

LAURIE R. KURTZWEG is an economist on the staff of the Foreign Demographic Analysis Division, BEA, U.S. Department of Commerce. She received a Ph.D. in economics from Duke University. Ms. Kurtzweg has contributed to a compendium on the Soviet economy published by the Joint Economic Committee of Congress and is specializing in international input-output comparisons.

ARTHUR L. MOSES is an economist with the secretariat of the United Nations Economic Commission for Europe in Geneva. He received his Ph.D. degree in economics from Duke University. Dr. Moses has worked in the field of Soviet input-output analysis for several years and is the author of several papers and monographs dealing with various aspects of Soviet transportation. He is currently engaged in research on long-term economic problems faced by industrialized countries.

PER O. STRANGERT is a senior researcher with the Research Institute for National Defense of Sweden. He has a M.Sc. degree from the University of Lund and a doctorate from the Stockholm School of Economics. Dr. Strangert's research interests cover econometrics, systems analysis, and planning models, and he has published several papers in these areas. He spent the 1974-75 academic year as a post-doctoral student at Duke University where he participated in the research program on Soviet input-output analysis.

*CHEMICAL AND PETRO-CHEMICAL INDUSTRIES OF
RUSSIA AND EASTERN EUROPE, 1960-1980
Cecil Rajana

ECONOMIC DEVELOPMENT IN THE SOVIET UNION
AND EASTERN EUROPE, Volume I: Reforms,
Technology and Income Distribution
edited by Zbigniew M. Fallenbuchl

ECONOMIC DEVELOPMENT IN THE SOVIET UNION AND
EASTERN EUROPE, Volume II: Sectoral Analysis
edited by Zbigniew M. Fallenbuchl

THE ESTIMATION OF SOVIET DEFENSE EXPENDITURES,
1955-75: An Unconventional Approach
William T. Lee

INPUT-OUTPUT ANALYSIS AND THE SOVIET ECONOMY:
An Annotated Bibliography
Vladimir G. Treml

SOVIET INDUSTRIAL IMPORT PRIORITIES: With
Marketing Considerations for Exporting to the USSR
Christopher E. Stowell

TECHNOLOGY AND COMMUNIST CULTURE
edited by Frederic J. Fleron, Jr.

*For sale in U.S. and Philippines